Also in the Variorum Collected Studies Series:

SEBASTIAN BROCK
Studies in Syriac Christianity

SEBASTIAN BROCK
Syriac Perspectives on Late Antiquity

HAN J.W. DRIJVERS
East of Antioch:
Studies in Early Syriac Christianity

W.H.C. FREND
Archaeology and History in the Study of Early Christianity

J.H.G.W. LIEBESCHUETZ
From Diocletian to the Arab Conquest:
Change in the Late Roman Empire

T.D. BARNES
Early Christianity and the Roman Empire

R.A. MARKUS
From Augustine to Gregory the Great:
History and Christianity in Late Antiquity

GERALD BONNER
God's Decree and Man's Destiny:
Studies on the Thought of Augustine of Hippo

HENRY CHADWICK
Heresy and Orthodoxy in the Early Church

FRANÇOIS HALKIN
Martyrs Grecs, IIe–VIIIe siècles

IRFAN SHAHÎD
Byzantium and the Semitic Orient before the Rise of Islam

IHOR ŠEVČENKO
Ideology, Letters and Culture in the Byzantine World

MICHEL AUBINEAU
Chryostome, Sévérien, Proclus, Hésychius et alii:
Patristique et hagiographie grecques

DAVID T. RUNIA
Exegesis and Philosophy:
Studies on Philo of Alexandria

JOHN DILLON
The Golden Chain:
Studies in the Development of Platonism and Christianity

Arabic Christianity in the Monasteries of Ninth-Century Palestine

Professor Sidney H. Griffith

Sidney H. Griffith

Arabic Christianity in the Monasteries of Ninth-Century Palestine

VARIORUM

Published by VARIORUM
Ashgate Publishing Limited
Gower House, Croft Road,
Aldershot, Hampshire GU11 3HR
Great Britain

Ashgate Publishing Company
Old Post Road
Brookfield, Vermont 05036
U S A

ISBN 0–86078–337–5

A CIP catalogue record for this book is available from the British Library and the US Library of Congress.

Printed by Galliard (Printers) Ltd
Great Yarmouth, Norfolk
Great Britain

COLLECTED STUDIES SERIES CS380

CONTENTS

This volume contains viii + 341 pages

PUBLISHER'S NOTE

The articles in this volume, as in all others in the Collected Studies Series, have not been given a new, continuous pagination. In order to avoid confusion, and to facilitate their use where these same studies have been referred to elsewhere, the original pagination has been maintained wherever possible.

Each article has been given a Roman number in order of appearance, as listed in the Contents. This number is repeated on each page and quoted in the index entries.

PREFACE

The history of Christian literature took a new turn in the eighth century when monks in the monasteries of Palestine began to write theology and saints' lives in the Arabic language of the *Qur'ān* and to translate the Bible, liturgical texts, hagiographies, patristic texts and other ecclesiastical works from Greek, and sometimes from Syriac, into the *lingua franca* of the Islamic caliphate. It is not too surprising in hindsight to see why these monastic communities were the first Christian groups to adopt the public language of the new body politic in the eighth century. For up to that time they had been centres of learning and piety for the Chalcedonians in the oriental patriarchates, and when Byzantine hegemony ended in those territories, so too did the numbers of readers and writers of Greek gradually diminish and then altogether disappear from the area, not to reappear in any appreciable numbers until political fortunes changed almost three centuries later. The Melkite communities, whose principal ecclesiastical language had hitherto been Greek, then became the first Christians in the caliphate to adopt Arabic as the language not only of their apologetic theology in the face of the new religious challenge, but they used it as their own preferred ecclesiastical and even liturgical idiom as well.

The studies which are gathered in the present volume investigate several issues in the transmission of Christian culture from Greek (and Syriac) into Arabic. The scene is set in article I, which sketches the broad outline of the Christian/Muslim confrontation in the first Abbasid century and a half, naming the principal apologists and their works. The subsequent studies focus on issues, persons and texts in the Melkite communities, for whom the monasteries of Palestine were intellectual and liturgical centres of influence. In article II there is a discussion of the earliest discoverable project to translate the Gospels into Arabic. This enterprise was part of a larger undertaking to translate Christian classics into the language of the caliphate, which is the subject of article III. A particular problem which arose in the Melkite communities in the ninth century was an argument over the legitimacy of the Christian practice of venerating icons, which articles IV and V address. A topic in the controversy between Muslims and Christians, particularly Melkites, was the freedom of the will. Theodore Abū Qurrah, the most prominent Melkite apologist of the era addressed it in an essay which is the subject of article VI. Article VII presents a monk of the monastery of Mar Chariton who played a major role in the transmission of Arabic Christian theology in the ninth century, Stephen of Ramlah. Articles VIII and IX introduce a major work of Christian apologetic theology from the second half of the ninth century, an exciting work here dubbed the *Summa Theologiae Arabica*. An original hagiographical text, telling the story of the martyr ʿAbd al-Masīḥ is the subject of article X. Finally, article XI presents a monk of Mar Sabas monastery who played a major role in copying monastic texts in Arabic translation, Anthony David of Baghdad.

The author would like to take this opportunity to thank the original publishers of these studies for their permission to reproduce them in this volume: Presses Universitaires de France, Paris (I); Otto Harrassowitz, Wiesbaden (II); Duncan Black Macdonald Center, Hartford, Connecticut (III); the editors of *Byzantion*, Louvain-la-Neuve (IV, VIII); The American Oriental Society, New Haven, Connecticut (V); the editors of *Parole de l'Orient*, Kaslik, Lebanon (VI); Cambridge University Press (VII); Pontificio Istituto Orientale, Rome (IX); the editors of *Le Muséon*, Louvain-la-Neuve (X); American Society of Church History, Chicago, Illinois (XI). Finally I would like to record a special expression of gratitude to Monica J. Blanchard, the librarian of the Institute of Christian Oriental Research at the Catholic University of America, without whose professional expertise these studies would have been much the poorer. I dedicate the collection of them to the memory of Msgr. Patrick Wm. Skehan, who was determined to support Christian Arabic studies at the Catholic University of America.

SIDNEY H. GRIFFITH

Institute of Christian Oriental Research
The Catholic University of America
Washington, D.C., 1992

I

THE PROPHET MUḤAMMAD HIS SCRIPTURE AND HIS MESSAGE ACCORDING TO THE CHRISTIAN APOLOGIES IN ARABIC AND SYRIAC FROM THE FIRST ABBASID CENTURY

The first Abbasid century was the period of time during which the first Christian apologies in Syriac and Arabic appeared, in response to the religious claims of Islam. The profile of Islam, and the Christian appraisal of Islamic teachings that the writers of this period proposed, effectively set the agenda for the future development of Christian apologetics within *dar al-islām*. The prophet Muḥammad himself, and the *Qur'ān*, were important topics of consideration in many of the treatises.

The purpose of the present investigation is to sketch the portrait of Muḥammad, and the estimation of the *Qur'ān*, that may be drawn from these works of Christian apology. The proper appreciation of the portrait requires one first of all to gain a knowledge of the scope of the works in question. Accordingly, the first part of the paper designates the apologists and the treatises that are available in modern published editions. The second part discusses Islam, Muḥammad, and the *Qur'ān* as they appear in these works.

I. — The Apologists and Their Works

The earliest Syriac apology, actually pre-dating the first Abbasid century by some forty years, is the brief report of a conversation between the Jacobite Patriarch John I (d. 648) and a Muslim official named 'Amr. The report is actually a letter from the patriarch that recounts the questions about Christianity which the Muslim official posed, along with an account of John's replies. The topics under discussion are the Gospel, the doctrines of the Trinity and the Incarnation, and the laws and statutes that govern Christian life.[1] The letter is in fact a miniature catechism of Christian beliefs, designed to furnish the reader with ready answers to the customary questions raised by Muslims. It offers no detailed arguments in favor of the Christian doctrines. Yet, one may recognize in this brief letter the outline of the topics of controversy that would become the standard table of contents for the later Syriac and Arabic apologetic treatises.

The first Syriac treatise that presents a more detailed apology for Christianity, against the standard Muslim objections to Christian doctrines, is chapter ten of Theodore bar Kônî's *Scholion*. This work, put forward by its author as an introductory and summary commentary on the Bible, based on the teachings of Theodore of Mopsuestia, is actually a manual of Nestorian theology, produced for use in the Nestorian school system. Chapter ten is a new feature of the second edition of the book. It is a dialogue between a master and his disciple, in which the disciple poses questions that reflect a Muslim point of view, and the master answers the questions with a defense of the Christian doctrines and religious practices which Muslims find objectionable.[2] Theodore completed his *Scholion* in the last decade of the eighth century. He was, therefore, a contemporary of the writer of the most well known Syriac, anti-Muslim apology, the Nestorian patriarch, Timothy I (d. 823).

Timothy's apology for Christianity is actually a letter from the patriarch, describing two interviews he had with the caliph al-Mahdī, in which the caliph asked questions about Christian doctrines, and the patriarch answered in defense of the doctrines. The letter became so popular that it circulated in the Christian community in a longer Syriac recension, and in an abridged

1. M. F. Nau, Un colloque du patriarche Jean avec l'émir des Agaréens et faits divers des années 712 à 716, *Journal asiatique*, 11th series, *5* (1915), pp. 225–79. Cf. also H. Lammens, A propos d'un colloque entre le patriarche jacobite Jean Ier et 'Amr ibn al-'Āṣ, *Journal asiatique*, 11th series, *13* (1919), pp. 97–110.

2. Cf. Addai Scher, *Theodorus bar Kônî Liber Scholiorum* (*CSCO*, vols. 55 and 69; Paris, 1910 and 1912). Chapter ten is in vol. 69, pp. 231–84. Cf. also Sidney H. Griffith, Chapter Ten of the *Scholion*: Theodore bar Kônî's Anti-Muslim Apology for Christianity, *Orientalia Christiana Periodica*, *47* (1981), pp. 158–188, to appear; and Theodore bar Kônî's *Scholion*, a Nestorian *Summa Contra Gentiles* from the First Abbasid Century, *East of Byzantium: Syria and Armenia in the Formative Period; Dumbarton Oaks Symposium*, May 9–11, 1980, forthcoming publication.

one, as well as in several Arabic versions.[1] The popularity of this letter-treatise was probably due as much to its simple, straightforward style, as to the fame of its author. The patriarch's answers to the caliph's questions are clearly intended to serve as ready replies that any Christian may use in response to the queries of curious Muslims.

Patriarch Timothy dealt more philosophically with the intellectual challenge of Islam in his as yet unpublished letter no. 40, which he addressed to Sergius, priest and doctor, sometime in the year 781. The letter recounts a discussion between the patriarch and an 'Aristotelian philosopher' at the caliph's court. The topics of the discussion are the oneness of God, the divine Trinity, and the doctrine of the Incarnation.[2] It is quite evident in this letter that Timothy is fully conversant with the current debates among the Muslim *mutakallimūn*. For example, he takes advantage of their concern with the divine attributes, to suggest that the Christian doctrine of the Trinity furnishes the only adequate approach to the description of God. In this, and in other respects, Timothy foreshadows the apologetic methodology of the Arabic Christian writers.

The Jacobite writer, Nonnus of Nisibis, composed an apologetical treatise in Syriac at the very end of the first Abbasid century. As in the instance of several other Christian writers in his time and place, Nonnus structured his treatise as a guide for someone who would be searching for the true religion among the several options available to him in the ninth century, in Iraq; but it is quite clear that the pressure of Islam is his primary concern. The unity of God, the divine Trinity, and the Incarnation are his major topics, along with a discussion of the motives of credibility that he believes should support one's allegiance to Christianity alone among the contemporary religions.[3]

For all practical purposes, during the first Abbasid century

1. A. Mingana, Timothy's Apology for Christianity, *Woodbrooke Studies, 2* (1928), pp. 1–162. Cf. the shorter Syriac rendition *in* A. Van Roey, Une apologie syriaque attribuée à Elie de Nisibe, *Le Muséon, 59* (1946), pp. 381–97. For the Arabic versions, cf. Hans Putman, *L'église et l'islam sous Timothée I* (Beyrouth, 1975); Robert Caspar, Les versions arabes du dialogue entre le Catholicos Timothée I et le calife al-Mahdī, *Islamochristiana, 3* (1977), pp. 107–75.

2. Cf. Raphael Bidawid, *Les lettres du patriarche nestorien Timothée I* (Studi e Testi, 187: Città del Vaticano, 1956), pp. 32–3, 63. An English translation of Timothy's letter no. 40, from MS Vat. Siriaco 605, ff. 216v–244v, is the master's thesis of Thomas Hurst at the Catholic University of America, Washington, DC, 1981.

3. Cf. A. Van Roey, *Nonnus de Nisibe; traité apologétique* (Bibliothèque du Muséon, v. 21; Louvain, 1948).

the most important apologists for Christianity who wrote in Arabic were three. As it happens, they represent the three major faith communities then composing the Christian population within *dār al-Islām.* Theodore Abū Qurrah (d. c. 820) was a Melkite; Ḥabīb ibn Ḫidmah Abū Rā'iṭah (d. after 828) was a Jacobite; and 'Ammār al-Baṣrī (d. c. 850) was a Nestorian.

Theodore Abū Qurrah was the most prolific of the Christian Arabic writers of the first Abbasid century. His published works include a long treatise in defense of the Christian practice of venerating images, some dozen theological treatises on topics such as the Trinity, the Incarnation, and the nature and structure of church government. His general apology for Christianity is called simply, 'On the Existence of the Creator and the Orthodox Religion.' For the rest, his surviving works include some few short Arabic essays, and forty-three treatises and *opuscula* preserved in Greek.[1]

The popularity of the apologetic works of Theodore Abū Qurrah among Arabic speaking Christians is attested to by the considerable number of manuscripts that have survived, containing the transcript of an alleged conference between Abū Qurrah and a Muslim official, usually designated as the caliph, al-Ma'mūn. The texts contain questions from the caliph, and replies from Abū Qurrah in justification of Christian beliefs and practices. None of the twenty some known manuscripts that present such reports have been edited in modern times, although in 1925 Alfred Guillaume published a *résumé* of the contents of

1. I. Arendzen, *Theodori Abu Kurra de cultu imaginum libellus e codice arabico nunc primum editus latine versus illustratus* (Bonn, 1877); Constantin Bacha, *Les œuvres arabes de Théodore Aboucara évêque d'Haran* (Beyrouth, 1904); Id., *Un traité des œuvres arabes de Théodore Abou-Kurra, évêque de Haran* (Tripoli de Syrie and Rome, 1905); Georg Graf, *Die arabischen Schriften des Theodore Abû Qurra, Bischofs von Ḥarrân (ca. 740–820)* (Forschungen zur christlichen Literatur-und Dogmengeschichte, X. Band. 3/4 Heft; Paderborn, 1910); Louis Cheikho, Mīmar li-Tadurus Abī Qurrah fī Wuǧūd al-Ḫāliq wa-d-Dīn al-Qawīm, *al-Machriq, 15* (1912), pp. 757–74; 825–42; Georg Graf, *Des Theodor Abû Kurra Traktat über den Schöpfer und die wahre Religion* (Beiträge zur Geschichte der Philosophie des Mittelalters. Texte und Untersuchungen, Band XIV, Heft. 1; Munster i.W., 1913); Ignace Dick, Deux écrits inédits de Theodore Abuqurra, *Le Muséon, 72* (1959), pp. 53–67; Sidney H. Griffith, Some Unpublished Arabic Sayings Attributed to Theodore Abū Qurrah, *Le Muséon, 92* (1979), pp. 29–35. For Abū Qurrah's works preserved only in Greek cf. J. P. Migne, *Patrologiae Cursus Completus, Series Graeca* (161 vols. *in* 166; Paris, 1857–87), vol. 97, cols. 1461–610. For a recent general study on Abū Qurrah cf. Ignace Dick, Un continuateur arabe de saint Jean Damascène: Théodore Abuqurra, évêque melkite de Harran, *Proche-Orient chrétien, 12* (1962), pp. 209–23, 319–32; *13* (1963), pp. 114–29.

the text preserved in Paris Arabic MS 70.[1] Following the judgment of Georg Graf, most modern scholars doubt the authenticity of these widely differing reports, concluding that later Christians in the Muslim *milieu* produced them, elaborating on Abū Qurrah's well known retorts to particular Muslim allegations about Christian beliefs or practices.[2]

Abū Qurrah's Jacobite rival, Ḥabīb ibn Ḫidmah Abū Rā'iṭah, was also a prominent Christian apologist of the first Abbasid century. His general apology for Christianity, called simply an epistle (*risālah*) 'on the substantiation of the Christian religion and the holy Trinity', is unfinished in the form in which it has come down to us. In addition to his apology, we have in a modern edition his treatises on the Trinity, the doctrine of the Incarnation, the refutation of the Melkites, the Jacobite addition to the *Trishagion*, and several smaller essays and reports.[3] A noticeable feature of Abū Rā'iṭah's works, especially in his discussion of the doctrine of the Trinity, is his knowledge of the current debates among the Muslim *mutakallimūn*, and his use of the Arabic idiom of these controversies to commend the Christian doctrines.[4] It is quite clear that in Iraq there was at this time a certain dialogue, or at least a dialectical relationship, between Christian and Muslim scholars about the implications of describing (*waṣf*) God in the Arabic language. Abū Rā'iṭah, like 'Ammār al-Baṣrī and other, later Christian apologists, followed these discussions with interest, and exploited them for their own apologetic purposes.

The Nestorian school system in Iraq was the context in which 'Ammār al-Baṣrī composed his Christian apologies in Arabic. His general apology for Christianity is entitled simply, *Kitāb al-burhān*, or 'proof-text', in an obvious reference to the *Qur'ān*'s injunction, repeated several times on occasions when the prophet Muḥammad met members of other religious communities, 'Produce your proof (*burhān*), if you speak truly', e.g., in *al-Baqarah* (2): 111). In addition to this general apology, 'Ammār also wrote a more detailed Arabic treatise, entitled

1. Alfred GUILLAUME, Theodore Abū Qurra as Apologist, *Moslem World*, *15* (1925), pp. 42–51.
2. Georg GRAF, *Geschichte der christlichen arabischen Literatur* (vol. 2, Studi e Testi, 133; Città del Vaticano, 1947), pp. 21–3.
3. Cf. Georg GRAF, *Die Schriften des Jacobiten Ḥabīb Ibn Ḫidma Abū Rā'iṭa* (*CSCO*, vols. 130 and 131; Louvain, 1951).
4. Cf. Sidney H. GRIFFITH, Ḥabīb ibn Ḫidmah Abū Rā'iṭah, A Christian *Mutakallim* of the First Abbasid Century, *Oriens Christianus*, *64* (1980), pp. 161–201.

Kitāb al-masā'il wa l-ağwibah, or 'book of questions and answers', in which he discusses the topics of controversy between Christians and Muslims with more refinement.[1] 'Ammār is thoroughly acquainted with the world of the Muslim *'ilm al-kalām*, and he exercises a considerable ingenuity in fashioning his arguments in favor of Christian doctrines, in terms which take advantage of the issues that interested the Muslim scholars.

There are two published Christian Arabic documents from the early ninth century that are incomplete in the form in which we presently have them. The first of them is an anonymous treatise on the Trinity, entitled *fī taṯlīṯ Allāh al-wāḥid*, which can be only approximately translated into English as 'on confessing the threeness of the one God'.[2] Only a portion of it has survived. It quotes passages from the Old and New Testaments, and from the *Qur'ān*, in favor of the doctrine of the Trinity. The other document is the account of a debate, allegedly held in Jerusalem in c. 815 A.D., between a monk named Abraham of Tiberias, and a Muslim official named 'Abd ar-Raḥmān ibn al-Malik ibn Ṣāliḥ. Unfortunately, the text of this account is published only in a German translation, and so its usefulness is limited.[3]

Just over the boundary of the first Abbasid century is the apologetic treatise of Ḥunayn Ibn Isḥāq (d. 873). The occasion for the composition of his treatise affords the modern reader a rare glimpse into the relationship between Christians and Muslims in mid-ninth century Baghdad. According to the story that has come down to us, Ḥunayn and his Muslim friend, Abū l-Ḥasan 'Alī ibn Yaḥyā al-Munağğim (d. 888), the son of al-Ma'mūn's court astronomer who had converted to Islam at the caliph's request, were present together in Baghdad at a *mağlis* hosted by Abū l-Ḥasan 'Abd Allāh ibn Yaḥyā al-Barmakī, somewhere around the years 861-862. The Muslim friend heard Ḥunayn claim that it is inexcusable for a man not to accept an obvious truth, or for him summarily to dismiss out of hand an

1. Michel HAYEK (ed.), *'Ammār al-Baṣrī, Apologie et Controverses*, Beyrouth, 1977). The French introduction and summary of the treatises also appears in *Islamochristiana, 2* (1976), pp. 69–113.

2. Cf. Margaret DUNLOP GIBSON, *An Arabic Version of the Acts of the Apostles and the Seven Catholic Epistles;... with a Treatise on the Triune Nature of God* (Studia Sinaitica, 7; London, 1899), pp. 75–107. Cf. also J. Rendel HARRIS, A Tract on the Triune Nature of God, *American Journal of Theology*, 5 (1901), pp. 75–86.

3. K. VOLLERS, Das Religionsgespräch von Jerusalem (um 800 D); aus dem Arabischen übersetzt, *Zeitschrift fur Kirchengeschiste*, 29 (1908), pp. 29–71, 197–221; and Graf, 1947, pp. 28–30.

argument which he knows will validate a position to which he is opposed. Thereupon, Ibn al-Munağğim sent Ḥunayn a note, arguing that he should accept Islam. Ḥunayn ignored the note. So Ibn al-Munağğim sent a formal *risālah*, entitled *al-burhān*, not only to Ḥunayn, but to his fellow Christian scholar. Qusṭā ibn Lūqā (d. 912). In his *risālah*, Ibn al-Munağğim argued that any open minded person should accept Islam because of Muḥammad's legitimate claim to prophecy. Ḥunayn and Qustā replied with the apologies that have survived under the names.[1] While to date, only a portion of Ḥunayn's apology has been published, the whole correspondence will shortly appear in *Patrologia Orientalis.*[2]

It remains only to consider the famous apology that circulates under the name of 'Abd al-Masīḥ ibn Isḥaq al-Kindī, perhaps the most well known of all the early apologies for Christianity. The apology is in the form of a letter from 'Abd al-Masīḥ, in reply to an earlier letter from a Muslim character named 'Abd Allāh ibn Ismā'il al-Hāšimī, in which 'Abd Allāh summons his correspondent to the profession of Islam. 'Abd Allāh's letter is a very summary statement of the Muslim *šahādah* and the five pillars of Islam. 'Abd al-Masīḥ's reply on the other hand is a long defense of the standard Christian doctrines and practices, according to the customary outline of topics in the more popular apologies for Christianity, along with a vigorous polemic against the *Qur'ān*' the prophet Muḥammad, and the teachings and practices that are characteristic of Islam. The two letters circulated as units of a single work, and the correspondents are presented as members of the court of the caliph al-Ma'mūn (813–833). There are a number of manuscripts of the correspondence, and considerable variation in the reported names of the correspondents. Unfortunately, there is not yet a satisfactory modern, critical edition of the Arabic text. The only published recension of the correspondence is one brought out by Christian missionaries at the end of the nineteenth century, using two unidentified manuscripts.[3] The work also played a role in western

1. Cf. Rachid Haddad, Ḥunayn ibn Isḥāq Apologiste chrétien, *Arabica, 21* (1974), pp. 292–302; Paul Nwiya, Un dialogue islamo-chrétien au ixe siècle, *Axes, 9* (1976–77), pp. 7–21.

2. For Ḥunayn's apology, cf. Louis Cheikho, *Vingt traités théologiques* (Beyrouth, 1920), pp. 143–46; and Paul Sbath, *Vingt traités philosophiques et apologétiques d'auteurs arabes chrétiens du IXe au XIVe siècle* (Cairo, 1929), pp. 181–5. For the whole correspondence, cf. Samir Khalil and Paul Nwiya, *Patrologia Orientalis, 40,* no. 183, to appear.

3. Cf. Anton Tien (ed.), *Risālat 'Abd Allāh b. Ismā 'īl al-Hāšimī ilā 'Abd al-Masīḥ ibn Isḥaq al-Kindī yad'ūhu bihā ilāl-Islām wa-Risālat 'Abd*

medieval, anti-Islamic polemic, due to the availability of a Latin version in Spain already in the time of Peter the Venerable (d. 1156).[1]

There has been a considerable amount of scholarly controversy about the date of composition of the correspondence, and also about the doctrinal persuasion of the Christian author. Regarding the date of composition, there are two points of reference that provide an upper and a lower limit for the period of time within which the work could have been written. On the one hand, it had to have been in existence by the beginning of the eleventh century, for al-Bīrūnī (d.c. 1050) refers to it in his *The Chronology of Ancient Nations.*[2] On the other hand, it cannot have antedated the circulation of Abū Rā'iṭah's treatise in defense of the doctrine of the Trinity, since the author of the correspondence quotes extensively from Abū Rā'iṭah's treatise.[3] Some have suggested that the borrowing may have been the other way about, i.e., that Abū Rā'iṭah may have quoted from the apology of al-Kindī. However, this suggestion is implausible since the tenor and tone of al-Kindī's letter is completely comparable to what one expects to find in popular tracts of apologetics and polemics, and it is not at all like the reasoned intellectual and theological arguments of the kind elaborated by Abū Rā'iṭah. In other words, the quoted passages in the al-Kindī *risālah* are somewhat out of their compatible context there, while they are perfectly tailored to the specifications of Abū Rā'iṭah's treatise.

Within the limits provided by the two points of reference that exist for the work, some scholars have opted for a date of composition within the tenth century, citing various historical allusions in the text and the level of the author's awareness of developments within the contemporary Muslim schools of religious

al-Masīḥ ilā al-Hāšimī yaruddu bihā 'alayhi wa-yad'ūhu ilā n-Naṣrāniyyah (London, 1885); Graf, 1947, pp. 135–45; G. Troupeau, al-Kindî, 'Abd al-Masīḥ b.Isḥāḳ, *EI*², vol. V., pp. 120–1. Summaries of the correspondence are available *in* William Muir, *The Apology of Al Kindy; written at the court of al-Mamun (c. A. H. 215; A. D. 830), in defense of Christianity against Islam* (London, 1887); Armand Abel, L'apologie d'al-Kindi et sa place dans la polémique islamo-chrétienne, *Atti della Accademia Nazionale dei Lincei, 361* (1963), pp. 501–23; Georges C. Anawati, Polémique, apologie et dialogues islamo-chrétiens. Positions classiques, médiévales et positions contemporaines, *Euntes Docete, 22* (1969), pp. 380–92. A forthcoming new edition of the text is announced by Pasteur G. Tartar of the Union des Croyants Monothéistes, Combs-La-Ville, France.

1. Jose Muñoz Sendino, Al-Kindi, Apologia del Cristianismo, *Miscelanea Comillas, 11* and *12* (1949), pp. 339–460; James Kritzeck, *Peter the Venerable and Islam* (Princeton, 1964), pp. 101–7.
2. Cf. Muir, *op. cit.*, pp. 13 ff.
3. Cf. Graf, *op. cit.*, 1951, vol. 131, pp. 32–6.

scholarship.[1] However, some scholars see no necessity in these arguments.[2] And, indeed, there really is no compelling reason to doubt the work's own testimony that its author took his inspiration from events he witnessed at the caliphal court of al-Ma'mūn (813–833). This caliph was famous for sponsoring just such exchanges as this correspondence records.[3] The contents of the correspondence are not such as should preclude their appearance in the first Abbasid century. Consequently, the author's testimony should be accepted, and the work dated to the second half of this century.

The author of the al-Hāšimī/al-Kindī correspondence is completely anonymous. In all likelihood, he was a Nestorian, a fact that would in no way prevent him from borrowing the Trinitarian arguments of the Jacobite, Abū Rā'iṭah. Moreover, it is highly unlikely that the names of the persons affixed to the

1. So, e.g., L. MASSIGNON, Al-Kindī, 'Abd al-Masīḥ b. Isḥāḳ, *EI*[1], vol. II, p. 1080; P. KRAUSS, Beiträge zur islamischen Ketzergeschichte, *Rivista degli Studi Orientali, 14* (1933), pp. 335–79. Kraus alleges a dependence of the al-Hāšimī/al-Kindī correspondence on the *Kitāb az-zumurrudh* of Ibn ar-Rawāndī (d. c. 910), a Mu'tazilite, who later became a *zindīq* and wrote a polemic against the prophethood of Muḥammad, and the authenticity of the *Qur'ān* as a book of divine revelation. Kraus' evidence consists of several topical parallels between the arguments employed in the al-Kindī letter and Ibn ar-Rawāndī's work. He suspects that the parellels may support the conclusion that the Christian author was dependent on the work of Ibn ar-Rāwandī. Kraus' views have been cited with apparent approval by G. GRAF, *GCAL, op. cit.*, vol. II, p. 143; G. TROUPEAU, al-Kindi, 'Abd al-Masīḥ b. Isḥāḳ, *EI*[2], vol. V, p. 120; and Robert CASPAR *et al.*, Bibliographie du Dialogue islamo-chrétien, *Islamo-christiana, I* (1975), p. 143.

A fresh reading of Kraus' arguments has persuaded the present writer that they are not convincing. In the first place, as Kraus is at some pains to point out, the parallels are merely topical. There is no question of direct quotation. And Kraus himself points out the many dissimilarities in the midst of the similarities that are to be found in the accounts of the two writers. Kraus' suggestion of dependence is based on his idea that before the time of Ibn ar-Rāwandī, there would have been no *Christian* context within which the work of the author of the al-Hāšimī/al-Kindī correspondence could have been at home. The evidence presented in this paper counters this suggestion. In fact, if there is to be an issue of dependence between these two authors, given the state of the development of Christian Arabic apologetics in the first Abbasid century, it seems more reasonable to suppose that Ibn ar-Rawāndī was influenced by the Christians. His arguments certainly have about them the ring of the Christian, anti-Muslim polemical pamphlets. Moreover, there is no known Muslim antecedent for such arguments. And Ibn ar-Rawāndī is known to have been under the influence of Abū 'Īsā al-Warrāq, a man who was certainly conversant with Christian works p. 112, n. 4 below. The conclusion should be that Ibn ar-Rawāndī was in debt to the Christian apologists, and not the other way about. Cf. P. KRAUS (G. Vajda), Ibn al-Rawāndī, *EI*[2], vol. III, pp. 905–6.

2. Cf. SENDINO, art. cit., pp. 346–7; HADAD, art. cit., p. 302, n. 1.

3. Cf. e.g., the account of al-Ma'mūn given in William Muir, *The Caliphate, Its Rise, Decline, and Fall; From Original Sources* (Edinburgh, 1915), pp. 506–8.

letters are authentic names of genuine persons. All three elements of each name amount to a neat statement of the two faiths, Christianity and Islam. While all of the elements of each name are quite commonly found among the names of contemporaries, their neat symmetry in the present instance suggests that they designate merely literary *personae.* Furthermore, it is hardly credible that any Muslim intellectual, even in the court of al-Ma'mūn, would be party to the summary portrait of Islam that is found here, a mere preface to al-Kindī's rebuttal; or who would be in any way associated with a work that so negatively depicts Islam, the *Qur'ān*, and the prophet Muḥammad. A distinguishing feature of the al-Kindī apology for Christianity, which makes it unique among the Syriac or Arabic apologies of the first Abbasid century, is the bluntness with which it dismisses the religious claims of Islam, in an impudent tone of voice that disparages the *Qur'ān* and the prophet in a way that is reminiscent of the Greek anti-Islamic polemical treatises.[1] For this reason, Armand Abel styled the author of this correspondence, 'le Nicétas du monde arabe.'[2]

Closely related to the apologetic treatises of the first Abbasid century is the Christian Syriac and Arabic apocalyptic tradition that first appeared at roughly the same time, in the form of the Christian legend of Baḥīrā. Baḥīrā is a name of the Christian monk who, according to Islamic tradition, recognized Muḥammad's prophethood when as a young teenager the future prophet visited Syria with a Meccan caravan.[3] And among Muslim polemicists of the first Abbasid century, Baḥīrā was put forward as the sort of Christian person who was commended to Muslims in the *Qur'ān* (*al-Mā'idah* (5):82), in contrast to the Christians represented by the current Nestorians, Jacobites, or Melkites, who were engaged in anti-Islamic polemics.[4] Accordingly, it is not surprising that Christian apologetic writers of the period, including the author of the al-Hāšimī/al-Kindī correspondence, argued that this monk was a heretic, and that he influenced Muḥammad only in terms of his heterodox religious notions. In the second half of the first Abbasid century, probably during the reign of al-Ma'mūn in the judgment of some modern scholars,

1. Cf. Adel-Théodore KHOURY, *Les théologiens byzantins et l'islam; textes et auteurs (VIIIe-XIIIe siècle)* (Louvain et Paris, 1969); ID., *Polémique byzantine contre l'islam (VIIIe-XIIIe siècle)* (Leiden, 1972).
2. ABEL, art. cit., p. 523.
3. For pertinent bibliography cf. A. ABEL, Baḥīrā, *EI*², vol. I, pp. 922–3.
4. Cf. the remarks of al-Ǧāḥiz in his refutation of the Christians, J. FINKEL *Three Essays of Abu 'Othman 'Amr ibn Baḥr al-Jaḥiz* (Cairo, 1926), p. 14.

this monk's story was woven into the Christian legend of a Danielesque, apocalyptic, even eschatological vision that interprets the rule of the Muslims as a phase of human history that should pass away in a future time when God will bring victory and peace to his own proper people[1]. Such an apocalyptic interpretation of the events of Islamic rule was also current in the Jewish community in the first Abbasid century, a fact which corroborates the dating of the Christian Baḥīrā legend to this same time.[2]

The Christian apologetic literature in Syriac and Arabic that appeared during the first Abbasid century has a unique importance. While many of the more renowned Christian religious thinkers who wrote in Arabic came from later times, e.g., writers such as Yaḥya ibn 'Adī (d. 974), Eutychius of Alexandria (d. 940), Ibn aṭ-Ṭayyib (d. 1043), Elias of Nisibis (d.c. 1049), or Severus ibn al-Muqaffa' (d.c. 1000), it was the achievement of the controversialists, both Christian and Muslim, of the first Abbasid century to determine the manner in which the standard topics of Christian/Muslim dialectic were to be proposed in Arabic, and to choose the style in which they would be discussed.

It is interesting to note that the first appearance of Christian theology in Arabic, which came about largely during the second half of the first Abbasid century, and principally in Mesopotamia and Iraq, corresponds to the period of time when, according to all accessible indications, large numbers of hitherto Christian people were becoming Muslims. There are a number of witnesses to the prevalence of this conversion phenomenon. The most

1. The Syriac and Arabic texts of this legend are published with an English translation *in* R. Gottheil, A Christian Bahira Legend, *Zeitschrift für Assyriologie, 13* (1898), pp. 189–242; *14* (1899), pp. 203–68; *15* (1900), pp. 56–102; *17* (1903), pp. 125–66. For commentary, and arguments for dating the composition of the legend to the time of al-Ma'mūn, cf. A. Abel, L'Apocalypse de Baḥîra et la notion islamique de Mahdî, *Annuaire de l'Institut de Philologie et d'Histoire orientales, 3* (1935), pp. 1–12; id., Changements politiques et littérature eschatologique dans le monde musulman, *Studia Islamica, 2* (1954), pp. 23–43. For an argument in favor of a later date, cf. Graf, *op. cit.*, 1947, pp. 145–9. In the 14th century the legend found its way into Latin. Cf. J. Bignami-Odier, and M. G. Levi della Vida, Une version latine de l'Apocalypse syro-arabe de Serge-Bahira, *Mélanges d'archéologie et d'histoire, 62* (1950), pp. 125–48.

2. For pertinent discussion and bibliography, cf. Bernard Lewis, An Apolcayptic Vision of Islamic History, *Bulletin of the School of Oriental and African Studies, 13* (1950), pp. 308–38. For a broader survey of this genre of literature, but favoring a much later date, cf. M. Steinschneider, Apolocalypsen mit polemischer Tendenz, *Zeitschrift der Deutschen morgenländischen Gesellschaft, 28* (1874), pp. 627–57; *29* (1876), pp. 162–6.

unambiguous of them is a passage quoted by J. B. Segal from an anonymous Syriac chronicle of the late eighth century. The chronicler complains:

The gates were opened to them to [enter] Islam. The wanton and the dissolute slipped towards the pit and the abyss of perdition, and lost their souls as well as their bodies—all, that is, that we possess . . . Without blows or tortures they slipped towards apostasy in great precipitancy; they formed groups of ten or twenty or thirty or a hundred or two hundred or three hundred without any sort of compulsion . . ., going down to Harran and becoming Moslems in the presence of [government] officials. A great crowd did so . . . from the districts of Edessa and of Harran and of Tella and of Resaina.[1]

Of course, the Christian community viewed the converts with contempt. They considered the conversions to be merely for the sake of personal power and social advancement. The author of the al-Hāšimī/al-Kindī correspondence, for example, puts this view into the mouth of al-Ma'mūn, when the caliph was confronted with the charge that the converts at his court were insincere. Al-Ma'mūn replies:

I certainly know that so and so, and so and so, were Christians. They became Muslims reluctantly. They are really neither Muslims nor Christians, but deceivers. What should I do? How should I act? God's curse be on them all.[2]

Further evidence of fairly widespread conversion to Islam from the Christian community during the first Abbasid century is available by inference from other sorts of information. Richard W. Bulliet, for example, on the basis of his statistical analysis of the rates of conversion to Islam in the medieval period, maintains that the second half of the century is the beginning of the first great wave of conversions in Iraq, Syria, and even in Egypt. According to his terminology, the years 791–888 comprise the period of the 'early majority', when up to thirty-four percent of the population may be estimated to have converted to Islam, in what he calls a 'bandwagon process.'[3]

Certainly these would be circumstances sufficient to encourage the Christian community to produce an apologetic literature

1. J. B. Segal, *Edessa, 'the Blessed City'* (Oxford, 1970), p. 206. Cf. also the threat of punishment against the 'renegades' in the Christian Baḥīrā Legend, Gottheil, art. cit., *13* (1898), p. 237, *14* (1899), pp. 229–30.
2. Tien, *op. cit.*, p. 112.
3. Cf. Richard W. Bulliet, ***Conversion to Islam in the Medieval Period; an Essay in Quantitative History*** (Cambridge, Mass., 1979).

that argues against the religious claims of Islam. And although these apologies may be, on the surface at least, adressed to Muslims, one must surmise that the Christian community itself is their primarily intended audience. Their purpose would be to stem the tide of conversion to Islam by arguing that Christianity and its doctrines are the only ones that are logically worthy of credence.

Conversely, the Christian apologetical efforts, once they began in earnest, drew the counter-fire of the Muslim intellectuals. In broad strokes, this reaction is visible in the growth and development, during the first half of the first Abbasid century, of the social disabilities that were theoretically to be imposed on the *ahl adh-dhimmah*, according to the terms of the so called 'Covenant of 'Umar.' By the year 800 or so this document had come through the process of elaboration by which the juridical scholars brought it to the form in which it became traditional.[1] And by the end of the first Abbasid century, the caliph al-Mutawakkil (847–861) was trying to make the provisions of this covenant the effective law of the land, in what was to be one of the few overt, anti-Christian, official government policies in the history of Islam.[2]

Some measure of the Muslim annoyance at the arguments of the Christian apologists of the first Abbasid century is recorded in the essay that al-Ǧāḥiẓ wrote against the Christians sometime prior to 847, and which found a role in al-Mutawakkil's anti-Christian campaign.[3] In the essay al-Ǧāḥiẓ asserts:

> This community has not been as sorely tried at the hands of the Jews, the Maǧūs, or the Sabaeans, as it has been tried with the Christians. The fact is that they ferret out the contradictory from our traditions, our reports with a weak chain of transmitters (*isnād*), and the ambiguous verses of our scripture. Then they busy themselves with the pusillanimous among us. They question our common people about these things, with whatever they happen to know of the questions of the renegades and

1. Cf. A. S. Tritton, *The Caliphs and their Non-Muslim Subjects, A Critical Study of the Covenant of 'Umar* (London, 1930); Antoine Fattal, *Le statut légal des non-musulmans en pays d'islam* (Beyrouth, 1958).

2. Cf. Dominique Sourdel, *Le Vizirat 'Abbāside de 749 à 936* (2 vols.; Damas, 1959), vol. I, pp. 271–86; id., The 'Abbasid Caliphate, *in* P. M. Holt *et al.* (eds.), *The Cambridge History of Islam* (2 vols.; Cambridge, 1970), pp. 126–7; F. E. Peters, *Allah's Commonwealth; a history of Islam in the Near East 600–1100 A. D.* (New York, 1973), pp. 450–3; M. A. Shaban, *Islamic History; a New Interpretation* (Cambridge, 1976), pp. 72–80.

3. Cf. Ch. Pellat, Ǧāḥiẓ à Bagdad et à Sāmarrā *Rivista degli Studi Orientali, 27* (1952), pp. 57–8; id., Ǧāḥiẓana III; essai d'inventaire de l'œuvre ǧāḥiẓienne, *Arabica, 3* (1956), p. 170.

the damned *zanādiqah*, even to the point that with this they often acquit themselves well, even toward our scholars and people of rank. They provide controversy among the powerful. They dupe the weak. A trying factor also is that every Muslim thinks that he is a *mutakallim* and that no one else is more adept at arguing against these deviants.[1]

Several of the Muslim *mutakallimūn* of the first Abbasid century even went so far as to write treatises against particular Christian apologists. According to reports preserved in Ibn an-Nadīm's *Fihrist*, 'Īsā b. Ṣubayḥ al-Murdār (d. 840) wrote an attack against Abū Qurrah while Abū l-Hudhayl al-'Allāf (d. 841/2) wrote a treatise against 'Ammār al-Baṣrī.[2] And from the same source we learn that the early Mu'tazilite, Ḍirār b. 'Amr (fl. 786–809), wrote a refutation of Christians in general, as did Abū 'Īsā Muḥammad b. Hārūn al-Warrāq (d. 861), in three different recensions.[3] Thanks to the refutations of Yaḥyā b. 'Adī, some of the work of al-Warrāq has survived. In his refutations, Yaḥyā quoted from it and rebutted it paragraph by paragraph, thereby allowing a portion of al-Warrāq's writing to be recovered for modern scholarship.[4]

Another noteable Muslim reaction to the apologetic efforts of the Christian writers was the refutation of Christians composed by the Zaydite *imām*, al-Qāsim ibn Ibrāhīm (d. 860).[5] The refutation is a product of al-Qāsim's stay in Egypt during the years 815–26, where he frequented the discussions of the Muslim *mutakallimūm*, in the company of a Copt named Salmūn.[6] And, of course, there is also the well known work of 'Alī ibn Rabbān aṭ-Ṭabarī, a Nestorian who converted to Islam as an elderly man, at some point between 838 and 848. His rebuttal of the Christian claim to be the only true religion includes a treatise against the doctrines of the Trinity and the incarnation, preserved only in an incomplete copy, and a work entitled *Kitāb ad-dīn*

1. J. FINKEL (ed.), *Three Essays of Abu 'Othman 'Amr Ibn Baḥr al-Jāḥiẓ* (Cairo, 1926), pp. 19–20.
2. Cf. J. W. FÜCK, Some Hitherto Unpublished Texts on the Mu'tazilite Movement from Ibn-al-Nadīm's *Kitāb-al-Fihrist*, *in* S. M. ABDULLAH (ed.), *Professor Muḥammad Shafi' Presentation Volume* (Lahore, 1955), pp. 57–8, 62.
3. *Ibid.*, pp. 69 and 72. Cf. also B. DODGE, *The Fihrist of al-Nadīm* (2 vols.; New York, 1970), vol. 1, pp. 388, 394, 415, 419.
4. Cf. the mimeo edition of Armand ABEL, *Abū 'Īsā Muḥammad B. Harran al Warraq; le livre pour la réfutation des trois sectes chrétiennes, texte arabe traduit et présenté* (Bruxelles, 1949).
5. Cf. Ignazio DI MATTEO, Confutazione contro i Cristiani dello Zaydita al-Qāsim b. Ibrāhīm, *Rivista degli Studi Orientali*, *9* (1921–3), pp. 301–64.
6. Cf. Wilfred MADELUNG, *Der Imām al-Qāsim ibn Ibrāhīm und die Glaubenslehre der Zaiditen* (Berlin, 1965), pp. 88–90.

wa d-dawlah, which is a scriptural argument in favor of the legitimacy of Muḥammad's claim to prophecy.[1] While there have been serious objections brought against the authenticity of the latter book it is nevertheless quite clear that in his writing 'Alī ibn Rabbān aṭ-Ṭabarī intended to counter the influence of the Christian apologists who were attempting to stem the tide of conversions to Islam, and at the same time he intended to give them a dose of their own medicine. In the introduction to his treatise against the Christian doctrines he says,

> No Muslim will examine my book without becoming happier with Islam. Nor will any Christian read it without being put into a difficult dilemma; either to leave his religion and trouble his conscience, or to be ashamed on account of his position and have doubts about it for as long as his life may last, because of the reasonable argument and the veracity of the account that will become clear to him.[2]

Finally, among the published Muslim, anti-Christian treatises of the ninth century, we may mention an anonymous pamphlet, of uncertain date, but which was copied in the late ninth century, or the early tenth, and which may, therefore, have been composed much earlier.[3] It is a popular apology for Islam, obviously written to equip the reader with ready responses to the common Christian allegations about Islam, and to furnish him with arguments against the Christian doctrines that Muslims find objectionable.

We have mentioned here only the published Christian and Muslim apologetic works which have a claim to date from the first Abbasid century. These works are, of course, the only ones available to us for the purpose of investigating the image of the prophet and of Islam in the Christian imagination of this early Islamic era. But we know of other writers and other works that have yet to come to light in modern times, except by way of being listed in manuscript catalogs.[4] The knowledge that

1. Cf. A. Khalifé et W. Kutsch, Ar-Radd 'Ala-n-Naṣārā de 'Alī aṭ-Ṭabarī, *Mélanges de l'Université de Saint-Joseph, 36* (1959), pp. 115–48; A. Mingana (ed.), *Kitāb ad-dīn wa d-dawlah* (Cairo, 1923); id. (trans.), *The Book of Religion and Empire; a semi-official defense and exposition of Islam written by order at the court and with the assistance of the caliph Mutawakkil* (A. D. 847–61) (Manchester, 1922). Regarding the authenticity of the second work cf. Maurice Bouyges, Nos informations sur 'Aliy . . . aṭ-Ṭabariy, *Mélanges de l'Université Saint-Joseph, 28* (1949–50), pp. 67–114.
2. Khalifé et Kutsch, art. cit., p. 120.
3. Cf. Dominique Sourdel, Un pamphlet musulman anonyme d'époque abbāside contre les chrétiens, *Revue des Etudes islamiques, 34* (1966), pp. 1-34.
4. Cf. the pertinent Muslim and Christian writers, *in* Robert Caspar *et al.*, Bibliographie du dialogue islamo-chrétien; auteurs et œuvres du VIIe au Xe siècle, *Islamo-christiana, 1* (1975), pp. 131–81; *2* (1976), pp. 188–95.

these other works existed, however, even without the availability of their texts, reinforces the depiction of the first Abbasid century as an era of major importance for understanding the growth of the Muslim/Christian religious controversies in Arabic.

II. — ISLAM, MUḤAMMAD, AND THE 'QUR'ĀN'

One of the provisions, customarily found among the conditions (*šurūṭ*) of the covenant that by the middle of the first Abbasid century theoretically governed the lives of the protected people (*ahl adh-dhimmah*) within the realm of Islam, stipulates, 'If any of you says of the Prophet, of God's book or his religion what is unfitting, he is debarred from the protection of God, the Commander of the Faithful, and all Muslims.'[1] One suspects that this stipulation arose from the exigencies of everyday life in the religiously pluralistic world of Islam in the eighth Christian century. As time went on after the first Arab conquest, one supposes, and as more people from the subject populations converted to Islam, the social circumstances conceivably would have favored the evolution of ever more specific regulations concerning the low social profile that the *Qur'ān* requires of the non-Muslim scripture people (*al-Tawbah* (9):29). Some such gradual development, at any rate, is suggested by the so-far meagre number of studies dealing with the *ḥadīth* reports that relate to the subject religious groups.[2] And, indeed, in *al-Ǧāḥiẓ'* polemical essay against the Christian community, there is some support for the supposition that such regulations came about gradually. He complains that the Christians in his time hardly ever abided by the conditions in fulfillment of which they would have a right to Muslim protection. In fact, he charges, such conditions as the one we have quoted above had no place in the earlier recensions of the covenant of protection because to have committed such a provision to writing would itself have been a manifestation of weakness and an inducement to the subject populations to test their limits. In his own time, however, the situation had deteriorated to such an extent that al-Ǧāḥiẓ alleged that Christians would defame the prophet's mother, and accuse her of immorality, and then claim that they had not

1. TRITTON, *op. cit.*, p. 12.
2. Cf. e.g., Georges VAJDA, Juifs et musulmans sélon le ḥadīṯ, *Journal asiatique, 229* (1937), pp. 57–127; R. MARSTON SPEIGHT, Attitudes Toward Christians as Revealed in the *Musnad* of al-Ṭayālisī, *Muslim World, 63* (1973), pp. 249–68.

thereby breached the covenant because the prophet's mother had not been a Muslim.[1]

Such a public defamation of the prophet as the one al-Ǧāḥiẓ alleges here is foreign to the tone of the Christian apologetic literature that is preserved in Syriac or in Arabic, from the first Abbasid century. On the other hand, his allegations are an accurate description of the temper of the Greek polemical writings against Muḥammad and Islam that began to appear at roughly the same time.[2] It may be that undercurrents of this hostile posture circulated in the Arabic speaking world as well as among the Greek, and later the Latin writers, who attempted to discredit the religious claims of Islam. Traces of such an attitude appear in the al-Hāšimī/al-Kindī correspondence. But for the most part, in the Arabic treatises there is an interest in religious dialogue. None of the writers expressed this conciliatory attitude more forthrightly than did Ḥabīb ibn Ḫidmah Abū Rā'iṭah. In his treatise on the Trinity, for example, he writes of his hopes for the dialogue, and he advises his readers to invite Muslims to the conversation on the Trinity with the following words of encouragement.

> The hope is that you will treat us fairly in the discussion and that you will bargain with us as brothers who share in the goods they inherit from their father. All of them share in them. Nothing belongs to one rather than to another. So we and you should be on a par in the discussion.[3]

One should not assume that such words as these were meant, in any modern sense, to encourage an ecumenical search for some sort of religious unity. It is quite clear that Abū Rā'iṭah hopes to press the claims of his own Christian faith as vigorously as he can. But his words remind us that his chosen forum in which to conduct his apology for Christianity, whether by literary artifice only, or in actual practice, is the scholarly *maǧlis*, in which the assembled *mutakallimūn* are expected to press their individual claims according to the conventions of the *'ilm al-kalām*. This undertaking, of course, is a far cry from the rude calumnies of which al-Ǧāḥiẓ complains, and it is also the very antithesis to the belligerent posture assumed by the writers of many of the Greek polemical tracts.

1. Cf. FINKEL, *op. cit.*, pp. 18 and 19.
2. For precisely this attack against the prophet's mother, cf. KHOURY, *op. cit.*, 1972, pp. 64–5.
3. GRAF, *op. cit.*, 1951, vol. 130, pp. 3 and 4.

All of the apologetical literature that has survived from the first Abbasid century, be it Muslim or Christian, in Syriac or Arabic, is dialogical in form. This is true not only of the reports of staged debates, such as those involving the patriarch Timothy and the caliph al-Mahdī, or the exchange of correspondence between Ibn al-Munağğim and Ḥunayn ibn al-Isḥāq, it is an equally accurate description of Theodore bar Kônî's 'Questions and Answers', and 'Ammār al-Baṣrī's very closely reasoned treatises. All of them, by convention, are addressed to an inquirer, either by name or merely in rhetorical style, in the introduction to the treatise. And the arguments are unfailingly carried forward with an eye to rebutting the thesis, i.e., in Arabic, *al-qawl*, the thesis statement, of 'those who disagree with us (*muḫālifūnā*)'. As Theodore Abū Qurrah reminds the reader in his Greek *opusculum* 34, this dialogical style, which has persuasion as its dominant note, represents a rhetorical choice on the part of the writer, who, according to Greek academic usages, may choose to argue either διαλεκτικῶς or ἀποδεικτικῶς.[1] But there is more to be said about such a style in an Arabic, Islamic milieu, than merely to cite these categorical designations recognized by Greek rhetoricians.

The Arabic *'ilm al-kalām* became a highly sophisticated expository technique among Muslim religious scholars. It is in all probability, the forerunner of the western medieval scholastic method.[2] In the first Abbasid century, this dialectical technique was the standard academic methodology for discussing religious questions in Arabic, be they completely Muslim questions, or questions involving the relationship of Islam to other religious communities. While there is much current scholarly debate about the origins of this technique in the Islamic milieu,[3] the

1. *PG*, 97, col. 1585.

2. Cf. George Makdisi, The Scholastic Method in Medieval Education: an Inquiry into its Origins in Law and Theology, *Speculum*, *49* (1974), pp. 640–61.

3. Cf. particularly the work of Josef Van Ess, The Logical Structure of Islamic Theology, *in* G. E. von Grunebaum (ed.), *Logic in Classical Islamic Culture* (Wiesbaden, 1970), pp. 21–50; id., The Beginnings of Islamic Theology, *in* J. Murdoch and E. Sylla (eds.), *The Cultural Context of Medieval Learning* (Boston, 1975), pp. 89–111; id., Disputationspraxis in der islamischen Theologie, eine vorläufige Skizze, *Revue des Etudes islamiques, 44* (1976), pp. 23–60. Cf. also Friedrich Niewöhner, Die Diskussion um den Kalām und die Mutakallimun in der europäischen Philosophergeschichtsschreibung, *Archiv für Begriffsgeschichte, 18* (1974), pp. 7–34. And here is the place to record the writer's inkling that the *kalām* style and practice owes more to the usages of the Syriac academies in Mesopotamia and Iraq than it does to the conventions of Greek theological writers. Cf. M. A. Cook,

point to be made in the present context is that the Christian apologists of the first Abbasid century, who wrote in Syriac and Arabic, were actual participants in formal scholarly conversations with Muslim intellectuals. They were not, as were the Greek polemicists, writing in isolation from Islam, without any appreciation for the intellectual acuity of the Muslim *mutakallimūn*, or any respect for their intellectual objections to Christian doctrines. The works of the Christian and Muslim scholars that have been cited in the first section of this study are themselves the evidence for the participation of these scholars in the written *kalām*. For example, no other interpretation can be put on such facts as that Abū Hudhayl wrote a treatise explicitly addressed to the views of 'Ammār al-Baṣrī, while the latter scholar directed his apology for the Trinity expressly against positions espoused by the former.[1] As for the participation of Christian scholars in the oral debates of the *maǧālis* of Muslim academicians, there are numerous remarks in both Muslim and Christian sources to substantiate the conclusion that such meetings occurred. First among them, of course, are the introductions to such works as Timothy's letters, the al-Hāšimī/al-Kindī correspondence, the report of Abraham of Tiberias' debate in Jerusalem, and the other reports of a similar nature that are listed above.[2] But in addition to these testimonies to the occurrence of scholarly discussions about religion between Christians and Muslims, which someone may consider to be of doubtful value as documentary evidence, since they often are said to be literary contrivances, there are remarks in other sources to the same effect.[3] Antonius Rhetor (d.c. 840–850), for example, in one of his letters alludes to the courteous discussions about religion that took place in Baghdad between Christians and Muslims in the time of al-Manṣūr (754–775).[4] We have already seen that in Egypt a Copt named Salmūn used to accompany al-Qāsim ibn Ibrāhīm to the *maǧlis* of the Muslim *mutakallimūn*.[5] And as a final

The Origins of Kalām, *Bulletin of the School of Oriental and African Studies, 43* (1980), pp. 32–43.

1. Cf. above, n. 36, and Sidney H. Griffith, *The Concept of al-uqnūm in 'Ammār al-Baṣrī's Apology for the Doctrine of the Trinity*, a paper read at the First Congress for Christian Arabic, Goslar, Sept. 11–3, 1980, *Orientalia Christiana Analecta* (1983), pp. 151-173.
2. Cf. above, nn. 3, 4, 13, 16.
3. Some scholars make a distinction between the *maǧālis* that may be literary inventions, and those that may be considered to have actually taken place. Cf., e.g., Joseph Nasrallah, Naẓīf ibn Yumn; médecin, traducteur et théologien melchite du xe siècle, *Arabica, 21* (1974), pp. 309–10.
4. Cf. the reference *in* J. M. Fiey, Tagrit, *L'Orient syrien, 8* (1963), p. 317.
5. Cf. above, p. 112, n. 6.

attestation to this practice we may cite the story preserved in Ibn an-Nadīm's *Fihrist* about Ibn Kullāb's talks with the Nestorian, Pethion, as recounted by a later Muslim, Abū al-'Abbās al-Baghawī, who also frequented the company of Christian scholars.[1]

The discussion of the *'ilm al-kalām* and its ideal *mağlis* setting is not a digression from the present paper's main purpose. Rather, keeping in mind this *Sitz im Leben*, and its associated literary genres, one gains an insight into the purposes of the Christian apologists as they attempted to reflect the facts of Islam in an idiom that is intelligible to Christians. Within the parameters of their own theological system, the writers hope to give their readers enough information to gain a debating advantage in their encounters with the Muslim *mutakallimūn*. So, from this perspective, we move on to sketch the portraits of the Islamic community, the prophet Muḥammad, and the *Qur'ān*, as we find them in the literature that is here under review.

A) *The Muslim Community*

There are considerable differences in the designations used for the Islamic community in Syriac on the one hand, and in Arabic on the other. Accordingly, in this section of the present inquiry the Syriac and the Arabic treatises will be considered separately.

1. *The Syriac Treatises.*—Undoubtedly, the most frequent designation for the Muslims in the Syriac apologetical treatises of the first Abbasid century is the term *ḥanpâ* (pl. *ḥanpê*), a Syriac word that in general may be said to mean 'pagan', or 'heathen'. Prior to the appearance of Islam in the Syriac speaking area, such a *ḥanpâ* seems most often to have been what the Greek fathers called a 'Hellene', i.e., a follower of the old 'pagan' religion who had not become Christian with the empire. Nonnus of Nisibis qualifies the term when he uses it to designate Muslims, calling them 'present-day (*d^ehāšâ*) *ḥanpê* or 'recent (*ḥadtê*) *ḥanpê*'.[2] Of course, in these contexts, the term does not mean simply 'pagans. It is used to designate Muslims by the Syriac writers, at least in part, because they would have been well aware of the fact that the Syriac word is cognate to the Arabic term *ḥanīf* (pl. *ḥunafā'*), which is used in the *Qur'ān*

1. Cf. DODGE, *op. cit.*, pp. 448–9.
2. VAN ROEY, *op. cit.*, pp. 9* and 12*.

some dozen times to describe a non-Christian, non-Jewish person who yet follows the true monotheistic religion. Most importantly, in *Āl 'Imrān* (3:67), the term *ḥanīf* is used in tandem with the adjective *muslim* to describe the religious posture of Abraham. Accordingly, in Arabic, on the face of it, the term seems to have a meaning that is the polar opposite to the sense of its Syriac cognate. But the matter is not quite so simple. Even in Arabic the term *ḥanīf* was used by medieval writers in a sense akin to the significance of the word *ḥanpâ* as the Syriac writers usually employed it. For example, the Sabaeans, the denizens of Ḥarrān, a city closely connected with Abraham in the scriptural traditions, were considered to be *ḥanpê*, or Hellenes, by the Syrian Christians, and later Muslim writers followed suit by calling them *ḥunafā'* in Arabic.[1] So one must wonder if even in the *Qur'an*, a scripture in which the Arabic diction often resembles Syriac usages, the primary sense of the term *ḥanīf* is not 'non-Christian', or 'non-Jew', with the important qualification that such a person is a monotheist (e.g. *al-Baqarah* 2:135), and, indeed, a monotheist who recognizes the truth of Muḥammad's preaching.[2] There is the story of Waraqah ibn Nawfal, for example, whom the Islamic traditions remember as one of the *ḥunafā'*, who was said to be thoroughly familiar with the Old and New Testaments. He apparently did become a Christian, according to the story, but he lived to recognize the legitimacy of Muḥammad's claim to prophecy.[3]

1. Cf. the discussion and bibliography, *in* Ḥ. A. Faris and H. W. Glidden, The Development of the Meaning of Koranic *Ḥanīf*, *The Journal of the Palestine Oriental Society, 19* (1939–40), pp. 1–13; S. M. Stern, 'Abd al-Jabbār's Account of How Christ's Religion Was Falsified By the Adoption of Roman Customs, *The Journal of Theological Studies, 19* (1968), pp. 159–64.

2. Some scholars, e.g., R. Bell and J. Horovitz, have insisted that the term *ḥanīf* has its own independent life in Arabic, related only etymologically to Syriac *ḥanpâ*, without a similarity of meanings, at least in the *Qur'ān* and other writings of that same age or earlier, where, says Horovitz, it means 'pious'. Cf. R. Bell, *The Origin of Islam in its Christian Environment* (London, 1926), pp. 57–9; J. Horovitz, *Koranische Untersuchungen* (Berlin and Leipzig, 1926), pp. 56–9. Noting the unlikelihood of such opposite meanings for two obviously related words, K. Ahrens surmised that maybe a Christian of the *Qur'ān*'s time could use the terms *ḥanpâ*/*ḥanīf*, without censorious intent, to designate an unbaptized monotheist. Cf. K. Ahrens, Christliches im Qoran, *Zeitschrift der Deutschen Morgenländischen Gesellschaft, 84* (1930), pp. 27–8. Such a usage as this, however, implies only that *ḥanpâ* simply means 'non-Christian' to the Christian ear. While for a Christian such a sense of the term is hardly laudatory, it is not unthinkable that Muḥammad would have found it to be a quite agreeable sense for what he had in mind. Cf. Arthur Jeffery, *The Foreign Vocabulary of the Qur'ān* (Baroda, 1938), pp. 112–5.

3. Waraqah's story appears in many Muslim accounts. Here we may mention only these few: Muḥammad 'Abd al-Malik ibn Hišām, *Sīrat an-nabī*

Perhaps because of the correlation between the adjectives *ḥanīf* and *muslim* in *Āl 'Imrān* (3:67), Muslims apparently fairly commonly called themselves *ḥunafā'*, and Islam *ḥanīfiyyah*, at least in the early years of the Islamic era. A testimony to this usage would be the occurrence of the term *al-ḥanīfiyyah* instead of *al-islām* in Ibn Mas'ūd's (d. 653) *Qur'ān*, at *Āl-'Imrān* (3):19 (viz., 'religion with God is *al-islām*').[1]

One must then conclude that the Syriac apologists of the first Abbasid century employed the term *ḥanpê* to designate the Muslims, first of all because of the simple fact that the term means 'non-Christians'. It does not mean, of itself, 'polytheists', or 'idolators', as these writers well understood, although the term may also be applied to these non-Christians. Secondly, knowing of the Muslim sense of the cognate Arabic term *ḥunafā'*, one might argue that the Syriac apologists wanted to call Muslims by one of their own names for themselves. But one's suspicion must be that these writers were pleased with the *double entendre* inherent in the meanings of the words in the two languages, and that they exploited the nuisance potential inherent in the mutually exclusive senses of the two nouns. Such was certainly the intent in several passages to be found in the Arabic Christian apologies. The author of the al-Hāšimī/al-Kindī correspondence, for example, has al-Kindī make the following declaration to his Muslim debate partner.

> Along with his fathers and grandfathers, and the people of his country, Abraham used to worship the idol, i.e., the one named al-'Uzzā in Ḥarrān, as a *ḥanīf*, as you agree, O you *ḥanīf*. . . . He abandoned *al-ḥanīfiyyah*, which is the worship of idols, and became a monotheist, a believer, because we find *al-ḥanīfiyyah* in God's revealed scriptures as a name for the worship of idols.[2]

The author who described the debate in Jerusalem between the monk, Abraham of Tiberias and the Muslim official, also brings the two senses of the term *ḥanīf* into the argument. His point, of course, is to suggest that the Muslims are unaware of the true meaning of this term, which, in his view, they naively use

(4 vols.; Cairo, 1356), vol. I, p. 256; ABŪ L-FARAĞ AL-ISBAHĀNĪ, *Kitāb al-aghānī* (20 vols.; Cairo, 1285), vol. III, p. 14; ABŪ 'ABD ALLĀH MUḤAMMAD IBN ISMĀ'ĪL AL-BUḪĀRĪ, *Kitāb al-ğāmi' aṣ-ṣaḥīḥ* (M. Ludolf KREHL, ed., 4 vols.; Leiden, 1862), vol. III, pp. 380–1, vol. IV, pp. 347–8.

1. Arthur JEFFERY, *Materials for the History of the Qur'ān; the Old Codices* (Leiden, 1937), p. 32. Cf. also the range of meanings to include Muslims *in* W. E. LANE, *An Arabic-English Lexicon* (7 vols.; London, 1863–93), vol. II, p. 658.

2. TIEN, *op. cit.*, p. 42.

in a positive sense.[1] Montgomery Watt has suggested that such a polemical Christian reaction to the Arabic use of *ḥanīf*, as a term suitable even to describe a Muslim, may have been responsible for the early diminution of the term's popularity in Islamic Arabic as a synonym for *muslim.*[2] However this may be, it is clear that the Syriac apologists did not think of the new *ḥanpê* as idolators, or as polytheists, or even as pagans. In fact within the limits imposed by their own task to commend the superiority of Christianity, these writers often went to some trouble to underline what they considered to be points in Islam's favor, by comparison with other religious systems.

Nonnus of Nisibis says that in what they believe about Christ, by comparison with the Jews or the Magians, 'the recent *ḥanpê* are more right minded than the others.'[3] And the patriarch, Timothy, echoes the same theme, when he speaks of the response to Muḥammad on the part of the Muslims, whom he calls 'Ishmaelites.' Their reaction is in stark contrast, he alleges, to the inimical response of the Jews to the prophets of the Old Testament. Timothy writes:

> The Jews are, therefore, despised today and rejected by all, but the contrary is the case with the [Ishmaelites], who are today held in great honour and esteem by God and men, because they forsook idolatry and polytheism, and worshipped and honoured one God; in this they deserve the love and praise of all.[4]

Theodore bar Kônî portrays the Muslims as a people who are in receipt of a peculiar 'tradition' (*mašl'ᵉmānûtâ*) or 'teaching' (*malpānûtâ*) about the Law and the Prophets, which their teacher, coming more than six hundred years after Christ, has handed over (*'ašlem*) to them.[5] They accept the Old Testament, and the fact that the Messiah has come, says Theodore, but they reject the genuine teachings of the scriptures. Theodore puts his theological judgment of Islam into the teacher's remark to the student toward the end of the dialogue. 'As I see it,' he says,

1. Cf. Vollers, art. cit., pp. 40 and 45. Note the author's mistaken idea that it is Christ, and not Abraham, who is mentioned in *Āl 'Imrān* (3), 67.
2. Cf. W. Montgomery Watt, Two Interesting Christian-Arabic Usages, *Journal of Semitic Studies, 2* (1957), 360–5; Id., Ḥanīf, *EI²*, vol. III, pp. 165–6.
3. Van Roey, *op. cit.*, p. 12*.
4. Mingana, art. cit., p. 59. Mingana translated the Syriac term *'išma'lāyê* in the text (cf. p. 131), by means of the word 'Arabs'. I have substituted Ishmaelites for his choice.
5. Cf. Scher, *op. cit.*, vol. 69, pp. 235, 246, 283.

'You are believing as a Jew.'[1] This judgment accords well with that of patriarch Timothy, who calls the Muslims, 'the new Jews' in his as yet unpublished letter no. 40.[2]

For the rest, the Syriac apologists refer to the Muslims with a selection of traditional epithets for Arabs and desert nomads that carry with them nuances of religious judgment. As mentioned above, a common one of them is 'Ishmaelites.' For the Muslims, of course, *Ismāʿīl* is Abraham's son of blessing and promise, who, they say, had a hand in the building of the *Kaʿbah*, and who even ranks ahead of Isaac in one place in the *Qur'ān* (i.e., *Ibrāhīm* (14):39).[3] But for the Christian writers, the texts of Genesis 21:9–21 and Galatians 4:21–31 are clearly what would be uppermost in their minds at the mention of the name of Hagar's son. As St. Paul puts it, 'The slave-woman's son was born in the course of nature. . . . She and her children are in slavery' (Gal. 5:23, 25). As for the Muslim accounts of Ismāʿīl's exploits, the apologists, such as the author of the account of the debate of Abraham of Tiberias, simply denied their accuracy.[4]

Hagar's name too appears in these same treatises. In the Syriac *Baḥīrā* legends, for example, Muḥammad's people are often called both 'Ishmaelites,' and 'Sons of Hagar.'[5] In the text that reports the Jacobite patriarch John's meeting with the Muslim official, the Muslims are called *Mahgᵉrāye/Mᵉhaggᵉrāye*, a term that was to be widely used in later Syriac writers.[6] The most obvious meaning of this term, observing the use of Hagar's name in a finite verbal form in later Syriac writings to mean 'he became a Muslim,' is 'devotees of Hagar,' or 'followers of the way of Hagar.'[7] This understanding of the term is spelled out quite clearly in what remains of a colophon, on what was probably the last leaf of a Syriac New Testament, from the year 682. It reads: 'This book of the New Testament was completed in the year 993 of the Greeks, which is the year 63 according to the *Mahgᵉrāye*, the sons of Ishmael, the son of Hagar, the son of

1 *Ibid.*, p. 235.
2. MS Vat. Siriaco 605, f. 216v. Cf. Bidawid, *op. cit.*, pp. 32 and 33.
3. The place of Ismāʿīl in *Qur'ān* and *ḥadīth* is fairly complicated to describe, and to examine critically. Cf. R. Paret, 'Ismāʿīl' *EI²*, vol. IV, pp. 184–5; Michel Hayek, *Le mystère d'Ismaël* (Paris, 1964).
4. Cf. Vollers, art. cit., p. 50.
5. Cf. Gottheil, art. cit., *13* (1898), p. 203, *et passim*.
6. Cf. Nau, art. cit., p. 248.
7. The verbal form is *ahgar*. Cf. its abundant appearance in later texts, e.g. '*in* Bar Hebraeus' chronicle, Paul Bedjan (ed.) *Gregorii Barhebraei Chronicon Syriacum* (Paris, 1890), p. 115 *et passim*.

Abraham.'[1] In the Islamic milieu, this comment reflects a religious judgment on the part of the Christian writers, of course, and not merely an ethnic or historical allusion. It parallels, and perhaps it even owes its inspiration to the Greek adjective οἱ Ἀγαρήνοι. This term, which was used already in the fourth century and earlier to mean simply 'Arabs,' came later to designate 'Muslims.'[2] It seems completely gratuitous, therefore, for a modern observer to notice a mere graphic, or etymological similarity between the Christian Syriac word *mahgerāye* and the Muslim Arabic word *muhāǧirūn*, and then, lacking any mutually acceptable context of meaning in which such a proposal might find a place, to suggest that Christian Syriac writers borrowed the Muslim Arabic word, and then used it in a completely different sense from the one intended by Muslims.[3] Meanwhile, contrariwise, there is abundant evidence indicating that Syriac writers commonly followed Greek Christian usages, and even borrowed Greek words, increasingly so after the seventh century. Clearly then, in Christian apologies, the Muslims are called οἱ Ἀγαρήνοι and *mahgerāye*, with the intention of communicating all that these terms suggest about the Christian evaluation of the religious

1. W. Wright, *Catalogue of Syriac Manuscripts in the British Museum* (3 vols.; London, 1870–2), vol. I, p. 92.

2. Cf. E. A. Sophocles, *Greek Lexicon of the Roman and Byzantine Periods* (2 vols.; New York, 1887), vol. I, p. 63. Epiphanius, e.g., refers to Hagar and Ishmael as the ancestors of the tribes of the Agarenes, Ishmaelites, and Saracens. Cf. K. Hall, *Epiphanius (Ancoratus und Panarion)* (*GCS*, vol. 25; Leipzig, 1915), p. 180.

3. Cf. Patricia Crone and Michael Cook, *Hagarism, the Making of the Islamic World* (Cambridge, 1977), pp. 8–9, 160–1. There is some merit to the suggestion that the Greek term 'Magaritai' may be derived from the Arabic term *muhāǧirūn*. Cf. Henry and Renée Kahane, Die Magariten, *Zeitschrift für Romanische Philologie*, *76* (1960), pp. 185–204. As for the verbal form *ahgar*, *mahgar* in Syriac, if it is to be related to the Muslim Arabic *haǧara*, *hiǧrah*, and not to the biblical Hagar, one suspects that the relationship should not be to Muḥammad's Meccan *muhāǧirūn* and their descendants. Rather, the reference should be to the *hiǧrah* itself. On this hypothesis, the verb *ahgar* in Syriac would mean 'to become a Muslim,' because the subject of the verb would be said to be joining the *hiǧrah*, i.e., leaving his own ancestral religion to join Muḥammad's company. Perhaps the Syrians would have utilized the Muslim Arabic expression in this fashion, having taken note of the Muslim habit of numbering the years by the *hiǧrah* of the prophet. That such a habit obtained already in the seventh century is attested to by the colophon to the Syriac. New Testament quoted above, which speaks of the 'year 63 according to the *Mahgerāyê*.' Cf. n. 1 above. Such an under standing would also make better sense of the expression, *namôsâ demahgrâ*, that appears in the letter describing patriarch John's interview with the *emir*. Cf. Nau, art. cit., p. 252. The phrase, which is awkward in the singular, would then mean not 'the law of the Hagarene,' but 'the law of the *Hiǧrah*,' or of 'one who follows or joins the *hiǧrah*'. The problem with this suggestion, of course, is that it is speculative, and it lacks documentary evidence, whereas the parallel, *mahgerāyê* ὁι ἀγαρήνοι, is well attested.

significance of Islam. John Damascene, for one, was very explicit about his intentions, in chapter 101 of his *De heresibus.* Having explained to his own satisfaction, why the Arabs are called Ishmaelites and Hagarenes, from an etymological point of view, he goes on to declare that it is to these people that Muḥammad gave as their religion, a 'heresy,' of his own making, after having come into contact with the Old and New Testaments, presumably as expounded by an Arian monk, according to John's theological judgment. Accordingly, in the Damascene's view, Islam is what he calls the 'currently prevailing, deceptive superstition of the Ishmaelites, the precursor of the Antichrist.'[1] This judgment is already compatible with his use of such epithets as 'sons of Ishmael', or 'sons of Hagar' to designate Muslims. For, as one learns from Nicetas Byzantinos, the point to insist upon with the Muslims is that already in the scriptures, Ishmael and Hagar are excluded from God's promise to Abraham.[2]

Finally, one may note that in the Syriac apologies the Muslims sometimes are called *Ṭayyāyê*, or even *sarqāyê.*[3] The former is an adjective derived from the name of a tribe of Arab nomads who had become friendly to Christianity even before the time of Islam. In its adjectival form, their name is a frequent term for Arab nomads in Syriac texts.[4] The term *sarqāyê*, on the other hand, seems to be related to the enigmatic Greek word for 'Arabs', viz. οἱ σαρακήνοι.[5]

There are very few doctrinal descriptions of Islam in the Syriac apologetic treatises from the first Abbasid century. Nonnus of Nisibis, as mentioned above, contents himself with some references to statements about Christ in the *Qur'ān.* But he quotes them out of context, and presents them as evidences of how closely Islam comes to what he regards as the truth about Christ. In fact, he says that the Muslims honor Christ so much that they will not accept it that he could have died by crucifixion.[6]

One may glean a very rudimentary description of some of the basic tenets of Islam from chapter ten of Theodore bar Kônî's

1. *PG*, vol. 94, cols. 764–5. Cf. Daniel J. Sahas, *John of Damascus on Islam, the 'Heresy of the Ishmaelites'* (Leiden, 1972), pp. 68–74.
2. *PG*, vol. 105, cols. 788–92. Cf. Khoury, *Les Théologiens byzantins, op. cit.*, pp. 159–60.
3. Cf., e.g., Gottheil, art. cit., *13*, (1898), p. 202.
4. Cf. Nau, art. cit., p. 251, and J. S. Trimingham, *Christianity Among the Arabs in Pre-Islamic Times* (London, 1979), p. 213.
5. Cf. Trimingham, *op. cit.*, pp. 213–4.
6. Van Roey, *op. cit.*, p. 12*.

Scholion. In the dialogue between the student and his master that Theodore presents there, the student repeats the objections of Muslims to those Christian doctrines and practices that were the standard topics of controversy between the two communities. Basically, of course, they amount to the charges that the doctrine of the Trinity compromises monotheism, and the doctrine of the Incarnation, both obscures the truth about Jesus, son of Mary, and attributes creaturely attributes to God. Theodore, on the other hand, suggests to his readers that Islam, the tradition (*mašlᵉmānûtâ*) that Muslims have inherited from their teacher, is essentially a mistaken doctrine (*malpanûtâ*) about the proper interpretation of the Torah and the Prophets.[1] This characterization of Islam is in contrast, of course, to Theodore's own presentation of Christianity and its four canonical Gospels, as the fulfillment of the promises of the Old Testament.

2. *The Arabic Treatises*.—Many of the Christian apologetic treatises in Arabic refer to the Islamic community very straightforwardly as *al-muslimūn*. 'Ammār al-Baṣrī, for example, does so regularly. Indeed, in the introduction to the *Kitāb al-masā'il wa l-aǧwibah* he dedicates his work to the *amīr al-mu'minīn*, whom, he says, God has empowered to investigate the allegations of those who disseminate erroneous religious opinions.[2] Unfortunately, however, the portion of 'Ammār's *Kitāb al-burhān* in which he may have ventured to give a brief sketch of the teachings of Islam, is missing from the manuscript in which his work is preserved.[3]

Theodore Abū Qurrah uses the terms *islām*, *muslimīn*, and the name Muḥammad, in only one place in all of his published Arabic works. They occur in the short paragraph in his general apology for Christianity, in which he described what he calls *dīn al-islām*, i.e., the Islamic religion. His description of the tenets of Islam is very summary. God has sent it, says Abū Qurrah, at the hands of his prophet, Muḥammad, who summons people to worship God alone and to associate nothing with him. Moreover, Abū Qurrah reports that Muḥammad encouraged good works and forbade what should be forbidden. The delights of heaven, the reward for doers of good works, are described with a tissue of quotations from the *Qur'ān*, depicting the

1. Cf. Griffith, Chapter Ten of the Scholion . . ., art. cit.
2. Cf. Hayek, *op. cit.*, pp. 93–5.
3. Cf. *Ibid.*, p. 31.

physical aspects of happiness there.[1] For the rest, however, Abū Qurrah's references to Islam are fairly oblique, except in those instances in which he quotes from the *Qur'ān*, or cites doctrinal formulations that are recognizably Islamic.

Among Abū Qurrah's circumlocutions for designating the Muslims are the following. He occasionally calls them 'people of faith' (*ahl al-'īmān*), or 'those who claim faith' (*man yadda'ī l-'īmān*).[2] One suspects that these expressions come from the *Qur'ān*'s description of Muslims as *al-mu'minūn*, a name also widely used in the early Muslim community.[3] Other expressions that Abū Qurrah employs to designate the Muslims, which also demonstrate his familiarity with the phraseology of the *Qur'ān*, are: 'those who claim to have a book sent down from God (*man yadda'ī 'anna biyadihi kitāban munzalan min Allāh*)', and, 'those who claim inspiration and communication from God (*man idda'ā al-waḥyā wa-r-risālata min Allāh*)'.[4] While these phrases reveal Abū Qurrah's familiarity with Muslim expressions, in their rhetorical context in his treatises they put the emphasis on the Muslim claim, and they do not suggest that Abū Qurrah thinks that the claim is legitimate.

Ḥabīb ibn Ḫidmah Abū Rā'iṭah several times refers to the Muslims as 'southerners' (i.e. *ahl at-tayman*).[5] With Abū Qurrah's usage in mind, one is initially tempted to amend Abū Rā'iṭah's text to read *ahl al-'īmān*. However, the reference actually seems to be to the *qiblah*, i.e., the direction to which Muslims turn when they pray, toward the *Ka'bah* in Mecca. There is some support for this suggestion in a latter west Syrian chronicle from the region of Edessa. It says that at their times of prayer, the Muslims perform their worship facing south.[6] Abū Rā'iṭah's location in Takrīt, in present day Iraq, would have put him in a position to observe the same phenomenon as did the author of the Syrian chronicle, i.e., Muslims facing south in prayer. In one of his letters, Jacob of Edessa (d. 708) explained this same matter, i.e., south as the direction of the *qiblah*.[7] So, in all

1. Cheikho, art. cit., *al-Machriq, 12* (1912), p. 770.
2. Cf. Bacha, 1904, *op. cit.*, p. 182; Arendzen, *op. cit.*, p. 7.
3. Cf. W. Montgomery Watt, The Conception of *īmān* in Islamic Theology, *Der Islam, 43* (1967), pp. 1–10; Frederick M. Denny, Some Religio-Communal Terms and Concepts in the *Qur'ān*, *Numen, 24* (1977), pp. 26–59.
4. Arendzen, *op. cit.*, p. 1, and Bacha, 1904, *op. cit.*, p. 9.
5. Graf, 1951, *op. cit.*, vol. 130, p. 1.
6. Cf. I.-B. Chabot (ed.), *Anonymi Auctoris Chronicon ad Annum Christi 1234 Pertinens* (*CSCO*, vol. 81; Paris, 1920), p. 230.
7. Cf. the passage quoted *in* Wm. Wright's, *Catalogue of the Syraic MSS*, *op. cit.*, vol. II, p. 604.

likelihood, Abū Rā'iṭah's designation of Muslims as 'southerners' is simply a reference to their *qiblah*.

There is some play with the word *muslim* in several of the Arabic apologies. The author of the al-Hāšimī/al-Kindī correspondence, for example, attempts to find a contradiction in the *Qur'ān* by pointing to the text in *Āl 'Imrān* (3):67, where Abraham is said to be 'a *ḥanīf*, a *muslim*', and relating it to the passage in *al-An'ām* (6:14), where Muḥammad is commanded to say, 'I shall be the first of those who have submitted.' Therefore, says the apologist, Abraham can have no part with the Muslims, since, by his own admission, Muḥammad is the first of them.[1] Taking another tack, the author of the Abraham of Tiberias debate capitalizes on the distinction between 'submission' (*islām*) and 'belief' (*'īmān*). Citing *Āl 'Imrān* (3:83), according to which 'whoever is in heaven or earth, willingly or unwillingly has submitted (*aslama*)', he argues that therefore all creatures, good and bad, are *muslims*, according to the *Qur'ān*, and men and angels have no edge over devils or beasts on that account. Moreover, says this Christian apologist, the text in *al-Ḥuǧarāt* (49):14 clearly distinguishes *islām* from *īmān*, in that even Bediun Arabs may be said to have the former without the latter. Subsequently, the Muslim in the debate claims that *islām* and *īmān* are the same, while the Christian monk counters with another quotation from the *Qur'ān* to the contrary, viz., *Āl 'Imrān* (3:102), where, he mistakenly says, believers are encouraged to fear God without becoming Muslims.[2]

The Arabic version of the Christian Baḥīrā legend adds yet another twist to this theme. Here the author speaks of *muslim* as an abbreviated religious name which the prophet's tutor-monk gave to him for his people, by which the monk meant, our author says, *muslim al-masīḥī*, or 'Christ's Muslim'. And a few pages later he explains what he means by this expression, in connection with a comment on *al-Ḥuǧurāt* (49:14): 'The Arabs say, 'We believe.' Say: 'You do not believe'; rather say, 'We submit'; for belief has not entered your hearts.' About this passage from the *Qur'ān*, the tutor-monk is presented in the legend as explaining to Muḥammad: 'By this I meant that the genuine faith is faith in Christ, and *islām* (i.e., submission) is the *islām* of one of his disciples.'[3] In the whole work, of course, God's command to Muḥammad as recorded in the *Qur'ān*, e.g.,

1. Cf. TIEN, *op. cit.*, pp. 46–7.
2. Cf. VOLLERS, art. cit., pp. 46 and 70.
3. GOTTHEIL, art. cit., *15* (1900), pp. 74 and 79.

'say', as in this verse from *al-Ḥuǧurāt*, is presented as the command of the tutor-monk. Submission consequently, comes to be seen as the only option within the power of the 'Sons of Ishmael', in contradistinction to the faith potential of the Christians.

Of all of the Christian Arabic apologies that have survived from the first Abbasid century, the longest description of Islam is in the al-Hāšimī/al-Kindī correspondence. It is the principal subject matter of the comparatively brief, first letter in the exchange, presented as the work of the Muslim correspondent.[1] However, as we shall see, it is quite clear that only a Nestorian Christian could have written this letter. Basically, in its essential outline, it is akin to the account of Islam that Abū Qurrah presented in his general apology for Christianity, with the difference that the author of the al-Hāšimī/al-Kindī correspondence provides a broad array of descriptive material, including liberal quotations from the *Qur'ān*, of the sort that play directly into the hands of the Christian apologists and polemicists. In fact, the al-Hāšimī letter is virtually a mere table of contents for the refutations that are the subject matter of the much longer al-Kindī letter. The author of the al-Hāšimī letter shows no interest at all in the topics that concern the authors of the few authentic Muslim apologies that we have from the first Abbasid century. It is undoubtedly, then, the work of the Christian author of the whole correspondence, and an integral part of his apology for Christianity.

There are three main sections in the al-Hāšimī letter. In the first of them, after the invocations and introductory remarks, the supposedly Muslim writer first of all situates Muḥammad in the sequence of prophets: Moses, Jesus, Muḥammad. This is in fact a standard Muslim proposition in the controversies of the first Abbasid century, which is found in a number of the treatises of the time that have survived.[2] In the present instance, the allegedly Muslim author moves quickly from this basic statement to a detailed account of his own knowledge of christianity, its scriptures and its usages, and he says that he learned much of it in debate (*munāẓarah*) with Timothy, the patriarch.[3] The Nestorians in general, he says, as opposed to Melkites and Jacobites, are the most respectable and intellectually acceptable of all the Christians. The Jacobites are the worst, according to

1. Cf. Tien, *op. cit.*, pp. 2–37.
2. Cf., e.g., the proposals of the caliph in his dialogue with Timothy, the patriarch, *in* Mingana, *op. cit.*, pp. 35 ff.
3. Tien, *op. cit.*, p. 7.

this writer's opinion.[1] Moreover, he goes on to argue at some length, that the Nestorians are the sort of Christians whose monks evangelized Muḥammad, and who even protected him from the Jews and the polytheists of the Quraysh, once the prophet's own revelations began to come down. For this reason, the writer alleges, Muḥammad offered the Christians the covenant of protection. All of this reminds the reader of no known Muslim account of the prophet's early experiences. And it is important to realize, as we shall see in more detail later, that the writer of the al-Hāšimī/al-Kindī correspondence was well acquainted with Muslim records of the life of the prophet and of the collection of the *Qur'ān*. The account in the al-Hāšimī letter does, however, bear a striking resemblance to the basic suggestions of the Christian Baḥīrā legend, according to which Muḥammad owed all of his acceptable religious insights to the care of a Christian monk.[2] Having made this point, the writer of the letter gives a fuller account of his knowledge of Christian usages, especially their liturgical calendar and daily *horarium* of prayer. Finally, in preparation for the main body of his letter, he sets forth some very equable and friendly rules for Christian/Muslim dialogue.

The main body of the al-Hāšimī letter is concerned with an exposition of the Muslim *šahādah* and the five pillars of Islam, with a concentration on *ǧihād*, and a statement of the basic Muslim objections to Christianity. By far the longest portion of this main body of the letter, however, amounting to almost half of the number of pages devoted to the whole letter in the 1885 Tien edition,[3] is taken up with a concrete description of the physical delights and appointments of paradise, and the agonies of Gehenna, along with the licenses enjoyed by true Muslims in this world—all composed in a *catena* of apt phrases and verses quoted from the *Qur'ān*.[4] Such an exposition plays straight into the hands of the Christian polemicists, who were in the habit of making much of precisely this aspect of the

1. *Ibid.*, p. 7: 'The Jacobites are the most unbelieving people, the most wicked in speech, and the worst in creed. They are the farthest from the truth, repeating the formulae of Cyril of Alexandria, Jacob Baradaeus, and Severus, the holder of the see of Antioch.' If authentic, this would certainly be a unique statement for a Muslim. The writer is clearly a Nestorian, as recognized by G. Graf, *GCAL*, vol. II, p. 143.

2. Cf. Gottheil, art. cit., and below, the discussion of the portrait of Muḥammad in the Christian apologies.

3. Tien, *op. cit.*, pp. 19–33.

4. Abū Qurrah weaves together a similar, but brief tissue of quotations from the *Qur'ān* to depict his idea of the Muslim paradise. Cf. Cheikho, art. cit., p. 770.

Islamic revelation, arguing that such a materialistic scenario is incompatible with true spiritual advancement, and inconceivable as an ingredient in a genuine, divine communication to men.[1] Moreover, such an exposition is never to be found in any known, contemporary Muslim commendation of Islam to Christians. Rather, these Muslim apologies, in addition to defending the legitimacy of Muḥammad's claim to prophethood, all concentrate on exposing what their authors consider to be the scriptural and conceptual inadequacies of the doctrines of the Trinity and the Incarnation, subjects which are only summarily and almost mutely dealt with in the al-Hāšimī letter, in two pages of the 1885 Tien edition, and then only with several well known quotations from the *Qur'ān*.[2] Clearly, therefore, this letter is the work of the Christian author of the whole correspondence. In fact, it merely offers the texts which this author exploits in the al-Kindī letter as prime exhibits of the insufficiency of Islam.

The third section of the al-Hāšimī letter contains a short, final recommendation of Islam, and a renewed assurance of the freedom within which Christian/Muslim dialogue might be conducted. With the contents of the al-Kindī letter in mind, one recognizes a certain wistfulness in the words of the author in the closing remarks of the al-Hāšimī *persona* to his Christian correspondent. He says:

> Argue then, God give you health, with whatever you wish, and speak however, you wish, say what you want. Expatiate on everything that in your opinion will bring you to a stronger argument. You are in the most abundant safety. But you owe it to us, God prosper you, since we have given you maximum freedom, and we have accorded your tongue a wide range, that you set up between you and us a just arbiter, that does no wrong, and that does not deal unjustly in verdict or decision, and that will not incline to anything other than the truth, whenever a change of the wind blows. Indeed, it is reason *(al-'aql)*, to which God himself adheres, be He respected and praised, and which he bestows.[3]

Such pleading is completely out of step with the confident tone of the Muslim, anti-Christian polemicists, such as 'Alī ibn

1. Cf. Vollers, art. cit., pp. 46–7, and also the Greek polemicists as described in Khoury, *op. cit.*, 1972, pp. 300–14. At least one Muslim apologist countered this charge by pointing to a similar materialism in Gospel accounts of the kingdom. Cf. Sourdel, art. cit., p. 31.
2. Tien, *op. cit.*, pp. 33–4.
3. *Ibid.*, pp. 36–7.

Rabbān aṭ-Ṭabarī, with his 'silencing questions', al-Qāsim ibn Ibrāhīm, with his sure footed demonstrations, and the sharp tongued self-assurance of al-Ǧāḥiẓ.

B) *The Portrait of Muḥammad*

As one should expect, the portrait of Muḥammad that is transmitted in the Christian apologetic literature of the first Abbasid century is very sketchy. Details of his biography are mentioned only to the extent that they serve some purpose in the author's overall intention to discredit the religious claims of Islam, where these claims are in opposition to the teachings of Christianity. The Christian authors of apologetic treatises in Syriac and Arabic were forthright in their rejection of Muslim claims that Muḥammad was in receipt of a revelation from God, that he was the Paraclete announced in the Gospel, or even that he should be considered a genuine prophet. That they were so open and clear in their disavowal of these Muslim tenets should not cause surprise. Muslims were well aware of the fact that Christians did not accept these things. It is true that the debate setting of some of the treatises, such as that of Abraham of Tiberias, or the al-Hāšimī/al-Kindī correspondence, fostered a certain aggressiveness in diction that Muslims must find offensive. Indeed, it may have been precisely such tracts as these, and such debates and discussions which were their occasions, or at least their inspirations, that elicited the stinging rebuke of al-Ǧāḥiẓ, to which we referred above, and that eventually led to the oppressive measures inaugurated at the end of the first Abbasid century by the caliph, al-Mutawakkil.

There was personal contact between Muslims and Christians within *dār al-Islām*. Christians were familiar with the *Qūr'an*, and with Muslim traditions. While they were the adversaries of the Muslims in the religious controversies, there was none of the personal isolation, at least in the first Abbasid century, of the sort that must have been a factor in provoking so many of the hostile fantasies that are found in the polemical works of Christians in other lands, who wrote in Greek or Latin, often depicting Muḥammad as demon possessed, an agent of the anti-Christ, or as personally morally depraved.[1] In the Syriac and

1. Cf. the works of Khoury cited above, and Norman Daniel, *Islam and the West, the Making of an Image* (Edinburgh, 1960); id., *The Arabs and Mediaeval Europe* (London, 1975); R. W. Southern, *Western Views of Islam in the Middle Ages* (Cambridge, Mass., 1962).

Arabic treatises, Muḥammad himself is a subject of discussion only to the degree that the authors refer to the facts of his life in an attempt to discredit the religious beliefs about him that the Muslims propound.

1. *Biographical Details.* — The Christian apologists mention the biographical details of Muḥammad's life in order to argue that he is not a prophet in the biblical sense of the term. In the first place they mention the facts of his early career so as to be able to argue that his religious vocation was part of a broader attempt on his part to gain power and preeminence among his own people. Secondly, they cite his encounter with a Christian monk in order to suggest that even his religious message is not original with himself, and that it does not come from God. Rather, they claim, Muḥammad owed what the apologists considered to be his errant religious views to the personal influence of a Christian monk.

Not all of the apologists explicitly mention any details of Muḥammad's biography. They are found only in the more popular, and more polemic, works, such as the al-Hāšimī/al-Kindī correspondence, and in the account of Abraham of Tiberias' debate before the Muslim emir in Jerusalem, and, in the instance of Muḥammad's encounter with the Christian monk, in the Christian Baḥīrā legends. For the rest, the more theologically inclined apologists concentrate on a discussion of the motives of credibility that should inform a person's acceptance of anyone who claims to have a revelation from God. In this way, it is quite clear, they intend to reject Muḥammad's claims to prophecy.

Abraham of Tiberias brings up Muḥammad's family history as an argument against the Muslim claim that Muḥammad is the Paraclete whose coming Jesus foretold in John's Gospel. His human genealogy, Abraham contends, precludes the possibility that he could be the heavenly paraclete that is described in the Gospel as the spirit of God. Muḥammad, Abraham says, 'is the son of 'Abdallāh ibn 'Abd al-Muṭṭalib, and his mother is Amīnah, the daughter of Wahb ibn 'Abd Manāf. He was born six hundred years after Christ and his ascension to Heaven'.[1]

Abraham's report is a straight forward statement of Muḥammad's family connections. Matters are not quite so simple in the much longer accounts of the author of the al-Hāšimī/al-Kindī

1. **Vollers, art. cit., p. 66.**

correspondence. Right from the beginning this author's controversial intentions are clear. He writes about the life of Muḥammad, and of the events in which the prophet was involved, with the avowed intention of demonstrating that his very biography is a testimony against the legitimacy of his claim to prophethood. From passages in the *Qur'ān*, and reports that can actually be found in the Muslim traditions and biographies of Muḥammad, the author of the al-Kindī letter takes the information to provide a personality profile of the prophet that, in the Christian apologetic context, negates his prophetic claims. Of all the Christian apologies in Syriac and Arabic this one comes closest to the disdainful spirit of the Greek and Latin polemical treatises. In this respect, it is unique among the treatises composed within *dār al-islām*, and a far cry from the respectful tones of such writers as Ḥabīb ibn Ḫidmah Abū Rā'iṭah, from whom the writer of the al-Kindī letter has actually quoted at length, as mentioned above.

The al-Kindī character frequently refers to Muḥammad in his letter to al-Hāšimī as 'your master (*ṣāḥibuka*)', and he never calls him by any title of a positive religious significance. His manner of dealing with the biography of the prophet may be made evident most quickly by quoting a rather long passage, in which his characteristic style is plain. He has his bare facts in order, but his interpretation of them paints a portrait of Muḥammad that is far from flattering.

This man was an orphan in the care of his paternal uncle, 'Abd Manāf, known as Abū Ṭālib, who had taken over his support at the death of his father. He used to provide for him and protect him. And he used to worship the idols, Allāt and al-'Uzzā, along with his uncle's people, and the people of his family in Mecca. . . . Then he grew up in that situation until he came into the service of the caravan that belonged to Ḥadīğah bint Ḫuwaylid. He worked for his wages at it, going back and forth to Syria, etc., up until what came about of his affairs and Ḥadīğah's, and his marriage to her for reasons that you will recognise. Then, when she had emboldened him with her wealth, his soul challenged him to lay claim to dominion and headship over his own clan and the people of his country. . . . And when he despaired of that to which his soul enticed him, he claimed prophethood, and that he was a messenger sent from the Lord of the worlds. . . . This was due to the instruction of the man who dictated to him, whose name and history we shall mention in another place in our book. . . . Then he took as his companions idle people, raider comrades, who used to attack the highway, according to the custom of the country and the practice of its people that is current among them even until now. This sort rallied to him. . . . He came with his companions to al-Madīnah. It was then a ruinous waste, in which there were only weak people, most of them Jews, in whom there was no liveliness. The first thing relating to justice, or the exhibiting of the legitimacy of prophethood and its signs, that his rule initiated there, was that he took over the drying floor that belonged to two orphan youths of the Banū n-Naǧǧār, and made it into a mosque.[1]

Much has been left out in this translation of al-Kindī's account of Muḥammad's early life and prophetic call. But enough is quoted to enable the reader to catch the drift of the apologist's polemical tone. From this point, he goes on to contrast Muḥammad's militarily unsuccessful early campaigns against the Meccan caravans, with the successful battles of biblical characters such as Joshua bar Nūn. Along the way he manages to paint Muḥammad in the colors of a brigand. Then the writer turns to Muḥammad's personal life. He makes his point quite bluntly.

We say in regard to this master of yours, that his actions are contrary to your statement that he has been sent to all humankind with mercy and compassion. Indeed, he was a man who had no care or concern except for a beautiful woman with whom he might be paired, or for a people whose blood he was zealous to shed, to take their wealth, and to marry their women.[2]

From here the writer goes on to speak with disapproval of Muḥammad's marriages, and of his wives, lingering over the account of 'Ā'išah's misadventure with Ṣafwān ibn al-Mu'aṭṭal as-Sulamī. Always the issue is that in the view of the writer, Muḥammad's conduct is unworthy of a genuine prophet.

Another incident in Muḥammad's biography that attracts several of the Christian apologists is the story of his encounter with the Christian monk, whose name is Baḥīrā in Muslim sources, and Sergius or Nestorius in Christian sources. According to the Muslim story, while on a trip to Syria with his uncle, Abū Ṭālib, Muḥammad met the monk at Buṣrā. Relying on the description of the future prophet which he found in his sacred books, the monk is said to have recognized 'the seal of prophethood between his shoulders in the very place described in

1. Tien, *op. cit.*, pp. 68–71. Muir thought that the report of the orphans' plot of land was simply an error on the author's part. Cf. Muir, *The Apology of al-Kindi*, *op. cit.*, p. 44, n. 1. But the author knew his Ibn Isḥāq. Cf. Guillaume, *op. cit.*, *in* n. 1, p. 134 below, p. 228.

2. *Ibid.*, p. 81.

his book'.[1] With an account such as this, as Armand Abel has explained, ‚both at the end of the 2nd/8th century and in the first part of the 3rd/9th century, the tradition, as it then stood, concurred in recognizing in the monk Baḥīrā, the witness, chosen at the heart of the most important scriptural religion, of the authenticity of the Prophet's mission'.[2] An important element in this tradition, that was not lost on the Christian apologists, as we shall see, is the advice the monk gives to Abū Ṭālib. According to Ibn Isḥāq, the monk said, 'Take your nephew back to his country and guard him carefully against the Jews, for by Allāh! if they see him and know about him what I know, they will do him evil.'[3]

The author of the al-Kindī letter presents a version of the story of Muḥammad's meeting with a Christian monk that has as its purpose the rejection of the idea that Muḥammad received revelations from God.[4] In this version the monk's name is given as Sergius. He is said to have met Muḥammad in Mecca, after having been banished from his own Christian people for some unspecified innovation; probably of a doctrinal nature. He repented of his error, however, as the story goes, and when he met Muḥammad he is said to have introduced himself to the future prophet under the name Nestorius, for purposes of affirming Nestorius' doctrinal point of view. We have already noticed above the author's intention to commend the Nestorians to the Muslims, in that the al-Hāšimī character finds the Nestorians to be the most acceptable Christians, approved already in the *Qur'ān*. The reference, of course, is to the passage in *al-Mā'idah* (5):82, according to which the friendliest people to the Muslims are those who call themselves Christians, 'among whom there are elders and monks'. The al-Kindī letter says that Muḥammad's meeting with Sergius/Nestorius is responsible for this verse, and for much else that is in the *Qur'ān* that accords with Christianity. Before, Muḥammad himself could actually become a Nestorian, however, according to the author of the al-Kindī letter, the monk died and his teaching was distorted by two learned Jews, 'Abd Allāh ibn Salām and Ka'b al-Aḥbar. Their influence, al-Kindī says, led ultimately to the errors one

1. A. Guillaume, *The Life of Muḥammad; a Translation of Isḥāq's Sīrat Rasūl Allāh* (Oxford, 1955), p. 80; F. Wüstenfeld, *Das Leben Muḥammad's nach Muḥammad Ibn Ishâk* (2 vols.; Göttingen, 1858), vol. I, pt. 1, pp. 115–7.
2. Armand Abel, Baḥīrā, *EI*², vol. I, p. 922.
3. Guillaume, *op. cit.*, p. 81; Wüstenfeld, *op. cit.*, vol. I, pt. 1, pp. 116–7.
4. Tien, *op. cit.*, pp. 128–9.

currently finds in the *Qur'ān*. According to Ibn Isḥaq's report, 'Abd Allāh ibn Salām, is remembered in Islamic traditions as a learned Jew of Medina who early on converted to Islam.[1] Ka'b, on the other hand, was a Yementie Jew who actually converted to Islam only after the death of Muḥammad.[2]

The story of Muḥammad's encounter with the monk also appears in the Christian apocalypses in Syriac and Arabic that first appeared in the first Abbasid century.[3] As they have come down to us, there are two Syriac versions of the apocalypse, and one in Arabic. While the major outlines of these versions are similar, they differ considerably in detail. Ironically, it is in the Syriac versions that the monk's story retains the most resemblance to the Muslim traditions about Baḥīrā. In all of the versions, however, the story is told by a traveling monk who is said to have met Baḥīrā in the latter's old age, as he is on the point of death. He recounts his apocalyptic vision of Muslim history to the visitor, including the story of his encounter with Muḥammad, and the young prophet's acceptance of his teaching. The account of the vision, apart from the elements of the Baḥīrā story, is in the apocalyptic tradition common to Christians and Jews at the time.[4] But it is the Baḥīrā story itself that is pertinent here.

In the Syriac versions (A&B) the monk's name is Sargīs (i.e., Sergius). But the writers know his Muslim name, and at one point in version A the author says, 'by the Hagar[enes] he was called *Beḥîrâ* and a prophet'.[5] And thereafter in his narrative he often refers to the monk by both names, i.e., *Sargīs Beḥîrâ*. The monk spent many years in the Ishmaelite territory, the texts say, because he was exiled from Bêt Armāyê on account of his opposition to the veneration of more than one simple cross in a church at any given time. The narrator of the story

1. Cf. Guillaume, *op. cit.*, pp. 240–1; Wüstenfeld, *op. cit.*, vol. I pt. 1, pp. 353–4.
2. Cf. M. Schmitz, Ka'b al-Aḥbār, *EI²*, vol. IV, pp. 316–7. Since Ka'b al-Aḥbār became a Muslim only after the death of Muḥammad, one is tempted here to think of Ubay b. Ka'b, one of the Anṣār, who was the prophet's secretary in Medina. Cf. Jeffrery, *Materials . . .*, p. 114.
3. For the text cf. Gottheil, art. cit. Regarding the dating, cf. the articles of Abel cited in p. 109, n. 1 above, and Graf's reservations in *GCAL*, *op. cit.*, vol. II, pp. 145–9. Graf is swayed by comparisons between the al-Kindi letter and the text in Gottheil. However now that we know of the extensive Christian scholarship in the first Abbasid century, it is not necessary to postulate the dependence of one work on another. There is no reason why one should not conclude that different writers dealt differently with similar themes, even within the same period.
4. Cf. p. 109, n. 2 above.
5. Gottheil, art. cit., *13* (1898), p. 203.

in version A, a monk named Īšo'yahb, says that he himself learned of Sargīs Beḥîrâ's first encounter with Muḥammad, from one of his early disciples, a man named Ḥakīm. Then the story picks up elements that are central to the Muslim version, as recounted by Ibn Isḥāq.[1] For Sargīs Beḥîrâ is said to have lived by a well where Arabs often stopped on their travels. One day, the story goes, he saw some Arabs coming in the distance, '—also Mohammed the youth who was coming with them. As soon as Sargis saw the youth Mohammed, he understood that the youth would become a great man; because he saw a vision above his head, the likeness of a cloud'.[2] The narrator goes on to say that since the Arabs left Muḥammad outside when they went in to visit the monk, 'then Sargis said to the Saracens (*sarqāyê*), a great man has come with you; let him enter! They answered, we have with us a boy, an orphan; he is silent and uncouth'.[3] Thereupon, of course, Muḥammad enters and the monk predicts his coming power, making no reference to prophethood, as should be expected in this Christian text. Following this incident in both Syriac versions, the accounts go on to describe Muḥammad's series of interviews with the monk, in which he learns the religious opinions of Sargis and accepts them. The purpose of these narratives, of course, is to designate Sargis, and not God, as the source of Muḥammad's preaching, and the real author of the *Qur'ān*. The writer of version A is quite explicit on this point. He says of Sargis Beḥîrâ: 'He taught the Ishmaelites and became a chief for them, because he prophesied to them the things they liked, he wrote and handed over (*'ašlem*) to them this scripture that they call *Qur'ān*.'[4]

It is in connection with the *Qur'ān* that the Syriac versions bring up the Jewish scribe (*sāprâ*), who, says the author of version B, 'confused and distorted everything that Sargīs said'.[5] This scribe is variously called 'Kaleb', 'Ka'f', 'Ka'b', 'Kālef', and 'Kāteb'. In all probability he is the same Ka'b al-Aḥbār mentioned by the author of the al-Kindī letter, to whom we referred above. Perhaps the Christian writer was aware of the accusation voiced by some Muslims, that Ka'b had introduced Jewish elements into Islam.[6] Whatever may be the truth of

1. Cf. GUILLAUME, *op. cit.*, pp. 79–81; WÜSTENFELD, *op. cit.*, vol. I, pt. 1, pp. 115–7.
2. GOTTHEIL, art. cit., *13* (1898), pp. 216 and 14 (1899), p. 216.
3. *Ibid.*, p. 216 and p. 217.
4. *Ibid.*, pp. 212 and 214.
5. *Ibid.*, pp. 240 and 250.
6. Cf. SCHMITZ, art. cit., p. 317.

this suggestion, it is clear that the point of the story for the Syriac writers is that Islam, religiously speaking, amounts to Judaism. The Christian Baḥīrā legend in Syriac closes on this note. The author says of the Muslims: 'Everything to which they adhere is from the doctrine of Ka'b. Sargīs handed over to them the New Testament, and Ka'b the Old Testament.'[1]

The Christian Baḥīrā legend in Arabic is a long confession of guilt on the part of the monk, who is called Baḥīrā here and not Sergius. He makes his confession to a young monk, Murhib, who comes to visit him when he is close to death.[2] The apocalyptic vision is recounted, as is the story of Muḥammad's meeting Baḥīrā. But none of the elements of Ibn Isḥāq's account of the meeting is to be found in the Christian Arabic version of the story, unless it would be the monk's obvious antipathy to the Jews. Rather, in the Christian Arabic version, Muḥammad appears in princely style at Baḥīrā's cell. He is the leader of his band of Arabs. He comes back many times to learn the monk's doctrines. The monk ultimately takes the responsibility for the very wording of many passages in the *Qur'ān*, explaining at each step the real Christian meanings that he intended to communicate, as it were subliminally, under the obvious sense of the text. He places an emphasis on what he considers to be the intellectual and moral disabilities of the Arabs, Muḥammad included. It is clearly the apologetic and polemic intent of the author, not only to prove that Muḥammad is not a prophet, but to suggest that Islam comes from a disgraced Christian monk, to whom the Muslims themselves refer in their traditions of the prophet.

2. *Muḥammad the Paraclete.*—The Syriac versions of the Christian Baḥīrā legends maintain that one of the changes introduced into the *Qur'ān* by Ka'b, the Jewish scribe, after the death of Sargīs Beḥīrā, is the notion that Muḥammad is the paraclete whom Jesus promised to send after going to hisf ather. The author of the Syriac version A puts the charge against Ka'b as follows:

> He changed whatever Sargīs wrote or taught, and he said to them that what he [i.e., Sargīs] had said to them about Christ, the son of Mary, viz., 'I shall go and I shall send to you the Paraclete', this one is Muḥammad.[3]

1. Gottheil, art. cit., *13* (1898), pp. 241–2; *14* (1899), p. 251.
2. Gottheil, art. cit., *15* (1900), pp. 56–102; *17* (1903), pp. 125–66.
3. Gottheil, art. cit., *13* (1898), p. 213; *14* (1899), p. 214.

The reference here is to St. John's Gospel, probably, more specifically, to John 16:7. And, from the Muslim side, in Ibn Isḥāq's biography of the prophet, there is a long quotation from John 15:23–16:2 to the same effect.[1] That is to say, Ibn Isḥāq claims that these verses refer to Muḥammad. The Gospel version from which Ibn Isḥāq's Arabic translation was made was undoubtedly the one that is represented in the Palestinian Syriac Lectionary. The evidence for this conclusion is, among other things, that Ibn Isḥāq's Arabic simply transliterates the Syriac term, *m*ᵉ*naḥḥ*ᵉ*mānâ*, which is a unique rendering among Syriac Gospel versions for the original Greek term, ὁ παράκλητος.[2] Ibn Isḥāq goes on to explain: 'The *Munaḥḥemanâ* (God bless and preserve him!) in Syriac is Muḥammad; in Greek he is the paraclete.'[3]

At this remove, it is difficult to understand how the term 'paraclete' came to be identified with Muḥammad. There is of course the passage in the *Qur'ān* to the effect that Jesus, son of Mary, spoke to the Israelites announcing 'a messenger who will come from me, whose name is Aḥmad' (*aṣ-Ṣaff* (61:6)). And so, on the strength of this statement, Muslims would have been searching the Gospels to find the announcement. Some modern interpreters have suggested that on the basis of the meaning of the name, Aḥmad, taken as a *Beiform* for Muḥammad, a connection with ὁ παράκλητος was made via a confusion with the Greek word ὁ περικλυτός, 'highly-esteemed'. This, however, seems to be an unlikely solution, since the term *aḥmad* was probably not a proper name at the time of the *Qur'ān*.[4] Rather, the *Qur'ān* phrase, in all likelihood, originally meant, 'whose name is praiseworthy', understanding *aḥmad* as an elative adjective. Later, of course, when the adjective was definitely used as a personal name, the *Qur'ān* phrase was understood accordingly.[5] But only a Muslim with a very good knowledge of Greek could have made the identification of Paraclete with Muḥammad on the basis of a confusion of Greek words. Taking his clue from

1. Cf. GUILLAUME, *op. cit.*, pp. 103–4; WÜSTENFELD, *op. cit.*, vol. I, pt. 1, pp. 149–50.
2. Cf. Anton BAUMSTARK, Eine altarabische Evangelienübersetzung aus dem Christlich-Palastinenischen, *Zeitschrift für Semitistik und verwandte Gebiete, 8* (1932), pp. 201–9; A. GUILLAUME, The Version of the Gospels Used in Medina c. A. D. 700, *Al-Andalus, 15* (1950), pp. 289–96.
3. GUILLAUME, *op. cit.*, p. 105; WÜSTENFELD, *op. cit.*, vol. I., pt. 1, p. 50.
4. Cf. W. MONTGOMERY WATT, His Name is Aḥmad, *Muslim World, 34* (1953), pp. 110–7.
5. Cf. Rudi PARET, *Der Koran, Kommentar und Konkordanz* (2nd ed.; Stuttgart, 1977), p. 476.

the passage we have quoted from Ibn Isḥāq, Joseph Schacht suggested that the identification was based simply on the assonance between the Palestinian Syriac word, *m^e^naḥḥ^e^mānâ* and the Arabic name, Muḥammad.[1] But this suggestion does not seem very convincing either. Perhaps the straightforward explanation is the best one. The *Qur'ān* says that Jesus foretold the coming of a messenger (cf. also *al-A'rāf* (7):157). The only person whose coming Jesus foretells in the Gospel is the Paraclete. Therefore, the paraclete must be Muḥammad.

Naturally, the Christian apologists of the first Abbasid century simply denied that the Paraclete could be Muḥammad, or that there is any other mention of Muḥammad in either the Gospels, or the Torah, or the books of the prophets. This was already a topic in the Muslim/Christian controversies in the time of Patriarch Timothy. In the report of his debate before the caliph al-Mahdī, the patriarch goes so far as to say:

> To tell the truth, if I had found in the Gospel a prophecy concerning the coming of Muḥammad, I would have left the Gospel for the Ḳur'ān, as I have left the Torah and the Prophets for the Gospel.[2]

Regarding the identity of the Paraclete, Timothy argues that it is the spirit of God, even God himself, and therefore, it can in no way be identified with Muḥammad. To this argument the caliph answers with the charge that the Christians are guilty of the alteration (*at-taḥrīf*) of the text of the scriptures, not only the Gospel, but also the Old Testament passages which Muslims take to refer to Muḥammad, e.g., Isaiah's vision of 'men mounted on donkeys, and men mounted on camels' (Isaiah 21:7). The caliph contends, 'The rider on the ass is Jesus and the rider on the camel is Muḥammad.' But Timothy won't allow any such interpretation, on the grounds that only the Medes and the Elamites are explicitly mentioned in the text.[3]

As for the Paraclete, and the Christian contention that the name can in no way refer to Muḥammad, the Muslim who debated with Abraham of Tiberias retorts that, 'After Christ's ascension into heaven, John and his associates revised the Gospel, as they wished, and they set down what is in your possession. So has our prophet handed it down.'[4] Here the

1. Cf. J. Schacht, Aḥmad, *EI*², vol. I, p. 267.
2. Mingana, art. cit., p. 36. Cf. also the Arabic version *in* Putman, *op. cit.*, p. 26 of the Arabic text.
3. Mingana, art. cit., pp. 32–9; Putman, *op. cit.*, pp. 21–31.
4. Vollers, art. cit., p. 62.

speaker is referring to the charge in the *Qur'ān*, which actually concerns the Jews, that 'they have perverted the words from their meanings' (*an-Nisā'* 4:46). Other works of the first Abbasid century also testify that Muslim scholars of the period pressed the charge of *at-taḥrīf* against the Christian apologists. In Theodore bar Kônî's anti-Muslim tract, for example, the student/Muslim has the following to say, transferring the charge from Jews to Christians, and citing the authority of his teacher, i.e., Muḥammad. He says.

> I adhere to all that is in the books of the Old Testament because I know that there is no addition or deletion in them, according to the saying of the one who has delivered this teaching to us. But in regard to what is written in the New Testament, I do not adhere to all of it, because there are many things in it that are falsified. He (i.e., Christ) did not bring them. Others have introduced and intermingled them for the purpose of deception.[1]

Other Christian apologists of the period also devote portions of their works to refuting the charge of *at-taḥrīf*.[2] The importance of bringing the matter up in the present connection is the evidence it brings to our attention of how much the Muslim/Christian controversies of the first Abbasid century were centered on the scriptures—in the works of both parties. For example, in regard to the Paraclete/Muḥammad identification, the Muslim apologist, 'Alī ibn Rabbān aṭ-Ṭabarī, argues at some length in favor of the Muslim interpretation of the Johannine passages in question, in the process refuting the usual Christian objections to the identification, and in particular Timothy's claim that the Paraclete is God's consubstantial Spirit. Aṭ-Ṭabarī, on the basis of further scriptural and *Qur'ānic* references, goes on to interpret the Spirit of God/Paraclete identification in a manner acceptable to Muslims.[3]

3. *Muḥammad and Miracles.*—Running like a refrain through all of the Christian apologies of the first Abbasid century is the contention that miraculous signs, worked by the prophets in the name of God, or by Jesus in his own name, are the only sufficiently reasonable warranty for accepting Christianity, or,

1. Scher, *op. cit.*, vol. 69, p. 235.
2. Cf., e.g., the arguments of 'Ammār al-Baṣrī, in his *Kitāb al-burhān*, Hayek, *op. cit.*, pp. 41–6.
3. Cf. Mingana, *The Book of Religion and Empire* (Manchester, 1923), pp. 118–24 (Arabic text).

indeed, any scripture, anyone claiming divine inspiration, or any body of religious doctrine. The reason for this insistence is the notable lack of personal miracles ascribed to Muḥammad, along with the *Qur'ān*'s rejection of miracles as a criterion for religious credibility. 'Ammār al-Baṣrī, for example, cites *al-An'ām* (6:109) to this effect. The verse says:

> They have sworn by God the most earnest oaths if a sign comes to them they will believe in it. Say: 'Signs are only with God.' What will make you realize that, when it comes, they will not believe? (Arberry).

'Ammār, claiming to be following an interpretation of 'Abd Allāh ibn al-'Abbās, says that the rejection of miraculous signs recorded in this verse, came down to Muḥammad on the occasion of an oath sworn by Christians, Jews and polytheists, that if they should see such a sign worked at the hands of Muḥammad they would put their faith in him.[1] 'Ammār's point is that even on an occasion such as this, Muḥammad rejects the very notion of miraculous signs. Therefore, in 'Ammār's view, in principle, Islam and Muḥammad have no reasonable claim to credibility.

The Christians and Jews are not in fact explicitly mentioned in the passage that 'Ammār quotes from *al-An'ām*, nor can I find any such interpretation of the verse attributed to Ibn al-'Abbās in a Muslim source. Nevertheless, it is clear that 'Ammār is aware of the *Qur'ān*'s negative view of personal evidentiary miracles in Muḥammad's instance.

The author of the al-Kindī letter also knew of the *Qur'ān*'s rejection of personal evidentiary miracles. He cites *al-Isrā'* (17):59 to this effect, a verse to which 'Amāmr al-Baṣrī also refers, in the passage of his *Kitāb al-burhān* cited above.[2] But in the al-Kindī letter the author goes on to enumerate a number of miracles, which, he says, later Muslim traditions have attributed to Muḥammad. People have alleged, he maintains, against Muḥammad's wishes, that these extraordinary incidents attest to the genuineness of his prophetic role. In fact, the writer concludes, Muḥammad's claims were accepted only by force of arms.[3]

1. Cf. HAYEK, *op. cit.*, pp. 31–32.
2. Cf. TIEN, *op. cit.*, p. 102.
3. Cf. TIEN, pp. 103–9. At one point the author of the al-Kindī letter cites one, Muḥammad ibn Isḥāq az-Zuhrī as the source of his information about one of Muḥammad's miracles. Cf. *ibid.*, p. 108. It is the miracle in which the prophet puts his hand into an empty water vessel, and enough water flowed out for men and beasts to drink. In the first place, it looks as if the Christian author has given the author of the *sīrah* the *nisbah* of the traditionist, Muḥammad b. Muslim b. 'Ubayd Allāh b. Šihāb az-Zuhrī, from

It is clear that most Christian apologists of the first Abbasid century believed that people accepted Islam, and Muḥammad's status as a prophet, not because of evidentiary miracles, but because of a number of other motives that the apologists consider to be unworthy. Theodore Abū Qurrah, Ḥabîb ibn Ḫidmah Abū Rā'iṭah, 'Ammār al-Baṣrī, and Ḥunayn ibn Isḥāq all have lists of such motives, which they explain in greater or less detail. While no two of the lists are exactly the same, they are very similar. 'Ammār al-Baṣrī, for example, gives the following list in one place in his *Kitāb al-burhān*: 'tribal collusion' (*al-tawāṭu'*), 'the sword', 'wealth, dominion and power', 'ethnic bigotry' (*al-'aṣabiyyah*), 'personal preference', 'licentious laws', and 'sorcery'.[1] The method then is to argue that all religions other than Christianity are accepted for one or more of these unworthy reasons. Whereas Christianity, the arguments go, especially *vis à vis* Islam, is accepted only because of the divine testimony of the miracles of Christ, and of the apostles, in the name of Christ.

C. *The Estimation of the* Qur'ān

Doubtless because of the polemic pressure exerted by the Christian apologists, Muslim scholars late in the first Abbasid century, and thereafter, elaborated the argument that the *Qur'ān* is Islam's evidentiary miracle. The inspiration for this doctrine is, of course, already to be found in the *Qur'ān*, e.g., in *al-Isrā'* (17:88), *al-Baqarah* (2:23), and *al-Ḥašr* (59:21). The author of the al-Kindī letter cites these verses as what the Muslim apologists bring forward in support of their contention that the *Qur'ān* itself is their most compelling argument (*al-ḥuǧǧah al-bāliḡah*, cf. *al-An'ām* (6:149), in favor of the claim that Muḥammad was in receipt of divine revelations, the same as were Moses, the prophets, and Jesus Christ. By comparison with the earlier divine messengers, the author of the al-Kindī letter contends, 'Your master was an *ummī* man, who had no

whom Ibn Isḥāq actually quotes fairly often. Secondly, Ibn Isḥāq's version of the al-Ḥudaybiyah miracle, which is presumably the one at issue here, involves digging in a dry well with one of Muḥammad's arrows. Cf. Guillaume, *op. cit.*, pp. 500–1; Wüstenfeld, vol. I, pt. 2, p. 742. There were several versions of this miracle in Islamic tradition. Cf. the references *in* A. J. Wensinck, *A Handbook of Early Muhammadan Tradition* (Leiden, 1927), p. 102.

1. Cf. Hayek, *op. cit.*, p. 33. For a discussion of these lists, and their role in apologetic argument, cf. Sidney H. Griffith, Comparative Religion in the Apologetics of the First Christian Arabic Theologians, *Proceedings of the PMR Conference*, *4* (1979), pp. 63-87.

learning, and no knowledge of these reports. And had it not been communicated to him by inspiration, and prophesied to him, from where would he have learned it, to the point of setting it down and bringing it forth?'[1] He answers his own question. He claims that the Christian monk, Sergius, i.e., Sargis Baḥīrā, taught Muḥammad the *Qur'ān*, which was subsequently distorted, according to al-Kindī, by the two Jews, 'Abd Allāh ibn Salām and Ka'b al-Aḥbār.

From this point, the author of the al-Kindī letter launches himself into a long discussion of the history of the putting together, or the collection (*al-ğam'*), of the text of the *Qur'ān* into the form in which it presently exists. He mentions the details of the recensions of Abū Bakr and 'Uthman, and cites Muslim disagreements over particular verses, words, and phrases. All of this, in his view, is evidence that the *Qur'ān* cannot be considered a book of divine revelation. At the end he comes back to the Arabic language of the *Qur'ān*, i.e., the claim that no one can imitate it. He attacks its Arabic style, and argues that not only is it not an evidence of divine revelation, but it is not worthy of the best Arab poets.[2]

There is no space here to analyze the al-Kindī letter's account of the collection of the *Qur'ān*. Unfortunately, thus far little scholarly attention has been paid to this valuable ninth century discussion of such an important issue. Perhaps the polemical character of the text makes it suspect as an historical document. But the fact remains that it is one of the earliest testimonies to the process of the *Qur'ān*'s canonization.

An interesting phrase in the al-Kindī letter's discussion of the *Qur'ān* is the characterization of Muḥammad as a *rağulun ummiyyun*. The adjective *ummī* occurs also in the *Qur'ān* as a description of the prophet, in *al-A'rāf* (7):157 and 158. There has been an enormous amount of discussion about its precise meaning.[3] It is quite clear in the passage quoted above that for the Christian apologist it means that Muḥammad was untutored and had no knowledge of the Jewish and Christian scripture narratives. There is no explicit suggestion that illiteracy is implied in the meaning of the term, as later Muslim usage would have it. But neither is the sense of the word excluded by what the al-Kindī character has to say. And it is clear from other

1. Tien, *op. cit.*, p. 126.
2. Cf. Tien, *op. cit.*, pp. 126–48.
3. Cf. Paret, *op. cit.*, pp. 21–2.

sources that the meaning of the adjective had a role to play in the growth of the doctrine of the *Qur'ān* as Islam's evidentiary miracle. A recent study suggests that in Muslim commentaries on the *Qur'ān*, the idea that the adjective primarily means illiteracy came into prominence only in the first Abbasid century.[1] This development would not be surprising, given the fact that this is also the period in which the Christian apologetic pressure began to build within *dār al-islām*. Furthermore, it is now clear that the elaboration of the formal doctrine of *i'ǧāz al-qur'ān*, i.e., the miraculous inimitability of the language of the *Qur'ān*, owes something to the pressures exerted within the community by Christian polemics. While it may not have come into full flower among the Muslim *mutakallimūn* until the tenth century, the doctrine clearly has its roots in the works of the very Muslim scholars who were in controversy with the Christian apologists, with their insistence on evidentiary miracles, already in the first Abbasid century.[2] The nature of the Christian pressure is evident in the following exchange between the caliph al-Mahdī and patriarch Timothy:

> And our King said to me: 'Do you not believe that Our Book was given by God?'—And I replied to him: ?It is not my business to decide whether it is from God or not. But I will say something of which your majesty is well aware, and that is all the words of God found in the Torah and in the Prophets, and those of them found in the Gospel and in the writings of the Apostles, have been confirmed by signs and miracles; as to the words of your Book they have not been corroborated by a single sign or miracle. . . . Since signs and miracles are proofs of the will of God, the conclusion drawn from their absence in your Book is well known to your Majesty.'[3]

For the rest, the Christian apologists of the first Abbasid century quoted the *Qur'ān* abundantly in their arguments, and not always negatively. It is quite clear, that whether or not they refer to it by some such expression as, 'your scripture', they mean to use its words and phrases because they are immediately familiar to Muslims, and the apologists hope thereby to purchase

1. Cf. I. GOLDFELD, The Illiterate Prophet *(Nabī Ummī)*, an inquiry into the development of a dogma in Islamic tradition, *Der Islam, 57* (1980), pp. 58–67.
2. Cf. Richard C. MARTIN, The Role of the Basrah Mu'tazilah in Formulating the Doctrine of the Apologetic Miracle, *Journal of Near Eastern Studies, 39* (1980), pp. 175–89.
3. MINGANA, art. cit., pp. 36–7.

some persuasiveness for their arguments. The anonymous Arabic treatise on the Trinity from Mt. Sinai, for example, quotes the *Qur'ān* by name, albeit not always exactly, right along with the other testimonies of the divine plural from scripture, in support of the doctrine of the Trinity![1] It is no wonder, then, that the Muslim jurist aš-Šāfi'ī (d. 820) held that a copy of the *Qur'ān* may not be sold to a Christian, and that a will should be void which bequeaths a *Qur'ān* or a collection of traditions to a Christian.[2]

1. Cf. Gibson, *op. cit.*, p. 77 (Arabic text).
2. Cf. Tritton, *op. cit.*, p. 101; Fattal, *op. cit.*, pp. 148–9.

II

The Gospel in Arabic: An Inquiry into its Appearance in the First Abbasid Century

I. *Apologetics and the First Abbasid Century*

With the success of the Abbasid revolution, and its espousal of the principle of the social equality of all Muslim believers, conversion to Islam became an attractive option to large numbers of upwardly mobile Christians in the conquered territories[1]. Prior to that time many Jews, Christians and Muslims altogether seem to have thought of Islam as the religion of the conquering Arabs, which made no special appeal for conversion to the "scripture people" (*ahl al-kitāb*), who theoretically were to become "protected people" (*ahl adh-dhimmah*) in return for their payment of a special tax (*al-ǧizyah*), and the maintenance of a low social profile (*at-Tawbah* (9):29)[2]. It was Abbasid policy on the other hand, with roots stretching back to the programs of the Umayyad caliph ʿUmar II (717-720), actively to summon the subject populations to Islam, and to promise full political and social participation to converted Jews, Christians and Magians[3]. Accordingly, it was in response to these inducements to convert to Islam, during the first Abbasid century, that the first Christian apologetic treatises in Syriac and Arabic appeared, having controversy with Muslims as their primary concern. Between the years 750 and 850 controversialists such as Theodore bar Kônî, Nonnus of Nisibis, Theodore Abū Qurrah, Ḥabīb ibn Ḫidmah Abū Rā'iṭah and ʿAmmār al-Baṣrī produced the apologetic essays that set the agenda for years to come in the Christian/Muslim religious dialogue[4]. In large part

1 Cf. M.A. Shaban, *The Abbasid Revolution* (Cambridge, 1970), esp. p. 168.

2 Cf. Claude Cahen, "Note sur l'accueil des chrétiens d'orient a l'islam", *Revue de l'Histoire des Religions* 166 (1964), pp. 51-58; Armand Abel, "La djizya: tribute ou rançon?" *Studia Islamica* 32 (1970), pp. 5-19.

3 Daniel C. Dennett, *Conversion and the Poll Tax in Early Islam* (Cambridge, Mass., 1950). Cf. H.A.R. Gibb, "The Fiscal Rescript of ʿUmar II", *Arabica* 2 (1955), pp. 1-16.

4 Cf. Sidney H. Griffith, "The Prophet Muḥammad, His Scripture and His Message, According to the Christian Apologies in Arabic and Syriac from the First Abbasid Century", in *La vie du prophète Mahomet; un colloque, Université des Sciences Humaines de Strasbourg, 23-24 Octobre 1980* (Strasbourg, 1982), pp. 99-146.

their effort was simply to translate Christianity into Arabic, the *lingua franca* of the new body politic.

We have ample evidence that contemporary Muslim *mutakallimūn* such as Ḍirār b. ʿAmr, ʿĪsā b. Ṣubayḥ al-Murdār, and Abū l-Hudhayl al-ʿAllāf, were deeply involved in the ensuing controversy. These three early Muʿtazilites all wrote refutations of Christianity, the latter two addressing their treatises by name against Abū Qurrah and ʿAmmār al-Baṣrī respectively[5]. So annoying did the campaign to explain Christianity in Arabic become to many Muslims that al-Ǧāḥiẓ was led to complain in his *Refutation of Christians*:

> This community has not been so tried at the hands of the Jews, the Mağūs, or the Sabaeans, as it has been tried at the hands of the Christians ... And due to the trial, every Muslim thinks that he is a *mutakallim*, and that there is no one more entitled to argue with these deviants[6].

Perhaps it was in response to this Christian apologetic offensive in Arabic that, in some of the renditions of the "Covenant of Umar" dating from the first Abbasid century, we find among the conditions which the Christians should observe, the agreement that they would not use the language of the Muslims[7]. Under the caliph al-Mutawakkil (d. 861) this stipulation was at least theoretically strengthened to the point of prohibiting Christians even from teaching Arabic to their children[8].

It is natural to suppose that the translation of the Gospels and the other Christian scriptures into Arabic would have been an important part of the first Christian apologetic campaign in that language. After all, it is the *Qur'ān*'s injunction that says, "Let the people of the Gospel judge by what God has sent down it it" (*al-Mā'idah* (5):47). Accordingly, the Christian apologists did make the Gospel the focal point of their attempts to demonstrate the credibility of the Christian doctrines in Arabic[9]. So it is not surprising to discover that the earliest unambiguous documentary evidence for the translation of the Gospel into Arabic dates from this era.

The scope of the present inquiry is to highlight the circumstances which fostered the translation of the Gospels into Arabic, with reference both

5 Cf. Bayard Dodge, *The Fihrist of al-Nadīm* (2 vols.; New York, 1970), vol. I, pp. 386-389, 393-395, 415-417.
6 J. Finkel, *Three Essays of Abu ʿOthman ʿAmr ibn Baḥr al-Jaḥiẓ* (Cairo, 1926), pp. 19-20.
7 Cf. A.S. Tritton, *The Caliphs and their Non-Muslim Subjects; a Critical Study of the Covenant of ʿUmar* (London, 1930), p. 7.
8 Cf. Antoine Fattal, *Le statut légal des non-musulmans en pays d'islam* (Beyrouth, 1958),
9 Cf. Sidney H. Griffith, "Comparative Religion in the Apologetics of the First Christian Arabic Theologians", *Proceedings of the PMR Conference* 4 (1979), pp. 63-87.

to the liturgical and to the apologetical requirements of the Christian community. Within the Islamic context the inquiry necessarily involves the definition of the Gospel involved, as well as a discussion of the references to the Gospel in Christian and Muslim sources prior to the ninth century. Inevitably the question of the translation of the Gospel into Arabic prior to the rise of Islam presents itself. The hypothesis suggested by the results of the present inquiry is that prior to the ninth century, no texts of the Gospel in Arabic were available to either Muslims or Christians. They became available for the first time, for both liturgical and apologetical purposes, in the ninth century, in Palestine, under Melkite auspices. Any earlier versions which may have been made in Arabia prior to Islam have left only faint traces behind them, and were unknown to Christians in the conquered territories.

II. *The Gospel in Arabic*

A. What is the Gospel?

Following the usage of the *Qur'ān*, the ordinary Arabic word for 'Gospel' is *al-inğīl*. In all likelihood it derives from the Greek τὸ εὐαγγέλιον, through the possible influence of the Ethiopic word *wangēl*[10]. As such the term occurs some dozen times in the *Qur'ān*, to designate what God has sent down to Jesus for the guidance of the "Gospel people" (*ahl al-inğīl*). "We gave him the Gospel", God says, and "in it is guidance and light, and it is a confirmation of the Torah that was before it" (*al-Mā'idah* (5):46). As a matter of fact, according to the *Qur'ān*, the Torah, the Gospel, and the *Qur'ān* itself are on a par as God's announcements of His reliable promise (*at-Tawbah* (9):111). Jesus, to whom God gave the Gospel, is a messenger of God (*an-Nisā'* (4):171), the Messiah, who is not God (*al-Mā'idah* (5):17), who is as human and as creaturely as Adam (*Āl 'Imrān* (3):59), and whom the Jews did not crucify (*an-Nisā'* (4):157).

Such has never been a Christian view of the Gospel. In the course of his Arabic apology in favor of the Christian doctrine of human redemption through Jesus' passion and death on the cross, Theodore Abū Qurrah undertook to explain more clearly the Christian understanding of the Gospel. It is Jesus' summons (*ad-da'wah*), he explains in Islamic flavored Arabic.

10 Cf. Arthur Jeffrey, *The Foreign Vocabulary of the Qur'ān* (Baroda, 1938), pp. 71-72; Carra de Vaux & G.C. Anawati, "Indjīl", *EI*², Vol. III, p. 1205.

"His summons is named a Gospel (*inǧīl*), i.e., an announcement of good news (*bišārah*), because it has announced to people Christ's salvation of them from what no one else could have saved them"[11]. Accordingly, in the Christian view, the Gospel is an announcement of what God has accomplished for mankind in Christ, written down under divine inspiration by the four canonical evangelists. To some of the Muslim scholars of Abbasid times and later, however, such a view seemed to be a distortion of the original facts, as reported in the *Qur'ān*. And the *Qur'ān* itself, originally in connection with the Torah, and the Jews' observance of its prescriptions, suggested what had happened. "A group of them used to attend to God's word. Thereafter they distorted it (*yuḥarrifūnahu*), after they had understood it. And they know it" (*al-Baqarah* (2):75).

The charge of *at-taḥrīf*, or 'distortion', that is brought against the scripture people already in the *Qur'ān*, has a long history of exegesis which it is not to the present purpose to rehearse here[12]. However, one of the consequences of the charge has to do with the proper identification of the authentic Gospel. As is evident from what has already been said, for Muslims the Gospel is the divine revelation which God gave to Jesus, and for Christians it is the good news of what God has done for mankind, written in Greek by four inspired evangelists. Accordingly, Christians speak of the Gospel in four Gospels. For some Muslims, however, the four Gospels in Greek already represent a distortion. By the first Abbasid century someone must already have formulated what was to be clearly described later by the great Mu'tazilite scholar, 'Abd al-Ǧabbār al-Hamḏānī (d. 1025), viz., the conviction that God originally delivered the Gospel to Jesus in Hebrew, his presumed native language, since, as 'Abd al-Ǧabbār points out, Jesus belonged to the Hebrew community. According to 'Abd al-Ǧabbār's logical conclusion, therefore, Jesus' fractious later followers must have been responsible for the Greek versions of the Gospels. The evidence he offers for this contention is the manifest difference in detail, and even the contradictions that are evident in the four Greek narratives of Matthew, Mark, Luke and John[13]. What makes one suspect that some earlier Muslim scholars

11 Constantin Bacha, *Les œuvres arabes de Théodore Aboucara* (Beyrouth, 1904), p. 90.

12 Cf. I. Goldziher, "Ueber muhammedanische Polemik gegen Ahl al-kitāb", *ZDMG* 32 (1878), pp. 341-387; I. Di Matteo, "Il *taḥrīf* od alterazione della Bibbia secondo i musulmani", *Bessarione* 38 (1922), pp. 64-111, 223-260; W. Montgomery Watt, "The Early Development of the Muslim Attitude to the Bible", *Glasgow University Oriental Society Transactions* 16 (1955-1956), pp. 50-62; J.-M. Gaudeul & R. Caspar, "Textes de la tradition musulmane concernant le *taḥrîf* (falsification) des écritures", *Islamochristiana* 6 (1980), pp. 61-104.

13 Cf. the English version of 'Abd al-Ǧabbār's views in S. M. Stern, "'Abd al-Jabbār's Account of How Christ's Religion Was Falsified By the Adoption of Roman Customs", *JThS*

shared ʿAbd al-Ǧabbār's conviction about the status of the Greek Gospels is the fact that already in the first Abbasid century such a writer as ʿAlī ibn Rabbān aṭ-Ṭabarī, from whom ʿAbd al-Ǧabbār quoted some of his information about Christians, as S. M. Stern has shown, was already busily pointing out some of the same inconsistencies in the four Gospels, and calling attention to the distorting influence of Paul, another theme that ʿAbd al-Ǧabbār himself was to follow up later[14].

While it is not within the purview of the present article to discuss the complicated Islamic doctrines of *at-taḥrīf*, or even to trace the history of the Islamic teaching about the original Gospel which the *Qur'ān* says that God gave to Jesus, it is important at the outset to make clear the ambiguity that adheres to the very term 'Gospel' in Arabic. In reading Islamic texts one must always ask himself which sense of the word is to be understood, the Gospel as Christians have it in the four Gospels, or the Gospel as Jesus received it from God, according to the Islamic view? The purpose of the present article is to search for the first Arabic version of the canonical four Gospels of the Christian community. Muslims were certainly well aware of these Gospels, as will become abundantly clear below. As for the Gospel which Muslims believe that God gave to Jesus, and the conviction of ʿAbd al-Ǧabbār and others that its original language was Hebrew, one may conclude only that the *Qur'ān* is the sole witness for the existence of such a Gospel. The suggestion of some Muslim scholars that it was originally in Hebrew is an obvious conclusion for them to draw from the data contained in their own divine revelation. Furthermore, given this notion of the Gospel revealed in the *Qur'ān* it is not surprising that in commenting on Christianity in the *Qur'ān* Abū Ǧaʿfar Muḥammad ibn Ǧarīr aṭ-Ṭabarī (d. 923) paid virtually no attention at all to what Christians would recognize as the Gospel according to Matthew, Mark, Luke or John. Rather, he was concerned only with the no longer available Gospel that the *Qur'ān* says God gave to Jesus[15].

19 (1968), pp. 133-137. Cf. also S.M. Stern, "Quotations From Apocryphal Gospels in ʿAbd al-Ǧabbār", *JThS* 18 (1967), pp. 34-57. T. Baarda, "Het ontstaan van de vier Evangelien volgense ʿAbd al-Djabbār", *Nederlands Theologisch Tijdschrift* 28 (1974), pp. 215-238. For the original text, cf. ʿAbd al-Ǧabbār ibn Aḥmad al-Hamḏānī, *Tathbīt dalā'il an-nubuwwah* (2 vols.; Beirut, 1966). In a recent article Patricia Crone proposes that ʿAbd al-Ǧabbār here records the views of a group of Judeo-Christians. Cf. P. Crone, "Islam, Judeo-Christianity and Byzantine Iconoclasm", *Jerusalem Studies in Arabic and Islam* 2 (1980), pp. 59-95.

14 Cf. A. Khalifé et W. Kutsch, "Ar-Radd ʿAla-n-Naṣārā de ʿAlī aṭ-Ṭabarī", *MUSJ* 36 (1959), pp. 115-148. Another, later Islamic scholar, Ibn Ḥazm (d. 1064), a younger contemporary of ʿAbd al-Ǧabbār, employed a similar line of argument. Cf. Gaudeu & Caspar, *art. cit.*, pp. 78-82.

15 Cf. A. Charfi, "Christianity in the *Qur'ān* Commentary of Ṭabarī", *Islamochristiana* 6 (1980), pp. 107-109.

There was, of course, the "Gospel of the Hebrews", once current in Hebrew, i.e., Aramaic, as the scripture of a group of Jewish Christians sometimes known as Ναζωραῖοι, the Arabic form of whose name is probably *an-Naṣārā*, the *Qur`ān*'s name for Christians. There is a record of the presence of Ναζωραῖοι in Syria, and it is not impossible that they were known in Mecca, and ultimately to Muḥammad himself[16]. However, after the Islamic conquest the religious conflict of the Muslims was with the Christians of the patriarchal sees of Constantinople, Antioch, and Jerusalem, whose Gospel was in Greek, or in Syriac derived from Greek, according to the Gospels of the four evangelists. While it is not inconceivable that the Ναζωραῖοι and their "Hebrew" Gospel somehow lie behind the *Qur`ān*'s view of the Gospel, it is unquestionable that the canonical Gospels were the focus of controversy in and after the first Abbasid century, and it is their first appearance in Arabic that is the subject of the present inquiry.

B. The Earliest Documentary Evidence

The ninth Christian century is the earliest time from which we have unambiguous, documentary evidence of Arabic versions of the four Gospels. The evidence is in the form of the actual manuscripts which contain these versions, which, as we shall see, have been transmitted in close association with anti-Muslim, Arabic apologies for Christianity; and reports, from both Christians and Muslims, dealing with the subject of Gospel translations into Arabic, or quoting passages from the Gospels in Arabic. We shall briefly survey both forms of this evidence.

1. Arabic Gospel Manuscripts

The oldest known, dated manuscripts containing Arabic translations of the New Testament are in the collections of St. Catherine's monastery at Mt. Sinai. Sinai Arabic MS 151 contains an Arabic version of the Epistles of Paul, the Acts of the Apostles, and the Catholic Epistles. It is the oldest of the dated New Testament manuscripts. The colophon of this

16 Regarding the Ναζωραῖοι, cf. the sources cited in G.W.H. Lampe, *A Patristic Greek Lexicon* (Oxford, 1961), p. 897. For the Greek name and its Syriac connections, cf. H.H. Schaeder, "Ναζαρηνός, Ναζωραῖος", in G. Kittel (ed.), *Theological Dictionary of the New Testament* (Trans. G.W. Bromiley, vol. IV; Grand Rapids, Mich., 1967), pp. 874-879. For "The Gospel of the Nazoraeans", cf. Edgar Hennecke, *New Testament Apocrypha* (W. Schneemelcher, ed., R. McL. Wilson, trans.; Philadelphia, 1963), vol. I, pp. 139-153. For the connection of the Arabic word *an-naṣārā* with οἱ Ναζωραῖοι, via the Syriac *naṣrāyê*, cf. A. Jeffery, *The Foreign Vocabulary of the Qur`ān* (Baroda, 1938), pp. 280-281. A recent writer has proposed a connection between Islam and the Ναζωραῖοι, viz., J. Dorra-Haddad, "Coran, prédication nazaréenne", *POC* 23 (1973), pp. 148-151. Cf. also M.P. Roncaglia, "Éléments Ébionites et Elkasaïtes dans le Coran", *POC* 21 (1971), pp. 101-126.

MS informs us that one Bišr ibn as-Sirrī made the translation from Syriac in Damascus during Ramaḍān of the Hiğrah year 253, i.e., 867 A.D.[17] The oldest, dated manuscript containing the Gospels in Arabic is Sinai Arabic MS 72. Here the text of the four canonical Gospels is marked off according to the lessons of the temporal cycle of the Greek liturgical calendar of the Jerusalem church. A colophon informs us that the MS was written by Stephen of Ramleh in the year 284 of the Arabs, i.e., in 897 A.D.[18]. Although this MS remains unpublished, we know that its text belongs to a distinct family of some half dozen Arabic Gospel manuscripts which contain a version of the Gospel rendered from the original Greek[19]. A recent study of the text of the Gospel according to Mark in these MSS shows that Sinai Arabic MS 72 is in all likelihood the latest of them all, textwise, featuring numerous improvements and corrections of earlier readings[20].

Vatican Arabic 13, which originally contained an Arabic version of the Psalms, the four Gospels, the Acts of the Apostles, and all of the Epistles, now has only Paul's Epistles and portions of the Gospels in what remains of the manuscript. It comes originally from the monastery of Mar Sabas in Judea. Modern scholars consider it to be one of the oldest surviving Arabic New Testament manuscripts. It carries no date, but is now generally reckoned to have been written in the ninth century[21].

There are, of course, many other manuscripts of the Gospels rendered into Arabic. We have mentioned here only the most notable early ones[22].

17 The Pauline epistles have been edited and translated into English. Cf. Harvey Staal, *Mt. Sinai Arabic Codex 151; I, Pauline Epistles* (CSCO, 452, 453; Lovanii, 1983). On Bišr ibn as-Sirrī, cf. J. Nasrallah, "Deux versions melchites partielles de la Bible du ixe et du xe siècles", *OrChr* 64 (1980), pp. 203-206.

18 Cf. the published photograph of this colophon in Constance E. Padwick, "Al-Ghazali and the Arabic Versions of the Gospels", *Moslem World* (1939), pp. 134ff.

19 For a description of these MSS cf. Graf, vol. I, pp. 142-147.

20 Cf. Amy Galli Garland, "An Arabic Translation of the Gospel According to Mark", (Unpublished M.A. Thesis, The Catholic University of America; Washingtonu 1979). M. Samir Arbache has a doctoral dissertation in preparation at Louvain on the Sinai Gospel MSS. Cf. *Bulletin d'arabe chrétien* 1 (1977), p. 82.

21 Cf. Graf, vol. I, pp. 115 & 138.

22 Cf. the list of Bible versions in Arabic in J. Blau, *A Grammar of Christian Arabic* (CSCO, vols. 267, 276, 279; Louvain, 1966-1967), vol. 267, pp. 29-34. For a general overview of the Arabic versions of the Gospels, cf. Ignazio Guidi, "Le traduzioni degli Evangelii in arabo e in etiopico", in *Reale Accademia dei Lincei* 285 (1888), pp. 5-37; Graf, vol. I, pp. 138-170; Bruce M. Metzger, *The Early Versions of the New Testament; their Origin, Transmission and Limitations* (Oxford, 1977), pp. 257-268. André Ferré, of the Pontifical Institute of Arabic Studies in Rome, is at work on a new survey of Arabic Gospel versions. Cf. *Bulletin d'arabe chrétien* 1 (1977), p. 84.

An interesting fact about the Sinai Gospel manuscripts in this group is that they were written by the same people who have transmitted some of the earliest Christian Arabic controversial treatises to us, and it is to them that we shall now turn our attention.

Stephen of Ramleh, the scribe who wrote Sinai Arabic MS 72, included two short treatises at the end of his Gospel text. One is an inspirational homily, attributed to Mar Basil. The other is a short apologetic treatise composed by Theodore Abū Qurrah. It is a dialogue between a Christian and a Muslim, about the alleged Jewish responsability for Christ's crucifixion[23]. This same Stephen of Ramleh also wrote a major portion of the British Museum MS Or. 4950. This important manuscript, written in the year 877/8, contains two long Christian Arabic apologetic treatises. One is a still largely unpublished treatise in 25 chapters that discusses and defends the major Christian doctrines about God and Christ. The other is Theodore Abū Qurrah's defense of the Christian practice of venerating images, against the objections to this practice generally voiced by Muslims and Jews[24].

Sinai Arabic MS 154 is another New Testament manuscript written in the ninth century that also contains the text of an apologetic treatise. In addition to Arabic versions of the Acts of the Apostles and the Catholic Epistles, the scribe has included an anonymous treatise in defense of the doctrine of the Trinity. A remarkable feature of this treatise is the large number of quotations from the *Qur'ān* which the author employs, in addition to his citation of the standard biblical testimonies that one usually finds cited in support of the doctrine[25].

From the little evidence we have presented here it is already clear that the earliest datable copies of the Gospel in Arabic are from Syria/Palestine,

23 Cf. Sidney H. Griffith, "Some Unpublished Arabic Sayings Attributed to Theodore Abū Qurrah", *Le Muséon* 92 (1979), pp. 29-35.

24 A page of MS 4950 is published in Agnes Smith Lewis and Margaret Dunlop Gibson, *Forty-One Facsimiles of Dated Christian Arabic Manuscripts* (Studia Sinaitica, XII; Cambridge, 1907), pp. 2-4. A portion of the first apologetic treatise was published in Louis Ma'luf, "The Oldest Christian Arabic Manuscript", (Arabic) *al-Machriq* 6 (1903), pp. 1011-1023. Cf. Graf, vol. II, pp. 16-19. For Abū Qurrah's treatise, cf. Ioannes Arendzen, *Theodori Abu Kurra de cultu imaginum libellus e codice arabico nunc primum editus latine versus illustratus* (Bonn, 1897); German translation: Georg Graf, *Die arabischen Schriften des Theodor Abū Qurra* (Paderborn, 1910), pp. 278-333. The present writer has prepared a new edition and English translation of Abū Qurrah's treatise, to appear soon, and is at work on Georg Graf's unfinished edition of the first apologetic treatise in BM Arabic MS 4950, the *Summa Theologiae* in 25 chapters.

25 Cf. Margaret Dunlop Gibson, *An Arabic Version of the Acts of the Apostles and the Seven Catholic Epistles From an Eighth or Ninth Century MS in the Convent of St. Catherine on Mount Sinai* (Studia Sinaitica, VII; Cambridge, 1899). Cf. also Graf, vol. I, pp. 172-173; vol. II, pp. 27-28.

largely from St. Catherine's and Mar Sabas' monasteries, in the ninth century. Furthermore, there is a clear relationship in the manuscript traditions between these earliest discoverable Arabic versions of the Gospel, along with the other New Testament writings, and the earliest Christian, apologetic treatises in Arabic — notably those of Theodore Abū Qurrah, himself a monk of Mar Sabas. These and other sources of information which we shall consider below support the conclusion that it was in the ninth century, or late eighth century, that a full edition of the Gospel appeared in Arabic, when this language became the common language for public affairs, even among the subject, non-Muslim populations in the Fertile Crescent whose original languages were Syriac, Greek or Coptic.

Here is the place to note in passing that the earliest extant manuscripts of the Old Testament in Arabic also date from Abbasid times. Perhaps the earliest surviving, integral manuscript is the Arabic version of the Wisdom of Jesus ben Sirach, contained in Sinai Arabic MS 155, which may date from the ninth century, and which is itself the product of re-copying[26]. But even more interesting than this Sinai MS, for reasons that will appear below, is the dual language MS fragment from Damascus which contains a large portion of Psalm 78 (LXX,77), vv. 20-31, 51-61, in the Greek of the LXX, accompanied by an Arabic version that is written in Greek script[27]. The fragment was discovered by Bruno Violet in Damascus, in the Umayyad mosque. Greek paleographical considerations show that the text was written in Syria at the end of the eighth century, or in the early ninth century[28].

Anton Baumstark, who was a notable proponent of the theory that the Gospel was translated into Arabic in pre-Islamic times, at one time also suggested that the Psalter was translated then too, even as far back as the fifth century, perhaps when Euthymius (377-473), the Palestinian monk, began his missionary work among the Arabs[29]. Baumstark based his proposal on what he took to be the archaic form of the Arabic text of a Psalter preserved as Zurich Or. MS 94. However, now one is in a position to recognize that this ninth or tenth century manuscript, which has been little studied beyond the small portion of it which Baumstark published (viz.

26 Cf. Richard M. Frank, *The Wisdom of Jesus ben Sirach (Sinai ar. 155. ixth/xth cent.)* (CSCO, vols. 357 & 358; Louvain, 1974).

27 Cf. B. Violet, "Ein zweisprachiges Psalmfragment aus Damaskus", *Berichtigter Sonderabzug aus der Orientalistischen Literatur-Zeitung, 1901* (Berlin, 1902). The text of the Psalm is also available in P. Kahle, *Die arabischen Bibelübersetzungen. Texte mit Glossar und Literaturübersicht* (Leipzig, 1904), pp. 32-35.

28 Cf. Violet, *art. cit.*, and Graf, vol. I, pp. 114-115; Blau, *op. cit.*, vol. 267, p. 31.

29 A. Baumstark, "Der älteste erhaltene griechisch-arabische Text von Psalm 110 (109)", *OrChr* 31 (1934), p. 62.

Ps. 110, LXX 109), actually seems to exhibit an Arabic text that is comparable to that which was written in southern Palestine in the ninth and tenth centuries[30].

Not only are the earliest dated biblical Arabic manuscripts from the ninth century, but even a cursory glance through Graf's or Blau's lists of manuscripts shows that this century witnessed a fairly prodigious amount of other non-biblical Christian writing in Arabic, especially in Palestine. However, one should not immediately conclude that the ninth century is the earliest time when Christians wrote in Arabic. Some works doubtless date back to the eighth century. Many of the ninth century manuscripts seem to be copies of works written earlier. As noted above, Sinai Arabic MS 72, the earliest dated manuscript of the Gospel in Arabic, is clearly an improvement on the text of the Gospel in the other manuscripts in its family. This fact argues that the text in the other manuscripts had an earlier origin[31]. The earliest date so far attested in a documentary source for Christian writing in Arabic is the report in British Museum MS or. 5019, written in the tenth or eleventh century, that the martyrology contained in the text was translated into Arabic in the year 772[32].

2. References to the Arabic Gospel

a. Christian References

The earliest occasion which later Christian writers remembered as concerned with a project to translate the Gospel into Arabic was originally described in an early 8th century Syriac chronicle, which reports an encounter between a Muslim official named ʿAmr, and the Jacobite Patriarch John I (d. 648), in the course of which the Muslim is said to have made inquiries about the contents of the Gospel[33]. According to Michael the Syrian, a twelfth century Jacobite chronicler, it was as a consequence of his meeting with ʿAmr[34] that the Patriarch John made arrangements for the first translation of the Gospel from Syriac into Arabic, with the con-

30 Cf. Graf, vol. I, p. 115. Cf. also the fragmentary, triglot Psalter, in Greek, Syriac, and Arabic published by N. Pigulevskaya, "Greco - Siro - Arabskaia Rukopis IXv", *Palestinskii Sbornik* 1 (63) (1954), pp. 59-90.

31 Cf. n. 20 above. Even one of the earliest dated Christian manuscripts in Arabic, viz., British Museum Or. MS. 4950, copied in 877, testifies that its text of Theodore Abū Qurrah's treatise on images was copied from an earlier manuscript.

32 Cf. Joshua Blau, *The Emergence and Linguistic Background of Judaeo-Arabic* (Oxford, 1965), pp. 5-6.

33 Cf. M.J. Nau, "Un colloque du patriarche Jean avec l'émir des agaréens et faits divers des années 712 a 716", *Journal Asiatique* 11th Series, 5 (1915), pp. 225-279.

34 Probably ʿAmr ibn Ṣaʿd ibn Abī Waqqāṣ, cf. J. Spencer Trimingham, *Christianity Among the Arabs in Pre-Islamic Times* (London & New York, 1979), p. 225.

sultation of men from those Christian, Arab tribes of Mesopotamia who knew both Syriac and Arabic. Following Michael's account, the Muslem official gave the patriarch clear orders to this effect.

> Thereupon he commanded him, "Translate your Gospel for me into the Saracen language, i.e., Arabic[35]; but do not mention Christ's name, that he is God, or baptism, or the cross." Fortified by the Lord, his Beatitude said, "Far be it that I should subtract a single *yod* or stroke from the Gospel[36], even if all the arrows and lances in your camp should transfix me." When he saw that he would not be convinced, he gave the order, "Go, write what you want". So, he assembled the bishops, and he brought help from the Tanûkāyê, the 'Aqûlāyê, and the Ṭu'āyê, who were knowledgeable in both the Arabic and in the Syriac language, and he commanded them to translate the Gospel into the Arabic language[37].

Michael the Syrian's list of the three Christian Arab tribes, whose members understood both Arabic and Syriac, calls one's attention to the fact that there were many Arab Christians prior to the rise of Islam, including not only these three groups in Mesopotamia, but also the many Christians among the Arabic speaking populations in Arabia proper, in the Sinai, and in Syria/Palestine, from at least as early as the fifth century[38]. However, Michael the Syrian's statement that the three groups in Mesopotamia were bilingual reminds the modern reader that every one of these Arabic speaking Christian communities, who were tribally organized and at least semi-noma-

35 Michael's Syriac expression is *lešānâ sarqāyâ awkēt ṭayyâyâ*. *Sarqāyâ* is simply an adjective derived from the transliteration of the enigmatic Greek word Σαρακηνοί, which originally designated nomadic Arabs, and in later Byzantine writers meant 'Muslims'. Cf. V. Christides, "The Names ΑΡΑΒΕΣ, ΣΑΡΑΚΗΝΟΙ etc., and their False Byzantine Etymologies", *ByZ* 65 (1972), pp. 329-333. It is curious that Christides does not seem to know of John Damascene's ideas about the etymology of Σαρακηνοί. Cf. Daniel J. Sahas, *John of Damascus on Islam; the "Heresy of the Ishmaelites"* (Leiden, 1972), p. 71. Cf. also Trimingham, *op. cit.*, pp. 312-313; and Louis Cheikho, "Al-'arab aw as-sarḥiyyūn", *Al-Machriq* 7 (1904), pp. 340-343, where the author suggests that the term might ultimately come from the name of the Yemenite province *as-Sarḥah*, whose inhabitants the sea-faring Greeks may have encountered, and whose name they may eventualy have applied to all Arabians, and all Arab nomads. The Syriac adjective *ṭayyāyâ* comes from the name of the Arab tribe, *aṭ-Ṭayy*, and it was widely used in Syriac texts of Byzantine times to designate Arabic speaking, bedouin nomads. Cf. Trimingham, *op. cit.*, pp. 146-312.

36 Cf. Mt. 5:18.

37 J.-B. Chabot, *Chronique de Michel le Syrien; patriarche jacobite d'Antioche (1166-1199)* (4 vols.; Paris, 1899-1910), vol. II, p. 432, vol. IV, p. 422.

38 Cf. the extensive bibliography in Trimingham, *op. cit.*, and particularly the work of Professor Irfan Shahid (Kawar). Of special interest for the present inquiry are his recent works: *The Martyrs of Najrān: New Documents* (Subsidia Hagiographica, 49; Bruxelles, 1971); "*The Martyrs of Najrān*: Miscellaneous Reflexions", *Le Muséon* 93 (1980), pp. 149-161; "Byzantium in South Arabia", *Dumbarton Oaks Papers* 33 (1979), pp. 25-94. Of decisive importance for the whole field of inquiry into Christianity among the pre-Islamic Arabs, will be Prof. Shahid's forth-coming three volumes, *Byzantium and the Arabs Before the Rise of Islam: from Constantine to Heraclius*.

dic, lived in association with a larger, ecclesiastically more dominant group, whose church language was either Greek, Syriac, or, in one known instance where a vernacular was employed in the liturgy, Palestinian Aramaic. The official Christian scriptures of the Arab tribes most likely remained in these ecclesiastical languages of the completely settled communities. If among the tribes any Arabic versions of the Gospel ever were made prior to the rise of Islam, an accomplishment that is not to be considered *a priori* impossible or even unlikely, all mention and all unambiguous evidence of them disappeared later.

As for what became of Patriarch John's Arabic version of the Gospel, no other mention of it seems to have survived. Presumably the patriarch used it in his discussions with Muslims. As for the Christian community, it was not yet that they had Gospel, liturgy and theology in Arabic.

b. Muslim References

i. Ibn Isḥāq

The earliest known extended quotation from the Gospel in an Islamic Arabic text, apart from some earlier allusions to Gospel stories which we shall mention below, is undoubtedly the passage from John 15:23 - 16:1 which Abū ʿAbd Allāh Muḥammad ibn Isḥāq (d.c. 767) included in his biography of the prophet Muḥammad, and which has been preserved in the later biography by Abū Muḥammad ʿAbd al-Malik ibn Hišām (d. 834). It is worth quoting Ibn Isḥāq's passage at some length, in order to appreciate the significance of his reference to St. John's Gospel[39].

> Ibn Isḥāq said, "Here is what has come down to me about the description of God's messenger, God's prayer and peace be upon him, in what Jesus, son of Mary, set down in the Gospel, for the people of the Gospel, which came to him from God, as Yuḥannis the apostle established it for them when he copied the Gospel for them at the commission of Jesus, son of Mary, peace be upon him; he said: (15:23) "Whoever has hated me, has hated the Lord. (15:24) Had I not performed in their presence such works as no one has performed before me, they would have no sin. But now they have become proud and they think that they will find fault with me and even with the Lord[40]. (15:25) However, it is inevitable that the saying concerning *an-Nāmūs* will be fulfilled, "They have hated me for nothing, i.e., in vain". (15:26) Had *al-Munaḥḥemānâ*, he whom God will send, already come to you from the Lord, and the spirit of truth[41], he who comes from God, he would have been a witness for me, and you too,

39 Abū Muḥammad ʿAbd al-Malik ibn Hišām, *Sīrat an-nabī* (ed. Muḥammad Muḥyī d-Din ʿAbd al-Ḥamīd, 4 vols.; Cairo, 1356), vol. I, p. 251; F. Wüstenfeld (ed.), *Das Leben Muhammeds nach Muhammed Ibn Ishâk* (Göttingen, 1858), pp. 149-150.

40 For this rendition of the enigmatic *y-ʾ-z-w-n-n-y*, cf. below.

41 Reading *wa rūḥi l-qisṭ* with Wüstenfeld, cf. the explanation below.

> because you have been with me from the beginning. (16:1) I have said this to you so that you may not be in doubt."
> *Al-Munaḥḥᵉmānâ* in Syriac is Muḥammad, and in Greek it is *al-baraqlitis*, God's prayer and peace be upon him.

The first thing that must strike the reader of this passage is the fact that Ibn Isḥāq is citing St. John's Gospel as a scriptural testimony to the future divine mission of Muḥammad. Indeed, in context in the *Sīrah* the passage occurs at the end of the first part of the book, just prior to the accounts of the first revelations to Muḥammad, in company with a number of other testimonies from Jews and Christians to Muḥammad's prophethood, culminating in the story of Waraqah ibn Nawfal, to which we shall return below. Secondly, it is easily recognizable that Ibn Isḥāq's idea of the Gospel is the Islamic, in fact the Qur'anic view that the Gospel is something which God gave to Jesus. Ibn Isḥāq says that the apostle John had merely copied it down on Jesus' commission. Furthermore, with reference to any known Christian version of the Gospel according to John, it becomes clear from what Ibn Isḥāq offers us here that he must also have been convinced that John's text as Christians have it has been altered[42]. For, in his quotation of John 15:23 - 16:1 there are a number of telling variants. The three occurrences of the phrase "my Father" in the passage as it appears in Christian texts, have here all become "the Lord," in accordance with the *Qur'ān*'s insistence that God has no son (*al-Iḫlāṣ* (112)), and that Jesus, son of Mary, is only God's messenger (*an-Nisā'*(4): 171), whom, as the Messiah, the Christians have said to be God's son, "imitating the doctrine of those who disbelieved earlier. ... They have taken their own scholars and their own monks as lords, in spite of God, or the Messiah, the son of Mary" (*at-Tawbah* (9):30-31). Clearly then, Ibn Isḥāq must have felt that he had ample divine authority in the *Qur'ān* to set matters aright in his quotation from the Gospel of John.

Both A. Baumstark and A. Guillaume, the two modern scholars who have most assiduously studied Ibn Isḥāq's quotation, have shown that the Christian text that underlies the quotation as we have it here in undoubtedly the version preserved now in the so called Palestinian Syriac Lectionary[43]. Their evidence for this conclusion is principally the un-

42 It is noteworthy that in Ibn Isḥāq's account of the conversion of the Persian Salmān, which just precedes the quotation of the John passage, Salmān was informed by his first respected Christian master that "men have died and have either altered (*baddalū*) or abandoned most of their true religion". Cf. ʿAbd al-Malik ibn Hišām, *op. cit.*, vol. I, p. 236.

43 Cf. A. Baumstark, "Eine altarabische Evangelienübersetzung aus dem Christlich-Palastinensischen", *ZSem* 8 (1932), pp. 201-209; A. Guillaume, "The Version of the Gospels Used in Medina c. A.D. 700", *Al-Andalus* 15 (1950), pp. 289-296. For the Palestinian text of the

mistakable appearance of the singular term *al-munaḥḥ^{e}mānâ*, the Comforter, in Ibn Isḥāq's quotation, as a rendering of the original ὁ Παράκλητος. The term is unique to the Palestinian Syriac version. Then there is the phrase, "the spirit of truth", in vs. 26, the original Arabic version of which in Ibn Isḥāq's quotation betrays its debt to the same Palestinian Syriac text[44]. Both scholars also mention a number of other, smaller pointers to the Palestinian version which it is not necessary to repeat here. Rather, what is important now is to call attention to those places in the text where Baumstark and Guillaume detected further deliberate Islamic alterations, or corrections to the Christian text, or where mistakes or textual corruptions seem to them to have crept into the quotation.

15:24b, "But now they have become proud and they think that they will find fault with me, and even with the Lord."

Both Baumstark and Guillaume argue that the Arabic text of Ibn Isḥāq is corrupt in this verse. They correct the rare word *baṭirū'*, "they have become proud," to *naẓarū'*, "they have seen", to agree with both the Greek and the Palestinian Syriac readings, and they mention the easy mistake it would have been to confuse the consonants of these two words in the Arabic script[45]. Further, Baumstark proposed a fairly complicated double textual corruption in Syriac to account for the last part of the verse, involving the introduction into the original text of a form of the Syriac root *ḥ-w-b*, "to be guilty", which he then supposed was subsequently misread to be a form of the root *ḥ-s-n*, "to be strong, to overcome", yielding the final reading, "they think that they will overcome me ..."[46], which, on Baumstark's view, Ibn Isḥāq would have found before him. Both Baumstark and Guillaume, therefore, understood Ibn Isḥāq's verb, *y-ʿ-z-w-n-n-y*, to be a form of the root *ʿ-z-z*, and Baumstark offered what seemed to him to be a plausible explanation of how a misunderstanding of the underlying Syriac could issue in such an errant Arabic version of John 15:24b.

The readings of Guillaume and Baumstark make sense of Ibn Isḥāq's quotation of vs. 15:24b by measuring it against the Palestinian Syriac *Vorlage*, and ultimately against the Greek original. This approach assumes that Ibn Isḥāq's intention was accurately to reproduce an Arabic version

passage under discussion, cf. A. Smith Lewis & M. Dunlop Gibson, *The Palestinian Syriac Lectionary of the Gospels* (London, 1899), pp. 24 & 187.

44 Wüstenfeld, following a better MS, preserves the original *wa rūḥi l-qisṭ*. Cf. Baumstark, *art. cit.*, p. 201; ʿAbd al-Malik ibn Hišām, on the other hand, follows the later 'correction' of the phrase to *rūḥi l-qudus*, *op. cit.*, p. 251. Cf. Guillaume, *art. cit.*, p. 293.

45 Baumstark, art. cit., p. 205; Guillaume, *art. cit.*, p. 294.

46 Baumstark, art. cit., pp. 205-206.

of the Palestinian Syriac text. However, on the evidence of his alteration of 'father' to 'Lord' throughout the passage, we have already seen that Ibn Isḥāq must rather have intended accurately to quote from John's copy of the Gospel as it would have been originally, when God gave it to Jesus, according to the *Qur'ān*'s teaching, and not to reflect what in his view would have to be instances of textual alterations introduced later by the Christian community in support of their unique doctrines about God and Jesus. Religious accuracy, and hence scriptural accuracy, for Ibn Isḥāq, would have been measured by the *Qur'ān*'s teachings, and not by Christian manuscripts in Greek, Syriac or Arabic.

Accordingly, in John 15:24b one should look for the religious accuracy which Ibn Isḥāq meant to reflect. In this connection one's attention is drawn immediately to the fact that the root *b-ṭ-r*, in the sense of "to be proud, vain," appears twice in the *Qur'ān*, in *al-Anfāl* (8):47 and *al-Qaṣaṣ* (28):58, and in both places it describes the state of mind of those who have in the past turned aside from God's way, or who have rejected His messenger. Clearly, this sense fits an Islamic understanding of the context of John 15:24. Furthermore, if the reader understands Ibn Isḥāq's verb, *y-ʿ-z-w-n-ny*, to be a form of the root *ʿ-z-w*, it may be understood to mean "to charge, to incriminate, to blame", in the first form, and "to comfort, to console" in the second and fourth forms. The first alternative fits well with an Islamic understanding of the present verse, and the second meaning, of course, is perfect for the Christian Palestinian understanding of the important term, *al-munaḥḥ^emānâ* in 15:26. In fact, the ninth century Christian Arabic translator of St. John's Gospel chose precisely the root *ʿ-z-w* to render the term in question, as we shall see below.

15:25, "The saying concerning *an-Nāmūs* will be fulfilled."

The translation of this phrase reflects the Islamic understanding of the term *an-Nāmūs* as referring not to the Torah, or to a law of Moses (*nāmûsâ d^eMôšê* in Syriac, e.g., in Luke 2:22), but to Gabriel, who brought it to Moses. As aṭ-Ṭabarī said, "By *an-Nāmūs* one means Ǧibrīl, who used to come to Moses"[47]. The evidence that such was also Ibn Isḥāq's understanding of *an-Nāmūs* is to be seen in his omission of the participle 'written' and the third person plural pronominal suffix from his Arabic rendering of the Palestinian Syriac reading, "The saying written in their law(s)"[48]. While Baumstark did not think that the omission of the pronoun or the participle was significant enough to warrant one's understanding Ibn Isḥāq to mean an-Nāmūs in the Islamic sense here, his cavil seems actually

47 M.J. De Goeje (ed.), *Annales quos Scripsit Abu Djafar Mohammed ibn Djarir at-Tabari* (Leiden, 1882-1885), 1st series, vol. III, p. 1151.

48 Lewis and Gibson, *op. cit.*, pp. 24, l. 22 and 287, l. 12.

to stem from his method of measuring Ibn Isḥāq's version of this passage of John's Gospel against Christian texts, rather than against Ibn Isḥāq's own Islamic understanding of what the Gospel should say. Baumstark confined his discussion to the missing pronoun and simply ignored the missing participle[49]. Guillaume, on the other hand, clearly recognized that "one cannot escape the conclusion that the alteration is deliberate"[50].

15:26, "*Al-Munaḥḥ^emānâ*, he whom God will send to you."

The Palestinian Syriac version of John 15:26, following the original Greek, speaks of "*al-munaḥḥ^emānâ*, whom I shall send to you". There are two subjects for discussion in this verse, the identity of *al-munaḥḥ^emānâ* himself, and the identity of the sender. In both instances Ibn Isḥāq's Islamic construction of the Gospel text is evident.

As all commentators on the Palestinian Syriac lectionary have observed, and as Baumstark and Guillaume have both rehearsed it, the term *al-munaḥḥ^emānâ*, which Ibn Isḥāq simply transliterated into Arabic characters, is a unique rendering of the original Greek term in John 15:26, ὁ Παράκλητος, in a sense unique in Syriac to the Palestinian Syriac deployment of the root *n-ḥ-m*, to mean "the comforter"[51]. For Christians, the Paraclete, the Comforter, is the Holy Spirit, or as St. John calls him, "the Spirit of truth", whom Jesus promises to send after his return to the Father.

For Ibn Isḥāq and the Muslims this idea is an instance of the distortion (*at-taḥrīf*) which Christians have introduced into the Gospel text, particularly at places where the coming of Muḥammad was foretold. According to the report of a Christian controversialist of the first Abbasid century, his Muslim interlocutor explicitly made this charge against John and his disciples after Christ's ascension. The Muslim said to the Christian:

49 A. Baumstark, "Eine altarabische Evangelienübersetzung ..., *art. cit.*, p. 206. In an earlier article Baumstark admits the Islamic understanding of *an-Nāmūs*, in connection with the story of Waraqah ibn Nawfal, as found in the *Sīrah* of Ibn Isḥāq/Ibn Hišām, and in support of it he cites some passages from the eastern liturgy in which the Greek ὁ νόμος seems to have an almost anthropomorphic, or angelomorphic sense. Cf. A. Baumstark, "Das Problem eines vorislamischen christlich-kirchlichen Schrifttums in arabischer Sprache", *Islamica* 4 (1929-1931), pp. 565-566.

50 Guillaume, *art. cit.*, p. 294.

51 As all the commentators have mentioned, the Palestinian Syriac use of the root *n-ḥ-m* to mean 'to give comfort' is comparable to the Jewish Aramaic deployment of the root. Cf., e.g., Guillaume, *art. cit.*, p. 293. However, the meaning 'comforter' for Παράκλητος, instead of the more likely 'advocate', poses yet another lexical problem, which need not detain us here. Cf. J. Behm, "Παράκλητος", in G. Kittel & G. Friedrich (eds.), G.W. Bromiley (trans. & ed.), *Theological Dictionary of the New Testament* (10 vols.; Grand Rapids, Mich., 1964-1976), vol. V, pp. 800-814.

What you have said, you report only from your Gospel and your new books. But we have the original, genuine Gospel. We have gotten it from our prophet, and it stands in opposition to what is in your possession; for John and his associates, after Christ's ascension to heaven, revised the Gospel and set down what is in your possession, as they wished. So has our prophet handed it down to us[52].

Ibn Isḥāq knew very well, on the authority of the *Qur'ān* itself, that Jesus said, "O Sons of Israel I am a messenger of God to you, confirming what was before me of the Torah, and announcing a messenger who will come after me, whose name is *aḥmad*" (*aṣ-Ṣaff* (61):5). Consequently, what John originally wrote down of the Gospel at Jesus' commission could only have been in accordance with what the *Qur'ān* says. So Ibn Isḥāq presented John 15:26 in an Islamically correct fashion which makes the Paraclete, the Comforter, a designation for Muḥammad, as he says explicitly at the end of the long passage translated above. Nor is he troubled by any necessity to explain the relationship between *aḥmad* and ὁ Παράκλητος/*al-munaḥḥ^{e}mānâ*[53]. The unquestionable assumption for Ibn Isḥāq was that Jesus predicted the coming of Muḥammad. John 15:26 says that Jesus said that the Paraclete will come. Therefore, the Paraclete designates Muḥammad. As for who will send the Paraclete/Muḥammad, it is clear that God is the one who sends His own messengers (cf., e.g., *G͟hāfir* (40):78: *arsalnā rusulan*). Therefore, the undistorted Gospel must have described *al-Munaḥḥ^{e}mānâ* as "He whom God will send", and so Ibn Isḥāq reports it. Baumstark's proposal that Ibn Isḥāq's report in this instance was based on a corruption of the Syriac phrase for "Whom I shall send"[54] once again, and not without ingenuity, measures Ibn Isḥāq's quotation against Christian texts, rather than against his own Islamic understanding of the matter in hand.

16:1, "So that you may not be in doubt."

The Palestinian Syriac lectionary, along with the original Greek, says "So that you might not be tripped up", that is to say, "scandalized", as the expression has universally been interpreted in Christian circles. Ibn Isḥāq has simply supplied an easily understood Islamic phrase here, the recognition of which removes the necessity to follow Guillaume in his search for dialectical understandings of the root *š-k-k* to mean 'to limp', or 'to fall'[55].

52 K. Vollers, "Das Religionsgespräch von Jerusalem", *ZKG* 29 (1908), p. 62.

53 Western scholars have long attempted to interpret *aḥmad* as a reflection of παράκλητος, misread as περικλυτός. Cf. Theodor Nöldeke, *Geschichte des Qorans* (vol. I, 2nd ed., F. Schwally; Leipzig, 1909), p. 9, n. 1. In all probability the *Qur'ān* passage has no reference to any particular Gospel passage. As for the relationship between *al-m^{e}naḥḥ^{e}mānâ* and Muḥammad/Aḥmad, one scholar has proposed that "this identification is based only on the assonance between the Aramaic word and the name Muḥammad, and seems to have been suggested by Christian converts to Islam". J. Schacht, "Aḥmad", *EI*^{2}, vol. I, p. 267.

54 Baumstark, "Eine altarabische Evangelienübersetzung...", *art. cit.*, pp. 206-207.

55 Guillaume, *art. cit.*, p. 295.

In the *Qur'ān*, the people to whom prophets have been sent, who have spoken against their prophets, are often said to be "*fī šakkin ... murībin*", i.e., "in suspicious doubt", as were the people to whom Ṣāliḥ was sent (*Hūd* (11):62), the people to whom Moses was sent (*Hūd* (11):110), and even the people to whom Muḥammad was sent (*Sabā'* (34):54). Indeed, at one place in the *Qur'ān* there is this specific advice: "If you are in doubt about what we have sent down to you, ask those who were reading scripture before you. The truth has come to you from your Lord, so do not be among the doubters" (*Yūnus* (10):94). Ibn Isḥāq's Islamic understanding of John 16:1 is, therefore, easily intelligible, as are the apologetical reasons for which he searched out this whole passage from the Gospel according to John[56].

Quite clearly Ibn Isḥāq's Arabic version of John 15:23 - 16:1 is dependent upon the version of the Gospel preserved in the Palestinian Syriac lectionary. There is every reason to believe that he found it in Syriac, and that he alone, or with the help of an Arabic speaking Christian, put it into an Arabic idiom that would be both comprehensible and doctrinally reinforcing to Muslim readers. There is no reason to believe that Ibn Isḥāq's quotation is dependent upon a pre-existent, Christian, Arabic version of the Gospel. He himself twice refers to his Syriac source, once to explain that Syriac *maǧǧānan* means *bāṭilan*, and once to claim that *al-Munaḥḥ*^{e}*mānâ* is Syriac for Muḥammad.

There is certainly no reason to propose a connection between Ibn Isḥāq's quotation from John, and the Palestinian Arabic Gospel text that is represented in the family of Arabic manuscripts mentioned above, which originate from the first Abbasid century[57]. A comparison between Ibn Isḥāq's quotation and the text of John 15:23 - 16:1 in Sinai Arabic MSS 72 and 74 makes this conclusion crystal clear. The one connection between the two versions of the passage from John is that both of them depend upon a Gospel text of the type that now remains only in the Palestinian Syriac lectionary. The translator of the texts in the Sinai MSS understood the Paraclete to be 'the Comforter', and he rendered this understanding into Arabic with a form of the root *'-z-w*, viz., *al-mu'azzī*[58]. Below we shall discuss further the relationship between the Palestinian Arabic Gospel text and the Palestinian Syriac lectionary.

56 Cf. John Wansbrough, *The Sectarian Milieu; Content and Composition of Islamic Salvation History* (Oxford, 1978).

57 Cf. nn. 19 & 20 above.

58 Sinai Arabic MS 72, f. 110r, l. 18, and Sinai Arabic MS 74, f. 238, l. 5.

ii. Waraqah ibn Nawfal

The story of Waraqah ibn Nawfal includes not so much a claim to the existence of an early Arabic version of the Gospel, as it does a testimony to the religious association and linguistic knowledge of Waraqah himself.

Waraqah ibn Nawfal was a cousin of Ḫadīğah, the wife of Muḥammad. Waraqah was a Christian, according to tradition, one of the handful of Meccans in the prophet's time who became monotheists prior to the preaching of Islam. He is remembered in Islamic tradition for his knowledge of the scriptures, both the Torah and the Gospel. It is in connection with him that we find in Islamic historical sources the only mention of the Gospel in Arabic in any form in pre-Islamic times.

In the several renditions in which it has come down to us, the constant features in Waraqah's story are that he had become a Christian in the *Ğāhiliyyah*, that he was learned in the scriptures, and that when the prophet had his inaugural revelation (*bad' al-wahy*) and described the experience to Waraqah at Ḫadīğah's instigation, Waraqah recognized immediately Muḥammad's prophetic vocation.

The details are not exactly the same in any two of the ten or so accounts of Muḥammad's meeting with Waraqah that are preserved in early Islamic sources. The most common form of the story, found in three places, may be quoted here from al-Buḫārī's collection of traditions. The scene is set as just following Muḥammad's disclosure of his first visionary experience to Ḫadīğah.

> Ḫadīğah hurried off with him until she brought him to Waraqah ibn Nawfal. He was the son of Ḫadīğah's uncle, her father's brother. He was a man who had professed Christianity in the time of ignorance. He used to write *al-kitāb al-ʿarabī*, and he would write down from the Gospel *bi l-ʿarabiyyah* whatever God wanted him to write. He was a very old man, now gone blind. Ḫadīğah said, "Uncle, listen to your brother's son". Waraqah said, "O son of my brother, what is it you see?" So the prophet, God's prayer and peace be on him, gave him the report of what he had seen. Waraqah said, "This is an-Nāmūs that was sent down to Moses"[59].

Two points in this account attract our attention, viz., that Waraqah copied passages from the Gospel, and that he told Muḥammad that an-Nāmūs had come to him. We shall discuss each of them in turn, citing the significant variations that occur in the other reports of this incident.

All of the sources insist that Waraqah was knowledgeable about the scriptures. In the form of the story about him that we have quoted above, it is his ability to write in Arabic that is emphasized. A slightly different

59 Abū ʿAbd Allāh Muḥammad ibn Ismāʿīl al-Buḫārī, *Kitāb al-ğāmiʿ aṣ-ṣaḥīḥ* (M. Ludolf Krehl, ed., 4 vols.; Leiden, 1862), vol. III, pp. 380-381. Cf. also vol. IV, pp. 347-348, and Muslim b. al-Haǧǧāǧ, *Ṣaḥīḥ Muslim* (8 vols.; Cairo, 1334), vol. I, pp. 97-98.

wording of this story says simply, "He used to read the Gospel *bi l-ʿarabiyyah*"[60]. Ibn Hišām, on the other hand, is content to say in his edition of Ibn Isḥāq's *Sīrah* of the prophet, "Waraqah had professed Christianity, and he read the scriptures, and heard from the people of the Torah and the Gospel"[61]. The striking variant in the telling of the story, however, is what we find in another place in al-Buḫārī's collection of traditions, as well as in the *Kitāb al-aghānī*. It says of Waraqah, "He used to write *al-kitāb al-ʿibrānī*, and he would write down from the Gospel *bi l-ʿibrāniyyah*"[62].

Already in the last century A. Sprenger noticed this discrepancy concerning the language in which Waraqah is said to have read and copied from the Gospel. Sprenger proposed that the "Hebrew" in question was actually the Aramaic script employed by Jews, and that in this story it means that Waraqah was writing Arabic in the Aramaic script. So in his view there is no real conflict between the two versions of the story. Nor is there, in his judgment, any unlikelihood that someone would write Arabic in non-Arabic characters. Historically there is not only the example of Arabic speaking Jews writing Arabic in "Hebrew" characters. Syriac speakers also employed their own alphabet to write Arabic, a writing called *Garšūnî* in Syriac[63]. But Waraqah, a Meccan and a native Arabic speaker, and not a Jew but an alleged Christian, would hardly have had any need to borrow the "Hebrew" script. By his time the north Arabic script, albeit with an obvious debt to the Syriac script in its origins, would certainly have been available to Waraqah[64].

There is nothing *a priori* unlikely about the arrival of Christianity in the environs of Mecca in the time of Waraqah ibn Nawfal. Indeed, in the sixth century the Ḥiğāz was virtually surrounded by Christian areas in Sinai, Syria/Palestine, the Syriac and Arabic speaking areas of Mesopotamia and Iraq, al-Ḥirā, Nağrān to the south of the Ḥiğāz, and across the sea in

60 Al-Buḫārī, *op. cit.*, vol. II, p. 352.

61 Ibn Hišām, *op. cit.*, vol. I, p. 256.

62 Al-Buḫārī, *op. cit.*, vol. I, p. 5; Abū Farağ al-Isbahānī, *Kitāb al-aghānī* (20 vols.; Cairo, 1285), vol. III, p. 14.

63 A. Sprenger, *Das Leben und die Lehre des Mohammad nach bisher grösstentheils unbenutzten Quellen* (3 vols.; Berlin, 1861-1865), vol. I, pp. 124-134.

64 Cf. Nabia Abbott, *The Rise of the North Arabic Script and its Kur'ānic Development, With a Full Description of the Kur'ān Manuscripts in the Oriental Institute* (Chicago, 1939), pp. 5-11; J. Starcky, "Petra et la Nabatene", *Dictionnaire de la bible. Supplement*, vol. VII, cols. 932-934; Janine Sourdel-Thomine, "Les origines de l'écriture arabe, à propos d'une hypothèse récente", *Revue des Études Islamiques* 34 (1966), pp. 151-157; *idem.*, "Khaṭṭ", EI^2, vol. IV, pp. 113-1122. Regarding the hypothesis that Christian literary use of Arabic was widespread before the rise of Islam, usually associated with the name of Louis Cheikho, cf. Camille Héchaïme, *Louis Cheikho et son livre "le christianisme et la littérature chrétienne en Arabie avant l'islam", étude critique* (Beyrouth, 1967).

Ethiopia[65]. Furthermore, the merchants of Mecca travelled in all of these areas and had commercial relations with them. Early Islamic tradition as well as Christian sources testify to the presence of Christians in the area, even among the nomadic tribes. So there is no reason to doubt the basic veracity of the reports that Waraqah ibn Nawfal was a Christian, and that he was familiar with both the Torah and the Gospel, as Ibn Isḥāq/Ibn Hišām have said, even given the evidently apologetical character of the *Sīrah*, and its requirement to present Muḥammad as affirmed by the scripture people[66].

The question before us concerns the language in which the Gospel arrived in Mecca, and the language in which Waraqah would have been likely to "write down from the Gospel ... whatever God wanted him to write". Two questions are actually involved here.

The straightforward answer to the first question is that in all likelihood the bearers of Christianity in the Ḥiğāz had their Gospel in Syriac, not because it would have been impossible for them to have had it in Arabic (or even in Greek), but because there is no evidence to support the conclusion that they did have it in Arabic, and what evidence there is points to Syriac. The answer to the second question is that in all likelihood Waraqah ibn Nawfal copied from the Gospel (and the Torah) in his own native, Arabic language, this accomplishment being among his notable achievements remembered in Islamic tradition. The answers to both questions require further elucidation.

The evidence that Syriac was the scripture language of the Christian Arabs in Muḥammad's lifetime is first of all the large number of expressions with a Syriac origin, having to do with Biblical and Christian religious concepts that are to be found in the *Qur'ān*, beginning with this very word itself, and extending to many other distinctive locutions[67]. Secondly, in

65 Cf. the studies and bibliographies in Trimingham, *op. cit.*, n. 34 above, and the works of I. Shahid, n. 38 above.

66 On the apologetic character of the *sīrah*, cf. J. Wansbrough, *op. cit.*, n. 56 above.

67 For the relationship between *qur'ān* and *qeryānâ*, cf. Arthur Jeffrey, *The Foreign Vocabulary of the Qur'ān* (Baroda, 1938), p. 234; R. Blachère, *Le Coran* ("Que sais-je?" no. 1245; Paris, 1966), pp. 15-16. For an extended lexical discussion of Quranic terms, cf. K. Ahrens, "Christliches im Qoran", *ZDMG* 84 (1930), pp. 15-68, 148-190. For historical considerations and analyses of Quranic passages in relationship to Christian diction in Syriac, cf., esp., Tor Andrae, *Les origines de l'islam et le christianisme* (Trans. J. Roche; Paris, 1955). Andrae originally wrote this study in German in 1923-1925, and published it in the journal, *Kyrkohistorisk Årsskrift*, which is not available to me. Regarding the Syriac origins of the *Qur'ān*'s name for Jesus, i.e., *'Isā al-Masīḥ*, cf. M. Hayek, "L'origine des terms 'Isâ-al-Masîḥ (Jésus-Christ) dans le Coran", *OrSyr* 7 (1962), pp. 227-254, 365-382. Cf. also John Bowman, "The Debt of Islam to Monophysite Syrian Christianity", in E.C.B. Mac Laurin (ed.), *Essays in Honour of Griffithes Wheeler Thatcher 1863-1950* (Sydney, 1967), pp. 191-216, and in *Nederlands Theologisch Tijdschrift* 19 (1964/5), pp. 177-201. For some relation-

Muḥammad's time Syriac speaking Christians seem to have exerted the strongest formative influence on the established Christian community nearest to the Ḥiğāz to the south, viz., Nağrān, with its ties to the church at al-Ḥirā; while to the north and east the Arabic speaking tribes which included Christians customarily moved freely in and out of the Syriac speaking areas, or had contacts with the churches of Syria/Palestine[68]. As we shall see below, the language of the vernacular scriptures in much of Syria/Palestine prior to the rise of Islam was the Aramaic dialect known as Palestinian Syriac.

The *Qur`ān* itself insists some dozen times that it is an Arabic *Qur`ān* (e.g., in *Yūsuf* (12); 2), as opposed to the lessons of the Jews and the Christians, which are in other languages. In his commentary on this verse, aṭ-Ṭabarī explains that it is as if God said about Muḥammad's Ḥiğāzī audience, "because their tongue and their speech is Arabic, we sent down this scripture in their own tongue so that they could understand it and gain knowledge from it"[69]. Presumably, among others, Christian preachers were about in the Mecca/Medina area whose scriptures were not in Arabic. Indeed, there is evidence of their presence in the *Qur`ān* itself, when it records the reaction of those members of Muḥammad's audience who doubted that it was really God's message that the prophet was preaching, but rather the teaching of someone else. They referred to the presence of some un-named person whose speech the *Qur`ān* says was not Arabic. Of the doubters *an-Naḥl* (16):103 says, "We know very well what they say, 'Only a mortal is teaching him'. The speech of him at whom they hint is barbarous; and this is speech Arabic, manifest" (Arberry). In his commentary on this verse, aṭ-Ṭabarī explains that Christians were the people at whom the suspicious Arabs were hinting. He records traditions that identify their barbarous speech as Byzantine Greek[70]. However, this identification may simply reflect the later Islamic awareness that the original Gospel as the Christians have it is Greek. In the Ḥiğāz, in the late sixth and the early seventh centuries, the barbarous, or non-Arabic (*a`ğamī*) speech of Christian monks and preachers was most likely Syriac.

What was remarkable about Waraqah ibn Nawfal's acquaintance with the scriptures was the fact that he copied from them in Arabic. The language in which he was able to write the scriptures is thus a focal point of the story

ships between passages from the *Qur`ān* and the Syriac liturgy, cf. Erwin Graf, "Zu den christlichen Einflüssen im Koran", in *Al-Bāḥith, Festschrift Joseph Henninger zum 70. Geburtstag am 12. Mai 1976* (Studia Instituti Anthropos, vol. 28; Bonn, 1976), pp. 111-144.

68 For Nağrān cf. the studies of Prof. Irfan Shahid, cited in n. 38 above; for the rest, cf. Trimingham, *op. cit.*, with a complete bibliography of earlier works.

69 Abū Ğa`far Muḥammad ibn Ğarīr aṭ-Ṭabarī, *Tafsīr al-Qur`ān* (30 vols. in 13; Cairo, 1321), vol., 12, p. 84.

70 *Ibid.*, vol. 14, pp. 109-111.

that is preserved about him. The fact that this language, or writing, is said to be "Hebrew" in some tellings of Waraqah's story underlines this point. As for the "Hebrew" itself, it is most easily explained as a later correction of the narrative, contributed by someone who thought he knew not only that the language of the Torah was Hebrew, but that Jesus' native language, and hence the language of the original, undistorted Gospel must also have been Hebrew[71]. For, it would have been a necessity for Islamic apologetic purposes, given Waraqah's role in recognizing Muḥammad's prophethood, that he have his testimony from the original, undistorted Gospel.

As for Waraqah's statement about the source of Muḥammad's revelations, viz., "This is *an-Nāmūs* that was sent down to Moses", one must recognize in this report the classical Islamic understanding of *an-Nāmūs* as a designation for the angel Gabriel, as discussed above[72]. Indeed this understanding of *an-Nāmūs* is clear in one version of Waraqah's story as preserved by al-Buḫārī, where an additional phrase explains that *an-Nāmūs* is "the master of the mystery, who would inform him (i.e., Moses) of what he would conceal from anyone else"[73].

It is understandable how Gabriel was thought of in association with the moment of revelation. There are Jewish traditions which record instances of Gabriel visiting Moses[74]. The *Qur'ān* too mentions Gabriel's role in the revelation to Muḥammad, "He is the one who brought it down to your heart, by God's permission, confirming what was prior to it, as guidance and good news for the believers (*al-Baqarah* (2):97). What is mysterious is how *an-Nāmūs* came to designate Gabriel. While it is not to the present purpose to pursue this question at any length, one cannot help but to observe the obvious similarity of the Arabic word to the Syriac *nāmôsâ*, the ordinary word for "law, ordinance, usage", as in a law of Moses (*nāmôsâ dᵉMôšê*, e.g., in Luke 2:22 *Peš*). Anton Baumstark, as we have seen, wondered if the identification of *an-Nāmūs* with Gabriel could have been due to an almost anthropomorphic, or angelomorphic, sense of the Greek word ὁ νόμος in the eastern liturgy[75]. While it is unlikely that a Greek liturgical phrase *per se* would have influenced the Islamic interpretation of *an-Nāmūs*, it is notable that in Syriac texts one finds a similar 'personalization' of *nāmôsâ*. In his *Sermon on Our Lord*, for example, Ephraem set a scene of punishment among the women in the Exodus who had given their jewelry

71 Cf. n. 13 above, and the attendant discussion in the text.
72 Cf. n. 47 above, and the attendant discussion in the text.
73 Al-Buḫārī, *op. cit.*, vol. II, p. 352.
74 Cf. the instances cited in Louis Ginzberg, *The Legends of the Jews* (7 vols.; Philadelphia, 1913-1938), vol. VII, pp. 173-174.
75 Cf., 49 above; M. Plessner, "Nāmūs", *EI*¹, vol. III, pp. 902-904.

for the manufacture of the golden calf (Ex. 32:15-29). According to the story, Moses crushed the calf, mixed its remains with water and forced them to drink it. Later he commanded the Levites to slay the men in the camp (vs. 27). Ephraem called these Levites 'avengers', and he pictured them as slaying the people who had given their jewelry for the calf. He said, "He made it (i.e., the community) drink the water of the trial so that the sign of the adultresses might appear. Thereupon this *nāmôsâ* assailed the women who had drunk the testing water"[76]. Perhaps it is not farfetched to think that Syrian preachers among the Arabs would have followed Ephraem's lead in speaking of *nāmôsâ* as virtually an avenging angel, and someone identified him as Gabriel.

There remains one more Christian, and probably Syriac element in Waraqah's story. In the version of his encounter with Muḥammad that we find in the *Sīrah*, Waraqah begins his testimony to Muḥammad's prophetic vocation with the exclamation, *quddūs quddūs*[77]. The expression puts one in mind of the triple *qadîšâ* one finds in the Syriac *Trishagion*. The form of the word, i.e., *quddūs*, comes from the *Qur'ān* (e.g., *al-Ḥašr* (59):23), but the exclamatory usage of it here recalls the Christian liturgy, a point already made by Baumstark[78].

iii. Wahb ibn Munabbih (d. 732)

Among the Muslim scholars of the first century of the *Hiğrah* there were those, notably Wahb ibn Munabbih, who were renowned for their knowledge of the traditions and scriptures of the ancients, including the Jews and Christians. Wahb himself, in his accounts of the earlier prophets, alluded to the Torah, the Psalms, and once or twice to the Gospel, including a long paraphrase of Jesus' sermon on the mount, following along the lines of Matthew 5-7[79]. R.G. Khoury has most recently studied these citations and allusions in the works of Wahb and others, and has signalled the two issues which they raise, viz., the obvious Islamicization of the accounts, and the question of their sources.

As a result of our previous study of Ibn Isḥāq's quotation from John 15:23 - 16:1, and the story of Waraqah ibn Nawfal, it comes as no surprise to learn that Wahb ibn Munabbih's accounts of the narratives in Torah

76 E. Beck, *Des heiligen Ephraem des Syrers Sermo de Domino Nostro* (CSCO, vol. 270; Louvain, 1966), p. 6.

77 Muḥammad ʿAbd al-Malik ibn Hišām, *Sīrat an-Nabī* (4 vols.; Cairo, 1356), vol. I, p. 256.

78 Cf. Baumstark, "Das Problem ...", *art. cit.*, p. 565.

79 Cf. the reference in R.G. Khoury, "Quelques réflexions sur les citations de la Bible dans les premières générations islamiques du premier et du deuxième siècles de l'hégire", *Bulletin d'Études Orientales* 29 (1977), p. 272, n. 13.

and Gospel are presented in a manner which accords with what the *Qur'ān* teaches about their message.

As for Wahb's sources, Khoury points particularly to early converts to Islam from Judaism for the Torah and Psalms, such as Ka'b al-Aḥbar and 'Abd Allāh b. Salām[80]. There is also the report from Mālik ibn Dīnār (d. 748) that he took a book that interested him from a Christian monastery. In reference to this report Khoury says, "If one can believe such texts, and basically what could be more natural than to think of such encounters all across the centuries, he could have come upon an Arabic version of the Old and of the New Testaments, or at least of a part"[81].

In the absence of any positive evidence to the contrary, however, the most likely construction to put upon the reports that have come down to us about scriptures in Christian monasteries, or in the possession of monks, even in pre-Islamic Arabia[82], is that they were in languages other than Arabic, most probably Syriac, and possibly some Greek. The people who read them in these languages would have transmitted their contents to inquiring early Muslims, possibly in writing; or Muslims with a scholarly inclination could have learned to read them for themselves, and to make their own notes. They certainly presented their references to Torah and Gospel, as we have seen, dressed in an Islamic guise. What is still lacking, with the dubious exception of Waraqah's story, is any explicit reference to Torah or Gospel in Arabic, even in the form of scholarly notes, prior to the first Abbasid century. Accordingly, it seems reasonable to assume that early Muslim writers learned of the contents of Torah or Gospel from Jews or Christians *viva voce*, without reference to an Arabic text, against which to measure the accuracy of their reference to them. Accuracy would have been measured, as we have seen, against the requirements of Islamic dogmatic ideas[83].

80 *Ibid.*, p. 272.

81 *Ibid.*, pp. 275-276.

82 Pre-Islamic poets refer to monks and their scriptures. Cf. the references in Tor Andrae, *Les origines*, *op. cit.*, pp. 42ff.

83 There is support for the idea that Muslims in the early eighth century learned about the Gospel from Christians *viva voce*, in a story about al-Aṣbagh, the son of 'Abd al-'Azīz ibn Marwān, the governor of Egypt. In his *History of the Patriarchs*, Severus ibn al-Muqaffa' described the anti-Christian behavior of al-Aṣbagh, and said of him: "At that time a deacon, named Benjamin, became attached to him and grew intimate with him; and al-Aṣbagh loved him more than all his companions. And he treacherously revealed to al-Aṣbagh the secrets of the Christians, and even expounded the Gospel to him in Arabic as well as the books of alchemy. For al-Aṣbagh sought out books that they might be read to him, and so for instance he read the Festal Epistles, in order that he might see whether the Muslims were insulted therein or not". B. Evetts, "History of the Patriarchs of the Coptic Church of Alexandria (III, Agathon to Michael I (766)", *PO* 5 (1910), p. (305), 51.

iv. The First Abbasid Century

From the first Abbasid century onward there is evidence of the existence of Arabic versions of the Gospels with which Muslims were familiar. In the first place there is the earliest explicit mention of a translation of them in the *Fihrist* of Ibn an-Nadīm (d. 995/8), concerning the work of Aḥmad ibn ʿAbd Allāh ibn Salām, a scholar of the time of Harūn ar-Rašīd (786-809). According to Ibn an-Nadīm, Salām said, "I have translated ... the Torah, the Gospels, and the books of the prophets and disciples from Hebrew, Greek and Sabian, which are the languages of the people of each book, into Arabic, letter for letter"[84]. Whether or not one is prepared to credit the extent of this claim, what is important for the present inquiry is the clear reference to a translation project for the scriptures in the late eighth century.

More important than this notice of Ibn Salām's translation project, however, are a number of Muslim writers from the late eighth and the ninth centuries, who quote from the Torah and the Gospel with a fidelity which shows that they must have had Arabic versions of these scriptures before them, to which they referred for their quotations, and from which they learned at first hand how the Christian account of the Gospel message differs from the Islamic one. As we have mentioned, this is the same period of time to which the available documentary evidence allows one to date the Christian program to translate the Gospel into Arabic.

The earliest Muslim scholar whose quotations from the Bible suggest that he had an Arabic version before him is Abū ar-Rabīʿ Muḥammad ibn al-Layth. He wrote a *risālah*, a letter-treatise, in the name of Harūn ar-Rašīd (786-809), addressed to the Byzantine emperor, Constantine VI (780-797), arguing in favor of the truth claims of Islam[85]. He quoted from the Old Testament and the New Testament, and it is particularly in his quotations from the former that it is clear that he was working with a version. Unfortuneately, his quotations from the Gospels of Matthew and John are too few, toọ allusive, and too fragmentary to allow the conclusion that he had an Arabic version of the Gospel before him[86]. But it is notable that these few references show no trace of the Islamicization one finds in the earlier Muslim references to the Gospel.

Other Muslim apologists and polemicists against Christianity in the ninth century quoted freely from the Gospels in Arabic. ʿAlī Rabbān aṭ-Ṭabarī,

84 Cf. Dodge, *op. cit.*, vol. I, p. 42.

85 Cf. D.M. Dunlop, "A Letter of Harūn ar-Rashīd to the Emperor Constantine VI", in Matthew Black & Georg Fohrer (eds.), *In Memoriam Paul Kahle* (Beiheft zur *ZAW*, no. 103; Berlin, 1968), pp. 106-115.

86 *Ibid.*, pp. 113-114.

who converted to Islam at an advanced age, was already well acquainted with the Gospels during his life as a Christian. He quoted extensively from them in his apologies for Islam[87]. But there were other Muslim apologists of the period who had no known Christian background, who made an equally copious use of Gospel quotations in their treatises. We may mention in this connection an anonymous early ninth century Muslim refutation of Christians, and the polemical treatise of the Zaydī scholar, al-Qāsim ibn Ibrāhīm[88].

By the end of the ninth century there were well known Muslim scholarly writers, such as Ibn Qutaybah (d. 889), and the historian al-Ya'qūbī, who were well acquainted with the Gospels and quoted from them in their works[89]. It is clear that they had versions before them, and did not have to rely solely on Islamic doctrines about the contents of the original Gospel before, in the Islamic view, it was distorted at the hands of the Christian evangelists[90].

By the tenth century, Muslim scholars were taking note of Arabic versions of the scriptures done by Christians. Ibn an-Nadīm, for example, reports that a priest named Yūnus informed him of the Christian writings available in Arabic, listing the books of the Old and New Testaments, along with collections of canons and the *synodicon*[91]. And al-Mas'ūdī (d. 956), in his *Kitāb at-tanbīh wa l-išrāf*, recorded it as his opinion that of the versions of the Torah in Arabic, the one by Ḥunayn ibn Isḥāq (d. 873) was the best according

87 Cf. Max Meyerhof, "'Alī ibn Rabbān aṭ-Ṭabarī, ein persischer Arzt des 9. Jahrhunderts n. Chr.", *ZDMG* 85 (1931), pp. 38-68; A. Khalifé et W. Kutsch, "Ar-Radd 'Alā-n-Naṣārā de 'Alī aṭ-Ṭabarī", *MUSJ* 36 (1959), pp. 115-148. Scripture quotations and their interpretation are the essence of the author's *Book of Religion and Empire*. Cf. A. Mingana (ed.), *Kitāb ad-Dīn wa d-Dawlah* (Cairo, 1923), Eng. trans. (Manchester, 1922). But the authenticity of this work has been questioned. Cf. Maurice Bouyges, "Nos informations sur 'Aliy ... at-Tabariy", *MUSJ* 28 (1949-1950), pp. 67-114.

88 Cf. Dominique Sourdel, "Un pamphlet musulman anonyme d'époque 'Abbasīde contre les chrétiens", *Revue des Études Islamiques* 34 (1966), pp. 1-34; Ignazio Di Matteo, "Confutazione contro i Cristiani dello Zaydita al-Qāsim b. Ibrāhīm", *Rivista degli Studi Orientali* 9 (1921-1923), pp. 301-364.

89 Cf. G. Lecomte, "Les citations de l'ancien et du nouveau testament dans l'œuvre d'Ibn Qutayba", *Arabica* 5 (1958), pp. 34-46. For Ibn Qutayba and the Old Testament, cf. also G. Vajda, "Judaeo-Arabica : observations sur quelques citations bibliques chez Ibn Qotayba", *Revue des Études Juives* 99 (1935), pp. 68-80. For al-Ya'qūbī cf. Dwight M. Donaldson, "Al-Ya'qūbī's Chapter About Jesus Christ", in *The Macdonald Presentation Volume* (Princeton, 1933), pp. 89-105; André Ferré, "L'historien al-Ya'qūbī et les évangiles", *Islamochristiana* 3 (1977), pp. 65-83.

90 Arthur Vööbus proposed that the Old Syriac version of the New Testament text lay behind the Arabic translations found in the works of these Muslim authors, as well as in those of some early Christian Arabic writers. Cf. A. Vööbus, *Early Versions of the New Testament; Manuscript Studies* (Stockholm, 1954), pp. 276-287.

91 Dodge, *op. cit.*, vol. I, pp. 45-46.

to most people[92]. Clearly by this time Christianity had found its tongue in Arabic, to the point that even the Muslims were noticing the fact.

One should not think that the scholarship displayed in the ninth century by Ibn Qutaybah or al-Ya'qūbī in regard to the text of the Christian Gospels brought an end to the Islamic dogmatic approach to the message of the Gospel, or the life and teaching of Jesus. Indeed, the textual approach of these two scholars to the subject was the exception. Such major figures as Abū Ğa'far aṭ-Ṭabari and al-Mas'ūdī still wrote fairly extensively of Jesus and Christianity without any reference at all to the Gospels of the Christians, or any evidence that they had consulted them[93]. The point to be made here is simply that by the ninth century it is clear for the first time from Muslim sources that Arabic versions of the Christian scriptures were available.

III. *The Gospel in Arabia Prior to Islam*

A number of prominent scholars have argued that it is likely that pre-Islamic, Christian Arabs would have been anxious to render the Gospels and other liturgical compositions from Greek and Syriac into their native Arabic. Given what can be discovered about the status of Arabic as a literary language prior to Islam, these scholars argue that it is probable that such a Gospel translation was in fact produced. There are two headings in particular under which to review these arguments. The one is the Palestinian Arabic Gospel text discussed earlier, which some scholars have considered to be pre-Islamic in its origins. The other is the history of Christianity in Arabia, in search of which at least one modern scholar considers that some clues for the existence of a pre-Islamic Gospel in Arabic can be found, particularly in Nağrān.

A. The Palestinian Arabic Gospel Text

Anton Baumstark was the first scholar to put forward the claim that the Palestinian Gospel text preserves an old, pre-Islamic version of the Gospel in Arabic. His hypothesis was that the translation was made in one of the Syrian centers of Christian Arab life, either in Ghassanid Sergiopolis, or in al-Ḥīrā to the east, and that this version was subsequently borrowed by the monks of Mar Sabas and St. Catherine's monasteries for use in the liturgy of the Word among the Palestinian Christian Arabs. After the rise of Islam, according to Baumstark's hypothesis, most of the Arabs on the

92 Abū al-Ḥasan 'Alī ibn al-Ḥusayn ibn 'Alī al-Mas'ūdī, *Kitāb at-tanbīh wa'l-ischrāf* (M.J. De Goeje (ed.), *Bibliotheca Geographorum Arabicum*, 8; Lugduni-Batavorum, 1894), p. 112.

93 Cf. Ferré, *art. cit.*, pp. 81-82.

borders of Palestine became Muslims and so the Arabic Gospel lectionaries became literary curiosities preserved by the monks, who were themselves Greek speaking[94].

The motivating factor in Baumstark's argument seems to have been his conviction that once the church was established in Arabic speaking areas, it would have been inconceivable that at least the lessons to be read at the divine liturgy would not have been translated into the Arabic language. Accordingly, at the beginning of his article on this subject he cited the practice of Christian missionaries in other areas, whereby the translation of the scriptures into the native language was the first order of business. For the rest, Baumstark's evidence consists of the following observations. He points to the report in Islamic traditions that the Meccan Waraqah ibn Nawfal, just prior to Muḥammad's call to prophecy, had become a Christian and was conversant with the scriptures. Secondly, he points to some phrases in the *Qur`ān* which seemed to him to be remarkably faithful renderings of some passages in the Psalms. Finally, and most importantly, he refers to the Arabic versions of the Gospels, marked with rubrics that indicate when they are to be read in the liturgy, which came originally from Palestine, but which were available to Baumstark in two different manuscripts, viz., Vatican Borgia Arabic MS 95, and Berlin Or. Oct. MS 1108, along with a few leaves from another, otherwise unknown manuscript. It was the rubrics in these manuscripts that interested Baumstark. He pointed out that they reflect the liturgical usage of the Jerusalem church prior to the rise of Islam, and not the Byzantine usage which became common after the Arab conquest. Therefore, Baumstark argued, it is probable that the Arabic Gospel text in these manuscripts itself comes from the same time as the rubrics — i.e., from before the time of Islam. More specifically, he argued that this Arabic version of the Gospels was probably made in the environs of the Arab city of al-Ḥirā in the sixth century[95].

Since Baumstark wrote his articles about the Palestine Gospel text it has become evident that his two manuscripts are members of the family of manuscripts from Palestine which contains basically the same Arabic version of the Gospels, made from a Greek *Vorlage*. Other members of the family, as mentioned earlier, are Sinai Arabic MSS 72 and 74. Sinai MS 72, as we have seen above, is the earliest dated Gospel MS known. It was written in 897. The other dated MS in the family is Berlin 1108. It was copied in 1046/47. Serious textual study of these MSS began in 1938, when the texts of Matthew

94 Anton Baumstark, "Das Problem eines vorislamischen christlich-kirchlichen Schrifttums in arabischer Sprache", *Islamica* 4 (1929-1931), pp. 562-575.

95 Anton Baumstark, "Die sonntägliche Evangelienlesung im vor-byzantinischen Jerusalem", *ByZ* 30 (1929/1930), pp. 350-359.

and Mark from Vatican Borgia 95 and Berlin 1108 were published and compared[96]. The Sinai MSS have not yet been published, but the researches of a number of scholars are sufficient to inform us of the general relationship of the manuscripts in the family.

What is immediately clear upon an examination of these texts is the care of the original translators and the subsequent copyists constantly to remain faithful to the original Greek, with a literalness that often makes the Arabic baffling. The practice of improving the Arabic text persists from copyist to copyist in such a way that it allows one to propose a relative chronology for the manuscripts. The texts of Vatican Borgia MS 95, Sinai MS 74, and Berlin MS 1108 most often agree with one another. While Sinai MS 72, which carries the earliest date of any known Arabic Gospel MS, shows most evidence of improvement in terms of Arabic expression, and corrections in many of the readings. Some marginal glosses that occur in Sinai MS 74 have even found their way into the text of Sinai MS 72. Therefore, one concludes that in terms of the relative age of the Gospel version in Arabic it offers, the earliest dated MS actually contains a later recension of the version in its manuscript family. And the latest dated MS and its allies contain an earlier exemplar of this particular translation tradition[97]. As if to underline the fact that this family of manuscripts played a definite role in a concerted attempt to render the Gospel into an intelligible Arabic, suitable to the sensitivities of the Arabic speakers within the *dar al-islām*, it appears that the considerably improved and corrected Arabic version of the Gospels in Sinai Arabic 75 is what Georg Graf called an *Ableger* from the text found in the family of manuscripts we have been discussing[98]. Sinai Arabic MS 75 thus represents the culmination of the attempt on the part of a group of Palestinian Christians to achieve an Arabic version of the Gospel in the early Islamic period which could pass for literary Arabic.

The milieu of these Gospel manuscripts is decidedly Palestinian. They reflect the Greek of the Caesarean Gospel text one should expect there. There is even an occasional reading reflecting expressions unique to the so-called Palestinian Syriac version of the Gospels, which also rests on a Greek *Vorlage*[99]. Consider, for example, the addition to Mt. 6:34, found only in our family of Arabic Gospel manuscripts and the Palestinian Syriac version : "Let the day's own trouble be sufficient for the day, and the hour's

96 Bernhard Levin, *Die griechisch-arabische Evangelien-Übersetzung; Vat. Borg. ar. 95 und Ber. orient. oct. 1108* (Uppsala, 1938).

97 Cf. Joshua Blau, "Über einige christlich-arabische Manuscripte aus dem 9. und 10. Jahrhundert", *Le Muséon* 75 (1962), pp. 101-108. Cf. also the study by Amy Galli Garland, cited in n. 20 above.

98 Graf, vol. I, p. 146.

99 Metzger, *op. cit.*, pp. 75-82.

difficulties for the hour". The last phrase is an *agraphon*, found in no Greek manuscript of the Gospel[100].

More to the point for the purpose of the present inquiry is the fact that the Arabic of these Gospel manuscripts, along with the Arabic of the many theological treatises coming from Palestinian monasteries in the same period, to which we alluded above, from the point of view of grammar, syntax, and even lexicography, is what Joshua Blau designates as a form of Middle Arabic. It represents a popular pattern of Christian Arabic speech which was at home in southern Palestine beginning in the eighth century. It is significant that the earliest date Blau can assign to any of the texts written in this veritable dialect, both biblical and non-biblical, as mentioned earlier, is the year 772[101]. So the conclusion must be that the early Palestinian Arabic Gospels are indigenous to Palestine, and a product of the Palestinian Christians' adjustment to the arrival of Arabic as a *lingua franca* within *dar al-islām*, probably beginning in their area with the reforms of ʿAbd al-Malik (685-705), as we shall argue below. The evidence of the language itself thus precludes a pre-Islamic date for the origin of the Palestinian Arabic Gospel text[102].

Baumstark's choice of al-Ḥirā as a likely place for the translation of the Gospels into Arabic, even prior to Islam, was not a completely groundless surmise on his part. Christianity was certainly well established there by the end of the sixth century[103]. By that time in al-Ḥirā written Arabic had achieved a sufficiently high degree of development to be capable to serve as a vehicle for the translation of the Gospels. Christian Arabs themselves probably used this written Arabic language at this early time[104]. The problem is that if they ever thought of translating the Gospels into Arabic, and we have no documentary evidence to support the surmise that they ever entertained such a thought, they almost certainly would have translated them from Syriac, which was the ecclesiastical language of the Nestorian and Jacobite Christian communities of the area. The early Palestinian Arabic Gospels on the other hand are definitely translated from Greek. The persons and monasteries with which they are associated are Melkite. The likelihood of an

100 The addition appears in Sinai Arabic MSS 72 and 74, Vatican Borgia Arabic MS 95, and Berlin Orient. Oct. 1108. It is absent in Sinai Arabic MS 75. Cf. Agnes Smith Lewis and Margaret Dunlop Gibson, *The Palestinian Syriac Lectionary of the Gospels* (London, 1899), p. 71. Cf. Metzger, *op. cit.*, p. 267.

101 Blau, *A Grammar of Christian Arabic*, *op. cit.*, vol. 267, pp. 19-38, esp. p. 20, n. 7.

102 Cf. J. Blau, "Sind uns Reste arabischer Bibelübersetzungen aus vorislamischer Zeit erhalten geblieben?" *Le Muséon* 86 (1973), pp. 67-72.

103 Cf. J. Spencer Trimingham, *Christianity Among the Arabs in Pre-Islamic Times* (London, 1979), pp. 188-202, including references to earlier bibliography.

104 Cf. the studies cited in n. 64 above.

Arabic Gospel text originating in al-Ḥīrā and finding its way to widespread acceptance in the monasteries of Palestine prior to the rise of Islam is highly improbable. Not only is the earliest dated manuscript which contains the early Palestinian Gospel text from the late 9th century; but all of the manuscripts in the family of them which carries the same Gospel text tradition are examples of the Christian Arabic dialect of the eighth and ninth centuries that was a stage in the rise of middle Arabic.

As for the evidence of the rubrics contained in the Palestinian manuscripts, which reflect the liturgical usage of the pre-Islamic Jerusalem church, and which were Baumstark's only plausible reason for assigning the Palestinian Gospel versions to pre-Islamic times, they need not be considered an obstacle to the later date of the Gospel text. As Georg Graf pointed out, the persistence of these rubrics, even after the time when the liturgical practices were supposed to have changed in Palestine, may only testify to the tenacity of earlier liturgical practices in Palestinian monasteries, as they affected the Arabic speaking, non-monastic population[105]. Furthermore, there is now evidence to suggest that Palestine, along with the other Oriental patriarchates, was virtually sealed off from effective direct communication with Constantinople from about 750 until the tenth century[106]. So the liturgical changes in question probably did not occur in Palestine until long after they were mandated in Byzantium.

B. Naǧrān

Himyarite Naǧrān is a likely place to look for a pre-Islamic, Arabic version of the Gospels. Christianity flourished there, due in no small part to the efforts of Simeon of Bêt Aršām who was active as a missionary during the first half of the sixth century[107]. It was Simeon in any case who furnished the evidence that may be construed as supportive of the surmise that there was in Naǧrān a pre-Islamic, Arabic version of the Gospels. Simeon wrote a letter in Syriac in 518/19 in which he tells the story of the Christian martyrs of Naǧrān who had been killed by the Jewish king of Himyar, D̲h̲u Nuwās, around the year 517. The letter speaks of reports of the massacre which circulated in documents written in the Naǧrānite language. Professor Irfan Shahid, who has edited, translated and extensively studied Simeon's letter and related documents, argues that this Naǧrānite language (*seprâ*

105 Cf. Graf, vol. I, pp. 143-146; Vööbus, *op. cit.*, p. 293.

106 Cf. Sidney H. Griffith, "Eutychius of Alexandria on the Emperor Theophilus and Iconoclasm in Byzantium: a Tenth Century Moment in Christian Apologetics in Arabic", *Byzantion* 52 (1982), pp. 154-190.

107 Cf. Trimingham, *op. cit.*, pp. 169, 195, 289, 294-307.

nîgrānāyâ) was Arabic[108]. The significance of this fact in regard to the present topic may be stated in Professor Shahid's words.

> The fact that these letters dispatched from Najrān were written in Arabic illuminates the obscurity which shrouds the problem of an Arabic liturgical language and Bible translation in pre-Islamic times. These letters are perhaps the single most important evidence that can be adduced in favor of an affirmative answer to this question[109].

Others may argue that Syriac was the ecclesiastical language of the Christians in Arabia. Professor Shahid does not deny its official presence there. But, on the basis of the geographical distance of Nağrān from the Syriac speaking areas, he presses his point, "For the devotional purposes of the Najrānites, Arabic must have been their principal language"[110]. No small part of his readiness to reach this conclusion is his conviction that "the feeling of the Arabs for their language and the spoken word was such as to make it completely incomprehensible that they would not have desired to express their religious sentiments through their own language, which had been so highly developed and refined by the great poets of pre-Islamic Arabia"[111]. When it comes to the specific point which most interests us here, Professor Shahid says, "The case for a pre-Islamic Arabic translation of the Bible or part of it is as strong as the case for the use of Arabic in church service and rests upon the same arguments that have been adduced above"[112].

What confirms the argument for Professor Shahid is aṭ-Ṭabarī's mention of the story that one of the Christians of Nağrān escaped the massacre of his people by Dhu Nuwās, and came with the report of it to the king of Abyssinia, bringing along with him a partly burned Gospel book[113]. "What is important in the reference", says Professor Shahid, "is its reflection of the fact that there was a Gospel in South Arabia around 520. Whether the whole of the Bible or only a part of it was translated is not clear; it is safe to assume that of the books of the Bible, the Gospels and the Psalms, and possibly the Pentateuch, were the first to be translated"[114].

108 Irfan Shahid, *The Martyrs of Najrān, New Documents* (Subsidia Hagiographica, 49; Bruxelles, 1971), pp. 242-250. Prof. Shahid has defended his argument that Arabic was the language of Nağrān, against the attack of G. Garbini in his review of *The Martyrs of Najrān* in *Rivista degli Studi Orientali* 52 (1978), pp. 111-112. Cf. Shahid, "*The Martyrs of Najran*: Miscellaneous Reflections", *Le Muséon* 93 (1980), pp. 154-157.

109 Shahid, *Martyrs*, *op. cit.*, p. 247.

110 *Ibid.*

111 *Ibid.*, p. 248.

112 *Ibid.*, p. 249.

113 Cf. Th. Nöldeke, *Geschichte der Perser und Araber zur Zeit der Sasaniden aus der arabischen Chronik des Ṭabari* (Leyden, 1879), p. 188.

114 Shahid, *op. cit.*, pp. 249-250.

C. The Argument for a Pre-Islamic Gospel in Arabic

Professor Shahid and Anton Baumstark share the conviction that it is inconceivable that Arab Christians prior to the rise of Islam should not have had an Arabic version of the Gospels, if for no other purpose, for use in the liturgy of the divine word. The arguments rest not so much on documentary evidence for the existence of any such Arabic versions, although some bits of evidence have been put forward, but on the above mentioned inconceivability, and on the fact that the Arabic language of the sixth century was certainly sufficiently well developed, in more than one place, to serve such a purpose. Furthermore, in his forthcoming *Byzantium and the Arabs before the Rise of Islam : from Constantine to Heraclius*, Professor Shahid will unfold a panorama of Arab Christian history which dates from the fourth century[115]. Naturally, he will argue that Arabic was the language of this Christianity.

Opposing the views of Professor Shahid are those of Professor J. Spencer Trimingham. Noting the lack of documentary evidence for the existence of a pre-Islamic, Arabic version of the Gospels and other scriptures, Professor Trimingham reaches the following conclusion :

> The fact that Aramaic was so widely understood hindered the translation of Christian writings into Arabic ... The Arab Church had no focus that could provide that sense of Christian-Arab unity that the Syriac Church had in its Syriac Bible and liturgy. The many translations of Christian writings from Syriac into Arabic that exist are all subsequent to the Muslim Arab conquest[116].

It becomes clear in his review of Professor Trimingham's book, that Professor Shahid will argue that documentary evidence for Christianity in Arabia will in large part come from the hints and clues of it which remain in the works of the pre-Islamic, Christian Arabic poets[117]. One can only await the publication of Professor Shahid's projected three volume study before any more can be said on the subject.

As for the thesis of the present study, it is that in the first Abbasid century an abundant Christian literature, including versions of the Gospels, began to appear in Arabic, without reference to any previous Arabic ecclesiastical archive. Rather, as mentioned above, the determining factor for this development was the arrival of Arabic as a *lingua franca* within *dar al-islām*. When the language of the *Qur'ān* became the language of empire, the Gospels were translated into Arabic. The project was first inaugurated in the monastic communities of Palestine.

115 Cf. Shahid, "... : Miscellaneous Reflections", *art. cit.*, p. 160.
116 Trimingham, *op. cit.*, pp. 225-226.
117 Irfan Shahid, review of J. Spencer Trimingham, *op. cit.*, *JSSt* 26 (1981), pp. 150-153.

IV. *Palestine and the Gospel in Arabic*

At the beginning of the present inquiry it was noted that the impetus to assimilate the subject peoples into the Islamic community was a feature of the Abbasid revolution, with roots in the policies of the Umayyad caliph, ʿUmar II (717-720). Even earlier, the impetus to Arabicize the administration of affairs in all the domains of the caliph began in the reign of ʿAbd al-Malik (685-705)[118]. The Arabicization involved not only a change of the language in which records were kept among the subject populations. An important feature of this administrative reformation was the public and official proclamation in Arabic of the basic tenets of Islam. No where is this more evident than in ʿAbd al-Malik's monetary reform. The iconographical formulae of his coinage went through a process of development whereby all notations in languages other than Arabic disappeared, along with their associated religious or imperial designs. No trace of Greek, or of Christian crosses and figural representations remained once the development found its conclusion. The new coinage carried only epigraphic designs, proclaming the truths of Islam, and claiming the authority of the caliph[119]. The same is to be said even for road signs; from the time of the reign of ʿAbd al-Malik one finds them in Arabic, announcing the *šahādah*[120]. As if to put the point clearly, in a Greek papyrus document from the time of ʿAbd al-Malik one finds the *basmallah* and the *šahādah* in Arabic, followed by a Greek translation[121]. And, of course, ʿAbd al-Malik's truly monumental statement of the truths of Islam in Arabic, in the public forum, is the Dome of the Rock in Jerusalem, with its emphatically Islamic inscriptions composed of phrases from the *Qurʾān*[122].

118 On this caliph and his reign, cf. ʿAbd al-Ameer ʿAbd Dixon, *The Umayyad Caliphate 65-86/684-705; a Political Study* (London, 1971).

119 Cf. Philip Grierson, "The Monetary Reforms of ʿAbd al-Malik, their Metrological Basis and their Financial Repercussions", *Journal of the Economic and Social History of the Orient* 3 (1960), pp. 241-264. Grierson's study is metrological and not iconographical, but he provides a full bibliography along with some important comments on iconography. For the latter concern cf. J. Walker, *A Catalogue of the Arab-Byzantine and Post-Reform Umaiyad Coins* (London, 1956); G.C. Miles, "The Iconography of Umayyad Coinage", *Ars Orientalis* 3 (1959), pp. 207-213; A. Grabar, *l'iconoclasme byzantin : dossier archéologique* (Paris, 1957), pp. 67-74.

120 Cf. Moshe Sharon, "An Arabic Inscription from the Time of the Caliph ʿAbd al-Malik", *Bulletin of the School of Oriental and African Studies* 29 (1966), pp. 367-372.

121 Cf. L. Mitteis & U. Wilcken, *Grundzüge und Chrestomathie der Papyruskunde* (2 vols. in 4; Leipzig-Berlin, 1912), vol. I, pt. 1, p. 135.

122 Cf. Oleg Grabar, "The Dome of the Rock in Jerusalem", *Ars Orientalis* 3 (1959), pp. 33-59, reprinted in the author's *Studies in Medieval Islamic Art* (London, 1976); K.A.C. Creswell, *Early Muslim Architecture : Umayyads A.D. 622-750* (2nd ed. in two parts, vol. I, part II; Oxford, 1969); E.C. Dodd, "The Image of the Word", *Berytus* 18 (1969), pp. 35-79;

The message was clear and unmistakable. The official deployment of Arabic in the conquered territories stated the religious and imperial claims of Islam. As if to leave no doubt about the effect of this policy on the Christian community, ʿAbd al-Malik, in what may be taken as a gesture symbolic of the new resolution publicly to promote Islam, attempted to expropriate the church of St. John in Damascus, to incorporate it into the mosque beside it [123]. In the spirit of these same affairs one must understand the caliph Yazīd's (720-724) reaction against the public declarations of Christian faith in the open display of crosses and icons [124]. It is no wonder that later Christian historians dated the beginnings of anti-Christian policies in Islamic government to the reign of ʿAbd al-Malik [125], in spite of this caliph's well documented benevolence to many individual Christians in his entourage, as well as in his administration [126].

The Arabicization of the Islamic government was not without its effects within the conquered Christian populations outside of Arabia. The policy effectively required the caliph's subjects to learn Arabic for the sake of their own civic protection, as well as in pursuit of upward social mobility. Eventually, within a century of the institution of ʿAbd al-Malik's policies, Christians were producing their own literature in Arabic.

It is not surprising that the earliest exemplars of Christianity in Arabic appeared in the Palestinian area. Here the ecclesiastical language had been Greek, with the exception of the local Syro-Palestinian dialect of Aramaic, often called Palestinian Syriac, which appears to have been used in church principally for the liturgy, but also for the more popular genres of religious writing, such as homilies and saints' lives [127]. After the Islamic conquest, and during the initial period of military occupation in Syro-Palestine, church life in the area doubtless continued as before, having adjusted itself to the new facts of civic life. With ʿAbd al-Malik's reforms and innovations, however,

C. Kessler, "ʿAbd al-Malik's Inscription in the Dome of the Rock: a Reconsideration", *The Journal of the Royal Asiatic Society* (1970), pp. 2-14.

123 Dixon, *op. cit.*, p. 23. Cf. the references to this and to a similar affair involving columns from the Basilica of Gethsemane, which ʿAbd al-Malik wanted to incorporate into the mosque at Mecca; in J. Nasrallah, *Saint Jean de Damas, son époque, sa vie, son œuvre* (Harissa, 1950), pp. 54-55.

124 A.A. Vasiliev, "The Iconoclastic Edict of the Caliph Yazīd II, A.D. 721", *Dumbarton Oaks Papers* 9 & 10 (1956), pp. 25-47.

125 J.B. Chabot, *Denys de Tell Maḥrē: Chronique* (Paris, 1895), vol. II, pp. 474-475.

126 Cf. Nasrallah, *op. cit.*, pp. 37-55.

127 Cf. the brief survey, with bibliography, in B.M. Metzger, *The Early Versions of the New Testament* (Oxford, 1977), pp. 75-82. Cf. also the comments and bibliography of M. Goshen-Gottstein, *The Bible in the Syropalestinian Version; Part I: Pentateuch and Prophets* (Jerusalem, 1973), pp. viii-xv.

the seeds were sown for an eventual ecclesiastical adaptation to the new linguistic, and the novel religious milieu in Arabic.

A fact that would have hurried the pace of adaptation in Syria/Palestine was that Greek had been the language of participation in the life of Byzantium. It had suited Melkite church life in the area, helped by the indigenous Aramaic dialect, as long as Palestine had been a province of the Byzantine empire, with strong ties to Constantinople. Afterwards, however, Syro-Palestinians, largely Melkite in religious confession, like their brothers in Alexandria, were left without the comforts of a full church life in an indigenous language, i.e., in Coptic or Syriac, as enjoyed by the largely Monophysite communities in Egypt and Syro-Mesopotamia, the Maronites in Syria, or the Nestorians and others in the Persian territories. This fact must have aided the Arabicization of Christianity in Palestine.

It was as an eventual consequence of the policies inaugurated by ʿAbd al-Malik that John Damascene, Palestine's greatest ecclesiastical writer in Greek, retired to the monastery of Mar Sabas, probably between 718 and 720, during the caliphate of ʿUmar II[128]. His scholarly achievement is still recognized as a major exponent of Byzantine Christianity. But a symbol of what was really happening in Palestine is to be seen in the fact that after 750, in the next generation of scholarship at Mar Sabas, John Damascene's disciple, Theodore Abū Qurrah, was writing in Arabic. One cannot be sure that Abū Qurrah ever wrote in Greek. Among the forty-three Greek *opuscula* preserved under his name, one of the longer ones was translated from Arabic[129], and one now has evidence that one of the shorter ones also circulated originally in Arabic[130].

Greek, of course, did not simply disappear from the Melkite church of Palestine. It was a language of liturgy and high church-manship. But not even all the monks of Mar Sabas could understand it by the end of the eighth century[131]. The time was ripe for the full appearance of Christianity in Arabic, obviously, by now, the daily language of many Christians in Palestine. The liturgy, and the pastoral effort to produce effective apologetical information in the new vernacular were the two areas in which Arabic first appears in the manuscript tradition.

128 Cf. Nasrallah, *op. cit.*, p. 81.

129 Abū Qurrah originally wrote his epistle-treatise against the "heretics" of Armenia in Arabic, at the behest of Patriarch Thomas of Jerusalem. The patriarch's *synkellos*, Michael, translated it into Greek, and it is preserved as Abū Qurrah's Greek *opusculum* IV. Cf. *PG*, vol. 97, col. 1504D.

130 Cf. Sidney H. Griffith, "Some Unpublished Arabic Sayings Attributed to Theodore Abū Qurrah", *Le Muséon* 92 (1979), pp. 29-35.

131 Cf. S. Vailhé, "Le monastère de saint Sabas", *Échos d'Orient* 3 (1899-1900), p. 22. On the swift Arabicization of life in Palestine beginning in the eighth century, cf. R.P. Blake, "La littérature grecque en Palestine au viiie siècle", *Le Muséon* 78 (1965), pp. 376-378.

A. The Liturgy

From as early as the fourth century there is evidence that in Palestine there was a need for the translation of the scripture lessons of the divine liturgy from Greek into the Aramaic vernacular. Both Eusebius and the western pilgrim, Etheria, provide the documentation for the employment of Aramaic translators in the liturgy, even in Jerusalem, at this early date[132]. This practice was presumably the situation which eventually gave birth to the Palestinian Syriac Version of the scriptures, a version which is preserved in notably liturgical manuscripts. While the date of the origin of this version is uncertain, with likely estimates ranging from the fourth century to the sixth[133], it is clear that the Melkite community of Palestine was its original home. Melkite groups in Egypt and Syria, perhaps refugees from Palestine, were still employing it as late as the twelfth century. Two of the most important manuscripts of the Gospel lectionary in this version were written in this century by Palestinian scribes, in a place called "Antioch of the Arabs"[134]. But the manuscripts themselves were found in the monastery of St. Catherine at Mt. Sinai[135]. The most plausible hypothesis is that this version of the Gospels grew out of the liturgical need for translations of the lessons in the vernacular, reaching back into the circumstances described by Eusebius and Egeria[136].

As it happens, the Arabic Gospel text of the family of manuscripts which includes Sinai Arabic MSS 72 and 74, along with Vatican Borgia MS 95 and Berlin Orient. Oct. MS 1108, as mentioned earlier, has marked affinities with the text of the Syro-Palestinian lectionary[137]. Here is not the place to pursue this relationship further, a task which must await the full scholarly edition of these important Arabic manuscripts. However, it is important to recall that these manuscripts present the four Gospels in a continous text, and not in a lectionary format. Nevertheless, the text is marked off with liturgical rubrics, assigning pericopes to the appropriate days in the temporal cycle of the liturgy. These circumstances argue that the origin of this text of the Gospel in Arabic, *mutatis mutandis*, answered the same need as did the earlier Syro-Palestinian version, and that in a certain sense it can be considered its successor.

132 Cf. the relevant passages noted and quoted in Vööbus, *Early Versions*, *op. cit.*, p. 126, nn. 2 & 3.
133 *Ibid.*, pp. 123-128.
134 Cf. Metzger, *op. cit.*, p. 79, and n. 1.
135 Cf. Agnes Smith Lewis & Margaret Dunlop Gibson, *The Palestinian Syriac Lectionary of the Gospels* (London, 1899).
136 Cf. M.-J. Lagrange, "L'origine de la version syro-palestinienne des évangiles", *Revue Biblique* 34 (1925), pp. 481-504.
137 Cf. n. 100 above, and B. Levin, *op. cit.*, p. 42.

It is striking that all of the early Arabic versions of the Bible from the ninth century which are actually extant, including the fragment of Psalm 78 in Greek characters from Damascus, come from the Syro-Palestinian area, and were seemingly all accomplished under Melkite auspices. The most likely hypothesis is that the reforms instituted by ʿAbd al-Malik eventually produced the circumstances which made necessary the first Arabic versions of the scriptures. The Melkites in Syria/Palestine, who had earlier experience with the necessity of providing for liturgical lessons in a vernacular language, met this new necessity in a similar spirit, and thus became the first Christian community to publish an Arabic Bible. A western pilgrim to Jerusalem, who around 808 A.D. wrote a *Memorandum on the Houses of God and Monasteries in the Holy City*, listed among the clergy of the church of St. Mary at Mt. Olivet, one "qui Sarracenica lingua psallit"[138].

B. Apologetics

At the beginning of the present article attention was called to the fact that the earliest Arabic manuscripts which contain Gospel texts often also contain apologetic tracts. The connection is not accidental. The Gospel in Arabic was a necessity in the first Abbasid century not only for liturgical purposes, but also for the purpose of defending Christian doctrines and practices against challenges to them coming from Muslims.

Since it was the conviction of the Islamic community that "the people of the Gospel should pass judgment according to what God has sent down in it" (*al-Māʾidah* (5):47), one is not surprised that the first Christian apologists to write in Arabic were concerned to set out in their treatises a careful explanation of how the Gospel provides testimonies to the truth of the standard Christian doctrines. In the first place the effort required a clear statement of what the Gospel is, in Christian eyes. As we have seen, the *Qurʾān* has it simply that God gave Jesus the Gospel, "confirming what was in the Torah before it" (*al-Māʾidah* (5):46). Secondly, the apologists had to explain their principles of exegesis, especially in regard to the relationship between the Torah and the Gospel. And finally, they had to argue that the Gospel alone, of all the sacred books, is the only one that warrants human faith, and that it sustains the religious doctrines propounded by Christians.

Here is not the place to examine these arguments. The central position which the Gospel holds in the apologetical treatises of the time may be

138 T. Tobler & A. Molinier, *Itinera Hierosolymitana et Descriptiones Terrae Sanctae* (Genevae, 1879), p. 302.

shown by two quotations from the works of Theodore Abū Qurrah, some of whose writings were transmitted by the same scribes who wrote the Biblical manuscripts described earlier[139]. The first quotation includes a neat description of a Bible in hand, with the Gospel in the central position. He says, "Christianity is simply faith in the Gospel and its appendices, and the Law of Moses and the books of the prophets in between"[140]. The Gospel's appendices are the books of the Acts of the Apostles, the Epistles, and Revelation — the books that make up the remainder of the New Testament. The books of the prophets "in between" are all the Old Testament books from Joshua to Malachi.

In his stylistically more popular tract "On the Existence of the Creator, and the True Religion", Abū Qurrah leaves no doubt about the Gospel's central position. He says,

> Were it not for the Gospel, we would not have acknowledged Moses to be from God. Rather, on reflection, we would have vigorously opposed him. Likewise, we have acknowledged the prophets to be from God because of the Gospel. It is not on the basis of reason, since we have acknowledged them because Christ has informed us that they are prophets. Also, because we have knowledge of Christ's whole economy, and having read their books and discovered that they had previously described his whole economy just as he accomplished it, we have acknowledged that they are prophets. At this point in time we do not acknowledge Christ and his affairs because of the books of the prophets. Rather, we acknowledge them because of Christ's saying that they are prophets and because of our own recognition that his economy is written in their books[141].

Earlier in this article Abū Qurrah was quoted as saying that the Gospel is Jesus' summons (*ad-da'wah*)[142] to people to accept the good news of the salvation he won for them. In this connection it is pertinent ro recall that both Abu Qurrah and other Christian apologists who wrote in Arabic were accustomed to argue that one of the motives for accepting the credibility of Christianity is that, alone among the messengers of the world's religions, Christian evangelists saw to it that the good news about Christ was proclaimed to each people in their own language[143].

139 Cf. nn. 22 & 23 above. See Sidney H. Griffith, "Stephen of Ramleh and the Christian Kerygma in Arabic, in Ninth Century Palestine", *Journal of Ecclesiastical History* 36 (1985), pp. 23-45.

140 Constantin Bacha, *Les œuvres arabes de Théodore Aboucara, évêque d'Ḥarān* (Beyrouth, 1904), p. 27.

141 Louis Cheikho, "Mīmar li Tādurus Abī Qurrah fī wuǧūd al-ḫāliq wa d-dīn al-qawīm", *al-Machriq* 15 (1912), p. 837.

142 Cf. n. 11 above.

143 Cf. Theodore Abū Qurrah's deployment of this argument in I. Dick, "Deux écrits inédits de Théodore Abuqurra", *Le Muséon* 72 (1959), p. 64; 'Ammār al-Baṣrī in M. Hayek, *'Ammār al-Baṣrī, apologie et controverses* (Beyrouth, 1977), pp. 128 & 131.

V. *Conclusion*

The conclusion to be drawn from our inquiry into the appearance of the Gospel in Arabic in the first Abbasid century is that it was in this century, in Syria/Palestine, as a pastoral project under Melkite auspices, that the first translation was made for general use in the church. Michael the Syrian's report of an earlier Arabic version of the Gospel made at the command of the Jacobite patriarch, John I, if it is reliable, concerns only a translation made in the seventh century for the consultation of a Muslim official. It had no discernible influence in the life of the church.

As for quotations from the Gospels in Islamic sources, it is clear from the foregoing inquiry that prior to the first Abbasid century Muslim writers spoke of the Gospel and it's message, primarily from the point of view of Islamic ideas about it's contents, and they worded their quotations accordingly. Only from the ninth century does one find evidence that allows the conclusion to be drawn that some Muslim writers had Arabic translations of the Gospels at their service, which they could use to document their references. Even then, as we have seen, only a few writers made use of the new resources. Earlier scholars, even someone of the stature of Ibn Isḥāq, apparently were dependent upon Christian informants about the Christian Gospels, or themselves learned enough of the requisite languages to find the places in the Christian scriptures which interested them. There is no evidence in their works of an existent Arabic version in the hands of Christians. Rather, the quotations in Arabic are all such as to betray the work of an Islamic interpreter, who most likely rendered only certain passages into Arabic, and then on an *ad hoc* basis, and in accordance with Islamic ideas about what is religiously correct. Such a procedure does not suggest that these writers were working with an Arabic version of the Bible. Rather, it suggests that there was no such version yet available.

All one can say about the possibility of a pre-Islamic, Christian version of the Gospel in Arabic is that no sure sign of it's actual existence has yet emerged. Furthermore, even if some unambiguous evidence of it should turn up as a result of more recent investigations, it is clear that after the Islamic conquest of the territories of the oriental patriarchates, and once Arabic had become the official and *de facto* public language of the caliphate, the church faced a much different pastoral problem than was the case with the earlier missions among the pre-Islamic Arabs.

The new pastoral problem asserted itself first in Syria/Palestine because it was here, in the Melkite community, that by the ninth century Arabic had become the only common language among Christians. In Mesopotamia and Iraq, on the other hand, the translation of the Bible into Arabic, at the hands of savants such as Ḥunayn ibn Isḥāq, appears to have been essentially a scholarly and apologetical activity. The Christian liturgy remained in Syriac, even as the apologists were beginning to write in Arabic. In Syria/Palestine, however, there was a pressing liturgical, as well as an apologetical need for the Gospel in Arabic. The dozen or so earliest manuscripts of the Christian scriptures translated into Arabic from Syriac and Greek all appeared in this milieu, as we have sketched it above. A symbol of the circumstances which evoked these first versions may be seen in the old bilingual fragment of Mt. 13:46-52 found at Sinai[144]. The text is in both Greek and Arabic, in eloquent testimony to the need which in Palestine prompted the first appearance of the Gospel in Arabic in the first Abbasid century. It was not until sometime later, even in the twelfth century, that a similar need was felt in other, linguistically more homogenous churches within *dār al-islām*.

144 Cf. Agnes Smith Lewis, *Catalogue of the Syriac MSS in the Convent of S. Catherine on Mount Sinai* (Studia Sinaitica, no. 1; London, 1894), pp. 105-106.

III

THE MONKS OF PALESTINE AND THE GROWTH OF CHRISTIAN LITERATURE IN ARABIC

Palestinian monasteries such as those of Mar Sabas, Mar Charitōn, and St. Catherine at Mt. Sinai are well known to historians of eastern Christianity as centers of notable Christian culture in the Holy Land. One has only to mention the names of the monasteries themselves, or of some of their more famous author-monks, such as John of Damascus or Anastasius of Sinai, to make the point. They all enjoy virtually instant name recognition among modern western scholars.[1] However, it is also true that because of their close association with Constantinople one almost automatically associates these monasteries and their scholar-monks with the history of Christianity in Byzantium, ignoring the fact that by the eighth century, the time of John of Damascus (d.c. 750) and the last years of Anastasius of Sinai (d.c. 700), one is actually speaking of the Islamic era, and of authors who lived under the authority of the caliphate. By the time John of Damascus had finished his career, the Holy Land had been under the rule of Muslims for more than a hundred years.[2] Of course, John and Anastasius had written their works in Greek, and the familiarity of this language itself allowed their compositions to play an important part in Byzantine church life, once they had been carried to Constantinople by refugee monks. For modern historians, however, this very familiarity has obscured the fact that in the patriarchate of Jerusalem, by the second half of the eighth century the readership of John of Damascus's works was being steadily restricted to an ever smaller circle of scholar-monks, who were themselves busy producing the first ecclesiastical literature in Arabic, the public language of the new Islamic society.

---

[1] For a guide to the early history of the Palestinian monasteries, see B. Flusin, *Miracle et histoire dans l'oeuvre de Cyrille de Scythopolis* (Paris: Etudes Augustiniennes, 1983); Derwas James Chitty, *The Desert a City: an Introduction to the Study of Egyptian and Palestinian Monasticism under the Christian Empire* (Oxford: Blackwell, 1966), pp. 101ff; H. Leclercq, "Laures palestiniennes," *DACL*, VIII, 2, cols. 1961-1988. See also the earlier landmark studies: A. Ehrhard, "Das griechische Kloster Mar-Saba in Palaestina," *Römische Quartalschrift*, XVII (1893), 32-79; S. Vailhé, "Les écrivains de Mar-Saba," *Échos d'Orient*, II (1898-1899), 1-11, 33-47, and his "Le monastère de saint-Sabas," *Échos d'Orient*, II (1898-1899), 332-41; III (1899-1900), 18-28, 168-77. For the Greek writers of the eighth century cf. R.P. Blake, "La littérature grecque en Palestine au VIIIe siècle," *Mus*, LXXVIII (1965), 367–80.

[2] See J. Nasrallah, *Saint Jean de Damas, son époque, sa vie, son oeuvre* (Harissa, 1950); Daniel J. Sahas, *John of Damascus on Islam, the "Heresy of the Ishmaelites"* (Leiden: E.J. Brill, 1972).

Accordingly, it is the purpose of the present communication to give an account of the growth and development of this new Arabic literature in the Palestinian monasteries. It first comes to light in the course of the first Abbasid century, and it represents the first fruits of what was to become a long-term project, carried out in many communities under the rule of the caliphate, to commend Christian faith in the *lingua franca* of the new socio-political reality brought about by the establishment of the *dār al-islām*. For the Palestinian monasteries themselves this project represents the continuation of a long-term devotion to scholarship, now turned to meet the intellectual challenge of Islam.

I.
The First Abbasid Century

Already under the Umayyad caliphs, and particularly during the reign of ʿAbd al-Malik (685–705), the Islamic government in Damascus had been taking steps to assimilate the conquered territories of the oriental patriarchates into a publicly recognizable Islamic realm.[3] A striking monumental symbol of this campaign was the construction under ʿAbd al-Malik of the shrine of the Dome of the Rock in Jerusalem.[4] Furthermore, during the reign of the same caliph the purpose was equally well served in numerous humbler instances, ranging all the way from the installation of road signs proclaiming the Islamic *shahāda*,[5] to the circulation of coinage stamped with an unmistakably Islamic iconography.[6] Under the caliph al-Walīd I (705-715) orders were given for all official records to be kept in the Arabic language.[7] ʿUmar II (717-720), in spite of his brief reign, eased the way for conversions to Islam by adjusting the tax laws, and by espousing the principle of the equality of all Muslim believers.[8] Yazīd II (720-724), although he too reigned only briefly, is on record as having given orders for the extirpation of the public symbols of Christianity, that is, crosses and images, even from private Christian premises.[9] The cumulative effect of these

[3] See ʿAbd al-Ameer ʿAbd Dixon, *The Umayyad Caliphate 65-86/684-705; a Political Study* (London: Luzac, 1971).

[4] See Oleg Grabar, "The Dome of the Rock in Jerusalem," *Ars Orientalis*, III (1959), 33-59, reprinted in the author's *Studies in Medieval Islamic Art* (London: Variorum Reprints, 1976); E.C. Dodd, "The Image of the Word," *Berytus*, XVIII (1969), 35-79; C. Kessler, "ʿAbd al-Malik's Inscription in the Dome of the Rock: a Reconsideration," *The Journal of the Royal Asiatic Society*, 1970, pp. 2-14.

[5] Cf. Moshe Sharon, "An Arabic Inscription from the Time of the Caliph ʿAbd al-Malik," *BSOAS*, XXIX (1966), 367-72.

[6] Cf. G.C. Miles, "The Iconography of Umayyad Coinage," *Ars Orientalis*, III (1959), 207-13.

[7] J.B. Chabot, *Anonymi Auctoris Chronicon ad Annum Christi 1234 Pertinens* [Corpus Scriptorum Christianorum Orientalium (CSCO), vol. 81] (Paris: J. Gabalda, 1920), pp. 298-99.

[8] See H.A.R. Gibb, "The Fiscal Rescript of ʿUmar II," *Arabica*, II (1955), 1-16; ʿAbd al-ʿAzīz Durī, "Notes on Taxation in Early Islam," *JESHO*, XVII (1974), 136-44. See also W.W. Barthold, "Caliph ʿUmar II and the Conflicting Reports of his Personality," *IQ*, XV (1971), 69-95—an English version of a Russian original, written in 1922.

[9] See A.A. Vasiliev, "The Iconoclastic Edict of the Caliph Yazīd II, A.D. 721," *Dumbarton Oaks Papers*, 9 and 10 (1956), pp. 25-47.

and similar measures over the first century of Islamic rule, taken together with the continuing success of Muslim arms in holding Byzantium at bay, prepared the way for the society of Abbasid times, which in theory had been built on the principle of the equality of all Muslim believers.[10] After the revolution of 750 all eyes in the caliphate, Jewish, Christian and Muslim alike, turned east, towards Baghdad as the new center of socio-political stability, and the source of religious and civil policy for the whole Islamic realm.[11] There ensued almost two centuries of virtual isolation from the Roman/Byzantine world, during which time the classical civilization of Islam came to fruition, without the interference of Byzantium, even in internal Christian concerns.[12] This state of affairs lasted until the second half of the tenth century, when Islamic military power was unable to stop the incursions of the crusading Byzantine emperor, Nicephorous Phocas (963–969), and his successor, and murderer, John Tzimisces (969–976).[13]

Official Islamic policy regarding the subject religious communities, that is to say the scripture people (*ahl al-kitāb*), who, according to the Qur'ān, *S. al-Tawba* (9):29, were supposed to receive state protection (*al-dhimma*) in return for the payment of a special poll tax (*al-jizya*), found its classic expression during the first Abbasid century, in the so-called "Covenant of ʿUmar."[14] This legal instrument was perhaps more ideal than real in the prescriptions it laid down for the government of Christian and Jewish life in the caliphate, but the very fact that it came to its final form around the year 800 is a testimony to the full development, at this mid-point in the first Abbasid century, of the classical ideal of the Islamic society. And the achievement of such an ideological coherence among Islamic jurists regarding the protected religious communities had obvious implications for the Christian church. As the present writer has argued elsewhere, it was at this time that conversion to Islam must have become more appealing to upwardly mobile Christians. So it is not surprising that it is also to this era, the first Abbasid century, that one must date the appearance of the earliest Christian Arabic literature, when Christians within dār al-islām must finally have realized that their lot for the foreseeable future was to live as a

[10] See M.A. Shaban, *The ʿAbbasid Revolution* (Cambridge: Cambridge University Press, 1970), p. 168.

[11] See Jacob Lassner, *The Shaping of ʿAbbāsid Rule* (Princeton: Princeton University Press, 1980).

[12] For a survey of government functions and policies during this period see Dominique Sourdel, *Le Vizirat ʿAbbāside de 749 à 936*, 2 vols. (Damas, 1959). Some hints regarding the ecclesiastical situation in Syria/Palestine are given in Hugh Kennedy, "The Melkite Church from the Islamic Conquest to the Crusades: Continuity and Adaptation in the Byzantine Legacy," in *The 17th International Byzantine Congress; Major Papers* (New Rochelle, N.Y.: A.D. Caratzas, 1986), pp. 325-43.

[13] See George Ostrogorsky, *History of the Byzantine State*, rev. ed. Tr. Joan Hussey (New Brunswick, N.J.: Rutgers University Press, 1969), pp. 288-98. Cf. also P.E. Walker, "The 'Crusade' of John Tzimisces in the Light of New Arabic Evidence," *Byzantion*, XLVII (1977), 301-27.

[14] See Arthur Stanley Tritton, *The Caliphs and their Non-Muslim Subjects; a Critical Study of the Covenant of ʿUmar* (London: Oxford University Press, 1930); Antoine Fattal, *Le statut légal des non-musulmans en pays d'islam* (Beyrouth, 1958); Bat Ye'or, *The Dhimmi; Jews and Christians under Islam* (Cranbury, N.J.: Fairleigh Dickinson, 1985).

subject population in an Islamic state.[15]

The earliest Christian Arabic literature may be divided into two broad categories. The first of them comprises what one might call "church-books," that is, works which Christians require for the ordinary conduct of their internal religious affairs. These writings would be the scriptures, patristic classics, inspirational homilies, lives of the saints, and such practical texts as creeds and canons, which govern the inner life of the community according to the decisions of the several major church councils. The second broad category of material which one might discern in the early Christian Arabic archive includes those works which one might loosely call apologetical treatises. The basic characteristic of these writings is that they were composed with an eye to the outside. In them the authors intend to bring the traditional theological considerations of their own Christian party to bear on the intellectual challenges of the day, in the very idiom of the current socio-political scene. Inevitably, of course, in the Christian Arabic literature of the first Abbasid century, Islam was the major horizon in view of which the Christian writers had to discuss not only their own internal differences, but their reactions to the claims of the newly established religion as well. Furthermore, in addition to the need to commend the credibility of Christian faith to the Muslims, in the first Abbasid century there was also the increasingly important requirement to furnish Christians themselves with persuasive reasons, stated in clear Arabic, for not heeding the evermore persistent call to Islam.

Chronologically, the monastic communities of Palestine seem to have led the way in the production of both categories of Christian Arabic literature. For even though the Abbasid revolution ushered in the era of the general Arabicization of Muslims and Christians alike in the Aramaic/Syriac speaking areas of the oriental patriarchates,[16] it was only in Melkite Palestine that the Christian "church-books" customarily had been kept in a non-Semitic language. Due perhaps to its strong ties with Constantinople, and to the triumph of Chalcedonian orthodoxy in the patriarchate of Jerusalem,[17] as well as to the fact that pilgrims flocked there from all over the Christian world,[18] Greek had

---

[15] See Sidney H. Griffith, "The Prophet Muḥammad, His Scripture and His Message, According to the Christian Apologies in Arabic and Syriac From the First Abbasid Century," in T. Fahd, ed., *La vie du prophète Mahomet* [Colloque de Strasbourg, 1980] (Paris: Presses Universitaires de France, 1983), pp. 99-146. See the author's further remarks in "The First *Summa Theologiae Arabica*, 877 A.D.," *Conversion and Continuity: Indigenous Christian Communities in Medieval Islamic Lands, a Colloquium* (The University of Toronto, 23-25 October, 1986), forthcoming.

[16] See A.N. Poliak, "L'arabisation de l'orient sémitique," *Revue des Études Islamiques*, XII (1938), 35-63.

[17] See the discussion and further bibliography in Christoph von Schönborn, *Sophrone de Jérusalem, vie monastique et confession dogmatique* [Théologie historique, 20] (Paris: Beauchesne, 1972).

[18] See J. Wilkinson, *Jerusalem Pilgrims Before the Crusades* (Warminster: Aris & Phillips, 1977); E.D. Hunt, *Holy Land Pilgrimage in the Later Roman Empire A.D. 312-460* (Oxford: Oxford University Press, 1982); P. Maraval, *Lieux saints et pèlerinages d'Orient* (Paris: Cerf, 1985).

remained the dominant ecclesiastical language of Palestine until the end of the Umayyad era.[19] It began to be replaced by Arabic in the first Abbasid century. While scripture and liturgy, along with the other "church-books," had long been in Syriac in much of Syria, Mesopotamia, and Iraq, and in Coptic in Egypt (outside Alexandria), in Palestine the custom had grown up from the fourth century to provide for the needs of the speakers of the vernacular languages through interpreters at the divine liturgy, but to preserve the basic rites and their texts in Greek. The earliest testimony to this practice in the Jerusalem church is to be found in the account of her journeys in the Holy Land left behind by the fourth-century pilgrim, Egeria. She visited Jerusalem in Holy Week of the year 381, and she recorded the following observation:

> In this province there are some people who know both Greek and Syriac, but others know only one or the other. The bishop may know Syriac, but he never uses it. He always speaks in Greek, and has a presbyter beside him who translates the Greek into Syriac, so that everyone can understand what he means. Similarly the lessons read in church have to be read in Greek, but there is always someone in attendance to translate into Syriac so that the people understand. Of course there are also people here who speak neither Greek nor Syriac, but Latin. But there is no need for them to be discouraged, since some of the brothers or sisters who speak Latin as well as Greek will explain things to them.[20]

Although there did eventually appear a small Christian archive of "church-books" in the Syriac language of which Egeria spoke, which is more accurately called Palestinian Aramaic,[21] its origins no doubt may be traced to the interpreters whom she mentioned.[22] This literature, even though it was still being copied by refugee Palestinians as late as the twelfth century,[23] never seriously challenged the hegemony of Greek in the ecclesiastical scholarship of Palestine, which had grown up from the earliest days in Caesarea, Gaza, Jerusalem, and, of course, in the Judaean monasteries. But then, once the speakers of Greek were effectively off the scene, that is by the middle of the first Abbasid century, Palestine, unlike the other oriental patriarchates, was ripe for a virtually complete conversion to Arabic. This state of affairs explains why one finds

---

[19] See Blake, "La littérature grecque." John of Damascus, the last notable Greek writer of Syria/Palestine died c. 749, around the very year when the first Christian Arabic writer of note was born, i.e., Theodore Abū Qurra, about whom see below.

[20] John Wilkinson, *Egeria's Travels to the Holy Land*, rev. ed. (Warminster: Aris & Phillips, 1981), p. 146.

[21] See the comment and bibliography of B.M. Metzger, *The Early Versions of the New Testament* (Oxford: Oxford University Press, 1977), pp. 75-82; M. Goshen-Gottstein, *The Bible in the Syropalestinian Version; Part I: Pentateuch and Prophets* (Jerusalem, 1973), pp. viii-xv. See also the bibliography in J. Barclay, "Melkite Orthodox Syro-Byzantine Manuscripts in Syriac and Palestinian Aramaic," *Studii Biblicii Franciscani Liber Annuus*, XXI (1971), 205-19.

[22] See the insightful remarks of M.-J. Lagrange, "L'origine de la version syro-palestinienne des évangiles," *Revue Biblique*, XXXIV (1925), 481-504.

[23] See Metzger, *The Early Versions*, p. 79, and n. 1

evidence of "church-books" in Arabic from Palestine already in the eighth century, as will appear below, with their incidence growing steadily throughout the ninth century; while in the other Syriac-speaking areas, where Greek was never so deeply embedded as it was in the Jerusalem patriarchate, the earliest Christian Arabic literature belongs almost exclusively to the second category of writings described above, and appears first in the ninth century.[24] In Egypt there is no appreciable Christian Arabic writing to speak of at all until the time of Eutychius of Alexandria (d. 940) and Severus b. al-Muqaffaʿ (d.c. 1000).[25] Their works, however, clearly belong to the second category of Christian Arabic literature, and do not include texts which Christians in Egypt in the first two Abbasid centuries would have employed in the daily exercise of their devotional lives.

II.
Old South Palestinian Arabic

Georg Graf was the first modern scholar to call attention to the fact that Palestine's early Christian Arabic archive, with its collection both of "church-books" and apologetical works, actually forms a distinctive literary ensemble, which was the product of the scholarly activity of the monks of the Holy Land's famous monasteries, from the eighth to the tenth centuries.[26] Following Graf some twenty years later, W. Heffening came to the same conclusion in the course of studying the origins of an Arabic version of one of Ephraem the Syrian's works hitherto known only in Greek.[27] According to Heffening, who paid special attention to codicological and linguistic considerations, by the end of the ninth century "one may speak of a scribal school of the Mar Saba cloister, and perhaps even of scribal schools of the cloisters of Sinai and Mār Ḥarīṭan."[28]

From the very beginning of the publication of Christian Arabic manuscripts from Palestine, scholars have commented upon the peculiarities of the morphology, grammar, syntax, and even the orthography, to be found in them. Joannes Arendzen called attention to these considerations in the very first publication of an integral work from the Palestinian Christian Arabic archive which he brought out in 1897, viz., Theodore Abū Qurra's tract on the Christian practice of venerating images. The work was copied by Stephen of Ramla at the

---

[24] See Griffith, "The Prophet Muḥammad." Even the versions of the scriptures in Arabic that may have been produced in Iraq by Ḥunayn b. Isḥāq (d. 873) and others were for scholarly, not liturgical, purposes. See the discussion in Sidney H. Griffith, "The Gospel in Arabic: an Inquiry into its Appearance in the First Abbasid Century," *Oriens Christianus*, LXIX (1985), 126-67.

[25] See Khalil Samir, "Arabic Sources for Early Egyptian Christianity," in B.A. Pearson & J.E. Goehring, eds., *The Roots of Egyptian Christianity* (Philadelphia: Fortress Press, 1986), pp. 82-97.

[26] See Georg Graf, *Die christlich-arabische Literatur bis zur fränkischen Zeit, eine literarhistorische Skizze* (Freiburg im Breisgau: Herder, 1905), pp. 8-21.

[27] W. Heffening, "Die griechische Ephraem-Paraenesis gegen das Lachen in arabische Übersetzung," *Oriens Christianus*, XXIV (1927), 94-119.

[28] Ibid., 102.

monastery of Mar Charitōn in the year 877.[29] In the light of earlier publications of specimens of texts from the same time and place, Arendzen noted in his introduction to Stephen of Ramla's manuscript that "one will easily be persuaded that the Christian Arabs, at least in Asia, intentionally preserved for themselves a peculiar manner of writing, and that while the Muslims were using a rounder, more cursive hand in the ninth, tenth and eleventh centuries, which is called *Nasḫī*, they [i.e., the Christians] were making use of the old square, angular forms of the letters, which in the first place remind one of Syriac, and which hold a place midway between old Kufic and *Nasḫī*."[30]

Arendzen was too hasty in assigning this Palestinian, monastic hand to all of the Christians of "Asia," over the three centuries he mentions. But it is true that, whether intentionally or not, the monks of the Holy Land employed a recognizably distinctive style of writing in the ninth and tenth centuries,[31] which is but one of a number of characteristics which set the Palestinian texts apart. Morphological, grammatical, and syntactical considerations also have a role to play among the distinctive traits of the Arabic written in the *scriptoria* of the Holy Land monasteries. And it is instructive to observe that already in the midst of the nineteenth century, when the texts themselves were first coming within the ken of western scholars, these linguistic considerations claimed their immediate attention.[32] By the century's end, largely on the basis of Palestinian texts, Arabists were speaking of the role of the Christians in the development of the modern "vulgar Arabic," as if there were indeed such a thing as a "christliches Arabismus."[33] And in 1905 Georg Graf published a linguistic study, again based largely on Palestinian manuscripts, the title of which clearly announces the scholarly consensus that had already developed: *Der Sprachgebrauch der ältesten christlich-arabischen Literatur, ein Beitrag zur Geschichte des Vulgär Arabisch.*[34] Thereafter, it became the practice in editing these manuscripts to

---

[29] Joannes Arendzen, *Theodori Abu Ḳurra de Cultu Imaginum Libellus e Codice Arabico Nunc Primum Editus Latine Versus Illustratus* (doct. diss., Bonn, 1897).

[30] Ibid., p. xvi.

[31] See, e.g., Agnes Smith Lewis and Margaret Dunlop Gibson, eds. and trs., *Forty-One Facsimiles of Dated Christian Arabic Manuscripts* [Studia Sinaitica, XII] (Cambridge: Cambridge University Press, 1907), plates II, III, IV, pp. 3-8; E. Tisserant, *Specimina Codicum Orientalium* (Bonn, 1914), plates 54, 55, 56, pp. xxxviii-xxxix. A change in hands, moving from Kufic to *naskhī* can actually be observed in Sinai Arabic MS 151, which contains dated texts written in the years 867, 1021 and 1025 A.D. See the remarks of Harvey Staal, "Codex Sinai Arabic 151, Pauline Epistles; Part I (Arabic Text), Part II (English Translation)," (Ph.D. Dissertation, University of Utah, 1968; Ann Arbor, Michigan: University Microfilms, 68-14, 443), Part II, pp. 9-10, and plates I-IV in appendix. Note that Staal mistakenly translates the Hijrī dates 412 and 416 to 1030 and 1035 A.D. on p. 16. Part I of this dissertation has now been published: Harvey Staal, *Mt. Sinai Arabic Codex 151; I, Pauline Epistles* [CSCO, vols. 452 and 453] (Louvain, 1983).

[32] Notice, e.g., H.L. Fleischer's attention to these matters in articles written in 1847, 1854, and 1864, in *Kleinere Schriften*, 3 vols. (Leipzig: S. Hirzel, 1885-1888), III, 378-99.

[33] J. Oestrup, "Über zwei arabische Codices sinaitici der Strassburger Universitäts - und Landesbibliothek," *ZDMG*, LI (1897), 469.

[34] Georg Graf, *Der Sprachgebrauch der ältesten christlich-arabischen Literatur. Ein Beitrag zur Geschichte des Vulgär-arabisch* (Leipzig: Harrassowitz, 1905). Palestinian MSS numbered twelve among the seventeen documents on which the study was based; cf. pp. 1-3.

catalog the ways in which the Palestinian texts exemplify the alleged tendency among Christian writers of Arabic to abandon standard linguistic usages in favor of what Bernhard Levin called, "die lebendige Mundart."[35]

One will quickly notice the tendency on the part of the earlier scholars to put forward their findings in the Palestinian manuscripts as general characteristics of all Christian speech in Arabic, almost as if their purpose was to isolate a single, distinctly Christian 'dialect' in the language. This tendency, which is perhaps more accurately to be described as a misapprehension due to the employment of the vague expression "Christian Arabic," is now discredited by the appearance of Joshua Blau's more orderly linguistic studies of the Palestinian texts. As irony would have it, however, Blau's own *chef d'oeuvre* in this line of inquiry is itself unqualifiedly, and therefore misleadingly, entitled, *A Grammar of Christian Arabic.*[36] Blau in fact is the scholar who has given a more precise focus to the study of Middle Arabic dialects, by defining more closely the several component speech groups, one of which he describes in this book. He does indeed often call this language "Christian Arabic (Ch A)," which for him is a broad term including a number of sub-groups. But he also, and more accurately, calls the principal subject of his study "Ancient South Palestinian (ASP)."[37] For, what he in fact describes here is the Arabic language of the manuscripts written by Christian monks in the ninth and tenth centuries in the Holy Land. Blau intends no more, and certainly does not claim that here we have the grammar of a universal, Christian Arabic language, as some may have taken the book's inaccurate title to imply.[38]

What made Blau's linguistic investigations possible, and what extended their range much beyond the limits under which earlier scholars labored, was the easy availability after 1950 of microfilm copies of the Arabic manuscripts preserved in the library of St. Catherine's monastery in Sinai.[39] Many of the manuscripts

---

[35] Bernhard Levin, ed. and tr., *Die griechisch-arabische Evangelien-Übersetzung* (doct. diss., Uppsala, 1938), pp. 18-19.

[36] J. Blau, *A Grammar of Christian Arabic* [CSCO, vols. 267, 276, 279] (Louvain: Secr. CSCO, 1966-1967). Other publications by Blau, pertinent to the present inquiry, are: "The Importance of Middle Arabic Dialects for the History of Arabic," in Uriel Heyd, ed., *Studies in Islamic History and Civilization* [Scripta Hierosolymitana, 9] (Jerusalem: Magnes Press, 1961), pp. 205-28; "Uber einige christlich-arabische Manuskripte aus dem 9. und 10. Jahrhundert," *Mus*, LXXV (1962), 101-108; "Uber einige alte christlich-arabische Handschriften aus Sinai," *Mus*, LXXVI (1963), 369-74; *The Emergence and Linguistic Background of Judaeo-Arabic; a Study of the Origins of Middle Arabic* [Scripta Judaica, 5] (Oxford: Oxford University Press, 1965); "Sind uns Reste arabischer Bibelübersetzungen aus vorislamischer Zeit erhalten geblieben?" *Mus*, LXXXVI (1973), 67-72; "The State of Research in the Field of the Linguistic Study of Middle Arabic," *Ar*, XXVIII (1981), 187-203.

[37] Blau, *Grammar*, p. 20.

[38] See the remarks of Kh. Samir in Kh. Samir, ed., *Actes du premier congrès international d'études arabes chrétiennes, Goslar, septembre 1980* [Orientalia Christiana Analecta, 218] (Rome: Pontifical Institute for Oriental Studies, 1982), pp. 52-59.

[39] The first catalog of St. Catherine's manuscripts was Margaret Dunlop Gibson, comp., *Catalogue of the Arabic MSS. in the Convent of S. Catherine on Mount Sinai* [Studia Sinaitica, III] (London: C.J. Clay & Sons, 1894). After the Library of Congress/University of Alexandria microfilming expedition in 1950 there appeared: K.W. Clark, ed., *Checklist of Manuscripts in St.*

housed there came originally from the monasteries of Mar Sabas and Mar Charitōn. These copies, taken together with the studies of earlier scholars, based on manuscripts preserved in other libraries, allowed Blau to compose a virtual catalog of all that now remains of the Christian literary production in Arabic in Palestine, in the ninth and tenth centuries.[40] His *Grammar*, is, therefore, a linguistic description of a rather precisely defined archive, from which certain historical extrapolations may legitimately be drawn. For comparative purposes, Blau also makes reference in his *Grammar* to Arabic texts composed by Christians elsewhere than in the Holy Land, at roughly the same period of time. These references are, however, for comparative purposes only, and the texts are not among those which exemplify the "Ancient South Palestinian" Arabic which is the focus of Blau's study.[41] But the very fact that these other texts are available for reference serves the useful purpose of more closely defining the Palestinian archive.

The "Ancient South Palestinian" archive is distinguished by an ensemble of linguistic features, including the handwriting as Arendzen had mentioned. Altogether they compose the recognizable stylistic profile of the Arabic written by the scholar monks of Palestine during the first two Abbasid centuries. It is precisely this composite profile, emerging from the ensemble of distinguishing linguistic features, that is important to notice. Any one of the distinguishing features taken singly, or even some few of them taken together, as Samir Khalil has reminded scholars, may be found elsewhere, in Arabic texts of different times and places, written by Christians, Jews, and Muslims alike.[42] This is not the place to rehearse once again the principal features in question because Blau's three volumes are easily available.[43] What is important for the present purpose, however, is to call attention to certain historical conclusions which one may draw from the linguistic investigations.

From a literary point of view, one of the most obvious facts is that out of the sixty some works in "Ancient South Palestinian" which Blau studied, he is sure of only five of them as original compositions in that language.[44] All of these are

---

Catherine's Monastery, Mount Sinai, Microfilmed for the Library of Congress, 1950 (Washington, D.C.: Library of Congress, 1952); Aziz Suryal Atiya, *The Arabic Manuscripts of Mount Sinai; a Hand-list of the Arabic Manuscripts and Scrolls Microfilmed at the Library of the Monastery of St. Catherine, Mount Sinai* (Baltimore: John Hopkins University Press, 1955). A revised numbering system has now been elaborated in Murad Kamil, *Catalogue of All Manuscripts in the Monastery of St. Catherine on Mount Sinai* (Wiesbaden: Harrassowitz, 1970). Yet more recent finds of Arabic manuscripts at Sinai are cataloged and described, with numberous specimen photographs, in I.E. Meïmarē, *Katalogos tōn neōn arabikōn cheirographōn tēs hieras monēs hagias aikaterinēs tou orous sina* [Greek and Arabic] (Athens, 1985).

[40] See the list of published and unpublished works on which the grammatical study was based, Blau, *Grammar*, pp. 21-33.

[41] Consult the list of pertinent non ASP texts, ibid., pp. 34-36.

[42] See Samir, *Actes du premier congrès*, p. 56, and n. 68.

[43] See esp. Blau, *Grammar*, pp. 42-54.

[44] Ibid., pp. 21-23. One suspects that the number should really be six, if not seven. The present writer believes that the *Kitāb al-burhān* which is usually ascribed to Eutychius of Alexandria, should properly be considered the composition of a Palestinian monk. See M. Breydy, *Études sur Saʿīd ibn Baṭrīq et ses sources* [CSCO, vol. 450] (Louvain: E. Peeters, 1983).

apologetical works. The remaining compositions, most of them translations, fall into the category of "church-books" described above. Among them is a group of thirty-five items, consisting mainly of homilies, saints lives, martyrdoms, patristic selections, and so forth,[45] while twenty-one pieces are Arabic versions of parts of the scriptures.[46] This ratio of original compositions to translations, leaving room for the reassignment of some of the hagiographical items to the status of originals, accords well with what one otherwise knows of the socio-historical situation of Christians in Syria/Palestine in the ninth and tenth centuries. The "church-books" would have served the ongoing needs of the members of the Melkite community, whose vernacular language would increasingly have been Arabic. The apologetic, original compositions in Arabic represent the first steps taken by Melkite Christians in Syria/Palestine to address themselves to issues beyond their own internal community life, issues which take into account questions raised by Muslims and others, and which inevitably would have been raised in Arabic. More will be said about these original Arabic works below.

Next, Blau's examination of the Palestinian texts highlights the linguistic features which he believes are sufficient in the aggregate to have played a role in bringing about a new linguistic type, viz., a dialect of Middle Arabic. However, Blau insists that the writers of these manuscripts were themselves intending to write Classical Arabic, an intention which is revealed in the numerous pseudo-correct forms to be found in the texts, either of what Blau calls the "hyper" correct, or the "hypo" correct variety.[47] They both reveal the writers' efforts to make a hitherto spoken fluency conform to the requirements of correct usage in a literary language. This conclusion involves the corollary that, contrary to the earlier assumption that the Palestinian writers were abandoning standard usage in favor of a more colloquial expression,[48] they were in fact laboring to write a more correct literary Arabic than they must have spoken. Their failures, or deviations from standard usage, are what reveal the burgeoning new linguistic type. Their efforts to write correctly call attention to the fact that the documents in the Palestinian archive furnish the evidence which allows one to infer that in the first two Abbasid centuries, Melkite Christians in the Holy Land, whose ecclesiastical language had been largely Greek, with a substratum of Syriac, were in fact now making the endeavor to produce a fluent Christian literature in Arabic. Again, this conclusion accords well with what one otherwise knows about the socio-historical situation of Christians in the Holy Land in the period between the Islamic conquest and the incursion of the crusaders.[49]

---

[45] Blau, *Grammar*, pp. 23-29. Blau lists all thirty-five of these works under "translations." The designation is not completely accurate. The story of ʿAbd al-Masīḥ (Christodoulos, p. 24), the account of St. Anthony Ruwaḥ (p. 26), a short response of Abū Qurra (p. 27), and maybe more, are surely original compositions in Arabic. See below.

[46] Ibid., pp. 29-33.

[47] Ibid., pp. 42-52.

[48] See above, and especially the views of B. Levin, n. 35 above.

[49] Consider Kennedy, "The Melkite Church," n. 12 above; Griffith, "The First *Summa*," n. 15 above.

Finally, Blau's study of the grammar of the Palestinian manuscripts puts into high-relief yet another feature of the Arabic language to be found there, which also accords well with what one knows from other considerations to have been an important bias, namely the influence of Aramaic and Syriac.[50] Most of the Palestinian texts in question were translated from Greek or Syriac originals, as the statistics cited earlier testify. In fact, the versions are sometimes so literal that "they are hardly worth being called Arabic at all (especially concerning word order)."[51] But even in those works which were written originally in Arabic, as Blau goes on to observe, Aramaic/Syriac influence is evident. This should not be a surprising circumstance when one recalls that not only was Palestinian Aramaic the ongoing vernacular language in the Holy Land until early Abbasid times and even later, but that once the Greek speakers virtually disappeared from the area, the writers in the Palestinian monasteries were themselves largely from Syriac-speaking communities. It is no wonder then that their Arabic hand reminded Arendzen of Syriac.[52] And this fact corroborates the historical point made on other grounds that during the first two Abbasid centuries even the Melkite Christians in the caliphate turned their eyes to the east, and had virtually no contact with Byzantium until the mid-tenth century.[53]

Before leaving the subject of the distinctive state of the Arabic language to be found in the South Palestinian Christian manuscripts from the ninth and tenth centuries,[54] it is instructive to take into account the additional fact that there is a notable difference to be observed between the states of the language in texts from different times and places, which carry the work of the same author. Here is not the place to develop this issue in any detail, but one must mention it briefly because it reinforces one's perception of the distinctiveness of what was written in Palestine during the period of time which is of present concern. The works of Theodore Abū Qurra (c. 750 - c. 825) provide the only real opportunity for such a comparison, because he is the only writer of the time and place whose works spread well beyond his own era, and are available in modern published editions. Abū Qurra's career will be discussed below. Here the only purpose is to call attention to the differences in the "state of the language" to be observed in the author's works published on the basis of Palestinian manuscripts of the ninth and tenth centuries, and those published on the basis of manuscripts from later times, or other places.

---

[50] See Blau, *Grammar*, pp. 54-55, and p. 628, where the index to the *Grammar* cites passages throughout the work which designate "Aramaic influence."

[51] Blau, ibid., p. 54.

[52] See n. 30 above.

[53] On this subject see Kennedy, "The Melkite Church," n. 12 above, and the following articles by Sidney H. Griffith: "Eutychius of Alexandria on the Emperor Theophilus and Iconoclasm in Byzantium: a Tenth Century Moment in Christian Apologetics in Arabic," *Byzantion*, LII (1982), 154-90; "Stephen of Ramlah and the Christian Kerygma in Arabic in Ninth Century Palestine," *The Journal of Ecclesiastical History*, XXXVI (1985), 23-45; and "Greek into Arabic: Life and Letters in the Monasteries of Palestine in the Ninth Century; the *Summa Theologiae Arabica*," *Byzantion*, to appear.

[54] Samir prefers to speak of the distinctiveness of this Arabic usage as "un état de langue." See Samir, *Actes du premier congrès*, p. 58.

The majority of the published Arabic works of Theodore Abū Qurra are based on manuscripts of relatively recent vintage. For the edition of ten of Abū Qurra's Arabic tracts, which Constantin Bacha published in 1904, he relied on a copy made in 1735, which the copyist himself said was made from yet another copy, written in 1051, which in turn was said to be based on an older manuscript kept at the monastery of Mar Sabas.[55] Similarly, Louis Cheikho published another work of Abū Qurra based on a unique manuscript, now said to date from the end of the seventeenth century.[56] When one compares the "state of the language" in these editions of the works of Abū Qurra with what one finds in the author's tract on the veneration of images, which Arendzen edited from the manuscript written by Stephen of Ramla in 877,[57] the distinctiveness of the earlier Palestinian Arabic is immediately evident, even to the casual reader. Clearly, over the centuries, Abū Qurra's diction must have been "improved" from copyist to copyist. This is in fact a process which one can observe beginning already in the Palestinian manuscripts of the ninth and tenth centuries. For example, in the tenth century another scribe copied Abū Qurra's tract on images in Sinai Arabic MS 330, making numerous orthographical and grammatical changes from what Stephen of Ramla had written, and not always for the better, from the point of view of the requirements of classical Arabic, but remaining within the range of usages characteristic of Palestine in early Abbasid times. Then one may observe a diverging trend in the "states of the languages," now leading away from the earlier Palestinian practice, in the text of the creed by Abū Qurra which Ignace Dick edited on the basis of two manuscripts, Sinai Arabic MSS 549 and 561, from, respectively, the tenth and thirteenth centuries. Almost all of the variants in the latter manuscript are of the "improving" variety. And now they veer away from the peculiar profile constituted by the ensemble of linguistic traits which characterized the earlier state of Arabic used in the Holy Land monasteries.[58]

Two historical conclusions may be drawn from observations such as these. The first of them is that the several "states of the language" which one may perceive in the transmitted works of Theodore Abū Qurra testify to the distinctiveness of the Arabic employed by the monks of Palestine in the ninth

---

[55] See Constantin Bacha, *Les oeuvres arabes de Theodore Aboucara, évêque d'Haran* (Beyrouth, 1904), p. 5; and his *Un traité des oeuvres arabes de Théodore Abou-Kurra, évêque de Haran* (Tripoli [Syria] and Rome, 1905), p. 8.

[56] L. Cheikho, "Mīmar li Tādurus Abī Qurra fī Wujud al-Khāliq, wa 'l-Dīn al-Qawīm," *al-Machriq*, XV (1912), 757-74, 825-42. See the new edition by I. Dick, *Theodore Abuqurra, Traité de l'existence du Créateur et de la vraie religion; introduction et texte critique* [Patrimoine Arabe Chrétien, 3] (Jounieh et Rome, 1982). Cheikho, in his *al-Machriq* article, XV, 757, dated the MS in question to the eighteenth century. Dick has revised the date to the seventeenth century. See Dick, "Le traité de Théodore Abū Qurra de l'existence du Créateur et de la vraie religion," in Kh. Samir, ed., *Actes du premier congrès*, p. 149.

[57] See no. 29 above.

[58] See I. Dick, "Deux écrits inédits de Théodore Abuqurra," *Mus*, LXXII (1959), 53-59. Dick is now preparing a new edition of the tract on images, to appear in the series "Patrimoine Arabe Chrétien."

and tenth centuries, as they were learning to write more felicitously in the language they had presumably been speaking fluently since the middle of the eighth century. Secondly, it is clear that this was not an inert state of the language. Rather, it is clear from manuscript to manuscript, as well as in the margins and between the lines of individual manuscripts, that in the Palestinian *scriptoria* there was an ongoing effort to write ever more correctly in Arabic.[59] Of course, Christian writers and copyists of later periods and other places developed their own characteristic "scribal errors," particularly writers whose real ecclesiastical language continued to be Syriac or Coptic (or even Greek, after the incursion of westerners into the territories of the caliphate in the eleventh century and later). In some places, some Christian writers and scribes wrote notably correct classical Arabic. But this is another story, and one which is not pertinent to the present inquiry.[60] It remains here only to draw the obvious corollary from all that has been said thus far. It is that the writers of the few original works preserved in "Ancient South Palestinian" Arabic, including Theodore Abū Qurra, actually wrote their compositions in this distinguishable dialect or 'state' of Middle Arabic, and that they did not employ the good classical usage which one might otherwise have presumed, especially for a writer such as Abū Qurra, who alone of the Syro-Palestinians achieved a widespread fame in the Arabic-speaking world of later times.

III.
The Earliest Christian Arabic Texts

After the middle of the first Abbasid century few if any original Greek writers remained in the monasteries of the Holy Land. There is a Greek account of the martyrdom of twenty monks of Mar Sabas monastery in the year 797, and a Greek life of St. Stephen the wonder-worker, from the same monastery, said to have been written by Leontius of Mar Sabas.[61] And sometime in the ninth century monks of Mar Sabas translated the ascetical homilies of Isaac of Nineveh from Syriac into Greek. But this is all there is to cite, until the eleventh

---

[59] The ongoing process can be observed in the 'states' of the language evident in a single family of Gospel MSS, mentioned in Georg Graf, *Geschichte der christlichen arabischen Literatur*, 5 vols. [Studi e Testi, 118, 133, 146, 147, 172] (Città del Vaticano, 1944-1953), I, 142-47. See Sidney H. Griffith, "The Gospel in Arabic," n. 24 above. Look for Samir Arbache's long-promised study of the Gospels in the Sinai MSS. See also evidences of the continuing efforts in the Palestinian monasteries to write "correct" Arabic, in S.H. Griffith, "The Arabic Account of ʿAbd al-Masīḥ an-Nağrānī al-Ghassānī," *Mus*, XCVIII (1985), 331-74.

[60] See Samir, *Actes du premier congrès*, pp. 60-68.

[61] See Vailhé, "Les écrivains," pp. 39-43; R.P. Blake, "La littérature grecque," p. 375; I. Ševčenko, "Constantinople Viewed from the Eastern Provinces in the Middle Byzantine Period," *Harvard Ukranian Studies*, III/IV (1979-1980), 735-37. See the editions of the Greek texts cited in F. Halkin, *Bibliotheca Hagiographica Graeca*, 3rd ed., 3 vols. [Subsidia Hagiographica, no. 8a] (Bruxelles: Société des Bollandistes, 1957), II, 96 [no. 1200] and 254 [no. 1670]. For Isaac of Nineveh's homilies see [Dana Miller], *The Ascetical Homilies of St. Isaac the Syrian* (Brookline, Massachusetts: The Holy Transfiguration Monastery, 1984).

century. An exception to prove the rule may be the work of Basil of Emesa, the alleged writer of the life of St. Theodore of Edessa.[62] This *Vita* has survived in Greek, in a manuscript dated to the year 1023, which belonged originally to the Georgian monastery, Iviron, on Mt. Athos.[63] It has also survived in Arabic, in a thirteenth-century Egyptian manuscript, now in the Bibliothèque National de Paris.[64] Modern scholars consider the *Vita* in its present form to have been written originally in Greek, and the Arabic accordingly is a translation.[65] This conclusion, plus the additional observation that the *Vita* contains such unlikely elements as an account of the alleged synod of the oriental patriarchs in Jerusalem in the year 836, which is supposed to have issued an anti-iconoclast letter to the emperor Theophilus,[66] the story of a supposed visit by Theodore to the court of Emperor Michael III (842-867), and tales about the conversion to Christianity of a "Persian King Mawijas," all conspire to prompt one to the further conclusion that the *Vita* itself, in its present form, was written in Byzantium, and is not at all the composition of any monk living in the Holy Land in the mid-ninth century.[67] However, this is not to say that the *Vita* has no relationship to the literary activity of the monks of Mar Sabas monastery. For, as Paulus Peeters reminded scholars in 1930, the *Vita* of Theodore of Edessa includes the story of St. Michael of Mar Sabas, the account of whose martyrdom at the hands of the Muslims is told independently in an eleventh-century Georgian manuscript.[68] And furthermore, Peeters was able to show that the Georgian account is in fact the translation of an Arabic original, in which Basil of Emesa is the narrator of the story about Michael. So the investigation has at this point come the full circle back to Basil of Emesa, who, if he is not

---

62 See Halkin, *Bibliotheca*, II, 274-75 [no. 1744, a-e].

63 See A. Vasiliev, "The Life of St. Theodore of Edessa," *Byzantion*, XIV (1942-1943), 167-69.

64 See G. Troupeau, *Catalogue des manuscrits arabes; première partie, manuscrits chrétiens* (Paris: Bibliothèque Nationale, 1972), MS 147, pp. 110-13, cf. p. 112, no. 12.

65 See G. Graf, *GCAL*, II, 24-25; Vasiliev, "Life of St. Theodore," 192-98.

66 On the probably fictional character of this event see Ševčenko, "Constantinople Viewed," 735, n. 36. See also the pertinent remarks and further bibliography in Sidney H. Griffith, "Eutychius of Alexandria on the Emperor Theophilus and Iconoclasm in Byzantium: A Tenth Century Moment in Christian Apologetics in Arabic," *Byzantion*, LII 1982), 154-90; and his "Greek into Arabic," n. 53 above.

67 See Vasiliev, "Life of St. Theodore," 199-210, 216-25 for a summary of these two topics. What highlights their fictional character is the otherwise well attested isolation of Syro-Palestine from Byzantium during the period in question. See Griffith's "Eutychius of Alexandria," and his "Stephen of Ramlah and the Christian Kerygma in Arabic," n. 53 above. Regarding the inauthenticity of the works attributed to Theodore in the *Vita*, see the article by Gouillard, n. 69 below, 138-57.

68 P. Peeters, "La passion de s. Michel le sabaïte," *Analecta Bollandiana*, XLVIII (1930), 65–98. Peeters proposed that the story of St. Theodore of Edessa was merely a calque on the biography of Theodore Abū Qurra, with the corollary that there never were two separate persons. Vasiliev, "Life of St. Theodore," no. 63, rejected this idea, and defended the historicity of Theodore of Edessa. But more recent scholars do not believe that Vasiliev made his case. See, e.g., Hans Georg Beck, *Kirche und theologische Literatur im byzantinischen Reich* (München: Beck, 1959), pp. 558-59. Regarding the Georgian MS itself, and its publication, see R.P. Blake, "Catalogue des manuscrits géorgiens de la bibliothèque de la laure d'Iviron au mont Athios," *Revue de l'Orient Chrétien*, XXIII, 3 ème sér., VIII (1931-1932), 324-25.

altogether a fictional character, emerges as a monk of Mar Sabas, later, perhaps the Melkite bishop of Emesa, and who now appears not as a writer of Greek, as the unknown Byzantine author of the *Vita* of Theodore of Edessa would have it, but as a hagiographic *raconteur* who probably spoke and wrote in Arabic, and who flourished around the mid-point of the first Abbasid century.[69]

As if to reinforce the idea that by the beginning of the ninth century Arabic was a living literary language for the monks of Mar Sabas, it now appears that there was a Georgian version of the martyrdom of the twenty monks of Mar Sabas in 797, which was translated not from the Greek text mentioned above, but from Arabic, and, as it turns out, the same might be true even of the *Vita* of Stephen the wonder-worker.[70] This observation raises the possibility that the Greek texts of these works may not have been the original ones, but that still missing Arabic narratives were the first written accounts of the martyrs of 797 and of the life of Stephen. What adds some verisimilitude to this possibility is the additional observation that there is yet another Georgian text with roots in Mar Sabas monastery, which is definitely a translation from Arabic, namely the *Vita* of St. Romanos the Neomartyr.[71] Sometime in the 780s, the writer, a monk of Mar Sabas, composed an account of Romanos's martyrdom at al-Raqqa in the year 780, after nine years spent as a prisoner in Baghdad.[72] Since no Greek *Vita* of St. Romanos has come to light, the most reasonable assumption to make is that Arabic was indeed its original language.

The fact that Georgian manuscripts have played such an important role in discovering the history of the appearance of the Arabic language in the literature of the Holy Land monasteries in the first Abbasid century should cause no

---

[69] See Peeters, "La passion de s. Michel," esp. 80 and n. 2. Therefore, Basil could not himself have been the author who invented Theodore of Edessa, as Gouillard would have it. Rather, the Byzantine author of the *Vita*, whoever he was, must have attributed his tale to Basil, who became Basil of Hieropolis when the story was later translated into Arabic. See J. Gouillard, "Supercheries et méprises littéraires; l'oeuvre de saint Théodore d'Edessa," *Revue des Études Byzantines*, V (1947), 137-38.

[70] See n. 61 above, and R.P. Blake, "Deux lacunes comblées dans la passio xx monachorum sabaitarum," *Analecta Bollandiana*, LXVIII (1950), 27-43; G. Garitte, "Un extrait géorgien de la vie d'Étienne le sabaïte," *Mus*, LXVII (1954), 71-92, esp. 77. There is in fact an Arabic life of St. Stephen of Mar Sabas, dated 902, among the newly discovered Sinai Arabic MSS, MS 66. See Meïmarè, *Katalogos tòn neòn arabikòn cheirographòn*, p. 35. The MS is a palimpsest, the Arabic written over an earlier Palestinian Syriac text.

[71] The text was published originally in 1910 by K. Kekelidze, and translated into Russian. For details see G. Garitte, "Bibliographie de K. Kekelidze (+ 1962)," *Mus*, LXXVI (1963), 447, no. 7.

[72] For the date of composition of the *Vita*, see P. Peeters, "S. Romain le néomartyr (+ 1 mai 780), d'après un document géorgien" *Analecta Bollandiana*, XXX (1911), 403. Note the *caveat* registered in I. Ševčenko, "Hagiography of the Iconoclast Period," in A. Bryer and J. Herrin, eds., *Iconoclasm* (Birmingham: University of Birmingham, 1977), p. 114, n. 9. There is really no reason, following Peeters, to set 787 as the year before which the *Vita* must have been written, just because the decrees of Nicea II forbade "double monasteries." On other grounds one knows that this council was virtually unknown in the territory of the oriental patriarchates during the ninth and tenth centuries. For pertinent bibliography and discussion see, in addition to the studies cited in n. 67 above, Sidney H. Griffith, "Theodore Abū Qurrah's Arabic Tract on the Christian Practice of Venerating Images," *JAOS*, CV (1985), 53-73.

surprise. There is a recorded presence of Georgian monks in Palestine almost continually from the fifth century until the sixteenth century.[73] This circumstance, taken in conjunction with the fact that the Georgians professed the same Chalcedonian convictions as did the Greek-speaking monks, explains the importance of the large Georgian archive associated with the Holy Land libraries. Both the Greek patriarchal library in Jerusalem and the library of St. Catherine's monastery at Mt. Sinai have significant collections of Georgian manuscripts. In the patriarchal library are assembled manuscripts from the Georgian monasteries around Jerusalem, dating from the eleventh century at the earliest.[74] This late date reflects the conditions in the Holy Land up until the reassertion of western power in the region, and it reminds one that during the two previous centuries Arabic had been gaining ground in the Palestinian monasteries. This latter phenomenon is reflected in the Georgian manuscripts of the tenth century preserved at the Iviron on Mt. Athos, which contain texts that are translations from Arabic.[75] The Georgian collection at Mt. Sinai on the other hand, while smaller than that in Jerusalem, contains among its eighty-five manuscripts some sixteen from the ninth and tenth centuries.[76] And all of them fall into the category of "church-books" described earlier. One does not find among them the apologetic texts which reflect a turn to the outside, Islamic society, such as are among the Arabic manuscripts from ninth- and tenth-century Palestine. Such texts as there are of this sort in Georgian are translations ultimately from Arabic, and here one thinks principally of the works of Theodore Abū Qurra, which for the most part came into Georgian via Greek in the twelfth century.[77] However, there is a report that in the early eleventh century the Georgian monk Euthymius Mtʿac'mideli (d. 1028) of the Iviron monastery translated a now unknown work by Abū Qurra from Georgian into Greek.[78] This notice prompts one to suppose that the Georgian text with which Euthymius worked was a direct translation from Arabic, probably made in the Holy Land, where in the monastic community at least there was still a Georgian readership, even during the ninth and tenth centuries,[79] to judge by the Sinai manuscripts, although there are no known original compositions in Georgian to record from this period.

---

[73] See the long survey, based largely on pilgrims' reports, by G. Peradze, "An Account of the Georgian Monks and Monasteries in Palestine," *Georgica*, I, 4 and 5 (1937), 181-246. On the significance of Georgian texts for the history of Christian texts in Arabic in the Holy Land, see Khalil Samir, "Les plus anciens homéliaires géorgiens et les versions patristiques arabes," *OCP*, XLII (1976), 217-31.

[74] See R.P. Blake, "Catalogue des manuscrits géorgiens de la bibliothèque patriarcale grecque à Jérusalem," *Revue de l'Orient Chrétien*, XXIII (1922-1923), 345-413; XXIV (1924), 190-210, 387-429; XXV (1925-1926), 132-55.

[75] See, e.g., the text cited in n. 68 above.

[76] See Gérard Garitte, *Catalogue des manuscrits géorgiens littéraires du mont Sinaï* [CSCO, vol. 165] (Louvain: L. Durbecq, 1956), p. 1.

[77] See M. Tarchnišvili, *Geschichte der kirchlichen georgischen Literatur* [Studi e Testi, no. 185] (Città del Vaticano, 1955), pp. 208-209, 370-71.

[78] See ibid., p. 129, and Graf, *GCAL*, II, 21.

[79] See the remarks of Heinrich Husmann, "Die datierten griechischen Sinai-Handschriften des 9. bis 16. Jahrhunderts, Herkunft und Schreiber," *Ostkirchliche Studien*, XXVII (1978), 143-44.

The same is to be said about the Greek manuscripts written in Palestine in the ninth and tenth centuries. As noted above, there are only two works which might be considered original compositions, and both of these, one learns from Georgian versions, may have had Arabic originals.[80] For the rest, the Greek manuscripts written in Palestine during the ninth and tenth centuries, all seemingly in the "church-book" category, must have served the needs only of a Greek readership, which would have been found exclusively in the monastic community.[81] Beginning in the eleventh century, of course, with the reinstatement of relatively free communications with Byzantium and the west, Greek culture in the Palestinian monasteries took out a new lease on life. But by that time Christian literature in Arabic had already achieved its majority, and no longer depended on the direct support of the older Christian cultures.

The earliest recorded date so far published from an early documentary source which refers to a Christian text in Arabic is contained in a note appended to the end of an Arabic version of the story of the "Fathers who were killed at Mount Sinai," which appears in two manuscripts, Sinai Arabic MS 542 (f. 15r) and British Museum Oriental MS 5019 (f. 58b). The wording of the note is slightly different in the two manuscripts, but they agree in stating that the text of the martyrdom was originally translated from Greek into Arabic in the Hijra year 155, which corresponds to 772 A.D.[82]

Among dated manuscripts, the earliest one so far reported is MS 16, one of the newly-discovered Sinai manuscripts. It is a Gospel manuscript, dated to 859.[83] Next is Sinai Arabic MS 151, which was written in Damascus, and not in one of the Palestinian monasteries. It contains an Arabic version of the Epistles of St. Paul, the Acts of the Apostles, and the Catholic Epistles.[84] However, it is important to note that the early date, "the month of Ramadhān, of the year two hundred and fifty-three," that is, Sept. 4 to Oct. 4, 867 A.D.,[85] refers only to the translation of the Pauline Epistles in the first portion of the manuscript, and not to other portions of the text, which date to later times. This fact made Blau wonder if a later scribe may not have simply copied the first portion of the manuscript, colophon and all, from an earlier *Vorlage* into a later text.[86] However this may be, the year 867 remains for now the date of the earliest dated

---

[80] See nn. 61 and 70 above.

[81] See, e.g., Husmann, "Die datierten griechischen Sinai-Handschriften," 145-47; D. Harlfinger, D.R. Reinsch, J.A.M. Sonderkamp, *Specimina Sinaitica; die datierten griechischen Handschriften des Katharinen-Klosters auf dem Berge Sinai, 9. bis 12. Jahrhundert* (Berlin: Dietrich Reimer, 1983).

[82] The note which mentions the date of the translation in BM 5019 has been published a number of times. It appeared first, in truncated form, in Ḥ. Zayyāt, "Shuhadā' al-naṣrāniyya fī 'l-islām," *al-Machriq*, XXXVI (1938), 462. J. Blau has published the note three times, twice in Arabic characters, once in transcription. See Blau's "The Importance of Middle Arabic Dialects," p. 219, n. 40 (Arabic); "Über einige christlich-arabische Manuskripte," 103 (transcription); and *Emergence and Linguistic Background*, p. 5, n. 7 (Arabic). For the full texts of both notes, plus discussion, see now S.H. Griffith, "The Arabic Account of ʿAbd al-Masīḥ," 337-42.

[83] Meimarē, *Katalogos tōn neōn arabikōn cheirographōn*, p. 27.

[84] See Atiya, *Arabic Manuscripts of Mt. Sinai*, p. 6; Kamil, *Catalogue of All Manuscripts*, p. 16.

[85] See Staal, "Codex Sinai Arabic 151," part II, p. 18.

[86] Blau, "Über einige christlich-arabische Manuscripte," 107.

and published Christian manuscript in Arabic. But soon the record will move more than a century earlier, with the new edition and publication of the full text of the anonymous treatise on "The Triune Nature of God," from Sinai Arabic MS 154. Although scholars have long dated this manuscript to "the eighth or ninth century," its new editor has reportedly found a date in the 740s written in an unpublished portion of the text of the anonymous treatise.[87]

Of all the manuscripts mentioned by Blau in his catalog of "Ancient South Palestinian" texts, only eleven actually mention the dates when they were written. And of these eleven, only four are from the ninth century.[88] British Museum MS 4950 was written in the year 877.[89] The six leaves of a manuscript of Mar Sabas, now in the Leningrad library, contain a work which the scribe says he wrote out in "the year 272 of the years of the Arabs," that is, somewhere between June 18, 885 and June 7, 886 A.D.[90] Vatican Arabic MS 71, according to its colophon, was written at Mar Sabas in the same year as the previous manuscript, viz., in 885/886.[91] And Sinai Arabic MS 72, according to its colophon, was written in the year 897.[92] For the undated manuscripts in Blau's catalog, dates in the ninth and tenth centuries have been assigned largely on the basis of paleographical considerations by the scholars who have studied the texts, and whose works Blau has noted.

Among the newly-discovered Christian Arabic manuscripts from Sinai not mentioned in Blau's list of old South Palestinian texts, at least three carry dates from the ninth century: MS 1, containing saints lives and martyrologies, was written in 868; MS 16, with the Gospels in Arabic, as already mentioned, was written in 859; and MS 46, which is a portion of Sinai Arabic MS 151, mentioned above, contains Arabic versions of some theological discourses, and was written in 867.[93]

In the absence of many dated manuscripts from the eighth century one must necessarily fall back on the only other available evidence, which is the evidence of paleography. Of course, there is also the biographical evidence of the only

---

[87] The major portion of the text is published in Margaret D. Gibson, *An Arabic Version of the Acts of the Apostles and the Seven Catholic Epistles, from an Eighth or Ninth Century MS. in the Convent of St. Catherine on Mount Sinai, with a Treatise 'On the Triune Nature of God'* [Studia Sinaitica, no. VII] (Cambridge: Cambridge University Press, 1899). The new edition is being prepared at Rome, in the Pontifical Institute of Oriental Studies, under the direction of P. Samir Khalil.

[88] See Blau, *Grammar*, pp. 21-33

[89] See the colophon to the first work in this MS (f. 197v) published in A.S. Lewis and M.D. Gibson, *Forty-One Facsimiles*, pp. 2-4; Arendzen, *Theodori Abu Ḳurra de Cultu Imaginum Libellus*, p. xv.

[90] See I. Krackovsky, "A New Testament Apokryphon in an Arabic MS of the Year 885-886," [Russian] *Vizantysky Vremennik*, XIV (1907), 261 (Arabic text).

[91] See the colophon published in E. Tisserant, *Specimina Codicum Orientalium* (Bonn: A. Marcus et E. Weber, 1914), pp. xxxviii-xxxix, pl. 54. Regarding both the Leningrad and the Vatican MSS see now S.H. Griffith, "Anthony David of Baghdad, Scribe and Monk of Mar Sabas; Arabic in the Monasteries of Palestine," to appear.

[92] See the colophon (f. 118v) published in C.E. Padwick, "Al-Ghazali and the Arabic Versions of the Gospels, an Unsolved Problem," *MW*, XXIX (1939), between 134 and 135.

[93] Meïmarē, *Katalogos tōn neōn arabikōn cheirographōn*, pp. 21, 27, 32.

Christian Arabic writer of the period whose name is known, that is, Theodore Abū Qurra (c. 750 - c. 825). But his biography, and his writings, are themselves known mostly from later witnesses.[94] And while the study of Arabic paleography in this early period is not yet on as sure a footing as one might wish, it nevertheless does provide some basis for the assumption that Syro/Palestinian Christians were actually writing Arabic in the eighth century. Concretely, in addition to Sinai Arabic MS 154, one may cite Sinai Arabic MS 514 as another case in point. This manuscript is a palimpsest. It originally came to the attention of Margaret Dunlop Gibson and Agnes Smith Lewis in 1902, who immediately noticed that the characteristic Christian Arabic hand of ninth- and tenth-century Palestine was superimposed on a much earlier Syriac hand.[95] When Aziz Suryal Atiya came upon the manuscript again in 1950, he was able to determine that it is in fact a "quintuple palimpsest." The lower two layers, containing Syriac texts of the Peshitta, are succeeded by a Gospel lectionary in Greek uncials of the seventh century, followed by an undetermined text in an archaic Kufic hand of the first century of the Hijra, which was in turn washed away to make room for what Atiya calls the "middle Kufic of the eighth to early ninth century."[96] In addition to some *memre* of James of Sarūg, this uppermost layer contains a collection of Arabic versions of martyrdoms and saints' lives of uncertain provenance. So this manuscript, which Atiya nicknamed "Codex Arabicus," is all by itself virtually a complete stratigraphic record of the Christian literary history of Palestine, up to the early Arabic period.

Another manuscript which provides paleographic evidence for Christian Arabic writing in the same period, although it comes, like Sinai Arabic MS 151, originally from Damascus, and not from the Palestinian monasteries, is the bilingual fragment of Psalm 78:20-61, in both Greek and Arabic, with the Arabic text appearing in Greek script.[97] On the basis of this Greek script, along with other considerations, the editor of the fragment dates it to the end of the eighth century.[98] In the same vein is the collection of fragments of a trilingual Psalter, in Greek, Syriac and Arabic, found at Mar Sabas monastery, and now in Leningrad.[99] On the basis of paleographic considerations, the manuscript, which contains Pss. 70:7-16, 73:4-14, 77:28-38, and 79:9-16, is dated to the ninth century.[100] Finally, from Sinai there is a bilingual Gospel lectionary in Greek

[94] The basic biographical study remains that of I. Dick, "Un continuateur arabe de saint Jean Damascene: Théodore Abuqurra, évêque melkite de Ḥarrān," *POC*, XII (1962), 209-23; 319-32; XIII (1963), 114-29.

[95] See Lewis and Gibson, *Forty-One Facsimiles*, frontispiece and pp. xvii-xviii.

[96] See Atiya, *The Arabic Manuscripts of Mount Sinai*, p. 19. Note also plates II-V, showing the Syriac, Greek, and Kufic palimpsests.

[97] See Bruno Violet, *Ein zweisprachiges Psalmfragment aus Damaskus* (offprint, with corrections, from the *Orientalistische Litteratur-Zeitung*, 1901; Berlin, 1902).

[98] Ibid., fol. 23.

[99] See N. Pigulevskaya, "A Greek-Syriac-Arabic Manuscript of the Ninth Century," [Russian] *Palestinskiy Sbornik*, LXIII (1954), 59-90.

[100] Ibid., 60.

and Arabic written by the monk John, son of Victor of Damietta, in the year 995/96.[101]

As Blau has observed, it stands to reason that some of the manuscripts copied in the ninth and tenth centuries in the Palestinian monasteries were actually composed in the eighth century, and he even questioningly mentions the seventh century.[102] Be that as it may, the available documentation now clearly shows that the first Christian texts in old Palestinian Arabic were written in the eighth century, and increasingly in the tenth century there was a concerted effort in the monasteries to provide ecclesiastical books of all sorts in Arabic. Thereafter, the spate of Christian publishing in Arabic never ceased, as the manuscripts of St. Catherine's alone make evident. So it now remains in the present study to describe briefly the original works in old South Palestinian Arabic with a view to highlighting the productivity and originality of the first Arabophone writer-monks of the Holy Land's monasteries.

IV.
The Monks of Palestine and Christian Kalām

By far the majority of the some hundred surviving Arabic texts which monks associated with the monasteries of Palestine wrote in the ninth and tenth centuries are translations of the scriptures and other "church-books" from Greek and Syriac originals. Gradually, modern scholars, in their studies of the Arabic versions of Biblical books and Patristic texts, are taking more account of these Palestinian materials.[103] There are also some saints' lives in the archive, which appear to be Arabic originals.[104] But among the most interesting of all these Arabic texts from the Holy Land monasteries are the few works of Christian *kalām*, or controversial, apologetic theology in the Islamic milieu, which are

---

[101] See Harlfinger et al., *Specimina Sinaitica*, pp. 17-18, and plates 18-22.

[102] See Blau, *Grammar*, p. 20, n. 7.

[103] Of studies not mentioned earlier, one might cite the following: R.M. Frank, *The Wisdom of Jesus ben Sirach (Sinai ar. 155, ixth/xth cent.)* [CSCO, vols. 357 and 358] (Louvain: Secr. CSCO, 1974); B. Knutsson, *Studies in the Text and Language of Three Syriac-Arabic Versions of the Book of Judicum, with Special Reference to the Middle Arabic Elements* (Leiden: E.J. Brill, 1974), for which see Samir Khalil, "Trois versions arabes du Livre des Juges," *Oriens Christianus*, LXV (1981), 87-101; F. Leemhuis, A.F.J. Klijn, and G.J.H. van Gelder, *The Arabic Text of the Apocalypse of Baruch* (Leiden: E.J. Brill, 1986). For patristic texts, see the recent publications of Jacques Grand Henry on the Arabic versions of the works of Gregory of Nazianzus, among which are the following: "Les discours de saint Grégoire de Nazianze dans le manuscrit arabe du Sinaï 274," *Mus*, XCIV (1981), 153-76; "La version arabe de quelques textes apocryphes attribués à Grégoire de Nazianze," *Mus*, XCVI (1983), 239-50; "La tradition manuscrite de la version arabe des 'Discours' de Grégoire de Nazianze," in J. Mossay, ed., *II. Symposium Nazianzenum; Louvain-la-Neuve, 25-28 Août 1981* (Paderborn: Ferdinand Schöningh, 1983), pp. 113–18. See also Samir Arbache, "Sentences arabes de saint Basil," *Mus*, XCVIII (1985), 315–29.

[104] See I. Dick, "La passion arabe de s. Antoine Ruwaḥ, néomartyr de Damas (+25 dec. 799)," *Mus*, LXXIV, (1961), 108-33; S.H. Griffith, "The Arabic Account of ʿAbd al-Masīḥ an-Naǧrānī al-Ghassānī," *Mus*, XCVIII (1985), 331-74.

truly original compositions. It is appropriate to bring the present essay to a close by giving some account of these important works.

It was in religious dialogue with Muslims, and in the apologetic effort to confirm the faith of Arabophone Christians challenged by the manifest success of Islamic thought and institutions, that the scholar-monks of the Holy Land monasteries showed the most ingenuity. For they took up the challenge to become *mutakallimūn*, religious controversialists, with the task of defending the faith in public argument, in the very language of Islam. Such works of Christian kalām are, to be sure, few in number by comparison to the majority of Arabic texts in the "church-books" category that have survived from the ninth and tenth centuries. But there can be no question that the kalām texts, the truly original Christian compositions in Arabic, show the most evidence of the resolve of the Holy Land monks seriously to meet the Qur'ān's criticisms of key Christian doctrines, in the very Arabic idiom which made them appear so plausible to their contemporaries, Christians and Muslims alike.

Perhaps the earliest text of Christian kalām so far known to survive from the old Palestinian archive is the treatise, "On the triune nature of God," in Sinai Arabic MS 154, published and translated into English already in 1899.[105] As noted above, there is reason to believe that the manuscript was written as early as the 740s, which means that it was composed even before the birth of Theodore Abū Qurra, the only Christian mutakallim of the early period whose name one now knows. As for the contents of the work, they are almost entirely given over to a presentation of scriptural testimonies from the Old and New Testaments, which the unknown author construes as evidences for the veracity of the doctrine of the Trinity. In this enterprise his work is utterly traditional, and may almost be styled a translation of customary testimony lists.[106] What is new in the work is the author's employment of quotations from the Qur'ān alongside the scripture testimonies to buttress his arguments. And the irony of this situation is that if the dating of the manuscript to the first half of the eighth century is secure, this Christian text is among the earliest surviving documents containing quotations from the Arabic text of the Qur'ān.

Another early work of Christian kalām, which survives now only in papyrus fragments dated to the eighth century, also contains quotations from the Qur'ān alongside testimonies from the scriptures to the standard Christian doctrines.[107]

---

[105] See the texts in M.D. Gibson, *An Arabic Version of the Acts*, pp. 2-36 (English), 75-107 (Arabic). Unfortunately, the published text stops short of the end of the work. In the Library of Congress/ University of Alexandria microfilm of Sinai Arabic MS 154 there are at least eleven more pages of text, which do not appear in Gibson's publication. And even in the microfilm, the text stops *in medias res*. One must wait for the new publication mentioned in n. 87 above for a fuller text.

[106] See Rendel Harris's review of Gibson's publication of the text, in the *American Journal of Theology*, Jan., 1901, pp. 75-86.

[107] See G. Graf, "Christlich-arabische Texte, zwei Disputationen zwischen Muslimen und Christen," in F. Bilabel and A. Grohmann, eds., *Griechische, koptische und arabische Texte zur Religion und religiösen Literatur in Ägyptens Spätzeit* (Heidelberg: Verlag der Universitäts Bibliothek, 1934), pp. 1-31.

And this coincidence reminds one that these two earliest Christian kalām texts together confirm the fact that in Arabic the first discussions between Christians and Muslims had to do with the interpretation of the scriptures, vis à vis the claims of the Qur'ān—a circumstance which accords well with what one knows from early Syriac texts related to Christian encounters with Muslims, but which stands in contrast to the polemics one reads about in Greek texts of the period.[108] Indeed, at one stage in the disputations between Christians and Muslims over scripture texts it apparently became customary even to include a Jewish interlocutor in the proceedings, for the purpose of verifying the quotations from the Bible. Such at least is the suggestion of a later Palestinian text which tells of a debate between a monk of Edessa named Abraham of Tiberias, who argues with a Muslim convert from Christianity in Jerusalem around the turn of the ninth century.[109]

It was not long, however, before Christian kalām texts from Palestinian monasteries moved beyond the stage of merely providing ready answers for Christians caught in controversy with Muslims. From the time of Abū Qurra through the tenth century there is ample evidence of a lively Christian intellectual life in Arabic, in Melkite circles in Jerusalem, Edessa, Ḥarrān, Baghdad, and Damascus, even Alexandria—all with some connection with the monasteries in Palestine, which seem to have served as the centers of Melkite scholarship.[110] To illustrate this, a brief review follows of three cases in point: the Arabic works of Theodore Abū Qurra, the now anonymous *Summa Theologiae Arabica*, and the *Kitāb al-burhān*, formerly ascribed to Eutychius of Alexandria. All of these works, at least in origin, properly belong to the archive of old South Palestinian texts described by Joshua Blau.

A. Theodore Abū Qurra

In all likelihood Abū Qurra was born and raised in Edessa, and his mother tongue was Syriac. In fact, he himself says that he wrote some thirty treatises in Syriac.[111] But his fame came from his fluency in Arabic. His career took him to the monastery of Mar Sabas in Judea, to the bishopric of Ḥarrān (795-812) in Syro-Mesopotamia, to the caliph's court at Baghdad, and finally back to Mar Sabas. In between these stations on the way of his life, Abū Qurra travelled to

---

[108] For further discussion and bibliography, see S.H. Griffith, "The Prophet Muḥammad, his Scripture and his Message," n. 15 above.

[109] See K. Vollers, "Das Religionsgespräch von Jerusalem (um 800 D) aus dem Arabischen übersetzt," *Zeitschrift für Kirchengeschichte*, XXIX (1908), 29-71; 197-221. For other MSS, see the entry in R. Caspar *et al.*, "Bibliographie du dialogue islamo-chrétien," *Islamo*, I (1975), 157-58. But see also the remarks of J. Nasrallah, "Dialogue islamo-chrétien à propos de publications récentes," *Revue des Études Islamiques*, XLIV (1978), 134. One should note another manuscript, from the twelfth century (1137-1139), Sinai Arabic MS 434, ff. 171v-181v, which also features a Palestinian monk's replies to a Muslim's questions.

[110] One may trace these connections through the prosopography of the old South Palestinian archive of Christian texts in Arabic. See S.H. Griffith, "Anthony David of Baghdad," n. 91 above.

[111] Bacha, *Les oeuvres arabes de Théodore Aboucara*, pp. 60-61.

Armenia and to Egypt as a mutakallim in the service of Chalcedonian orthodoxy.[112] He made a name for himself that amounted to notoriety among his adversaries. The Jacobite, Ḥabīb b. Khidma Abū Rā'iṭa, complained about what he perceived to be Abū Qurra's sophistries;[113] the Muslim mutakallim, ʿIsā b. Ṣabīḥ al-Murdar wrote a tract, "Against Abū Qurra, the Christian";[114] and three and a half centuries afterwards, the Jacobite patriarch of Antioch, Michael I (d. 1199), recorded what the Jacobites thought of Abū Qurra, that "because he was a sophist, and engaged in dialectics with the pagans [*ḥanpê*, i.e., the Muslims], and knew the Saracen language, he was an object of wonder to the simple folk."[115]

Due to the industry of his fellow monks in Palestine, some of Abū Qurra's writings were translated into Greek and circulated in Byzantium. But it is doubtful if Abū Qurra himself ever wrote in Greek.[116] His own industry seems to have been consumed in composing the sixteen or so Arabic works we have from his hand, and the thirty Syriac works he says he wrote—not to mention his long and busy career as a controversialist.[117] In fact, his career in controversy is what puts its stamp on his writings. In them he addresses the concerns of his own Arabophone Melkite community, who required support in their faith, and who needed help to formulate responses to their adversaries. These adversaries were both Christian and non-Christian; the former included Monophysites, Nestorians, and Monothelites; the latter were comprised of Jews and, of course, Muslims. Abū Qurra's purposes were to answer the objections of the adversaries, and, perhaps most importantly, to make a clear statement of Christian faith in Arabic.[118] The latter achievement is what put him in the vanguard of the movement toward a fully Arabophone Christianity in the caliphate, a movement which had its earliest life-giving roots in the monasteries of Palestine.

---

[112] See Dick, "Un continuateur arabe de St. Jean Damascène," n. 94 above.

[113] See G. Graf, *Die Schriften des Jacobiten Ḥabīb Ibn Ḫidma Abū Rā'iṭa* [CSCO, vols. 130 and 131] (Louvain: L. Durbecq, 1951), Arabic text (vol. 130), p. 73.

[114] See Bayard Dodge, ed. and tr., *The Fihrist of al-Nadīm; a Tenth-Century Survey of Muslim Culture*, 2 vols. (New York: Columbia University Press, 1970), I, 394.

[115] J.-B. Chabot, *Chronique de Michel le syrien; patriarche jacobite d'Antioche (1166-1199)*, 4 vols. (Paris: Ernest Leroux, 1899-1910), III, 32 (French), IV, 495-96 (Syriac).

[116] See the arguments in S.H. Griffith, "Stephen of Ramlah," n. 53 above.

[117] For the published works of Abū Qurra in Arabic, see above notes 29 (Arendzen), 55 (Bacha), 56 (Cheikho and Dick), 58 (Dick), as well as G. Graf, *Die arabischen Schriften des Theodor Abu Qurra, Bischofs von Ḥarran (ca. 740-820)* [Forschungen zur christlichen Literatur- und Dogmengeschichte, Band X, Heft 3/4] (Paderborn, 1910), G. Graf, *Des Theodor Abu Kurra Traktat über den Schöpfer und die wahre Religion* [Beiträge zur Geschichte der Philosophie des Mittelalters. Texte and Untersuchungen, Band XIV, Heft 1] (Münster, Westphalia: Aschendorff, 1913), and S.H. Griffith, "Some Unpublished Arabic Sayings Attributed to Theodore Abū Qurrah," *Mus*, XCII (1979), 29-35. For Abū Qurra's works preserved only in Greek, see *PG*, vol. 97, cols. 1461-1610. For the manuscripts of unpublished works attributed to Abū Qurra, see Graf, *GCAL*, II, 7-16, and Nasrallah, "Dialogue islamo-chrétien" in *Revue des Etudes Islamiques*, XLVI (1978), 129-32.

[118] See S.H. Griffith, "The Controversial Theology of Theodore Abū Qurrah (c. 750 - c. 820 A.D.); a Methodological, Comparative Study in Christian Arabic Literature" (Ph.D. Thesis; Washington, D.C.: The Catholic University of America, 1978)—available from University Microfilms International, Ann Arbor, Michigan; no. 78-19874.

B. The *Summa Theologiae Arabica*

The Palestinian Arabic manuscript which contains the earliest surviving text of one of the works of Theodore Abū Qurra, British Library Oriental MS 4950, written by Stephen of Ramla at the monastery of Mar Charitōn in 877 A.D.,[119] also contains the single most comprehensive statement of Christian faith in Arabic from the ninth century. It was composed, or maybe compiled, by a now unknown scholar monk in the generation after Abū Qurra, somewhere between the years 850 and 870.[120] The *Summa* stands complete in twenty-five chapters, the headings for which have long been published,[121] while the work as a whole still awaits publication in a critical edition of the Arabic text, with a translation into English by the present writer.

It is clear that the compiler of the *Summa* drew on a tradition of a century or more of Christian theology in Arabic for his work, including the treatises of Theodore Abū Qurra, as well as the growing library of scriptures and other Christian classics which the monks of Palestine had long been busy translating into the newly enfranchised language of the caliphate. It makes most sense to think of there having been a 'school' of Christian theology in Arabic, centered in the monasteries of Mar Sabas and Mar Charitōn in Judea in the ninth century, which was largely under the influence of the accomplishments of Theodore Abū Qurra in the previous generation.[122] Notably different, however, from the practice of Abū Qurra is a new sense of what one might call Christian ecumenism in the *Summa*. The author/compiler was obviously concerned to play down the differences among Christians, without at all denying them, for the sake of presenting a more effective argument in support of Christian doctrines against the challenges of Jews and Muslims.[123]

The full title of the *Summa* reads:

> The summary of the ways of faith in the
> Trinity of the unity of God, and in the
> incarnation of God the Word from the pure
> virgin Mary.[124]

Appropriately enough in a work of kalām, the "ways of faith" mentioned in this title refer to the creedal statements (*aqāwīl*), the modes of verbal expression,

[119] See S.H. Griffith, "Stephen of Ramlah," n. 53 above.

[120] See now Khalil Samir, "Date de composition de la 'Somme des aspects de la foi,' " *OCP*, LI (1985), 352-87.

[121] See G. Graf, *GCAL*, II, 17-18.

[122] See S.H. Griffith, "A Ninth Century Summa Theologiae Arabica," in Khalil Samir, ed., *Actes du deuxième congrès international d'etudes arabes chrétiennes* [Orientalia Christiana Analecta, 226] (Rome: Pontifical Institute for Oriental Studies, 1986), pp. 123–41. In the same volume see also Kh. Samir," "La 'Somme des aspects de la foi,' oeuvre d'Abū Qurrah?"

[123] See S.H. Griffith, "A Ninth Century *Summa Theologiae Arabica* and the 'Sectarian Milieu,' " *Jerusalem Studies in Arabic and Islam*, to appear.

[124] BL MS 4950, f. 2r.

in which Christians confess their faith. The *Summa* also includes a chapter (XIV) which states and then refutes what the author calls "the ways which exclude their proponents from Christianity,"[125] and each one of these "ways" is characterized as an allegation (*zaʿm*) made by an adversary who somehow contradicts an important thesis or doctrinal proposition (*qawl*) espoused in Melkite orthodoxy. For the rest, the chapters of the *Summa* set out reasoned statements of the Christian articles of faith, buttressed by numerous testimonies from the scriptures. Indeed, several chapters are devoted almost exclusively to the quotation of testimonies from scripture (XII and XIII), and these are the chapters which one finds copied several times in the manuscript tradition, even apart from the *Summa* as a whole.[126]

Special features of the *Summa*, in addition to the traditional doctrinal discussions of Trinity and Incarnation which it contains, are the chapters devoted to issues which arose in the controversies of the day as a direct result of the Islamic hegemony under which the Melkite community now lived. Among these is chapter XVIII, which provides tailor-made rebuttals, so to speak, against challenges to Christian doctrines which Muslims customarily posed in the course of day-to-day arguments about religion. Included in the chapter are also answers to objections to Christian ideas posed by Manichaean dualists.[127] Then there is a chapter devoted to proving that Christianity is the true religion of Abraham, and indeed of Adam before him (chap. XIX). And there are several chapters (XX - XXII) devoted to setting forth the position of Jews in the Christian scheme of things, which explain that the gentiles have now become heirs of the promise which God had once made to the Israelite people. The latter is a particularly intriguing theme because it suggests that in the increasingly Islamic cultural milieu of the first Abbasid century or so, Jews, Christians, and Muslims were all concerned to review and revise their conflicting religious claims. And it suggests that Jews and Christians in particular, being *ahl al-dhimma* and without political power, were now required to argue their differences with one another in open appeals to exegetical reason, without recourse to imperial power, be it Roman or Persian, to advance their interests in the public domain.[128]

The *Summa* is distinguished from other works of Christian apologetics in Arabic of the early Abbasid era by the breadth of its scope, and by the comprehensiveness of its coverage of issues of importance to the Melkite community, including even an Arabic translation of the so-called "Apostolic

---

[125] BL MS 4950, f. 76r.

[126] See the convenient chart displaying the relationship of the chapters of the *Summa* and the contents of the MSS where portions of the *Summa* appear, in Samir, "Date de composition," 355.

[127] The contents of chapter XVIII are listed in Khalil Samir, "Kitāb ǧāmiʿ wuǧūh al-īmān wa muǧādalah Abī Qurrah ʿan ṣalb al-Masīḥ," *al-Maçarrat*, LXX (1984), 411-27; Rachid Haddad, *La trinité divine chez les théologiens arabes (750-1050)* (Paris: Beauchesne, 1985), p. 60; Griffith, "A Ninth Century *Summa*," n. 123 above.

[128] For the earliest Jewish *kalām* see now Sarah Stroumsa, "Dawūd ibn Marwān al-Muqammiṣ and his ʿIshrūn Maqāla" (Unpublished Ph.D. dissertation; The Hebrew University of Jerusalem, 1983).

Canons," along with some other canonical provisions which date from the early church synods (chap. XXV). In fact, the *Summa* by itself matches and surpasses the range of topics which one finds addressed in the full bibliographies of the known works of early Christian mutakallimūn such as Theodore Abū Qurra, Ḥabīb b. Khidma Abū Rā'iṭa, and ʿAmmār al-Baṣrī.

Finally, a striking feature of the *Summa* is the fact that the kalām itself, the Arabic language of the discourse in this work of Christian apologetics, is replete with Islamic religious vocabulary, and with Arabic expressions which put the apologetic arguments in the *Summa* squarely within the framework of a reply to the Qur'ān's rhetorical challenges to the Christians.[129]

C. The *Kitāb al-burhān*

An important manuscript in the archive of old South Palestinian texts is Sinai Arabic MS 75 (Kamil, 68). On the basis of paleographical considerations, scholars have assigned it to the turn of the ninth and tenth centuries, but dates written on the last leaf of the manuscript clearly place it well within the tenth century.[130] It is important because it contains texts in both categories of works which the monks of the Holy Land were busy producing in Arabic from the ninth through the eleventh centuries: translations and original compositions.

The scribe of this manuscript left neither his own name nor the date when he wrote. But he named his monastery as that of Mar Charitōn.[131] His manuscript contains a version of the Gospels in Arabic which is seen to be a much improved offshoot of the text in the early Palestinian family of Arabic Gospel manuscripts such as Stephen of Ramla had copied and revised in Sinai Arabic MS 72.[132] The text of the Gospels in Sinai MS 75 is complete with a double set of rubrics, indicating the lectionary usages both of Jerusalem and Constantinople, and suggesting thereby an increased awareness in Palestine in the tenth century of what was happening liturgically and otherwise in Byzantium, a state of affairs in marked constrast to what one learns from ninth century texts.[133]

Of the two other works in the manuscript, one is a copy of what many scholars have long thought of as Eutychius of Alexandria's *Kitāb al-burhān*.[134] The attribution is made largely on the basis of the fact that portions of the work

[129] See S.H. Griffith, "The First Christian *Summa Theologiae* in Arabic," n. 15 above.

[130] See Graf, *GCAL*, I, 146; Blau, *Grammar*, p. 30. Atiya, *The Arabic Manuscripts of Mount Sinai*, p. 4, and Kamil, *Catalogue of All Manuscripts*, p. 14, both prefer to date the MS to the ninth century. For the dates in the MS, see Cachia and Watt, *Eutychius of Alexandria* (n. 134 below), CSCO, vol. 192, pp. i and ii.

[131] Colophon, Sinai Arabic MS 75, f. 222r.

[132] See Graf, *GCAL*, I, 146.

[133] Ibid., 140, and see Blau, "Über einige christlich-arabische Manuscripte" (n. 36 above), 107. See also A. Baumstark, "Die sonntägliche Evangelienlesung in vorbyzantinischen Jerusalem," *BZ*, XXX (1929/1930), 350-59.

[134] The work is published, with an English translation, in P. Cachia, ed. and W. Montgomery Watt, tr., *Eutychius of Alexandria, the Book of the Demonstration* [CSCO, vols. 192, 193, 209, 210] (Louvain: Secr. CSCO, 1960-1961).

appear in Eutychius's chronicle of world history, quoted quite faithfully; and in another instance, the same words are attributed explicitly to Saʿīd b. Baṭrīq, the physician who is none other than the patriarch Eutychius himself.[135] However, there is now every reason to doubt the correctness of attributing this work to Eutychius.[136] Linguistically, it has many affinities with the group of Palestinian texts studied by Blau; the writer is quite familiar with Palestinian holy places, which he describes at length.[137] Moreover, since he was a Melkite himself, Eutychius, or anyone writing in his name, would have had every encouragement to quote from the scholarly works of the monks in the Palestinian monasteries. It is consistent with what one knows of the scholarship cultivated at Mar Charitōn to propose that the *Kitāb al-burhān* is the work of a monk who wrote in the tradition of the author/compiler of the *Summa Theologiae Arabica.* In fact, like the *Summa*, the *Kitāb al-burhān* is best thought of as a compilation of earlier doctrinal works, together with some original compositions in Arabic.[138]

The title of the *Kitāb al-burhān* is well chosen. In the Qurʾān there is the record of God's instruction to Muḥammad, in reference to his dealings with the religious claims of Jews and Christians, to say to them, "Produce your proof (*burhānakum*) if you are people who speak the truth"; S. *al-Baqara* (2):111. It is not unlikely that it is because of the influence of this phrase, which is repeated four times in the Qurʾān in several different contexts, that the title *Kitāb al-burhān* was a popular one among Christian apologists for their treatises in Arabic.[139] In the Palestinian text under consideration here, the apologetic topics are the standard ones: the doctrines of the Trinity, the Incarnation, and a number of typically Christian religious observances and practices. In addition, there are numerous quotations from works attributed to early fathers of the church, such as Athanasius of Alexandria, and long lists of scripture testimonies. A particularly interesting feature of the work, to which an allusion was made above, is the long section listing Palestinian holy places, which may itself be a separate work included in the *Kitāb al-burhān.* In it the author encourages pilgrimage to these holy places associated with the life of Christ, and he claims that they should always remain in Christian hands.

> Wherever there is a place that God glorified and hallowed by the appearance in it of His Christ and the presence of His Holy Spirit, be it plain or mountain, wherever there is a place in which God spoke to any of His prophets before that or in which His wonders were seen, He has set all these places in the hands of those who believe in Christ, to pass as an inheritance from fathers to sons for ever, until He brings them the kingdom of heaven which does not perish . . . .

---

[135] See G. Graf, "Ein bisher unbekanntes Werk des Patriarchen Eutychios von Alexandrien," *Oriens Christianus* n.s. I (1911), 227-44.

[136] See Breydy, *Études sur Saʿīd ibn Baṭrīq* (n. 44 above), pp. 88-94.

[137] See Cachia and Watt, *Eutychius of Alexandria*, Part I, Arabic text (vol. 192), pp. 165-97.

[138] See Breydy, *Études*, pp. 88-89.

[139] Michel Hayek cites seven other Christian Arabic writers, who composed treatises under this same title, in his *ʿAmmār al-Baṣrī, apologie et controverses* (Beyrouth, 1977), pp. 32-33.

> God did not give the sites of the prophets and the relics of Christ and the places of the apostles and martyrs to any people save the Christians. It is they who sought them out, and honoured them and built churches upon them. That was done by their Christian kings and, beneath the kings, by governors and others, out of their eagerness, on account of their great faith and their desire for good, through the working of God in them (or what He did for them) in respect of that, and His strengthening them for it.[140]

It is interesting to note, at the end of the author's list of holy places, references to a church of the Theotokos in Constantinople, St. Peter's in Rome, St. Paul's in Kawkab, near Damascus, and finally, a reference to the *mandylion* in Edessa.[141] Clearly, the author of this work had a cosmopolitan view of Christianity. But he also clearly had an interest in securing the rights of the Christian shrines in the Holy Land.

As for the Holy Land monks, the three collections of original compositions in Arabic which are briefly reviewed here are not the sum total of their creative literary achievements. One knows, for example, of other works of Christian kalām from tenth-century Palestine which have not survived in full, or which have not been studied by modern scholars.[142] Furthermore, it is clear from the studies of Michel Breydy that in Palestine and elsewhere Melkite monks were busy enhancing the history of Christianity in the caliphate, an accomplishment which is usually attributed in its entirety to Eutychius of Alexandria.[143] But enough has been said here to give one some sense of the scope of the accomplishments of the Arabophone church in one quarter of its enclave in the Muslim world—the Melkite patriarchate of Jerusalem, and specifically the monasteries of the Holy Land.

---

[140] Cachia and Watt, *Eutychius of Alexandria,* Part I, Trnsl. (vol. 193), pp. 134 and 162.

[141] Ibid., pp. 152, 153, 162.

[142] Consider, for example, the tenth-century upper text on a palimpsest manuscript from Sinai, which is a "Disputation between a Christian and an Unbeliever." Only one page of it has been published, in Agnes Smith Lewis, *The Forty Martyrs of the Sinai Desert and the Story of Eulogios* [Horae Semiticae, IX] (Cambridge: Cambridge University Press, 1912), pp. 52-53, and the plate facing p. 69.

[143] Breydy, *Études*, passim.

IV

EUTYCHIUS OF ALEXANDRIA ON THE EMPEROR THEOPHILUS AND ICONOCLASM IN BYZANTIUM : A TENTH CENTURY MOMENT IN CHRISTIAN APOLOGETICS IN ARABIC

I

Eutychius, known in Arabic as Saᶜīd ibn Biṭrīq, was born in Cairo in the year 877. He became the Melkite patriarch of Alexandria on February 7, 933, and he retained this position until his death in 940 (1). Eutychius' fame is built not on his career as a patriarch, but on his accomplishments as an author in the Arabic language. And in the fulfillment of this vocation his most ambitious work is undoubtedly a history of the world, which he composed in an annalistic style that he probably borrowed from the Byzantine Greek chronographers. According to the Muslim biographer, Ibn Abī Usaybiᶜah (1194-1270), Eutychius named his history *The String of Pearls* (2), but it has been preserved in the Arabic manuscript tradition under the simple title, *The Book of History Compiled on the Basis of Verification and Authentication* (3), suggesting Eutychius' critical concerns. He says in his introduction, "I have made it a brief summary ..., having composed it concisely and carefully from the

(1) Eutychius himself reports the bare facts of his biography. Cf. L. CHEIKHO et al. (eds.), *Eutychii Patriarchae Alexandrini Annales* (CSCO, vols. 50 & 51 ; Beirut & Paris, 1906 & 1909), vol. 51, pp. 69-70. 'Eutychius' was his throne name as patriarch. Cf. *ibid*., p. 86.

(2) Cf. August MÜLLER, *Ibn Abī Useibia, ᶜUyūn al-Anbā' fī Tabaqāt aṭ-Ṭibbā* (2 vols. in 1 ; Königsberg, 1884), vol. II, p. 86.

(3) *Kitāb at-tārīḫ al-maǧmūᶜ ᶜalā t-taḥqīq wa t-taṣdīq*. CHEIKHO, vol. 50, p. 3. The only version of Eutychius' history in a western language is the one done in Oxford in the 17th century, viz., John SELDEN & Edward POCOCKE, *Contextio Gemmarum sive Eutychii Patriarchae Alexandrini Annales* (Oxford, 1658), available in *PG*, vol. CXI, cols. 889-1232.

Torah and the Gospel, and the extant, ancient and modern books" [4].

Eutychius explains that the range of his history is "from the age of Adam until years of the Islamic *Hiğrah*" [5]. In fact he brings his chronicle to a close in the year 938, during the reign of the Caliph, ar-Rāḍī (934-940) [6]. His purpose in composing it in the first place, he says in his introduction, is a practical one. People should have a reference source, to which they may refer when they engage in conversation about any one of the sciences. As a matter of practical observation, Eutychius says, "People differ very much about history. After long research and much effort, what seems right to me in this regard is that I make a compendium of what is in the Torah and other reliable books. I shall put it together in brief, concise accounts. As a result, my book should be sufficient in itself, leaving no need for referral to anyone else for knowledge of anything in history" [7].

The evidence suggests that Eutychius began work on his world history even before his elevation to the patriarchate. He dedicated it to his brother, a physician named ᶜĪsā ibn Biṭrīq, precisely the sort of learned person, one may presume, who would have been involved in conversations of the kind that Eutychius thought should profit from the availability of a handy reference source in Arabic. In Eutychius' day, in the fourth century of the *Hiğrah*, Arabic was certainly already the language of daily life in Egypt, even among Melkite Christians, whose Greek was getting rusty in spite of their allegiance to the creeds and the six councils approved by the patriarchs of Constantinople. The fact of the matter was, as the topic of the present article will allow the reader to observe in a specific instance, that Melkite Christians who lived within the realm of Islam, were not only losing their Greek, but they lost contact with

(4) CHEIKHO, vol. 50, p. 5.

(5) *Ibid.*, p. 3.

(6) After Eutychius' death, his history was continued by Yaḥyā ibn Saᶜīd ibn Yaḥya al-Anṭākī, up to the year 1027/1028. Cf. the Arabic text in CHEIKHO, *op. cit.*, vol. 51, pp. 89-273. Another edition, with a French translation, is available in I. KRATCHKOVSKY & A. VASILIEV, *Histoire de Yahya-ibn-Saᶜīd d'Antioche, continuateur de Saᶜīd-ibn-Bitriq*, in *Patrologia Orientalis*, 18 (1924), pp. 699-834 ; 23 (1932), pp. 345-520.

(7) CHEIKHO, vol. 50, p. 5.

events in Byzantium, even though their confessional preferences disposed them to an interest in Byzantine ecclesiastical affairs. They had no choice but to create for themselves an ecclesiastical life in Arabic, complete with liturgical texts, and a whole complement of ancillary compositions in philosophy, theology, history and hagiography (8).

Eutychius was not alone in the late ninth and early tenth centuries in the task of putting Christian history into Arabic dress. Contemporary with him was his fellow Melkite, Agapius, or Maḥbūb ibn Qusṭanṭīn, the bishop of Manbiǧ, i.e., Syriac Mabbūg and Greek Hieropolis, in the former Byzantine province of Osrhoene. Like Eutychius in Egypt, Agapius in Syria found it opportune to compose a world history in Arabic. The name of his book is *Kitāb al-ᶜunwān*, i.e., "the book of the title" (9). Agapius explained that his purpose was to produce in Arabic the sort of book that was called *ḫrūniqūn*, i.e., *Χρονικόν*, in Byzantine Greek. Speaking of the first day of creation, which he takes to be the 18th of Adar (*i.e.*, Nīsān, March), he says, "From this day, and month and year, begins the account of the times and years of the history of the world. It reports and gives notice of what happened in them. It is the sort of book that is named *ḫrūniqūn* in Byzantine Greek. In Arabic its interpretation is the cycle of the years and the procession of time and epochs" (10). In the form in which it has reached modern

(8) Significantly, the earliest dated version of the Gospel in Arabic is a Lectionary, preserved in Sinai *Arabic MS*, 72, copied by Stephen of Ramleh in 897. Cf. Georg GRAF, *Geschichte der christlichen arabischen Literatur* (vol. I, *Studi e Testi*, vol. 118 ; Città del Vaticano, 1944), pp. 142-147. On the Gospel, cf. Sidney H. GRIFFITH, *The Gospel in Arabic and the Christian / Muslim Controversies of the First Abbasid Century*, to appear. For other genres of Christian literature in Arabic at this time, cf. Gérard TROUPEAU, *La littérature arabe chrétienne du Xᵉ au XIIᵉ siècle*, in *Cahiers de Civilisation Médiévale Xᵉ-XIIᵉ siècle*, 14 (1971), pp. 1-20 ; and Robert CASPAR et al., *Bibliographie du dialogue islamo-chrétien ; auteurs et œuvres du VIIᵉ au Xᵉ siècle*, *Islamochristiana*, 1 (1975), pp. 131-181 ; 2 (1976), pp. 188-195.

(9) Cf. the Arabic edition by L. CHEIKHO, *Agapius Episcopus Mabbugensis Historia Universalis* (CSCO, vol. 65 ; Paris, 1912), and the Arabic edition, with a French translation, by A. VASILIEV, *Kitab al-ᶜUnvan, histoire universelle écrite par Agapius (Mahboub) de Menbidj*, in *Patrologia Orientalis*, 5 (1910), pp. 557-692 ; 7 (1911), pp. 457-491 ; 8 (1912), pp. 397-550.

(10) VASILIEV, *art. cit.*, 5 (1910), pp. 571-572.

readers, Agapius' history extends only as far as the caliphate of al-Mahdī (776 A.D.), although originally it extended to the year 941 ([11]). Both Agapius and Eutychius are careful to explain how the Arabic, Muslim numbering of the years intersects with the earlier chronological reckonings ([12]). Clearly their readers are presumed to be more familiar with the *Hiğrah* dating, and more knowledgeable about the historical events associated with Muslim rule in their homelands, than they would be with the current religious and political history of Byzantium and her neighbors. Accordingly, in both chronicles, from the rise of Islam the *Hiğrah* dating and the reigns of the Caliphs are the backbone of the narratives. By contrast with the detailed account of events in Byzantium before the rise of Islam, and especially the theological movements, disputes, and ecumenical councils, the references to Byzantium and her affairs become more exiguous in these chronicles as the reigns of the caliphs unfold. Even such a major religious controversy as was stirred up over the issue of iconoclasm in Byzantium received but scant attention from these two Melkite chroniclers, who lived under Muslim rule less than a century following the last of the iconoclast emperors ! The silence on this issue is particularly surprising since Melkites from Palestine played such a prominent role, as shall appear below, in the elaboration of iconophile theory.

One is naturally curious about the sources utilized by these first two Christian historians to write in Arabic. Both of them claim to have used the biblical books, and both of them make reference, to borrow Eutychius' phrase, "to other reliable books" ([13]). But they rarely designate their sources more exactly. In his account of the Roman destruction of Jerusalem, Agapius refers to what "Josephus, the Hebrew, mentions in the book he wrote on the ruin of Jerusalem" ([14]). And in connection with his narration of the Abbasid revolution, Agappius quotes from Theophilus, the astronomer, *i.e.*, Theophilus of Edessa (d. 785), another Melkite savant, who wrote a

(11) Cf. Georg GRAF, *GCAL* (vol. 2, *Studi e Testi*, vol. 133 ; Città del Vaticano, 1947), p. 39.

(12) Cf. VASILIEV, *art. cit.*, 8 (1912), pp. 455-456 ; CHEIKHO, *Eutychii ... Annales*, vol. 51, p. 1.

(13) *Ibid.*, vol. 50, p. 5.

(14) Cf. VASILIEV, *art. cit.*, 7 (1911), p. 497.

chronicle in Syriac (15). Agapius says explicitly about his reliance on Theophilus' work, "We have taken these reports from what Theophilus, the astronomer, said. ... He wrote much, but we have only summarized it in this book" (16). From all of this one might conclude that Agapius relied on available Syriac and Greek sources for his chronicle (17). And one suspects that following the Islamic conquest, there were few documents available to him that reported current events in Byzantium, hence the very cursory attention Byzantine affairs receive, once the policies of the Muslim rulers became more important for the Christians living in the so-called 'Oriental Patriarchates'. Eutychius, on the other hand, while he mentions a number of earlier Christian writers (18), says nothing very specific about the sources he used in composing his chronicle. As noted above, he mentions certain "reliable books", and at some points in his narrative it was perhaps Eutychius himself, and not a later scribe working with variant copies of the patriarch's chronicle, who occasionaly includes parenthetical remarks in the narrative that report what is "in another copy (*fī nusḫatin uḫrā*)" (19). If these remarks do come from Eutychius, they suggest that he consulted different documentary sources in the compilation of his chronicle, and was attentive to their variations. The impression that he did in fact use different sources is confirmed in the two accounts he gives of the coming to power of the emperor Nicephorus, as will appear below.

The historical works of both Eutychius and Agapius must be appreciated against the background of the growth of Christian literature in Arabic that had been underway for more than a century before their time. Leaving aside the vexing and doubtful question about whether or not there was a pre-Islamic Christian literature in

(15) *Ibid.*, 8 (1912), p. 525. Cf. also A. BAUMSTARK, *Geschichte der syrischen Literatur* (Bonn, 1922), pp. 341-342.

(16) VASILIEV, *art. cit.*, 8 (1912), p. 525.

(17) Cf. E. W. BROOKS, *The Sources of Theophanes and the Syriac Chroniclers*, in *Byzantinische Zeitschrift*, 15 (1906), pp. 578-587 ; S. GERO, *Byzantine Iconoclasm During the Reign of Leo III ; with particular reference to the oriental sources* (CSCO, vol. 346 ; Louvain, 1973), pp. 199-205.

(18) Cf. the indices of the writers mentioned by Eutychius in *PG*, vol. 111, cols. 1231-1232.

(19) Cf. *e.g.*, CHEIKHO, *Eutychii ... Annales*, vol. 51, pp. 63 & 82.

Arabic (20), it is quite clear that after the rise of Islam the Abbasid revolution ushered in the era that prompted the first efforts on the part of Christians to express their religious convictions in "an Arabic language manifest", to borrow the *Qur'ān*'s own characterization of the revelation that God sent down to Muḥammad (*an-Naḥl* (16): 103). It seems that a determining factor for the beginning of Christian literary life in Arabic during the first Abbasid century (750-850) was a shift in the prevailing Islamic consensus for governing. It had appeared already under the Umayyads, in the policies of the caliph Umar II (717-720) and his successor Yazid II (720-724) (21), but it came into bolder expression in the rhetoric that

(20) Louis Cheikho was a notable proponent of the thesis that there was a pre-Islamic Christian Arabic literature. Cf. Camille HECHAÏMÉ, *Louis Cheikho et son livre 'le christianisme et la littérature chrétienne en Arabie avant l'islam', étude critique* (Beyrouth, 1967). Regarding the thesis that there was a pre-Islamic, Arabic version of the Gospel, cf. Irfan SHAHID, *The Martyrs of Najran, New Documents* (Subsidia Hagiographica, 49 ; Bruxelles, 1971), pp. 242-250.

(21) Umar II seems to have been the first caliph after the conquest to be seriously interested in the conversion of non-Arabs to Islam. In the first place one might cite his social and financial reforms, to stop the payment of the *Ǧizyah* on the part of converts to Islam. Cf. W. W. BARTHOLD, *Caliph ᶜUmar II and the Conflicting Reports on his Personality*, in *The Islamic Quarterly*, 15 (1971), pp. 82-83, 87-88 (originally written in Russian in 1922) ; H. A. R. GIBB, *The Fiscal Rescript of ᶜUmar II*, in *Arabica*, 2 (1955), pp. 1-16 ; A. A. DURI, *Notes on Taxation in Early Islam*, in *Journal of the Economic and Social History of the Orient*, 17 (1974), pp. 140 & 143 ; M. A. SHABAN, *Islamic History, A.D. 600-750, a new interpretation* (Cambridge, 1971), pp. 131-137. Secondly, Agapius records the caliph's dispatch of a letter to the Byzantine emperor, Leo III, summoning him to Islam, and debating the truth claims of his religion. And Agapius also says that Leo replied in defense of Christianity, "with arguments from the revealed scriptures, demonstrations from reason, and adductions from the *Qur'ān*". VASILIEV, *art. cit.*, 8 (1912), p. 503. There is a considerable controversy about the authenticity of the works that have survived as versions of this correspondence. For the texts, cf. Adel-Théodore KHOURY, *Les théologiens byzantins et l'Islam (VIIIe-XIIIe s.)* (Paris, 1969), pp. 200-218 ; Arthur JEFFERY, *Ghevond's Text of the Correspondence between ᶜUmar II and Leo III*, in *The Harvard Theological Review*, 37 (1944), pp. 269-232. For a critical discussion, cf. S. GERO, *Byzantine Iconoclasm during the Reign of Leo III, with particular attention to the oriental sources* (CSCO, vol. 346 ; Louvain, 1973), pp. 153-171. There seems to be only one modern scholar who straightforwardly accepts the authenticity of the Armenian text of the correspondence, viz., L. W. BARNARD, *The Graeco-Roman and Oriental Background of the Iconoclastic Controversy* (Leiden, 1974), p. 23, n. 28. The fact of ᶜUmar's summons to Leo to embrace Islam, however, is not in

accompanied the Abbasid revolution. The new course was the active concern to promote conversion to islam among the subject populations, and to foster the assimilation of all Muslims into an equal participation in the social and religious life of the islamic community (22). To judge by the Christians recation, the policy must have been effective. For, it is in the first Abbasid century that the first Christian apologetical texts in Arabic appeared, in the works of the Melkite, Theodore Abū Qurrah, the Jacobite, Ḥabīb ibn Ḫidmah Abū Rā'iṭah, and the Nestorian, ᶜAmmār al-Baṣrī, to name only the most prominent writers of the period. From this point forward, Christianity sprang to life in Arabic. By the end of the ninth century there were numerous works of Christian apologetics in Arabic, Arabic versions of the scriptures become available, and everywhere, among Melkites, Jacobites, and Nestorians, an effort was made by Christians to provide the Arabic reading public with an ongoing acquaintance with Christian beliefs and practices. Eutychius himself participated in the apologetical enterprise with his book entitled *Kitāb al-burhān*, an attempt to explain Christianity in an Arabic idiom suitable to answer the difficult challenges to Christian doctrines posed by Muslims (23).

It is not an accident that the first Christian chronicles in Arabic were composed under Melkite auspices. While some Melkites spoke

doubt, and is characteristic of the resolve of this caliph actively to preach Islam. It is within the context of this resolve, that doubtless was widespread among other Muslims as well, that one should interpret the so-called 'iconoclastic edict' of ᶜUmar's successor, Yazid II. Cf. A. A. Vasiliev, *The Iconoclastic Edict of the Caliph Yazid II, A.D. 721*, in *Dumbarton Oaks Papers*, 9 & 10 (1956), pp. 25-47. This edict, as the first of a number of such governamental measures, is in every way comparable to similar Islamic attempts to regulate Christian behavior at later times, by way of the 'Covenant of ᶜUmar'. Cf. A. S. Tritton, *The Caliphs and their Non-Muslim Subjects ; a Critical Study of the Covenant of ᶜUmar* (London, 1930). For a more up-to-date bibliography, cf. J. M. Fiey, *Chrétiens syriaques sous les Abbasides surtout à Bagdad (749-1258)* (CSCO, vol. 420 ; Louvain, 1980), pp. 4 & n. 15, 87-90.

(22) M. A. Shaban, *The ᶜAbbasid Revolution* (Cambridge, 1970), p. 168.

(23) Pierre Cachia & W. Montgomery Watt, *Eutychius of Alexandria, The Book of the Demonstration (Kitāb al-Burhān)* (CSCO, vols. 192, 193, 209, 210 ; Louvain, 1960 – 1961). On the attribution of this work to Eutychius, cf. G. Graf, *Ein bisher unbekanntes Werk des Patriarchen Eutychius von Alexandrien*, in *Oriens Christianus*, 1 (1911), pp. 227-244.

and wrote in Syriac, by and large the ecclesiastical language of the Melkite church was Greek, particularly in Palestine, where ecclesiastical life was under the strong influence of the monasteries of Mar Sabas, Mar Charitōn, and St. Catherine at Mt. Sinai. These monasteries had long been centers of Chalcedonian power, with strong ties to Constantinople. They radiated their influence throughout the Melkite world. Theodore Abū Qurrah, for instance, who was Melkite bishop of Ḥarrān, and who by his own testimony wrote some thirty treatises in Syriac ([24]), was a monk of Mar Sabas. With the Islamic conquest, however,and particularly with the policies that came into vogue with the success of the Abbasid revolution, the Melkite community faced a social situation in which an important factor was the declining currency of the Greek language in the population at large, even in cities like Alexandria, Jerusalem and Antioch. While the Jacobites, the Nestorians, and the Chalcedonian Maronites could preserve their ecclesiastical life in Syriac, employing Arabic in early Abbasid times largely only for apologetic purposes, and the Copts of Egypt could do the same in their own language, the Melkites of Syria/Palestine had no such indigenous linguistic home to which they could withdraw. They had not cultivated the intellectual life in Palestinian Aramaic, but in Greek ([25]). Not surprisingly, therefore, a Palestinian Melkite Monk, Theodore Abū Qurrah (d. c. 820), is the earliest Christian writer in Arabic. The first systematic projects to translate the new Testament into Arabic from Syriac or Greek took place in Syria and Palestine, under Melkite auspices ([26]). The earliest dated Arabic manuscript of Christian theology in Arabic was copied in the monastery of Mar Charitōn in Judea in the year 877 ([27]).

(24) Constantin BACHA, *Les œuvres arabes de Théodore Aboucara, évêque d'Haran* (Beyrouth, 1904), pp. 60-61.

(25) The scriptures were the only significant writings in Palestinian Syriac. Cf. Bruce M. METZGER, *The Early Versions of the New Testament* (Oxford, 1977), pp. 75-82.

(26) Cf. n. 8 above. *Sinai Arabic MS*, 151 contains an Arabic version of the epistles of Paul, the Acts of the Apostles, and the catholic epistles. It is actually the oldest dated New Testament MS. One Bišr ibn as-Sirrī made the translation from Syriac in the year 867. Cf. Harvey STAAL, *Codex Sinai Arabic 151 Pauline Epistles ; Part I (Rom., I & II Cor., Phil.), Arabic Text ; Part II, English Translation* (Unpublished Ph. D. dissertation, University of Utah ; Salt Lake City, 1968).

(27) It is *British Museum Or., MS. 4950*. For a facsimile of the colophon

As the works of Eutychius and Agapius show, by the beginning of the ninth century, Melkites in Egypt, as well as in Syria, also required Arabic texts for their everyday life. They were becoming less preoccupied with Byzantium, except as the place of origin of their creeds, and they lost touch with even the religious controversies of contemporary Constantinople. By the second half of the ninth century, even the Copts, in the person of Severus ibn al-Muqaffa^{c}, were pressing for the expression of their faith in Arabic (28).

An interesing fact in the Arabicization of Melkite church life in Palestine in the ninth century is that the Arabic Gospel lectionary, as preserved in the ninth century family of manuscripts containing the Gospels in Arabic, is marked off in pericopes for the Gospel lessons for the temporal cycle of the divine liturgy, according to the old Jerusalem liturgical calendar, and not according to the Byzantine calendar, adopted in Constantinople after the middle of the ninth century (29). This fact in itself suggests a lack of attention to, if not a lack of knowledge of the ecclesiastical affairs in Byzantium, on the part of the Melkites in Palestine at this time.

A symbol of what was happening in the oriental patriarchates may be seen in the fact that in the early eighth century, a scholar such as John Damascene was writing in Greek and playing a role in the life of the Byzantine church, participating in the controversy over images, and even being anathematized by name by the council of Hieria in 754 as "one who is Saracen-minded, ... who insults

bearing the date, cf. Agnes SMITH LEWIS & Margaret DUNLOP GIBSON, *Forty-One Facsimiles of Dated Christian Arabic Manuscripts* (*Studia Sinaitica*, 12 ; Cambridge, 1907), pp. 2-4.

(28) Severus said that he composed his *History of the Patriarchs* from earlier Greek and Coptic sources because in his day Arabic was the language of most of the people, "most of whom are ignorant of the Coptic and the Greek". Quoted in K. SAMIR, *Un traité inédit de Sawīrus Ibn al-Muqaffa^{c} (Xe siècle) 'Le flambeau de l'intelligence'*, in *Orientalia Christiana Periodica*, 41 (1975), p. 156, n. 1 ; cf. also p. 160, n. 2.

(29) The family of MSS is composed of *Sinai Arabic MSS 72 & 74*, *Vatican Borgia Arabic MS 95*, *Berlin Or. Oct. MS 1108*, along with a few leaves from another MS. Cf. GRAF, *GCAL*, vol. I, pp. 142-147. Regarding the pericopes, cf. A. BAUMSTARK, *Die sonntägliche Evangelienlesung in vorbyzantinischen Jerusalem*, in *Byzantinische Zeitschrift*, 30 (1929-1930), pp. 350-359.

Christ and plots against the empire" [30]. By the end of the eighth century, John Damascene's younger confrere at Mar Sabas' monastery, Theodore Abū Qurrah, wrote in Arabic, and relied on the services of a translator for Greek versions of his work [31]. He wrote an Arabic treatise in defense of the practice of venerating images, drawing heavily on John Damascene's orations on the same subject, but making no reference at all to the Byzantine controversy, or to the iconodule council of 787 [32] ! Rather, Abū Qurrah was concerned with problems raised by Muslims and Jews in regard to religious images. And this disregard for Byzantine concerns, and particularly the iconoclastic controversy, leads one directly to the strange treament of this subject in the chronicle of Eutychius of Alexandria, from the point of view of a western reader.

II

Eutychius of Alexandria mentions Byzantine iconoclasm only once in his chronicle. He tells the story under the entry devoted to events in the reign of the caliph, al-Mutawakkil (847-861), in connection with the Byzantine emperor Theophilus (829-843), the

(30) Cf. the translation of the passage from the acts of the council of Hieria in S. GERO, *Byzantine Iconoclasm during the Reign of Constantine V, with Particular Attention to the Oriental Sources* (CSCO, vol. 384 ; Louvain, 1977), p. 94.

(31) The superscription to Abū Qurrah's Greek *opusculum*, 4 informs the reader that it is a letter on the Orthodox faith, from Patriarch Thomas of Jerusalem (807-821) to the 'heretics' in Armenia. It was composed by Theodore Abū Qurrah in Arabic, according to the superscription, and translated into Greek by Michael Synkellos. Cf. *PG*., vol. 97, col. 1504. At least one other Greek *opusculum*, viz., no. 9, *ibid*., col. 1529, was also translated from Arabic into Greek. Cf. Sidney H. GRIFFITH, *Some Unpublished Arabic Sayings Attributed to Theodore Abū Qurrah*, in *Le Muséon*, 92 (1979), pp. 29-35. For a brief discussion of the languages of Christian Palestine at this time, cf. G. EVERY, *Syrian Christians in Palestine in the Early Middle Ages*, in *The Eastern Churches Quarterly*, 7 (1946), pp. 363-372.

(32) Cf. Ioannes ARENDZEN, *Theodori Abu Kurra de Cultu Imaginum Libellus e Codice Arabico nunc Primum Editus Latine Versus Illustratus* (Bonn, 1897). For a German translation, cf. Georg GRAF, *Die arabischen Schriften des Theodor Abû Qurra, Bischofs von Ḥrrân (ca. 740-820)* (Paderborn, 1910), pp. 278-333. Cf. also Sidney H. GRIFFITH, *Theodore Abū Qurrah's Arabic Treatise on Bowing Down to the Images of Christ and the Saints : a Christian Apologetic Tract of the First Abbasid Century*, forthcoming publication.

last iconoclastic emperor. The asynchrony between the reigns of the two sovereigns is typical of the arrangement of the text in this latter portion of Eutychius' annals. He obviously squeezes in the Byzantine emperors and patriarchs, not without some surprising errors, as will become apparent, where he finds the space. His interest is more involved with the events in the caliph's realm, the chronological succession of whose reigns is the organizing principle of his narrative once Eutychius begins to follow the Islamic chronology of the *Hiğrah* (33).

The procedure here will be to present an English translation of the entry that deals with Theophilus, to discuss this account, and then, in a third section of the article to relate Eutychius' discussion of Byzantine iconoclasm to other Arabic and Syriac reports of this controversy, and to advance an hypothesis to explain the image issue in Syriac and Arabic sources from early Abbasid times.

A. Eutychius' Text

Of the events in al-Mutawakkil's reign, Eutychius mentions only the caliph's arrangement for the construction of a new Nilometer in

(33) Eutychius assigns the first year of the *Hiğrah* to the first year of the reign of the emperor Heraclius (610-641), and he explains that the term *Hiğrah* refers to the flight of Muḥammad to Medina. When he reconciles the *Hiğrah* chronology with the other chronologies of his times, Eutychius offers the following correspondences: "There were 338 years from Diocletian to the *Hiğrah*, 614 years from Christ our Lord to the *Hiğrah*, 933 years from Alexander to the *Hiğrah*, ..., 6, 114 years from Adam to the *Hiğrah*". Cheikho, *Eutychii ... Annales*, vol. 51, p. 1. What immediately strikes the modern reader of this passage is the fact that Eutychius designates the Gregorian year 614 as the first year of the *Hiğrah*, while the other dates, viz., the Diocletian year 338, the Seleucid year 933, and the Alexandrian year of the world 6114, all correspond to the Gregorian year 622, to which year the first year of the *Hiğrah* is generally ascribed. Cf. V. Grumel, *la Chronologie* (Traité d'études byzantines ; Paris, 1958), p. 246. Eutychius is no doubt following the reckoning of the Alexandrians, according to which Christ was born in the year 5501, which corresponds to the Gregorian year 9. Cf. V. Grumel, p. 223. As for his statement that the first year of the *Hiğrah* corresponds to the first year of the emperor Heraclius, one can only cite it as one more instance in which Eutychius' sources failed him. Agapius, on the other hand, assigns the beginning of the *Hiğrah* chronology to the Seleucid year 933, which he says is the eleventh year of Heraclius. Cf. Vasiliev, *art. cit.*, 8 (1912), p. 456.

Cairo, his building of a new city called al-Ǧaᶜfariyyah in Iraq, and his employment of harsh measures against Christians in his realm. On the latter subject, Eutychius says of al-Mutawakkil.

> He got angry at Buḫtīšūᶜ, the physician. He prescribed for all the countries that the Christians should put on the dress of the vagrant, patches on their outer graments, a patch on the front and a patch on the back ; and that they should be forbidden to ride on horses, that balls be put on their saddles, that they ride with wooden stirrups, that images of satans (in one copy, of pigs and apes) be put on the doors of their dwellings. From this the Christians acquired sore trouble, grief and affliction (34).

The physician is the Nestorian Buḫtīšūᶜ ibn Ǧibrīl (d. 870), a one-time intimate friend of the caliph, who eventually fell out of his favor (35). Buḫtīšūᶜ was a contemporary, and a rival, of another famous Nestorian physician, Ḥunayn ibn Isḥāq (d. 873). Interesting in the present context is the story preserved in Ibn Abī Uṣaybiᶜah's *ᶜUyūn al-anbā' fī ṭabaqāt aṭ-ṭibbā'* (36) about a quarrel between Buḫtīšūᶜ and Ḥunayn over the practice of venerating images. The story is told in the first person, as if by Ḥunanyn himself. However, there is some controversy over its authenticity (37). In the story, Buḫtīšūᶜ is said to have tricked Ḥunayn into denouncing the Christian practice of venerating images in the presence of al-Mutawakkil, to the point of desecrating an image of Mary and the Christchild. Subsequently, according to the story, the caliph, acting on the advice of the Nestorian *catholicos*, imprisoned Ḥunayn and confiscated his goods because he had disavowed a true Christian practice ! Only later did Ḥunayn achieve freedom, and that only when the caliph's illness required his medical expertise.

(34) CHEIKHO, *Eutychii ... Annales*, vol. 51, p. 63. On al-Mutawakkil's well known anti-Christian policies, cf. TRITTON, *op. cit.* ; D. SOURDEL, *Le vizirat ᶜabbāside de 749 à 936 (132 à 324 de l'hégire)* (2 vols. ; Damascus, 1959-1960), vol. I, pp. 271-286 ; FIEY, *op. cit.*, pp. 83-90.

(35) Cf. D. SOURDEL, *Bukhtishuᶜ*, *EI²*, vol. I, p. 1298, and GRAF, *GCAL*, vol. II, pp. 110-111.

(36) Cf. MUELLER, *op. cit.*, vol. II, pp. 191-197.

(37) Cf. B. HEMMERDINGER, *Ḥunain ibn Isḥāq et l'iconoclasme byzantin*, in *Actes du XIIᵉ Congrès International d'Études Byzantines* (Beograd, 1964), vol. II, pp. 467-469 ; G. STROHMAIER, *Ḥunain ibn Isḥāq und die Bilder*, in *Klio*, 43-45 (1965), pp. 525-533 ; FIEY, *op. cit.*, p. 104.

There are many problems connected with this story, the pursuit of which would not be pertinent here. In the present context, however, it is interesting to note that in the story it is Buḫtīšūᶜ who is the defender of the practice of venerating images. He is able to bring down his rival, Ḥunayn, because of the latter's alleged unorthodox views on this subject.

Whether or not Eutychius knew of this story, or whether there was any connection in his mind between the Buḫtīšūᶜ/Ḥunayn incident, with its focus on the question of the legitimacy or illegitimacy of venerating images among Christians, and the introduction of al-Mutawakkil's anti-Christian policies, he definitely seems to associate the caliph's anger at Buḫtīšūᶜ with the initiation of these policies. It is almost as if al-Mutawakkil's program reminds Eutychius of a similar repressive policy on the part of the Byzantine emperor. For, it is precisely at this point in his narrative that he records what he knows about the iconoclastic policy of the emperor, Theophilus. It is one of the longest entries to be devoted to Byzantine affairs in this portion of Eutychius' chronicle. This fact is itself noteworthy, given the chronicler's predominant concern with events within the *dar al-islām*. The text of the entry follows [38] :

> Michael, the son of Theophilus, the king of the Byzantines, died and after him his son Theophilus became king of the Byzantines. He removed the images from the churches, effaced them, broke them, and commanded that there be no images in churches at all. The reason that prompted him to remove the images from the churches was that one of his ministers reported to him that in a certain place in Byzantine territory there was a church belonging to Lady Mary in which there was an image. On her feast day, a drop of milk would come out of the breasts of the image. King Theophilus refused to acknowledge this, and he undertook an investigation into the matter. The custodian of the church was found to have drilled a hole into the wall behind the image. He made a perforation into the breasts of the image and introduced a small, thin tube of lead into it. Then he smeared the place over with clay and lime so that it would not be noticed. On the feast day of Lady Mary he would pour milk into the perforation, and a small drop would come out of the breasts of the image. People used to come on pilgrimage to this church, and so for

(38) Cheikho, *Eutychii ... Annales*, vol. 51, pp. 63-64.

this reason the administrator acquired enormous wealth. King Theophilus sent and tore down this image, and repaired the site, and ordered that in churches there should be no image at all. He beheaded the administrator of that church. He removed the images from the churches, and he said that images are the equivalent of idols, and that whoever bows down to an image is like one who bows down to idols. A controversy arose among the Byzantines over the matter of images, to the point that some of them were calling others unbelievers. Some said whoever bows down to an image has disbelieved. Others said that whoever does not bow down to images has disbelieved.

Sophronius, the patriarch of Alexandria, heard about this, so he wrote an extensive treatise, in which he upholds bowing down to images, and he provided argumentation for it. He said, "God, praise and glory be to Him, and hallowed he His names, commanded Moses to make golden images of the Cherubim on the Ark of the Covenant, and to put it inside the sanctuary". He also argued, "Solomon, the son of David, when he labored to build the temple, put a golden image of the Cherubim in it". And he said, "Whenever a document from the king arrives, sealed with the king's seal, and the official (39) is told, 'This is the king's seal, and his document', does he not rise to take the document in his hand, to kiss it, to put it to his head and his eyes ? His standing, and his kissing the document, is not to honor the scroll, or the wax that is sealed on the scroll, or the ink that is inside the scroll ; nor is his standing or his honor for the document. It is certainly not for any one of these features. It is only to honor the king and the king's name, since this is his document. So, from this perspective it is necessary for us to kiss this image, and to bow down to it, since our kissing it and our bowing down, is not like our bowing down to idols. Our honor and reverence are only for the name of this martyr, whose image is here portrayed in these colors". He dispatched the book to King Theophilus. The king received it, took delight in it, and abandoned his disapproval of images.

Abū Qurrah was also among those who supported bowing down to images. He wrote a book on this, and he named it, "Sermons on Bowing Down to Images".

From this point in his entry under the name of al-Mutawakkil, Eutychius goes on to speak of the succession of patriarchs in

(39) The text has *lilᶜālim*, but it is quite clear that it should be *lilᶜāmil*, to correspond to the previous *ᶜammāl*. Cf. *ibid*., p. 64, l. 5.

Alexandria and Jerusalem. He mentions the murder and burial of the caliph, in the city which he had named *al-Ǧa*ᶜ*fariyyah*. He describes al-Mutawakkil's physical appearance, and brings the narrative to a close with a brief account of the caliph's courtiers.

B. Commentary

Even the casual reader will instantly spot items requiring commentary in Eutychius' unique story. An important point to notice initially, however, is that the chronicler offers this narrative to the reader as his sole account of Byzantine iconoclasm! The notice of Theodore Abū Qurrah's treatise on images, which comes at the end, is for the benefit of the Christian reader of Arabic, who requires such a text not for the purpose of responding to Byzantine iconoclasts, but as a defense of the Christian practice of venerating images of Christ and the saints, in the face of the Muslim claim, shared with Byzantine iconoclasts, that such a practice is tantamount to idol worship. The similarity of the two counterpositions is perhaps the reason for Eutychius' comparatively long digression on this subject in his history. He is not so much interested in Byzantine affairs, which he reports with surprising inexactitude, but in the topic of the dispute which divided the Byzantine church, a topic which was relevant to him as an apologist for Christianity who, in his own quite different social circumstances, must take account of Muslim objections to the religious legitimacy of the Christian habit of venerating images. This aspect of the matter will be discussed below, but first certain curiosities in Eutychius' narrative must be explored.

1) *The Succession of Byzantine Emperors*.

From the point of view of Byzantine history, Eutychius' most surprising misconception, aside from missing virtually the entire iconoclastic crisis of more than a century, is undoubtedly his complete confusion about the origins of the Amorian dynasty. The reader is alerted to this situation immediately upon seeing the statement, "Michael, the son of Theophilus, the king of the Byzantines, died, and after him his son, Theophilus, became king of the Byzantines" (40). Eutychius means here Michael II (820-829), the

(40) *Ibid*., p. 63.

founder of the Amorian dynasty, and the father of the emperor Theophilus (829-842). It is the statement that Michael was the son of Theophilus that attracts one's attention, and is the clue that leads one to the discovery that Eutychius was completely confused about the whole succession of Byzantine emperors between Nicephorus (802-811) and the emperor Theophilus, a period of some nine years. He speaks of the death of Nicephorus and the imperial succession after him in two places in the chronicle. First, in his entry under the reign of the caliph al-Amīn (809-813), he says: "Nicephorus, son of Istibrāq ([41]), king of the Byzantines, died, and after him Istibrāq, son of Nicephorus, son of Istibrāq, became king over the Byzantines" ([42]). Then, a few pages later, toward the end of his presentation of the events in the reign of the caliph al-Ma'mūn (813-833), he says: "Constantine defeated Nicephorus, son of Istibrāq. He overthrew him and Constantine became king over the Byzantines" ([43]). In this entry he skips Stauracius (811), Michael I Rangabe (811-813), and Leo V (813-820), and introduces into their places two otherwise unknown persons. First, as mentioned in the quotation above, he introduces an unknown Constantine, who, according to Eutychius, defeated and supplanted Nicephorus ([44]). Then he mentions as Constantine's son, another man named Theophilus, who is said to have succeeded his father on the throne ([45]), and whom Eutychius designates as the father of the first Amorian emperor, Michael II ([46]), and consequently, the grandfather of the known emperor Theophilus (829-842) ([47]). Further, following up his account of how Nicephorus became emperor, one discovers that Eutychius also skipped over the interval between Nicephorus and the earlier emperor Leo IV (775-780), including the reigns of Constantine VI (780-797), and Irene (797-802), a period of some twenty-two years. He makes Nicephorus succeed Leo IV: "Leo, son

(41) *Istibrāq* is the Arabic transcription of Σταυράκιος, Stauracios. It is written *Istīrāq*, once at p. 51, elsewhere, consistently, *Istibrāq*.

(42) *Ibid.*, p. 54.

(43) *Ibid.*, p. 59.

(44) *Ibid.*, p. 59.

(45) *Ibid.*, p. 60.

(46) *Ibid.*, p. 61.

(47) *Ibid.*, p. 67.

of Constantine, son of Leo, died. After him Nicephorus, son of Istibtāq became king over the Byzantines" (48). And earlier in the list of emperors, in the section of his chronicle that is arranged by the *Hiğrah* years and the reigns of the caliphs, Eutychius also skips Philippicus (711-713) and Anastasius II (713-715), the two rulers who came between the second reign of Justinian II (705-711) and Theodosius III (715-717). He lists Artabasdus as a legitimate emperor between Leo III (717-741) and Constantine V (741-775).

After Theophilus, Eutychius records the accession of the emperor's son Michael III (842-867) to the throne, and he also notes the beginning of the Macedonian dynasty, with the usurpation of power by Basil I (867-886). From here to the end of his chronicle he has the emperors in order, with the curious twist that in the several places where Romanus I Lecapenus (920-944) is clearly meant, the Arabic text has the consonants *dmtyws* (49). In all likelihood, these consonants are a corruption from *rwmnws*, or some such more likely transcription of the Greek name Romanos. The consonants involved could easily be confused in the Arabic script.

These mistakes in recording the succession of the Byzantine emperors indicate that the sources of information about Byzantine affairs that were available to Eutychius were very unreliable for the period of time ranging from the beginning of the eighth century to the first quarter of the ninth century. He is particularly at a loss for the years between Leo IV and Michael II, i.e., between 780 and 820. For the earlier years, it is only a matter of skipping two emperors, Philippicus and Anastasius II. After the reign of Leo IV, however, Eutychius not only skips any mention of four emperors, viz., Constantine VI, Irene, Michael I, and Leo V, but he follows two apparently different accounts of how Nicephorus came to power, and he introduces three otherwise unknown individuals, viz., the Stauracius whom he calls the father of Nicephorus, and the grandfather of the emperor Stauracius (811) ; the Constantine whom he calls the father of Theophilus, and the grandfather of Michael II ; and the Theophilus whom he calls the father of Michael II, and the grandfather of the emperor Theophilus. It now becomes evident that these three "invented" emperors are all "made-to-order" grandfa-

(48) *Ibid.*, p. 51.
(49) *Ibid.*, p. 82.

thers for three actual emperors, to whom, in two instances, Eutychius has given the names of their grandsons (i.e., Stauracius and Theophilus), and one of whom, Constantine, carries the name of the successor of Leo IV, i.e., Constantine VI, whom Eutychius had skipped over earlier in his narrative. Eutychius, therefore, was acutely aware of the gaps in his knowledge about the succession of the emperors in Constantinople. And he devised a formula for filling in the *lacunae* with names that were at least recognizably Byzantine imperial names.

It is worth noting here that there is evidence that Agapius also had some difficulty in gathering reliable information about the succession of the Byzantine emperors in the eighth century. Although, in the form in which it has survived, his chronicle reaches only as far as the beginning of the reign of Leo IV (775-780), in the sequence of emperors from the time of Heraclius he leaves out Leontius (695-698), and fails to mention that Justinian II had a second reign (705-711). Rather, he lists Tiberius II (698-705) as a co-emperor with Justinian. Therefore, Agapius too must have had some little difficulty finding sources for his history of this period, and this fact corroborates the conclusion that one would reach on other grounds, viz., that beginning in the eighth century even Melkite Christians living in the Arabic speaking milieu were losing contact with Byzantium.

When one turns to Eutychius of Alexandria's accounts of the succession of the patriarchs of Constantinople, he discovers that the chronicler had even less information about them at his disposal than he had about the emperors ! All goes well enough until in his narrative Eutychius comes to the second half of the seventh century. Between the patriarchs Peter (655-666) and George I (679-686), he skips over the four intervening patriarchs : Thomas II (667-669), John V (669-675), Constantine I (675-677), and Theodoros I (677-679). But then, after the death of George I, whom Eutychius correctly names as the one who presided over the sixth ecumenical council, Constantinople II (680-681) [50], he introduces the four patriarchs whom he had skipped earlier, in their proper sequence of succession, but now as successors to George I [51]. Finally, at the

(50) *Ibid.*, p. 34.
(51) *Ibid.*, pp. 38, 40, 45, 49.

point where he assigns Theodoros I to the time of the caliph Ǧaᶜfar al-Manṣūr (754-775), the second Abbasid caliph, Eutychius makes his confession of the fact that the modern reader of his chronicle has already suspected to have been the case. He says, "The names of the patriarchs of Constantinople have not reached me since Theodoros died, until I have written this book. Likewise, in regard to the patriarchs of Rome, from the time of Agabius (i.e., Agatho, 678-691), patriarch of Rome, the names of the patriarchs of Rome and reports of them have not reached me" (52). But in his own day, as Eutychius says, he knows about the conflict between Patriarch Nicholas (901-907) and the emperor Leo VI (886-912), in the course of which Leo VI replaced Nicholas with Euthymius (907-912) (53). And Eutychius correctly reports that before his death Leo VI returned Nicholas to the throne for a second term as patriarch (911-925) (54). After Nicholas' second term, Eutychius reports the succession of Stephen II (925-928), Tryphon (928-931), and Theophylaktos (933-956) as patriarchs. He closes his chronicle with the following notice : "In the year 326 (i.e., 937 A.D.) a gratifying peace came about between the Byzantines (and the Muslims). And in that year, Theofilaks, patriarch of the city of Constantinople, sent a messenger to the patriarchs of Alexandria and Antioch asking them to mention his name in their prayers and in their liturgies because this had been cut off since the era of the Umayyads. They complied with him in this" (55).

Clearly, then, and in plain words in relationship to the patriarchs, Eutychius testifies to the scarcity of information in the Arabic speaking world about Byzantine ecclesiastical affairs, especially after the Abbasid revolution. It is interesting to note in passing, that for the same period Eutychius' knowledge of affairs in the oriental patriarchates is fairly well *au courant*, at least in regard to the events he chooses to narrate.

Turning again to Agapius' narative one is startled to discover that he never mentions a single patriarch of Constantinople from the reign of the emperor Heraclius, to that of Constantine V ! His last

(52) *Ibid.*, p. 49.
(53) *Ibid.*, pp. 73-74.
(54) *Ibid.*, p. 81.
(55) *Ibid.*, pp. 87-88.

mention of a patriarch was the following notice, under the reign of the emperor Justinian I (527-565) : "And Epiphanius, patriarch of Constantinople, died after ruling for seven years. After him, Anthimius took over for ten years" (56). Actually, Epiphanius rules for sixteen years, and Anthimius for only one !

While he says nothing about the patriarchs of Constantinople after Anthimius, Agapius does mention that Agatho, the patriarch of Rome, agreed with the doctrine of the sixth ecumenical council (681), but he neglects to mention the council's president, patriarch George I (679-686) (57). He mentions that Gregory, the patriarch of Rome, was angry at the emperor Leo III for ordering the removal of images of the martyrs from churches, without saying a word about the struggles of patriarch Germanos I (715-730), or even the opposition of John Damascene (58). And finally, he mentions the iconoclastic council of the emperor Constantine V, i.e., the council of Hieria (754), and its anathemas, reporting without objection that the fathers of the council "promulgated many canons and named it the seventh council" (59).

Clearly, Agapius as well as Eutychius had trouble finding sources of information about Byzantine ecclesiastical affairs. One must then conclude that following the Islamic conquest, and particularly following the Abbasid revolution, Melkite Christians in the oriental patriarchates were increasingly cut off from their co-religionists in Byzantium, and their own affairs, *vis-à-vis* the Islamic establisment, became more all absorbing, until the political and military circumstances of the late ninth century once again allowed easier contacts with Byzantium.

A particularly striking evidence of the east's isolation from Byzantine ecclesiastical affairs can be seen in Eutychius' failure to mention two events which involved the oriental patriarchs themselves, according to Byzantine sources. The first of them is the letter addressed to the emperor Theophilus by the three oriental patriarchs, Christopher of Alexandria (817-849), Job of Antioch (814-845), and Basil of Jerusalem (821-839), arguing against the

(56) Vasiliev, *art. cit.*, 8 (1912), p. 428.
(57) Cf. *Ibid.*, p. 473.
(58) Cf. *Ibid.*, p. 506.
(59) *Ibid.*, p. 533.

emperor's iconoclastic policies (60). More will be said below about this letter. The second event is the Photian controversy. Eutychius makes no mention of this affair, nor of the encyclical letter that Photius sent to the oriental patriarchs in the year 867 (61) nor of the participation of the legates of these same patriarchs in the council of 869 (62).

One must conclude that Eutychius either did not know of these events in the life of the Byzantine church, with their direct reference to the oriental patriarchates, or that he did not consider them to be sufficiently interesting, or even important enough to be mentioned in his chronicle. Both events transpired during the fifty years that preceded his birth. Perhaps he did not mention them, in part, for both reasons. Documentation may have been scarce, and, after all, the problems of the church within the *dar al-islām* were of another sort than those that worried the churches of Byzantium and Rome. So it need not be surprising that Eutychius was more concerned with the activities of the islamic governments than he was with even the ecclesiastical affairs of Byzantium.

2. *The Story of the Lactating Virgin*.

A curious feature of Eutychius' report about the motives that induced the emperor Theophilus to adopt an iconoclastic policy is his proposal that the emperor's moral outrage at the charlantanry of an ecclesiastical official was at the root of it. It is as if, in Eutychius' view, the emperor's reaction was perfectly understandable, and even laudable, in view of the reprehensible practices he had uncovered. The only problem was that the emperor went too far with his corrective measures, but even these, according to Eutychius, were set aright by the intervention of the Alexandrian patriarch, Sophronius. As it stands, Eutychius' report is unique among the documents known to this writer in assigning the origins of Byzantine iconoclasm to an emperor's outrage, not at the practice of

(60) Cf. L. Duchesne, *L'iconographie byzantine dans un document grec du IXe siècle*, in *Roma e l'Oriente*, 5 (1912-1913), pp. 222-239, 273-285, 349-366.

(61) Cf. V. Grumel, *Le patriarcat byzantin ; les regestes des actes du patriarcat de Constantinople* (2 vols. ; Paris, 1932-1936), vol. I, pp. 88-89 ; F. Dvornik, *The Photian Schism, History and Legend* (Cambridge, 1948), p. 119.

(62) Cf. Dvornik, *op. cit.*, p. 193.

venerating images itself, but at the criminally fraudulent behavior of an ecclesiastic who contrived miracles in association with an image, for the purpose of his own financial gain.

As for the image of the lactating virgin, she seems truly to be at home in Egypt. Prior to the time of iconoclasm this particular iconographic motif seems to have been appreciated especially in Egypt (63). The best known exemplars of the genre, which modern art historians trace back in part to the Isis/Horus motif in pre-Christian Egyptian representations, come from the Fayyum and Saqqara in lower Egypt, and perhaps even from Melkite circles (64). So, in Eutychius' story of ecclesiastical charlatanry, the *virgo lactans* should put the reader in mind of Egypt, and it should not at all remind him of Byzantium proper. Perhaps, with this Egyptian flavor to the story, Eutychius intended to appeal to his original readership's immediate experience of Mary images, in order to make more concrete his views of the emperor's provocation to formulate his iconoclastic policies.

Eutychius' report of the iconoclasts' conviction about images is accurate enough, as far as it goes, i.e., that images are equivalent to idols, and that whoever bows down to an image is like one who bows down to idols (65). Such a sentiment was not unique to iconoclasts, however, but was deeply rooted in an earlier Christian antipathy to religious images, based on Bible passages such as *Exodus*, 20 : 4-5 and *Deuteronomy*, 5 : 8-9 (66). In fact, iconoclastic

(63) Cf. G. A. Wellen, *Das Marienbild der frühchristlichen Kunst*, in *Lexicon der christlichen Ikonographie* (Freiburg, 1971), vol. 3, cols. 158-159.

(64) Cf. especially K. Wessel, *Eine Grabstele aus Medinet al-Fajum, zum Problem der Maria Lactans*, in *Wissenschaftliche Zeitschrift der Humboldt Universität zu Berlin*, 4 (1954/1955), pp. 149-154 ; Idem, *Koptische Kunst, die Spätantike in Ágypten* (Recklinghausen, 1963), pp. 17-18, 130-133, 156 ; *Idem*, in Gertrud Schiller, *Ikonographie der christlichen Kunst* (Band 4, 2, "Maria" ; Gütersloh, 1980), pp. 22, 180. Cf. also A. Effenberger, *Koptische Kunst, Ägypten in spätantiker, byzantinischer und frühislamischer Zeit* (Wien, 1975), pp. 156-158, 213-214.

(65) Cf. H. von Campenhausen, *Die Bilderfrage als theologisches Problem der alten Kirche, in the author's Tradition und Leben, Kräfte der Kirchengeschichte, Aufsätze und Vorträge* (Tübingen, 1960), pp. 241-242 ; S. Gero, *Notes on Byzantine Iconoclasm in the Eighth Century*, in *Byzantion*, 44 (1974), p. 27.

(66) Cf. E. Kitzinger, *The Cult of Images in the Age Before Iconoclasm*, in *Dumbarton Oaks Papers*, 8 (1954), pp. 93, 131, 133.

theory was much more developed than this simple identification of images with idols, even in the declarations of the iconoclastic councils [67]. But in the form in which Eutychius' readers would have encountered the antipathy to religious images, the biblically inspired identification of images with idols would have been right on the mark, as shall appear below.

3. *The Patriarch Sophronius.*

Sophronius I was patriarch of Alexandria from 836 to 859 [68]. Theophilus was emperor from 829-842. Eutychius says that Patriarch Sophronius wrote a treatise in defense of the practice of venerating images and sent it to the emperor, who promptly repented of his iconoclastic policies.

As for the contents of Sophronius' treatise, which, by the way, is known only from Eutychius' report of it, the three topics which it discusses are standard iconodule arguments in justification of image veneration. They are that in the Old Testament God commanded Moses and Solomon to make images ; that one venerates the image of the emperor without fear of being charged with idol-worship ; and that in venerating the image of a saint, one is actually honoring the saint and not his image [69].

While Sophronius' treatise written for the emperor Theophilus is known only from Eutychius' report about it, in Byzantine Greek sources there is the record of a letter sent to the same emperor by the

(67) Paul J. ALEXANDER, *The Iconoclastic Council of St. Sophia (815) and its Definition (*Horos*)*, in *Dumbarton Oaks Papers*, 7 (1953), pp. 35-66 ; IDEM, *Church Councils and Patristic Authority, the Iconoclastic Councils of Hiereia (754) and St. Sophia (815)*, in *Harvard Studies in Classical Philosophy*, 63 (1958), pp. 493-505 ; M. V. ANASTOS, *The Ethical Theory of Images Formulated by the Iconoclasts in 754 and 815*, in *Dumbarton Oaks Papers*, 8 (1954), pp. 151-160 ; IDEM, *The Argument for Iconoclasm as Presented by the Iconoclast Council of 754*, in *Late Classical and Medieval Studies in Honor of Albert Mathias Frank Jr.* (Princeton, 1955), pp. 177-188.

(68) Following here the dates of J. FAIVRE, *Alexandrie*, in *DHGE*, vol. II, col. 366. They differ considerably from Grumel's dates for Sophronius' reign, viz., 848-860. Cf. V. GRUMEL, *La chronologie*, *op. cit.*, p. 443.

(69) Cf. the general survey of the arguments on Jaroslav PELIKAN, *The Spirit of Eastern Christendom (600-700)*, (The Christian Tradition, a History of the Development of Doctrine, vol. II ; Chicago, 1974), pp. 91-145.

three Oriental Patriarchs on the same theme, of which Eutychius makes no mention at all in his history, as was noted above. The letter is said to have been the product of a synod, attended by the patriarchs or their representatives, and numerous other persons, held at Jerusalem, in the Church of the Resurrection, in April of the year 836, the year when Christopher of Alexandria is supposed to have died. In the form in which the letter has survived, expressing the longing on the part of the patriarchs for the return of Byzantine rule, it invites doubts about its authenticity (70). One wonders if such an account of the opposition of the Oriental Patriarchs to iconoclasm was not composed completely within the Greek speaking realms of the emperor, having as its kernel of fact merely the known support of *iconodulia* within the Oriental patriarchates ?

Finally, in reference to Eutychius' statement that when Theophilus received Sophronius' treatise he foreswore his iconoclastic policies, one is reminded that this reversal of policy is generally ascribed not to Theophilus at all, but to Theodora, the regent for Michael III (842-867), at a synod held in March 843, under the presidency of Patriarch Methodius (843-847) (71). However, it is interesting to note that in later Byzantine literature Theophilus was remembered for his sense of justice, and, at least in part, somewhat excused for his iconoclastic policies (72). There is also a report in an account of the life of Theodora, probably written during the reign of Basil I (867-886), to the effect that the empress agreed to reestablish the veneration of images, if all the clergy prayed for the absolution of the sins of her deceased husband. Subsequently, the story goes, she and Patriarch Methodius were assured in a vision of Theophilus' absolution, and the narrative proceeds to recount the noble deeds of the emperor (73).

(70) Cf. A. Vasiliev, *The Life of St. Theodore of Edessa*, in *Byzantion*, 16 (1942-1943), pp. 216-225 ; H. G. Beck, *Kirche und theologische Literatur* (München, 1959), p. 496.

(71) Cf., in general, G. Ostrogorsky, *History of the Byzantine State* (Trans. J. Hussey, rev. ed. ; New Brunswick, N.J., 1969), pp. 217-219.

(72) Cf. Ch. Diehl, *La légende de l'empereur Théophile*, *Seminarium Kondakovianum*, 4 (1931), pp. 33-37.

(73) Cf. W. Regel, *Analecta Byzantino-Russica* (Petropoli, 1891), pp. xiii, xviii, 19-39.

Emperor Theophilus was also remembered in Greek hagiography for his cruelty. There is, for example, the story of his treatment of Sts. Theodore and Theophane, two monks from the monastery of Mar Sabas in Judea, who were called 'Graptoi' because of the abuse they received at the emperor's hands in the year 836. In response to what he perceived to be their stubborn refusal to desist from spreading iconodule propaganda, the emperor caused a twelve line iambic poem, charging them with criminal religious behavior, to be branded onto their faces (74). Eutychius makes no mention of these Palestinian monks from the monastery of Mar Sabas.

4. *Theodore Abū Qurrah's Treatise.*

It is notable that on the subject of image veneration, Eutychius names only Theodore Abū Qurrah as an earlier scholar whose writings might interest the reader of his history. Abū Qurrah's treatise, which was written in Arabic, survives in only two known manuscripts (75). As far as can be determined in the present state of scholarship, Abū Qurrah wrote his treatise while he was the Melkite bishop in Ḥarrān, somewhere between the years 800 and 812 (76). He composed it, as he says, in response to a particular state of affairs between Christians and Muslims.

> Many Christians are abandoning bowing down (*as-suǧūd*) to the image of Christ, our God, ..., and to the images of his saints, ... because the non-Christians, and especially those who claim to have a scripture sent down from God, rebuke them for their bowing down to these images, and on account of it they mock them and ascribe to them the worship of idols, contravening what God commanded in the Torah and the prophets (77).

That such was in fact the charge that Muslims brought against Christians can be seen in the following passage from an anonymous

(74) Cf. P. O. Vailhé, *Saint Michel le Syncelle et les deux frères Grapti, Saint Théodore et Saint Théophane*, in *Revue de l'Orient Chrétien*, 9 (1901), pp. 313-332, 610-642.

(75) As published in Arendzen, *op. cit.*, cf. n. 32 above, the treatise is from the *British Museum Or. MS 4950*. It is also contained in *Sinai Arabic MS 330*.

(76) Cf. Sidney H. Griffith, *Theodore Abū Qurrah's Treatise* ..., work in progress.

(77) Arendzen, *op. cit.*, p. 1.

Muslim, apologetic pamphlet of the ninth Christian century. The author writes,

> You extol the cross and the image. You kiss them, and you prostrate yourselves to them, even though they are what people have made with their own hands. They neither hear, nor see, nor do harm, nor bring any advantage. The most estimable of them among you are made of gold and silver. Such is what Abraham's people did with their images and idols (78).

Two things are remarkable in connection with Eutychius' mention of Abū Qurrah's treatise in defense of image veneration. The first of them is the fact that Eutychius mentions only Abū Qurrah, and not his fellow monk and mentor from St. Sabas monastery in Judea, St. John Damascene, who wrote three very influential treatises in Greek in defense of *iconodulia* (79), and who was even anathematized by name in the acts of the council of Hiereia in 754, as mentioned above. Of course, the most obvious reason for Eutychius' failure to mention John Damascene's treatises is that they were in Greek, and Arabic was the language of the readers of Eutychius' history.

The second thing to note in connection with Eutychius' mention of Abū Qurrah's treatise is the fact that this staunchly Melkite writer, who also wrote a noteworthy Arabic treatise in defense of the dogmatic definitions of the first six ecumenical councils (80), neglected to mention the second council of Nicea (787) at all in his treatise in defense of images ! Initially this omission caused Georg Graf to postulate the year 787 as the *terminus ante quem* for Abū Qurrah's composition of the treatise on images (81). But now Ignace

(78) D. Sourdel, *Un pamphlet musulman anonyme d'époque ʿabbāside contre les chrétiens*, in *Revue des Études Islamiques*, 34 (1966), p. 29.

(79) Cf. the new edition, B. Kotter, *Die Schriften des Johannes von Damaskos* ; III, *Contra Imaginum Calumniatores Orationes Tres* (Berlin & New York, 1975).

(80) Cf. C. Bacha, *Un traité des œuvres arabes de Théodore Abou-Kurra, évêque de Harran ; publié et traduit en français pour la première fois* (Tripoli de Syrie & Rome, 1905) ; C. A. Kneller, *Theodor Abucara über Papsttum und Konzilien*, in *Zeitschrift für katholische Theologie*, 34 (1910), pp. 419-427 ; H. J. Sieben, *Zur Entwicklung der Konzilsidee, achter Teil*, in *Theologie und Philosophie*, 49 (1974), pp. 489-509.

(81) Georg Graf, *Die arabischen Schriften des Theodor Abû Qurra, Bischofs von Ḥarrân (ca. 740-820)* (Paderborn, 191), pp. 4-5.

Dick has shown conclusively that Abū Qurrah must have written the treatise in question after the year 799, because in it he tells the story of an Arab Muslim who became a convert to Christianity, and who was executed under the caliph Harūn ar-Rašīd (786-809) on December 25, 799 ([82]).

Not only are Eutychius and Abū Qurrah silent about the council of 787, and about Byzantine iconoclasm in general, but most of the Christians who wrote chronicles in Arabic and Syriac in the early period fail to mention the council, and they refer to iconoclasm only very summarily, if at all, as the misguided policy of this or that Byzantine emperor. Agapius' account of the measures adopted by Constantine V, and the council of 754, were mentioned above. To this one may add Michael the Syrian's (d. 1199) contention that the Greeks alleged that they disliked Constantine V because of his policy in regard to images, whereas really it was because he held 'orthodox', *i.e.*, Monophysite, views ([83]). Sebastian Brock has shown that Michael is referring here to the council's rejection of John Damascene, who was a defender of Maximist theology ([84]). The anonymous Syriac chronicle '*ad annum 1234*' takes note only of the council of 754, and later of the fact that Theodora, the mother of the emperor Theophilus, as regent after the death of her son, put an end to his iconoclastic policies ([85]). Bar Hebraeus (d. 1286), a Jacobite, likens the policy of Leo III to that of the caliph Yazīd II (720-724) ([86]), but he does not mean it as a compliment.

Finally, it should be said that, outside of Armenia ([87]), there was no iconoclastic movement east of Byzantium, beyond the reaches of

(82) Cf. Ignace DICK, *Un continuateur arabe de saint Jean Damascène : Théodore Abuqurra, évèque melkite de Harran*, in *Proche Orient Chrétien*, 13 (1963), pp. 116-118.

(83) Cf. J. B. CHABOT, *Chronique de Michel le syrien, patriarche jacobite d'Antioche (1166-1199)* (4 vols. ; Paris, 1899-1910), vol. II, pp. 489-521.

(84) S. BROCK, *Iconoclasm and the Monophysites*, in A. Bryer & J. Herrin (eds.), *Iconoclasm* (Birmingham, 1977), p. 55.

(85) Cf. J. B. CHABOT (& A. Abouna), *Anonymi Auctoris Chronicon ad Annum Christi 1234 Pertinens* (4 vols., CSCO, vols. 81, 82, 109, 354 ; Paris & Louvain, 1916, 1920, 1952, 1974), vol. 109, p. 263.

(86) Cf. E. A. W. BUDGE, *The Chronography of Gregory Abû 'l Faraj, ... commonly known as Bar Hebraeus* (2 vols. ; Oxford, 1932), vol. I, p. 109.

(87) Cf. entry no. VII, with updated bibliography, in Paul J. ALEXANDER, *Religious and Political History and Thought in the Byzantine Empire, Collected Studies* (London, 1978).

the imperial power in the 8th and 9th centuries. Certainly this was the case among the Melkites. Sebastian Brock has shown that there was no Syrian monophysite policy of iconoclasm (88). And the report quoted above about the conflict between Ḥunayn ibn Isḥāq and Buḫtīšūᶜ ibn Ǧibrīl presupposes that Ḥunayn was unique among the Nestorians for his views about images. Indeed, modern studies show that images were common among the Nestorians in the ninth century (89). And, beginning in the late eighth century, the scholars of all of these groups were concerned about justifying the veneration paid to images, or to symbols such as the cross, in response to the objections to these practices voiced by the Muslims in the contemporary debates about religion.

In this connection, it is instructive to take a quick glance at Eutychius' own apologetic treatise, entitled *Kitāb al-burhān* (90). Following the example of the apologists of the previous generation, Eutychius includes a defense of the symbol of the cross in his treatise, in the section that deals with other Christian sacraments and ritual practices, such as the Eucharistic liturgy, Baptism, Sunday as the holy day, and facing east in prayer. But unlike his co-religionist, Theodore Abū Qurrah, Eutychius pays no explicit attention to images. Rather, he presents a long discussion, of some forty pages in Cachia's edition (91), describing what he calls "the vestiges and locations (*āṯār wa amākin*)" (92) of Christ's holiness in this world. He means the churches which, as he says, emperors and other officials have built in the holy places associated with Christ's life. Eutychius speaks of some thirty churches, principally in the Holy Land, but including the mention of a church of St. Mary the Theotokos in Constantinople, the church of St. Peter in Rome, the

(88) Cf. Brock, *art. cit.*, and M. Mundell, *Monophysite Church Decoration*, in A. Bryer & J. Herrin, *op. cit.*, pp. 59-74.

(89) Cf. J. Dauvillier, *Quelques témoignages littéraires et archéologiques sur la présence et sur le culte des images dans l'ancienne église chaldéenne*, in *L'Orient Syrien*, 1 (1956), pp. 297-304 ; E. Delly, *Le culte des saintes images dans l'église syrienne orientale*, in *L'Orient Syrien*, 1 (1956), pp. 291-296.

(90) Cf. Pierre Cachia & W. Watt, *Eutychius of Alexandria, the Book of the Demonstration (Kitāb al-Burhān)* (CSCO, vols. 192, 193, 209, 210 ; Louvain, 1960 & 1961).

(91) Cachia, vol. 192, pp. 165-207.

(92) *Ibid.*, p. 165.

church of St. Paul in Kawkab, near Damascus, and finally the church at Edessa [93], in which, he says, is located, "the most marvelous of the vestiges which Christ has bequeated to us, the *mandylion* (*mandīlan*) ... with which Christ wiped his face, on which there is affixed an unchanging, clear adornment (*ḥilyah bayyinah*), without depiction (*ṣūrah*), drawing (*raqm*), or painting (*naqš*)" [94]. This is curious language with which to describe the famous image of Edessa. It is clear that Eutychius is accenting its stature as an *acheiropoiēton*, or image not made by human hands. But it is curious that he refrains from calling it an image (*ṣūrah*) as such. Rather, like all of the churches he has listed, it is a 'vestige' (*aṯar*) [95], he says, that Christ has left us.

It is difficult to avoid what one might call the iconic function of these 'vestiges and locations', of which Eutychius speaks. He says of them,

> By these vestiges and locations which he has bequeathed to us, Christ gave us altogether a blessing (*baraqah*), a sanctification, an approach to him, pardon for sins, feasts in which men come together in his name, spiritual joy without end, and testimonies (*šahādāt*) bearing witness to all that the book of the Gospel says of his story and his acts, and also what the books prior to the Gospel said of the affairs of the prophets [96].

Eutychius' obvious avoidance of any explicit discussion of images, even in the churches that he mentions, which must have contained numerous icons, mosaics, and frescoes, could lead one to the conclusion that for Eutychius' purposes in the *Kitāb al-burhān*, the issue of images and their veneration was not a point of

(93) Eutychius' list of churches in the Holy Land and elsewhere, and their proper identification, is the subject of another article with which the author is engaged.

(94) CACHIA, vol. 192, p. 207.

(95) Theodore Abū Qurrah was perfectly willing to speak of the "image of Christ (*ṣūrat al-masīḥ*)" in Edessa. Cf. ARENDZEN, *op. cit.*, p. 26, It is instructive that Eutychius speaks of a *mandilān*, and not an image. On the significance of this term, and for bibliography on Edessa's famous portrait, cf. Averil CAMERON, *The Sceptic and the Shroud*, An Inaugural Lecture in the Department of Classics and History, King's College, London, 29 April 1980.

(96) CACHIA, vol. 192, p. 165. The translation is adapted from the version presented by Watt in vol. 193, p. 134.

significant controversy between Christians and Muslims. But there is also another dimension to Eutychius' argument. He presents the churches as places of pilgrimage for Christians, and thereby he must certainly have intended to put the reader of Arabic in mind of the obligatory Islamic pilgrimage (*al-ḥaǧǧ*) to Mecca. Here is not the place in which to pursue further this aspect of Eutychius' apologetics. The point at issue presently is that in his own apologetic work, unlike Theodore Abū Qurrah, who wrote in the previous century, Eutychius sees no need especially to defend the practice of venerating images. This fact, taken in connection with the author's very summary discussion of Byzantine iconoclasm in his account of world history, might suggest that by Eutychius' day the issue of images had already been settled between Muslims and Christians. However, as it will be argued below, the truth of the matter seems to be that while images were often occasions of controversy, and even of violence between Christians and Muslims, explicit discussion of them was pushed to the background in most of the Christian apologetical works that were written within the realm of Islam, because, unlike in Byzantium, the practice of venerating images was never challened by Christians themselves in the oriental patriarchates. Hence it never assumed importance as one of the basic elements of Christian life which must be defended at all costs. Rather, it was part and parcel of the on-going Christian *modus vivendi*, and the apologetical energy of the community was expended in defense of the more fundamental doctrines of their faith, which the images themselves proclaimed.

III

The preceding analysis of Eutychius of Alexandria's discussion of Byzantine iconoclasm offers the modern reader of the patriarch's history the opportunity to raise some fundamental questions of interpretation about the work itself, and its role in the inception of Christian intellectual life in Arabic ; and it provides the historian of Christian apologetics in Arabic with the occasion to sketch in the place occupied by the veneration of images as a topic of controversy between Muslims and Christians in the medieval period. By now the conclusions reached by the present writer on these subjects may easily be inferred from the discussion that has gone before. However, clarity will better be served if these conclusions are drawn out more explicitly.

A. Byzantine Iconoclasm

While it may be true that among western historians of Byzantium, as Peter Brown says, "the Iconoclast controversy is in the grip of a crisis of over-explanation" (97), as much could certainly not be said for the same topic at the hands of the historians who lived in the oriental patriarchates during and after the period of Byzantine iconoclasm. Even though Stephen Gero has devoted two volumes to the study of iconoclasm during the reigns of Leo III and Constantine V, "with particular attention to the oriental sources", in fact the oriental sources in Syriac and Arabic have helped him only marginally, usually negatively, and then only in support of arguments first drawn from Greek texts, to conclude that "Byzantine iconoclasm in the eighth century, as it is described in the sources, was emphatically an imperial heresy, so to speak, born and bred in the purple" (98). To judge only by the record of it in Syrian and Arabic chronicles, one would have to conclude that there was no crisis of iconoclasm in Byzantium at anything like the magnitude of social and religious significance at which the modern historian is accustomed to think of it. And what is more to the point, even the Melkite writers of the first Abbasid century and a half, as we have seen, have nothing to say about the second council of Nicea in 787, let alone do they add it to the list of the six councils whose teachings they uphold (99). There simply was no policy of iconoclasm in the

(97) Peter Brown, *A Dark-Age Crisis : Aspects of the Iconoclastic Controversy*, in *The English Historical Review*, 88 (1973), p. 3.

(98) S. Gero, *Byzantine Iconoclasm during the Reign of Constantine V, with Particular Attention to the Oriental Sources* (CSCO, vol. 384 ; Louvain, 1977), p. 168.

(99) Even Theodore of Studios reported, twenty years after Nicea II, that the Oriental Patriarchs took no notice of the council at the time of its meeting, or later. Cf. Patrick Henry, *Initial Eastern Assessments of the Seventh Ecumenical Council*, in *The Journal of Theological Studies*, 25 (1974), p. 77. As late as the eleventh century, al Bīrūnī (d. 1084) lists a feast of the 'six councils' in the Melkite calendar. Cf. R. Griveau, *Les fêtes des melchites par Abou Rihân al-Birouni*, in *Patrologia Orientalis*, 10 (Paris, 1915), pp. 304-305. And much later, among 21 Arabic

oriental patriarchates. To the degree that such a policy in the Greek speaking world is mentioned at all in oriental sources, such as in Eutychius' chronicle, it is to explain it as an aberrant imperial policy in Byzantium itself, as Gero points out.

But what is to be said about the accuracy, or lack of it, in Eutychius' narrative ? Iconoclasm in Byzantium was certainly not limited to the reign of Theophilus. There is no other record of this emperor's repentance for having instigated or continued such a policy. There is no other record of an iconodule treatise written by Patriarch Sophronius, let alone that this Alexandrian patriarch singlehandedly changed the attitude of the emperor Theophilus. The fraudulently lactating virgin, whose story Eutychius repeats, seems to reflect an iconographic style that would have been at home in Alexandria, but foreign to Byzantium, where Eutychius' narrative places it. The succession of Byzantine emperors was certainly not as Eutychius presents it, and he himself confesses his lack of knowledge about the succession of the patriarchs of Constantinople for almost a century and a half. What is one to make of all of this ?

The first and most obvious conclusion to draw is that Eutychius lacked the proper documentary sources for both the civil and the ecclesiastical affairs of Byzantium from the early eighth century to well into the tenth century. His own admission aids this conclusion, as well as his errors in listing the emperors from Nicephorus to Michael II. However, it seems unlikely that he would completely lack documentary sources for the accomplishments of Sophronius, his own predecessor on the patriarchal throne of Alexandria by only some seventy years. And, as mentioned above, one knows of the reports in Greek sources of Sophronius' predecessor, Christopher's participation, at least by proxy, in a meeting of the oriental patriarchs held in Jerusalem in the year 836, at which a letter was allegedly drafted to admonish the emperor Theophilus to foreswear iconoclasm. So, it is not unlikely that the patriarchs of Alexandria, Christopher, Sophronius, and later Eutychius, at least were somewhat concerned about iconoclasm in Byzantium, even if they did

manuscripts of the Melkite collection of canons dating from the 13th to the 17th centuries, only 7 of them include a reference to Nicea II. Cf. J. B. DARBLADE, *La collection canonique arabe des melkites (XIIIe-XVIIe siècles)* (S. Congregazione Canonica Orientale, Fonti, serie II, Fascicolo XIII ; Harissa, 1946).

not know about, or deliberately chose to underplay, the true extent of it.

If one changes his perspective, and looks at Eutychius' report not from the point of view of the historian of Byzantium, but from the viewpoint of the historian of Christian literature in Arabic, another conclusion is possible. It is clear from Eutychius' own introduction to the *String of Pearls*, as noted at the beginning of the present article, that his intention in composing his history was to provide a reliable reference source in Arabic for persons who engage in conversations about history. So his purpose was first of all to serve the needs of Arabic speaking Christians who lived within the *dar al-islām*. By Eutychius' day, Christians in this realm had lived under Islamic rule for about three hundred years. So the political affairs of contemporary Byzantium would not have been among their primary interests. But the history of Byzantine ecclesiastical affairs prior to the consolidation of Islamic rule under the Abbasids was of paramount concern to Eutychius and to his readers, and to judge by the way in which Eutychius presents the story, this was because Byzantine history, right up to the last quarter of the seventh century, was largely the history of the developments that led to the calling of the six ecumenical councils, according to whose pronouncements the Melkite creed was defined. Not surprising then is Eutychius' promise in the introduction to his history, "I vouch for this book of mine. I have made it the best in terms of research,and most reliable in doctrine (*maḏhhab*)" ([100]). Doctrine was, of course, a major reason for writing history, not only for Eutychius, but for the very first Christian historians ([101]). By Eutychius' time, and in Alexandria, where by the mid-tenth century there were not only the monophysite Copts for the Melkites to contend with, but the Muslims as well, one might surmise that religious apologetics was the major reason for an interest in earlier Byzantine history on the part of the Arabic speaking Melkites. This point was not lost on the later Muslim religious polemicist, Ibn Taymiyya (d. 1328), who

(100) CHEIKHO, *Eutychii ... Annales*, vol. 50, p. 3.

(101) G. Glenn F. CHESNUT, *The First Christian Histories, Eusebius, Socrates, Sozomen, Theodoret, and Evagrius* (Paris, 1977).

devoted considerable space in his refutation of Christianity to the criticism of passages from Eutychius' history (102).

Apart from the controversies involving Patriarch Photius of Constantinople (858-867, 877-886), about which Eutychius has nothing at all to say in his history, the iconoclastic controversy was the only major religious movement with doctrinal significance in Byzantine history between the rise of the Abbasid caliphate and Eutychius' lifetime. Whereas the Photian affair had essentially to do with a quarrel between Rome and Constantinople, the issue of the veneration of sacred images had immediate relevance to the oriental patriarchates because it was an issue in the day to day controversies between Muslims and Christians. Since the Byzantine controversy lasted for more than a century, and since Palestinian monks played such a notable role in it, and some Christian pilgrims from the West traveled to the Holy Land during this period (103), Christians living within the realm of Islam must at least have heard of the controversy. Therefore, the pastoral problem of the eastern bishops, living in an area where even a smattering of knowledge about the facts of such a controversy among Byzantine Christians could only have a frustrating effect on their own apologetical efforts, would have been to put an acceptable construction upon what they knew of these events in Byzantium. For his part, Eutychius explained Byzantine iconoclasm as a case of mistaken enthusiasm on the part of the emperor, Theophilus, seeking to rectify abuses that grew up in at least one church in connection with image veneration. The fact that the image in question is Egyptian in style does not necessarily detract from what Eutychius may have honestly thought to have been the cause of Byzantine, imperial iconoclasm, viz., justified moral outrage on the emperor's part. Patriarch Sophronius may well have written a treatise in defense of the practice of venerating images, and he may even have sent it to the emperor. What remains curious is that Eutychius reports only about Theophilius' policies,

(102) G. TROUPEAU, *Ibn Taymiyya et sa réfutation d'Eutyches*, in *Bulletin d'Études Orientales*, 30 (1978), pp. 209-220.

(103) Documents survive of the travels of some half-dozen pilgrims to Egypt and the Holy Land during the Iconoclastic period and shortly thereafter. Cf. John D. WILKINSON, *Jerusalem Pilgrims before the Crusades* (Warminster, 1977), pp. 11-13.

and not those of his predecessors. One may conclude that even if he knew about them, to rehearse the whole affair in Arabic would have been counterproductive to the Christian apologetic requirements of Eutychius' time and place.

B. Images and Symbols : Muslim Polemic and Christian Apology

Muslims objected to the Christian practice of venerating the cross and images of Christ and the saints on the grounds that such a practice amounts to the idolatry that is expressly forbidden in the scriptures, as is clear from the passage quoted above from the anonymous Muslim polemical pamphlet from the ninth century (104). Correspondingly, the Christian apologists who answered the Muslim challenges to Christianity, in treatises written in Syriac and Arabic in the ninth century, never failed to include in their tracts intended for more popular consumption, a section that dealt with aspects of the public exercise of Christian faith that often attracted Muslim opposition. In addition to subjects such as Baptism, the eucharist, and facing east in prayer, the symbol of the cross and the practice of venerating it are inevitably topics of discussion in these treatises. But only Theodore Abū Quarrah among the first generation of Christian apologists in Arabic wrote expressly in defense of the veneration of images of Christ and the saints. Nevertheless, from other sources, such as lives of the saints and various chronicles in Syriac and Arabic, as well as in Muslim reports of Christian misbehavior, one learns that Christian images were often occasions of friction with Muslims.

The account of St. Anthony Ruwaḥ is a good case in point (105). Before his conversion to Christianity, and his subsequent martyrdom in 799, this young man of Qurayš, as the story goes, was fond of tearing down crosses from churches, and otherwise harassing the Christian community. The occasion of his conversion was a miracle that took place when he shot an arrow at the image of St. Theodore. The arrow was deflected from the image and it miraculously returned to pierce the archer's hand. This event was the first of a

(104) Cf. n. 78 above.

(105) Cf. I. Dick, *La passion arabe de S. Antoine Ruwaḥ, néomartyr de Damas († 25 déc. 799)*, in *Le Muséon*, 74 (1961), pp. 109-133.

series of miracles in attestation of the truth of Christianity that the young man witnessed. It initiated his conversion (106).

On another tack, Eutychius himself reports the story of a border conflict between Muslims and Christians in the days of the conquest, under the caliph ᶜUmar ibn al-Ḫaṭṭāb (634-644), that was occasioned when some Muslims allegedly defaced an image of the Byzantine emperor, Heraclius (610-641), that was affixed to a pillar used as a boundary marker near Qinnasrīn. According to the story, the quarrel was settled only when the Christians were allowed similarly to deface an image of the caliph, ᶜUmar (107). While this story seems a bit far-fetched in terms of its verisimilitude, it nevertheless records the Christian concern for images, and the Muslim disregard for their special character. And it shows the image as an occasion of controversy between Muslims and Christians, already from the first years of Islamic rule.

Even more specific in regard to the Islamic antipathy to Christian images is a story found in Severus ibn al-Muqaffaᶜ's *History of the Patriarchs of Alexandria*. It concerns the actions of one, al-Aṣbağh, who was the eldest son of the governor of Egypt, ᶜAbd al-ᶜAzīz ibn Marwān (d. 754), whom his father had put in charge of a particular district of the country. According to Severus, al-Aṣbağh was notorious for his ati-Christian behavior. The following is one of the episodes Severus recounts in evidence of his allegation.

> When on the great Sabbath, the Sabbath of the holy resurrection, he entered the monastery of Ḥulwān, he looked at the icons (*aṣ-ṣuwar*), adorned as they should be, with the veils over them and incense. There was the image of the pure Lady Mary, and the Lord at her breast. When he had looked at her, and pondered over her, he said to the bishops and the group with him, 'Who is this so ?'. They said, 'This is Mary, the mother of Christ'. He then hawked, and filled his mouth with spittle, and spat into her face. And he said, 'If I find the moment, I shall wipe the Christians out of this district. Who is Christ that you should worship him as God ?' (108).

This account, with its closing question, aptly puts the finger on the root of the Muslim antipathy to the omnipresent Christian

(106) Cf. *ibid.*, pp. 120-121, 127-129.

(107) CHEIKHO, *Eutychii ... Annales*, vol. 51, pp. 19-20.

(108) C. F. SEYBOLD, *Severus ibn al-Muqaffaᶜ, Alexandrinische Patriarchengeschichte von S. Marcus bis Michael I, 61-767* (Hamburg, 1912), p. 134.

crosses and images. Not only do they smack of idolatry to Muslim sensibilities, but the most common of them, in this instance the virgin and child, proclaim the very doctrines about Christ and his mother that the *Qur'ān* flatly denies, viz., that he is divine (cf. e.g., *al-Ma'idah* (5) : 75), and, in the instance of the cross, the Christian claim that Christ was crucified at the instigation of the Jews (cf. *an-Nisā'* (4) : 157). This is the most creditable reason not only for al-Aṣbaḡh's behavior, but also for the caliph al-Yazīd's much discussed order that Christian crosses and images should be destroyed, and even for the many traditions that are said to go back to the prophet Muḥammad, prohibiting images in Islam, not to mention the stipulations in the covenant of ᶜUmar against the public showing of a cross, or the 'display of idolatry' (109).

Here is not the place to discuss these issues in detail. The point to be made is that crosses, images and icons were constant occasions for controversy between Christians and Muslims, for doctrinal reasons as much as for any other cause. The cross and the icon bespoke the very doctrines that were the major topics of controversy between the two religious communities, in addition to their susceptibility to the charge that they were no better than idols.

For all of these reasons, one may easily see that Patriarch Eutychius would not have been anxious to present Byzantine iconoclasm in his history as anything more than a passing phase in one emperor's over zealous attempt to insure the purity of the church's life and practice.

(109) For al-Yazid's decree, and the wide attention it has attracted in connection with Byzantine iconoclasm, cf. A. A. Vasiliev, *The Iconoclastic Edict of the Caliph Yazid II, A.D. 721*, in *Dumbarton Oaks Papers*, 9 & 10 (1956), pp. 25-47. On the traditions going back to Muḥammad, cf. the list of them in A. J. Wensinck, *A Handbook of Early Muhammadan Tradition* (Leiden, 1927), p. 108 ; and the interpretation in R. Paret, *Die Entstehungszeit des islamischen Bilderverbots*, in *Kunst des Orients*, 11 (1976-1977), pp. 158-181. For the Islamic point of view in regard to images and the arts, cf. O. Grabar, *The Formation of Islamic Art* (New Haven, 1978), pp. 76-101 ; and *idem*, in *Islam and Iconoclasm*, in A. Bryer & J. Herrin, *Iconoclasm* (Birmingham, 1977), pp. 45-52. For the stipulations in the covenant of ᶜUmar, cf. A. S. Tritton, *The Caliphs and their Non-Muslim Subjects ; a Critical Study of the Covenant of ᶜUmar* (London, 1930) ; A. Fattal, *Le statut légal des non-musulmans en pays d'Islam* (Beyrouth, 1958).

V

THEODORE ABŪ QURRAH'S ARABIC TRACT ON THE CHRISTIAN PRACTICE OF VENERATING IMAGES

Between the years 795 and 812 A.D., Theodore Abū Qurrah served as the Melkite bishop of Ḥarrān. During this period he composed in Arabic a pamphlet in which he justified the Christian practice of venerating images of Christ and the saints, against objections coming from Jews and Muslims. He wrote the pamphlet in response to a request from an individual named Yannah, who was an official at the "Church of the Image of Christ" in Edessa. The review of Abū Qurrah's arguments in this pamphlet provides evidence for the study of contemporary Jewish and Islamic attitudes to public Christian devotional observances, as well as to pictorial artwork in the religious milieu in general. Furthermore, the consideration of the socio-historical context of the tract allows one to gain a new perspective on the progress of the public promotion of Islam in the territories of the caliphate during the early Islamic centuries. And it offers yet another perspective from which to consider the relationship of Islamic attitudes concerning religious art to iconoclasm in Byzantium.

A NEGLECTED SOURCE OF HISTORICAL INFORMATION about the early Islamic period in the Near East is the body of Christian religious literature in Arabic which began to appear toward the middle years of the first Abbasid century. Although this literature is for the most part concerned with arguments about religion among Christians, Jews, and Muslims, the discussions contained in the polemic and apologetic texts often provide unexpected bits and pieces of historical information or offer a new perspective from which a fresh consideration may be given to old historical problems. Theodore Abū Qurrah's Arabic tract on the Christian practice of venerating images of Christ and the saints is a case in point. While this work is an exercise in religious apologetics, a consideration of its contents from the point of view of social and religious history provides one with a rare glimpse into certain aspects of the relationships among Jews, Christians, and Muslims in the Abbasid caliphate during the early years of the ninth Christian century. Moreover, a consideration of the historical background of these relationships from the perspective of Abū Qurrah's tract on images offers one a new view of the well known Islamic campaign for the public display of the symbols of Islam in the conquered territories, beginning already in the reign of the caliph ᶜAbd al-Malik (685–705). In many places in his tract, Abū Qurrah also affords the reader an insight into how much was known among the *ahl adh-dhimmah* of this early period about the *Qurʾān*, the *ḥadīth*, and a number of Islamic religious practices. And finally, one may learn from a study of Abū Qurrah's tract how surprisingly little concerned the Christian community living within *dar al-islām* was with iconoclasm and other policies in contemporary Byzantium.

I. THEODORE ABŪ QURRAH: A CHRISTIAN *mutakallim*

Theodore Abū Qurrah (c. 750–c. 820) was a native of Edessa in Syria, who came to the monastery of Mar Sabas in Palestine to become a monk. Once there he became involved in the intensive intellectual life that had been set in motion in the monastery in the previous generation by St. John Damascene.[1] The project which this Greek-speaking Palestinian monk had undertaken was no less than to produce a systematic summary of Christian doctrine in its Chalcedonian and Maximist phase. It seems likely that the Islamic conquest, which claimed Palestine definitively in the year 638, was a major factor among the circumstances

[1] Ignace Dick, "Un continuateur arabe de saint Jean Damascène: Théodore Abuqurra, évêque melkite de Harran," *Proche Orient Chrétien* 12 (1962), pp. 209–223, 319–332; 13 (1963), pp. 114–129.

which prompted John to produce a compendium of the faith in the first place, along with an epitome of the ecclesiastical philosophy which supported it.[2] The need for a convincing apologetic in the face of a strong non-Christian intellectual challenge had not been so strong since the days of the early Greek apologists. Certainly, for Abū Qurrah, who popularized much of John's thought, the hegemony of the Muslims was a deciding factor among the circumstances which prompted him to write.

John Damascene wrote in Greek and his works were carried to Constantinople by refugee monks from Palestine.[3] In due course, his writings became well known all over Byzantium, and he was eventually said to be the last father of the church in the east. Theodore Abū Qurrah, on the other hand, wrote principally in Arabic and his works circulated within the Chalcedonian communities under Islamic rule. While a number of his treatises were translated into Greek, and so circulated in Byzantium, for the most part he was unknown outside of the Islamic world.[4] Yet his works are a mine of information for the historian who wants to learn about the life of the Christian community under Islamic rule, once all meaningful contact with Constantinople had come to a halt.

Abū Qurrah was no sedentary monk. He was a controversialist, who travelled from Egypt to Armenia, and in the territories in between, preaching the Chalcedonian message and arguing with Jews, Muslims, and Jacobites alike.[5] Michael the Syrian, a Jacobite chronicler writing in the twelfth century, recorded the memory in his community that Abū Qurrah was a sophist who had excited the minds of simple folk, being especially successful since he knew Arabic.[6]

While religious controversy was his stock in trade and, in addition to preaching and debate, he wrote a number of apologetical tracts in defense of Christianity, Abū Qurrah was also for a time a bishop. Between the years 795 and 812, he served as the Melkite bishop of Ḥarrān, a suffragan see to the metropolitan of Edessa, located only about twenty-five miles away. For some reason which has not been mentioned in the sources, except for Michael the Syrian's remark that it was because of "charges" brought against him, the Melkite patriarch of Antioch, Theodoret (795–812) removed Abū Qurrah from his bishopric in the year 812.[7] Afterwards he set out on the journeys which

---

[2] J. Nasrallah, *Saint Jean de Damas, son époque, sa vie, son oeuvre* (Harissa, 1950). See also the extensive bibliography in M. Geerad (ed.), *Clavis Patrum Graecorum* (vol. III; Brepols, 1979), pp. 511–536.

[3] For a discussion of the isolation of Palestine from Byzantium during the 8th, 9th, and most of the 10th centuries, see Sidney H. Griffith, "Stephen of Ramlah and the Christian *Kerygma* in Arabic in Ninth Century Palestine," to appear.

[4] The published works of Abū Qurrah are: I. Arendzen, *Theodori Abu Ḳurra de Cultu Imaginum Libellus e Codice Arabico Nunc Primum Editus Latine Versus Illustratus* (Bonn, 1897); Constantin Bacha, *Les oeuvres arabes de Théodore Aboucara évêque d'Haran* (Beyrouth, 1904); idem, *Un traité des oeuvres arabes de Théodore Abou-Kurra, évêque de Haran* (Tripoli de Syrie & Rome, 1905); Georg Graf, *Die arabischen Schriften des Theodor Abu Qurra, Bischofs von Ḥarran (ca. 740–820)* (Forschungen zur christlichen Literatur- und Dogmengeschichte, X. Band, 3/4 Heft; Paderborn, 1910); Louis Cheikho, "Mīmar li Tadūrūs Abī Qurrah fī Wuǧūd al-Ḫāliq wa d-Dīn al-Qawīm," *al-Machriq* 15 (1912), pp. 757–774, 825–842; Georg Graf, *Des Theodor Abu Kurra Traktat über den Schöpfer und die wahre Religion* (Beiträge zur Geschichte der Philosophie des Mittelalters. Texte und Untersuchungen, Band XIV, Heft 1; Münster i.W., 1913); Ignace Dick, "Deux écrits inédits de Théodore Abuqurra," *Le Muséon* 72 (1959), pp. 53–67; Sidney H. Griffith, "Some Unpublished Arabic Sayings Attributed to Theodore Abū Qurrah," *Le Muséon* 92 (1979), pp. 29–35. For Abū Qurrah's works preserved only in Greek, see J. P. Migne, *Patrologiae Cursus Completus, Series Graeca* (161 vols. in 166; Paris, 1857–1887), vol. 97, cols. 1461–1610. For the MSS of unpublished works attributed to Abū Qurrah, see Graf, *GCAL*, vol. II, pp. 7–26; and J. Nasrallah, "Dialogue Islamo-Chrétien a propos de publications récentes," *Revue des Études Islamiques* 46 (1978), pp. 129–132. On his own testimony one knows that Abū Qurrah also wrote some thirty treatises in Syriac, of which no trace has yet appeared to modern scholars. See Bacha, 1904, op. cit., pp. 60–61.

[5] Sidney H. Griffith, "The Controversial Theology of Theodore Abū Qurrah (c. 750–c. 820 A.D.), a Methodological, Comparative Study in Christian Arabic Literature," (Ph.D. Dissertation; The Catholic University of America, Washington, D.C., 1978; Ann Arbor, Michigan, University Microfilms International, no. 7819874. See abstract in *Dissertation Abstracts International* 39, no. 5 (1978), pp. 2992–2993.

[6] J.-B. Chabot, *Chronique de Michel le Syrien; patriarche Jacobite d'Antioche 1166–1199* (4 vols.; Paris, 1899–1910), vol. IV, p. 496.

[7] Ibid., vol. III, p. 32. On the date of this patriarch, see the discussion in Dick, art. cit., 13 (1963), p. 119. The fact that Byzantine historians like Theophane did not speak of Theodoret is entirely consistent with the isolation of the eastern patriarchates from Byzantium, up to the end of the tenth century.

made his reputation as a controversialist, perhaps even reaching the caliph's court in Baghdad. Theodore Abū Qurrah died sometime between the years 820 and 825, but no one knows for sure whether or not he ever returned to Mar Sabas monastery.[8]

Abū Qurrah's activities did not escape the notice of the Islamic scholarly establishment. His name appears in at least two places in the *Fihrist* of the Muslim bio-bibliographer, Ibn an-Nadīm (d. 995). In one place, he lists Abū Qurrah among the few Christian scholars whose works he knows; again he mentions that the Mu^{c}tazilite *mutakallim*, ^{c}Īsā ibn Sabīḥ al-Murdār (d. 840), wrote a treatise "against Abū Qurrah, the Christian."[9]

Most of Abū Qurrah's treatises deal with the standard topics of controversy among Jews, Christians, and Muslims, which the Christians felt a particular need to defend, viz., the doctrines of the Trinity and the Incarnation, as well as various practices of church life, such as the sacraments, the habit of facing east to pray, and the veneration of the cross. Almost all of the Christian apologists who were active in the first Abassid century discussed these topics.[10] However, aside from his own genius and originality, what is unique among Abū Qurrah's publications is his tract on the Christian practice of venerating images. Outside of Byzantium, where the iconoclastic crisis flared up intermittently for a century and more and which elicited at home a spate of books and letters on the subject of images, there was nothing much written about icons and the practice of venerating them, except in Palestine, in the monastery of Mar Sabas by John Damascene, and in Syria, by the erstwhile monk of Mar Sabas, Theodore Abū Qurrah.

John Damascene's three discourses *Contra imaginum calumniatores* are now well known.[11] And being in Greek, they eventually came to enjoy a wide popularity in Byzantium. Theodore Abū Qurrah's tract, however, being in Arabic, was comprehensible only in a milieu in which there had never been any Christian iconoclasm. Moreover, since its author was a Melkite, living in *dār al-islām*, where most Christians were either Monophysites or some sort of Nestorians, Abū Qurrah's tract on venerating images seems to have had but a limited appeal. Only two copies of it, both of them early, have survived, and only one other early writer mentioned it, namely Eutychius, the Melkite patriarch of Alexandria, who died in the year 940.[12]

The earliest manuscript containing a copy of Abū Qurrah's tract on images is British Museum Oriental MS 4950, which the monk Stephen of Ramlah wrote at the Judean monastery of Mar Charitōn in the year 877.[13] John Arendzen published it, with a Latin version, in Bonn, in 1897.[14] In 1910, Georg Graf published a German version of this tract along with his translations of ten other Arabic treatises by Abū Qurrah, which Constantine Bacha had brought out in 1904.[15] In 1959, Ignace Dick announced the discovery of another copy of the tract on images in Sinai Arabic MS 330 (ff. 315r–357r).[16] It is an undated manuscript which the catalogers of the Sinai manuscripts have assigned to the tenth century on the basis of paleographical considerations.[17]

---

[8] See the biographical resumé in Dick, art. cit., 13 (1963), pp. 121–129.

[9] Bayard Dodge, *The Fihrist of al-Nadīm; a Tenth Century Survey of Muslim Culture* (2 vols.; New York, 1970), vol. I, pp. 46 & 394. At p. 46 Dodge failed to notice that Abū ^{c}Izzah is to be read as Abū Qurrah. See I. Krackovskij, "Theodore Abū Qurrah in the Muslim Writers of the Ninth–Tenth Centuries," (Russian) *Christianskij Vostok* 4 (1915), p. 306. See also Dick, art. cit., 12 (1962), p. 328, n. 40, who comes to the same conclusion independently of Krackovskij, whom he does not cite.

[10] For a survey of the Christian apologists writing within *dār al-islām* during the first Abbasid century, see Sidney H. Griffith, "The Prophet Muḥammad, His Scripture and His Message, According to the Christian Apologies in Arabic and Syriac From the First Abbasid Century," in *La vie du prophète Mahomet* (Paris, 1983), pp. 99–146. On the topics see G. Graf, "Christliche Polemik gegen den Islam," *Gelbe Hefte* 2 (1926), pp. 825–842.

[11] See the critical edition by B. Kotter, *Die Schriften des Johannes von Damaskos; III, Contra Imaginum Calumniatores Orationes Tres* (Berlin & New York, 1975).

[12] L. Cheikho et al. (eds.), *Eutychii Patriarchae Alexandrini Annales* (CSCO, vols. 50 & 51; Paris, 1906 & 1909), vol. 51, p. 64. Sidney H. Griffith, "Eutychius of Alexandria on the Emperor Theophilus and Iconoclasm in Byzantium: a Tenth Century Moment in Christian Apologetics in Arabic," *Byzantion* 52 (1982), pp. 154–190.

[13] On this manuscript and its writer see Sidney H. Griffith, "Stephen of Ramlah and the Christian *Kerygma* in Arabic in Ninth Century Palestine," to appear.

[14] Joannes Arendzen, *Theodori Abu Ḳurra de Cultu Imaginum Libellus e Codice Arabico Nunc Primum Editus Latine Versus Illustratus* (Bonnae, 1897).

[15] G. Graf, *Die arabische Schriften . . .*, op. cit., pp. 278–333; Bacha, *Les oeuvres arabes . . .*, op. cit.

[16] Dick, "Deux écrits . . . ," art. cit., p. 54.

[17] A. S. Atiya, *The Arabic Manuscripts of Mount Sinai* (Baltimore, 1955), p. 9.

To date, no systematic study of Abū Qurrah's tract on images has been published. The purpose of the present essay is very briefly to outline the argument of the tract and then to pass on to a consideration of the socio-religious circumstances in which it was written, including a discussion of the Islamic prophetic tradition against images of living things, which Abū Qurrah quotes. Finally, some questions are posed about iconoclasm in Byzantium, on the basis of a consideration of Abū Qurrah's tract.

II. THE ARGUMENT OF THE TRACT ON IMAGES

Doctrinally, Theodore Abū Qurrah was a student of John Damascene. In his tract on images, as indeed in all of his works, there is no appreciable progression of ideas beyond what his master had achieved. Abū Qurrah's originality consists in the genius with which he expressed John's arguments in Arabic. On every page of the tract on images, one finds the arguments of the earlier scholars deployed to meet the needs of the new generation of Christians, who spoke Arabic, and who were more evidently in debate with Muslims than were their parents. References to Muslims and to their ideas, allusions to the *Qurʾān* and to the Islamic tradition are the novelties in Abū Qurrah's tract, from the point of view of its intellectual content. What these have to reveal about the difficulties which plagued the Christian community in Abū Qurrah's day will be the subject of the next section of this article. First, one must recall the rather simple outline of the arguments as Abū Qurrah presented them.

It is clear that in the twenty-four chapters of the tract under review, Abū Qurrah was concerned to reinforce the conviction of his Christian readers of the rectitude of their habitual practice of venerating images. He also intended to furnish them with ready replies with which they might defend themselves against the charge that the veneration of images is no more than idolatry. Furthermore, following John Damascene, he argued that any Christian who would give up the veneration of images, for fear of being accused of idolatry, must logically give up all forms of the public exercise of his religion.

Abū Qurrah presented his arguments in five broad strokes.[18] First, he argued that it is not a valid contention against images to allege that they imply the attribution of bodiliness to God. All scriptural language, be it in the Old Testament, the Gospel, or the *Qurʾān*, speaks of God in terms that of themselves imply bodiliness, because human knowledge proceeds necessarily from the sensible to the intelligible. Images are the writing of the illiterate. Therefore, the bodiliness which images imply is no more attributable to God than is the bodiliness which the language of the scriptures implies.

Secondly, even though the veneration of images is not enjoined on Christians in the Bible, Abū Qurrah argues that the practice must be apostolic in origin, because images are found in all of the churches of every country. To reject them because there is no mention of them in the New Testament would require one logically to reject other things not mentioned there, concerning the apostolic foundations of which no one has a doubt—e.g., the eucharistic formulae and various other liturgical practices.

In the third place, Abū Qurrah cites passages from three of the fathers, the "teachers" of the church, as he calls them, which, he says, attest to the early presence of images in the church, and to the legitimacy of venerating them. He cites passages from the pseudo-Athanasian *Quaestiones ad Antiochum Ducem*, which both Abū Qurrah and John Damascene took to be authentic; from Eusebius of Caesarea's report in the *Ecclesiastical History* about the image of Christ at Baniyas, erected by the woman whom Christ had cured of the issue of blood; a story from the "fathers of Jerusalem" about an image of Mary which allayed a monk's tempations; and finally some sentences from Gregory the Theologian about the venerability of Christ's cradle and the stone on which he was laid in Bethlehem. The argument here is simply that anyone who would depart from the practice (*aš-šarīʿah*) of these Christian teachers, has in effect departed from Christianity.[19]

By far the longest set of arguments in the tract is the one which comprises the fourth step, in which Abū Qurrah spends ten of his twenty-four chapters explaining how the Christian habit of venerating images

[18] The brief analysis of the tract on images which is presented here follows the scheme originally put forward in Griffith, "The Controversial Theology . . . ," op. cit., pp. 248–270.

[19] Abū Qurrah's argument from the fathers is presented in chapter 8 of the tract: Arendzen, op. cit., pp. 10–14 (Arabic), pp. 12–15 (Latin); Graf, *Die arabische Schriften*, op. cit., pp. 289–293. He found all of these stories in John Damascene's discourses, save the latter one from Gregory the Theologian. See Kotter, op. cit., pp. 124, 169, 173, 191. The use of the term *aš-šarīʿah* reflects the Islamic ambience. See *SEI*, pp. 524–529.

does not come under the ban against idols which is recorded in Exodus 20:2–5 and in Deuteronomy 6:13 (10:20). There is nothing new in the argument, which goes beyond what John Damascene had to say on the subject, except that there is a considerably heightened anti-Jewishness in Abū Qurrah's deployment of his master's argument that images are not idols. The adoration or the honor which one's act of προσκύνησις (*as-suğūd*) expresses, Abū Qurrah contends, is addressed either to God, who deserves adoration, or to his saints who deserve honor. This practice is in accord with the actions of David, Solomon and other scriptural characters. Consequently, says Abū Qurrah, the scriptural prohibition of idolatry is addressed to the ancient Israelites, who had a constant proclivity to indulge in it, and not to the Christian practice of venerating images of Christ, and the saints, which is simply a way of giving adoration to God, to whom alone it is due, and honor to the saints, to whom it is appropriate.[20]

Finally, at the end of the tract Abū Qurrah takes up some particular challenges which the opponents employ in justifying their rejection of the veneration of images. It is a matter of applying the reasoning already elaborated earlier in the treatise to these specific objections, which are simply variations on the basic theme that venerating images is tantamount to idolatry.

For the purposes of the present essay, there is no need to sketch further the arguments Abū Qurrah deploys in his tract on images. One may read them independently, in the Latin, German, and soon the English, versions, if not in the original Arabic, while a more detailed summary is available elsewhere.[21] If these ideas are readily familiar from John Damascene's discourses on the same subject, what is more noteworthy in the tract are the remarks the author makes about his occasion for writing it in the first place, and his reference to the concrete, socio-religious circumstances in which he found himself. These are the facts which are pertinent to the topic under consideration here, the role of Jews and Muslims in the rise of iconophobia among Christians living under Islamic rule.

III. THE SOCIAL, HISTORICAL, AND RELIGIOUS CONTEXT

A. TIME AND PLACE OF COMPOSITION

For a long time after the discovery of Abū Qurrah's tract on images, scholars were of the opinion that he must have composed it before the year 787, since he no where in it mentioned the second council of Nicea, which took place in that year. What made this conclusion attractive was the fact that Abū Qurrah himself, in another treatise, *On the Law, the Gospel, and the Orthodox Faith*,[22] made much of the teaching of the previous six ecumenical councils, as the only sure yardstick of the teaching of the Holy Spirit. Accordingly, it seemed highly improbable that Abū Qurrah would not have cited the teaching of Nicea II, had he written his tract on images after the council was held and its acts promulgated. What is more, in chapter six of the tract on images he alluded to the earlier treatise, in which he had developed his ideas on conciliar authority.[23] To Georg Graf, therefore, the question seemed closed. Abū Qurrah wrote the treatise before 787.[24]

In 1963, Ignace Dick was able to show that Abū Qurrah could not have written his tract until after the year 799. What makes this conclusion certain is the fact that in chapter sixteen of the tract on images Abū Qurrah alludes to the story of the Muslim convert to Christianity, St. Anthony Ruwaḥ, who was killed at Raqqah, not far from Ḥarrān, by the order of the caliph, Harūn ar-Rašīd (786–809), on December 25, 799.[25] Dick discovered the date of the martyrdom in the course of editing the account of it contained in

[20] In these chapters of his treatise, Abū Qurrah echoes many themes that seem first to have been sounded in Leontius of Neapolis' (d. c. 650) "Sermo Contra Judaeos." See *PG*, vol. 93, cols. 1597–1610; and Norman H. Baynes, "The Icons Before Iconoclasm," *Harvard Theological Review* 44 (1951), pp. 93–106. See also Sidney H. Griffith, "The Christian *Adversus Judaeos* Tradition and 'the new Jews,' a Polemical Characterization of Muslims in the Christian Apologies in Syriac and Arabic of the First Abbasid Century," to appear.

[21] Griffith, "The Controversial Theology . . . ," op. cit., pp. 248–270, and the brief summary in G. Dumeige, *Nicée II* (Histoires des Conciles Oecumeniques, 4; Paris, 1976), pp. 158–159.

[22] Bacha, *Un traite* '. . . , op. cit.

[23] Arendzen, op. cit., p. 9 (Arabic), p. 10 (Latin); Graf, *Die arabischen Schriften* . . . , op. cit., p. 287.

[24] Ibid., p. 5.

[25] Arendzen, op. cit., p. 33 (Arabic), pp. 34–35 (Latin); Graf, *Die arabischen Schriften* . . . , op. cit., p. 314. Dick, "Un continuateur arabe . . . ," art. cit., 13 (1963), pp. 116–118.

Sinai Arabic MS 513, which was written in the tenth century.[26]

What the new date for Abū Qurrah's tract brings to mind is the fact, now corroborated in many other places, that there was virtually no knowledge of the proceedings of Nicea II in the oriental patriarchates during Abū Qurrah's lifetime, and probably not until the tenth century.[27] However, there were many refugee monks from Jerusalem in Constantinople in 787, some of whom participated in the council as "legates" of their patriarchs. But even Theodore of Studios, as he says in his letter to the monk Arsenius, was aware that these refugees did not really represent their patriarchs.[28] The refugees apparently had no contact with home. There is no record of any one of them ever returning to Jerusalem. The council seemingly had no relevance to the east, at the time of its convention.

The new *terminus a quo* for dating Abū Qurrah's tract on images reminds one that its context was not iconoclasm in Byzantium, a frame of reference to which one all too readily turns. Rather, in Abū Qurrah's lifetime and within the parameters of his own pastoral experience, the milieu in which he wrote his tract had Edessa as its point of reference, as will become clear, and his concern was to shore up the confidence of Christians who were developing a case of iconophobia due to the attacks against their traditional religious practices coming from Jews and Muslims, as his own words will make clear when quoted below.

Ignace Dick has shown that Abū Qurrah probably served as Melkite bishop of Ḥarrān between the years 795 and 812, as well as that he could not have written his tract on images until after the year 799.[29] Therefore, given the frame of reference of the treatise, about which more will be said, it seems reasonable to propose that Abū Qurrah wrote it while he was still bishop of Ḥarrān, that is between the years 800 and 812. Afterwards he travelled to Armenia, and his controversial projects became involved in refutations of the Monophysites and debates with Muslims, concerns that seem to have dominated his scholarship during his final years.

The copyists of Abū Qurrah's tract on images captured its topic sentence in the title paragraph they gave to it: "A discourse . . . in which Abū Qurrah affirms that prostration to the image of Christ, our God, who became incarnate from the Holy Spirit and from the pure virgin Mary, as well as to the images of his saints, is incumbent upon every Christian."[30] And the copyist of British Museum Oriental MS 4950, Stephen of Ramlah, immediately identifies one of Abū Qurrah's main arguments, viz., that anyone who disavows prostration to these images, has acted out of ignorance of the Christian tradition, and should logically disavow all of the Christian mysteries.[31]

It is Abū Qurrah himself who pinpoints more closely the occasion for writing his treatise. He has written it, he says in chapter one, at the request of "our brother, Abba Yannah," who had informed him of an unacceptable state of affairs. "You . . . have informed us," Abū Qurrah wrote, "that many Christians are abandoning prostration to the image of Christ . . . and to the images of his saints . . . because non-Christians, and especially those who claim to be in possession of a scripture sent down from God, rebuke them for their prostration to these images, and because of it impute to them the worship of the idols, and the infringement of what God commanded in the Torah and the prophets, and they sneer at them."[32]

In this introductory statement, Abū Qurrah has identified two important features of his tract. The first is its connection with problems in the church at Edessa. The second is the designation of the non-Christians who have caused the problem by accusing the Christians of idolatry, namely the Jews and the Muslims. Each feature must be discussed in more detail.

One discovers the tract's connection with Edessa in the name of the person to whom it is addressed. Indeed, Sinai Arabic MS 330 (f. 515v, 1.3) adds after the name Yannah, the phrase, "you who are here with us in Edessa." But more important, one knows from an eighth century Syriac document from Edessa, that the name Yannah was a common name in a family of

[26] I. Dick, "La passion arabe de S. Antoine Ruwaḥ, néomartyr de Damas (+ 25 déc. 799)," *Le Muséon* 74 (1961), pp. 109–133.

[27] Sidney H. Griffith, "Eutychius of Alexandria . . . ," art. cit.

[28] P. Henry, "Initial Eastern Assessments of the Seventh Oecumenical Council," *Journal of Theological Studies* 25 (1974), p. 77. For a resumé of the communications of the alleged "legates" of the oriental patriarchs see Dumeige, op. cit., pp. 112–114.

[29] Dick, "Un continuateur arabe . . . ," art. cit., 13 (1963), pp. 116–120.

[30] Arendzen, op. cit., p. 1 (Arabic), p. 1 (Latin); Graf, *Die arabischen Schriften* . . . , op. cit., p. 278.

[31] Ibid.

[32] Ibid.

persons who were in charge of the famous "Church of the Image of Christ" at Edessa.[33] Furthermore, in chapter twenty-three of his tract, Abū Qurrah applies the lesson to be learned from his previous twenty-some chapters of argumentation, specifically to what must have been a current of iconophobia in the congregation of this famous church. He says:

> As for the image of Christ, our God incarnate from the virgin Mary, we mention it here of all the images because it is honored by prostration especially in our city, Edessa, the Blessed, at definite times, with its own feasts and pilgrimages. If there is any Christian opposed to making prostration to it, I would like an image of his father to be painted by the door of the Church of the Image of Christ. I would then invite everyone who makes prostration to the image of Christ, when he comes out from its presence, to spit in the face of the image of the father, especially if his father was the one who bequeathed it to him that he should not make prostration to the holy image—until I see if he gets angry or not.[34]

Abū Qurrah's point is clear, as is the connection with Edessa. It is also clear that his pastoral problem is the fact that some members of the Christian community, for a generation or more, have refused to make prostration to the holy images, even to the renowned image of Edessa. This image was doubtless the famous *acheiropoiētos*, which John Damascene had mentioned twice in his remarks on images, in two different works, although Abū Qurrah himself does not speak of this miraculous quality of the Edessa image.[35]

It is evident from Abū Qurrah's first chapter, as we have seen, that both he and Abba Yannah, who had commissioned the tract in the first place, believed that the reason some Christians refused to make a prostration to the holy images was "because non-Christians . . . rebuke them for their prostration to these images . . . and they sneer at them."[36] These non-Christians, it is clear from the persons against whom Abū Qurrah addresses his arguments, were the Jews and the Muslims. One must then inquire into what Jews and Muslims had to say about Christians and their crosses and images, which caused some Christians to give up the practice of venerating them in public.

B. THE JEWS

1. The Jews and Christian Images

Here is not the place to pursue the matter in detail, but it is clear that beginning already with the Persian conquest and occupation of most of the territory of the oriental patriarchates in the late sixth and early seventh centuries, and continuing into the Islamic period, there was a renewed polemic between Christians and Jews, and for the first time it included arguments about the Christian practice of venerating the cross and the images of Christ and the saints. For the Greek-speaking world, the evidences of this polemic are to be seen in such works as the *Adversus Judaeos* sermons of Stephen of Bostra, of which some fragments only remain, and those of Leontius of Neapolis, and in the pertinent sections of the Pseudo-Athanasian *Quaestiones ad Antiochum Ducem.* John Damascene quoted from these works in his third discourse on images.[37] In addition, there are the *Doctrina Jacobi Nuper Baptizati, The Trophies of Damascus*, and the *Dialogue of Papiscus and Philo.* All of these

---

[33] R. W. Thompson, "An Eighth Century Melkite Colophon from Edessa," *Journal of Theological Studies* 13 (1962), pp. 249–258. The final consonant in the name of the official in Arabic and Syriac, 'h' and 'y' respectively, do not bespeak a difference in the name. For Syriac *yani* = John, see R. Payne Smith (ed), *Thesaurus Syriacus* (2 vols.; Oxford, 1879), vol. I, col. 1607. In Arabic the same name appears as *y-n-h/y-n-y*. Cf. G. Graf, *Verzeichnis arabischer kirchlicher Termini* (2nd ed., CSCO, vol. 147; Louvain, 1954), p. 120.

[34] Arendzen, op. cit., p. 46 (Arabic), p. 48 (Latin); Graf, *Die arabischen Schriften* . . . , op. cit., pp. 328–329.

[35] Kotter, *Contra Imaginum Calumniatores*, op. cit., pp. 145–146, and in B. Kotter, *Die Schriften des Johannes von Damaskos*; II, Expositio fidei (Berlin & New York, 1973), p. 208. The classic discussion of the Edessa image is E. von Dobschütz, *Christusbilder; Untersuchungen zur christlichen Legende* (Texte und Untersuchungen zur Geschichte der altchristlichen Literatur, vol. 18; Leipzig, 1899), pp. 102–196. For the current scholarly discussion see Averil Cameron, "The Sceptic and the Shroud," (An Inaugural Lecture in the Departments of Classics and History, King's College, London, 29 April 1980).

[36] See n. 32 above.

[37] Kotter, *Contra Imaginum Calumniatores*, op. cit., p. 174 for Stephen of Bostra, pp. 169 & 191 for the *Quaestiones*, and the index on p. 208 for the numerous citations from Leontius.

works include references to the new topics of controversy between Jews and Christians, *viz.*, the Christian practice of venerating the cross and images.[38] In the Syriac-speaking world, the *Disputation of Sergius the Stylite Against a Jew*, which was written in the neighborhood of Emesa somewhere between the years 730 and 770, also enlarges on this new topic of debate.[39] And Christian historians and apologists who wrote in Arabic, other than Abū Qurrah, such as Agapius of Manbiğ, Eutychius of Alexandria, and Severus ibn al-Muqaffaᶜ in the tenth century,[40] recorded numerous instances of clashes among Jews, Christians, and Muslims, often instigated by some alleged abuses of crosses or icons at the hands of Jews. Of course, this was to become a fairly constant theme in both Arabic and Syriac chronicles. Typical of such notices is the following account of measures directed against Christians in Damascus in the time of the caliph ᶜUthmān (644–656), recorded in the anonymous Syriac chronicle *Ad Annum 1234 Pertinens*. It will be useful to translate the entire passage here, in spite of its length, because it includes many elements relevant to the discussion which will follow.

> At that time there was an Arab military commander named ᶜAmr bar Saᶜd. Motivated by the influence of the evil men who advised him, he armed himself against the Christians in his jurisdiction, and he set himself up to humiliate them, and to blot out the honor of their estate. He gave the order that the crosses were to be pulled down, and effaced from walls, streets, and conspicuous places, and that the emblem of the cross was not to be displayed on feast-days or rogation days. When this was tyranically decreed by the king, it very much delighted the Jewish people. They began running around taking down the precious crosses from the rooves of the holy shrines and churches, and effacing those in the streets and on walls. Thereupon, since the Christians were aggrieved, one of the Christian notables, a believing God-fearer who had access to the emir, ᶜAmr, went into him and said: "O good emir, it is not just that you have given the accursed Jews, the enemies of our faith, power over us that they should go up, onto our churches, and insult our symbols and crosses." Thereupon that emir, when God inspired him, replied: "I commanded only that the crosses in the streets be effaced, the ones we constantly see when we are passing through." And he ordered one of those standing in attendance upon him to go out and to throw down head first any Jew he could find on the roof of a church. Now there was a Jew who had gone up onto the roof of the shrine of John the Baptist, and he was carrying a cross he had broken off the roof, and he was coming down the stairway. The officer who had been sent by the emir, when he saw the Jew, took the cross away from him, and hit him over the head. His brains came out through his nostrils, and he fell down dead. So the vehemence of the decree was eased.[41]

2. Abū Qurrah's Tract and the Jews

Abū Qurrah's tract on venerating images is replete with arguments directed against Jews. He uses here some of the strongest anti-Jewish language to be found in Christian Arabic literature.[42] Throughout the tract he often rhetorically addresses his arguments to an unnamed Jew (*yā yahūdī*). He weaves into the fabric of his apology essentially the program of the *Adversus Judaeos* tracts of the sort originally appearing in the work of Leontius of Neapolis at the beginning of the

[38] See the survey of these works in A. L. Williams, *Adversus Judaeos, a Bird's-Eye View of Christian Apologiae Until the Renaissance* (Cambridge, 1935), pp. 151–180.

[39] A. P. Hayman, *The Disputation of Sergius The Stylite Against a Jew* (CSCO, vols. 152 & 153; Louvain, 1973).

[40] A. Vasiliev, "Kitab al-ᶜUnvan, histoire universelle écrite par Agapius (Mahboub) de Menbidj," *Patrologia Orientalis* 5 (1910), pp. 557–692; 7 (1911), pp. 457–491; 8 (1912), pp. 397–550). L. Cheikho, *Eutychii Patriarchae Alexandrini Annales* (CSCO, vols. 50 & 51; Beirut & Paris, 1906 & 1909), with a Latin version in *PG*, vol. CXI, cols. 889–1232. For the chronicle of Severus, see B. Evetts, "History of the Patriarchs of the Coptic Church of Alexandria," *Patrologia Orientalis* 1 (1907), pp. 99–124; 5 (1910), pp. 1–215; 10 (1915), 357–551.

[41] I.-B. Chabot, *Anonymi Auctoris Chronicon ad Annum Christi 1234 Pertinens* (CSCO, vol. 81; Paris, 1920), pp. 262–263. In spite of the late date of the final form of this chronicle, it is clear that its compiler used earlier chronicles as sources. S. P. Brock, "Syriac Sources for Seventh-Century History," *Byzantine and Modern Greek Studies* 2 (1976), p. 22. For a brief survey of incidents similar to the one recounted here, see the discussion of friction between Christians, Muslims, and Jews occasioned by crosses, images, and the ringing of the *nāqūs* in A. S. Tritton, *The Caliphs and their Non-Muslim Subjects* (London, 1930), pp. 100–114.

[42] Griffith, "The Christian *Adversus Judaeos* Tradition . . . ," art. cit.

seventh century.[43] The program involves refuting the absolutist interpretation of passages in scripture such as Exodus 20:4–5, by reference to other passages which record actions of patriarchs, prophets and kings that would be in violation of the commandment if it is understood absolutely. Abū Qurrah makes the by now familiar argument that Exodus 20:4–5 and similar passages must be interpreted as addressed to the particular situation of the Israelites at the time of Moses, which was characterized by a proclivity on their part to polytheism and the worship of idols. Therefore, after fairly lengthy arguments in several chapters, he concludes that one cannot argue from Exodus 20:4–5, or from any other place in the scriptures, that it is God's command that no image ever be made, and that one should never make an act of prostration to any being other than God.[44] To think that such is the meaning of the scriptures is to read them as the Jews read them, with darkened minds, who without the light of Christ cannot understand their own texts.[45] Abū Qurrah makes his point quite clearly, regarding Christians who have become convinced that making images and venerating them are unscriptural practices. He says,

> The marvel of those of us who are ignorant is that if the Christians, with the subtlety of their spiritual minds, did not present the Jewish scriptures in a favorable light, they would be the laughing stock of all people. The Jews have no doubt about this because people do call them foolish. Will (people) then turn their faces away from prostration to the holy images because the Jews and others find them repugnant?[46]

What is to be noticed here is that Abū Qurrah quite clearly maintains that fear of the Jews, and of Jewish polemics, is responsible for iconophobia among some Christians. The Christians so influenced by the Jews are the object of his amazement, even more than the Jews themselves. As he says,

> There should be no astonishment at the Jew when he does not understand these matters, because he is coarse, stupid, as the prophets have testified about him, and blindness is deep seated in his heart. . . . Rather, the astonishment is at those insane Christians who turn away from offering prostration to the image of Christ, and to the images of the saints.[47]

Abū Qurrah next argues that even though Christians generally have no need for evidentiary miracles in connection with the mysteries of their faith, nevertheless "in the instance of the 'outsiders,' or because of the dullness of the lowest rank of the Christians in their religion, God has often manifested the glory of the mysteries of Christianity, as we hear every day," Abū Qurrah says, "from reports about which a reasonable man should have no doubts once he has dealt with them properly."[48] And by way of providing examples he recounts two instances in which a Muslim and a Jew, respectively, have desecrated a Christian image, and have been converted as a result of a consequent miracle.[49] St. Anthony, the converted Muslim who was killed in 799, is said to have become a Christian when he shot an arrow at the image of St. Theodore, only to have it rebound to wound himself.[50] And a certain blind Jew of Tiberias reportedly became a Christian when he regained his sight, having wiped a bit of the blood over his eyes which had miraculously exuded from an image of Christ crucified, that some of his co-religionists had been abusing.[51] In view of all of this, as well as his arguments

[43] See n. 20 above.

[44] See in particular, chaps. 9–15, 18 & 19, in Arendzen, op. cit., pp. 14–32, 35–41 (Arabic), 15–33, 37–43 (Latin); Graf, *Die arabischen Schriften* . . . , op. cit., pp. 293–312, 317–323.

[45] Abū Qurrah also develops this theme in other works, particularly in connection with the typological interpretation of the scriptures; see, e.g., Bacha, *Un traité*. . . , op. cit., pp. 10–14.

[46] Arendzen, op. cit., p. 9 (Arabic), p. 9 (Latin); Graf, *Die arabischen Schriften* . . . , op. cit., p. 286.

[47] Ibid., pp. 31 (Arabic), 33 (Latin); 312.

[48] Ibid., pp. 33 (Arabic), p. 34 (Latin); p. 313.

[49] Ibid., pp. 33 (Arabic), 34–35 (Latin); 313–314.

[50] Dick, "La passion arabe . . . ," art. cit.

[51] Abū Qurrah probably found this story in a Syriac source. His account is an abbreviated version of a story told in a Syriac MS containing "Histories of the Apostles, Saints and Martyrs," one of which is told by a certain Philotheus, "The History of the Likeness of Christ, and of How the Accursed Jews in the City of Tiberias Made a Mock Thereof in the Days of the God-Loving Emperor Zeno." The manuscript and an English version are presented in E. A. Wallis Budge, *The History of the Blessed Virgin Mary and the History of the Likeness of Christ* (2 vols.; London, 1899), vol. II, pp. 171ff. Unfortunately one cannot now determine the era in which this story arose. Budge's manuscript is a copy, made for him in Iraq in 1892, from an original of an unspecified

from scripture, Abū Qurrah concludes that "any Christian who is not satisfied with it should better become a Jew because of the dullness of his mind."[52]

In one instance Abū Qurrah turns what he represents as the Jewish argument against Christians back against the Jews themselves. In chapter seventeen of the tract, after upbraiding the Jewish adversary for failing to understand his own scripture (which he will never do so long as he remains a Jew, Abū Qurrah says parenthetically),[53] he turns the argument around to cite the inconsistency of Jewish practice with the Jewish argument against paying veneration to any material thing.

Abū Qurrah refers to the *ʾeben šᵉtiyyah* in Jerusalem, which since the time of ʿAbd al-Malik had been enclosed under the Dome of the Rock, and to the former Jewish practice of honoring it. He says to the Jew whom he constantly addresses in his tract:

> The reader should understand in regard to your devotion to the rock in Jerusalem, that, were you allowed access to it, when you arrived you would kiss it and anoint it out of honor for it. . . . But tell us, what obliges you to do this to this rock? I know that you say that it has come from the Garden, and therefore one makes the effort to honor it. But your statement that it has come from the Garden is not a proof of it. It is not mentioned in any of your prophets . . . . For the same reason, honor and make prostration to the Euphrates, the Tigris, and the other two rivers of which the scripture does say that they come from the Garden.[54]

Abū Qurrah goes on to say to his imaginary Jewish interlocutor that "it is due to the blindness that has sway over your heart"[55] that such an inconsistency in religious practice is allowed. And with this argument he finds the only point that allows him to abandon his apologetics and to take the offensive against the Jews, whose polemics he has blamed for turning some Christians away from their prostrations to the cross and to images of Christ and the saints.

It remains only to note that there is evidence of a tightening of the Jewish attitude to images, beginning in Palestine in the sixth century,[56] precisely in the period which witnessed a crescendo in the Christian devotion to religious images.[57] It seems clear that the images themselves then became occasions of controversy between Christians and Jews and the outward symbols of all that divided the two communities. Particularly at the end of the century was this the case, when under the Persian hegemony, the political power no longer gave any special protection to the Christians or to the objects which publicly proclaimed their faith. And this same state of affairs obtained under the Muslims, with the difference that, like the Christians before them, but unlike the Persians, the Muslims too came to the point of insisting that public monuments should proclaim only what the rulers considered to be the true religion. This campaign also induced iconophobia in some Christians, as Abū Qurrah makes clear, and it is to this Islamic challenge that one must turn next.

C. THE MUSLIMS

1. The Muslims and Christian Images

By Abū Qurrah's day, the Muslims were already on record as being opposed to Christian crosses and images. One of the earliest Christian memories of the Islamic invasion of Sinai, written in the mid-seventh century, makes a special note of the antipathy of the

---

date. Ibid., vol. I, p. vi. Among the spurious works attributed to St. Athanasius are six versions of a similar incident said to have taken place in Berytus. See *PG*, vol. XXVIII, cols. 797–824.

[52] Arendzen, op. cit., p. 34 (Arabic), p. 36 (Latin); Graf, *Die arabischen Schriften . . .*, op cit., p. 315.

[53] Ibid.

[54] Ibid., pp. 34–35 (Arabic), 36–37 (Latin); pp. 315–317. On the rock in Jewish tradition see Hans Schmidt, *Der heilige Fels in Jerusalem; eine archäologische und religionsgeschichtliche Studie* (Tübingen, 1933), pp. 96–102. According to the report of some fourth century pilgrims to Palestine from Bordeaux, Jews used to come yearly to the stone to anoint it, and to conduct mourning ceremonies there. See the discussion and bibliography in Th. A. Busink, *Der Tempel von Jerusalem von Salomo bis Herodes* (2 vols.; Leiden, 1970 & 1980), vol. I, p. 6; vol. II, pp. 904–914. On ʿAbd al-Malik's shrine, see the bibliography in O. Grabar, "Ḳubbat al-Sakhra," *EI*², vol. V, pp. 298–299.

[55] Arendzen, op. cit., p. 35 (Arabic), p. 37 (Latin); Graf, *Die arabischen Schriften . . .*, op. cit., p. 317.

[56] J.-B. Frey, "La question des images chez les juifs à la lumière des récentes découvertes," *Biblica* 15 (1934), pp. 298–299; A. Grabar, *L'iconoclasme byzantin; dossier archéologique* (Paris, 1957), pp. 99–103.

[57] See the classic survey in E. Kitzinger, "The Cult of Images in the Age Before Iconoclasm," *Dumbarton Oaks Papers* 8 (1954), pp. 83–150.

"Saracens" to the cross.[58] And, the Syriac account given by Abraham of Bêt Ḥâlê (early eighth century?) of a dispute between a monk and an Arab, reportedly contains a challenge from the latter, specifically about the practice in Edessa of venerating the Abgar image, in view of the Bible's prohibition of idolatry.[59] By the time of the reign of the caliph ᶜAbd al-Malik (685–705), a governmental policy for the public display of Islam in the conquered territories was set on a collision course with the already widely exhibited public symbols of Christianity. Nowhere is the policy more evident than in the caliph's monetary reforms. The iconographic formulae of his coinage went through a process of development whereby all notations in languages other than Arabic eventually disappeared, along with their associated Christian or imperial designs. No trace of Greek or Christian crosses and figural representation remained. The new coinage carried only epigraphic designs, proclaiming the truths of Islam and claiming the authority of the caliph.[60] The same is to be said even for road signs; from the time of the reign of ᶜAbd al-Malik, one begins to find them in Arabic, announcing the Islamic *šahādah*.[61] But, of course, ᶜAbd al-Malik's truly monumental public statement of the truths of Islam was the Dome of the Rock in Jerusalem, with its emphatically Islamic inscription, which is composed of phrases from the *Qurᵓān*, and which virtually assumes the role of images in comparable Christian structures.[62] The Islamic message proclaimed in ᶜAbd al-Malik's public statements was directly contrary to what the usual Christian crosses, icons, and frescoes announced. The *Qurᵓān* explicitly teaches that Jesus and his mother Mary were but human beings (see *al-Māᵓidah* (5): 17, 72–75, 116) and that, contrary to their boast, the Jews neither killed nor crucified Jesus (see *an-Nisāᵓ* (4): 157). Accordingly, it is not surprising to discover reports in Christian histories which assign the date of the beginning of Christian troubles under Islam to the reign of ᶜAbd al-Malik, including the enactment by this caliph of a policy of knocking down the publicly displayed crosses in his realm.[63]

According to a report in the *History of the Patriarchs of Alexandria*, the caliph ᶜAbd al-Malik's brother, ᶜAbd al-Azīz, who was the governor of Egypt, "commanded to destroy all the crosses which were in the land of Egypt, even the crosses of gold and silver. So the Christians in the land of Egypt were troubled. Moreover, he wrote certain inscriptions and placed them on the doors of the churches at Miṣr and in the

---

[58] F. Nau, "Le texte grec des récits du moine Anastase sur les saints pères du Sinai," *Oriens Christianus* 2 (1902), p. 82.

[59] P. Crone, "Islam, Judeo-Christianity and Byzantine Iconoclasm," *Jerusalem Studies in Arabic and Islam* 2 (1980), p. 68, n. 41.

[60] On this caliph and his reign, see ᶜAbd al-Ameer ᶜAbd Dixon, *The Umayyad Caliphate, 65–86/684–705; a Political Study* (London, 1971). On the monetary reform, see Philip Grierson, "The Monetary Reforms of ᶜAbd al-Malik, their Metrological Basis and their Financial Repercussions," *Journal of the Economic and Social History of the Orient* 3 (1960), pp. 241–264. Grierson's article is primarily concerned with metrology, but he provides a full bibliography, with some important comments on iconography. For the iconography of the coinage in particular, see J. Walker, *A Catalogue of the Arab-Byzantine and Post-Reform Umaiyad Coins* (London, 1956); G. C. Miles, "The Iconography of Umayyad Coinage," *Ars Orientalis* 3 (1959), pp. 207–213; A. Grabar, *L'iconoclasme byzantin: dossier archéologique* (Paris, 1957), pp. 67–74.

[61] Moshe Sharon, "An Arabic Inscription from the Time of the Caliph ᶜAbd al-Malik," *Bulletin of the School of Oriental and African Studies* 29 (1966), pp. 367–372.

[62] Oleg Grabar, "The Dome of the Rock in Jerusalem," *Ars Orientalis* 3 (1959), pp. 33–59, reprinted in the author's *Studies in Medieval Islamic Art* (London, 1976); K. A. C. Creswell, *Early Muslim Architecture: Umayyads A.D. 622–750* (2nd ed. in 2 parts, vol. I, pt. II; Oxford, 1969); E. C. Dodd, "The Image of the Word," *Berytus* 18 (1969), pp. 35–79; C. Kessler, "ᶜAbd al-Malik's Inscription in the Dome of the Rock: a Reconsideration," *The Journal of the Royal Asiatic Society* (1970), pp. 2–14. See also S. D. Goitein, *Studies in Islamic History and Institutions* (Leiden, 1966), pp. 135–148. Gibb's argument that the Dome of the Rock was constructed with the help of Byzantine artisans and materials, acquired by trade between otherwise hostile powers in no way militates against the fact that the structure was an item in ᶜAbd al-Malik's program for the Islamicization of public life in the caliphate. See H. A. R. Gibb, "Arab-Byzantine Relations Under the Umayyad Caliphate," *Dumbarton Oaks Papers* 12 (1958), pp. 221–233. The Dome of the Rock clearly played an important role in what Oleg Grabar has called Islam's "symbolic appropriation of the land." O. Grabar, *The Formation of Islamic Art* (New Haven, Conn., 1973), pp. 48–67.

[63] ᶜAbd al-Malik ordered a census for the purpose of enforcing the payment of the *ǧizyah*. Cf. J.-B. Chabot, *Chronique de Denys de Tell-Maḥré, quatrième partie* (Paris, 1895), p. 10. And he ordered that the crosses be pulled down, and that all the pigs in his realm be killed. See Chabot, *Chronique de Michel le Syrien*, op. cit., vol. II, p. 475.

Delta, saying in them, 'Muhammad is the great Apostle of God, and Jesus also is the Apostle of God. But verily God is not begotten and does not beget.'"[64]

The spirit of ᶜAbd al-Malik's reforms is certainly evident in this story. However, an even finer point is put on the matter in another story, involving the son of ᶜAbd al-ᶜAzīz, one al-Aṣbagh, who was notoriously anti-Christian and whom his father had put in charge of a certain district in Egypt. Severus ibn al-Muqaffaᶜ preserved the following anecdote about him:

> On the Saturday of Light he entered the Monastery of Ḥulwan, and looked at the pictures being carried in procession according to the rule. And there was a picture of our pure lady Mary and of the Lord Christ in her lap; so when he looked at it and considered it, he said to the bishops and to several people who were with him: 'Who is represented in this picture?' They answered: 'This is Mary, the mother of Christ.' Then he was moved with hatred against her, and filled his mouth with saliva and spat in her face, saying: 'If I find an opportunity, I will root out the Christians from this land. Who is Christ that you worship him as a God?'[65]

The caliph Walīd I (705–715), ᶜAbd al-Malik's successor, continued the project of erecting mosques, often at the expense of existing Christian churches, to judge by Christian reports.[66] But his most significant contribution was to enforce the use of Arabic in public administration. This adjustment is reported in the anonymous Syriac chronicle *Ad Annum Christi 1234 Pertinens*:

> Walīd, the king of Ṭayyāyê, ordered that in his chancery, i.e., the treasury, which these Ṭayyāyê call the *dīwān*, one should not write in Greek, but in the Arabic language, because up to that time the ledgers of the kings of the Ṭayyāyê were in Greek.[67]

Some twelve years after the time of ᶜAbd al-Malik, the caliph ᶜUmar II (717–720) took the next logical step in the campaign to Islamicize the realm and instituted a policy of summoning the subject populations to Islam, by insisting in certain circumstances on the cancellation of poll taxes for those who converted.[68] According to Severus ibn al-Muqaffaᶜ, ᶜUmar II also subscribed to the policy of leaving no publicly displayed cross unbroken.[69] Such policies were entirely consistent with ᶜAbd al-Malik's earlier reforms. And consequently it is not surprising to learn that ᶜUmar's successor, Yazīd II (720–724) elevated the by then well attested Islamic antipathy to Christian crosses and images to a government policy for the destruction of these objects wherever they were to be found. According to Severus' report, Yazīd "issued orders that the crosses should be broken in every place, and that the pictures which were in the churches should be removed."[70] And indeed there is archaeological evidence that in several places in Syria/Palestine in the early

---

[64] Evetts, art. cit., 5 (1910), p. (279) = 25. The last sentence of this quotation alludes to *al-Iḫlāṣ* (112): 3.

[65] Ibid., p. (306) = 52. Later in his history Severus ibn al-Muqaffaᶜ recounts a similar incident in which it is clear that it is the Christian doctrine which the images proclaim that most annoys the Muslims. In this account a young Muslim is converted to the confession of Christianity after abusing a picture of Christ crucified and being miraculously punished for it. Ibid., pp. (403) = 149–(404) = 150.

[66] See, e.g., Eutychius' account of Walīd's reign in Cheikho, op. cit., vol. 51, pp. 41–42.

[67] Chabot, *Anonymi Auctoris Chronicon . . .*, op. cit., vol. 81, pp. 298–299.

[68] D. C. Dennett, *Conversion and the Poll Tax in Early Islam* (Cambridge, Mass., 1950); H. A. R. Gibb, "The Fiscal Rescript of ᶜUmar II," *Arabica* 2 (1955), pp. 1–16.

[69] Evetts, op. cit., 5 (1910), p. (326) = 72. Interesting in connection with ᶜUmar II is a tenth century Armenian version of a letter which the Byzantine emperor Leo III (717–741), the first iconoclast emperor, is supposed to have sent in reply to the caliph's letter summoning him to Islam. In it Leo III justifies the practice of venerating images, against ᶜUmar II's charge of idolatry. A. Jeffrey, "Ghevond's Text of the Correspondence Between ᶜUmar II and Leo III," *The Harvard Theological Review* 37 (1944), pp. 322–323. Some scholars defend the authenticity of this correspondence, e.g., L. W. Barnard, *The Graeco-Roman and Oriental Background of the Iconoclastic Controversy* (Leiden, 1974), pp. 23–25; idem, "Byzantium and Islam, the Interaction of Two Worlds in the Iconoclastic Era," *Byzantinoslavica* 36 (1975), pp. 31–32. However, serious, and in the end telling objections have been raised against the authenticity of the correspondence by Stephen Gero, *Byzantine Iconoclasm During the Reign of Leo III, with Particular Attention to the Oriental Sources* (CSCO, vol. 346; Louvain, 1973), pp. 153–171.

[70] Evetts, art. cit., 5 (1910), pp. (326) = 72–(327) = 73. Yazīd's policy is widely discussed in Christian literature, but generally in isolation from a consideration of the program initiated in ᶜAbd al-Malik's time for promoting the public display of Islam. See the standard discussion in A. A. Vasiliev, "The Iconoclastic Edict of the Caliph Yazid II, A.D. 721," *Dumbarton Oaks Papers* 9 & 10 (1956), pp. 25–47.

eighth century the destruction was carried out as ordered.[71]

By the ninth century, in Islamic scholarly circles the position was formulated that the Christian veneration of crosses and images was tantamount to the idolatry which had already been forbidden by the Torah. An anonymous Muslim writer of an anti-Christian pamphlet that dates from the ninth century summed up the Islamic argument in the following words addressed to the Christians:

> You extol the cross and the image. You kiss them, and you prostrate yourselves to them, even though they are what people have made with their own hands. They neither hear, nor see, nor do harm, nor bring any advantage. The most estimable of them among you are made of gold and silver. Such is what Abraham's people did with their images and idols.[72]

The phraseology of this Muslim writer's accusation against the Christians echoes the judgment which the *Qur'ān* passed on the idols worshipped by Abraham's ancestors (see, e.g., *aš-Šuʿarā'* (26): 69–73). According to the *Qur'ān*, it is to God alone that people are commanded to bow down in worship (see *an-Nağm* (53): 62). Consequently the Christian practice of bowing down before crosses and images of Christ and the saints struck the Muslims as tantamount to idolatry.

It is in the context of this understanding of the action of "bowing-down" to mean "adoration," along with the Islamic rejection of the truth of what Christian crosses and images proclaimed in the first place, that one must understand two provisions of Islamic customary law which came to the fore in the first Abbasid century. The first of them is the prohibition in the "Covenant of ʿUmar" against displaying a cross on church buildings and against parading "idolatry" in companies of Muslims.[73] The second provision is the Islamic rule against making figural representations of living things in religious contexts. The traditions supporting this prohibition came into particular prominence during Abū Qurrah's lifetime and, as a matter of fact, as will appear below, Abū Qurrah's citation of the prohibition in his apologetic tract on images is one of the earliest documentary evidences of an official Islamic stance against figural representations in art.

The record of the Islamic campaign against the public display of crosses and icons; the charge against the Christians that the veneration of these objects is idolatry; and the fact that by the ninth century the Muslims were in full political and social control of Egypt, Palestine, Syria, Mesopotamia, and Iraq, the homelands of eastern Christianity—all go to give an ample explanation of why Abū Qurrah should have identified the Muslims as a principal cause of Christian iconophobia. One must now turn to an examination of Abū Qurrah's references to the Muslims in his tract on images.

2. Abū Qurrah's Tract and the Muslims

Throughout his Arabic works, Abū Qurrah demonstrates his familiarity with Islam and its teachings by quoting from the *Qur'ān*, alluding to characteristically Islamic notions or citing typically Islamic practices.[74] This is his habit, even in works which are devoted to exclusively Christian topics or which concern debates between rival Christian denominations. For within the boundaries of the Caliphate, all Christian discussion which was conducted in Arabic was open to the scrutiny of Muslim scholars. And there is ample evidence that at certain times and places the *mutakallimūn* of both communities attempted to purchase some credibility in the rival's camp.[75] But for the Christian writers, one suspects, the major concern was to prevent conversions to Islam on the part of upwardly mobile young Christians. Apologetics of this sort not only involved commending the truth of Christian doctrines

---

[71] R. DeVaux, "Une mosaïque byzantine à Maʿin (Transjordanie)," *Revue Biblique* 47 (1938), pp. 255–258. DeVaux was unaware of the Arabic documentation for Yazīd's decree. The archaeological facts speak for themselves. Furthermore, if the mosaics in the church of the Nativity in Bethlehem can be dated to the eighth century, their unique depiction of the teachings of the ecumenical councils in inscriptions, with no accompanying representations of persons, plus their similarities to other examples of Umayyad art, might be taken as evidence of the influence of the growing Islamic aniconic attitude, even on Christian church decoration in the period under discussion. See A. Grabar, *L'iconoclasme byzantin . . .*, op. cit., pp. 57–61.

[72] Dominique Sourdel, "Un pamphlet musulman anonyme d'époque ʿAbbaside contre les chrétiens," *Revue des Études Islamiques* 34 (1966), p. 29.

[73] A. S. Tritton, op. cit., pp. 6–7.

[74] See the survey of his references to Muslims in Griffith, "The Controversial Theology . . . ," op. cit., pp. 41–47, 105–111, 241–244.

[75] See the discussion of this aspect of Christian apologetics in Arabic in Sidney H. Griffith, "ʿAmmār al-Baṣrī's *Kitāb al-burhān*: Christian *kalām* in the First Abbasid Century," *Le Muséon* 96 (1983), pp. 145–181.

in an Arabic idiom that mirrored the intellectual concerns of the day, but it also involved demonstrating the inadequacy of the Islamic alternative. This is the method which Abū Qurrah employed in his tract on the Christian practice of venerating images. His purpose, he said, was "to bring back the hearts of those who are frightened away from prostration to these holy images to the practice of making prostration to them in the manner our fathers established and approved."[76]

Already in the first chapter of the tract, Abū Qurrah enrolls the Muslims in the group of non-Christians whom he calls *al-barrāniyyūn*, that is to say "the outsiders," a designation that was particularly appropriate to the region of Edessa in that it reflects the old Syriac word *barrānāyê*, which was used already in Ephraem's day to designate the wandering nomads of the desert regions, who almost by definition were considered uncivilized.[77]

One of Abū Qurrah's first arguments against the Christians who allow themselves to be talked out of their habit of venerating images because it is an ignominy in the eyes of the "outsiders," is to point out that these same "outsiders" have in their own scriptures statements which seem equally ridiculous to the worldly minded. To prove the point, he then heads a list of some seventeen instances taken from the Old Testament, which of course the Muslims also profess to accept, with the following statement which incorporates a quotation of the *Qur*ʾ*ān*: "For who of those whose minds are too haughty for faith would not laugh to hear that God created things from nothing, and that when He wanted to make something, *innamā yaqūlu lahu kun fayakūnu.*"[78] (See *al-Baqarah* (2): 117)

The next explicit reference to Muslims comes when Abū Qurrah cites a whole list of passages from the Bible which he says clearly attribute bodiliness to God, along with other things which some people might also think it appropriate to affirm of God. His argument here, addressed at first to the Jews, is that persons whose scriptures say such things about God as do these scripture passages are in no position to accuse the Christians of mischief in what they say about Christ, that he is the Son of God, or about Mary his mother, that she is the Mother of God. These of course were the most prominent messages proclaimed by most crosses, images, and icons.[79] And then Abū Qurrah turns his argument against the scripture of the Muslims. This time, he calls them people "other than Jews who lay claim to faith."[80] If one of these people should plead that he does not accept what the Christians say about Christ because it is an abomination, Abū Qurrah claims of such a one that "he himself, without a doubt says that God sits on the throne, and he says that God has hands and a face, and other such things which we cannot be bothered to pursue here."[81] Quite obviously this remark refers to the standard Qurʾānic *topoi*, e.g., *Yūnus* (10): 3, *Āl* ʿ*Imrān* (3): 73, *ar-Rūm* (30): 38, which were customarily cited in the discussions among the Muslim *mutakallimūn* about the *ṣifāt Allāh*, discussions which Abū Qurrah exploits elsewhere for his own apologetic purposes.[82] Here, in the tract on images, his claim is simply that persons with such statements in their scriptures have no business objecting to the bodiliness which Christians attribute to God in Christ, whom they maintain they can portray in an image.

Abū Qurrah's next citation from the *Qur*ʾ*ān* comes in a chapter in which he is arguing that in spite of what one might think on first reading biblical passages such as Exodus 20:2–5 and Deuteronomy 6:13, it is not God's will that the act of prostration (*as-suǧūd*) be made exclusively to Himself. Moreover, there are others than the Jews, Abū Qurrah points out, who say:

> It is not permitted that prostration be made to anything other than to God, and they mock the Christians for their prostrating to the images and to people. They maintain that the act of prostration is an act of worship, all the while themselves recalling that "God commanded all the angels to prostrate themselves to Adam, and they prostrated themselves, except Iblīs

[76] Arendzen, op. cit., p. 2 (Arabic), p. 2 (Latin); Graf, *Die arabischen Schriften* . . . , op. cit., p. 279.

[77] R. Payne Smith, *Thesaurus Syriacus* (2 vols.; Oxford, 1879), vol. I, col. 578.

[78] Arendzen, op. cit., pp. 5–6 (Arabic), p. 6 (Latin); Graf, *Die arabischen Schriften* . . . , op. cit., pp. 283–284.

[79] See, e.g., the passage cited in n. 65 above.

[80] Arendzen, op. cit., p. 6 (Arabic), p. 7 (Latin); Graf, *Die arabischen Schriften* . . . , op. cit., p. 284.

[81] Ibid., p. 7 (Arabic), p. 9 (Latin); pp. 285–286.

[82] Abū Qurrah, like the other Christian apologists of the period, took advantage of the discussions among Muslims about the *ṣifāt Allāh* in his apology for the doctrine of the Trinity. Griffith, "The Controversial Theology . . . ," op cit., pp. 136–172.

> refused, and came to be among the *kāfirīn*." If the prostration was an act of worship, then inevitably, according to what you say, God commanded the angels to worship Adam. Far be it from God to do this.[83]

One easily recognizes the Iblīs passage from *al-Baqarah* (2): 34 in this quotation, and Abū Qurrah immediately follows it up with another quotation from the *Qur'ān*. He argues that Muslims should not mock the Christians for making an act of prostration before one of their bishops, since the Muslim himself should recall that Jacob and his sons "bowed down to Joseph as ones making prostration (*suǧǧadan*)."[84] With the exception of Joseph's name, Abū Qurrah has here quoted literally from *Yūsuf* (12): 100. His purpose is to argue that the act of prostration may be a gesture of honor and not exclusively one of adoration.

Satisified that he has shown that in His scriptures, including even the *Qur'ān*, God could not have intended to forbid all gestures of prostration not directed to Himself, Abū Qurrah turns next to argue that neither did God mean to forbid men absolutely never to make images of anything at all, as the words of Exodus 20:2–5 may seem to say. It is in this connection that he refers to the much discussed Islamic *ḥadīth* which records Muḥammad's words about the punishment due to an image maker on the last day. In chapter ten of his tract on images, Abū Qurrah thought it necessary to provide his Christian readers with an argument against "those who say that anyone who has made an image of a living thing will be obliged on resurrection day to blow the spirit into his image."[85] It is worth quoting Abū Qurrah's argument against this challenge in full, in spite of its length.

> Where are those who say that whoever fashions a likeness of any living thing will be obliged to blow the spirit into it on resurrection day? Do they think that Solomon and Moses will be obliged to blow the spirit into the likenesses which they made? God would then have willed them evil when He let them make them, and far be it from God to will evil on His friends. The marvel of those who make this statement is that they themselves make images of plants, but they do not know that if those who make images of living things are to be obliged to blow spirits into the images they have made, then they too are obliged to paint their images, making them grow, bearing fruit. Both of these matters are the same in respect to human ability.
>
> These people would have to be punished forever for making images of plants, since they would not have the power to deal with these images in accordance with what we have cited, and their judgment would be valid against themselves, not against us. They must know that, according to their own conception, in making images of plants they are at variance with God's statement in the Law, "Do not make for yourself a likeness of anything in heaven, or on the earth, or in the waters under the earth": For God did not say, "Do not make for yourself a likeness of anything living." Rather, everything to do with likenesses is included. They blame others for the same thing they do themselves, but they do not even notice it.[86]

One knows of course that the judgment against image makers recorded here is the same, and is almost in the same words, as the prophet Muḥammad's dictum preserved in the Islamic *ḥadīth*.[87] What is more, it is important for a full understanding of the argument to notice the context in which the particular prophetic tradition cited by Abū Qurrah actually appeared in Islamic sources. The report preserved not only the prophet's *dictum* but, in some versions, it includes also the advice given to an erstwhile, professional image maker by ᶜAbd Allāh ibn ᶜAbbās, who is credited as the original reporter of the *dictum* in the chain of authorities who transmitted it. As the story goes, a man had come to Ibn ᶜAbbās to say that image making was his livelihood. When Ibn ᶜAbbās informed him of the prophet's *dictum*, the man paled with fear. So Ibn ᶜAbbās said: "If you insist on doing it, available to you are the plants, or anything in which there is no spirit."[88] Abū Qurrah, therefore, was not only taking issue with the Islamic notion of the punishment due the image makers. But in light of the Islamic practice of employing floral decoration on the walls of mosques and elsewhere and the legitimation of this

---

[83] Arendzen, op. cit., p. 17 (Arabic), p. 18 (Latin); Graf, *Die arabischen Schriften . . .*, op. cit., p. 296.

[84] Ibid.

[85] Ibid., p. 17 (Arabic), p. 18 (Latin); p. 297.

[86] Ibid., p. 19 (Arabic), p. 20 (Latin); pp. 298–299.

[87] The congruence was pointed out by K. A. C. Creswell, "The Lawfulness of Painting in Early Islam," *Ars Islamica* 11 & 12 (1946), pp. 159–166.

[88] M. L. Krehl, *Le recueil des traditions Mahométanes par Abou Abdallah Mohammad ibn Ismaîl el-Bokhâri* (4 vols.; Leyde, 1862–1908), vol. II, pp. 40–41.

practice in the traditions, he believes that he has uncovered a basic inconsistency in the Islamic reasoning about figural images. At the end of his argument, he boasts: "They are now unmasked who deride Christians for making images of Christ and the saints in their churches, and for making prostration to people."[89]

According to Abū Qurrah, Muslims also objected to the Christian practice of touching and kissing the icons of Christ and the saints. They argued that the legitimacy of putting images in churches is one thing, but to touch them and kiss them in veneration is something unseemly. Abū Qurrah countered with the argument that the veneration of worship is paid not to the image which one touches, i.e., the paints and panels, but to Christ or the saint represented there. He bolstered his argument by referring to the Muslim's own manner of praying. He says: "Tell us, regarding the act of prostration, do you make it only to the thing onto which you put your knees and forehead, or to what your intention wills by putting down your knees and forehead in bowing?"[90] The purpose of the argument is evident, namely, to draw a parallel between the Muslim's postures in prayer and the Christians' ritual in connection with the icons. Abū Qurrah puts it straightforwardly:

> Everyone who makes prostration to God touches at least either the ground or a carpet with his knees, but his prostration is conducted only according to his intention to make a prostration to God. So also with the Christians, their touching of the image in the prostration is in accordance with their intention thereby to honor Christ, their God, or his saints, or the prophets, the apostles, the martyrs and others.[91]

By now enough has been said to make clear the method of Abū Qurrah's apology. He deploys many arguments in his treatise and all of them are designed to convince recalcitrant Christians of the legitimacy of their traditional practice of venerating images. His purpose is to rebut the Islamic arguments against the images by discovering inconsistencies in them. But at the end of his tract, he calls the readers' attention to the positive value of the images in proclaiming Christian faith, and thereby allowing the faithful Christian, in suffering rebuke for it, to have a share in Christ's passion, and by accepting it to deserve his reward. Abū Qurrah contends:

> If anyone says that the "outsiders" already rebuke us in regard to Christ's cross without even seeing these images, he should understand that if these images were not in our churches, most of what we have in mind would not occur to the hearts of those of them who come into our churches. The images are what arouse them to rebuke us.[92]

With this frank testimony, Abū Qurrah suggests what indeed seems to have been the case, namely, that what most annoyed the Muslims and the Jews about Christian images was not simply the fact that they were images or even that Christians venerated them, but that most of them proclaimed about Jesus and Mary precisely what the *Qur'ān* denied about them. And this was no reason, according to Abū Qurrah, for Christians to abandon their images: because the Muslims rebuke them or sneer at them because of what the images proclaim.

D. IMAGES AND ISLAMIC TRADITIONS

The Muslims of Abū Qurrah's day were not only opposed to the public display of Christian crosses and icons; they were also convinced that no representations of living things other than plants should have a place in any religious art or be displayed in Islamic premises. There has been a considerable amount of modern scholarly discussion about the significance and development of this Islamic attitude to religious images[93] and, as noted above, in his tract on images Abū Qurrah took notice of one of the more popular prophetic traditions in Islam which reject religious images. Abū Qurrah's reference to this tradition, in chapter ten of his tract, is thus one of the earliest documentary evidences of its currency. It was written perhaps fifty years prior to the first of the canonical collections of Islamic traditions which began to appear only in the second half of the ninth Christian century.

Rudi Paret, in an historical analysis of the chains of authorities who transmitted the several forms of the Islamic traditions about images, has now shown that

[89] Arendzen, op. cit. p. 19 (Arabic), pp. 20–21 (Latin); Graf, *Die arabischen Schriften* . . . , p. 299.

[90] Ibid., p. 20 (Arabic), p. 21 (Latin); pp. 299–300.

[91] Ibid., p. 22 (Arabic), p. 23 (Latin); p. 302.

[92] Ibid., p. 49 (Arabic), p. 51 (Latin); p. 332.

[93] See the discussion and selected bibliography on this issue in O. Grabar, *Formation*, op. cit., pp. 75–103, 222–223.

the period of time to which one may date the earliest occasions when these traditions were brought forward in public discourse was earlier than Abū Qurrah's day.[94] They first appeared during the last quarter of the seventh century, according to Paret's analysis roughly in the period of the reign of the caliph ᶜAbd al-Malik (685–705). In fact, Paret expressly relates the first appearance of the Islamic scholarly concern with prophetic traditions about images to the efforts being made during ᶜAbd al-Malik's reign to Arabicize and to Islamicize public life in the caliphate.[95] In other words, the first view of the development of an official Islamic antipathy to images of living things may be dated to the very period of the initial Christian/Muslim clash over Christian images and the doctrine which they proclaim, as outlined earlier in the present article.

According to Paret, the Islamic attitude to image making did not grow all at once to the form in which Theodore Abū Qurrah took notice of it. Rather, it was not until the first quarter of the eighth century, after some controversy on the subject, that the injunction against making images of living things came to be focused on representations of those beings in which there is the breath of life (*ar-rūḥ*) and to exclude from the general Islamic disapproval of images, representations of trees or plants.[96] The very existence of controversy on this subject, highlighted by the social problem involving the plight of the image maker, as in the story told about Ibn ᶜAbbās, suggests that there was a period of time during which the theological rationale for the official Islamic antipathy to images underwent a process of adjustment. By Abū Qurrah's day, the development was complete and, by then, Muslims were already threatening the Christians with punishment on the last day for their use of images of living beings.

It is important to note that the theological rationale for the disapproval of making images of living things, as it first came into view at the time of ᶜAbd al-Malik, is thoroughly Islamic in conception. While this aspect of the rationale is not immediately evident in the form of the tradition quoted by Abū Qurrah, it is nevertheless quite evident in other forms of the tradition that are of an equal age; and indeed it is already assumed as the warranty for the punishment which is said to be due to an image maker in the tradition quoted by Abū Qurrah. This rationale is most clearly voiced in a tradition which is traced back to Abū Hurayrah (d. 679) as its original reporter. It is a tradition which reports a divine judgment (*ḥadīth qudsī*) on the matter of image making and not simply Muḥammad's considered opinion. The setting involves a scenario in which one Abū Zurᶜah walked into a dwelling in Medina along with Abū Hurayrah and they saw "an image maker at work (*muṣawwiran yuṣawwiru*)" aloft. Abū Hurayrah said: "I heard the messenger of God, prayer and peace be on him, say 'Who is more infamous than those who set out to create (*yaḫluqu*), like my act of creating (*kaḫalqī*)? Let them create a grain; let them create a tiny atom!"[97]

Clearly, in this tradition the act of making an image (*at-taṣwīr*) is expressly associated with the divine activity of creating (*al-ḫalq*). The roots of the association are in the *Qurᵓān*. As Paret has shown, even the introductory phrase "who is more infamous (*man aẓlam*)" is a familiar Qurᵓānic expression, which occurs some fifteen times in the revelation.[98] Furthermore, and more important, every use of the second form of the verbal root *ṣ-w-r* in the *Qurᵓān* to mean "to form, to fashion," has God as the subject and refers to His creation. God is "the creator, the fashioner" (*al-ḫāliq al-bāriᵓ al-muṣawwir*) *al-Ḥašr* (59): 24. Obviously, to the Muslim ear, because it is so in the *Qurᵓān*, *at-taṣwīr* is an activitiy which is proper to God, and it must have been this idea which found its way into the traditions about image making and became the most basic theological rationale for the Islamic antipathy to image making.

In all but one of the instances of the appearance of the second form of the verbal root *ṣ-w-r* in the *Qurᵓān* to mean the act of creating, it describes God's activity in creating mankind. And it is in connection with accounts of the creation of men (Adam–Jesus) that the other element of the tradition quoted by Abū Qurrah is found to have Qurᵓānic roots. According to the *Qurᵓān*, when He created Adam, God breathed into him His own spirit (*ar-rūḥ*) of life (*al-Ḥiǧr* (15): 26–29; *as-Saǧdah* (32): 7–9; *Ṣād* (38): 71–72). Further, when Mary became pregnant with Jesus, it was because God blew His spirit into her (*al-Anbiyāᵓ* (21): 91). And then, among Jesus' evidentiary miracles the *Qurᵓān* tells of his creation (*ḫalq*) of birds from clay, into which, by God's permission, he breathed and they became real birds. (*Āl ᶜImrān* (3): 49; *al-Māᵓidah*

[94] Rudi Paret, "Die Entstehungszeit des islamischen Bilderverbots," *Kunst des Orients* 11 (1976–1977), pp. 158–181.

[95] Ibid., pp. 177–178.

[96] Ibid., pp. 166–167.

[97] Krehl, op. cit., vol. IV, p. 104.

[98] Paret, art. cit., pp. 164–165.

(5): 110). It is clear from passages such as these that according to the *Qur᾿ān*, to breathe in the spirit of life is the unique prerogative of God to create living beings.[99]

It is not, of course, surprising that the basic terms of the Islamic traditions against images and image makers should echo conceptions deeply embedded in the *Qur᾿ān*. Nor is it surprising that when questions about images arose in the early Islamic community, they evoked answers which put together several strands of Qur᾿ānic thought to meet the challenge. What is interesting in the context of the discussion of Theodore Abū Qurrah's Arabic tract on images is to inquire further into the circumstances which posed a problem of images for Muslims in the first place, and which elicited the formulation of a distinctly Islamic policy regarding them. Since this policy seems first to have come into the realm of public discourse at the very time of ᶜAbd al-Malik's campaign for the public display of Islam in the caliphate and since this campaign was itself conducted in an atmosphere of reaction against the public display of Christianity, as documented in the present article, it seems reasonable to propose that a certain anti-Christian impulse was also a factor in the scheme of things which fostered the first popularity of the aniconic traditions in Islamic discourse at that same time. After all, Christian crosses and images announced doctrines which the *Qur᾿ān* said were false.

While the mere mention of otherwise unspecified images and image makers in aniconic Islamic traditions does not of itself make the case that Christians and their doctrines were among the circumstances which first elicited the enunciation of these traditions, the mention of crosses in the same accounts certainly suggests Christians. For example, a number of the traditions which in the canonical collections are traced back to ᶜĀ᾿išah, the prophet's wife, record her memory of Muḥammad's antipathy to crosses and his determination to disallow them, even as designs on fabric.[100] Such an antipathy to crosses on Muḥammad's part or on the part of any later Muslim, is intelligible only in terms of what a Muslim would consider to be the objectionable Christian doctrine which the crosses signify.

A further evidence in the traditions which indicates an anti-Christian background for the growth and popularity of the Islamic antipathy to religious images is the story told originally by ᶜĀ᾿išah about Muḥammad's reaction to the report of churches in Ethiopia with images in them. The story involves two women who had returned from their exile there, when the early Muslims had been persecuted in Mecca. As ᶜĀ᾿išah told it, "Umm Ḥabībah and Umm Salamah remembered a church they had seen in Ethiopia, in which there were images. They mentioned it to the prophet. . . . He said, 'Those people, when a virtuous man among them dies, build a place of prayer (*masǧid*) over his grave, and they paint these images on it. Those will be the worst people (*al-ḫalq*) on resurrection day.' "[101]

One notices in the accounts of the Islamic aniconic traditions that the circumstance which often evokes a traditionist's memory of the prophet's disapproval of images of living things is the sight of an image maker (*al-muṣawwir*) plying his trade in Islamic premises.[102] On the one hand, this observation prompts the reader to suppose that there was already in the traditionist's mind an idea that somehow an image maker is not altogether a religiously wholesome character.[103] But since manifestly Muslims were themselves employing image makers on a grand scale in such enterprises as ᶜAbd al-Malik's projects, there obviously had to be some rationale for determining what program of images would be deployed in such structures as the Dome of the Rock or later, under Walīd I, the Umayyad mosque in Damascus. In other words, it seems plausible to propose that with the Islamic campaign for the public display of the symbols of Islam, beginning in the late seventh and early eighth centuries, and considering the attendant necessity to supplant the public display of Christianity in many of the conquered territories,[104] that Muslim thinkers consequently elaborated a rationale for the decoration of Islamic structures which both undercut the previous Christian practices and also provided a justification for the use of vegetal and calligraphic designs in Islamic monuments. In doing so, of course, these thinkers relied on the *Qur᾿ān* and on what could be culled from the memories of the earlier generations of

[99] T. O'Shaughnessy, *The Development of the Meaning of Spirit in the Koran* (Orientalia Christiana Analecta, 139; Rome, 1953), esp. pp. 25–33.

[100] Krehl, op. cit., vol. I, pp. 106–107; vol. IV, p. 104. See also Aḥmad ibn Ḥanbal, *Musnad* (6 vols.; Beirut, 1969 [Cairo, 1894]), vol. VI, p. 140.

[101] Krehl, op. cit., vol. I, p. 119; vol. III, p. 28.

[102] See n. 97 above.

[103] See the observations of Marshall G. S. Hodgson, "Islam and Image," *History of Religions* 3 (1964), pp. 220–260.

[104] See the important remarks of Oleg Grabar in his notes to Hodgson's essay, art. cit., pp. 258–260.

Muslims about the prophet's reactions in analogous situations.

Theodore Abū Qurrah's Arabic tract on venerating images provides documentary evidence that by the early ninth Christian century, Christians not only had to contend with charges of idolatry made against them by Jews and Muslims, and with the campaign of Muslim authorities to remove the public displays of Christianity. They also had to deal with the charge, already elaborated in Islamic circles, that the very making of images of living beings constituted an affront to the Creator. Both Abū Qurrah's reference to this Islamic tradition and his polemic defense against it testify to the fairly widespread popularity of this Islamic rationale for the decorative programs in Islamic premises by the beginning of the ninth century.

IV. THEODORE ABŪ QURRAH AND ICONOCLASM IN BYZANTIUM

Thus far in the present article nothing has been said about Christian iconoclasm in Byzantium. The reason is simply that in his apologetic tract on images, Abū Qurrah had nothing whatever to say on the subject. However, given the prominence of the iconoclastic controversy in histories of Byzantium,[105] and the fact that this quarrel was current in Abū Qurrah's own lifetime, his failure even to mention it is itself intriguing. Either he did not know about it or he was of the opinion that the debate over images in the patriarchate of Constantinople was simply irrelevant to the troubles of the Melkite Christians living within *dār al-islām*. He may have thought that the very existence of such a controversy in Byzantium was an embarassment to the church under Islam and that any mention of it would only further mislead, in his view, those Christians who were already growing shy of the practice of publicly venerating images because of the challenges to this practice being voiced at home by Jews and Muslims.

One really may not conclude that Abū Qurrah knew nothing at all about iconoclasm in Byzantium. John Damascene had mentioned the emperor Leo III (717–741) in his second discourse on images and he recorded the fact that partriarch Germanos I (715–730) was exiled for opposing the emperor's policies.[106] Moreover, Agapius of Manbiğ, the tenth century Melkite historian who wrote in Arabic, knew about Leo III's policies and he even mentioned the iconoclastic council of 754.[107] However, nothing more is said on the matter in the Melkite community within *dār al-islām* until Patriarch Eutychius of Alexandria wrote in his chronicle about the policies of emperor Theophilus (829–842). Eutychius thought that Theophilus had reformed his ways, after receiving instructions in the error of iconoclasm from Patriarch Sophronius I (829–842) of Alexandria![108] The patriarch's motives in this account may have been apologetical.[109] He referred his Arabic readers to Theodore Abū Qurrah's tract on images for more detail in the argumentation in defense of image veneration.

Abū Qurrah, therefore, probably knew about the policies of emperor Leo III. He may have known about the policies of emperor Constantine V (741–775) and the council of 754, although he said nothing about them. He probably did not have any accurate information about affairs in Byzantium from after the time when the Abbasid caliphate was firmly established under the caliph Abū Ğaᶜfar al-Manṣūr (754–775). As Eutychius of Alexandria reported, once the Abbasids established their power, until the tenth century the Melkites did not even know the names of the patriarchs of Constantinople.[110] Throughout Abū Qurrah's lifetime, therefore, the church in the east was virtually *incommunicado* with the church in Byzantium and iconoclasm there was irrelevant to the controversy in which Abū Qurrah was actually involved. In Byzantium the crisis concerned much more than the scriptural prohibition of idolatry. It was an ideological and theological problem among Christians. In Edessa, on the other hand, as Abū Qurrah posed it, the problem was simply that some Christians were abandoning the practice of venerating images because of the success of the Jewish and Islamic polemic against the practice as idolatrous and blasphemous.

Now, in view of Patricia Crone's recent renewal of the contention that "Byzantine Iconoclasm was a response to the rise of Islam,"[111] one must ask if Abū Qurrah's Arabic tract on venerating images offers any support for the contention. On the surface, it would seem that the tract explicitly endorses it, because Abū Qurrah says a number of times that some Christians have given up image veneration because of the attacks

---

[105] See "Orientations bibliographiques," in G. Dumeige, *Nicée II*, op. cit., pp. 278–287.

[106] Kotter, *Contra Imaginum Calumniatores*, op. cit., pp. 103, 113, 117.

[107] Vasiliev, art. cit., 8 (1912), p. 533.

[108] Cheikho, op. cit., vol. 51, pp. 63–64.

[109] Griffith, "Eutychius of Alexandria . . . ," art. cit.

[110] Cheikho, op. cit., vol. 51, pp. 49, 87–88.

[111] Crone, art. cit., p. 59.

of Jews and Muslims. However, one must remember that Abū Qurrah is talking about Christians living within *dār al-islām* and not about Christians in Byzantium.

To substantiate her contention, Crone points to the chronological sequence of caliph Yazīd II's well known decree for the destruction of Christian images in 721, bishop Constantine of Nacoleia's negative denunciation of images in 724, and then to the inception of an active, anti-image movement in Constantinople in 726, sponsored by emperor Leo III. Furthermore, she points to the accounts in Byzantine sources which associate the origins of iconoclasm with the pernicious influences of Jews conniving with Muslims, and argues that the Jewish polemic against Christian images itself arose only after the coming of the Muslims.[112] Earlier in the article, she had sketched an account of the socio-historical growth of Christianity, based on a highly idiosyncratic analysis of almost Hegelian proportions, according to which the history of Jews, Christians, and Muslims is seen to have progressed in a neat two-step waltz, based on a challenge/response model of sociological theorizing. The analysis pictures Christianity just waiting for Islam to trigger iconoclasm,[113] a set-up which then allowed the following conclusion.

> In sum, we have a general expectation that Islam might provoke iconoclasm, a perfect chronological sequence, explicit contemporary testimonia and striking parallels—a cluster of evidence which is all the more impressive for coming from a period for which most of the source material has been lost. To dismiss all this as accidental would require a skepticism verging on the fideist.[114]

In order to forge a connection between Christian iconoclasts in Byzantium and persons across the border in *dār al-Islām*, through whom influence could be carried, Crone postulates a newly enlivened Judeo-Christianity associated with a group called the *Athinganoi*.[115] This Jewish Christianity *redivivus* is said to have exerted a particular influence in Mesopotamia, as Crone creates their story, conveniently located then to affect people living in Phrygia and Amorium.

The scenario for the outbreak of Byzantine iconoclasm, in Crone's reconstruction, next envisions a Phrygian *Athinganos* who begins to voice iconoclastic sentiments, which, in Crone's words, must be considered in connection with "a short anti-Christian blast among the Arabs, and an enormous explosion burning up the accumulated qualms of the Greeks."[116] The qualms in question, according to Crone, were the Greeks' lack of nerve to smash up the "idolatrous" religious pictures, about which, in her reconstruction, they had long had an endemic bad conscience. The endemic bad conscience is perceived on the basis of Crone's aforementioned socio-historical analysis of the growth of Christianity.

Here is not the place to engage in a detailed debate with Crone's long and involved article. Its weakest point, in addition to the tortuously contrived theorizing mentioned earlier, is the postulation of a new Jewish Christianity grown up in association with the *Athinganoi*, which is then thought to have somehow influenced the Iconoclast bishops in Byzantium.[117]

---

[112] Ibid., pp. 68–70.

[113] Ibid., p. 64. The language is Crone's.

[114] Ibid., p. 70.

[115] On this group see J. Starr, "An Eastern Christian Sect: the Athinganoi," *Harvard Theological Review* 29 (1936), pp. 93–106.

[116] Crone, art. cit., p. 80.

[117] Crone herself writes, "The case for the survival of the Judeo-Christian tradition rests entirely on the Judeo-Christian writings, in particular the account preserved by ᶜAbd al-Jabbār." Art. cit., p. 94. However, it must be said that the account of the Christians preserved by ᶜAbd al-Ǧabbār ibn Aḥmad al-Hamadhānī in his *Tathbīt dalāʾil an-nubuwwah* (2 vols.; Beirut, 1966), vol. I, pp. 91–209 is part and parcel of his apology for Islam and for the prophethood of Muḥammad, which involves the rejection of Christian proposals, and the development of polemical arguments against them. There is no reason to suppose that ᶜAbd al-Ǧabbār is reporting Jewish Christian views when he rejects Christian doctrines and proposes that Jesus was an observant Jew, who himself taught none of what ᶜAbd al-Ǧabbār viewed as the aberrant doctrines of later Christians. ᶜAbd al-Ǧabbār did not invent this line of argument. Earlier polemicists also employed it. See S. M. Stern, "ᶜAbd al-Ǧabbār's Account of How Christ's Religion Was Falsified By the Adoption of Roman Customs," *The Journal of Theological Studies* 19 (1968), pp. 128–130. To propose that ᶜAbd al-Ǧabbār, or any other Jewish or Muslim polemicist, was merely reporting what some otherwise unattested Jewish Christian documents had to say, is willfully to refuse to consider the fact that ᶜAbd al-Ǧabbār was himself a skillful polemicist, who did his homework and knew what the Qurʾān's teachings required a Muslim to think about the veracity of Christian doctrines. The evidence for thinking that there ever were the "Judeo-Christian writings" of which

Nevertheless, there remains Crone's valid reminder that the Islamic antipathy to Christian crosses and images was indeed a situation that came into view at relatively the same time, and a bit previous to the first iconoclastic stirrings in Byzantium. But this temporal sequence is a far cry from evidence for assigning a cause for the rise of iconoclasm in Byzantium, or for alleging that it was a response to Islam. *Post hoc ergo propter hoc, non valet illatio.*

There is an element of *a priori* plausibility to be found in the suggestion that the polemics of Jews and Muslims may have played a role in prompting some Christians to re-evaluate a practice that some people in the church had always found only dubiously acceptable. However, the only explicit piece of documentary evidence for maintaining such a provocative role for Jews and Muslims at all in this matter is Theodore Abū Qurrah's tract on images, which Crone never mentions. In any event, the evidence applies to a re-evaluation of image veneration among Christians living in *dār al-Islām*, who had little or no contact with Byzantium. There is no mention of Judeo-Christians, or *Athinganoi* in Abū Qurrah's tract. Certainly, there is not here sufficient evidence to ground the judgment that iconoclasm in Byzantium was in effect a reaction to Islam. Such a conclusion would amount to reducing the whole intellectual and political struggle of more than a century in Byzantium to the dimensions of Abū Qurrah's pastoral problem in Edessa, where no Christian iconoclasm ever came about.

If one is to grant that there is an element of *a priori* plausibility in the suggestion that Jewish or Islamic polemics may have played a catalytic role in the rise of iconoclasm in Byzantium, one must also grant that it was only one of a number of conditions among which the movement developed. And if one wants to account for the "perfect chronological sequence" of events to which Crone has called attention, the most reasonable construction to put upon it is not that Yazīd II's decree in 721 somehow laid the groundwork for Leo III's actions in 726 or 730, but merely to notice that the caliphal program to Arabicize and Islamicize public life in the conquered territories came slightly earlier in time than did the imperial program to reform Christianity in Byzantium. After all, the two programs were different, as well as being in different places. Images and crosses were only incidental to Yazīd's purposes; they were the substance of Leo's efforts. Such at least is what is suggested by a view from Abū Qurrah's Arabic tract on venerating images.

Crone speaks turns out to be only Crone's notion (following the lead of S. Pines, in art. cit., p. 76 & nn. 90 & 91) that ʿAbd al-Ǧabbār would not have had the wit to develop these arguments himself, in reliance on earlier Islamic scholarship, and the consultation of Christian sources. Given what we have of the *qāḍī*'s scholarly output, this is the least likely conclusion of all to make in regard to his brilliant anti-Christian polemic.

VI

FREE WILL IN CHRISTIAN KALĀM: THE DOCTRINE OF THEODORE ABŪ QURRAH

Few issues loom so large in the scholarly discussions of the early years of the Islamic *'ilm al-kalām* than does the debate about human free will and divine predestination*. Not only were there different schools of thought on the subject among the medieval Muslim *mutakallimūn*, but modern historians are now involved in controversy about how the several Islamic doctrines evolved, at what period of time they appeared, and under what set of influences they were first put forward [1]. But in spite of this controversy, a number of commentators on the subject think that somehow, however elusively, Christian thought in Greek or Syriac was a factor behind the irruption of these topics into the public discourse of Islam during the Umayyad caliphate.

The very mention of the names of such shadowy figures in Islamic heresiography as Ma'bad al-Ǧuhānī (d. 703), Ghaylān al-Dimašqī (d. 743), Ǧahm ibn Ṣafwān (d. 745), and Wāṣil ibn 'Aṭā (d. 748), reminds one that from the point of view of some later Islamic scholars, these early innovators of doctrine were supposed to have been inspired to their allegedly novel ideas as a result of their association with Christian

---

* Special abbreviations used in this article:
— BACHA, *Les œuvres arabes* (see note 9);
— COOK, *Early Muslim Dogma* (see note 1);
— SAHAS, *John of Damascus* (see note 11);
— WATT, *The Formative Period* (see note 1).

[1] See W. Montgomery WATT, *The Formative Period of Islamic Thought* (Edinburgh, 1973), a work to be taken in conjunction with the author's earlier *Free Will and Predestination in Early Islam* (London, 1948). Regarding developments in the early Islamic period see Josef VAN ESS, *Zwischen Ḥadīṯ und Theologie; Studien zum Entstehen prädestinationischer Überlieferung* (Berlin and New York, 1975); *Anfänge muslimischer Theologie; zwei antiqadaritische Traktate aus dem ersten Jahrhundert der Higra* (Beirut, 1977). For an unsympathetic reaction to Van Ess' findings see Michael COOK, *Early Muslim Dogma* (Cambridge, 1981). For a review of the free will/predestination problem in the later schools of *kalām* see Cheikh BOUAMRANE, *Le problème de la liberté humaine dans la pensée musulmane (solution mu'tazilite)* (Paris, 1978); Daniel GIMARET, *Theories de l'acte humain en théologie musulmane* (Paris, 1980).

teachers. Morris S. Seale has done as much as any modern writer to call the attention of scholars to the charges of association with Christians which were sometimes levelled against these early Muslim innovators, and he has himself gone to considerable lengths to examine what is reported of their beliefs, with a view to documenting what he calls «certain parallelisms which betray dependence» on earlier Christian thought[2].

Not surprisingly, among the topics Seale examines he highlights the parallels that are to be observed between Christian ideas about the freedom of the human act of willing, especially as these ideas had been expressed in writings attributed to John of Damascus (d.c. 750), and similar ideas which are reported to be those of the early Muslim *Qadariyyah*, the partisans of free will[3]. And in this connection, Harry Austryn Wolfson even goes so far as to propose that the origins of the use of the Arabic term, *al-qadariyyah*, to designate the Muslim libertarians, as he calls them, are to be sought in the Arabic translation of the Greek word for someone endowed with free will, which is used in the text attributed to John of Damascus, i.e., αὐτεξούσιος. Wolfson says,

> We may assume that in the debates between Muslims and Christians on the problem of freedom of the will the term αὐτεξούσιος was translated into Arabic by *ḳādir bi-nafsihi*, «powerful by his own self». Once the term *ḳādir*, «powerful», was thus used in a phrase describing man's own power it was quite natural to use the term *ḳadariyyah* as a description of those who believed in man's own power to determine his actions[4].

Meanwhile, from the determinist side of the issue in Islam, after a cursory examination of one of the Syriac letters of Jacob of Edessa (d. 708), Michael Cook has recently suggested that perhaps there was a «widespread determinist mood» abroad in the world in late Umayyad times, even in Christian circles, which might help to explain the

---

[2] Morris S. SEALE, *Muslim Theology; a Study of Origins with Reference to the Church Fathers* (London, 1964), see p. 74. On the «heresiarchs» themselves see the studies of Van Ess listed in n. 1 above, and J. VAN ESS, *Les Qadarites et la Ġailanīya de Yazid III*, in *Studia Islamica* 31 (1970), pp. 269-286; «Maʿbad al-Ǧuhanī», in Richard GRAMLICH (ed.), *Islamwissenschaftliche Abhandlungen: Fritz Meier Z. 60. Geburtstag* (Wiesbaden, 1974), pp. 49-77. See also Richard M. FRANK, The Neoplatonism of Ǧahm ibn Ṣafwan, in *Le Muséon* 78 (1965), pp. 395-424.

[3] SEALE, *Muslim Theology* (note 2 above), pp. 16-35. See also Armand ABEL, *La polémique damascénienne et son influence sur les origines de la théologie musulmane*, in *L'élaboration de l'islam; colloque de Strasbourg, 12-14 juin 1959* (Paris, 1961), pp. 61-85.

[4] Harry Austryn WOLFSON, *The Philosophy of the Kalam* (Cambridge, Mass., 1976), p. 620.

appearance of the more determinist, or predestinarian ideas espoused by the anti-*qadarite* Muslim intellectuals of the period[5].

Of course, not all scholars accept the suggestion that one must have reference to Christian sources in order to appreciate the growth and development of the Islamic *kalām*, even where parallels abound[6]. Nor is it the purpose here to argue for or against any such Christian influences. Clearly the question of influences is a delicate one, and inevitably in any given instance the matter comes down to the historian's judgment about how much colloquy between Muslim and Christian intellectuals the available evidence will allow him to posit at any given time or place, or to what degree the obvious parallels in their thinking are to be attributed to a shared cultural history, and ultimately to a shared humanity. But if it is unclear how much Christian thought may be said to have affected the early Islamic *kalām*, there can be no doubt that by the late eighth century, Islamic thought was exerting a major influence on the way Christian writers living within the Islamic world were presenting their traditional beliefs. And it is this issue which is the focus of the present inquiry, particularly in regard to the topics of free will and divine predestination.

While his name is often invoked in favor of the thesis that Christian thought influenced the growth and development of the *Qadariyyah* in Islam[7], C. H. Becker is in fact the first modern scholar who pointed out, in regard to what is usually considered to be John of Damascus' argument with Islam over the human power to choose good or evil, that «the controversy over the whole question had first been registered in Islam, for John of Damascus designated Determinism simply as the Islamic doctrine, which he contrasted with free will (τὸ αὐτεξούσιον) as the specifically Christian one»[8]. Becker's insight is an important one, and it sets the agenda for the present inquiry. For the purpose here is to examine one Christian reaction to the ideas about human willing which were current in the Islamic world in the ninth century. More specifically,

---

5 COOK, *Early Muslim Dogma*, p. 151.

6 See, e.g., WATT, *The Formative Period*, pp. 98-99; Richard M. FRANK, *Beings and Their Attributes; the Teaching of the Basrian School of the Mu'tazila in the Classical Period* (Albany, N.Y., 1978), p. 5; J. VAN ESS, *Ḳadariyya*, in *EI*², vol. IV, pp. 371-372.

7 See WATT, *The Formative Period*, p. 98; J. VANESS, «Qadariyya», p. 371.

8 Carl H. BECKER, *Christliche Polemik und islamische Dogmenbildung*, in *Vom Werden und Wesen der islamischen Welt* (Hildesheim, 1967), p. 439. Article published originally in *Zeitschrift für Assyriologie* 26 (1911), pp. 175ff.

the present aim is to study Theodore Abū Qurrah's Arabic treatise on human freedom [9].

The discussion of Abū Qurrah's treatise on human freedom, however, requires some attention to be paid to the broader context of his work [10], and particularly to the text usually ascribed to John of Damascus, the *Disputatio Christiani et Saraceni* [11]. And several new ideas, or new emphases put on older ideas, will be brought forward in connection with it. Accordingly, the three sections of the article will consider in order, the *Disputatio*, Abū Qurrah's treatise, and a brief third section devoted to the conclusions which might be drawn from the foregoing considerations.

I. The Disputatio Christiani et Saraceni

The text which is most often mentioned in evidence of the Christian reaction to Islamic ideas about free will and predestination is the *Disputatio Christiani et Saraceni*, which is usually attributed to John of Damascus. John, who died in Mar Sabas monastery near Jerusalem c. 749/750 A.D., had quit the caliphal service in Damascus some twenty-five years earlier [12]. However, he did not go into simple monastic retirement. Rather, on his arrival in Palestine, John of Damascus took up a new career of Christian scholarship. And he produced there, in the Greek language, among many other works, a monumental synthesis of Christian thought, his *Pēgē Gnoseos*, which eventually achieved great fame throughout Christendom. Islam's intellectual challenge to

---

[9] Constantin BACHA, *Les œuvres arabes de Théodore Aboucara, évêque d'Haran* (Beyrouth, 1904), pp. 9-22. German version: Georg GRAF, *Die arabischen Schriften des Theodor Abu Qurra, Bischof's von Ḥarran (ca. 740-820); literarhistorische Untersuchungen und Übersetzung* (Paderborn, 1910), pp. 223-238.

[10] For a fuller discussion of the broader context see Sidney H. GRIFFITH, *The Controversial Theology of Theodore Abū Qurrah (c. 750-c. 820), a Methodological, Comparative Study in Christian Arabic Literature*, (Ph. D. Dissertation; The Catholic University of America, Washington, D.C. 1978).

[11] See Daniel J. SAHAS, *John of Damascus on Islam, the «Heresy of the Ishmaelites»* (Leiden, 1972), pp. 97-122, with the Greek text from *PG*, vol. 94, cols. 1336-1348, and an English version, pp. 142-155. A new critical edition of the text is available in Bernhard KOTTER (ed.), *Die Schriften des Johannes von Damaskus, IV, Liber de haeresibus. Opera polemica* (Berlin and New York, 1981), pp. 420-438. See also the outline of the work in Adel-Théodore KHOURY, *Les théologiens byzantins et l'islam: textes et auteurs* (VIIIe-XIIIe s.) (Louvain and Paris, 1969), pp. 68-82.

[12] There is some controversy over the date of John's withdrawal from Damascus, and his move to Palestine. See SAHAS, *John of Damascus*, pp. 43-45; Joseph NASRALLAH, *Saint Jean de Damas, son époque, sa vie, son œuvre* (Harissa, 1950), p. 81.

Christians may well have been among the background factors which inspired John to his accomplishment. But it must be said, especially in the present context, that of all he wrote, very little of it in fact has anything explicitly to do with Islam. And even that little bit has been subject to many questions about its authenticity [13]. As we shall see, such is the case particularly with the *Disputatio*.

One will notice immediately that the years of John of Damascus' monastic career coincide with the years during which Muslim controversialists such as Ġaylān al-Dimašqī and Ǧahm ibn Ṣafwān, not to mention the renowned al-Ḥasan al-Baṣrī (d. 728), were putting forward their own mutually exclusive ideas about how human beings can be said to choose the good or the evil which they perform. This coincidence has often been observed, and it is in fact one reason for the frequent allegation of John's influence on this argument among the Muslims. But there is another way to construe the coincidence, and it is that John's very removal to monastic life in Palestine should have precluded his participation in any arguments about religion which came to the attention of the members of the caliph's court in Damascus. Indeed, to judge by the enormous literary output of his years at Mar Sabas monastery, John of Damascus was in fact exclusively concerned with the Greek expression of Christianity. He seems to have turned his back on Damascus. The controversy which attracted his attention most insistently was the iconoclastic struggle in Byzantium [14], and nothing explicitly to do with the problems of the first generation of the Muslim *mutakallimūn*. Even the well known chapter 100/101 of the *De Haeresibus*, which describes and rejects the «deceptive superstition of the Ishmaelites», is simply a polemical pamphlet for Christian eyes alone [15]. And the ready

[13] SAHAS, *John of Damascus*, discusses the relevant texts, as well as the question of their authenticity. He favors the authenticity of chap. 100/101 of the *De Haeresibus*, pp. 60-66, and so does KHOURY, *Les théologiens byzantins* (note 11 above), pp. 50-55. But one should still consider the arguments of Armand ABEL, *Le chapitre CI du livre des hérésies de Jean Damascene: son inauthenticité*, in *Studia Islamica* 19 (1963), pp. 5-25.

[14] See Bernhard KOTTER, *Die Schriften des Johannes von Damaskos; III, Contra Imaginum Calumniatores Orationes Tres* (Berlin and New York, 1975). The idea that John's orations against the iconoclastic policies of Leo III were written in Damascus comes from the Greek *Vita* of the saint. It serves as the basis for the legend that the emperor had his revenge on the saint's opposition to his policies by arranging for the caliph to become suspicious of John's loyalty, through the receipt of a forged letter, supposedly written by John to Leo III. The easiest construction to put upon this account is to suggest that it expresses the iconophile hagiographer's contempt for Leo III, and that it has no basis in fact. See n. 12 above.

[15] See SAHAS, *John of Damascus*, pp. 58-95, 132-141; Bernhard KOTTER, *Die Schriften*

rebuttals which the author puts forward for Christians caught in disputes with Muslims are not free of such caricatures of Islamic beliefs and practices as John of Damascus himself should have had every reason to know to be unfair. There are no reasoned arguments here. The author's allegations merely repudiate Islam by way of ridicule, presumably to the satisfaction of a Christian believer[16]. In any case, the controversy over free will and divine predestination found no place in chapter 100/101 of the *De Haeresibus*.

As for the *Disputatio Christiani et Saraceni*, it seems not to belong to John of Damascus at all. The contents of the work have been transmitted in the manuscript tradition among the writings of John of Damascus, but they have also been transmitted piecemeal among the Greek *opuscula* attributed to Theodore Abū Qurrah (d.c. 825)[17]. This fact, taken together with a notice at the head of yet another one of Abū Qurrah's polemical Greek *opuscula*, to the effect that it was drawn «from his rebuttals to the Saracens in the words (διὰ φωνῆς) of John of Damascus»[18], encourages one to discount John's direct responsibility for the *Disputatio*. Indeed, on the face of it, to judge by the probable sense of the expression ἀπὸ φωνῆς after the ninth century[19], it seems more reasonable to suppose that the *Disputatio* presents Theodore Abū Qurrah's refutation of certain Islamic ideas, using John of Damascus' teachings for the purpose. And this conclusion has much to recommend it, both from what one knows of Abū Qurrah's career as a religious controversialist within the realm of Islam[20], and from the fact that he was certainly accustomed to put forward the doctrine of John of Damascus, who preceded Theodore as a monk at Mar Sabas by a generation[21].

---

des Johannes von Damaskos; IV, Liber de haeresibus. Opera polemica (Berlin and New York, 1981), pp. 60-67.

16 See the insightful discussion of Paul KHOURY, *Jean Damascène et l'islam*, in *Parole de l'Orient* 7 (1957), pp. 44-63; 8 (1958), pp. 313-339.

17 See the references cited in n. 11 above.

18 *PG*, vol. 94, col. 1596B.

19 See Marcel RICHARD, ΑΠΟ ΦΩΝΗΣ, in *Byzantion* 20 (1950), pp. 191-222.

20 See Sidney H. GRIFFITH, *The Controversial Theology of Theodore Abū Qurrah (c. 750-c. 820 A.D.); a Methodological, Comparative Study in Christian Arabic Literature*, (Ph. D. Dissertation; Washington, D.C.: The Catholic University of America, 1978; Ann Arbor, Michigan: University Microfilms, 78-19874).

21 See Ignace DICK, *Un continuateur arabe de saint Jean Damascène: Théodore Abuqurra, évêque melkite de Ḥarrān*, in *POC* 12 (1962), pp. 209-233, 319-332; 13 (1963), pp. 114-129.

What gives one some hesitation about simply ascribing responsibility for the *Disputatio* in its present form to Theodore Abū Qurrah without further ado is the fact that some questions might be raised about the authenticity even of the thirty-four Greek *opuscula* which are usually ascribed to him. For Syriac and Arabic seem to have been Abū Qurrah's preferred languages, and there is some evidence that the Greek works ascribed to him are a collection of translations of pieces which he wrote originally in Arabic[22], plus reports of his responses to questions put to him which he answered in Arabic or Syriac, but which others rendered into Greek[23]. Here is not the place to pursue this issue any further. But the mention of the problem reminds one that with Abū Qurrah there appears a new dimension to the Christian reaction to Islamic teaching. For Abū Qurrah did not simply turn his back to the Muslims, to address the Christian community in their own language, as John of Damascus did. Rather, as we shall see below in regard to the issues of free will and predestination, Abū Qurrah became the first Christian whose name we know to take notice of the religious ideas of interest to Christians which were current in the Islamic world, and to respond to them with reasoned arguments in Arabic, following the scholarly conventions of the Muslim *mutakallimūn*.

As for the *Disputatio*, then, given the present state of research into the works of Theodore Abū Qurrah which are preserved in Greek, one might reasonably prefer a scenario which envisions this dialogue in *Erotapokrisis* style as a report of Abū Qurrah's customary deployment of John of Damascus' doctrines, in arguments against various Islamic beliefs, or apologies for Christian teachings challenged by Muslims. One might even advance the thesis that the *Disputatio* owes its present format to the industry of a now unknown person who was reporting Abū Qurrah's debates with Muslims, and publishing the more successful arguments, for a Greek speaking audience. And one further suspects that this report was prepared outside of Syria/Palestine, by monks who were refugees from the Islamic world, and who lived as emigrés in

---

[22] See, e.g., Greek *opusculum* IV, *PG*, vol. 97, cols. 1504-1521, which Abū Qurrah wrote in Arabic, and Michael Synkellos translated into Greek. See the superscription to the work on col. 1504D.

[23] An example is Greek *opusculum* IX, *PG*, vol. 97, col. 1529, which reports two short responses from Abū Qurrah to a particular question, which had already circulated in Arabic. See Sidney H. GRIFFITH, *Some Unpublished Arabic Sayings Attributed to Theodore Abū Qurrah*, in *Le Muséon* 92 (1979), pp. 29-35. See also Khalil SAMIR, *Kitāb ǧāmi' wuǧūh* (n. 79 below).

Constantinople, after the model of the career of Michael Synkellos[24]. In this manner, the contents of the *Disputatio* would have come to circulate in Byzantium under the names of both John of Damascus and of Theodore Abū Qurrah. But the latter would have been ultimately the one reponsible for construing John's doctrines into replies suitable to particular issues in the controversy with the Muslims. And the emigré monks would have been responsible for the circulation of the Greek reports of these debates in Byzantium[25].

If this scenario may be considered to be a plausible construction to put upon the evidence in hand, then the topics under discussion in the *Disputatio* should reflect the actual debate topics between Christians and Muslims in Syria/Palestine just before, and during the first half of the ninth century, as well as the topics of discussion among the Muslim *mutakallimūn* of the same period, which might be likely to come to the notice of the Christians. And from this point of view, the correlation of topics is indeed notable. The *Disputatio*, of course, is only a brief work, and not a fully developed treatise, or even a full-dress polemical tract by the standards of the Christian writers in the eastern patriarchates at the time. But the topics it does contain are certainly to be found in contemporary Christian tracts in Syriac and Arabic[26]. And as the scholars who have studied the *Disputatio* have been quick to point out, several of the passages in this work which purport to advance the claims of Muslims can in fact be verified in Islamic sources of this period, and even earlier[27]. The issue of free will versus predestination is a case in point.

The available evidence shows, as was mentioned above, that Muslim scholars were actively discussing among themselves issues connected with the human ability to choose good or evil behavior during the very years

[24] For the biography of Michael see the texts cited by François HALKIN, in *BHG*, vol. II, p. 123. See also Siméon VAILHÉ, *Saint Michel le syncelle et les deux frères Grapti, saint Théodore et saint Théophane*, in *ROC* 9 (1901), pp. 313-323; 610-642.

[25] On the relative isolation of the church in Syria/Palestine from the church in Byzantium at this time see Sidney H. GRIFFITH, *Eutychius of Alexandria on the Emperor Theophilus and Iconoclasm in Byzantium: a Tenth Century Moment in Christian Apologetics in Arabic*, in *Byzantion* 52 (1982), pp. 154-190; *Stephen of Ramlah and the Christian Kerygma in Arabic in Ninth-Century Palestine*, in *Journal of Ecclesiastical History* 36 (1985), pp. 23-45.

[26] See Sidney H. GRIFFITH, *The Prophet Muḥammad, his Scripture and his Message according to the Christian Apologies in Arabic and Syriac from the First Abbasid Century*, in Toufic FAHD (ed.), *Vie du prophète Mahomet* (Colloque de Strasbourg, 1980; Paris, 1982), pp. 99-146.

[27] See SAHAS, KOTTER and KHOURY, cited in n. 11 above.

when John of Damascus was busy with his own scholarly projects in Mar Sabas monastery. It is not surprising, therefore, that by the next generation Christian controversialists were taking note of the general consensus that was already emerging among Muslims, to the effect that in view of God's omnipotence and omniscience, human beings could not really be said to have the power to determine the being, or ultimately even the quality of their own actions. For by the first half of the ninth century, during the very years when many Muʿtazilite *mutakallimūn* were championing various ideas of human free choice, under the patronage of the caliph's court in Baghdad, the movement was already well under way, symbolized by the name of Aḥmad ibn Ḥanbal (d. 855), which insured the victory of predestinarian views in the Muslim community at large. And these views must at first have seemed to be notably at variance with what Christians officially taught on the subject of human moral choice. So it should not be surprising to find a Christian polemicist at the turn of the ninth century representing Muslims simply as determinists, whose views would take away all human moral responsibility, and make a mockery of the biblical commandments to do good and avoid evil.

What is striking in the Christian polemical and apologetical texts from the first Abbasid century which discuss the free will issue, especially in view of what so many modern scholars have had to say about the Christian influence on the *Qadariyyah* in Islam, is the fact that these Christian tracts, on the first reading, seem not to mention at all any Muslims who are not predestinarians. Perhaps this one-sided view has its explanation in the argumentative character of these tracts, whose authors scarcely intended to put forward a dispassionate account of Islamic doctrines. Rather, their purposes were to represent Islam to their fellow Christians as an unacceptable religious option, and to furnish them with persuasive arguments to that effect. So one should not expect to find in them any account of Islamic doctrines agreeable to the Christians. But this fact in turn reminds one that not all of the Christian apologies from the first Abbasid century even raise the issue of free will. Indeed, in the Arabic apologies, one finds it discussed in any detail only in works which come from the Palestinian monastic milieu, and which have some connection with Theodore Abū Qurrah[28]. For the rest, the Arabic

[28] In Syriac theological literature, as will be mentioned below, the freedom of human beings for the moral choice was a persistent theme from the time of Ephraem onwards. It came up with explicit reference to the Muslims in Discourse I, chapter 6, of Moshe bar Kephâ's treatise on free will. See William WRIGHT, *Catalogue of Syriac Manuscripts in the British Museum* (3 vols.; London, 1870-1872), vol. II, p. 854.

apologists largely ignore the issue. This circumstance in turn suggests that for most Christian tractarians the charge of moral determinism could not be made to stick to the Muslims, either because the latter could point to the teachings of the *qadariyyah*, or because after the heat of the initial controversies, Muslim scholars did in fact come up with ways to preserve the moral accountability of individuals, even in the face of their predestinarian ideas, resulting from their views on the divine omnipotence and omniscience[29].

Even Theodore Abū Qurrah did not say that all Muslims are determinists, nor did he imply it. Rather, he simply combatted those determinist ideas which came to the fore in the course of the controversies over human moral responsibility which arose initially among the Muslims. And, as we shall see below, he combatted this moral determinism, as much as possible, in the very Arabic terms which recall nothing so much as the idiom of the *kalām* the Muslims themselves came to employ to reject the same determinist ideas. So the matter came full circle, and it soon disappeared as a significant topic of Muslim/Christian debate in Arabic. Among the Greek speakers, on the other hand, and those influenced by them outside of the realm of Islam, who did not keep up with developments in Islamic thought after the early ninth century, the issue of free will persisted as a minor topic in the ongoing campaign to discredit Islam[30].

One recension of the *Disputatio* attributed to John of Damascus, the so called Galland text, puts the issue of the human power to determine good or evil behavior in the first place among the topics of dispute between Christians and Muslims. This position in the text for such a relatively minor topic, even coming ahead of the discussion of Christ, is eccentric by comparison with any other Christian polemical tract. It calls one's attention once again to the fragmentary origins of the *Disputatio*, among the *disjecta membra* of the Greek reports of Theodore Abū Qurrah's answers to Islamic challenges to Christian beliefs[31].

Daniel J. Sahas, the most recent scholar to tabulate the correspondences between the issues raised in the *Disputatio* and issues which one can

---

[29] One thinks in particular of the Asharite doctrine. See GIMARET, *Théories de l'acte humain* (n. 1 above).

[30] See Adel-Théodore KHOURY, *Polémique byzantine contre l'islam* (VIIIe-XIIIe s.) (Leiden, 1972), pp. 323-338.

[31] *PG*, vol. 94 (Lequien), cols. 1585-1596; *PG*, vol. 96 (Galland), cols. 1335-1348; SAHAS, *John of Damascus on Islam*, pp. 142-149; KOTTER, *Die Schriften* (n. 11 above), IV, pp. 425-432. See the remarks of John MEYENDORF, *Byzantine Views of Islam*, in *Dumbarton Oaks Papers* 18 (1964), p. 117.

also document in early Muslim religious texts, lists six such correspondences which appear in the course of the debate about the human choice of good or evil: God's omnipotence, man's power of self determination (τὸ αὐτεξούσιον) or lack thereof, God's justice, creation versus the natural generation of the child resulting from immoral sexual behavior, God's fore-knowledge, and God's long-suffering patience with human disobedience to His will[32]. Sahas' purpose is to demonstrate that the *Disputatio* in fact reflects actual subjects of discussion among the Muslims. As we mentioned above, others such as Morris Seale or Harry Austryn Wolfson have been anxious to see in these same passages evidence of the Christian thought which in their view underlies the development of the *qadariyyah* in Islam[33]. Becker noted that the discussion of these issues in the *Disputatio* is predicated on the assumption that the controversy had already been registered in Islam, and that determinism was simply the Islamic doctrine[34].

Relying on the insights of all these earlier scholars, and seeing no need once again here to rehearse the arguments of these passages in the *Disputatio*, what the present writer wishes to suggest is a new hypothesis for their interpretation. Suppose that the arguments in the *Disputatio* were designed to oppose one current of ideas in Islam, that of the predestinarians, and to rebut them with traditional Christian teachings, by presenting these teachings in language which summons up yet another current of ideas in Islam, ideas more compatible with Christianity, those of the *Qadariyyah*, or the early *Mu'tazilah*. This is an apologetical method, as we shall see below, which is entirely characteristic of Theodore Abū Qurrah's manner of arguing. With it, one may suppose, Abū Qurrah, or whoever else employed it in the *Disputatio*, would have intended to commend the credibility of the Christian teachings on human willing, in phrases which he hoped would find a modicum of plausibility with some Muslims, or among those under the influence of Islamic intellectual life. For his theses mirror the ideas of some influential Muslim thinkers on the same subject. And in the *Disputatio* this mirroring effect, in a couple of instances, even survives the translation into Greek, or the Greek report of the Christian arguments. This has been the phenomenon which has been responsible for prompting Morris Seale and others to speak of «certain parallelisms which betray depen-

---

[32] SAHAS, *John of Damascus on Islam*, pp. 103-112.
[33] See nn. 2 and 4 above.
[34] See n. 8 above.

dence»[35], when they have read the *Disputatio* with particular Islamic texts mind.

Concretely, it is clear that of the six theses characteristic of the *Qadariyyah* which the Muslim heresiographer Muḥammad ibn Aḥmad ibn ʿAbd ar-Raḥmān al-Malaṭī (d. 987) found refuted in the earlier work of Ḫušayš ibn Aṣram Abū ʿĀṣim (d. 867), at least four of them can also be found affirmed in some fashion in the *Disputatio*[36]. Moreover, and perhaps more importantly, one can even find substantial agreement with most of the ideas about human moral determining power affirmed in the *Disputatio*, in the influential letter-treatise of al-Ḥasan al-Baṣrī (d. 728), who flourished as early as the days when John of Damascus himself had barely begun to think of a monastic career[37]. Given this coincidence of agreement, *mutatis mutandis*, of the theses espoused in the *Disputatio* with those held by some important Muslim intellectuals whose ideas were prized in the eighth and ninth centuries, it is difficult to avoid the conclusion that the Christian apologist in the *Disputatio* was purposefully taking advantage of the currency of certain ideas among Muslims to enhance the credibility of similar Christian ideas, over against the incompatible suggestions of yet another set of Islamic, predestinarian ideas which were rapidly gaining ground in the first Abbasid century.

In the context of the present study it is important to notice that there is in fact no explicit mention of «freedom» or «free choice» in the *Disputatio*. The Christian apologist here deals with some troublesome Islamic ideas about human moral determination in the very terms in

---

[35] SEALE, *Muslim Theology* (see note 2 above), p. 74.

[36] See Muḥammad ibn Aḥmad ibn ʿAbd ar-Raḥmān al-Malaṭī, *At-tanbīh wa r-radd ʿalā ahl al-ahwāʾ wa l-bidaʿ* (Muḥammad Zāhid ibn al-Ḥasan al-Bakūtharī, ed.; Cairo, 1949), pp. 157-167. See Ḫušayš' project mentioned on p. 91. The six theses are translated into English in WATT, *The Formative Period*, pp. 94-95. For the parallels with the *Disputatio* see especially SAHAS, *John of Damascus on Islam*, pp. 103-112.

[37] See the text of the letter in Helmut RITTER, *Studien zur Geschichte der islamischen Frömmigkeit*, in *Der Islam* 21 (1933), pp. 67-82. Ritter's discussion of «das *Qadar*problem» appears on pp. 57-64. See also Michael SCHWARZ, *The Letter of al-Ḥasan al-Baṣrī*, in *Oriens* 20 (1967), pp. 15-30; J. VAN ESS, *Anfänge muslimischer Theologie* (note 1 above), pp. 27-29. Michael COOK, *Early Muslim Dogma*, pp. 117-123, attacks the arguments advanced by Van Ess for assuming the authenticity of the letter and for dating it to the time of ʿAbd al-Malik, and wants to leave open the possibility for a date later in the Umayyad period, when the letter may have been forged. A date anywhere in the first half of the eighth Christian century is not incompatible with the ideas espoused in the present article. John Wansbrough's ascription of the letter to the end of the eighth Christian century puts it precisely in the milieu in which Theodore Abū Qurrah worked. See John WANSBROUGH, *Quranic Studies; Sources and Methods of Scriptural Interpretation* (London, 1977), pp. 160-164.

which the issue is discussed among Muslims. In particular, as both Daniel J. Sahas and Harry Austryn Wolfson have shown[38], there is a parallel significance to be observed in the meaning of the terms *al-qadar* and τὸ αὐτεξούσιον, in certain contexts. The virtual identity of significance to be seen in the deployment of some forms of these two terms, when they are used in the discussion of human choice, should not be overlooked. The debate among Muslims arose precisely over who had the ultimate determining power (*al-qadar*) in the good and evil doings of human beings, God or the humans involved in them. And in the *Disputatio* one finds a Christian response to just this dilemma, put forward within a set of distinctions which evokes traditional Christian ideas on the subject, and which also manages to state them in terms well calculated to take sides in the current debates among Muslims. However, the issue of «freedom» as such did not come up in the course of this controversy. It was not raised by the Muslims, nor does it appear in the *Disputatio*.

Theodore Abū Qurrah was the writer who introduced the concept of «freedom» into the discussion of human moral responsibility, when this issue became a point of controversy between Christians and Muslims. A consideration of his Arabic tract on this subject is the set purpose of the next section of this article.

II. Theodore Abū Qurrah's Arabic Tract on Human Freedom

Among the Arabic works of Abū Qurrah which Constantin Bacha edited in 1904 there appears one which is devoted exclusively to affirming the thesis that «from God man has in his created nature a steadfast freedom (*ḥurriyyah*), and that no constraint overcomes man's freedom in any way whatever»[39]. This tract is included in a manuscript copied as recently as the year 1735. But its copyist testifies that he worked from a text written in the year 1051 by a monk named Agapius, who in turn testified that he had as his exemplar an old manuscript written at Mar Sabas monastery[40]. Since we have the tract on human freedom from no

---

[38] Sahas, *John of Damascus on Islam*, p. 104, n. 6; Wolfson, *Philosophy of the Kalām*, p. 620.

[39] Bacha, *Les œuvres arabes*, p. 9. The entire tract appears on pp. 9-22. See the German translation in Graf, *Die arabischen Schriften* (see note 9 above), pp. 223-238.

[40] See Bacha's discussion in *Un traité des œuvres arabes de Théodore Abou-Kurra* (Tripoli de Syrie and Rome, 1905), p. 8.

other manuscript tradition than this one, it is important to observe that its pedigree in fact stretches back to Abū Qurrah's, and John of Damascus', old monastery in Palestine. For it was only among the monks of Palestine that human freedom of choice seems to have found its way into Christian Arabic literature, as a set topic of controversy between Christians and Muslims.

Abū Qurrah proceeds in a very orderly fashion in this tract on human freedom to combat what he views to be the errors of those who would deny either freedom's very existence, or its effectiveness. It will become clear in the review of his arguments below that Muslims were among his adversaries, although he never names them as such. The reason must be that in this matter not all Muslims propounded the views against which Abū Qurrah argued, but only those whom their own Muslim opponents dubbed «*al-Muğbirah*»[41], along with those whose predestinarian views, Abū Qurrah argued, were liable to precipitate them into the deeper errors of Manichaeism. For the rest, it will become clear, Abū Qurrah hopes to persuade them of the Christian point of view, arguing in an Arabic idiom which is full of words and phrases familiar to the Muslims, including at least one quotation from the *Qur'ān*.

Of course, one must suppose that the Arabic speaking Christian community was Abū Qurrah's primary audience. Nevertheless, there is some reason to believe that at least some Muslims became familiar with his thought, perhaps even with his ideas on free will. And in this connection one would love to know at least the table of contents of the now lost work of the Baghdadī Mu'tazilite writer, 'Īsā ibn Ṣubayḥ al-Murdār (d. 840), «Against Abū Qurrah, the Christian»[42].

From the point of view of the Christian intellectual heritage, it will become clear in what follows that Abū Qurrah is strongly indebted to the Syriac doctrinal tradition. For his insistence on the human freedom (*al-ḥurriyyah al-insiyyah*) that is proper to authentic moral responsibility has its roots in the concern for freedom (*ḥêrûtâ*) which is evident in the Syriac tradition, reaching all the way back to St. Ephraem[43], and finding expression as late as the ninth century in the work of the monophysite bishop of Mossul, Moshe bar Kephâ (d. 905)[44]. One should not be

---

[41] See WATT, *The Formative Period*, p. 118.

[42] Bayard DODGE, *The Fihrist of al-Nadīm* (2 vols.; New York, 1970), vol. I, p. 394.

[43] On this important subject see now T. BOU MANSOUR, *La liberté chez saint Ephrem le syrien*, in *ParOr* 11 (1983), pp. 89-156, to be continued.

[44] See n. 28 above. Moshe bar Kephâ's tract is the subject of a study on its own merits. In the present connection it will be important for its testimony that Muslims do believe in

surprised that Abū Qurrah owes his intellectual formation on this subject to the Syrians and not to the Greeks. After all, he was an Edessan by birth. Moreover, it is becoming increasingly clear that the Syrian heritage played a prominent role in the Arabicization of life in the Melkite monasteries in Palestine from the late eighth century onward[45]. So Abū Qurrah must not be thought of merely as «un continuateur arabe de saint Jean Damascène»[46], but also as an original thinker in his own right, indebted to his Syriac heritage as well as to what he learned of the Greek tradition at Mar Sabas monastery.

A. *Status Quaestionis*

At the very beginning of the tract on freedom Abū Qurrah makes it clear that solicitude for moral probity is his major concern. And in particular his aspiration is to refute the pretexts of those who allege that they are in some way compelled to commit the sins of which they are guilty. As Abū Qurrah himself puts it:

The one who seeks pretexts for sin says that he is compelled (*maqhūr*) to follow his desire, even if following it is morally wrong (*qabīḥ*). He is one of two: he is either the one who maintains that he has no freedom, and he says that he is constrained (*mağbūr*) by his creator to do whatever he does of good or evil; or he is the one who says that God created freedom for him, but that for some reason a compulsion (*al-qahr*) has been introduced into his freedom, and so it is constrained to do what it does of good or evil[47].

The principal burden of the tract then is to reject the allegations of those whom Abū Qurrah includes in either one of these two categories: those who say they have no freedom of moral action, but are constrained by God; and those who say that a compulsion (*al-qahr*) has overcome their freedom.

Abū Qurrah also mentioned two categories of opponents to the idea of human freedom in his treatise on the death of Christ. There, of course, the principal purpose was to explain the doctrine of the redemption, and to refute the Nestorians and the Monophysites. But it also entailed a statement of the Christian view of human moral responsibility. Abū Qurrah said:

---

freedom, but also say that good and evil are prescribed by God. See WRIGHT, *Catalogue* (see note 28 above), vol. II, p. 854.

[45] See Sidney H. GRIFFITH, *Greek into Arabic: Life and Letters in the Monasteries of Palestine in the Ninth Century*, to appear.

[46] See the title of P. Ignace DICK's important articles, cited in n. 21 above.

[47] BACHA, *Les œuvres arabes*, p. 9.

Regarding the doing of good or evil, the Church says that God created man having freedom (*ḥurriyyah*), and empowered him to choose what he wanted of good or evil, and to do it ... The Church's doctrine (*qawl*) has duly taken into account two other doctrines, each one of which differs from the other, and both of which differ with the doctrine of the Church. The first of them is the doctrine of those who say that God fashioned every single human being, and constrained him to do good or evil; He created some unhappy and some happy. The other doctrine is the doctrine of the Manichaeans ... They forge Satan into another god, along with God; they make God the cause of every good, and they make Satan the cause of every evil[48].

In the milieu in which Abū Qurrah pursued his career as a controversialist, one does not have to look far to discover the evidence that Muslims were in fact among the adversaries against whose teachings he supported the doctrine of human freedom. In the first place there were the so called *Muğbirah* among the Muslims, as mentioned above, including the followers of Ğahm ibn Ṣafwān, according to the Muslim heresiographers[49]. One will recall that in the account of such things which was to become traditional for Muslims, ash-Shahrastānī attributes the following view to Ğahm:

Man does not have determining power over anything, nor may he be described with any capability. Rather, he is constrained (*mağbūr*) in his actions; he has no determining power, no will, and no choice. Rather, God Most High creates actions in him commensurate with what He creates in all the inanimate bodies, and they are ascribed to him metaphorically, just as they are ascribed to the inanimate bodies[50].

But Ğahm ibn Ṣafwān and his followers were not the only Muslims included among the *Muğbirah*. One will recall that the Mu'tazilite scholars so characterized the predestinationists among the ancestors of the *ahl al-ḥadīṯ wa s-sunnah*[51]. And Abū Qurrah himself must have had this latter group of Muslims in mind when in his treatise on the death of Christ he reported that those who say that man is constrained to do good or evil are also the ones who say of God that «He created some unhappy and some happy»[52]. The latter phrase is an allusion to a passage in the *Qur'ān, Hūd* (11):105[53], whose terms appear in a number of traditions customarily quoted by the predestinationists. One such tradition which

48 Bacha, *Les œuvres arabes*, p. 50.

49 See Watt, *The Formative Period*, p. 148.

50 Muḥammad ibn 'Abd al-Karīm ash-Šahrastānī, *Kitāb al-milal wan-niḥal* (Cairo: al-Azhar, 1328/1910), p. 136.

51 See Watt, *The Formative Period*, pp. 117-118.

52 See n. 48 above.

53 *Hūd* (11):105, فمنهم شقيّ وسعيد.

was popular among them pictures God in dialogue with an angel at the creation of a man in the womb of his mother. At the end of the process there is the report: «Then God makes him unhappy or happy»[54]. So one may readily see in Abū Qurrah's words a clear reference to issues which were before the minds of the Muslim intellectuals of his day.

As for those in Abū Qurrah's milieu who held that men do have freedom, but that in real life there is a compulsion (*al-qahr*) which overcomes it, one is put first of all in mind of the title of chapter six of Moshe bar Kephâ's second discourse on human freedom, «Against the Muslims, who, even they, believe in freedom (*ḥêrûtâ*), but they say that good or evil is prescribed for them by God»[55]. Then, to judge by Abū Qurrah's own arguments, as they will appear below, the prescription claimed by the Muslims in his day must have been not only the predetermination of some to be happy and others to be unhappy, but God's foreknowledge of the good or evil in human behavior. For some of Abū Qurrah's adversaries seem to have argued that it is divine foreknowledge which in the end provides the compulsion (*al-qahr*) which should override any freedom enjoyed by men. And, as a matter of fact, among Muslim thinkers one finds references to God's foreknowledge (*sābiq ʿilm Allāh*) as such a determinant already in the epistle treatise attributed to the caliph ʿUmar ibn ʿAzīz (d. 720) against the Qadarites[56].

Both the treatise on Christ's death and the tract on human freedom name Mani and the Manichaeans among the adversaries against whom the case for freedom must be made. At first sight, the modern scholar may be inclined to think that Abū Qurrah brought the Manichaeans into the argument only for traditional reasons. Ephraem the Syrian had combatted them when he was championing the doctrine of human freedom[57]. Among the polemical works ascribed to John of Damascus there is a dialogue *Contra Manichaeos*, in which a case is made for the human power of moral determination[58]. So one might initially think that Abū Qurrah named the Manichaeans as adversaries simply out of respect for his intellectual masters. But there is more to it than this simple

[54] See VAN ESS, *Zwischen Ḥadīṯ und Theologie* (note 1 above), pp. 24-32.

[55] WRIGHT, *Catalogue* (see note 28 above), vol. II, p. 854. Moshe bar Kephâ's term for the Muslims is *Mahgrāyê*.

[56] See the text, translation, and commentary in VAN ESS, *Anfänge* (note 1 above), pp. 113-176, ٥٤ - ٤٣ ; and Cook's comments, *Early Muslim Dogma*, pp. 124-136.

[57] See Edmund BECK, *Ephräms Polemik gegen Mani und die Manichäer* (CSCO, vol. 391: Louvain, 1978), pp. 143-149.

[58] See KOTTER, *Die Schriften des Johannes von Damaskus* (note 15 above), IV, pp. 334-398, esp. p. 388. *PG*, vol. 94, cols. 1503-1584, esp. col. 1568.

anachronism. Since both Christians and Muslims rejected Manichaeism[59], Abū Qurrah could argue that to deny human freedom would logically leave open an option for Manichaean dualism. Furthermore, as Abū Qurrah himself noted in another treatise[60], the Manichaeans were among the so called *zanādiqah*, the misbelievers who proved to be so troublesome to the Abbasid court in Baghdad during the very years when the scholarly monk of Mar Sabas was busy writing his apologies for Christian doctrine[61]. So it is clear that when Abū Qurrah wrote his tract on human freedom, the Manichaeans were a present danger on the intellectual horizon, even for the Muslims. And the Christian apologist could reasonably pose the threat of a logical opening toward Manichaean dualism in the denial of human freedom to support his case in favor of the traditional Christian doctrine.

As for Abū Qurrah's purpose in writing his tract on human freedom, he states it himself in the introduction, with a reference to the overall apologetical goal which he had addressed in another treatise. He says,

> In this *mīmar* our purpose is not to prove that of all that is ascribed to God, the Gospel is the true, perfect Law. Nor is it that we would make the nay-sayers (*ahl al-ǧuḥūd*) acknowledge its truth. We have already done this in another place[62]. Our purpose is only to affirm that there is freedom (*al-ḥurriyyah*) in man's character (*ṣibġati l-insān*), and that there is no compulsion (*al-qahr*) put upon it from any cause, that it should yield spontaneously (*ṭaw'an*) to that cause[63].

B. *The Muǧbirah*

Against the adversaries who maintained that man has no freedom because he is constrained (*maǧbūr*) to the good or evil he performs Abū Qurrah advanced arguments from a consideration of divine justice, taken in conjunction with the divine command and prohibition addressed to men in the scriptures.

---

[59] See Georges VAJDA, *Le témoignage d'al-Māturidī sur la doctrine des Manichéens, des Daysanites et des Marcionites*, in *Arabica* 13 (1966), pp. 1-38, 113-128.

[60] See Ignace DICK, *Théodore Abuqurra, traité de l'existence du Créateur et de la vraie religion, introduction et texte critique*, (coll. *PAC* 3; Jounieh and Rome, 1982), pp. 205-208.

[61] See Georges VAJDA, *Les zindiqs en pays d'islam au début de la période abbaside*, in *RSO* 17 (1938), pp. 173-229.

[62] A reference to the author's earlier apologetic treatise: «On the authentication of the holy law of Moses and of the prophets who prophesied about Christ, and the holy Gospel which Christ's disciples transmitted to the gentiles — he being born of the virgin Mary; also the authentication of the orthodoxy which people ascribe to Chalcedon, and the invalidation of every creed which Christians profess except this one». BACHA, *Un traité* (note 40 above), p. 7.

[63] BACHA, *Les œuvres arabes*, p. 10.

Abū Qurrah assumes that his adversary will agree that God is just (*'adl*). So he proceeds to define the issue of justice as follows.

It is of justice (*'adl*) that of his own accord one who is just (*'ādil*) puts equal things equally, according to the state of their equality[64].

Accordingly, the argument goes, if man is constrained (*maǧbūr*) to what he does of good or evil he must be like one of the irrational animals. And the question becomes, «How then has God in His justice deemed it right to command and prohibit man, to promise him a reward for obeying Him, and a punishment for disobeying Him, and not done the same for the rest of the animals»[65]? Furthermore, «How could it be correct for God, that is to say just, to ordain for man something of which he is incapable (*lā yuṭīq*)»[66]? «Far be it from God», says Abū Qurrah with the Qur'ān, «to impose a task on a soul, except to its capacity»[67].

If the adversary suggests that God has issued commands and prohibitions to men «to have an argument (*al-ḥuǧǧah*) against them when He punishes them»[68], Abū Qurrah replies that as such it would be an unjust argument. For men who would be constrained to what they did of good or evil would have been «innately disposed» (*maǧbūl*), without having the ability (*istiṭā'ah*) to shrink back, or to stretch forward»[69], i.e., to shy away from or to welcome a given course of action. And this circumstance in turn should pose the following choice, says Abū Qurrah, for anyone who advocates such a doctrine of innate disposition (*al-ǧabl*): «You should either deny any command or prohibition from God, since you advocate innate disposition; or you should confess that God has given human beings commands and prohibitions, since you disavow innate disposition, and advocate freedom»[70].

---

[64] ان من العدل ان ينزل العادل من نفسه الاشياء المستوية بالسواء فى حال استوائها. BACHA, *Les œuvres arabes*, p. 10, 11. 7 and 8. See the same definition, only very slightly altered on l. 12.

[65] BACHA, *Les œuvres arabes*, p. 10.

[66] BACHA, *Les œuvres arabes*, p. 10.

[67] BACHA, *Les œuvres arabes*, p. 10. The allusion to the *Qur'ān* at the end of the quotation refers to a phrase which appears five times in the *Qur'ān*, with only slight variations: *al-Baqarah* (2):233, 286; *al-An'ām* (6):152; *al-A'rāf* (7):42; *al-Mu'minūn* (23):62. Al-Ḥasan al-Baṣrī also cited it in much the same sense as did Abū Qurrah. See RITTER, *Studien zur Geschichte* (note 37 above), p. 77.

[68] BACHA, *Les œuvres arabes*, p. 11. Abū Qurrah employes the word 'argument' (*al-ḥuǧǧah*) in a sense in which one finds it in the *Qur'ān*, of people having an 'argument', or a reason for dispute, against the believers (*al-Baqarah* (2):150), against God, (*al-Nisā'* (4):165), or of God having an 'argument' *vis à vis* human beings, (*al-An'ām* (6):149).

[69] BACHA, *Les œuvres arabes*, p. 11.

[70] BACHA, *Les œuvres arabes*, p. 11.

Finally, in his argument against the idea that men are somehow constrained to the good or evil they perform, Abū Qurrah appeals to the common experience of people, outside of the religious context of divine command or prohibition. He points to the fact that in both the civil and military spheres of life, the forms of social organization presume freedom in man's character (*ṣibġah*). As much may be seen in a king's government of his army, or a community's (*ummah*) appointment of judges (*al-quḍāh*) to administer its law (*šarīʿah*). So in the light of this experience, Abū Qurrah concludes that «people will not have agreed unanimously to this unless the human character (*aṣ-ṣibġah al-insiyyah*) was silently summoning them and notifying them that in it there is an ability (*istiṭāʿah*), a freedom (*ḥurriyyah*), which prompts the soul (and the body which subjugates it) to what it wants of what suits it or disgusts it»[71].

C. *A Compulsion on Freedom?*

Against those whom he presents as holding that God created man with freedom, but that now there is an unwonted compulsion (*al-qahr*) placed upon it, Abū Qurrah deploys a simple set of disjunctive propositions which demand an either/or response. It is a rapid argument, which in the theistic context has a foregone conclusion. Abū Qurrah is anxious merely to provide a logical transition to the subject which really attracts him, Manichaeism.

Such a compulsion, Abū Qurrah says, could derive only from God, or from another than God. If it would be from God himself, inevitably it would mean that God would have acted out of ignorance in creating freedom in the first place, or He would have changed His mind after seeing how men used it, or He would initially have given men freedom out of malevolence and voided it after repentance. It is evident that none of these options could be acceptable to any Jew, Christian, or Muslim.

If the compulsion in question must therefore come from another than God, Abū Qurrah claims that this other source would have to be either of God's creation, or of other than God's creation. The first option is impossible, Abū Qurrah argues, because it pits God in opposition to Himself. Consequently the source of this compulsion would have to be something other than God's creation, which has attacked it and despoiled it without God's permission. And this is the point to which Abū

---

[71] BACHA, *Les œuvres arabes*, p. 12. The phrase «and the body which subjugates it» is in parentheses in the text. One may doubt its authenticity. It resembles Abū Qurrah's description of Mani's teaching, see p. 13.

Qurrah wants to bring the argument. He now charges that «the holder of this thesis has fallen back onto the likes of the thesis of the stupid Mani, which introduces two beings (*kawnayn*), one good, one evil»[72].

D. *Manichaeanism*

Two things in particular strike the reader about Abū Qurrah's discussion of Manichaeanism in the tract on human freedom. The first of them is the fact that he devotes more space to this subject than he does to any other single issue which comes up for consideration in the tract[73]. And the second thing is the ridiculing, almost vulgar tone of voice which Abū Qurrah adopts in the course of his arguments against Mani, as if the heresiarch were not dead for almost six hundred years, but actively espousing his views in the writer's own milieu. In these pages Abū Qurrah addresses Mani directly (*yā Mānī*), calls him 'stupid' (*al-aḥmaq*), dubs his mission an utter flop (*al-ḥaybah*), and characterizes his doctrine as the utmost in ugliness and stupidity (*asmaǧ as-samāǧah wa aḥmaq al-ḥumq*). This approach contrasts notably with the sober tones of Abū Qurrah's description of Manichaeanism in his treatise on «The Existence of the Creator and the True Religion»[74]. One can only conclude that the intellectual threat of Manichaean doctrines to both Christians and Muslims must have been sufficiently real in Abū Qurrah's day for him to be able to use Mani so prominently as a foil in the defense of the Christian position on the doctrine of the human freedom to choose good or evil behavior.

To begin with Abū Qurrah reminds the reader of the Manichaean idea that on its own the human soul is free of evil, but that in its present state the body has subjugated (*qahara*) the soul, since on the cosmic scale Satan has captured the souls of men from God and has imprisoned them in bodies. For Abū Qurrah this should mean that Mani's mission should be to release the captive souls. Instead Mani preaches virtue to souls which *ex hypothesi*, being in a state of captivity, should be incapable of it!

Abū Qurrah professes himself to be astounded that Mani cites a Gospel text in support of his views: «The good tree cannot produce bad fruit, nor can the bad tree produce good fruit» (Mt. 7:18). For the Manichaean doctrine in fact has the innately good soul inevitably doing

---

[72] BACHA, *Les œuvres arabes*, p. 13.
[73] BACHA, *Les œuvres arabes*, pp. 13-18.
[74] See n. 60 above.

evil actions with the body which imprisons it. And, on Mani's own premises, the body, being innately evil, should be radically incapable of doing good deeds. No moral change therefore should be possible. Pointing out this logical dilemma for the Manichaeans gives Abū Qurrah the opportunity to advance his own interpretation of the Gospel passage, «By the Gospel saying, Christ our God means only the good intention and the bad intention»[75].

The intention (*an-niyyah*) is changeable, Abū Qurrah says, but from a good intention only good works can follow, and from a bad intention only bad works can follow. So, claims Abū Qurrah, John the Baptist said to the Jewish scholars, «You offspring of vipers, who has guided you to flee from the wrath to come? Do works suitable to repentance (*at-tawbah*)». (Mt. 3:7-8) «Do you not see», Abū Qurrah then asks, «that he named them the offspring of vipers, and that he demanded from them works of repentance, because by their own willing (*bimašī'atihim*) they became the offspring of vipers, and by their own willing they can change their state (*ḥāl*) and do works of repentance»[76]?

Abū Qurrah proposes that his own biblical exegesis shows clearly the weakness of Mani's ideas, and that they are in fact self contradictory. And then Abū Qurrah engages in further arguments *ad hominem*, claiming that Mani's own bodiliness, according to his own doctrines, should invalidate his teachings. He contrasts the sinful lives of Manichaeans with the virtuous lives of the orthodox Christians, who, due to their good intentions (*liḥusni niyyātihim*)[77], are in fact able to bring their bodies into submission to their souls. Such a person «sets his intention (*an-niyyah*)», Abū Qurrah explains, «by the true teaching which is the holy Gospel of Christ, the son of the virgin Mary»[78].

The intention, therefore, is the very epicenter of free choice for Abū Qurrah. Good works are dependent on good intention (*ḥusnu n-niyyah*) for their goodness, and they are recompensed according to intention, not according to their outward appearances. Such is Abū Qurrah's teaching in a number of places in his writings, not just in the tract on human freedom[79]. And in the present context this doctrine is particularly

---

[75] BACHA, *Les œuvres arabes*, p. 14.

[76] BACHA, *Les œuvres arabes*, p. 15.

[77] BACHA, *Les œuvres arabes*, p. 17.

[78] BACHA, *Les œuvres arabes*, p. 17.

[79] See the relevant texts cited in GRIFFITH, *The Controversial Theology* (note 10 above), pp. 84-85. The apologetical success of Abū Qurrah's emphasis on the «intention» for which an action is performed may be seen in one instance in particular. It is his insistence that the

significant because it is in the free play of human intentionality that Abū Qurrah finds not only a counter argument to the Manichaeans, but the focal point of his reply to anyone who would diminish man's radical moral freedom. As he says in regard to his somewhat lengthy rebuttal of Mani, «We have given his doctrine so close an opposition only because of its similarity to the doctrine of whoever wants to invalidate freedom by putting a compulsion (*al-qahr*) upon it»[80]. To allow any such compulsion, Abū Qurrah clearly argues, logically leaves open the possibility for Mani's radical dualism. Whereas the proper appreciation of the function of human intentionality may adequately explain the appearance of moral evil in the world, as well as man's responsibility for it.

This emphasis on the intention is not without roots in the Christian tradition. The Greek word which the translator chose for Abū Qurrah's *an-niyyah* in his Greek *opusculum* IX is προαίρεσις[81], a term which had appeared already in Aristotle's ethics and which the Fathers of the Church had employed in the same sense the word has when used to express Abū Qurrah's thought[82]. What is significant in the milieu in which the tract on human freedom appeared, however, is not this Greek resonance of the vocabulary but the fact that the concept of intention (*an-niyyah*) played an important role in contemporary Islamic thought. It does not appear in the *Qur'ān* to be sure, but much is said about intention in the *ḥadīth* literature, and for this reason the concept of intention was important in both law and piety, as one learns from Abū Qurrah's younger contemporary, Ḥāriṯ al-Muḥāsibī (d. 857)[83]. So one may conclude here that Abū

Jews may rightly be blamed for Christ's crucifixion, in spite of it being his major redemptive act, because of their malevolent intention toward him. See the argument as attributed to Abū Qurrah, and preserved both in Arabic and Greek, in Sidney H. GRIFFITH, *Some Unpublished Arabic Sayings Attributed to Theodore Abū Qurrah*, in *Le Museon* 92 (1979), pp. 29-35. It reappears in the *Summa Theologiae Arabica*, a work of the second half of the ninth century, copied by Stephen of Ramlah in the year 877 in BM Or. MS 4950, ff. 119r-119v. See SAMIR Khalil, *Kitāb ğāmi' wuğūh al-īmān wa muğādalat Abī Qurrah 'an ṣalb al-Masīḥ*, in *al-Maçarrat* 70 (1984), pp. 411-427. This concern for the responsibility for Christ's crucifixion also appears in the *Disputatio Saraceni et Christiani*, at the very end of the section which has to do with the discussion of the origin of evil, and the role of human willing in its appearance in the world. But here there is no explicit mention of the role of «intention». See SAHAS, *John of Damascus on Islam*, pp. 146-149; KOTTER, *Die Schriften* (note 11 above), IV, pp. 431-432.

[80] BACHA, *Les œuvres arabes*, p. 18.

[81] *PG*, 97, col. 1529C.

[82] See the entry in G. W. H. LAMPE, *A Patristic Greek Lexicon* (Oxford, 1961), pp. 1133-1134.

[83] See Margaret SMITH, *An Early Mystic of Baghdad: a Study of the Life and Teaching*

Qurrah's own emphasis on intention in his Arabic apologies was due to this currency of the term in the Islamic milieu in which he was busy commending the truthfulness of Christian doctrines. He relied on the conviction this term already carried in this milieu, and so he apparently felt no need to define it in any great detail.

E. *God's Foreknowledge*

But what was the compulsion (*al-qahr*) which some people put upon human freedom, which Abū Qurrah claimed should logically force them unwittingly into the errors of Manichaeism? It was God's foreknowledge (*sābiq ʿilm Allāh*). Abū Qurrah explained the reasoning of such a person in this way: «He says that God's knowledge of affairs comes first, and what comes first in God's knowledge must inevitably come to be. And the doer of what must inevitably come to be is compelled (*maqhūr*) to do it. Therefore, human freedom (*al-ḥurriyyah al-insiyyah*) is constrained (*maqhūr*) to do what it does of good or evil»[84].

Abū Qurrah's immediate answer to this proposal is that the first one on whom it would put a compulsion is God himself, an obviously unacceptable position. «If what comes first into God's knowledge must inevitably come to be, and the doer of what must inevitably come to be is compelled to what he does, as you have maintained, then God has become compelled to do what was first in His mind that He would do. But this is the ugliest thing that has ever occurred to anyone's mind, that God should be compelled»[85].

From this point it follows for Abū Qurrah that neither does God's foreknowledge put a compulsion on human freedom. For if it did so it would effectively nullify God's will for men freely to follow His commands and prohibitions. And this state of being would in turn also put a compulsion on God, which is admittedly an unacceptable option. So the choices are only three: to deny God's foreknowledge, an obvious absurdity; to say that God is compelled, which is the greatest fabrication against God (*al-iftirāʾ ʿalā Allāh*, see *an-Nisāʾ* (4):50); or to admit that God's knowledge puts no constraint, either on God Himself, or on human freedom. And the latter can be the only true option, says Abū Qurrah.

---

of Ḥārith b. Asad al-Muḥāsibī A.D. 781-857 (Cambridge, 1935), pp. 105-106; J. VAN ESS, *Die Gedankenwelt des Ḥāriṯ al-Muḥāsibi* (Bonn, 1961), pp. 145-146.

[84] BACHA, *Les œuvres arabes*, p. 18.

[85] BACHA, *Les œuvres arabes*, p. 18.

As for how this can be so, Abū Qurrah explains that «God does what He has foreknown; He has the power (*yaqduru*) not to do it. Human freedom will do what God foreknows of it; it has the power (*qādirah*) not to do it»[86]. And then Abū Qurrah spells out what he means:

You should not think that God will do what He has foreknown just because His foreknowledge precedes His acting, or that human freedom will do what God has foreknown of it, due to God's foreknowledge of what it is going to do. No, God, may He be blessed, will do what He wants (*šā'*) by perfect power (*al-qudrah at-tāmmah*), no less than what He would have done, had He not had foreknowledge of what He was going to do. So also human freedom manages as it wants (*šā'at*), by the power (*al-qudrah*) which God has given it concerning what He has commanded it, and what He has prohibited to it, no less than how it would have managed had God had no foreknowledge about anything to do with it[87].

Nothing less than this way of thinking will avoid putting a compulsion upon God himself according to Abū Qurrah, so it must be the true doctrine. That he is speaking to an issue which was already confronting the Muslim scholars, and in much these same terms, is clear from such texts as the predestinarian letter against the Qadarites which is usually ascribed to the caliph Umar II[88]. And what is more to the point, Abū Qurrah's position bears a striking resemblance to the line of thought elaborated on this very issue by al-Ḥasan al-Baṣrī, who clearly made the point that God's knowledge cannot be said to force the unbelief of one who has the power (*qādir*) not to disbelieve[89]. So once again Abū Qurrah may be seen to be making an appeal to a current of thought already familiar to Muslims, in a bid to purchase credibility for the Christian doctrine he has to defend.

F. *The Limits of Freedom*

The freedom which Abū Qurrah defends in his tract has its own proper sphere of operation. And its limits are essentially two: its authority (*sulṭān*) concerns what God has ordered and prohibited (*amr wa nahy*); and its province is this world (*ad-dunyah*). A brief word might be said about each of these limits.

[86] BACHA, *Les œuvres arabes*, p. 19.

[87] BACHA, *Les œuvres arabes*, p. 19.

[88] See n. 56 above.

[89] See RITTER, *Studien zur Geschichte*, pp. 77-78, and the English translation of the pertinent passage in SCHWARZ, *The Letter of al-Hasan al-Baṣrī*, pp. 29-30. For both, see note 37 above.

Abū Qurrah explains that it belongs to freedom «to intend what it wants of obedience to Him, or disobedience to Him»[90]. Even if one's will (*mašī'ah*) fails to achieve its effect because of bodily defect or some outward constraint, «this does not prevent freedom from intending what it wills of obedience to God or disobedience to Him, for which it is praised or blamed. For all of its works, it is recompensed for them commensurate with its intention in these works, not commensurate with what the eye sees of the externals of the works»[91].

It is in freedom's interiority, in its intentionality one might say, impervious to outside force, that Abū Qurrah finds the referent for its very name. «Freedom is named freedom», he explains, «because it has authority over itself always, since it inclines where it wills by its act of the will (*irādah*). And this authority (*sulṭān*) is what will not pass away, nor will a compulsion (*al-qahr*) be put on it in any way»[92]. And finally, Abū Qurrah claims, it is a matter of God's justice (*'adl*) that since freedom has authority over its intention, its rewards are «according to the reckoning of its intention»[93].

Once this world has passed away, however, there is no longer the possibility for recompense according to intention. Everything then becomes unalterable (*ġayr mutaġayyar*), Abū Qurrah explains. So one's imperative should now be to exercise his freedom in the work of repentance (*at-tawbah*)[94].

G. *To Deny God's Foreknowledge?*

There must have been some people in the Christian community who thought that to affirm God's foreknowledge of human affairs was effectively to vitiate any real freedom of moral determination on man's part. So they simply denied God's knowledge of future free acts. Abū Qurrah addressed himself to this proposal at the very end of his tract on human freedom, almost as an afterthought. He had already discussed God's foreknowledge earlier in the work. Now his concern was with those who «flee from saying that God has foreknowledge, out of a repugnance for being obliged on its account to put a compulsion on human freedom»[95].

---

[90] BACHA, *Les œuvres arabes*, p. 20.
[91] BACHA, *Les œuvres arabes*, p. 20.
[92] BACHA, *Les œuvres arabes*, p. 20.
[93] BACHA, *Les œuvres arabes*, p. 20.
[94] BACHA, *Les œuvres arabes*, p. 21.
[95] BACHA, *Les œuvres arabes*, p. 21.

Abū Qurrah's rebuttal of this new proposal consists in putting forward a selection of quotations from the Scriptures, mostly from the Gospels (e.g., Jn. 6:70, Mt. 26:34, Mk. 14:21, Mt. 25:41), in which one finds references to future human actions, whose agents, on the presumption of freedom, must nevertheless have been radically able not to perform them. What interested Abū Qurrah in the citation of these passages were their clear testimonies to the fact of divine foreknowledge, particularly in the person of Jesus, the Christ, «our Lord» and «our God», (*rabbunâ ilāhunā*) as Abū Qurrah was careful to specify in his Islamic milieu. So there could be no question of the fact of divine foreknowledge. And once this point is made Abū Qurrah is content to refer the reader back to his earlier discussion about how this foreknowledge cannot be said to put any compulsion (*al-qahr*) on human freedom. For if such would be the case, then God would be unjust in blaming or punishing any malefactor, even Judas or Satan and his angels, whose blameworthy behavior the Scriptures show God foreknew. Far be this from God, says Abū Qurrah[96].

To deny that God has foreknowledge of future free actions seems a strange position to find affirmed by Christians, even for the purpose of defending human freedom. But the fact that Abū Qurrah bases his refutation of this position so largely on quotations from the Gospels makes one conclude that he did mean to argue with Christian opponents on this point. And it is just possible that in the arguments about religion which flourished in the eighth and ninth centuries some Christians adopted formulae which on the face of it seemed to sacrifice divine foreknowledge to the dogma of human freedom. One will recall, however, that Abū Qurrah did not say that his opponents outright denied it, but that they «flee from saying that God has foreknowledge»[97].

In this connection it is instructive to notice that the caliph Umar II's letter against the Qadarites sets out to refute the position of people whose views seemed to be «a rejection of God's knowledge (*radd 'ilm Allāh*)»[98]. And later on the account of the theses of the Qadariyyah preserved by al-Malaṭī says that some of them «deny that knowledge is prior to what

[96] BACHA, *Les œuvres arabes*, pp. 21-22.

[97] See n. 95 above.

[98] See VAN ESS, *Anfänge* (note 1 above), p. ٤٣, and the discussion in COOK, *Early Muslim Dogma*, pp. 124-136.

creatures will do, or to what they will become»[99]. So perhaps one should not be too surprised to discover that similarly some Christians seemed to put the divine foreknowledge in jeopardy, in the course of the same controversy.

III. Conclusion

The *Disputatio Saraceni et Christiani*, in the form in which it has been preserved among the works of John of Damascus and Theodore Abū Qurrah, preserves the gist of some of the arguments which Christians deployed against Muslim determinists and predestinarians during the first Abbasid century. In all probability the work is a Greek report of these arguments as Theodore Abū Qurrah used them, with a demonstrable reliance on the doctrines of John of Damascus, and perhaps with the purposeful intention of echoing the thought of the master. What is striking about the arguments is the fact that the rejection of determinism and predestination is accomplished by adopting positions which also had a currency in the Islamic milieu, among the Qadarites and the *Muʿtazilah*. And this is the hallmark of Theodore Abū Qurrah's apologetical method. But the fact remains that only a few ready arguments are preserved in the *Disputatio*, probably due to their evident compatibility with the works of John of Damascus. These works were just beginning what would become a mass circulation in Byzantium, due to the initial efforts of the refugee monks from Palestine, who must have brought them along when they fled to Constantinople, perhaps during the first decades of the ninth century.

The Arabic tract on human freedom is a more unified essay on the problem of moral determinism, and the appropriate Christian response to it. There can be no doubt about the Islamic milieu in which Abū Qurrah wrote it. As the foregoing analysis has shown, the very diction of the tract demonstrates that the author was speaking the language of the *mutakallimūn*. And there is little or no trace of John of Damascus to be found in it. Rather, in this tract the Abū Qurrah who on his own testimony wrote some thirty treatises in Syriac[100], relied on a tradition of Christian thought with its roots in the works of Ephraem the Syrian.

---

[99] Al-Malaṭī, *At-tanbīh wa r-radd*, p. 165. See this passage also discussed in Cook, *Early Muslim Dogma*, pp. 132-133.

[100] Bacha, *Les œuvres arabes*, pp. 60-61.

Here the emphasis is on freedom (*ḥēruta/al-ḥurriyyah*), a concept which as such found no place in John of Damascus' work.

It is important to take into account this Syriac dimension of Abū Qurrah's thought. One cannot examine it in detail here. But perhaps enough has been said to call attention to its significance. Its influence is an important dimension, which sets Abū Qurrah's work off from anything that is to be found in Greek. It is indigenous to the world of the oriental patriarchates, and, along with the influence of the Muslim *mutakallimūn*, it marks an area of theological development in Abū Qurrah, which, as was said above, makes him more than simply an Arabic continuator of the projects of John of Damascus. He was the first creative theologian whose name we know who wrote in Arabic.

As for the topic of free will, Abū Qurrah's tract remains one of the few Christian statements in Arabic on the subject. It seldom appears in the standard apologetic works which circulated within *dār al-islām*. An exception to this statement is the *Summa Theologiae Arabica*. In the apologetic catechism which comprises chapter XVIII of this work, one may find sections «On *al-qadar*», «On *al-ǧabr*», and «On *qaḍā' Allāh*»[101]. The examination of these sections must await another occasion. But what can be said here about it is that while the work as a whole is not without the influence of Theodore Abū Qurrah[102], these three sections in fact show little debt to his thought. Nevertheless, together with Abū Qurrah's tract on human freedom, both the *Summa*, and even the *Disputatio Saraceni et Christiani*, show a role for Christian thought on the subject of free will in the debates which flourished within the «Sectarian Milieu»[103], which was the caliphate during the centuries prior to the crusades. And that role consisted in the project to state the traditional Christian faith in an Arabic idiom, in which all the problems were set according to the agenda of the Muslim *mutakallimūn*. Yet one can see here the emergence of a truly Christian *'ilm al-kalām*.

---

[101] BM Or. MS 4950, ff. 126v-129v. See n. 79 above.

[102] See SAMIR Khalil, *Notes sur les citations bibliques chez Abū Qurrah*, in *OCP* 44 (1983), pp. 184-191. Look for Sidney H. GRIFFITH, *A Ninth Century Summa Theologiae Arabica*, and SAMIR Khalil, *La «Somme des aspectes de la foi» œuvre d'Abū Qurrah?*, in Khalil SAMIR (Ed.), *Actes du deuxième congrès d'études arabes chrétiennes (1984)*, coll. *OCA* 226 (Rome 1985).

[103] The phrase belongs to John WANSBROUGH, *The Sectarian Milieu; Content and Composition of Islamic Salvation History* (Oxford, 1978), where the influences go all the other way, from Judaism and Christianity to Islam.

VII

Stephen of Ramlah and the Christian Kerygma in Arabic in Ninth-Century Palestine

In the period of time between the Islamic conquest and the coming of the crusaders to Palestine in 1099, Christian pilgrims from East and West continued to visit the Holy Land, and particularly Jerusalem, by the licence of the Islamic government. Among the western visitors during this period at least half a dozen of them published accounts of their journeys.[1] However, these accounts tell one virtually nothing about the life of the local Church, beyond the occasional list of shrines, churches, monasteries and the number of personnel assigned to them.[2] As one modern scholar has remarked, 'In the Patriarchate of Jerusalem the indigenous element is always half-hidden behind the crowds of pilgrims of every nationality... In the Holy City the resident aliens often outnumbered the Christian natives of Jerusalem, but in Palestine taken as a whole, the Syrians must always have been a majority.'[3]

By 'Syrians' the author means Aramaic-speaking, native Syro-Palestinians, among whom the educated also spoke and wrote Greek, the ecclesiastical language of the Byzantine, imperial Church, with which the Jerusalem patriarchate had enjoyed strong ties. As it happened, these native Christians, along with the permanently resident monks who came originally from many different countries, became the first of their creed

[1] J. Wilkinson, *Jerusalem Pilgrims before the Crusades*, Warminster 1977. Regarding pilgrimages to the Holy Land from the Christian East during the period, see J. M. Fiey, 'Le Pèlerinage des Nestoriens et Jacobites à Jérusalem', *Cahiers de Civilisation Médiévale*, xii (1969), 113–26.

[2] Such, for example, is the *Commematorium*, or *Memorandum on the Houses of God and Monasteries in the Holy City*, an anonymous publication written *c.* A.D. 808. T. Tobler and A. Molinier, *Itinera Hierosolymitana et Descriptiones Terrae Sanctae*, 2 vols., Geneva 1879, i. 301–5.

[3] G. Every, 'Syrian Christians in Palestine in the early Middle Ages', *Eastern Churches Quarterly*, vi (1946), 363.

in the Islamic world to adopt Arabic as their ecclesiastical language, in the time following the Abbasid revolution in the year 750.[4]

In view of this early adoption of Arabic among Christians in Syria–Palestine, the purpose of the present essay is first of all to highlight the Palestinian Church's increasing isolation from the Greek-speaking world of Byzantium after the Islamic conquest, and, secondly, to outline the chronological framework within which Greek (and Syriac) eventually gave way to Arabic as the ecclesiastical language of the Melkite community. A consideration of the works of Theodore Abū Qurrah will serve this purpose. Thirdly, and most pertinently, the aim is to sketch a portrait of Stephen of Ramlah and to call attention to the scholarly activity in Arabic at the monastery of Mar Charitōn, during the last quarter of the ninth century. Stephen, a Christian scholar who wrote in Arabic, and his monastery played an important role in ushering in the era of the Christian *kerygma* in Arabic, and he belonged to the generation of Christian scholars in the East whose careers went unnoticed beyond the boundaries of the Caliphate until curious westerners came upon their manuscripts in modern times.

I

Indications coming from a number of sources converge to prompt one to the conclusion that after the Islamic conquest, and particularly after the rise of the Abbasid caliphate, the Church in the Holy Land, along with the other oriental patriarchates, was virtually cut off from effective communication with Rome or Constantinople. The evidence is that between the conquest and the Byzantine reassertion of power in the area in the late tenth century,[5] the local churches conducted their affairs largely without knowledge of events in Byzantium or in the West. In turn, due to the same scarcity of current information, the Romans and the Byzantines seemingly paid no attention to the efforts of the Palestinian Church to accommodate itself to the reality of the new, Arabic-speaking Islamic polity. Rather, in the surviving documents of the period, the westerners refer to the Church of Jerusalem only in regard to matters which impinged upon their own affairs, and even then, as it will appear below, there is often something suspect about the authenticity of some of the documents reporting their alleged communications with the oriental patriarchates, or there is some doubt about the arrival of official letters addressed to these sees.

First of all, it is notable that the western pilgrims to the Holy Land did not take much notice even of the Muslims, on the *beneplacitum* of whose

[4] Cf. the remarks of R. P. Blake, 'La Littérature grecque en Palestine au viiie siècle', *Le Muséon*, lxxviii (1965), 376–8.

[5] For a sketch of the Byzantine re-assertions of power in the East in the century prior to the crusades, J. Prawer, *Histoire du royaume latin de Jérusalem* (trans. G. Nahon), 2 vols., Paris 1969 and 1970, i. 89–120.

leaders they were dependent for their rights to travel there in the first place. As John Wilkinson has put it:

> Despite occasional expressions of gratitude for courtesy and kindness, most of our pilgrims appear to regard local people with curiosity and little more. Thus up till the time of Caliph Hakim (996–1021) they express no hostility to the 'Saracens', whether they use the word in the sense of 'beduin', or of 'Muslims', even though they are barbarians who are always likely to attack Roman or Christian outposts.[6]

Sir Steven Runciman has had the most recent authoritative word to say about the two topics relating to Palestine in this period before the crusades, which are often discussed by modern historians, namely Charlemagne's foundations for pilgrims in Jerusalem, and the alleged Byzantine protectorate in the area in the eleventh century.[7] Neither of these issues, however, offers one much insight into the church life of the indigenous Christian community. They are concerned explicitly with the interest of foreign Christian governments to maintain pilgrims' rights in the Holy Land.

In Byzantine sources relating to the Jerusalem patriarchate after the Islamic conquest, every reference to church councils, church doctrines or practices, holy men, or even complaints about the Muslims, has a primary relevance to internal Byzantine affairs, while the domestic life of the Church in Palestine itself, especially after the Abbasid revolution, goes virtually unnoticed. One hears about it in Byzantine sources only to the degree that stories which are of interest in Constantinople have a Palestinian setting. These are particularly the lives of saints, a number of whose stories actually seem to have had roots in Arabic sources.[8]

On the other hand, matters which are of some importance in Byzantium – such as the question of the delegates of the oriental patriarchs to the council of 787, the Byzantine report of an alleged synod of the three oriental patriarchs in Jerusalem in 836 to discuss iconoclasm and Photius's famous letter to the oriental patriarchs about the *filioque* – all go without notice in what has come down to us of the historical documents of the oriental patriarchates themselves.[9] The fact of the matter seems to be that after the Islamic conquest, and particularly after the inception of the Caliph 'Abd al-Malik's (685–705) programme to assimilate the body politic in

[6] Wilkinson, *Jerusalem Pilgrims*, 32.

[7] S. Runciman, 'Charlemagne and Palestine', *English Historical Review*, l (1935), 606–19; idem, 'The Byzantine "Protectorate" in the Holy Land in the XI century', *Byzantion*, xviii (1948), 207–15; idem, *The Historic Role of the Christian Arabs of Palestine* (Carreras Arab Lecture, 1968), London 1970, text in English and Arabic.

[8] E.g. S. Vailhé, 'Saint Michel le syncelle et les deux frères Grapti, saint Théodore et saint Théophane', *Revue de l'Orient Chrétien*, ix (1901), 313–32, 610–42; P. Peeters, 'La Passion de S. Michel le sabaïte', *Analecta Bollandiana*, xlviii (1930), 65–98; A. Vasiliev, 'The Life of St. Theodore of Edessa', *Byzantion*, xvi (1942–3), 165–225; J. Featherstone, 'Theophane of Caesarea, Encomium of Theodore Graptos', *Analecta Bollandiana*, xcviii (1980), 93–150. See also n. 38 below.

[9] See the discussion of these issues in S. H. Griffith, 'Eutychius of Alexandria on the Emperor Theophilus and Iconoclasm in Byzantium: a tenth century moment in Christian apologetics in Arabic', *Byzantion*, lii (1982), 154–90.

the conquered areas to an Arabic and Islamic manner of public life,[10] contact with Byzantium, even in the Melkite Christian community, began to wane and was virtually broken off by the beginning of Abbasid times, not to be renewed until the tenth century, when Byzantine military power once again made inroads into the territories of a weakened caliphate.

Particularly telling in regard to the relative isolation of the oriental patriarchates are the remarks of Eutychius of Alexandria (877–940), who wrote in his World History: 'The names of the patriarchs of Constantinople have not reached me since Theodoros died (i.e. 679) at the time of writing this book. Likewise, in regard to the patriarchs of Rome, the names of the patriarchs of Rome and reports of them have not reached me.'[11] And further along Eutychius says: 'In the year 326 [i.e. A.D. 937] a gratifying peace came about between the Byzantines [and the Muslims]. And in that year, Theofilaks, patriarch of the city of Constantinople, sent a messenger to the patriarchs of Alexandria and Antioch asking them to mention his name in their prayers and in their liturgies because this had been cut off since the era of the Umayyads.'[12] Even a century later Yaḥyā Ibn Sa'īd al-Antākī (d. *c.* 1040), the scholar who continued Eutychius's history, remarked at the beginning of his own contribution that in his day there was still a lack of news in Egypt and Syria about ecclesiastical affairs in Byzantium and Rome. Therefore, he said, he had to abandon his earlier intention to update and to correct Eutychius's narrative, for lack of sources.[13]

In the meantime, of course, Greek-speaking Christianity in the patriarchate of Jerusalem enjoyed one last season of efflorescence which was in many ways its apogee. The name and work of John Damascene (d. *c.* 750), the scholar monk of Mar Sabas monastery and retired civil servant of the Umayyad caliphate, spring immediately to mind.[14] His *Fountain of Knowledge* in particular exerted a profound influence in Byzantium, once it was spirited out of Palestine. Being the first ever summary of patristic thought, the *Fountain* quickly became a sourcebook for Byzantine theologians.[15]

[10] The evidence for the Umayyad programme for the Islamicisation of public life is discussed in S. H. Griffith, 'Theodore Abū Qurrah's Arabic tract on the Christian practice of venerating images', *Journal of the American Oriental Society*, forthcoming.

[11] L. Cheikho *et al.* (eds.), *Eutychii Patriarchae Alexandrini Annales* (CSCO, vols I and II.), Beirut and Paris 1906 and 1909, li. 49.

[12] Ibid., 87–8.

[13] I. Krachkovsky and A. Vasiliev, 'Histoire de Yahya-ibn-Sa'id d'Antioche, continuateur de Sa'id-ibn-Bitriq', *Patrologia Orientalis*, xviii (1924), 706–9. On al-Anṭākī and his sources, cf. now J. H. Forsyth, 'The Byzantine-Arab Chronicle (938–1034) of Yaḥya b. Sa'īd al-Anṭākī', 2 vols. (Ph.D. dissertation, University of Michigan 1977), Ann Arbor, Michigan: University Microfilms International 1978.

[14] J. Nasrallah, *Saint Jean de Damas, son époque, sa vie, son oeuvre*, Harissa 1950; J. M. Hoeck, 'Stand und Aufgaben der Damaskenos Forschung', *Orientalia Christiana Periodica*, xvii (1951), 5–60. Full bibliography in M. Geerad (ed.), *Clavis Patrum Graecorum*, Turnout 1979, iii. 511–36. On John Damascene and the Muslims, D. J. Sahas, *John of Damascus on Islam, the 'Heresy of the Ishmaelites'*, Leiden 1972.

[15] B. Studer, *Die theologische Arbeitsweise des Johannes von Damaskus*, Ettal 1956, 132.

It served as a manual of theology for centuries in the ecclesiastical, educational establishment of the Greek-speaking world.[16] The first-known Arabic versions of John Damascene's work are of the tenth century, yet most of the extant manuscripts date only from the thirteenth century.[17] In spite of this relatively late date of the known Arabic versions of the Damescene's work in Palestine, and particularly in Mar Sabas monastery, the spirit of scholarly accomplishment lived on there after his death. The striking difference is that by the next generation the language of scholarship at Mar Sabas is not Greek, but Arabic.

Of course, John Damascene was not the only important Greek writer in Palestine from the time of the Islamic conquest until the Abbasid revolution; nor was he the only Syro-Palestinian from this period, or even from the ninth century, to exert an important influence in Constantinople and elsewhere in the Greek-speaking world. However, here is not the place to rehearse the history of Greek literature in Palestine.[18] The instant name recognition of John Damascene, along with a brief account of his scholarly accomplishments, are sufficient to call attention to the importance of Palestinian Greek scholarship, even for the world beyond *dār al-islām*, in the century following the Islamic conquest. Surprising as it may seem, however, the influence of the scholarly monks of Palestine in Byzantium was a one-way street: the monks travelled to Constantinople, carrying with them the Greek literature of the Holy Land, but until the tenth century they never seem to have returned to Jerusalem, bringing with them news of affairs in the Christian world beyond the reach of Islamic power.

There are passages in some documents dealing with people in the ninth century which do say that Christians from the Islamic world travelled to Byzantium and subsequently returned to their homes. The *Vita* of Theodore of Edessa, for example, says that he visited Constantinople during the reign of Michael III and Theodora (842–56), and returned.[19]

[16] Only such a role can explain the extraordinarily large number of MSS of this work and of its several parts which have survived to modern times. B. Kotter, *Die Überlieferung der Pege Gnoseos des h. Johannes von Damaskos*, Ettal 1959.

[17] Georg Graf, *Geschichte der christlichen arabischen Literatur* (hereafter cited as *GCAL*) (5 vols.), Vatican City 1944–53, i. 377–9; Nasrallah, *Saint Jean de Damas*, 179–89; Kotter, op. cit., 217–18; A. S. Atiya, 'St. John Damascene: survey of the unpublished Arabic versions of his works in Sinai', in G. Makdisi (ed.), *Arabic and Islamic Studies in Honor of Hamilton A. R. Gibb*, Cambridge, Mass. 1965, 73–83.

[18] Blake, 'La Littérature grecque', and the works cited in n. 8 above. Also A. Ehrhard, 'Das griechische Kloster Mar-Saba in Palaestina, seine Geschichte und seine litterarischen Denkmäler', *Römische Quartalschrift für christliche Alterthumskunde und für Kirchengeschichte*, vii (1893), 32–79; S. Vailhé, 'Les Écrivains de Mar-Saba', *Échos d'Orient*, ii (1898–9), 1–11, 33–47. One should also note the work of Anastasius of Sinai, now being brought to the attention of scholars by Karl-Heinz Uthemann, *Anastasii Sinaitae Viae Dux*, Corpus Christianorum, Series Graeca, 8, Leuven 1981: and J. Munitz, who is at work on a critical edition of Anastasius's *Quaestiones et Responsiones*. Uthemann, op. cit., p. ccxiii, n. 56. On Anastasius and the Muslims, S. H. Griffith, 'Anastasius of Sinai and the Muslims', forthcoming publication; see abstract in *Byzantine Studies Conference: Abstracts of Papers*, vii (1982), 13.

[19] A. Vasiliev, 'St. Theodore of Edessa', 171.

However, there are many unsolved problems with this *Vita*, which put its allegations in considerable doubt. Not least among the problems is the determination of its original language. Vasiliev thought the *Vita* was originally written in Greek, a judgement with which Georg Graf agreed.[20] If so, the *Vita*, given its date, must be a product of Byzantium and not of the Arab world. Hence it would not be a reliable indication of how well informed the Christians in Edessa might have been about Church life in Constantinople on the basis of news brought back by travellers.

Another story of an eastern Christian who travelled to Byzantium and back has similar problems. Some sources say that Ḥunayn ibn Isḥāq (d. 877), the famed Nestorian physician, travelled to the 'land of the Romans (*bilād ar-rūm*)', presumably Byzantium, and sojourned there to search out Greek books.[21] And some modern scholars have gone further, to propose that while he was there, Ḥunayn was influenced by the iconoclasts, a circumstance which in their view would explain an incident involving the court physician in later years when he allegedly desecrated an icon of the virgin Mary.[22] However, the trouble here is that there are serious problems both with the sources of Ḥunayn's biography and with the precise location of the *bilād ar-Rūm* he is said to have visited.[23] There is no report that Ḥunayn came home with news of ecclesiastical affairs in Byzantium.

So while there are these few reports of Christians from *dār al-islām* visiting Byzantium and returning home, one is still left facing the fact that the local Christian historians who wrote in Syriac and Arabic had only a meagre amount of information to record about Byzantine ecclesiastical affairs in the eighth and ninth centuries, even about a phenomenon as prominent as the iconoclastic controversy. Monks originally from Mar Sabas, such as Theodore and Theophane Graptoi, played a role with a high social profile in the second phase of this very controversy, yet no word is spoken about it in oriental sources.[24] The only conclusion one can draw from the silence is that few if any refugee monks from the Palestinian monasteries ever came back to the Holy Land to inform their *confrères* about ecclesiastical affairs in Byzantium. Certainly, documentary sources for the historian were wanting, as Yaḥyā ibn Sa'īd al-Antākī discovered when he searched for them in the eleventh century.[25]

The virtual isolation of the Syro-Palestinian Church from Byzantium

[20] G. Graf, *GCAL*, ii. 24.

[21] August Müller, *Ibn Abī Useibia*, *'Uyūn al-Anbā' fī Tabaqāt aṭ-Ṭibbā*, 2 vols. in 1, Königsberg 1884, ii. 187; J. Lippert, *Ibn al-Qifṭī's Ta'rīḫ al-Hukamā'*, Leipzig 1903, 174.

[22] On this incident cf. B. Hemmerdinger, 'Ḥunain ibn Isḥāq et l'iconoclasme byzantin', in *Actes du XIIe Congrès International d'Études Byzantines*, Belgrade 1964, ii. 467–9; G. Strohmaier, 'Ḥunain ibn Isḥāq und die Bilder', *Klio*, xliii–xlv (1965), 525–33.

[23] G. Strohmaier, 'Ḥunayn b. Isḥāḳ al-'Ibādī' *Encyclopedia of Islam* (hereafter cited as *EI*), 2nd edn, iii. 578–81.

[24] Griffith, 'Eutychius of Alexandria', and, for the earlier period of iconoclasm, S. Gero, *Byzantine Iconoclasm during the reign of Leo III, with particular Reference to the Oriental Sources* (CSCO, ccclxvi; Louvain, 1973), appendix A, 'Arab and Syriac accounts of early Iconoclasm', 199–205.

[25] Above, and n. 13.

was of decisive importance among the conditions which fostered the first appearance of Christian literature in Arabic, during the first Abbasid century. It appeared first in Palestine, among the Melkites, because in Palestine, where the ecclesiastical language had been largely Greek, with some Syriac,[26] there was no significant scholarship in the indigenous Aramaic dialect, sometimes called Palestinian Syriac, to compare with what Syriac- or Coptic-speaking Christians could claim in Egypt and in the vast territories nominally attached to the patriarchate of Antioch.[27] Once Palestine was definitively cut off from Byzantium, and Arabic became the *lingua franca* of the Islamic polity, Arabic also became the language of the local Christian community. Ironically, as a result of this development, for the first time since the earliest Christian presence in Palestine both the educated and the common people now spoke the same language, even for scholarly and ecclesiastical purposes.

Meanwhile, in Byzantium, to judge by the reports one finds in some Byzantine sources, ecclesiastical affairs in Constantinople were still being conducted with reference to the oriental patriarchates, through legates and intermediaries, as if the communication gap documented in Arabic and Syriac sources did not in fact exist.

In the eighth and ninth centuries Byzantine ecclesiastical functionaries continued to issue official letters to the oriental patriarchs in connection with the crises which beset the Church. Theodore of Studios (759–826), for example, sent letters to Alexandria and to Antioch, as well as to the Palestinian monasteries of St Sabas, St Charitōn and St Euthymius, informing persons there of the iconoclastic problem and soliciting their prayers.[28] Somewhat later Patriarch Photios issued letters to the oriental patriarchs in connection with his troubles with the bishop of Rome over the *filioque*.[29] Yet no mention of the receipt of these letters is to be found in eastern sources. And in one instance there are even reports in Byzantine

[26] Regarding Melkite documents in Syriac, R. W. Thompson, 'The text of the Syriac Athanasian Corpus', in J. N. Birdsall and R. W. Thompson (eds.), *Biblical and Patristic Studies in Memory of Robert Pierce Casey*, Freiburg 1963, 250–64. Melkite liturgical documents have also survived: S. P. Brock, 'A short Melkite baptismal service in Syriac', *Parole de l'Orient*, iii (1972), 119–30. With some documents it is difficult to tell which was their original language, Greek or Syriac. S. P. Brock, 'A Syriac fragment on the sixth council', *Oriens Christianus*, lvii (1973), 63–71; idem, 'An early Syriac life of Maximus the Confessor', *Analecta Bollandiana*, xci (1973), 299–346. See also J. M. Fiey, '"Rūm" à l'est de l'Euphrate', *Le Muséon*, xc (1977), 365–420, with its rich bibliography. Theodore Abū Qurrah said in one of his Arabic works that he had written some thirty treatises in Syriac. C. Bacha, *Les Oeuvres arabes de Théodore Aboucara, évêque d'Haran*, Beirut 1904, 60–1.

[27] Regarding Palestinian Syriac, see the bibliographic orientation available in B. M. Metzger, *The Early Versions of the New Testament*, Oxford 1977, 75–82; also the comments and bibliography of M. Goshen-Gottstein, *The Bible in the Syro-palestinian Version: Part I: Pentateuch and Prophets*, Jerusalem 1973, viii–xv.

[28] P.G. xcix. 1155–74.

[29] V. Grumel, *Le Patriarcat byzantin; les regestes des actes du patriarcat de Constantinople*, 2 vols., Paris 1932–6, i. 88–9; F. Dvornik, *The Photian Schism. History and legend*, Cambridge 1948, 119 and 193.

documents of a synod which was supposedly held in Jerusalem in the year 836, in which all three oriental patriarchs condemned iconoclasm in Byzantium and sent a letter to that effect to the Emperor Theophilus.[30] Again, no mention of this synod, or of its letter, is to be found in the East, not even in the work of Eutychius of Alexandria, who could hardly have failed to mention it had he known of such a synod.[31] Indeed, modern historians of Byzantium now seem to be convinced that the story of this synod was told in Constantinople in support of the iconophile cause, and that it has no value at all as documentary evidence for the ecclesiastical history of Jerusalem.[32]

At least one motive for this continued reference to the oriental patriarchates in Byzantine sources, during an era when few if any ecclesiastical communiqués from beyond *dār al-islām* seem actually to have arrived in Antioch, Alexandria or Jerusalem, must have been the issue of canonical legitimacy. This issue arose particularly in reference to the Council of Nicaea II in 787. To be truly ecumenical, there theoretically should have been in attendance at the council at least plenipotentiary legates from the oriental patriarchates, if not the patriarchs themselves. As if in testimony to the isolation of the East, it appears that refugee monks living in Byzantium were chosen on the spot to act as proxies for their patriarchs at this council. Not all iconophiles approved of the arrangement, and no less a figure than Theodore of Studios complained about it in a letter to a monk named Arsenius. Theodore wrote:

> As for those from the East, they were persuaded and induced by people here and were not sent by the patriarchs who because of their fear of the heathen, took no notice of it (i.e. the council) either then or later. The people did this in order to persuade the heretical populace more easily to come over to Orthodoxy on the pretence of there being an ecumenical council.[33]

In this passage Theodore, who had himself written to the oriental patriarchates to inform them about the government's iconoclastic policy and to seek prayerful support for the iconophiles, straightforwardly admits the absence of any real contact with them, and in doing so he also provides the evidence that in Constantinople the refugees spoke for the East without any immediate authorisation from home. Patrick Henry doubts Theodore's allegations on this point, citing the fact that a synodical letter from Patriarch Theodore of Jerusalem (745–67) was read at the council, having been brought by the legates.[34] However, Henry seems to have taken no notice of the additional fact that the patriarch in question

[30] L. Duchesne, 'L'Iconographie byzantine dans un document grec du ixe siècle', *Roma e l'Oriente*, v (1912–13), 222–39, 273–85, 349, 366.

[31] Griffith, 'Eutychius of Alexandria'.

[32] The remarks of Ihor Ševčenko, 'Constantinople viewed from the eastern provinces in the middle Byzantine period', *Harvard Ukrainian Studies*, iii–iv (1979–80), 735 n. 36.

[33] Quoted from P. Henry, 'Initial eastern assessments of the seventh oecumenical council', *JTS*, 2nd ser., xxv (1974), 77.

[34] Ibid., 77 and 78, esp. n. 1.

died twenty years before the council. This fact actually supports Theodore of Studios's contention, and also serves the point of the present argument. For Palestine at least, the delegates and intermediaries at the council of 787 were from among the refugees who represented their patriarchate in Constantinople on a more or less permanent basis. They probably had permanent residence in exile in the capital.[35]

The only traffic from Byzantium to *dār al-islām* from early in the eighth century until late in the tenth century, aside from military incursions, appears to have been strictly commercial adventures, pilgrimages to the Holy Land and imperial, diplomatic missions, all of which conducted their business without reference to the local Church. With all of these undertakings, as one modern scholar has observed concerning this period, 'annual warfare or seasonal raiding remained the main characteristic of Arab Byzantine relations'.[36] And in these circumstances the community life of the Church in Palestine, once it found its tongue in Arabic, went largely unnoticed in Byzantium.

A token of this lack of attention to Palestinian affairs may be seen in the work of the Byzantine monk, Epiphanius, who wrote a guidebook to the Holy Land some time between the years 750 and 800. He mentioned the monasteries of Mar Sabas and Mar Charitōn, well known in Constantinople because of the refugee monks, but he took no notice of the scholarly activity of the monks who remained behind, which at that time already was beginning to be conducted in Arabic.[37] And, on the other side, a token of the sketchy knowledge of Byzantine affairs that was available to the monks who lived in Palestine at the time may be seen in the vague ideas about iconoclasm and its adherents in the time of Constantine V which was available to the Arabic writer of the life of St Romanos. The writer was a monk from Mar Sabas monastery, and he was apparently dependent on Byzantine prisoners in Baghdad for what information he had about the controversy in Constantinople.[38] He wrote his life of Romanos in Arabic between the years 780 and 787, at the very time when his *confrère* at Mar Sabas, Theodore Abū Qurrah, would have been

[35] J. Gouillard, 'Un 'Quartier' d'émigrés palestiniens à Constantinople au ixe siècle?', *Revue des Études Sud-Est Européennes*, vii (1969), 73–6.

[36] Ahmad M. H. Shboul, *Al-Mas 'ūdī and His World; a Muslim Humanist and his Interest in Non-Muslims*, London 1979, 227. Cf. also this author's rich documentation for the state of affairs between the caliphate and Byzantium between the years 813 and 959, in his chapter, 'Al-Mas'ūdī on the Byzantines', 227–84. Also H. A. R. Gibb, 'Arab-Byzantine relations under the Umayyad caliphate', *Dumbarton Oaks Papers*, xii (1958), 221–33; A. A. Vasiliev, *Byzance et les Arabes*, 4 vols., Brussels 1935–68; V. Christides, 'The raids of the Moslems of Crete in the Aegean Sea, piracy and conquest', *Byzantion*, li (1981), 76–111.

[37] H. Donner, 'Die Palästinabeschreibung des Epiphanius Monachus Hagiopolita', *Zeitschrift des deutschen Palästina-Vereins*, lxxxvii (1971), 71; comment in Wilkinson, *Jerusalem Pilgrims*, 11 and 119.

[38] P. Peeters, 'S. Romain le néomartyr (1 mai 780), d'après un document géorgien', *Analecta Bollandiana*, xxx (1911), 393–427, and the remarks of Ihor Ševčenko, 'Hagiography of the Iconoclast period', in A. Bryer and J. Herrin (eds.), *Iconoclasm*, Birmingham 1977, 114–15.

preparing for his career as the first Christian *mutakallim* to make a name for himself in the Arab world, and the only one of a number of later Christian *mutakallimūn* to gain a reputation beyond the borders of the caliphate.[39] His career in fact marked the definitive turning point from Greek to Arabic in the Melkite community of Syria-Palestine.

II

Theodore Abū Qurrah (*c*. 750–*c*. 825) is the best-known scholar of the first generation of Christians in the Palestinian monastic communities to write theology in Arabic. As a monk of Mar Sabas, he was quite clearly indebted to the scholarly accomplishments of the earlier generation of Greek-speaking scholar monks in Palestine, and to John Damascene in particular.[40] However, a new frame of reference appeared in the works of Abū Qurrah, which was to become a standard feature of almost every Christian text in Arabic thereafter. This new feature is a distinctive apologetic purpose, in view of which Abū Qurrah and the other Christian writers in Arabic laboured to state their religious convictions, and even to argue among themselves about them, with an acute awareness of the presence of the Muslims, whose language of revelation they had adopted as their own. The Arabic which became the public language of the Islamic caliphate was the Arabic inspired by the *Qur'ān*. Accordingly, Christian writers were faced with the threefold task of learning to deploy the idiom of the *Qur'ān* to clarify Christian thought in the Christian community; to commend Christian thought to Muslims; and to discount the Islamic bent of the Arabic language they had assimilated. This apologetic purpose is never far from view in any of the Christian Arabic literature written from the first Abbasid century onward. The Arabic works of Theodore Abū Qurrah are the earliest texts in which this new programme appeared, and they provide an excellent vantage point from which to observe the changeover from Greek to Arabic in the ecclesiastical literature of Syria–Palestine.[41]

[39] On the terms *mutakallim* and *kalām*, F. Niewöhner, 'Die Diskussion um den Kalām und die Mutakallimūn in der europäischen Philosophiegeschichtsschreibung', *Archiv für Begriffsgeschichte*, xviii (1974), 7–34; J. Van Ess, 'Disputationspraxis in der islamischen Theologie, eine vorläufige Skizze', *Revue des Études Islamiques*, xliv (1976), 23–60; M. A. Cook, 'The Origins of Kalam', *Bulletin of the School of Oriental and African Studies*, xliii (1980), 32–43.

[40] I. Dick, 'Un Continuateur arabe de saint Jean Damascène: Théodore Abuqurra, évêque melkite de Ḥarran', *Proche-Orient Chrétien*, xii (1962), 209–23, 319–32; xiii (1963), 114–29.

[41] S. H. Griffith, 'The controversial theology of Theodore Abū Qurrah (*c*. 750–*c*. 820 A.D.), a methodological comparative study in Christian Arabic literature', (Ph.D. dissertation; The Catholic University of America, Washington, D.C., 1978), Ann Arbor, Michigan University Microfilms International, no. 7819874. Cf. abstract in *Dissertation Abstracts International*, xxxix, (1978), 2992–3. The influence of the apologetic dimension can also be discerned in early Islamic religious writing. See J. Wansbrough, *The Sectarian Milieu, content and composition of Islamic salvation history*, Oxford 1978.

Abū Qurrah himself testified that he wrote some thirty treatises in Syriac.[42] Unfortunately, none of them is known to have survived until modern times. What have survived of his works are in Arabic, Greek and Georgian. The latter are mostly translations from Greek.[43] In the early twelfth century Arsen Iqalt'oeli included a selection of nine such pieces attributed to Abū Qurrah in his *Dogmatikon*. This work was an influential compilation of dogmatic and polemical tracts, almost all of them translated from Greek into Georgian, in defence of the orthodox Chalcedonian cause, against Jacobites, Nestorians, Jews and Muslims.[44] However, there is also a report that in the early eleventh century the Georgian monk Euthymius Mt'ac'mideli (d. 1028), working the other way about, translated a now unknown work by Abū Qurrah from Georgian into Greek.[45] It is not impossible, therefore, that the document which Euthymius translated into Greek had originally been translated from Arabic or Syriac into Georgian, and for this reason was not already available in Greek. The life of St Romanos, one will remember, is another example of a Palestinian work which in the first Abbasid century was translated directly from Arabic into Georgian, bypassing Greek.[46]

So far some fourteen works in Arabic attributed to Abū Qurrah have been published, and forty-three in Greek.[47] On the face of it, then, one might conclude that Abū Qurrah wrote freely in Syriac, Arabic and Greek. That he wrote in Syriac is no surprise since his own testimony to this fact is available and, in all probability, Edessa, the cultural capital of the Syriac speakers, was his native city.[48] Arabic, of course, was the language of the dominant Islamic polity, and his own works which have survived in this language are the primary testimony to Abū Qurrah's mastery of

[42] Bacha, *Les Oeuvres arabes de Théodore Aboucara*, 60–1.

[43] Graf, *GCAL*, ii. 20–1; R. Gvaramia, 'Bibliographie du dialogue islamo-chrétien: auteurs chrétiens de langue géorgienne', *Islamochristiana*, vi (1980). 290–1.

[44] M. Tarchnišvili, *Geschichte der kirchlichen georgischen Literatur* (Studi e Testi, no. 185), Vatican City 1955, 208–9, 370–1.

[45] Ibid., 129, and Graf, *GCAL*, II, 21.

[46] Peeters, 'S. Romain', 403–9.

[47] The published works of Abū Qurrah in Arabic are: I. Arendzen, *Theodori Abu Kurra de Cultu Imaginum Libellus e Codice Arabico nunc Primum Editus Latine Versus Illustratus*, Bonn 1897; Bacha, *Les Oeuvres arabes de Théodore Aboucara*; idem, *Un Traité des oeuvres arabes de Théodore Abou-Kurra, évêque de Haran*, Tripoli, Syria and Rome 1905; G. Graf, *Die arabischen Schriften des Theodor ʾAbu Qurra, Bischofs von Ḥarran (ca. 740–820)* (Forschungen zur christlichen Literatur- und Dogmengeschichte, Band X, Heft 3/4, Paderborn 1910); Louis Cheikho, 'Mīmar li Tadūrūs Abī Qurrah fī Wuǧūd al-Ḫāliq wa d-Dīn al-Qawīm', *al-Machriq*, xv (1919), 757–74; 825–42; G. Graf, *Des Theodor Abu Kurra Traktat über den Schöpfer und die wahre Religion* (Beiträge zur Geschichte der Philosophie des Mittelalters. Texte und Untersuchungen, Band XIV, Heft 1), Münster, Westphalia 1913; I. Dick, 'Deux écrits inédits de Théodore Abuqurra', *Le Muséon*, lxxii (1959), 53–67; S. H. Griffith, 'Some unpublished Arabic sayings attributed to Theodore Abū Qurrah', *Le Muséon*, xcii (1979), 29–35. For Abū Qurrah's works preserved only in Greek, see P.G. xcvii. 1461–610. For the MSS of unpublished works attributed to Abū Qurrah, cf. Graf, *GCAL*, ii. 7–16 and J. Nasrallah, 'Dialogue islamo-chrétien à propos de publications récentes', *Revue des Études Islamiques*, xlvi (1978), 129–32.

[48] Dick, 'Un Continuateur arabe, xiii (1963), 121–2.

this new *lingua franca* in the lands under the control of the caliphate. As Georg Graf has shown, these works are not translations from any other language, although one can here and there detect the influences of the writer's native Syriac.[49] A further indication of Abū Qurrah's proficiency in Arabic is the complaint recorded by Michael the Syrian about him that: 'because he was a sophist, and engaged in dialectics with the pagans [*ḥanpê*, i.e. the Muslims], and knew the Saracen language, he was an object of wonder to the simple folk'.[50] In fact, Arabic seems to have been a preferred language for Abū Qurrah. The title paragraph to his long epistle-treatise against the Monophysites of Armenia, which is preserved as his Greek *opus* IV, says that Abū Qurrah first wrote the work in Arabic, at the request of Patriarch Thomas of Jerusalem (807–21). Subsequently, the patriarch's *synkellos*, Michael (d. 846), translated it into Greek.[51] This translator was none other than the same Michael Synkellos who later left Palestine and lived as a refugee in Constantinople, where, along with his *confrères* from Mar Sabas, Theodore and Theophane Graptoi, he opposed the policies of the iconoclasts.[52]

The question now is: did Abū Qurrah ever actually write in Greek any of the other works preserved under his name in that language or, like *opus* IV, are they all likely to have been translations? No final answer can yet be given to this question. It certainly seems likely that Abū Qurrah would have had at least a reading knowledge of Greek. However, the information in the title paragraph to *opus* IV suggests that he was reluctant to write in Greek. And there is now some corroborating evidence for this suggestion in that one of his shorter Greek *opuscula*, no. IX, is also seen to be a translation from Arabic, and not an original composition in Greek.[53] One must take into account the fact that of the forty-three published works in Greek attributed to Abū Qurrah, only three of them are full treatises in any meaningful sense of the word. They are the Greek *opera* II, IV and the final, or forty-third work, *De unione et incarnatione*, which was added at the end of Jakob Gretser's edition when the latter was included in Migne's *Patrologia Graeca*.[54] For the rest, there are some fifteen Greek reports of dialogues in which Abū Qurrah is featured as getting the best of his adversaries in Socratic-style arguments presented in the *Erōtapokrisis* format. And the remaining twenty-five pieces are almost all short records of Abū Qurrah's answers to this or that controversial issue that customarily arose in the arguments about religion which took place in his day.[55]

Both Georg Graf and Adel-Théodore Khoury have written of their impressions of the good quality of the Greek style of Abū Qurrah's treatises

49 Graf, *Die arabischen Schriften*, 20–5.

50 J.-B. Chabot, *Chronique de Michel le syrien; patriarche jacobite d'Antioche* (*1166–1199*) (4 vols.), Paris 1899–1910, iii. 32 (French), iv. 495–6 (Syriac).

51 P.G. xcvii. 1504D.

52 Vailhé, 'Saint Michel le syncelle'; Ševčenko, 'Hagiography of the Iconoclast period', 116, esp. n. 19.

53 Griffith, 'Some unpublished sayings'.

54 P.G. xcvii. 1601–10.

55 Graf's analysis, *Die arabischen Schriften*, 67–77.

and dialogues preserved in that language. They notice few infelicities or awkward expressions which would encourage one to think of these writings as translations. Graf, however, recalls the testimony of the title paragraph to *opus* IV, with its explicit statement that the work is a translation, and he is inclined to entertain the possibility that all the Greek works, including the treatises and the dialogues, were likewise translations, probably from Arabic originals.[56] Khoury on the other hand opts for Greek as the original language, even of the shorter pieces. In these *opuscula* Abū Qurrah several times speaks of Muslims in ways that it would be dangerous to do in Arabic, Khoury thinks. And for him this circumstance becomes a *suasio* in favour of the thesis that Abū Qurrah himself wrote in Greek all of the works attributed to him in that language.[57]

The disclosure of the Arabic antecedents of Greek *opusculum* IX prompts one to raise the issue anew. Graf had classed this piece in his group of the Greek *opuscula* which contain short subjects and extracts, both from Abū Qurrah's genuine works, and from the collection of unauthentic responses attributed to him, particularly in the many Arabic accounts of his supposed dialogue before a caliph, or other high Muslim official.[58] The Arabic original of *opusculum* IX, however, copied by Stephen of Ramlah in A.D. 897, is explicitly attributed to Abū Qurrah in Sinai Arabic MS 72, where it appears on one page (i.e. fo. 117r), as a short report following an Arabic translation of the four Gospels. This information allows one to see that the process of writing down the more successful Christian responses to particular challenges coming from Muslims or other adversaries and attributing them to Abū Qurrah was a practice which had begun already in the Arabic-speaking world. As a matter of fact, the gist of the argument preserved in Greek *opusculum* IX, and in Sinai Arabic MS 72, appears in yet another work written down by Stephen of Ramlah some twenty years earlier.[59] The details of the argument vary considerably in this earlier witness, and it is not explicitly attributed to Theodore Abū Qurrah, so one may consider it to have been a standard item in the Christian polemical repertory of the time.

All of this allows one to put forth the hypothesis that there probably were Arabic antecedents for the other twenty-four short items in the group of Greek *opuscula* categorised by Graf as of doubtful authenticity, as there were for *opusculum* IX. There seems to be no reason to doubt that refugee monks from Palestine, such as Michael Synkellos, the undoubted translator of Greek *opus* IV, could also have put the rest of these particularly trenchant polemical responses into Greek. And it is not unreasonable to propose that, following the Palestinian Arabic usage, the translator also attributed the responses to Abū Qurrah. The question of the authenticity

[56] Ibid., esp. 71.

[57] A. T. Khoury, *Les Théologiens byzantins et l'Islam*, Louvain and Paris 1969, 86–7.

[58] Graf, *Die arabischen Schriften*, 71–7. Regarding the 'debate' reports preserved in Arabic MSS, concerning which Graf had doubts about their authenticity, cf. Graf, *GCAL*, ii. 21–3.

[59] British Library Oriental MS 4950, fo. 119r–119v. On this MS see below.

of the attribution must await further textual studies, particularly in the Arabic manuscripts which report Abū Qurrah's debates in the presence of Muslim officials. As for the few longer treatises and dialogues preserved in Greek, it seems most reasonable to assume that they too were translated from Arabic by a particularly adept translator. There is no compelling reason to believe that Abū Qurrah himself wrote them in Greek. With the exception of a smooth Greek style, what concrete evidence there is, meagre at that, suggests that all of the Greek works attributed to Abū Qurrah are translations from Arabic. And, what is more to the present point, it appears that this handful of mostly short responses, with a few longer dialogues, and only three actual treatises which are attributed to Theodore Abū Qurrah in Greek, were the last works of a Syro-Palestinian monk to be translated into that language. In Byzantium, Abū Qurrah's translated works in Greek, along with a few pieces attributed to John Damascene, became the first in a long line of Greek, anti-Islamic tracts.[60]

In Palestine, Theodore Abū Qurrah's Arabic works were the first fruits of the new scholarship cultivated at Mar Sabas monastery. It seems likely that, beginning in the eighth century, this monastery, along with Mar Charitōn and the monastery at Sinai, made Palestine a centre for the intellectual life of all the Melkites in the Arabic-speaking world of the caliphate. There is evidence of an influx of originally Syriac-speaking monks to the monastery population in the late eighth and ninth centuries.[61] In the first half of the ninth century at least two monks, both originally from Edessa, Theodore Abū Qurrah and Theodore of Edessa, went from Mar Sabas to become Melkite bishops in Ḥarrān and Edessa respectively, thereby underlining the connection of the Palestinian monasteries with the Melkite community in Mesopotamia.[62]

Here is not the place to discuss the Palestinian hagiographic literature in any detail. It has a complexity all its own, due to that fact that the contents of the Arabic originals have been transmitted, and often transformed, at first through Georgian and later through Greek versions.[63] Suffice it to say now that there is evidence that by the eighth century the daily language of the monks was not Greek and was probably Arabic. The negative documentary evidence for this conclusion is the remark made in Leontius Sabaita's biography of St Stephen Sabaita to the effect that the saint addressed a visitor to his cave in Greek, as if the use of this language was something extraordinary.[64] The positive evidence is the production in the same period, by these same monks, of the aforementioned saints'

[60] Khoury, *Les Théologiens byzantins*, 83–105; idem, *Polémique byzantine contre l'islam*, Leiden 1972; idem, 'Apologétique byzantine contre islam (viiie–xiiie siècle)', *Proche Orient Chrétien*, xxix (1979), 242–300; xxx (1980), 132–74; xxxii (1981), 14–47.

[61] S. Vailhé, 'Le Monastère de saint-Sabas', *Echos d'Orient*, iii (1899–1900), 22. Cf. also Every, 'Syrian Christians in Palestine'.

[62] Dick, 'Un Continuateur arabe', 328–30; Vasiliev, 'St. Theodore of Edessa'.

[63] Nn. 8 and 38 above. The original, Arabic *vita* of John Damascene was also written in this period, cf. Sahas, *John of Damascus*, 32–5. Peeters and Sahas ascribe the author's motive for using Arabic to his presumed fear of the iconoclastic authorities in Byzantium.

[64] Cf. the passage quoted and discussed in Sahas, op. cit., 47 n. 1.

lives in Arabic rather than in Greek. Furthermore, these saints' lives often depict their heroes in dialogue with Muslims, providing a living example, so to speak, of how one might meet the religious challenges of Islam with apologetical arguments designed to defend the truth of Christian doctrines.[65] This feature of the saints' lives reminds one that in addition to hagiography, the two most important genres of Christian writing to appear in Arabic in the Palestinian monasteries, beginning from the eighth century, were apologetic tracts and versions of the scriptures, particularly the Gospels. These items make up the bulk of the Arabic manuscripts which have survived from Palestine from the ninth and tenth centuries, and to these we must now turn our attention.

III

While Theodore Abū Qurrah's name and works have been known to scholars for a long time, relatively little attention has been paid to the collection of Christian Arabic manuscripts from Palestine from the ninth and tenth centuries, with a view to going yet a step further in recovering the history of the Christian community in the Holy Land in the generations following Abū Qurrah's lifetime. The trouble has been that few of the manuscripts carry the names even of the scribes who wrote them, and precise dates for the writing are likewise scarce. Nevertheless, recent scholarship has made it possible to define more closely the body of material which is the only surviving documentation for the history of Christianity in Palestine in this period. Consequently, a new chapter may be opened in the history of Christian Arabic writing and a better idea may be had about the early role of the Melkite monks of Palestine in the eventually successful project to translate Christianity into Arabic.

Relying on the scholarship of many individuals who had earlier published Christian Arabic works from the ninth and tenth centuries, and taking advantage of the accessibility to the manuscripts of Sinai which the Library of Congress/University of Alexandria microfilm project afforded him,[66] Joshua Blau has succeeded in identifying and defining a distinct body of Christian literature in Arabic, with its own grammatical and syntactical peculiarities, native to Syria–Palestine.[67] Blau's principal concern is with the growth of a colloquial, middle Arabic dialect, which he discerns in the attempts of the Palestinian monks to express themselves in the language of the *Qur'ān*.[68] A by-product of this study in Arabic historical linguistics is Blau's annotated list of documentary sources for his

[65] E.g., A. Abel, 'La Portée apologétique de la "vie" de St. Théodore d'Edesse', *Byzantinoslavica*, x (1949), 229–40.

[66] A. S. Atiya, *The Arabic Manuscripts of Mount Sinai; a handlist of the Arabic manuscripts and scrolls microfilmed at the library of the monastery of St. Catherine, Mount Sinai*, Baltimore 1955.

[67] J. Blau, *A Grammar of Christian Arabic, based mainly on South Palestinian texts from the first millennium*, CSCO, cclxvii, cclxxvi, cclxxix, Louvain 1966–7.

[68] Cf. his recent discussion of his linguistic concerns in J. Blau, 'The state of research in the field of the linguistic study of middle Arabic', *Arabica*, xxviii (1981), 187–203.

study. It is a veritable catalogue of the literary efforts of the Palestinian monks in the ninth and tenth centuries to translate the scriptures and other Christian classics into Arabic, as well as to write saints' lives, homilies, works of apologetics and other ecclesiastical literature in the *lingua franca* of the new Islamic political order.[69] While translations are by far the most numerous items in this catalogue, there are some important original works as well, as will appear below.

Blau's studies should not be taken to mean that there is, or ever was, a peculiarly 'Christian' Arabic.[70] The Palestinian texts which were the subject matter of his study represent the earliest surviving documentary evidence of the efforts in the Christian community outside Arabia proper to produce an ecclesiastical literature in the Arabic language. The persons who wrote these texts, while they were Arabic-speakers, had obviously been educated in Greek and in Syriac, a circumstance that affected their writing in Arabic and may have been responsible for some of the peculiar features of their diction. A symbol of the state of affairs in this early period of Melkite Christianity in Arabic may be seen in the surviving fragment of an Arabic version of Psalm 78, probably from the late eighth century. It was written in Greek characters.[71]

Stephen of Ramlah is one of the few monks of the period, who laboured to produce some twenty Christian Arabic manuscripts which survive from the ninth century, whose name has come down to us.[72] As an added bonus, Stephen's manuscripts, which he wrote in the years 877 and 897 respectively, are among the earliest dated Christian manuscripts in Arabic to survive anywhere.[73] The manuscripts are Sinai Arabic MS 72 and British Library Oriental MS 4950. The contents of these manuscripts are discussed below. The first concern, however, is with their colophons, all three of which have been published, even though most of the other contents of these manuscripts remain unpublished.[74] The fullest statement about

[69] Blau, *Grammar*, cclxvii. 21–36.

[70] On the so-called 'Christian Arabic', see the remarks of Kh. Samir, *Le Traité de l'unité de Yaḥyā ibn 'Adī (893–974), étude et édition critique*, Jounieh and Rome 1980, pp. xv–xvii, 72–91; idem (ed.), *Actes du Premier Congrès International d'Études Arabes Chrétiennes–Goslar, septembre, 1980* (Orientalia Christiana Analecta, 218), Rome 1982, 52–9.

[71] B. Violet, 'Ein zweisprachiges Psalmfragment aus Damaskus', *Berichtiger Sonderabzug aus der orientalistischen Litteratur-Zeitung, 1901*, Berlin 1902, cols. 1–52. Melkites seem never to have used Karšūnī/Garšūnī, i.e. the system of writing Arabic in Syriac characters. Cf. G. Troupeau, 'Karshūnī, *EI*, iv, 671–2.

[72] Another such scholar–monk of the ninth century is Bišr ibn Sirrī, who wrote the earliest dated MS of the period, Sinai Arabic MS 151, written in A.D. 867. J. Nasrallah, 'Deux versions melchites partielles de la Bible du ixe et du xe siècles', *Oriens Christianus*, lxiv (1980), 203–6.

[73] The year A.D. 772 is actually the earliest date mentioned in a documentary source with reference to a Christian text in Arabic, although the MS itself has not yet come to light. Blau, *Grammar*, cclxvii. n. 7.

[74] The colophon of Sinai Arabic MS 72 (fo. 118v) is published in C. E. Padwick, 'Al-Ghazali and the Arabic versions of the Gospels, an unsolved problem', *The Moslem World*, xxix (1939), betw. pp. 134 and 135; and in Atiya, *The Arabic Manuscripts of Mount Sinai*, pl. vi. A re-cataloguing of the Sinai MSS has changed their traditional numbers.

Stephen himself is in the first colophon in BL 4950: 'The book is finished ... Stephen ... son of Ḥakam, known as ar-Ramlī, wrote it in the *laura* of Mar Charitōn, for his teacher ... Anba Basil.'[75] The other colophons add no different personal information about Stephen.

The colophon of Sinai Arabic MS 72 and the first colophon in BL 4950 give the dates when Stephen finished writing them. The former one states that Stephen wrote it 'on the first month of Adhar, among the months of the non-Arabs (*fī ašhur al-ağam*); and, according to the reckoning of the years of the world (as the church of Jerusalem, the Glorious Resurrection, reckons), in the year 6389, and of the years of the Arabs, in the month of Muḥarram, of the year 284'.[76] The non-Arab date corresponds to 1 March A.D. 897.[77] The Arab date, which mentions no specific day, corresponds to the period between 8 February and 9 March A.D. 897.[78] As for the first treatise in BL 4950, Stephen says he finished it 'on the first day of December, according to the reckoning of the years of the world which is accepted in the church of the Resurrection, Jerusalem, in the year 6369; and of the years of Alexander, the year 1188; that is, of the year of the Arabs in the month Rabīʿ I, of the year 264'.[79] The years of the world and the Seleucid system called the 'years of Alexander' translate into 1 December A.D. 877.[80] The date of the Arabs, which again mentions no specific day, corresponds to the period between 11 November and 10 December A.D. 877.[81]

It is interesting to note in these colophons that, in the late ninth century, it was the Alexandrian system of computation of the years of the world that was acceptable in Jerusalem and not the newer Byzantine system of computation, which in the ninth century was just beginning to make headway in Byzantium itself, although it was not to take a definitive hold there until the end of the tenth century.[82] Of course, Palestine was cut off from effective communication with Byzantium at this time, but one is drawn to observe that George Synkellos (d. between 810 and 814), whose *Chronicle* Theophanes, the noted Byzantine chronicler (d. 818) continued, had been a monk in Palestine prior to becoming Patriarch Tarasius's (d. 806) *synkellos*. Both of these chroniclers employed the Alexandrian

According to the new system, MS 72 is MS 65. Cf. Murad Kamil, *Catalogue of all Manuscripts in the Monastery of St. Catherine on Mount Sinai*, Wiesbaden 1970, 14. The two colophons in British Library MS 4950, one following each of the two works contained in the manuscript, are published in the following places: (fo. 197v), in A. S. Lewis and M. D. Gibson, *Forty-one facsimiles of dated Christian Arabic Manuscripts* (Studia Sinaitica, no. 12), Cambridge 1907, 2–4, including a photograph, a transcription and an English version; also in Arendzen, *Theodori Abu Kurra*, the photograph as a frontispiece for the volume and the transcription and commentary on p. xv; (fo. 237r), in Arendzen, op. cit., 50 (Arabic), 52 (Latin version).

[75] Fo. 197v, cf. Lewis and Gibson, op. cit. p. 3. The second two ellipses in the quotation indicate the omission of honorific adjectives. The first one marks the omission of the date, which will be supplied below.

[76] Padwick, 'Al-Ghazali'.

[77] The method of reckoning the years of the world which Stephen used is the one called 'Alexandrian', V. Grumel, *La Chronologie*, Paris 1958, 252.

[78] Ibid., 285.

[79] Lewis and Gibson, *Forty-one Facsimiles*, 3.

[80] Grumel, op. cit., 251.

[81] Ibid., 284.

[82] Ibid., 124–8.

chronology, while Theophanes's own continuator (tenth century) had to abandon it.[83]

As coincidence would have it, the Palestinian monastery which George Synkellos often visited on pilgrimage during his own sojourn as a monk in the Holy Land was none other than the *laura* of St Charitōn,[84] then known as the 'old *laura*', or 'the old Souka', which St Charitōn had founded in the mid-fourth century.[85] Before anyone paid attention to the colophons of the Sinai manuscripts, and particularly to the two by the hand of Stephen of Ramlah, virtually all that was known of the activity at the monastery of Mar Charitōn after the sixth century came from reports in the works of the Byzantine chroniclers, George Synkellos and his follower Theophanes, and the hagiographical writings attributed to Stephen, the Sabaite. However, most of the references to the monastery in these works confine themselves to reporting occasions when the premises were sacked and the monks killed, first by the Persians, then at the hands of the Arabs.[86] Even later visitors, including the Russian Abbot Daniel, who came to the monastery in the twelfth century, did little more than refer to the bare fact of the monastery's presence – in the vicinity of that of St Sabas.[87] Now, thanks to Stephen of Ramlah's colophons, one knows that in the last quarter of the ninth century, at least, the *laura* of Mar Charitōn was a centre of Christian scholarship in Arabic.

Stephen's own sobriquet, *ar-Ramlī*, must mean that he was a native of the town of ar-Ramlah, which had been established by the future Umayyad caliph, Sulayman ibn 'Abd al-Malik (715–17), when he was governor of Palestine, to serve as the Islamic capital of that province-like military district (*al-ğund*) which included Jerusalem and the Judean desert.[88] One knows from remarks made by the Muslim scholar al-Ya'qūbī (d. 897), who was a contemporary of Stephen of Ramlah, that when ar-Ramlah was built the city of Lydda was wrecked, and its population was transferred to the new town, the inhabitants of which were thus a mixture of 'Arabs and non-Arabs', as al-Ya'qūbī says, 'and the Samaritans

[83] Ibid., 95–7, 126.

[84] Cf. the Greek text cited in the anonymous article, 'Les Premiers Monastères de la Palestine', *Bessarione*, iii (1897–8), 54.

[85] For a sketch of the history of the monastery, anon. 'Les Premiers Monastères, 50–8; and S. Vailhé, 'Repertoire alphabétique des monastères de Palestine', *Revue d l'Orient Chrétien*, iv (1899), 524–5; H. Leclercq, 'Laures palestiniennes', *DACL*, viii, 2, cols. 1970–73. On St Charitōn himself, the brief sketch and bibliography in G. Garitte, 'Charitōn (Saint)', *DHGE*, xii, cols. 421–3.

[86] Cf. the passages cited in anon. 'Les Premiers Monastères', 54–5.

[87] Ibid., 56.

[88] E. Honigmann, 'Al-Ramla', *EI*, 1st edn, iii. 1193–5. For a selection of passages in translation from the works of Arab geographers and travellers, pertaining to ar-Ramlah, Guy Le Strange, *Palestine under the Moslems. A description of Syria and the Holy Land from A.D. 650 to 1500*, Boston 1890, 303–8; and A. S. Marmardji, *Textes géographiques arabes sur la Palestine*, Paris 1951, 81–6.

were its protected population'.[89] Since ar-Ramlah became a town of some distinction, one may assume that while he lived there Stephen of Ramlah came to know Muslims and the Islamic objections to Christian doctrines at first hand. According to tradition, the city had been the scene, some 150 years earlier, during the reign of Patriarch John V of Jerusalem (705–35), of the martyrdom of the Sinai monk, 'Abd al-Masīḥ an-Nağrānī. This monk, who had once been among the Muslims, sought a confrontation with the Islamic authorities in ar-Ramlah in order publicly to affirm his Christian faith. As a consequence, he was beheaded there on the orders of the provincial governor, and the account of his martyrdom appeared among the earliest Christian documents in Arabic.[90]

The contents of the manuscripts which Stephen of Ramlah wrote reveal the Palestinian Church's basic requirements in the area of ecclesiastical books in Arabic. Of first importance was the Gospel, both for liturgical purposes and for scholarly concerns. Stephen's Sinai Arabic MS 72 is the oldest, dated manuscript of the Gospel in Arabic known to modern scholars. It belongs to a family of Arabic Gospel manuscripts, the origins of which are to be sought earlier in the ninth century. In all probability the text put forward in this manuscript family represents the earliest project anywhere systematically to translate the Gospel into Arabic.[91] The translation was made from a Greek original, with a close affinity to the text which at an earlier time in Palestine was translated into the Aramaic dialect that is usually called Palestinian Syriac.[92] The lessons of the Greek liturgy of the Jerusalem Church were read in this language, for the benefit of the non-Greek-speaking, indigenous population, as far back as the fourth century.[93] So the Arab translators of Stephen's day were building on a practice that had already become habitual in the Palestinian Church.

The text of the Gospel in Sinai Arabic MS 72 is a continuous text of the four Gospels in their canonical order. It is not in the format of a lectionary. Nevertheless, the pericopes appointed to be read at the liturgies in the temporal cycle are marked off with rubrics in the manuscript, designating the passages according to the usages of the old Jerusalem Church.[94] The format of this Gospel manuscript, then, with its continuous text and liturgical rubrics, allowed it easily to serve both scholarly and devotional

[89] Ahmed ibn Abî Jakûb ibn Wâdhih al-Kâtib al-Jakûbî, *Kitāb al-Boldân*, in M. J. De Goeje (ed.), *Bibliotheca Geographorum Arabicorum*, Leiden 1892, viii. 328. Le Strange presumes too much in translating *al-'ağam* as 'Greeks', op. cit., 303. In the colophon to Sinai Arabic MS 72, Stephen of Ramlah used the term to refer to the usage of Aramaic speakers. Cf. n. 76 above. Al-Ya'qūbī probably means 'Muslims and non-Muslims'.

[90] H. Zayat, 'Šuhadā' an-Naṣrāniyyah fī l-Islām', *al-Machriq*, xxxvi (1938), 459–65.

[91] For bibliography and discussion, S. H. Griffith, 'The Gospel in Arabic: an inquiry into its appearance in the first Abbasid century', *Oriens Christianus*, forthcoming.

[92] Metzger, *Early Versions of the New Testament* 75–82.

[93] Cf. the remark made by the pilgrim Egeria (*c.* 384), quoted in Metzger, op. cit., 77.

[94] A. Baumstark, 'Die sonntägliche Evangelienlesung in vorbysantinischen Jerusalem', *Byzantinishe Zeitschrift*, xxx (1929–30), 350–9.

purposes. This feature is common to all of the manuscripts in this early Palestinian text-family of the Gospels in the Arabic Bible.

It is evident from an examination of the text, and a comparison of it with the texts of the other manuscripts in its family, that in Sinai Arabic MS 72 Stephen of Ramlah was not content simply to copy the Gospel in Arabic from another manuscript. For, although Stephen's manuscript is the earliest known dated manuscript of the Gospel in Arabic, the text which he wrote in MS 72, taken in comparison with the other manuscripts in the same text-family, shows evidence of improvement in terms of Arabic expression, and corrections in many of the readings.[95] Stephen, therefore, was not simply a copyist. He was a scholar-monk who played an active role in the attempt to improve the diction and textual fidelity of the Gospel in Arabic.

Two short treatises are appended to the end of Sinai Arabic MS 72. The first of them, reflecting the Islamic presence, occupies a single page (fo. 117r). As was mentioned earlier, it reports Theodore Abū Qurrah's responses to a Muslim's enquiry about why Christians blame the Jews for the death of Christ.[96] The second piece, probably reflecting Stephen's own monastic environment, fills some three pages (fos. 117v–118v) with spiritual aphorisms which are attributed to a certain Mar Basil, who in all likelihood is the same person as the Anba Basil, the teacher to whom Stephen has dedicated his copy of the first work in BL Or. MS 4950.[97]

The first 197 leaves of MS 4950 contain twenty-five chapters of a veritable *summa theologiae* in Arabic. Although the first leaf of the manuscript is missing, the copyist repeated the title of the work at the end of the table of contents at the front of the book: 'A Summary of the Ways of Faith in Confessing the Trinity of the "One-ness" of God, and the Incarnation of God, the Word, from the Pure Virgin Mary'.[98] The *Summa* is not confined simply to the discussion of the doctrines of the Trinity and the Incarnation, as one might think from a consideration of the title alone. Rather, the subject matter of the twenty-five chapters includes everything from the definitions of highly technical theological terms to an Arabic version of the conciliar and other canons which govern the everyday life of the Church. There are chapters which include long lists of scriptural testimonies to the Christian view of Christ's economy of salvation, as well as discussions of the proper manner of interpreting the Bible. A distinctive feature of the language of this *Summa* is its obvious accommodation to the religious diction of Muslims and the attention paid to answering typically Islamic objections to Christian doctrines. Indeed, one whole chapter of the *Summa*, i.e. chapter XVIII, comprises a primer of some thirty-four

[95] Griffith, 'The Gospel in Arabic'; J. Blau, 'Über einige christlich-arabische Manuscripte aus dem 9. und 10. Jahrhundert', *Le Muséon*, lxxv (1962), 101–8; Amy Galli Garland, 'An Arabic translation of the Gospel according to Mark', unpublished M.A. thesis, The Catholic University of America; Washington, D.C., 1979.

[96] S. H. Griffith, 'Some unpublished sayings'.

[97] Above, n. 75.

[98] British Library Oriental MS 4950, fo. 2r.

responses which deal with the common apologetical and polemical topics which had a place in the contemporary arguments about religion between Christians and Muslims.[99] Clearly then, the *Summa* is an important document in testimony to the day-to-day issues which concerned the Christian community in Palestine in the late ninth century. There is evidence that it had a considerable success on a wider scale, since extracts from it appear in a number of other manuscripts, from different times and places.[100]

The author of this treatise is not named in Stephen of Ramlah's colophon. Some scholars have suggested that he was none other than Theodore Abū Qurrah.[101] This identification is unlikely, as Blau has shown, because in the text the author mentions that more than 800 years have elapsed since the destruction of Jerusalem, a calculation which puts the date of composition somewhere between the year 870, counting from A.D. 70, and the year 877 when Stephen copied it.[102] Abū Qurrah died *c*. 820–5. Furthermore, as a number of scholars have noticed in the only four chapters of the work yet to be published,[103] although many of the illustrative arguments are similar to those employed by Abū Qurrah, on stylistic and lexical grounds one should conclude that the author of the work was someone else.[104] As noted above, even when the author of the *Summa* employs an argument which is essentially the same as one attributed to Abū Qurrah, the details differ considerably, suggesting a different writer for the *Summa*.[105] Perhaps it is not far-fetched to propose that there was a Palestinian 'school' of Christian thinkers who worked in Arabic, to which Abū Qurrah and others belonged, one centre of which was located at Mar Charitōn and one of whose monks wrote this treatise. As a matter of fact, it does not seem implausible to the present writer, given the earliest possible date for the composition of the text, i.e. after 870, and the date of the manuscript, i.e. 877, to suggest that Stephen of Ramlah was himself the author, or perhaps the compiler of this variegated work. When he simply copied the work of others he clearly said so, as he did at the beginning and end of the next work in BL 4950, and he did not dedicate work of another person to his teacher, Mar Basil, as he did the *Summa*. Of course, the crucial first two leaves of MS 4950 are missing, where

99 Cf. the discussion in Graf, *GCAL*, ii. 16–19, including a table of contents of the entire *Summa*.

100 Nasrallah, 'Dialogue islamo-chrétien', 131–2.

101 Kh. Samir, 'Notes sur les citations bibliques chez Abū Qurrah', *Orientalia Christiana Periodica*, xliv (1983), 184–91.

102 J. Blau, 'The importance of Middle Arabic dialects for the history of Arabic', in U. Heyd (ed.), *Studies in Islamic History and Civilization* (Scripta Hierosolymitana, IX), Jerusalem 1961, 208 n. 9; idem, 'Über einige christlich-arabische Manuscripte', 102.

103 L. Ma'lūf, 'Aqdam al-Maḫṭūṭāt an-Naṣrāniyyah al-'Arabiyyah', *al-Machriq*, vi (1903), 1011–23. The present writer is now preparing Graf's edition of this important treatise for publication.

104 Cf. Griffith, 'The controversial theology', 7–10. I no longer think that the term *al-bašar* hints at a Monophysite writer. It is simply a lexical difference from Abū Qurrah's usual vocabulary.

105 Above, n. 59.

Stephen may well have mentioned the author of the *Summa*. But if someone other than himself was to be named, it is surprising that the name was not repeated in the colophon at the end of the *Summa* (fo. 197v), where so much other information is given. Even Joshua Blau was tempted to conclude that Stephen was the author of the work, but he hesitated to do so because of what he observed to be a copyist's error at fo. 71r, l. 1.[106] However, since the error in question is simply a misplaced diacritical point, a common error, it is not really inconsistent with the proposal that Stephen was writing his own composition. But the fact remains that the question of authorship is an open one.

The second work which Stephen wrote in BL 4950 is Theodore Abū Qurrah's apologetic tract on the Christian practice of venerating images, which was published by John Arendzen in 1897.[107] Stephen's inclusion of Abū Qurrah's apologetic tract here, taken together with the few responses in Sinai 72, testifies to Abū Qurrah's popularity at Mar Charitōn in the late ninth century, and it suggests that he was one of the inspiring geniuses behind the Christian publishing enterprise in Arabic in the Palestinian monasteries. Furthermore, it is indicative of the fact that he exerted a strong influence on Stephen of Ramlah in particular, a fact which may account for why the *Summa* at the beginning of BL 4950 reminds so many modern scholars of Theodore Abū Qurrah's style of argumentation.

Abū Qurrah's treatise on the Christian practice of venerating images is an apologetic tract which furnishes Christians with arguments opposing the charge made against them by Jews and Muslims that such veneration is tantamount to the idolatry forbidden in the Bible. While this issue was not a constant topic in the religious arguments between Christians and Muslims everywhere in the East, as was the practice of venerating the cross, nevertheless, in the first Abbasid century it was an important topic, especially in the Melkite community. Eutychius of Alexandria mentioned Abū Qurrah's tract on images in his chronicle of world history,[108] and another monk in the tenth century wrote a copy of it in Sinai Arabic MS 330 (fos. 315r–357r). Unlike Abū Qurrah's other Arabic works, however, his treatise on images does not seem to have enjoyed a wide popularity among Arab Christians in the medieval period. It was not widely copied. But for the modern historian of the Church in *dār al-islām*, this apologetic tract reveals the dimensions of the controversy over religious images that occurred in the first Abbasid century, among Jews, Christians and Muslims, in the very era when iconoclasm was a policy adopted by the imperial government in Byzantium. It is the only document known to the present writer in which it is clear that the Melkites had a pastoral problem in regard to the practice of venerating images because some Christians

[106] Blau, 'Über einige christlich-arabische Manuscripte', 102.

[107] Arendzen, *Theodori Abu Kurra.*

[108] Cheikho *et al.*, *Eutychii Patriarchae Alexandrini Annales*, li. 64; Griffith, 'Eutychius of Alexandria'.

were abandoning the practice in the face of objections coming from Jews and Muslims.[109]

Stephen of Ramlah closed BL 4950 with another quotation from his teacher: 'the holy Mar Basil'.[110] At this time the identity of Mar Basil is still unknown and his few remarks, piously transmitted by Stephen, remain unstudied. At the very least Stephen's inclusion in his manuscripts of Mar Basil's spiritual teachings testifies to the lively state of monastic spirituality in the monasteries of Palestine in the late ninth century, and Stephen himself emerges as an important figure in the history of the Palestinian Church at that time. He played a major role in the Church's successful campaign to come to terms with life within *dār al-islām*, and he seems to have been in the forefront of the programme to publish the Christian *kerygma* in Arabic. His name and works deserve to take their place in the history of the Christian Church in the Holy Land.

109 S. H. Griffith, 'Theodore Abū Qurrah's Arabic tract', forthcoming.
110 British Library Oriental MS 4950, fo. 237v.

Additional Note

In the course of preparing a new edition of the text of the Arabic *Vita* of 'Abd al-Masīḥ al-Ghassānī, the author has been convinced of the need to revise H. Żayat's dating for the martyr's *floruit*. See n. 90 above. It seems likely that 'Abd al-Masīḥ met Patriarch John VI of Jerusalem, rather than John V, as Zayat thought, and that the martyrdom occurred *c*.860, presumably in the lifetime of Stephen of Ramlah. See S. H. Griffith, 'The Arabic account of 'Abd al-Masīḥ an-Nağrānī al-Ghassānī', forthcoming.

VIII

GREEK INTO ARABIC : LIFE AND LETTERS IN THE MONASTERIES OF PALESTINE IN THE NINTH CENTURY ; THE EXAMPLE OF THE *SUMMA THEOLOGIAE ARABICA*

Most western historians of the Christian east seem to think that the Abbasid revolution among the Muslims in the year 750 sounded the death knell for creative intellectual life in the hitherto famous Palestinian monasteries of St. Sabas, St. Charitōn, and the monastery of the Mother of God at Sinai. For the first century or so of Arab rule, everyone admits, Christian culture persisted in the Holy Land, and even achieved notable success, as is evident in the works of Anastasius of Sinai and John of Damascus, to mention only the two writers with the most immediate name recognition among western scholars. But after the Abbasid revolution, when the Islamic world turned its back on the Mediterranean, and Baghdad became the focus of culture in the Arabic speaking caliphate, the conventional view of historians has it that the monasteries of Palestine were wrecked as a result of the social upheavals of the times, the monks fled, and consequently that all intellectual and cultural life at these erstwhile lively centers of Christianity came to a halt ([1]).

One does not have to look far to discover the roots of this point of view. It was put forward in the first instance by the Byzantine historian, Theophanes the Confessor (d.c. 818) towards the end of his *Chronographia.* Under the heading of the 'Year of the World' 6305, or 805

(1) See, *e.g.*, R. P. Blake, "La littérature grecque en Palestine au VIIIe siècle", *Le Muséon,* 78 (1965), pp. 367-380, and C. Mango, "Who Wrote the Chronicle of Theophanes ?", *SRPSKA Academia Nauka, Zbornik Radova Vizantoloskog Instituta,* 18 (1978), p. 14 ; Michael Borgolte, *Der Gesandtenaustausch der Karolinger mit den Abbasiden und mit den Patriarchen von Jerusalem* (Münchener Beiträge zur Mediävistik und Renaissance-Forschung, 25 ; München, 1976), pp. 17-34.

A.D., as the author reckoned it, but 812/813 in the correct reckoning, Theophanes wrote :

> In the same year many Christian monks and laity from Palestine and all Syria reached Cyprus, fleeing the boundless evil of the Arabs. For general anarchy had seized Syria, Egypt, Africa, and their entire empire : in villages and cities their people, cursed by God, murdered, robbed, committed adultery and acts of licentiousness, and did all sorts of things hateful to God. The revered sites in the vicinity of the holy city of Christ our God, the Anastasis, Golgatha, and others, were profaned. In the same way, the famous *lauras* of Sts. Khariton and Sabas in the desert, as well as other churches and monasteries, were devastated. Some men became martyrs ; others got to Cyprus, and from it to Byzantium ([2]).

Theophanes' remarks give one the impression that there was no one left in the monasteries of Palestine much after the first decade of the ninth century. And there is no other Greek source available which one might consult to correct this mistaken scenario. From the Byzantine point of view, after the arrival of the final wave of Palestinian emigres in Constantinople in the reign of Michael I (811-813), the patriarchate of Jerusalem seems to have slipped entirely out of mind as a functioning center of Christian thought. There remained only the *loca sancta*, in which Christian governments had a diplomatic interest and which the pilgrims visited. And when these travellers mention the famous old monasteries of Mar Sabas or Mar Charitōn in passing, they leave no record at all of any new Christian culture thriving there ([3]).

The mistake here, of course, is that western scholars have been slow to take into account what can be learned about the fortunes of Christian culture in the Holy Land, and elsewhere in the caliphate,

(2) Carolus DE BOOR (ed.), *Theophanis Chronographia* (2 vols. ; Lipsiae, 1883 & 1885), vol. I, p. 499. The English translation is adapted from Harry TURTLEDOVE, *The Chronicle of Theophanes ; an English Translation of anni mundi 6095-6305 (A.D. 602-813), with Introduction and Notes* (Philadelphia, 1982), p. 178. Unfortunately, Turtledove's version must be used with care, and only with reference to the original, due to the translator's unpredictable omissions, and misreadings.

(3) See, *e.g.*, H. DONNER, "Die Palästina-beschreibung des Epiphanius Monachus Hagiopolita", *Zeitschrift des Deutschen Palästina-Vereins*, 87 (1971), p. 71. Cf. also John WILKINSON, *Jerusalem Pilgrims Before the Crusades* (Warminster, 1977). On the diplomatic interests see now M. BORGOLTE, *Der Gesandtenaustausch*, with its full bibliography.

from the abundant testimony of contemporary Christian texts in Arabic, which survive from the very monasteries whose demise the historians have often proclaimed, as a result of reading only Greek sources. Accordingly, the purpose of the present communication is somewhat to redress the balance of historical inquiry in this area by discussing an important Christian text in Arabic which was written in its present form at the monastery of Mar Charitōn in the year 877 A.D. As will become clear in the course of the discussion, the religious challenge of Islam was one of the primary motivating influences for the author of this work, which I call, with some justification in the text : *Summa Theologiae Arabica.*

The political and religious hegemony of Islam had by the end of the first Abbasid century brought about a civil culture in the Oriental Patriarchates, in which Arabic was the standard language, and everywhere the signs and symbols of the Islamic society held the public eye ([4]). This socio-political reality, in which Christians, Jews, and other religious minorities held a subordinate role as "protected people" (*ahl adh-dhimmah*), left them free to argue with one another about religion, but it presented them with the need to apologize for their faith in a language already laden with a bias for Islam – a situation vastly different from anything with which the citizens of Byzantium were yet familiar ([5]). So perhaps it is no wonder that even the Holy Land pilgrims from the west, who at least saw the famous monasteries of Palestine in those times, failed to mention the burgeoning scholarly activity going on in them because it was quite simply beyond their comprehension both linguistically and conceptually. But the result of their inattention has been that western historians have for the most part been content to allow the Christian history of the Holy Land to end with the eighth century, not to begin again until the time when Byzantine armies once more appeared in the area in the reigns of the emperors Nicephoros Phocas (963-969) and John Tzimisces

(4) Cf. Sidney H. GRIFFITH, "Theodore Abū Qurrah's Arabic Tract on the Christian Practice of Venerating Images", *Journal of the American Oriental Society*, 105 (1985), pp. 53-73.

(5) Protected, second-class citizenship for Christians, Jews and others under Islamic domination was theoreticaly governed by the "Covenant of Umar". Cf. A. S. TRITTON, *The Caliphs and their Non-Muslim Subjects, a Critical Study of the Covenant of ᶜUmar* (London, 1930) ; A. FATTAL, *Le statut légal des non-musulmans en pays d'Islam* (Beyrouth, 1958).

(969-976), and one could read about their exploits in Greek. A century later the crusaders from the patriarchate of Rome arrived, and then for a time the Holy Land became yet again a part of the history of the west, a story told in Greek and Latin chronicles. But still the story of the indigenous Christian communities remained largely untold. Nowadays, with attention paid to Christian Arabic texts, even we westerners can see that Christian culture continued to grow in Syria/Palestine in the ninth century and beyond, and found a new voice, in a new *lingua franca*, suitable for the life within *dār al-islām*. The *Summa Theologiae Arabica* which is the focus of this communication is a striking case in point, coming as it does from the very earliest period of Christian literature in Arabic. As we shall see, by the time the *Summa* was written, Christians living in the caliphate had been writing in Arabic for a century or more. So it is an appropriate document to put forward as an example of a new trend in the life and letters of the Palestinian monasteries.

The *Summa Theologiae Arabica*, which was written in its present form in the year 877 A.D. at the monastery of Mar Charitōn in the Judean desert, is preserved in its entirety in *British Library Oriental MS* 4950 ([6]). This manuscript also contains another original composition in Arabic by a Christian author, namely, Theodore Abū Qurrah's (d.c. 825) apologetic tract on the Christian practice of venerating images of Christ and the saints. John Arendzen published this text, with a Latin version, in 1897, so it has long been available to scholars ([7]). The *Summa*, on the other hand, has not yet been published in its entirety, but it will appear in the not too distant future in an updated edition of the Arabic text prepared originally by Msgr.

(6) A. G. ELLIS & Edward EDWARDS, *A Descriptive List of the Arabic Manuscripts Acquired by the Trustees of the British Museum since 1894* (London, 1912), p. 69. The contents of the *Summa* are described in George GRAF, *Geschichte der christlichen arabischen Literatur* (5 vols. ; Città del Vaticano, 1944-1953), vol. II, pp. 16-19.

(7) Cf. I. ARENDZEN, *Theodori Abu Kurra de Cultu Imaginum Libellus e Codice Arabico nunc Primum Editus Latine Versus Illustratus* (Bonn, 1897). A new edition of the text, on the basis not only of *BM* 4950, but also *Sinai Arabic MS* 330, which contains the only other known text of Abū Qurrah's tract, is now ready for publication, along with an English version and notes by the present writer. Ignace Dick has also prepared a new Arabic edition to appear in the series, Patrimoine Arabe Chrétien.

Georg Graf. Now it will be accompanied by an English version and explanatory notes by the present writer.

Before discussing the *Summa* in any further detail, it is first necessary to describe, at least in cursory fashion, the historical and cultural milieu in which both works contained in *BL* 4950 first appeared.

The most prominent feature of *BL* 4950, aside from a consideration of the merits of the two works it contains, is the fact that linguistically speaking it belongs to a family of Arabic manuscripts, all of which were written in Syria/Palestine in the ninth and tenth centuries. The texts which belong to this family of manuscripts share a set of linguistic and scribal idiosyncrasies, which altogether describe a certain state of the Arabic language, which has been seen to represent a stage in the growth of what the scholars of linguistics call "Middle Arabic" ([8]). While there is some controversy involved in the precise significance of such a characterization of this group of Christian Arabic manuscripts ([9]), the very existence of this definable archive of literary material from the Holy Land monasteries from the ninth and tenth centuries, affords the historian an opportunity to refer to these texts in his search for information about what constituted the scholarly activities of "Orthodox" or "Melkite" oriental Christians at this period, and what were their intellectual preoccupations, once the

(8) The state of the Arabic language displayed in these texts is described in Joshua Blau, *A Grammar of Christian Arabic* (CSCO, vols. 267, 276, 279 ; Louvain, 1966-1967). Blau's point of view, with reference to the Christian Arabic texts of Palestine, is also put forward in the following publications by the author : "The Importance of Middle Arabic Dialects for the History of Arabic", in U. Heyd (ed.), *Studies in Islamic History and Civilization* (Scripta Hierosolymitana, 9 ; Jerusalem, 1961), pp. 205-228 ; "Über einige christlich-arabische Manuskripte aus dem 9. und 10. Jahrhundert", *Le Muséon*, 75 (1962), pp. 101-108 ; "Über einige alte christlich-arabische Handschriften aus Sinai", *Le Muséon*, 76 (1963), pp. 369-374 ; *The Emergence and Linguistic Background of Judaeo-Arabic ; a Study of the Origins of Middle Arabic* (Scripta Judaica, 5 ; Oxford, 1965 ; "Sind uns Reste arabischer Bibelübersetzungen aus vorislamischer Zeit erhalten geblieben ?", *Le Muséon*, 86 (1973), pp. 67-72 ; "The State of Research in the Field of the Linguistic Study of Middle Arabic", *Arabica*, 28 (1981), pp. 187-203.

(9) See Kh. Samir (ed.), *Actes du premier congrès international d'études arabes chrétiennes, Goslar, septembre 1980* (Orientalia Christiana Analecta, 218 ; Rome, 1982), pp. 52-68. See also the review of this publication by J. Grand Henry, *Le Muséon*, 96 (1983), pp. 341-346.

regular contacts with Byzantium were broken. Furthermore, the manuscripts and their few surviving colophons also give one the opportunity to gain some understanding of the origins of the writers themselves, and some sense of the scope of their influence among the Christians living in the caliphate. For all of these issues, the list of "Old South Palestinian" texts studied by Joshua Blau for his *Grammar of Christian Arabic* may serve as the register of the primary documentary sources for the historian's quest ([10]).

Here, of course, is not the place for a detailed rehearsal of the historical information which one may acquire from the texts listed by Blau. But it is appropriate to highlight some general historical observations, based on such a detailed study ([11]). They will serve to provide a framework within which to appreciate more fully the significance of the *Summa Theologiae Arabica.*

The first general historical observation of importance is one which Blau himself has emphasized. Of the sixty some works in "Old South Palestinian" Arabic which he studied, only five or six of them are original compositions in arabic ([12]). Leaving aside some saints' lives, which Blau did not consider to be Arabic originals, but which may indeed have been so ([13]), all of these original works are doctrinal in character, with a controversial, or apologetical dimension. The *Summa* is preeminent among them. For the rest, the preponderant majority of known Christian Arabic texts from Palestine in the ninth and tenth centuries are translations from Greek or Syriac, and they

(10) BLAU, *Grammar,* vol. 267, pp. 21-33. Blau's list is not, of course, complete. One must also take into account the manuscript studies of Samir Khalil and J.-M. Sauget.

(11) More substantive study of the historical information which can be drawn from the "Old South Palestinian Texts" will appear in Sidney H. GRIFFITH, "Greek into Arabic : the Monks of Palestine and the Growth of Christian Literature in Arabic". For the broader context in which such issues must be studied, see Samir KHALIL, "La tradition arabe chrétienne et la chrétienté de terre-sainte", in D.-M. A. JAEGER, *Papers Read at the 1979 Tantur Conference on Christianity in the Holy Land* (Studia Oecumenica Hierosolymitana, 1 ; Jerusalem,1980), pp. 343-432.

(12) BLAU, *Grammar,* vol. 267, pp. 21-23. The *Kitāb al-burhān* usually ascribed to Eutychius of Alexandria, cf. GRAF, *GCAL,* vol. II, pp. 35-38, is probably also the composition of a Palestinian monk. See now the remarks of Michel BREYDY, *Études sur Saʿīd ibn Baṭriq et ses sources* (CSCO, vol. 450 ; Lovanii, 1983), pp. 88-94.

(13) See Sidney H. GRIFFITH, "The Arabic *Vita* of ʿAbd al-Masīḥ an-Nağrānī al-Ghassānī", *Le Muséon,* in press.

belong to the category of "church-books", or texts which Christians require for the ordinary conduct of their internal religious affairs, as opposed to works of scholarship or apology. There is a group of some thirty-five items, consisting mainly of homilies, saints' lives, martyrdoms, and selections from the writings of the fathers ; while twenty-one pieces are Arabic versions of parts of the scriptures ([14]). The simplest construction to put upon these facts is that in the ninth and tenth centuries in Syria/Palestine, the Melkite community increasingly required Church books in Arabic because this language had already become the daily language of most of the Melkites.

All of the Melkite "church books" in the "Old South Palestinian archive" are translations from Greek and Syriac. The earliest documentary reference to a date for such a translation project is the notice appearing in both *Sinai Arabic MS* 542 and *British Library Oriental* MS 5019 in regard to the translation of the account of the Sinai martyrs, which is usually ascribed to one Ammonios. The notice says, "This document was translated into Arabic from Greek ... in the year two hundred and fifty-five of the years of the Arabs" ([15]) – that is to say, in the year 772 A.D. Otherwise the earliest dated manuscript now available containing translations of "church books" into Arabic is almost a century later. Bišr ibn as-Sirrī says in the colophon to his translation of the Pauline epistles, "These fourteen epistles have been rendered from Syriac into Arabic ... in the month of Ramaḍān, of the year two hundred and fifty-three, in the city of Damascus" ([16]) – that is to say, in the year 867 A.D. The next oldest dated Christian Arabic

(14) BLAU, *Grammar*, vol. 267, pp. 23-33.

(15) See *British Library Oriental MS* 5019, f. 58v, and *Sinai Arabic MS* 542 (Kamil, 576), f. 15r. Both texts are quoted in Sidney H. GRIFFITH, "The Arabic Account of ʿAbd al-Masīḥ an-Naǧrānī al-Ghassānī", to appear. For the quotation of the text in *BL* 5019, see H. ZAYAT, "Shuhada' an-Naṣrāniyyah fī l-Islām", *al-Machriq*, 36 (1938), p. 462 ; J. BLAU, "The Importance of Middle Arabic", p. 219, n. 40 ; *idem*, "Über einige christliche-arabische Manuskripte", p. 103 ; *idem*, *The Emergence ... of Judaeo-Arabic*, p. 5, n. 7. For Ammonios and his narrative see the notice in H.-G. BECK, *Kirche und theologische Literatur im byzantinischen Reich* (Byzantinisches Handbuch ; Munich, 1959), p. 413.

(16) Harvey STAAL, *Mt. Sinai Arabic Codex 151 ; I, Pauline Epistles* (CSCO, vols. 452 & 453 ; Lovanii, 1983), vol. 452, p. 248; n. 23 (Arabic) ; vol. 453, p. 260, n. 23 (English). On *Bišr ibn as-Sirrī*, cf. J. NASRALLAH, "Deux versions melchites partielles de la Bible du IXᵉ et du Xᵉ siècles", *Oriens Christianus*, 64 (1980), pp. 203-206.

manuscript is *British Library Oriental MS* 4950, which contains the *Summa Theologiae Arabica.* As mentioned above, this manuscript was written at the Judean monastery of Mar Charitōn, in 877 A.D., by Stephen of Ramlah ([17]). For the rest, the "Old South Palestinian" archive, as it appears in Blau's list, features some twenty-five items dated to the ninth century. Most, but not all, of them lack more specific information, and they are assigned to the ninth century chiefly on the basis of paleographical considerations ([18]).

The year 772 A.D., one should note at this juncture, comes close to what must have been the beginning of the literary career of the earliest Christian Arabic writer known by name, Theodore Abū Qurrah (d.c. 825) ([19]). And a significant fact about the works of Abū Qurrah is that one knows of them in four languages. Some fourteen works survive in Arabic, and forty-three in Greek ([20]). Abū Qurrah

(17) See n. 6 above, and Sidney H. GRIFFITH, "Stephen of Ramlah and the Christian Kerygma in Arabic in Ninth-Century Palestine", *Journal of Ecclesiastical History,* 35 (1985), pp. 23-45.

(18) See Blau's brief discussion of each item, *Grammar,* vol. 267, pp. 21-33.

(19) See I. DICK, "Un Continuateur arabe de saint Jean Damascène : Théodore Abuqurra, évêque melkite de Harrān", *Proche-Orient Chrétien,* 12 (1962), pp. 209-233, 319-332 ; 13 (1963), pp. 114-129 ; Sidney H. GRIFFITH, "The Controversial Theology of Theodore Abū Qurrah (c. 750-c. 820 A.D.), a Methodological, Comparative Study in Christian Arabic Literature", (Ph. D. Dissertation ; The Catholic University of America, Washington, D.C., 1978), Ann Arbor, Michigan, University Microfilms International, no. 7819874.

(20) The published works of Abū Qurrah in Arabic are : I. ARENDZEN, *Theodori Abu Kurra de Cultu Imaginum Libellus e Codice Arabico nunc Primum Editus Latine Versus Illustratus* (Bonn, 1897) ; C. BACHA, *Les œuvres arabes de Théodore Aboucara évêque d'Haran* (Beirut, 1904) ; *idem, Un traité des œuvres arabes de Théodore Abou-Kurra, évêque de Haran* (Tripoli, Syria & Rome, 1905) ; G. GRAF, *Die arabischen Schriften des Theodor Abu Qurra, Bischofs von Ḥarran (ca. 740-820)* (Forschungen zur christlich Literatur- und Dogmengeschichte, Band X, Heft 3/4 ; Paderborn, 1910) ; L. CHEIKHO, "Mīmar li Tadūrūs Abī Qurrah fī Wuǧūd al-Ḫāliq wa d-Dīn al-Qawīm", *al-Machriq,* 15 (1912), pp. 757-774 ; 825-842 ; G. GRAF, *Des Theodor Abu Kurra Traktat über den Schöpfer und die wahre Religion* (Beiträge zur Geschichte der Philosophie des Mittelalters. Texte und Untersuchungen, Band XIV, Haft 1), Münster, Westphalia, 1913) ; I. DICK, "Deux écrits inédits de Théodore Abuqurra", *Le Muséon,* 72 (1959), pp. 53-67 ; S. H. GRIFFITH, "Some Unpublished Arabic Sayings Attributed to Theodore Abū Qurrah", *Le Muséon,* 92 (1979), pp. 29-35 ; I. DICK, *Théodore Abuqurra, Traité de l'existence du Créateur et de la vraie religion ; introduction et texte critique* (Patrimoine Arabe Chrétien, 3 ; Jounieh & Rome, 1982). For Abū Qurrah's works preserved only in Greek, see *PG,* vol. 97,

himself says that he wrote thirty treatises in Syriac ([21]), but none of these are known to have survived. Finally, some of Abū Qurrah's works have come down to us in Georgian. For the most part the latter are translations from Greek, done in the twelfth century ([22]). But it is worth noting that Euthymius, a Georgian monk who died c. 1028, worked the other way around, translating a now unknown work by Abū Qurrah from Georgian into Greek ([23]). The original could have been either Arabic or Syriac. In fact, there are several other well known instances, such as the *Life of St. Romanos the Neomartyr*, in which early Christian Arabic compositions have been preserved only in Georgian translation ([24]). And this circumstance reminds the historian both of the isolation of the oriental patriarchates from Byzantium in the ninth century, and of the continued presence of the Georgians among the Melkites of Syria/Palestine throughout the period ([25]).

cols. 1461-1610. For the manuscripts of unpublished works attributed to Abū Qurrah, see GRAF, *GCAL*, vol. II, pp. 7-16, and J. NASRALLAH, "Dialogue islamo-chrétien à propos de publications récentes", *Revue des Études Islamiques*, 46 (1978), pp. 129-132.

(21) BACHA, *Les Œuvres arabes*, pp. 60-61.

(22) See M. TARCHNISVILI, *Geschichte der kirchlichen georgischen Literatur* (Studi e Testi, 185 ; Vatican City, 1955), pp. 208-209, 370-371 ; R. GVARAMIA, "Bibliographie du dialogue islamo-chrétien : auteurs chrétiens de langue géorgienne", *Islamochristiana*, 6 (1980), pp. 290-291. See also *GCAL*, vol. II, pp. 20-21.

(23) TARCHNISVILI, *Geschichte*, p. 129, and GRAF, *GCAL*, vol. II, p. 21.

(24) See P. PEETERS, "S. Romain le néomartyr (1 mai 780), d'après un document géorgien", *Analecta Bollandiana*, 30 (1911), pp. 393-427 ; R. P. BLAKE, "Deux lacunes comblées dans la passio monachorum Sabaitorum", *Analecta Bollandiana*, 68 (1950), pp. 27-43 ; Gérard GARITTE, "Un extrait géorgien de la vie d'Étienne le Sabaite", *Le Muséon*, 67 (1954), pp. 71-92.

(25) See G. PERADZE, "An Account of the Georgian Monks and Monasteries in Palestine", *Georgica*, 1 (1937), pp. 181-246 ; R. P. BLAKE, "Catalogue des manuscrits géorgiens de la bibliothèque patriarcale grecque à Jérusalem", *Revue de l'Orient Chrétien*, 23 (1922-1923), pp. 345-413 ; 124 (1924), pp. 190-210, 387-429 ; 25 (1925-1926), pp. 132-155 ; G. GARITTE, *Catalogue des manuscrits géorgiens littéraires du mont Sinai* (CSCO, vol. 165 ; Louvain, 1956) ; Michel VAN ESBROECK, *Les plus anciens homéliaires géorgiens* (Publications de l'Institut Orientaliste de Louvain, 10 ; Louvain-La-Neuve, 1975) ; Kh. SAMIR, "Les plus anciens homéliaires géorgiens et les versions patristiques arabes", *Orientalia Christiana Periodica*, 42 (1976), pp. 217-231.

Abū Qurrah's surviving works show that Greek, Syriac, Georgian, and Arabic were all languages of the Melkite community in the Holy Land at the turn of the ninth century. Of the four of them, Georgian was not an indigenous language, and neither Abū Qurrah nor any other person of Syro-Palestinian origin is known to have employed it. It was the language of a group of foreign monks who generation after generation came on permanent pilgrimage to the Holy Land. But neither do translations prove their active involvement in the Melkite community life there.

For reasons put forward elsewhere, it seems unlikely to the present writer that Abū Qurrah himself ever wrote in Greek. Like his works preserved in Georgian, those which have survived in Greek may all be considered to be translations from Syriac or Arabic ([26]). For, Theodore Abū Qurrah was the harbinger of the new thing that was coming into its own at the turn of the ninth century. From the modern historian's point of view his is the prominent name associated with the first efforts to put Byzantine orthodoxy into Arabic. This project was the long range undertaking which in due course was responsible for the production of all the items in the "Old South Palestinian" archive. So while Abū Qurrah may well have known Greek, and have done his research in this traditional scholarly language of his Melkite community, he did his writing in his native Syriac, and in the new *lingua franca* of the caliphate. Years later, Michael the Syrian recorded the memory of Abū Qurrah preserved in the Syrian Orthodox community, "Because he was a sophist, and engaged in dialectics with the pagans [*ḥanpê*, *i.e.*, the Muslims], and knew the Saracen language, he was an object of wonder to the simple folk ([27])".

Greek, of course, had long been the language of the Jerusalem patriarchate. Although since the fourth century there had been the need in some circumstances to translate at least the lessons of the divine liturgy into the Aramaic vernacular of Palestine, and a relatively small collection of other Church books were also produced in that language ([28]), Greek remained the ecclesiastical language of the

(26) See GRIFFITH, "Stephen of Ramlah", n. 17 above.

(27) J.-B. CHABOT, *Chronique de Michel le syrien ; patriarche jacobite d'Antioche (1166-1199)* (4 vols. ; Paris, 1899-1910), vol. 3, p. 32 (French) ; vol. 4, pp. 495-496 (Syriac).

(28) See the famous passage from Egeria's travel journal in which she tells of the role of the Syriac interpreter at the liturgies she attended, John WILKINSON, *Egeria's*

Chalcedonian communities and the usual medium of scholarship. By the ninth century, however, there were persons associated with Mar Sabas monastery who had difficulties with the mastery of Greek. For example, toward the end of his account of the twenty martyrs of this monastery who suffered at the hands of the "Saracens" in the year 797, Stephen of Mar Sabas told the story of a Syrian priest who only with great difficulty had learned the recitation of the Psalter in Greek, and who now wanted to learn to speak the language idiomatically. As the story goes, his prayer was fulfilled in a dream, in which he had a vision of one of the martyred monks ([29]). One may suppose that the situation of this Syrian priest, who felt an acute lack of ability in Greek, was not uncommon in the early ninth century in Chalcedonian circles in Syria/Palestine. Such a circumstance would go a long way to explain how it came about that Michael Synkellos found it necessary around the year 810, before he joined the Palestinian emigre community of Constantinople, to compose his now well known basic introduction to Greek grammar and syntax. Michael was a monk of Mar Sabas, who had been born in Jerusalem around the year 761. Citing his own letters, one of his biographers described Michael as having been born of Persian-stock (*περσογενής*) ([30]). Perhaps this epithet means only that Michael's ancestors were originally east Syrian Christians. Many of them are known to have made pilgrimages to the Holy Land ; some

Travels to the Holy Land (Revised ed. ; Jerusalem & Warminster, 1981), p. 146. See also M.-J. LANGRANGE, "L'origine de la version syro-palestinienne des évangiles", *Revue Biblique*, 34 (1925), pp. 481-504 ; M. Goshen GOTTSTEIN, *The Bible in the Syropalestinian Version ; Part I : Pentateuch and Prophets* (Jerusalem, 1973), esp. pp. VIII-XV ; B. M. METZGER, *The Early Versions of the New Testament* (Oxford, 1977), pp. 75-82. Many useful bibliographical entries are recorded in J. BARCLAY, "Melkite Orthodox Syro-Byzantine Manuscripts in Syriac and Palestinian Aramaic", *Studi Biblicii Franciscani, Liber Annuus*, 21 (1971), pp. 205-219.

(29) See the story translated from Greek into Latin in J. BOLLANDUS et al., *Acta Sanctorum Martii* (vol. III ; Paris & Rome, 1865), p. 176.

(30) *περσογενὴς δὲ ὑπῆρχεν ἐκ προγόνων, καθὼς αὐτὸς ἐν ταῖς αὐτοῦ ἐπιστολαῖς διαγορεύων γράφει. Vita Sancti Michael Syncelli*, in Th. N. SCHMIDT, *Kahriedzami, Izvestija-Bulletin de l'Institut Archéol. Russe, 11 (1906), p. 227. Russian title transliteration from F. HALKIN, Bibliotheca Hagiographica Graeca* (Subsidia Hagiographica, 8A ; Bruxelles, 1957), vol. II, p. 123. See also P. O. VAILHÉ, "Saint Michel le syncelle et les deux frères Grapti, saint Théodore et saint Théophane", *Revue de l'Orient Chrétien*, 9 (1901), pp. 313-332, 610-642.

even stayed there ([31]). Furthermore, if one may believe the information transmitted in the title paragraphs of some of the manuscripts of Michael's treatise on Greek grammar and syntax, he composed this work at Edessa, on the request of a deacon named Lazarus ([32]). So one may suppose, on this basis, that Michael, like others at Mar Sabas, enjoyed regular contacts with the church at Edessa. Theodore Abū Qurrah, for example, was born there ([33]).

Michael Synkellos' Edessa connection, the fact that he was of Persian stock, the fact that he could serve as a translator from Arabic into Greek for Patriarch Thomas of Jerusalem, as he did in the instance of Abū Qurrah's letter against the Monophysites of Armenia ([34]), are all items which invite one to observe that Michael shared more than tri-lingualism with Theodore Abū Qurrah, his fellow monk of Mar Sabas. They both had a role to play in a new Melkite scholarly project which came to the fore in the monasteries of Palestine during the first Abbasid century, when Greek was losing its hold over the community. The scholars were required to turn their efforts on the one hand to the task of teaching Greek as a foreign language, and on the other to the project of translating the "church books" from their original Greek and Syriac into Arabic. The apologists were faced with the task of making a renewed statement of Christian religious claims, in the *lingua franca* of the new Islamic socio-political hegemony.

A fact not to be missed in the study of this Melkite *risorgimento* in Arabic, and one which is amply borne out in the contents of the "Old South Palestinian" archive, is the community's continued reliance on its Syriac heritage, a reliance which has been long overshadowed in the minds of western scholars by the community's habitual production of theological and liturgical books in Greek. But when the first Abbasid century brought about the circumstances which required the Melkites to adopt Arabic as an ecclesiastical language, they translated the

(31) See J. M. Fiey, "Le pèlerinage des nestoriens et Jacobites à Jérusalem", *Cahiers de civilization médiévale, x^e-viie siècles,* 12 (1969), pp. 113-126.

(32) The most common form of the title paragraph says that the treatise "was written in Edessa of Mesopotamia, at the request of the deacon, Lazarus". For the complete text of the title, with its variations, see D. Donnet, "Le traité de grammaire de Michel le Syncelle, inventaire préalable à l'histoire du texte", *Bulletin de l'Institut Historique Belge de Rome,* 40 (1969), pp. 38-39.

(33) See Dick, "Un continuateur arabe", 13 (1963), pp. 121-122.

(34) See the title to Abū Qurrah's Greek *opus,* IV, *PG,* vol. 97, col. 1504D.

scriptures and other Christian classics from Syriac as well as from Greek, including works of Ephraem and James of Sarūg, along with those of the Cappadocians and John Chrysostom ([35]). It is true, of course, and J.-M. Sauget has shown, that the earliest Arabic versions of works attributed to Ephraem in the Palestinian archive are translated from Greek, and not from Syriac ([36]). But this circumstance once again highlights the dual allegiance of the Melkite community. And in the instance of the Arabic versions of the works of the other classical Syriac poet, James of Sarūg, the matter is the other way about ([37]). Moreover, even the Arabic diction of the original writers in Arabic in this period, such as that of the Edessan, Theodore Abū Qurrah, preserves many idiosyncrasies of the Syriac speaker, when one can read the texts unaffected by the "improving" attentions of later copyists ([38]). Some scribes of the period went so far as to present their Arabic texts construed with the customary punctuation employed by writers of Syriac ([39]). It is clear therefore, here and elsewhere, that

(35) John Chrysostom was a favourite Greek author for the translators, and for the author of the *Summa Theologiae Arabica.* They provided more versions of homilies attributed to him, then to any other Greek father. Some sense of the range of the patristic works quoted in the Palestinian archive may be had simply by consulting the indices of Aziz S. ATIYA, *The Arabic Manuscripts of Mount Sinai ; a handlist of the Arabic Manuscripts and Scrolls Microfilmed at the Library of the Monastery of St. Catherine, Mount Sinai* (Baltimore, 1955). A full examination of the patristic texts preserved in the Palestinian archive has yet to appear.

(36) See J.-M. SAUGET, "Le dossier Ephrémien du manuscrit arabe Strasbourg 4226 et de ses membra disiecta", *Orientalia Christiana Periodica,* 42 (1976), pp. 426-458. For further bibliography on Arabic Ephraem, see also Samir KHALIL, "L'Ephrem arabe, état des travaux", in *Symposium Syriacum 1976 célébré du 13 au 17 septembre 1976 au Centre Culturel "Les Fontaines" de Chantilly* (Orientalia Christiana Analecta, 205 ; Rome, 1978), pp. 229-240.

(37) See Khalil Samir, "Un exemple des contacts culturels entre les églises syriaques et arabes : Jacques de Saroug dans la tradition arabe", in *III 5e Symposium Syriacum 1980. Les contacts du monde syriaque avec les autres cultures (Goslar, 7-11 septembre 1980)* (Orientalia Christiana Analecta, 221 ; Rome, 1983), pp. 213-245).

(38) Compare the diction of the words of Abū Qurrah published in BACHA, *Les œuvres arabes,* with that of the treatise on the veneration of images, from *BL Or.* MS 4950, in ARENDZEN, *Theodori Abu Kurra de Cultu Imaginum.* The former has been much "improved" ; the latter is characteristic of the older Palestinian texts.

(39) For such conventions employed by the writer of Sinai Arabic MS 542, see S. H. GRIFFITH, "The Arabic Account of ᶜAbd al-Masīḥ an-Naǧrānī al-Ghassānī", to appear.

Syriac was a language of the Melkite community, and not a monopoly of the non-Chalcedonian churches, as is sometimes thought ([40]).

One might reasonably ask about the fate of Greek Christian literature in Syria/Palestine from the ninth to the eleventh centuries. And the reply is that for all practical purposes during these centuries compositions in Greek ceased to be written in the Oriental Patriarchates, for the lack of an audience to appreciate them. Greek Christian classics survived, of course, in the monastic libraries, as the sources which provided the biblical and liturgical texts, and the teachings of the fathers for the new generation of writers in Syriac and Arabic ([41]). But there is no indication of any continued composition in Greek, other than such texts as Michael Synkellos' translation of Theodore Abu Qurrah's letter to the Armenians ([42]), or Michael's own very basic

(40) A growing number of studies emphasize the continued Melkite presence among speakers of Syriac after the Islamic conquest. See A. VAN ROEY, "Le lettre apologétique d'Elie à Léon, syncelle de l'évêque chalcédonien de Ḥarran", *Le Muséon*, 57 (1944), pp. 1-52 ; R. W. THOMPSON, "The Text of the Syriac Athanasian Corpus", in J. N. Birdsall & R. W. Thompson (eds.), *Biblical and Patristic Studies in Memory of Robert Pierce Casey* (Freiburg, 1963), pp. 250-264. Melkite liturgical documents have also survived, *e.g.*, S. P. BROCK, "A short Melkite Baptismal Service in Syriac", *Parole de l'Orient*, 3 (1972), pp. 119-130. In the area of history one might cite *Sinai Syriac MS* 10, and the important studies relating to this document by André DE HALLEUX, "Une notice syro-chalcédonienne sur Sévère d'Antioche", *Parole de l'Orient*, 7 (1976), pp. 461-477 ; *idem.*, "À la source d'une biographie expurgée de Philoxène de Mabbog", *Orientalia Lovaniensia Periodica*, 6-7 (1975-1976), pp. 253-266 ; *idem.*, "Trois synodes impériaux du VIe s. dans une chronique syriaque inédite", in Robert H. FISCHER, *A Tribute to Arthur Vööbus* (Chicago, 1977), pp. 295-307 ; *idem.*, "La chronique melkite abrégée du *MS. Sinai Syr.* 10", *Le Muséon*, 91 (1978), pp. 5-44. With some documents it is difficult to tell which was their original language, Greek or Syriac. See S. P. BROCK, "A Syriac Fragment on the Sixth Council", *Oriens Christianus*, 57 (1973), pp. 63-71 ; IDEM., "An Early Syriac Life of Maximus the Confessor", *Analecta Bollandiana*, 91 (1973), pp. 299-346. See also J. M. FIEY, "'Rūm' à l'est de l'Euphrate", *Le Muséon*, 90 (1977), pp. 365-420.

(41) See, *e.g.*, the appropriate items in the catalogs of the MSS microfilmed from Sinai and the Library of the Greek Orthodox Patriarchate in Jerusalem. K. W. CLARK, *Checklist of Manuscripts in St. Catherine's Monastery, Mount Sinai ; Microfilmed for the Library of Congress, 1950* (Washington, D.C., 1952) ; IDEM., *Checklist of Manuscripts in the Libraries of the Greek and Armenian Patriarchates in Jerusalem ; Microfilmed for the Library of Congress, 1949-50* (Washington, D.C., 1953).

(42) See n. 34 above.

Greek grammar mentioned above ([43]). The translation of Abū Qurrah's letter was done at the behest of Patriarch Thomas of Jerusalem, presumably for the benefit of the Byzantines, among whom reports of the writer's polemics seen to have been popular. The grammar, on the other hand, is best explained as being itself a testimony to the waning of Greek competence, even among the monks and other church officials, who now seemed to require an introductory textbook to study the language. And facility in Greek became something to boast about, a scholarly accomplishment.

If this assessment of the disappearance of Greek composition in the Oriental Patriarchates is to succeed, some account must be given of several Greek works which do purport to come from the area in the ninth century. They are the letter of the three oriental patriarchs to the emperor Theophilus, allegedly composed at a synod in Jerusalem in 836 ([44]) ; the *Life of Theodor of Edessa,* said to have been written at Mar Sabas by Basil of Emesa (d.c. 860) ([45]) : and the fable of *Barlaam and Joasaph* ([46]), often attributed to John of Damascus, but which at least one modern authority convincingly ascribes to one John, the monk of Mar Sabas named as the translator of the work in the manuscript tradition, whose *floruit* is now assigned to the turn of the ninth century ([47]).

Here is not the place to study these three Greek works, and time and space permit only a clue to be given as to how the present writer is inclined to deal with them in the context of the concerns of this article. In short, the most commendable hypothesis seems to be that in fact all three of these works are products of Byzantium, perhaps

(43) See n. 32 above.

(44) See the text in L. DUCHESNE, "L'iconographie byzantine dans un document grec du IXe siècle", *Roma e l'Oriente,* 5 (1912-1913), pp. 222-239, 273-285, 349-366.

(45) I. POMIALOVSKII, *Zhitie izhe vo sviatykh itca našego Feodora Arkhiepiskopa Edesskago* (St. Petersburg, 1892), pp. 1-220.

(46) Most readily available in G. R. WOODWARD & H. MATTINGLY, with introduction by D. M. LANG, *[St. John Damascene] ; Barlaam and Ioasaph* (Loeb Classical Library ; Cambridge, Mass., 1967).

(47) Alexander KAZHDAN, "Who, Where and When : the Greek Barlaam and Ioasaph ?" Privately circulated research paper ; Washington, D.C., Dumbarton Oaks, 1984. One should be alert for the coming publication of this important paper.

with the active assistance of emigre Palestinian monks living in Constantinople ([48]).

The letter which is supposed to have come from a Jerusalem synod held in 836 is now seen by at least one prominent Byzantinist to be a document produced in Constantinople in support of the iconophile side of the Byzantine controversy over the legitimacy of image veneration ([49]). The *Vita of Theodore of Edessa,* in its present form, is a composite document, a fact which in itself raises questions about its authenticity. Vasiliev argued that the presumed historicity of its report of the Jerusalem synod allegedly held in 836, and its mention of Theodore's visit to emperor Michael I should be taken as evidences of the *Vita*'s authenticity ([50]). But both of these arguments may now be seen to rest on unlikely presumptions. The letter from the Jerusalem synod probably was composed in Constantinople, the visit to the emperor appears to be unlikely on historical grounds ([51]). And as Paulus Peeters argued so long ago, Theodore's career in the *Vita,* in fact seems to be patterned on the biography of Theodore Abū Qurrah ([52]). So the most likely account to give of the *Vita of Theodore of Edessa* in its present form is to maintain that its several parts were assembled in Byzantium, probably at the hands of the emigre monks from Palestine who would have been the persons most likely to have been in possession of the materials from which the work was composed.

Even the Greek version of the fable of *Barlaam and Joasaph,* if it truly belongs to the ninth century, may most easily be explained as a product of Byzantium. On this hypothesis, John, the monk of Mar Sabas to whom the manuscript tradition attributes the translation, may be seen as a member of the Palestinian emigre community in

(48) See J. Gouillard, "Un 'quartier' d'émigrés palestiniens à Constantinople au IXe siècle ?", *Revue des Études Sud-Est Européennes,* 7 (1969), pp. 73-76.

(49) See Ihor Ševčenko, "Constantinople Viewed from the Eastern Provinces in the Middle Byzantine Period", *Harvard Ukranian Studies,* 3-4 (1979-1980), p. 735, n. 36.

(50) A. Vasiliev, "The Life of St. Theodore of Edessa", *Byzantion,* 16 (1942-1943), pp. 165-225.

(51) See S. H. Griffith, "Stephen of Ramlah".

(52) P. Peeters, "La passion de s. Michel le sabaïte", *Analecta Bollandiana,* 48 (1930), pp. 80-82.

Constantinople, where there would also have been a ready audience for the work. For the rest, this hypothesis in no way infringes upon the substance of Alexander Kazhdan's dating of the Greek *Barlaam and Joasaph* ([53]). And it leaves unaffected the Georgian tradition of the work, as well as its presumed Arabic origins ([54]). In fact, the Arabic origins of the fable should go a long way toward explaining why its Greek version might appear in Byzantium at the very time when emigre monks were also making Greek versions of extracts from the works of Theodore Abū Qurrah.

Enough has been said to make the point, and one must not tarry much longer before considering the *Summa Theologiae Arabica*, which is the parade example of early Christian Arabic literature to be introduced here. One might summarize what has so far been said about the circumstances in which this literature first appeared by saying that all of it is the product of the industry of the members of the Melkite community in Syria/Palestine in the eighth, ninth, and tenth centuries, who had a Syrian background, and who were well versed in the Christian classics in Syriac, as well as in the Greek liturgy and theology which dominated their church. To judge by what has remained of it the centers for the production of this early Christian Arabic literature were the monasteries of Palestine. But it is clear from the manuscripts themselves that Edessa and Damascus were also important intellectual centers for the community. Moreover, the scribes and writers had associations much wider then this. Their biographies, and sometimes the colophons of the manuscripts they wrote, as well as the translations of their works into other languages, such as Georgian, reveal that their world stretched from Egypt in the south, to Armenia and Georgia in the north, as well as to Baghdad, and the centers of Islamic culture in the east. Moreover, as we learn from Eulogius of Toledo, George of Bethlehem, one of the monks of

(53) See KAZHDAN, "Who, Where and When ...", n. 47 above.

(54) See the introductory essay by D. M. LANG, which argues for the origin of the Greek text from Georgian, in G. R. WOODWARD & H. MATTINGLY, *[St. John Damascene] ; Barlaam and Ioasaph.* It seems *a priori* likely that the Georgian "original" would have been a translation from a Christian Arabic text. For the story as it circulated in the Islamic community, see Daniel GIMARET, *Le livre de Bilawhar et Buḏasf, selon la version arabe ismaélienne* (Paris, 1971), IDEM., *Kitāb Bilawhar wa Būḏāsf* (Beyrouth, 1972).

Mar Sabas, even got as far as Cordoba where he died in 852. He told Eulogius that there were 500 monks in his monastery ; and Eulogius himself was impressed that George was proficient in Greek, Latin, and Arabic ([55]).

As for the *Summa Theologiae Arabica,* it is the first of the two works in *BL Oriental MS* 4950. It is composed of twenty-five chapters, which fill the first 197 leaves of the manuscript, 394 pages as we would count them. There is a table of contents at the beginning of the *Summa,* but since the first leaves of the manuscript are missing, the table effectively begins only with the contents of chapter ten. By a stroke of good fortune, however, the writer of the manuscript, Stephen ar-Ramlī, saw fit to repeat the title of the work at the end of the table of contents. He wrote, "Here is complete the naming of the twenty-five chapters belonging to the book, to the Summa (*ǧumlah*) of the ways (*wuǧūh*) of the faith in affirming the trinity of the oneness of God, and the incarnation of God the Word from the pure virgin, Mary" ([56]). By the phrase "ways of the faith", it becomes clear later in the work, the writer means the formulaic ways in which people express their faith ([57]).

The title of the *Summa,* and the table of contents, along with the chapter headings, give one a fair idea of the scope and compass of the work. It would be tedious to repeat all of this information here. But it is worth calling attention to the fact that the obviously apologetical agenda of the writer of the *Summa* prompts him to include in this one work a range of considerations which is well beyond the scope of any other single work in the whole library of Christain apologetical works in Arabic from the frist Abbasid century. In fact, the scope of the *Summa,* in terms of the range of topics it addresses, is comparable only to the complete apologetic bibliography of writers such as Ḥabīb

(55) See EULOGIUS OF TOLEDO, *Memoriale Sanctorum, Documentum Martyriale, Apologeticus Martyrum, PL,* vol. 115, cols. 777-792. See also Edward P. COLBERT, *The Martyrs of Cordoba (850-859) : a Study of the Sources* (The Catholic University of America Studies in Medieval History, New Series, vol. XVII ; Washington, D.C., 1962).

(56) *BL* 4950, f. 2 r, ll. 9-11.

(57) See the chapter heading for chapter 14 of the *Summa,* which discusses sixteen ways, *i.e., formulae,* which put their upholders outside of the Christian community, *BL* 4950, f. 86[r].

ibn Ḫidmah Abū Rā'iṭah ([58]), ᶜAmmār al-Baṣrī ([59]), or even the usual list of published treatises attributed to Theodore Abū Qurrah ([60]). And, of course, it goes much beyond the scope of the several records of debates between Christians and Muslims which are available from the period ([61]). The scale of the *Summa* is not completely dissimilar to that of the *Expositio Fidei* section of John of Damascus' *Πηγὴ γνώσεως*, produced at Mar Sabas monastery just over a century previously.

In the first chapter of the *Summa* the author provides an apologetically conditioned, historical sketch of the growth and expansion of Christianity among the peoples of the world. He puts into high relief the situation that obtains in his own time and place. This situation is, of course, dominated by the consolidation of the new Islamic socio-political hegemony, and the *de facto* establishment of Arabic as the public language of the caliphate. More will be said about this aspect of the work below. Then, for the next twelve chapters the author's accent is on the discussion of the standard doctrinal issues : the unity and Trinity of God, the incarnation, Christology, salvation history, and scriptural testimonies to these doctrines from the Old and New Testaments. All of this discussion is conducted in a language which reveals a deep concern with the major intellectual issues of the day among the *mutakallimūn*, both Christian and Muslim. Then, in chapter fourteen, the author provides something of a negative summary of the doctrines he has been explicating in the previous chapters. In an heresiographical style he explains sixteen ways of speaking about the faith which in his view should put a person outside of Christianity.

The final eleven chapters of the *Summa* are concerned mostly with practical issues stemming from the doctrines set forth in the earlier chapters. There are discussions of the duties of charity, of the role of

(58) See Georg GRAF, *Die Schriften des Jacobiten Ḥabīb ibn Ḫidma Abū Rā'iṭa* (CSCO, vols. 130 & 131 ; Louvain, 1951).

(59) See Michel HAYEK, *ᶜAmmār al-Baṣrī, apologie et controverses* (Beyrouth, 1977).

(60) See the list of Abū Qurrah's published works in n. 20 above.

(61) See S. H. GRIFFITH, "The Prophet Muḥammad, his Scripture and his Message According to the Christian Apologies in Arabic and Syriac from the First Abbasid Century", in T. FAHD (ed.), *La vie du prophète Mahomet ; colloque de Strasbourg (octobre 1980)* (Paris, 1983), pp. 99-146.

the Virgin Mary in salvation history and Christian piety, and a whole chapter devoted to the solution of difficult passages in the Gospels. Chapter eighteen is concerned with answering challenging questions which Muslims and Dualists pose for the Christians. It is in fact a full dress apologetic catechism for Christians who live in the world of the Muslims. The following four chapters of the *Summa* are essentially concerned with explaining the theoretical and historical relationships which in the author's view have obtained between the Jewish and Christian communities, and the pagans. Finally the author turns his attention to the duties of Christians in prayer, a discussion of how God is present in the world, which is in fact a disquisition on the relationship between faith and reason, and a concluding chapter of scriptural, patristic, and canonical rules which record the church's dispositions for practical life in the world.

Such a quick overview of the contents of the *Summa* hardly does justice to any part of it. But at least it may give some idea of the broad scope of the work. Already it will be clear that the author intends the *Summa* to be a practical manual to instruct the faith of his contemporaries, and he intends it to be a comprehensive catechism available for consultation.

One would have expected the copyist of the *Summa* to have set down the name of the author of the work, at least at the beginning, if not also at the end of the copy. Stephen of ar-Ramlah, for example, the scribe of *BL* 4950, mentioned the name of Theodore Abū Qurrah both at the beginning and at the end of his copy of the author's treatise on the practice of venerating images. But the beginning of the *Summa* is missing. At the end Stephen said only,

> The volume is complete, ..., and the completion of its writing was on the first day of September ..., of the years of the Arabs, Rabīᶜ I, 264. The poor, miserable sinner Stephen, son of Ḥakam, known as ar-Ramlī, wrote it in the *laura* of Mar Charitōn, for his teacher, ... Abba Basil, God grant him long life ([62]).

A number of scholars have proposed that Theodore Abū Qurrah was the author of the *Summa*. Most recently Samir Khalil, S. J., of Rome's Pontifical Institute of Oriental Studies has defended this

(62) *BL* 4950, f. 197v ; ARENDZEN, p. XV.

idea ([63]). But for reaons which the present writer has put forward in detail elsewhere, this suggestion really cannot be sustained ([64]).

In 1962 Joshua Blau called the attention of scholars to a line in the text of the *Summa* which, in his judgment, makes the authorship of Abū Qurrah impossible to maintain ([65]). The line in question appears in chapter twenty-one, where the discussion is directed to the Jews, concerning what the author considers to be the proper interpretation of those passages from the Prophets which predict the return of the exiled Jews to their ancestral home in the Holy Land. The text says,

> These prophets of God testify to God's loyalty to you, O community of Jews, in the building of the spotless temple, and in your return altogether from all the far away places, and your settlement in your own country. But subsequently you were exiled and scattered to all the far away places. The temple was destroyed and it has remained in ruins for eight hundred years and more ([66]).

As Blau explained, the "eight hundred years and more" recorded here should date the writing of the *Summa* after the year 870 A.D., and therefore more than fifty years after the death of Abū Qurrah around 825 ([67]). Moreover, Blau found it to be unlikely that the number of years elapsed from the time of the destruction of the temple under the emperor in 70 A.D., would have been adjusted higher by a later copyist of the *Summa.* Therefore, with a *terminus post quem* of 870, and a *terminus ante quem* of 877, contributed by the date of the completion of the writing of the *Summa* in *BL* 4950, Blau was tempted to identify Stephen ar-Ramlī, the writer of the manuscript, as the very author of the *Summa*, with the consequence that the text in *BL* 4950 would be the autography copy.

Elsewhere the present writer had put forward the suggestion that serious consideration should be given to the possibility that Stephen ar-Ramlī himself was the author, or at least the compiler, of the

(63) Khalil ṢAMIR, "Note sur les citations bibliques chez Abū Qurrah", *Orientalia Christiana Periodica*, 49 (1983), pp. 184-191.

(64) See S. H. GRIFFITH, "A Ninth Century *Summa Theologiae Arabica*", *Proceedings of the Second Symposium on Christian Arabic ; Groningen, 1984*, in press.

(65) BLAU, "Über einige christlich-arabische Manuskripte", p. 102.

(66) *BL* 4950, f. 154r ; *Sinai Arabic MS* 483, ff. 118r-118v.

(67) See DICK, "Un Continuateur arabe", 13 (1963), p. 120.

Summa Theologiae Arabica (68). There is evidence of compilation in the *Summa* (69). And such a process would also explain how portions of the text which sound so much like Abū Qurrah could be found in a work with so much else that is at variance with what one knows of this writer. One should perhaps think in terms of a school of writers with a base in the Palestinian monasteries, of whom Theodore Abū Qurrah may well have been the earliest and most influential. For now, however, it seems to the present writer, that no more can usefully be said about the authorship of the *Summa*, until the publication of the complete, critical edition of the text.

The very fact that the *Summa* was written in Arabic, and not in Greek, or Coptic, or Syriac, is a testimony to the successful Arabicization, and even the Islamicization, of the caliphate by the 870's when the *Summa* was written. By this time the Melkite community in Syria/Palestine had been producing church books and theological treatises in Arabic for about a century. And the time was ripe for a comprehensive presentation of the Christian point of view, taking into account the new socio-political realities of life under the rule of the Muslims. Among the Melkites, the *Summa* was the fruit of one hundred years of Christian doctrinal development in the Islamic milieu. And as such it is a fitting exemplar of the passage of life and letters from Greek into Arabic in ninth century Palestine.

(68) S. H. GRIFFITH, "Stephen of Ramlah", n. 17 above.

(69) Chapter eighteen, for example, is made up of two independent pieces. And, as Arendzen pointed out in 1897, there are additions in chapter 25 as well. See ARENDZEN, *Theodori Abu Kurra de Cultu Imaginum*, p. XIV. Other evidences of the composition of the work will be put forward in the full edition of the *Summa*.

IX

A NINTH CENTURY SUMMA THEOLOGIAE ARABICA *

I. BRITISH LIBRARY ORIENTAL MS 4950

The *Summa Theologiae Arabica* which is the subject of the present communication was written in its present form by Stephen of Ramlah in the year 877 A.D. at the monastery of Mar Charitōn in the Judean desert. It is preserved in its entirety in British Library Oriental MS 4950. This manuscript also contains another original composition in Arabic by a Christian author, namely, Theodore Abū Qurrah's apologetic tract on the practice of venerating images of Christ and the saints. John ARENDZEN published this text, with a Latin version, in 1897, so it has long been available to scholars.[1] The *Summa*, on the other hand, has not yet been published in its entirety, but it will appear in the not too distant future in an updated edition of the Arabic text prepared originally by Msgr. Georg GRAF. Now it will be accompanied by an English version and explanatory notes by the present writer.

* Special abbreviations used in this article:
ARENDZEN : see note 1.
ATIYA : see note 15.
BACHA : see note 12 (beginning).
BL = British Library.
KAMIL : see note 15.
MA'LŪF : see note 4.
NASRALLAH : see note 12 (at the end).

[1] Iohannes ARENDZEN, *Theodori Abu Kurra de Cultu Imaginum Libellus e Codice Arabico nunc Primum Editus Latine Versus Illustratus* (Bonn. 1897). A new edition of the text, on the basis not only of *BL Or. 4950*, but also *Sinai Arabic MS 330*, which contains the only other known text of Abū Qurrah's tract, is being prepared by Fr. Ignace DICK. See his communication in this volume.

The *Summa Theologiae Arabica* appears as the first of the two works in BL Oriental MS 4950. Its twenty-five chapters fill the first 197 leaves of the manuscript. The earliest available notice in modern times concerning the provenance of BL 4950 is the remark penned on the inside front cover to the effect that it was "bought of the Rev. C. Marsh, Oct. 14, 1895". In conversation with the Keeper of Oriental Manuscripts at that time, a Mr. Cl. DOUGLAS, John ARENDZEN learned that the manuscript had recently been brought to Britain from the east, but he was unable to discover any further details about its origins.[2] Within two years ARENDZEN had published ABŪ QURRAH's treatise on the veneration of images, which is, as mentioned above, the second of the two works contained in the manuscript. But he had little to say about the *Summa*, beyond copying its colophon. ARENDZEN also published a photostatic copy of ff. 197v + 198r as a frontispiece to his dissertation. It includes the *Summa*'s colophon, f. 197v, and the first page of Abū Qurrah's treatise. The photostat thus provided the earliest glimpse the scholarly community at large got of BL 4950. It was some years later before a photostat of f. 197v, with an Arabic transcription and an English version, appeared in LEWIS and GIBSON's album of Christian Arabic manuscripts.[3]

II. PUBLICATION OF THE SUMMA

A. Maʿlūf-s Edition

Father Louis MAᶜLŪF, S. J.,was the first modern scholar to devote attention to the *Summa Theologiae Arabica* in its own right. In 1903 he wrote an article entitled, "The Oldest Christian Arabic Manuscript", in which, after some introductory discussion, he published some sample passages of the text of the *Summa*. The sample consists of most of the text of the four chapters, five through eight, in which the author gives an account of the reasons why God became incarnate.[4] MAᶜLŪF did

[2] ARENDZEN, p. xiii.

[3] Agnes Smith LEWIS & Margaret Dunlop GIBSON, *Forty-One Facsimiles of Dated Christian Arabic Manuscripts*, coll. *Studia Sinaitica*, no. XII (Cambridge, 1907), pl. II, pp. 3 & 4.

[4] Luwīs MAᶜLŪF, *Aqdam al-maḫṭūṭāt n-naṣrāniyyah al-ᶜarabiyyah*, in *al-*

not copy the text of these chapters as he found it in the manuscript. Rather, as he says, citing some examples of the peculiarities of spelling and orthography in the writing, "we are content to call attention to these errors, and we have corrected them in the sample which we have set forth here."[5]

To date, MAᶜLŪF's sample of four chapters remains the only published portion of the *Summa Theologiae Arabica.* It appeared again in 1906, and once more in 1920, in anthologies of Christian Arabic texts published by Louis CHEIKHO, S.J.[6] And now the whole work awaits publication in GRAF's edition, as explained earlier.

B. Graf's Study

The next step forward in the study of the *Summa* came with the publication of the second volume of GRAF's *Geschichte der christlichen arabischen Literatur* in 1947. Here for the first time there appeared an analysis of the contents of the twenty-five chapters of the *Summa.*[7] For the most part the analysis reflects the table of contents which introduces the *Summa* in BL 4950, and the headings which introduce each chapter. However, since the first leaves of the manuscript are missing, the table effectively begins only with the contents of chapter ten. But by a stroke of good fortune, the writer of the manuscript, Stephen ar-Ramlī, saw fit to repeat the title of the work at the end of the table of contents. He wrote, "Here is complete the naming of the twenty-five chapters belonging to the book, to the *Summa* (*ǧumlah*) of the ways (*wuǧūh*) of the faith in affirming the trinity of the oneness of God, and the incarnation of God the Word from the pure virgin, Mary"[8]. By the phrase "ways of the faith", it becomes clear later in the work, the writer means the formulaic ways in which people express their faith.[9]

Machriq 6 (1903), pp. 1011-1023. The sample includes the text from ff. 29ʳ-39ᵛ. excluding f. 35ʳ, and ten lines on f. 39ᵛ.

[5] MAᶜLŪF, p. 1013.

[6] Louis CHEIKHO, *Seize traités théologiques d'auteurs arabes chrétiens (ixᵉ-xiiiᵉ siècles)* (Beyrouth, 1906), pp. 87-99; *Vingt traités théologiques* (Beyrouth, 1920), pp. 108-120.

[7] GCAL, vol. II, pp. 17-19.

[8] *BL Or. 4950,* f. 2ʳ, 11. 9-11.

[9] See the chapter heading for chapter 14 of the *Summa,* which discusses sixteen ways, i.e., formulae, which, in the writer's judgment, put their upholders outside of the Christian communtity, BL Or. 4950, f. 86ʳ.

The title of the *Summa*, and the table of contents, along with the chapter headings, provided by GRAF, give one a fair idea of the scope and compass of the work. It would be superfluous to repeat all of this information here. But it is worth calling attention to the fact that the obviously apologetical agenda of the writer of the *Summa* prompts him to include in this one work a range of considerations which is well beyond the scope of any other single work in the whole library of Christian apologetical works in Arabic from the first Abbasid century. In fact, the scope of the *Summa*, in terms of the range of topics it addresses, is comparable only to the complete apologetic bibliography of writers such as Ḥabīb ibn Ḫidmah ABŪ RĀ'IṬAH[10], ᶜAMMĀR AL-BAṢRĪ[11], or even the usual list of published treatises attributed to Theodore ABŪ QURRAH[12]. And, of course, it goes much beyond the scope of the several records of debates between Christians and Muslims which are available from the period.[13]

[10] See Georg GRAF, *Die Schriften des Jacobiten Ḥabib ibn Ḫidma Abū Rā'iṭa*, coll. CSCO 130 & 131 (Louvain, 1951).

[11] See Michel HAYEK, *'Ammār al-Baṣrī, apologie et controverses*, coll. *Rech-beyr* 85 (Beyrouth, 1977).

[12] The published works of Abū Qurrah in Arabic are: ARENDZEN; Constantin BACHA, *Les Oeuvres arabes de Théodore Aboucara évêque d'Haran* (Beirut, 1904); IDEM, *Un Traité des œuvres arabes de Théodore Abou-Kurra, évêque de Haran* (Tripoli, Syria & Rome, 1905); Georg GRAF, *Die arabischen Schriften des Theodor Abu Qurra, Bischofs von Ḥarran (ca. 740-820)*, coll. *Forschungen zur christlich Literatur - und Dogmengeschichte.* Band X, Heft 3/4 (Paderhorn, 1910); Louis CHEIKHO, *Mīmar li-Tadūrūs Abī Qurrah fī Wuǧūd al-Ḫāliq wa d-Din al-Qawim*, in *al-Mašriq* 15 (1912), pp. 757-774; 825-842; Georg GRAF, *Des Theodor Abu Kurra Traktat über den Schöpfer und die wahre Religion*, coll. *Beiträge zur Geschichte der Philosophie des Mittelalters.* Texte und Untersuchungen, Band XIV, Heft 1, (Münster, Westphalia, 1913); Ignace DICK, *Deux écrits inédits de Théodore Abuqurra*, in *le Muséon* 72 (1959), pp. 53-67; Sidney H. GRIFFITH, *Some Unpublished Arabic Sayings Attributed to Theodore Abū Qurrah*, in *le Muséon* 92 (1979), pp. 29-35; Ignace DICK, *Theodore Abuqurra, Traité de l'existence du Createur et de la vraie religion; introduction et texte critique*, coll. PAC 3 (Jounieh & Rome, 1982).

For Abū Qurrah's works preserved only in Greek, see *PG*, vol. 97, cols. 1461-1610. For the manuscripts of unpublished works attributed to Abū Qurrah, ses GCAL II, pp. 7-16, and Joseph NASRALLAH, *Dialogue islamo-chrétien. À propos de publications récentes*, in *Revue des Etudes Islamiques* 46 (1978), pp. 129-132.

[13] See Sidney H. GRIFFITH, *The Prophet Muhammad, his Scripture and his Message According to the Christian Apologies in Arabic and Syriac from the First*

C. The Manuscripts

On the face of it, one would find it surprising if such an *opus* as the *Summa* did not exercise a considerable influence in the world of Arab Christians, much beyond the confines of the Palestinian monastic community, or even of the closed society of the Melkites. But the fact of the matter is that to date there are only six manuscripts, other than BL 4950, in which scholars so far have recognized substantial portions of the *Summa*[14]. This number may well increase in the future, as the *Summa* itself becomes more well known, and as the contents of the many, already inventoried Christian Arabic manuscripts are more accurately analyzed. But for the present, the text in BL 4950 remains both the earliest, and the only complete copy of the *Summa Theologiae Arabica* known to scholars.

Apparently there was once a complete copy of the *Summa* in Sinai Arabic MS 483 (Kamil, 418), which was written in the year 1178 A.D.[15]. But now chapters one, two, and the first portion of chapter three are missing from this manuscript. For the rest, one finds only copies of chapters, or portions of chapters. The earliest copy, other than the one in BL 4950, appears to be the four leaves which comprise Munich Arab. MS 1071. The text is ascribed to the ninth century, and it contains extracts from chapters twelve and thirteen of the *Summa*[16]. From the tenth century there is a copy of chapters three to nine, and fourteen to seventeen in Sinai Arabic MS 431 (Kamil, 488)[17]. From the tenth or the eleventh centuries, Sinai Arabic MS 330 (Kamil, 457)

Abbasid Century, in Toufic FAHD (ed.), *La vie du prophète Mahomet; colloque de Strasbourg (octobre 1980)* (Paris, 1983), pp. 99-146.

[14] See NASRALLAH, p. 131.

[15] The year is given as 1177 in Aziz S. ATIYA, *The Arabic Manuscripts of Mount Sinai*, (Baltimore, 1955), p. 17; Murad KAMIL, *Catalogue of All Manuscripts in the Monastery of St. Catharine on Mount Sinai* (Wiesbaden, 1970), p. 33. The colophon to the MS says, "This book was completed... on Wednesday, the seventh of the month, *ḥazīrān* (i.e., June), of the year 1489, according to Alexander, the son of Philip, the Greek (*ar-rūmī*)" (Sinai Arabic MS 483, f. 380v). The year 1489 of the Seleucid era corresponds to the year 1178 of the modern Dionysian era, cf. Venance GRUMEL, *La Chronologie* (Paris, 1958), p. 257.

[16] Georg GRAF, *Christlich-arabische Handschriftenfragmente in der Bayerischen Staatsbibliothek*, in *OC* 38 (1954), pp. 131-132.

[17] NASRALLAH, p. 131; ATIYA, p. 12; KAMIL, p. 39. See also J BLAU, *Über*

contains a copy of chapters twelve, thirteen and seventeen[18]. Sinai Arabic MS 448 (Kamil, 495) has a copy of chapters five to eight, along with chapter eleven, done in the thirteenth century[19]. And finally, there is a copy of chapter eighteen of the *Summa* in Beirut Arabic MS 552, copied in the year 1718[20].

III. THE AUTHOR OF THE SUMMA

One would have expected one of the copyists of the *Summa* to have set down the name of the author of the work, at least at the beginning, if not also at the end of his copy. STEPHEN AR-RAMLĪ, for example, the writer of BL 4950, mentioned the name of Theodore ABŪ QURRAH both at the beginning and at the end of his copy of the author's treatise on the practice of venerating images.[21] But the beginning of the *Summa* is missing, both in BL 4950 and in Sinai Arabic MS 483. And at the end of it in BL 4950, Stephen said only,

> The volume is complete, ..., and the completion of its writing was on the first day of September..., of the years of the Arabs, Rabīᶜ I, 264. The poor, miserable sinner Stephen, son of Ḥakam, known as ar-Ramlī, wrote it in the *laura* of Mar Charitōn, for his teacher, ...Abba Basil, God grant him long life.[22]

At the end of the copy of the *Summa* in Sinai Arabic MS 483, the scribe says only, "By the help of our Lord and Savior, Jesus Christ, the twenty-five chapters are completed, as they were listed in the first one"[23]. The last phrase probably means only that the chapters were copied as they had been listed in a table of contents of the sort which one finds on the first leaves of BL 4950. But the author still remains unnamed.

einige alte christlich-arabische Handschriften aus Sinai, in *Le Muséon* 76 (1963), pp. 369-370.

[18] NASRALLAH, p. 131; ATIYA, p. 9; KAMIL, p. 37.

[19] NASRALLAH, p. 131; ATIYA, p. 14; KAMIL, p. 40.

[20] GCAL, II, p. 19; Louis CHEIKHO, *Catalogue raisonné des manuscrits de la Bibliothèque Orientale*, in *MUSJ* 11 (1926), p. 242.

[21] *BL Or. 4950*, f. 198ʳ and f. 237ʳ; ARENDZEN, pp. 1 & 50 (Arabic), 1 & 52 (Latin).

[22] *BL Or. 4950*, f. 197ᵛ; ARENDZEN, p. xv; LEWIS & GIBSON pl. II & p. 3.

[23] Sinai Arabic MS 483, 149, 11. 20 & 21.

A. Early Proposals

Initially, John ARENDZEN ventured the guess that the author of the *Summa* was a Monophysite, to judge by certain modes of expression which he employed to express his Christology[24]. More will be said about these expressions below. But beginning with the publication of the four chapters of the *Summa* in 1903, Theodore ABŪ QURRAH's name has consistently been put forward by scholars, with one notable exception, as the most likely candidate for the authorship of the work. Louis Maᶜlūf espoused this view when he published chapters five through eight, citing the similarity of Arabic style and diction, as well as the preferred manner of argument by examples, both in the known works of ABŪ QURRAH and in the *Summa.*[25] But Constantine BACHA, the editor of the Arabic works of ABŪ QURRAH, quickly challenged this view, citing the differences to be observed in the texts of the same Biblical quotations found both in the *Summa*, and in the works of ABŪ QURRAH. He also questioned the alleged similarity of style and argument.[26]

BACHA then proposed that the writer of the *Summa* may have been a Nestorian! In support of this suggestion he made reference to a note which Louis CHEIKHO had appended to MAᶜLŪF's discussion of the authorship of the *Summa.* CHEIKHO agreed with MAᶜLŪF that ABŪ QURRAH was the author of the work, but in his note he also advanced the theory there had once been two bishops named ABŪ QURRAH, one a Melkite, and one a Nestorian. CHEIKHO devised this theory to explain the confusing notices one finds in the Arabic manuscripts which purport to provide the transcript of a debate featuring ABŪ QURRAH before a Muslim official[27]. In later years CHEIKHO seems to have abandoned the theory of two bishops named ABŪ QURRAH, but he retained his conviction that Theodore ABŪ QURRAH was the author of the *Summa*[28]. In the meantime, however, BACHA had reproduced CHEIKHO's

[24] ARENDZEN, p. xiv.

[25] MAᶜLŪF, p. 1013.

[26] BACHA, pp. 188-190.

[27] See the text of the note in MAᶜLŪF, p. 1013. On the debate reports involving ABŪ QURRAH, see GCAL, II, pp. 21-23; DICK, "Un Continateur arabe," 12 (1962), pp. 330-332.

[28] See Louis CHEIKHO, *Mīmar li-Tadūrūs Abī Qurrah* (*supra*, note 12), p. 758, and IDEM, *Catalogue raisonné* (*supra*, note 20), p. 242.

note to MAᶜLŪF's publication of the four chapters[29]. And BACHA now argued that perhaps the author of the *Summa* was CHEIKHO's Nestorian ABŪ QURRAH. As a *suasio* for this suggestion, BACHA cited a line from chapter eight of the *Summa* which seems to locate Christ's tomb in the west (*fī arḍ al-maġrib*)[30], from the point of view of the writer and the original readers of the *Summa*. So, according to BACHA's interpretation, these people must have lived so far to the east of Palestine that they required an explanation of «western» burial customs to understand the Gospel's report that Joseph of Arimathea had laid Jesus' body «in a rock-hewn tomb, where no one had ever yet been laid.» (Lk. 23:54). So BACHA concluded that the writer of the *Summa* must have been an easterner, even the Nestorian ABŪ QURRAH to whom CHEIKHO had referred.

In whatever way one might explain the Summa's reference to the burial customs "in the land of the west", it is clear that this expression in no way makes the author a Nestorian. As Msgr. NASRALLAH has pointed out, the patristic citations, the creed, the Christology and the canonical material in the *Summa* all require the author to have been a Melkite[31]. Moreover, while there is a certain measure of Christian ecumenism evident in the text, in that no personal anathemas are uttered, e.g., against Nestorius, it is nevertheless clear that the author is not a Nestorian. On the key issue of Mariology, for example, the author of the *Summa* devotes the whole of chapter sixteen to the proposition that the virgin Mary gave birth to God. According to the writer one might say that she gave birth to the Messiah, a favorite Nestorian expression, only if by this expression one intends to say that she gave birth to the incarnate Son, God the Word[32]. Not surprisingly then, no subsequent scholar has ever defended BACHA's proposal that the author of the *Summa* was a Nestorian.

Georg GRAF seems not to have made a final decision about the authorship of the *Summa*. In the pertinent section of the GCAL he lists it as an "uncertain" work of Abū Qurrah, noting that the definitive ascription of authorship must await the full publication and study of the *Summa*[33]. He was himself engaged in this task, and left it

29 BACHA, pp. 189-190.
30 MAᶜLŪF, p. 1023; *BL Or. 4950*, f. 39ʳ.
31 NASRALLAH, p. 132.
32 See *BL Or. 4950*, ff. 91ʳ-96ʳ.
33 GCAL, II, pp. 16-17.

almost finished at his death. The present writer is in a position to be able to say that in his private papers connected with this effort, Msgr. Graf referred to the work as "Theol. Summa des Theodor A. Qurra."

B. Recent Proposals

In 1962 Joshua BLAU called the attention of scholars to a line in the text of the *Summa* which, in his judgment, makes the authorship of ABŪ QURRAH impossible to maintain[34]. The line in question appears in chapter twenty-one, where the discussion is directed to the Jews, concerning what the author considers to be the proper interpretation of those passages from the Prophets which predict the return of the exiled Jews to their ancestral home in the Holy Land. The text says,

> These prophets of God testify to God's loyalty to you, O community of Jews, in the building of the spotless temple, and in your return altogether from all the far away places, and your settlement in your own country. But subsequently you were exiled and scattered to all the far away places. The temple was destroyed and it has remained in ruins for eight hundred years and more[35].

As Blau explained, the "eight hundred years and more" recorded here should date the writing of the *Summa* after the year 870 A.D., and therefore more than fifty years after the death of ABŪ QURRAH around 825.[36] Moreover, BLAU found it to be unlikely that the number of years elapsed from the time of the destruction of the temple under the emperor in 70 A.D., would have been adjusted higher by a later copyist of the *Summa*. Therefore, with a *terminus post quem* of 870, and a *terminus ante quem* of 877, contributed by the date of the completion of the writing of the *Summa* in BL 4950, BLAU was tempted to identify STEPHEN AR-RAMLĪ, the writer of the manuscript, as the very author of the *Summa* with the consequence that the text in BL 4950 would then be the autograph copy. What gave him pause in this suggestion was an instance of what he took to be a typical copyist's error,

[34] Joshua BLAU, *Über einige christlich-arabische Manuskripte aus dem 9. und 10. Jahrhundert*, in *le Muséon* (1962), p. 102.

[35] *BL Or. 4950*, f. 154ʳ; *Sinai Arabic MS 483*, ff. 118ʳ-118ᵛ.

[36] See Ignace DICK, *Un continuateur arabe de saint Jean Damascène, Théodore Abuqurra, évêque melkite de Harran. La personne et son milieu*, in POC 13 (1963), pp. 114-129, see p. 120.

a case of misplaced diacritical points, *ḫaṭāyāki* for *ḥīṭāniki*, in chapter thirteen[37]. Such errors, in BLAU's view, should not be expected from the pen of the author of a work, while they may be expected from a copyist.

Most recently Father SAMIR has deftly disposed of the old objection to Theodore ABŪ QURRAH's authorship of the *Summa* on the basis of the dissimilarity of the biblical quotations[38]. SAMIR has convincingly shown that ABŪ QURRAH never quoted the scriptures absolutely literally, nor did he quote the same verse the same way twice, nor did he have a standard Arabic version of the Bible to hand. Then, at the end of this article, SAMIR announced that on the basis of internal criteria, "we will show that the *Summa of the Ways of the Faith* was in fact composed by Theodore ABŪ QURRAH in the year 825."[39]

In the meantime, however, further study of the internal criteria has led SAMIR to modify his original suggestion about ABŪ QURRAH's proposed authorship of the *Summa*, as one may read in his article in the present volume. And his new proposal in fact comes remarkably close to the substance of what the present writer had come to think independently. The basic contention which one wishes to foster here is that Theodore ABŪ QURRAH was not in fact the author of the *Summa*. A number of considerations work together in support of this contention, and in the first place must come BLAU's postulate that the work has to be dated after the year 870. The only way around this objection would seem to be the allegation that the writer of BL 4950, STEPHEN AR-RAMLĪ, altered the number of years elapsed since 70 A.D. to suit the requirements of his own time. But this allegation stands opposed to what one would expect to be the normal scribal practice. And, as a matter of fact, one finds the same "eight hundred years and more" from BL 4950 in Sinai Arabic MS 483, with a difference of some three hundred years between the two manuscripts.[40]

[37] *BL Or. 4950*, f. 71ʳ. It is interesting to note that the "error" in question, *ḫaṭāyāki*, appears also in the copy, *Sinai Arabic MS 330*. f. 215ʳ, line 1.

[38] Khalil SAMIR, *Note sur les citations bibliques chez Abū Qurrah*, in OCP 49 (1983), pp. 184-191.

[39] Samir, *Note sur les citations*, p. 191. Earlier Samir ascribed the *Summa* to Pseudo-Abū Qurrah. See SAMIR Khalil. *La tradition arabe chrétienne et la chrétienté de Terre-Sainte*, in David-Maria A. JAEGER (ed.), *Papers Read at the 1979 Tantur Conference on Christianity in the Holy Land* (Jerusalem, 1981), p. 415.

[40] See the texts cited in n. 35 above.

C. Reasons Against Abu Qurrah's Authorship

1. From the point of view of external criteria, it is striking that no where in the manuscript tradition is there any mention of Abū Qurrah's name in connection with the transmission of portions of the *Summa.* This is an especially notable omission, given the fact that one of the problems constantly facing the student of Abū Qurrah's works is the opposite state of affairs. That is to say, works are attributed to Abū Qurrah in the manuscript tradition which can only doubtfully be traced back to him, or which are certainly inauthentic, but which nevertheless have long circulated under his famous name. Those texts which purport to be transcripts of debates in which Abū Qurrah was involved, usually in the presence of Muslim officials, are cases in point.[41] Therefore, if portions of the *Summa* are never attributed to Abū Qurrah in the manuscript tradition, this fact should militate against his authorship of the work.

2. In this connection there immediately comes to mind an instance in which it has been proposed that a portion of the text of the *Summa* was in fact quoted and attributed to Abū Qurrah in another manuscript[42]. Sinai Arabic MS 72, which is another text written by Stephen ar-Ramlī, twenty years after BL 4950, in 897 A.D., and which contains an Arabic version of the four Gospels, includes at the end of the Gospels Abū Qurrah's answer to the Islamic challenge that Christians should thank the Jews, rather than to revile them, for their role in Christ's crucifixion, since they helped him achieve his purposes in the Christian economy of salvation. Abū Qurrah's answer here is substantially the same as what is reported in a Greek version, and attributed to him, in his Greek *opusculum* IX.[43] However, while the gist of this same argument is also found in the *Summa*[44], the details of the text are somewhat different, suggesting a different author to the present writer. The employment of the same basic argument in these two places should not be used to prove Abū Qurrah's authorship of the *Summa.* Abū Qurrah may in fact have been responsible for the argu-

[41] See the citations in n. 27 above.

[42] Nasrallah, p. 132.

[43] See Sidney H. Griffith, *Some Unpublished Arabic Sayings Attributed to Theodore Abu Qurrah*, in Le 92 (1979), pp. 29-35.

[44] *BL Or. 4950*, ff. 119^{r}-119^{v}.

ment, but it must have become a common item in the apologetical repertory, and its occurrence cannot be used to assign authorship of a work unless the details of its deployment are exactly the same, and then one may be dealing with a quotation. In the present instance one notices that the argument is attributed to ABŪ QURRAH in Sinai Arabic MS 72, but not in the considerably different text of the same basic argument in BL 4950! Father SAMIR brings up some important considerations regarding this argument in his article in the present volume.

3. All of those who have argued in favor of ABŪ QURRAH's authorship of the *Summa* have in the end based their contentions on internal criteria. And the internal criteria in question which have been mentioned so far, have to do with ABŪ QURRAH's preferred style of argument, with a plentiful use of similes, examples, and extended allegories, often involving a king, his son, and the royal advisors.[45] But similarities of this sort cannot be used to establish authorship since they involve styles of arguing which might be shared by many writers in a given time and place. Furthermore, there is nothing more likely to be borrowed by one writer from another than a good exemple, or an allegory. And the argument discussed above provides a good case in point.

4. To argue on the basis of internal criteria that ABŪ QURRAH wrote the *Summa* one should have to document correspondences of vocabulary, modes of expression, and characteristic turns of phrase, between the *Summa* and other works certainly by ABŪ QURRAH, which would reveal the same general profile of thinking. So far, on this level, the present writer can find only differences.

An example of such a difference is the contrast between the use of the term *al-bašar*, in its several variations, in the Christological sections of the *Summa* published by MAᶜLŪF, and in ABŪ QURRAH's customary Christological vocabulary.[46]

Another such difference is to be seen in the author of the *Summa*'s willingness to use the Arabic term *al-ašẖāṣ* to designate the per-

[45] See MAᶜLŪF, p. 1013; CHEIKHO, *Catalogue raisonné* (*supra*, note 20), p. 242.

[46] See Sidney H. GRIFFITH, *The Controversial Theology of Theodore Abu Qurrah (c. 750 – c. 820), a Methodological, Comparative Study in Christian Arabic Literature*, (Ph. D. Dissertation; The Catholic University of America, Washington, D.C., 1978), (Ann Arbor, Michigan, University Microfilms International, no. 78-19874), pp. 8-10.

sons of the Trinity, in contrast to ABŪ QURRAH's avoidance of the word.[47] The list of these sorts of differences could easily be prolonged, but here is not the place for it. Suffice it to say, that if internal criteria are to be found to link ABŪ QURRAH to the *Summa*, they must be of this detailed sort, where, so far, only differences seem to be found.

5. Another notable difference between the acknowledged works of Theodore ABŪ QURRAH and the *Summa* is the absence of *ad hominem* heresiographical argument in the latter work, while ABŪ QURRAH's works are full of arguments against non-Melkite Christian groups, particularly the Jacobites. And on the sectarian level, the *Summa* is much more informed with Islamic learning and lore than are the acknowledged works of ABŪ QURRAH. All of these considerations argue for another author for the *Summa*.

6. Elsewhere the present writer has put forward the suggestion that serious consideration should be given to the possibility that STEPHEN AR-RAMLĪ, the copyist, was also the author, or at least the compiler, of the *Summa Theologiae Arabica*[48]. There is evidence of compilation in the *Summa*[49]. And such a process would also explain how portions of the text which sound so much like ABŪ QURRAH could be found in a work with so much else that seems at variance with what one knows of the works of this writer. One should perhaps think in terms of a school of Christian writers in Arabic with a base in the Palestinian monasteries in the eighth and ninth centuries, of whom Theodore ABŪ QURRAH may well have been the earliest known and the most influential writer. For now, however, it seems that no more can usefully be

[47] See, e.g., chapter three, f. 23^v, et *passim*. See also GRIFFITH. *The Controversial Theology of Theodore Abū Qurrah*, pp. 156-158; and *The Concept of* al-uqnūm *in ʿAmmār al-Basrī's Apology for the Doctrine of the Trinity*, in Khalil SAMIR (ed.). *Actes du Premier Congrès International d'Études Arabes Chrétiennes*, coll. *OCA* 218 (Rome, 1982), pp. 187-191. Unavailable to me, in spite of repeated attempts to secure a copy, is Rachid HADDAD, *La Trinité chez les théologiens arabes (750-1050)*, a typewritten doctoral thesis.

[48] Sidney H. GRIFFITH. *Stephen of Ramlah and the Christian Kerygma in Arabic in Ninth-Century Palestine*, in *Journal of Ecclesiastical History* 36 (1985), pp. 23-45.

[49] Chapter eighteen, for exemple, is made up of two independent pieces, *BL Or. 4950*, ff. 114^r 130^v. And, as ARENDZEN pointed out in 1897, there are additions in chapter 25 as well. See ARENDZEN, p. xiv. Other evidences of the composition of the work will be put forward in the full edition of the *Summa*.

said about the authorship of the *Summa*, until the publication of the complete, critical edition of the text.

IV. THE ISLAMIC CONTEXT OF THE SUMMA

The very fact that the *Summa* was written in Arabic, and not in Greek, or Coptic, or Syriac, is a testimony to the successful Arabicization, and even the Islamicization, of much of the caliphate by the mid-ninth century. By this time the Melkite community in Syria/Palestine had been producing church books and theological treatises in Arabic for about a century. And the time was ripe for a comprehensive presentation of the Christian point of view, taking into account the new socio-political realities of life under the rule of the Muslims. Among the Melkites, the *Summa* was the fruit of one hundred years of doctrinal development in Arabic under Islamic rule.

It is interesting to note that as this scenario unfolds in the *Summa*, one notices little or no inter-Christian rancor, no *ad hominem* argumentation. To be sure, in chapter fourteen the author lists those propositions which in his judgment should put anyone who maintains them outside the Christian fold.[50] And it is likewise true that anyone with Melkite sympathies might easily find a way to include his own Christological adversaries among the upholders of one or another of the proscribed propositions. But in the *Summa* no names are named. It is clear overall that in the author's mind the major intellectual challenge of the day comes from the Muslims. And the last rejected proposition in chapter fourteen reflects that challenge when it rejects the thesis of those who would say, "Christ is God, but God is not Christ"[51]. For it seems clear that Christians who would make such a statement as this one, must have been seeking an accommodation with the *Qur'an*'s *dictum*, "They have already disbelieved who say God is Christ, Mary's son" (*al-Mā'idah* 5:17).

For the author of the *Summa*, there can be no doubt that the arrival of the Muslims is the event that has changed the course of history, interrupting what he pictures to have been the previously inexorable

[50] The title of the chapter is "A Statement on the ways which should put anyone who holds them outside of Christianity. Sixteen sections." *BL Or. 4950*, f. 76r.

[51] *BL Or. 4950*, f. 86r.

spread of Christianity. Now the Christians must restate their own traditional religious convictions in a new idiom, and they must also re-articulate their position *vis à vis* the Jews. Under Islam, when both Christians and Jews had to live as tolerated foreigners under the protection of the new body politic, the changed circumstances required both groups to re-think, and to express anew, in the idiom of a new day, their traditional doctrinal positions in regard to one another.[52] So, in his first chapter the author of the *Summa* explained the new historical *scenario*, and in the subsequent chapters he offered a summary of the new ways of expressing the traditional faith of his community, as they had been elaborated in Arabic, in response to Islamic challenges. In chapter eighteen he provided his readers with a primer for religious dialogue with the Muslims, and also with the Dualists.[53]

One may discover the occasion for the composition of the *Summa*, and the audience for whom it was intended, in the first chapter. Islam, it is clear, is what the author views as the principal challenge to Christians. And his audience is that group of Christians who in his own day were tempted to seek some religious accommodation with the new creed. One may bring this communication to a close with a few observations on these two issues.

The author of the *Summa* finds the principal challenge of Islam in its creedal simplicity. Straightaway he points out that by comparison with the doctrinal obscurity of previous, non-Christian religions, "The language (*kalām*) of this community about God is a clear language, which the common people may understand. I mean their statement, "There is no god but God"[54].

Here one quickly recognizes the first of the two phrases in the Islamic *šahādah*, "There is no god but God, and Muḥammad is his messenger (*rasūl*)". While the first phrase of the whole statement appears in the *Qur'ān* (*aṣ-Ṣāfāt* 37:35), the second phrase is attested only in the Islamic *ḥadīṯ*, which is also the warranty for the employment of the two phrases together to form Islam's characteristic confessional statement, or creed. According to modern students of Islam, the use of

[52] For the new Jewish apologetic, in the period under discussion here, see now the doctoral thesis of Sarah STROUMSA, *Dawūd ibn Marwān al-Muqammiṣ and His ʿIshrūn Maqāla*, 2 vols. (The Hebrew University, Jerusalem, 1983).

[53] *BL Or. 4950*, ff. 114ʳ-137ᵛ.

[54] *BL Or. 4950*, f. 5ᵛ.

the entire formula came into prominence only after the year 700, when many Christians and Jews were becoming Muslims.[55] So in this connection one must observe that contrary to what one might expect, given the prominence of the concern among contemporary Christian apologists to deny the status of prophet to Muḥammad, no mention of his name, or clear reference to his career, is to be found anywhere in the *Summa Theologiae Arabica.*

The author of the *Summa* concentrates his attention on the first phrase of the Islamic *šahādah,* and he immediately points out to the reader that by the employment of this phrase, its proponents are not thereby in agreement with the Christians. Rather, he says, "they mean a god other than the Father, Son, and Holy Spirit. According to their own statement, "God is neither a begetter, nor is He begotten". [...] Their statement, "There is no god but God", and our statement, are one in words (*al-alfāẓ*), but different in meaning (*al-maᶜnā*)"[56].

In this quotation one readily recongizes the author's reference to the *Qur'ān, al-Iḫlāṣ* (112):3. And he goes on to argue that the Christian doctrine of the Trinity, with its affirmation of divine generation, alone of the two creeds, really asserts a belief in a truly living and rational God who is one. But then, for the rebuttal of any further objections to Christian faith on the part of the Muslims, and for answers to their many questions about Christianity, the author refers the reader forward to chapter eighteen of the *Summa.* In chapter one he now turns his attention away from the Muslims, whom he has not yet explicitly named, to address himself to those Christians who in his own day used to let themselves appear to accept the simple creed that "there is no god but God". And in the author's reaction to this group of Christians the modern reader may gain an insight into the circumstances which composed the original occasion for the composition of the *Summa Theologiae Arabica.*

V. CHRISTIAN "MUNĀFIQĪN"

In chapter one the author of the *Summa* expresses his astonishment that in his own day, after centuries of Christian history had

[55] See W. Montgomery Watt, *The Formative Period of Islamic Thought* (Edinburgh, 1973), pp. 128-129.

[56] *BL Or. 4950,* f. 5ᵛ.

elapsed, during which, according to him, the faithful believers of every land and culture had fearlessly and yet clearly expressed their faith in Christ, there should now be

> ... a party (*qawm*) in the midst of the people of this community who rule over them, a party born among them, raised within them, and educated in their culture (*ta'addabū bi'adabihim*), and they hide their faith, and they divulge to them what suits them[57].

On the face of it, this passage identifies a group of Christian people who by the time of the author of the *Summa* had become so acculturated to life in the Islamic caliphate that they were dissembling their Christian faith. And the author minces no words in making the further charge that with this behavior, these same people were practicing a forbidden evasion of their confessional duty, which evasion, he said, they had learned from their ancestors. Moreover, there are now among them, the author charges, those who impede anyone else who openly attests his faith. All of them, claims the author of the *Summa*, take the easy way, "and they stray off the road which leads its people to the kingdom of heaven, in flight from giving testimony (*tašahhud*) to the doctrine of the trinity of the one-ness of God, and His incarnation, because of what strangers say in reproach to them"[58]. And this behavior, in the judgment of the author, is characteristic of "the hypocrites (*munāfiqīn*) who are among us, marked with our mark, standing in our congregations, contradicting our faith; those forfeiters of themselves (*al-ḫāsirīn*), who are Christians in name only"[59].

The reader of the *Summa* does not have long to wait before the author identifies more specifically the doctrinal aberrance which concerns him. He is angry at those who give voice to faith in Christ, but who then say in public only what agrees with what their Islamic overlords themselves would say about Jesus, the son of Mary. And in such a fashion, says the author, these nominal Christians, in what they say to please the Muslims, "are at variance with those Christians who in their (i.e., the Muslims') scripture are characterized by unbelief (*al-kufr*) and enmity toward God in what they say: "They have disbelieved who say that God is the Messiah, ᶜĪsā, the son of Mary" (*al-Mā'idah*

[57] *BL Or. 4950*, f. 6ʳ.
[58] *BL Or. 4950*, ff. 6ʳ-6ᵛ.
[59] *BL Or. 4950*, f. 6ᵛ.

(5):17); and "They have disbelieved who say that God is one of three" (*al-Mā'idah* (5):73), or the Messiah is the son of God"[60].

In conclusion, the author of the *Summa*, echoing the language of both *Qur'ān* and *Ḥadīṯ*, says of the Christian *munāfiqīn* he has been describing, "They are neither-Christians, nor are they *ḥunafā'*, Muslims, but in the meantime they are waverers (*mudabdabīn*)"[61]. One appreciates this remark to the full only when he recognizes in it an allusion both to the *Qur'ān*'s juxtaposition of the terms *ḥanīf* and *muslim* in describing Abraham in *Āl ᶜImrān* (3):67 on the one hand, and on the other, an echo of the significance of the term *mudabdabīn* in the *Ḥadīṯ*. In the latter instance, the identification of the Christian dissemblers by the author of the *Summa* as "waverers" takes its sense from Muḥammad's reported use of this word, in a tradition preserved by AḤMAD IBN ḤANBAL, to designate people who were neither Muslim nor Christian. According to the story, one ᶜUKKĀF ibn Bišr at-TAMĪMĪ, a celibate, was advised by the prophet to marry because his unmarried state made him an anomaly. Among Christians he should have been a monk, whereas among the Muslims, the *sunnah* prescribed marriage. ᶜUKKĀF being neither a monk nor, presumably, a Christian, nor married, was advised by MUḤAMMAD, "You should marry, lest you come to be among the waverers (*al-mudabdabīn*)"[62]. So, in its religious applications the Arabic lexicographers defined the latter term by reference to the *Ḥadīṯ*, along with the etymological suggestion that persons so described should be driven away[63], a nuance which must have been in the mind of the author of the *Summa*.

VI. PASTORAL SITUATION OF SUMMA'S AUTHOR

The interlude in the first chapter of the *Summa*, in which the author sets out and rejects the position of those who sought some doctrinal accommodation with the Muslims, must describe the pastoral situation which the church authorities faced in the ninth century among

[60] *BL Or. 4950*, ff. 7ʳ-7ᵛ.

[61] *BL Or. 4950*, f. 7ᵛ.

[62] Aḥmad IBN ḤANBAL, *Musnad*, 6 vols. (Beirut, 1389/1969), vol. V, pp. 163-164.

[63] See W. E. LANE, *An Arabic-English Lexicon*, 7 vols. (London, 1863-1893), vol. III, p. 953.

the Arabophone, upwardly mobile Christians in the caliphate. The author, as we have seen, attributes their attitude to fear of reproach. And his only advice to such persons is as follows:

> Whenever anyone reproaches them, or speaks ill of them, let them recall God's saying in His scripture, "Blessed are you whenever they reproach you, or expel you, or hate you falsely on my account. Rejoice at it and be happy. Your reward will be great in heaven" (Mt. 5:10-12)[64].

However, while the author of the *Summa* will allow no doctrinal accommodation with the Muslims, it must be readily apparent to anyone who reads his work that he has in fact undertaken to set out the traditional Christian faith in Arabic terms which owe much of their religious value to the *Qur'ān*, and to the usages of the *mutakallimūn* of his day, both Muslim and Christian. There is no time now to point out the details of this methodology, since to do so will be the burden of future studies of the many chapters of the *Summa*. Suffice it to say that one already has the evidence of such a method in the Arabic words quoted above in passages from chapter one (e.g., *munāfiqin, ḫāsirīn*, etc.). And if there could be any lingering doubt about it, the matter is resolved when one reads further in chapter one, to discover the author's re-affirmation of Christ's full divinity, whom he now, and often throughout his work, calls Christ, *rabb al-ʿālamīn.*[65]

[64] *BL Or. 4950*, f. 7r.
[65] See, e.g., *BL Or. 4950*, f. 7r and *passim*.

X

THE ARABIC ACCOUNT OF 'ABD AL-MASĪḤ AN-NAĞRĀNĪ AL-GHASSĀNĪ

When Christian groups living in the Holy Land under the rule of Islam first began to employ Arabic as an ecclesiastical language, their efforts were principally expended in the project to make available in the vernacular language of the caliphate those church books which people required for the exercise of their everyday religious life. This circumstance explains why translations of biblical books, lives of the saints, and the homilies of the fathers figure so largely in the Christian manuscripts in Arabic which were written in the monasteries of Palestine during the ninth and tenth centuries. Among the sixty some works from this archive which Joshua Blau listed in his catalog of texts exhibiting what he regarded to be a distinctive «Middle Arabic» dialect of South Palestine, he designated only five original compositions in Arabic [1]. And this circumstance, plus various linguistic peculiarities to be found in these texts, in turn have prompted scholars to think of the whole corpus as a monastic translation literature, with little or no relevance to the eventual growth of the large body of Christian literature in Arabic which appeared later for the most part, and outside the narrow confines of the Palestinian monastic communities [2].

While one may readily admit the peculiarities of these earliest dated manuscripts of Christian writing in Arabic, the fact remains that it was in the monasteries of Palestine, from the eighth through the tenth centuries that Arabic found its first employment as an everyday ecclesiastical language. The monks who wrote the manuscripts, and who composed those few original pieces that are preserved in this archive, were all Melkites, and for the most part, although they would have been educated in Greek, they were native speakers of Syriac. They spoke and wrote Arabic because by the late eighth century it was fast becoming the public language of Syria/Palestine [3]. From what one may discover in the sources about their careers, these monks were

[1] Cf. J. BLAU, *A Grammar of Christian Arabic* (*CSCO*, 267, 276, 279), Louvain, 1966-1967, vol. 267, p. 21-33 (quoted BLAU).

[2] Cf. Kh. SAMIR (ed.), *Actes du premier congrès international d'études arabes chrétiennes*, Goslar, septembre 1980 (*Orientalia Christiana Analecta*, 218), Rome, 1982, p. 52-59.

[3] Cf. Sidney H. GRIFFITH, «Greek into Arabic: the Monks of Palestine and the Growth of Christian Literature in Arabic», forthcoming.

not retired ascetics, but following the custom set already in the patriarchate of Jerusalem in Byzantine times, they took an active part in the pastoral mission of the patriarchate[4]. Theodore Abū Qurrah, for example, the one person of their number with some name recognition in modern times, gained a reputation as a difficult adversary among the rival Jacobites precisely because, as Michael the Syrian recorded three centuries later, «he was a sophist, and engaged in dialectics with the pagans [i.e., the Muslims], and knew the Saracen language, and was an object of wonder to the simple folk»[5].

In this same vein, the five original works which Blau noted among the Arabic productions of the *scriptoria* of the Palestinian monasteries in the ninth and tenth centuries are all apologetico/polemical works[6]. The religious claims of the Muslims, and of the newly enfranchised Jewish communities, along with the new sociopolitical realities which the Islamic caliphate presented, shaped the intellectual milieu in which these five works were composed. They are all tracts for use in arguments about religion, both within and without the Christian community. The one of them which is the most easily available at present for scholarly scrutiny is Theodore Abū Qurrah's tract in defense of the Christian practice of venerating images of Christ and the saints[7].

In addition to the five apologetic works which Blau singled out as original compositions, among the mass of texts in the Palestinian monastic archive, there are in fact some other texts there which also contain Arabic originals. They are contributions to the already well established literary genre of hagiography, and they concern persons who gave notable public testimony to their adherence to Christianity, in the face of determined opposition from the Islamic authorities. They are the stories of the martyrdoms of St. Anthony Ruwaḥ, and of ʿAbd al-Masīḥ an-Nağrānī al-Ghassānī.

[4] For an introduction to the distinctive monasticism of the patriarchate of Jerusalem, cf. the pertinent sections of Derwas J. CHITTY, *The Desert a City*, Oxford, c. 1966; Crestwood, New York, 1977.

[5] J.-B. CHABOT, *Chronique de Michel le syrien, patriarche jacobite d'Antioche (1166-1199)*, 4 vols., Paris, 1899-1910, vol. III, p. 32 (French), vol. IV, p. 495-496 (Syriac).

[6] Cf. BLAU, p. 21-23.

[7] Cf. I. ARENDZEN, *Theodori Abu Kurra de Cultu Imaginum Libellus e Codice Arabico nunc Primum Editus Latine Versus Illustratus*, Bonn, 1897. There is a German version in Georg GRAF, *Die arabischen Schriften des Theodor Abu Qurra, Bischofs von Ḥarrān (ca. 740-820)* (Forschungen zur christlichen Literatur- und Dogmengeschichte, X. Band, 3/4 Heft), Paderborn, 1910, p. 278-333. For commentary cf. Sidney H. GRIFFITH, «Theodore Abū Qurrah's Arabic Tract on the Christian Practice of Venerating Images», *Journal of the American Oriental Society*, 105 (1985), p. 53-73. A new edition of the tract, plus an English version with extensive commentary, will soon appear in the *CSCO* series.

The story of St. Anthony Ruwaḥ has long been known to scholars, and in 1961, Ignace Dick published a critical edition of the Arabic text of the martyrdom, based on *Sinai Arabic MS* 513, a production of the tenth century[8]. So far, however, no scholarly attention has been paid to the story of 'Abd al-Masīḥ an-Nağrānī, beyond Ḥabīb Zayāt's publication of the text as it appears in *BM Or. MS* 5019, which was written around the eleventh century[9]. Accordingly the purposes of the present article are first of all to publish the Arabic text of the martyrdom in its earliest available form, along with an English version of the account, and to discuss the text from three further points of view: the history of the Christian Palestinian manuscripts; the hagiography of encounters between Christians and Muslims; and the history of ecclesiastical life in the Holy Land during the time between the Islamic conquest and the coming of the crusaders.

I. The Text

A. *Summary of the Martyrdom*

At the outset of the inquiry it will be more convenient to provide a summary of the martyrdom, saving the Arabic text and English translation for a full exposition in an appendix. It is the story of a young man of Nağrān named Rabī' ibn Qays ibn Yazīd al-Ghassānī[10], who was brought up as a Christian, knowledgeable in the lore of his religion. When he was twenty years old he wanted to visit Jerusalem to pray at the holy places. Accordingly, he joined up with a group of Muslims from Nağrān who were setting out on a raiding expedition into Roman country (*arḍ ar-rūm*). However, as the hagiographer puts it, «ignorance, youth and bad companions» brought al-Ghassānī to make common cause with the raiders. For thirteen years, according to the

[8] Ignace Dick, «La passion arabe de s. Antoine Ruwaḥ, néomartyr de Damas (+ 25 dec. 799)», *Le Muséon*, 74 (1961), p. 108-133.

[9] Ḥabīb Zayāt, «Shuhadā' an-Naṣrāniyyah fī l-Islām», *al-Machriq*, 36 (1938), p. 463-465. Note Zayāt's error in citing *BM Or. MS* 5019 as 5091, a mistake repeated in Georg Graf, *Geschichte der christlichen arabischen Literatur* (5 vols.), Città del Vaticano, 1944-1953, vol. I, p. 489, 516, 520. Notice of the mistake was first published by Joshua Blau, «The Importance of Middle Arabic Dialects for the History of Arabic», in Uriel Heyd (ed.), *Studies in Islamic History and Civilization* (*Scripta Hierosolymitana*, vol. IX), Jerusalem, 1961, p. 219, n. 39. Cf. also Michel Van Esbroeck, «Un recueil prémétaphrastique arabe du XIe siècle (*Brit. Mus. Add.* 26.117 et *Or.* 5019)», *Analecta Bollandiana*, 85 (1967), p. 143-164, esp. p. 149.

[10] For variations in the name cf. below, n. 1 and 5 to the English translation.

account, he continued every year to go on expeditions, taking part in all the brutal mayhem these excursions involved. Furthermore, he used to pray with his Muslim companions. But finally, while passing the winter in the environs of the cities of Syria, he came one day to Baalbek, and entered a church there. He encountered a priest reading the Gospel, and in due course he confessed to the priest, «I once was of the adherents of this Gospel. But today I am of its enemies». After some encouragement, the priest was able to receive al-Ghassānī back into the church, and presently, once again, as a new convert he set off for a visit to Jerusalem.

In Jerusalem, al-Ghassānī visited the patriarch, a man named John, according to the narrative, who, after hearing his story, sent him off with a recommendation to the superior of Mar Sabas monastery to accept the penitent as a monk. And he stayed in that monastery for five years. Thereafter al-Ghassānī made a tour of the Palestinian monasteries, ending his journey at Mount Sinai, where he remained some years, serving the monks in an administrative capacity. In particular, he dealt with the authorities in Aylah with regard to the taxes (*al-ḫarāǧ*) due from the Mount, as well as those from the Christians in the towns of Pharan and Ra'yah. In view of this service, the monks made al-Ghassānī their *oeconome*, an office he filled for five years.

At this point in his career, al-Ghassānī was overcome with the desire to divulge his reconversion to Christianity to the Muslim authorities. Since his apostasy from Islam was punishable by death, this desire was really one for martyrdom. So he set out with a group of like minded monks for ar-Ramlah, the capital city of Palestine. When he arrived, he threw into the mosque a note describing his conversion and announcing that he was awaiting his fate in the lower church of St. Cyriacus. But when the Muslims came to get him, he was hidden from their sight by God's own action, according to his fellow monks, who were thus able to convince al-Ghassānī to give up his martyr's quest. So he left ar-Ramlah, paid a visit to Edessa, and came eventually back to Sinai.

When al-Ghassānī returned to Sinai, the superior of the monastery had died, and his confreres straightaway chose their returning brother to fill the vacant office. He accepted the new role, changed his name to 'Abd al-Masīḥ, and held office for seven years.

Next it happened that some difficulties arose concerning the taxes on the Sinai monastery which required 'Abd al-Masīḥ and several other monks once again to travel to the provincial capital at ar-Ramlah, because, as the hagiographer records it, «At that time their tax went to Palestine». But on the way the monks met a band of Muslims returning from their pilgrimage to Mecca, and one of them recognized ʿAbd al-Masīḥ as his old raiding companion, al-Ghassānī. The Muslims arrested the monks, and the one who recognized ʿAbd al-Masīḥ hurried ahead to ar-Ramlah to denounce him to the governor. In due course ʿAbd al-Masīḥ was interviewed twice by the governor, and when he refused to renounce Christianity, he was beheaded. His body was burned in a ruined well in Baliʿah, a suburb of ar-Ramlah.

After nine months, the monks contrived to retrieve ʿAbd al-Masīḥ's skeleton from the bottom of the ruined well, and after considerable haggling his remains were portioned out between the church of St. Cyriacus and the monastery at Sinai.

B. *Text History*

The story of ʿAbd al-Masīḥ an Nağrāni survives in four known manuscripts. The earliest of them is *Sinai Arabic MS* 542 (Kamil, 576), which, on the basis of paleographic considerations, is dated to the ninth century[11]. Accordingly, for reasons that will become clear as the discussion goes forward, the base text of the edition given in the appendix below is taken from this Sinai manuscript, and variants are cited from the «corrected» recension of the account of ʿAbd al-Masīḥ found in the *British Museum Oriental MS* 5019, from which Ḥabīb Zayat derived the text he published in *al-Machriq* in 1938[12].

In addition to the two manuscripts just mentioned, the story of ʿAbd al-Masīḥ reportedly appears in two other manuscripts, which are both unavailable to the present writer. The earliest of these is in all probability the manuscript described as no. 14 in the 1922 catalog of the Leipzig dealer in antique books, Karl W. Hiersemann[13]. The manuscript, which eventually perished in a fire at Louvain, is advertised as dating from the tenth century[14]. To judge by its contents as described

[11] Cf. Aziz SURYAL ATIYA, *The Arabic Manuscripts of Mount Sinai; a Hand-List of the Arabic Manuscripts and Scrolls Microfilmed at the Library of the Monastery of St. Catherine, Mount Sinai*, Baltimore, 1955, p. 22; Murad KAMIL, *Catalogue of All Manuscripts in the Monastery of St. Catherine on Mount Sinai*, Wiesbaden, 1970, p. 50.

[12] Cf. n. 9 above.

[13] *Orientalische Manuskripte; arabische, syrische, griechische, armenische, persische Handschriften des 7.-18. Jahrhunderts* (Katalog 500), Leipzig: Karl W. Hiersemann, 1922, no. 14, p. 10-12, f. 163v-167r.

[14] *Ibid.*, p. 10. Anton Baumstark was the scholar who authenticated Hiersemann's MSS. In an «*Avis*» included with the catalog. Baumstark wrote, «Le manuscrit No. 14,

in the firm's catalog, the missing index to Hiersemann Arabic MS 14 may be *Mingana Arabic MS* 248. The latter comprises two leaves, said to «contain the index to a MS of Mount Sinai». The leaves carry no date, but on the basis of paleographical considerations Mingana assigned them to «a Naskhi hand of about A.D. 1400»[15]. The leaves list the contents of a manuscript which match those of the Hiersemann MS in the order of their occurrence in nineteen out of twenty-three entries, and the four discrepancies may in fact not be found to be such if one could inspect the Hiersemann manuscript firsthand. The difference in dating between the index and the manuscript need not pose a problem, since it is not improbable that the index was supplied at a later time, when librarians at the monastery would have been putting some order into the earlier manuscript collections. Other Sinai manuscripts exhibit the same phenomenon, including *BM Oriental MS* 5019, as will appear below.

The fourth manuscript which includes the story of ʿAbd al-Masīḥ an-Nağrānī is *Sinai Arabic MS* 396 (Kamil, 156). The text is a *Menologion* for the month of November, which is assigned by Kamil to the thirteenth century[16]. Since this manuscript was not microfilmed in the Library of Congress/University of Alexandria expedition to Sinai in 1950, it is presently unavailable to scholars.

Although the edition of the story of ʿAbd al-Masīḥ an-Nağrānī given below rests on only two of the three extant manuscripts known to include it, one may be fairly confident that the base manuscript, *Sinai* 542, is the earliest available text of the story. Furthermore, the corrections and improvements which the writer of *BM* 5019 contributed to the text afford the modern reader a rare glimpse of the process by which the Palestinian monastic scribes over the years improved the Arabic diction of the texts which their communities most often employed.

grâce à sa date incontestable est un document de tout premier ordre pour l'histoire de la bibliographie, qui jusqu'ici n'avait coutume de prendre en consideration des manuscrits de papier coton aussi vieux». See also B. Outtier, «Le sort des manuscrits du 'Catalog Hiersemann 500'», *Analecta Bollandiana*, 93 (1975), p. 377-380.

[15] A. Mingana, *Catalogue of the Mingana Collection of Manuscripts* (vol. III, Additional Christian Arabic and Syriac Manuscripts), Cambridge, 1939, p. 52.

[16] Cf. Kamil, *op. cit.*, p. 18; Margaret Dunlop Gibson, *Catalogue of the Arabic MSS in the Convent of S. Catherine on Mount Sinai* (Studia Sinaitica, III), London, 1894, p. 65. Later Melkite calendars assigned the feast of ʿAbd al-Masīḥ to 9 March. Cf. J.-M. Sauget, *Premières récherches sur l'origine et les caracteristiques des synaraires melkites (XIe-XVIIe siècles)* (*Subsidia Hagiographica*, 45), Bruxelles, 1969, p. 366-367.

Since the aim of textual criticism must inevitably be to put forward a given text in a form that approaches as closely as possible to what in all likelihood left the pen of the original author of any given piece, the present edition of ʿAbd al-Masīḥ's story provides the text of *Sinai Arabic MS* 542 and the variants in *BM* 5019, along with all of their lexical, grammatical, syntactical, and orthographic idiosyncrasies. Punctuation, diacritical points, paragraphing, and vowelling, on the other hand, are supplied by the editor, in an attempt to ease the way for the modern reader. The resultant textual hybrid, which conforms neither to the usages of the Palestinian scribes and authors themselves, nor to modern ideas of Arabic readability, from the point of view of the standard literary language, should serve to highlight for the reader the peculiarity of Palestinian monastic Arabic in the period when ʿAbd al-Masīḥ's story was first written.

II. Palestinian Christian Texts in Arabic

Ḥabib Zayat's 1938 article in *al-Machriq* has often been quoted in subsequent scholarly literature, not because of his publication there of the story of ʿAbd al-Masīḥ an-Nağrāni, from the *British Museum Oriental MS 5019* (f. 103v-105v), but because of his discovery on an earlier folium (f. 58v) in the manuscript of one of the earliest known documentary references to Christian literature in Arabic[17]. For, at the conclusion of his copy of the Arabic account of some martyrs killed at Mt. Sinai and nearby Rāʾyah, the scribe of *BM* 5019 remarked that «this book was translated into Arabic from Greek, in the month of *Rabīʿ*, of the year 155 of the years of the Arabs»[18]. This date corresponds to the period of time between February 10 and March 11, 772 A.D., assuming that the month *Rabīʿ* I is meant, as will be shown below[19]. However, Zayat published only a portion of the scribe's note. Later, in three different places, Joshua Blau published the rest of the note, which contains further specifications regarding the date of the translation, but even Blau left out the final phrase[20]. Since the note is nowhere published in its entirety, it will be useful to provide it here.

[17] Cf. *art. cit.*, n. 9 above, p. 462.

[18] *Ibid.*

[19] Cf. V. Grumel, *La Chronologie* (*Traité d'Études Byzantines*, I), Paris, 1958, p. 282.

[20] J. Blau, «The Importance of Middle Arabic ...», *art. cit.*, n. 9 above, p. 219, n. 40; *idem*, «Über einige christlich-arabische Manuskripte aus dem 9. und 10. Jahrhundert», *Le Muséon*, 75 (1962), p. 103; *idem*, *The Emergence and Linguistic Background of Judaeo-Arabic*, Oxford, 1965, p. 5, n. 7.

شهدوا هاولى القديسين فى زمان دقليطانوس الملك الرومى الكافر. ولدقليطانوس مذ مات الى فسر هذا الكتاب بالعربية اربع مائة واربعة وسبعين سنة. فسر هذا الكتاب بالعربية من الرومية فى شهر ربيع سنة خمسة وخمسين ومائة من سنى العرب. فمن قراه او نسخه فليستغفر للذى فسر ولمن كتب غفر الله لهما[21].

These saints were martyred in the time of Diocletian, the pagan, Roman king. Since Diocletian died, until the translation of this document into Arabic, there have been four hundred and seventy-four years. This document was translated into Arabic from Greek in the month of *Rabi'*, of the year 155 of the years of the Arabs. Whoever reads it or copies it, should pray for forgiveness for the one who translated it, and for whoever has written it down. God forgive them both.

Joshua Blau noticed that on the face of it, there is a discrepancy of as much as eighteen years between the reckoning according to the years of the Arabs, and dating the translation 474 years from Diocletian's death, assuming the latter event occurred in 316 A.D. To follow this calculation is to move the date of the translation up to 790 A.D. Blau suggests several other options, such as the proposal that the text be amended to speak of Diocletian's coming to power (*m-l-k*) rather than to refer to his death (*m-'-t*), but anyway the matter is construed, there remains a discrepancy of fourteen to eighteen years[22].

Blau has not been the only person to notice the discrepancy between the two dates put forward in the scribe's note for the translation of the account of the Sinai martyrs into Arabic. Already in medieval times, someone at the Sinai monastery wrote a brief note in the right-hand margin of f. 58v, opposite the line, «since Diocletian died, until the translation of this document», to the effect that «in the account of George there is 'until here'»[23]. One may take it from this remark that the writer has discovered in an Arabic version of the account of St. George, the notice that the version of this saint's story was made in 790 A.D., counting four hundred and seventy-four years from the death of Diocletian «until here». Although there are five accounts of St. George in the Sinai Arabic manuscripts, as of the present writing, one has yet to come across the notice in question[24]. But the easiest construction to put upon the marginal comment in *BM* 5019 is that someone working with the manuscripts already in medieval times took notice

[21] *British Museum Oriental MS* 5019, f. 58v.

[22] Cf. passages cited in Blau's articles, n. 20 above.

[23] F. 58v, lower right hand margin : من قصة جرجس الى هاهنا

[24] Cf. ATIYA, *op. cit.*, n. 11 above, under MSS 153, 426, 474, 507, 523. There is the «good news» (*bišārah*) of George, bishop of Alexandria, in the unavailable *Sinai Arabic MS* 396. Cf. LEWIS, *op. cit.*, n. 15 above.

of the problematic dating and made reference to a similar observation which an Arabic translator had included in his version of the account of St. George, done in the year 790.

There is now more evidence to show that the writer of *BM 5019* was a compiler and redactor of earlier material, who did not hesitate to contribute his own observations on the material he transmitted. For *Sinai Arabic MS* 542 also includes the Arabic version of the Martyrs of Sinai, complete with the notice that the Arabic translation was made from Greek at a date which works out to be the year 772 A.D. The scribe's notice in *Sinai* 542 is as follows :

وكانت شهادة هولا القديسين على عهد ديقليطيانوس الملك الكافر. وفسر هذا الكتاب من الرومية الى العربية فى شهر ربيع الاول سنة خمسة وخمسين ومابة لله التسبحة وعلينا رحمته الى دهر الدهرين[25].

What one immediately notices in this earlier scribal note is the confirmation of the year 772 as the year in which the Arabic translation was made. Furthermore, it is clear that while the writer of Sinai Arabic *MS* 542 mentions Diocletian's reign as the time when the martyrs suffered, the computation of the number of years from the death of Diocletian to the date of the Arabic translation is a contribution from the later scribe of *BM* 5019. Subsequently, as mentioned above, already in medieval times someone noticed the discrepancy of the two dates, and in the margin of *BM* 5019 he put the information that in the story of St. George, who is also known to have been martyred in the time of Diocletian, it is said that there have been 474 years from the death of the Roman emperor «until now», i.e., presumably the year 790, when perhaps the story of St. George was first translated into Arabic. Maybe the scribe of *BM* 5019 simply borrowed the computation of the number of years from Diocletian, from an earlier manuscript containing the account of St. George, making the assumption that it was of the same age as the translation of the account of the martyrs of Sinai, who were said to have suffered under the same emperor. He did not notice the discrepancy of eighteen years, but a later reader observed it, and supplied in the margin the true reading from the account of St. George.

But, what about the dates of the manuscripts *BM* 5019 and *Sinai Arabic* 542? In the first place, the British Museum catalog simply

[25] *Sinai Arabic MS* 542 (Kamil, 576), f. 15r.

reports that *Or.* 5019 is dated to the year A.H. 568 [26]. Already in 1938, Zayat pointed out that the date in question, which he figured to correspond to December 12, 1166, belonged to the table of contents only, and not to the body of the manuscript. The latter, according to Zayat, must be dated to the tenth or eleventh centuries, on the basis of paleographical considerations [27]. Subsequently, Blau pointed out that Zayat erred in figuring the corresponding Julian date for 16 Ṣafar A.H. 568, which is actually October 7, 1172 [28]. But Blau accepted the ascription of the contents of the manuscript to an earlier time. Specifically, he noted that the language of the account of the Sinai martyrs, making an exception for later scribal corrections, accords well with the language of *British Museum Arabic MS* 4950, which is explicitly dated in the scribe's colophon to the year 877 A.D. [29].

The table of contents of *BM* 5019 lists a series of *mayāmir*, mostly attributed to John Chrysostom. But, as a matter of fact, the manuscript contains, almost exclusively, a selection of some twenty-five *qiṣāṣ* or «accounts» of the lives and accomplishments of holy men and women, none of which are mentioned in the table of contents. Michel Van Esbroeck solved this mystery regarding *BM* 5019 when he showed that the manuscript must be taken together with *BM Add.* 26.117. The latter is an eleventh century text written by the same scribe who wrote *BM* 5019, and together the two manuscripts preserve what is left of what was originally a two-fold anthology, comprising a collection of homilies, and a collection of saints' lives. The homilies survive only in fragments, but the collection of saints' lives is virtually complete, and Van Esbroeck has published a detailed analysis of the contents as they appear in the two British Museum manuscripts [30].

Blau, however, was quite right to have noticed that the account of the martyrs of Sinai in *BM* 5019 seems to be a corrected copy of a narrative written originally in the language of BM 4950. For in Sinai Arabic MS 542 there is available not only a recension of the account of the martyrs in the colloquial Arabic style of the Palestinian

[26] A.G. Ellis and E. Edwards, *A Descriptive List of the Arabic Manuscripts Acquired by the Trustees of the British Museum* (Since 1894), London, 1912, p. 70. A handwritten note on the MS itself says, «Bought of Mr. Butze, May 22, 1896». Cf. Van Esbroeck, *art. cit.*, n. 9 above.

[27] Zayat, *art. cit.*, p. 462.

[28] Cf. Blau, n. 20 above.

[29] Cf. Blau, «The Importance», *art. cit.*, n. 20 above, p. 219, n. 41; and «Über einige», *art. cit.*, n. 20 above, p. 104. On *MS* 4950 cf. Sidney H. Griffith, «Stephen of Ramlah and the Christian Kerygma in Arabic in Ninth Century Palestine», *The Journal of Ecclesiastical History*, 36 (1985), p. 23-45.

[30] Cf. Van Esbroeck, *art. cit.*, n. 9 above.

monasteries of the ninth and tenth centuries, but it is even written in the characteristic hand of the same time and place as well. And these same traits are also visible in the story of 'Abd al-Masīḥ an-Nağrānī in the two manuscripts. These features may easily be compared, from the linguistic point of view, in the edition given below of 'Abd al-Masīḥ's story.

Here is not the place to enter into a discussion of the typical Arabic usages of the Palestinian monastic scribes of the ninth and tenth centuries. The matter has all been rehearsed elsewhere[31]. What it is important to note here, however, is the fact that what was written in Arabic in the earlier period underwent a process of correction and improvement in later times, in what amount to later recensions of the same earlier material. In the instance of the story of 'Abd al-Masīḥ, what left the pen of the first Arabic writer was a somewhat infelicitously written specimen of the vernacular language of the Melkite community in Syria/Palestine in the eighth or ninth centuries. The story may have been copied in the ninth century by the scribe of *Sinai Arabic MS* 542 from yet an earlier exemplar. Together with the story of the martyrs of Sinai, the story of 'Abd al-Masīḥ was again copied, and revised from a linguistic point of view, in *BM* 5019.

The story of the martyrs of Sinai, as the manuscripts themselves testify, was a translation from Greek, done in the year 772. The writer of the Greek account is an otherwise unknown monk of Sinai named Ammonius[32]. While a considerable amount of scholarly controversy has attended the story of these martyrs, it need not detain one now, beyond the observation, recorded already by Blau[33], that Diocletian's name and date came to be associated with the story because Ammonius' account seems to have been modelled in part on events recorded by earlier church historians, in connection with martyrdoms suffered in the reign of the well known persecuting emperor of pre-Constantinian times[34]. Here one might only make the further observation that at Sinai, at some point in the tenth century, a seventh century Syriac version of Ammonius' account of the martyrs at Raithō,

[31] Cf. BLAU, *Grammar*, *op. cit.*, n. 1 above, and other references cited in GRIFFITH, «Greek into Arabic», *art. cit.*, n. 3 above.

[32] For the Greek texts and discussions about them cf. «Monachi in Sina et Raithu mm. saec. iv-v. — I an. 14», in F. HALKIN, *Bibliotheca Hagiographica Graeca* (*Subsidia Hagiographica*, 8a), 3 vols., Bruxelles, 1957, vol. II, p. 126-127; H.G. BECK, *Kirche und theologische Literatur im byzantinischen Reich*, München, 1959, p. 413.

[33] Cf. BLAU's references cited above in n. 29 and 20.

[34] Cf., e.g., R. DEVREESSE, «Le Christianisme dans la péninsule sinaïtique des origines à l'arrivée des Musulmans», *Revue Biblique*, 49 (1940), p. 216-220.

to adopt the Syriac spelling, was erased so that the vellum could be used again to carry what appears to be an original apologetic work, written in Arabic[35]. This manuscript, therefore, is itself a physical evidence of the social changes in the Christian community, which had been underway in Palestine at least since 772, and probably earlier. The Melkites were moving steadily away from their former employment of Greek and Syriac, toward a full scale adoption of Arabic as their everyday ecclesiastical language.

The movement to Arabic involved a large scale project to translate church books into the vernacular language of the caliphate. As noted at the very beginning of the present article, initially there were very few original compositions, and most of these were works of apologetics. But hagiography too was a genre in which new works appeared. The story of St. Anthony Ruwaḥ has already been mentioned as the most well known contribution to the genre[36]. And others are known from translations made already in medieval times from Arabic into a western language, notably Georgian. For example, there is the relatively well known story of Romanos, the captive Byzantine monk who was executed at ar-Raqqa in the time of the caliph al-Mahdī (775-785). His story was written originally in Arabic by his contemporary Stephen of Damascus, a monk of the Palestinian monastery of Mar Sabas. While Romanos' story remained unknown in Greek hagiography, it was translated into Georgian in the tenth century[37]. And there are other instances of a similar sort which it would be too much of a digression to mention here[38]. Suffice it now simply to remind the reader that even the life of St. John Damascene, which is so well known in Greek, had its roots in an Arabic original of the tenth century[39].

The Arabic account of ʿAbd al-Masīḥ an-Nağrānī appears in its earliest available form in *Sinai Arabic MS* 542, in all probability a product of the late ninth century. One knows from the testimony included in the same manuscript, at the end of the story of the Sinai

[35] Cf. Agnes Smith LEWIS, *The Forty Martyrs of the Sinai Desert, and the Story of Eulogios*, *Horae Semiticae*, 9, Cambridge, 1912, p. ix-xi.

[36] Cf. I. DICK, *art. cit.*, n. 8 above.

[37] Cf. P. PEETERS, «S. Romain le néomartyr († 1 mai 780) d'après un document georgien», *Analecta Bollandiana*, 30 (1911), p. 393-427.

[38] Cf. the references in Griffith, forthcoming article cited in n. 3 above.

[39] Cf. C. BACHA, *Biographie de saint Jean Damascène; texte original arabe*, Harissa, 1912; G. GRAF, «Das arabische Original der Vita des hl. Johannes von Damaskus», *Der Katholik*, 12, 4th series (1913), p. 164-190, 320-331; B. HEMMERDINGER, «La *Vita* arabe de saint Jean Damascène et BHG 884», *Orientalia Christiana Periodica*, 28 (1962), p. 422-423.

martyrs, that hagiographies in Arabic were available already a century earlier, at the very latest. So the question arises, is the story of ʿAbd al-Masīḥ an Arabic original, or is it a translation? Georg Graf stated unequivocally that it was a translation from Greek, and cites as evidence the presence of Greek words in the text, and the fact that the story has survived in a compilation of other Greek stories translated into Arabic[40]. However, one might take note of a few other pertinent facts as well. And the first of them is that no memory of the martyrdom of ʿAbd al-Masīḥ of Sinai seems to have survived in Greek, a fact that is remarkably at variance with what one would expect if the story had first been told in that language. There are accounts in Greek of other events in Palestine under the caliphate. For example, there are Greek accounts of the twenty monks killed at Mar Sabas monastery in 797, but it now appears, on the basis of modern studies of the Georgian version of this event, that the original may have been in Arabic[41]. Similarly, it is not only possible, but increasingly probable, that Arabic could have been the language of the original, as well as the language of the only known copies of the account of the exploits of ʿAbd al-Masīḥ an-Nağrānī.

It is undeniable that the Arabic diction of the account of ʿAbd al-Masīḥ in *Sinai Arabic MS* 542 is crude. The variants in *BM* 5019, one will observe in the notes to the Arabic text, are almost all of a lexical and grammatical character, clearly chosen to improve the clumsy Arabic expression of the original, which syntactically reminds the reader of nothing so much as the usages of Syriac. Moreover, the Arabic text in *Sinai* 542 is characteristic of the practices of writers of Syriac, complete with the accustomed punctuation marks for pause (:) and period(*). And this circumstance is itself characteristic of what we know about the earliest writers of Arabic in the Melkite community of Palestine. Modern scholars speak of 'Syriacisms' in their work; many of them were in fact from Syria[42]. Theodore Abū Qurrah, for example, the earliest known of them all, was from Edessa, and

[40] GRAF, *GCAL*, *op. cit.*, n. 9 above, vol. I, p. 517 and n. 1.

[41] For the Greek texts cf. F. HALKIN, *Bibliotheca Hagiographica Graeca*, *op. cit.*, n. 32 above, vol. II, p. 96. Regarding the Georgian version, and the possibly Arabic original, cf. R.P. BLAKE, «Deux lacunes comblées dans la passio xx monachorum sabaitarum», *Analecta Bollandiana*, 68 (1950), p. 27-43.

[42] Cf. the remarks of BLAU, *Grammar*, *op. cit.*, n. 1 above, vol. 267, p. 54; I. ARENDZEN, *Theodori Abu Ḳurra de Cultu Imaginum Libellus e Codice Arabico Nunc Primum Editus Latine Versus Illustratus*, Bonnae, 1897, p. xvi. For a list of the known Syro-Arab writers in Palestine at the time, cf. Griffith, forthcoming article mentioned in n. 3 above.

by his own testimony he wrote thirty some treatises in Syriac, just about double the number of Arabic works known from his pen[43]. So the simplest likely construction to put upon these facts is to suppose that the original writer of the Arabic story of ʿAbd al-Masīḥ was a native speaker of Syriac, for whom to learn to speak in Arabic would have been no great imposition, given the history of Syriac/Arabic bilingualism which was already a characteristic of life in an area where contact with Arabic speaking bedouin would have been of long standing duration[44]. But to write in Arabic would have been an altogether more difficult undertaking for the members of the Melkite community, whose traditions were rooted in Greek and Syriac. The record of their first efforts in this enterprise is what the Palestinian Christian Arabic archive from the ninth and tenth centuries provides. Hence the desirability of editing the texts in a manner which puts in high relief what initially left the pens of the first generations of writers in the new vernacular, and which shows how later scribes learned to improve the texts with an eye to the usages of the standard literary language. The whole process is an important part of the history of Christianity in Arabic.

As for Greek, its influence is never far from the surface of either Syriac or Arabic texts from the Melkite community, especially in the matter of ecclesiastical terminology, the only area in ʿAbd al-Masīḥ's story where Greek terms appear, e.g., ἁγιασμός, οἰκονόμος, διακονικόν. Their presence is not of itself a sufficient reason to propose that the story was written originally in Greek and later translated into Arabic. What might, however, initially be thought to favor such a conclusion is the circumstantial evidence of chronology.

From what one can glean from his story, the earliest time when ʿAbd al-Masīḥ could have come to Jerusalem was during the reign of patriarch John V (705-735), the first patriarch of this name after the Islamic conquest. Later, ʿAbd al-Masīḥ twice visited ar-Ramlah, because it was the residence of the Muslim governor of Palestine. Now ar-Ramlah was built, as an Islamic city, partly from materials taken from the wreckage of nearby Lydda, for the future caliph Sulayman

[43] Cf. Constantin BACHA, *Les œuvres arabes de Théodore Aboucara, évêque d'Haran* Beyrouth, 1904, p. 60-61.

[44] Cf. the remark of Michael the Syrian to this effect, in regard to a translation of the Gospel into Arabic arranged for by the Monophysite patriarch John I, J.-B. CHABOT, *Chronique de Michel le Syrien; patriarche jacobite d'Antioche (1166-1199)*, 4 vols., Paris, 1899-1910, vol. II, p. 342; vol. IV, p. 422. Cf. also M.J. NAU, «Un colloque du patriarche Jean avec l'émir des agaréens et faits divers des années 712 à 716», *Journal Asiatique*, 11th series, 5 (1915), p. 225-279.

ibn 'Abd al-Malik (d. 717), when he was governor of Palestine[45]. These factors taken together could possibly date the life and martyrdom of 'Abd al-Masīḥ an-Nağranī to the first half of the eighth century.

Indeed, the copyist of the martyrdom of 'Abd al-Masīḥ in *BM* 5019 assumed that the martyr met patriarch John V because he wrote at the head of his text that 'Abd al-Masīḥ was «martyred at ar-Ramlah, during the reign of the Umayyad kings»[46].

There were still Greek writers in Palestine at this time, including John Damascene himself (d. 749)[47]. Theodore Abū Qurrah (c. 750-c. 825), the earliest known Christian writer in Arabic had not even been born yet. The earliest attested date for the translation of Christian texts from Greek into Arabic is 772, well into the second half of the eighth century. It is clearly possible, therefore, on chronological grounds alone, to maintain that the first account of 'Abd al-Masīḥ an-Nağrānī was written in Greek, if one assumes that it was written shortly after the earliest possible date for his death. Relying on the computations of the years he spent in the several phases of his life, as found in the Arabic account of his exploits, the earliest possible date for 'Abd al-Masīḥ's execution would be the early 750's, counting some seventeen years from the last year when he possibly could have met patriarch John V (d. 735). More than a century, therefore, would have elapsed between the earliest possible date for the death of 'Abd al-Masīḥ an-Nağrānī and the writing of *Sinai Arabic MS* 542, which paleographically is in all likelihood a product of the second half of the ninth century.

But there is another chronological scenario, which, for reasons which will be explored below, seems more likely to the present writer. Another Patriarch John presided over the church in Jerusalem during the years when 'Abd al-Masīḥ's adventure could have transpired. He was John VI (839-843), and counting seventeen years from the last year when 'Abd al-Masīḥ could have met him, would put the martyr's execution in the early 860's, well within the period when Christians were writing in Arabic in Palestine, and well beyond the time when Greek was flourishing there. This circumstance, taken together with the fact that

[45] Cf. E. Honigman, «Al-Ramla», *EI*[1], vol. III, p. 1193-1195; Guy Le Strange, *Palestine Under the Moslems, a Description of Syria and the Holy Land from A.D. 650-1500*, Boston, 1890, p. 303-308; A. S. Marmardji, *Textes géographiques arabes sur la Palestine*, Paris, 1951, p. 81-86.

[46] Cf. n. 1 to the Arabic text edited in the appendix below.

[47] Cf. the brief survey in R. P. Blake, «La Littérature grecque en Palestine au viiie siècle», *Le Muséon*, 78 (1965), p. 367-380.

no memory of the man has survived at all in known Greek sources, or even in Georgian ones, would preclude the likelihood of a Greek original for the story of ʿAbd al-Masīḥ an-Nağrānī. Unlike its nearest analogue, the story of St. Anthony Ruwaḥ, with which it is transmitted in *BM* 5019, the memory of ʿAbd al-Masīḥ did not spread beyond Palestine, or, indeed, beyond Sinai, among whose manuscripts alone is the story found[48].

Finally, it does not seem reasonable, although once again it is not utterly impossible, to propose that the story of ʿAbd al-Masīḥ an-Nağrānī was originally written in Syriac. While Syriac seems to have been the mother-tongue of the first Christian writers of Arabic in the Palestinian monasteries, and its influences are everywhere to be seen in the manuscripts of the period, especially in the original Arabic compositions, there is no record of original writing in Syriac at Sinai during the period in question[49]. As a matter of fact, in the ninth and tenth centuries at Sinai, Syriac manuscripts are being erased so that Arabic texts may be written over them[50]. So the most probable conclusion remains that the story of ʿAbd al-Masīḥ an-Nağrānī was first written in Arabic, leaving open the possibility that it could well have circulated among the monks orally in Syriac, as well as in Arabic. Following this scenario, the multiple linguistic infelicities found in the Arabic diction of *Sinai* 542 are not to be attributed to the ineptitude of a maladroit translator. Rather, they are to be explained by

[48] Cf. I. DICK, *art. cit.*, n. 8 above. In *British Museum Or. MS* 5019, the story of St. Anthony Ruwaḥ appears on f. 100r-103v, with the story of ʿAbd al-Masiḥ an-Nağrānī following immediately on f. 103v-105v. On the eclipse of Greek in Palestine from the eighth to the tenth centuries, cf. GRIFFITH, «Stephen of Ramlah», *art. cit.*, n. 29 above. In later Melkite synaxaries in Arabic and Syriac the exploits of ʿAbd al-Masīḥ are told in one sentence referring to 9 March: «On it is the commemoration of ʿAbd al-Masīḥ, who was the superior of Mt. Sinai who was martyred in the city of ar-Ramlah», SAUGET, *op. cit.*, n. 16 above, p. 366. VAN ESBROECK, *art. cit.*, n. 9 above, p. 158, is mistaken to refer to the Georgian martyrdom of saint ʿAbd al-Masīḥ published by G. GARITTE, *Le Muséon*, 79 (1966), p. 187-237, in connection with the story of ʿAbd al-Masīḥ in *BM* 5019. Garitte's study concerns ʿAbd al-Masīḥ de Singar in Mesopotamia, a converted Jew, who was beheaded by his father.

[49] Cf. H. HUSMANN, «Die syrischen Handschriften des Sinai-Klosters, Herkunft und Schreiber», *Ostkirchlische Studien*, 24 (1975), p. 281-308.

[50] For the tenth century, cf. LEWIS, *op. cit.*, n. 35 above. For the ninth century, cf. Atiya's remarks on *Sinai Arabic MS* 514 (Kamil. 507), a quintuple palimpsest, A. S. ATIYA, *The Arabic Manuscripts of Mount Sinai; a Hand-list of the Arabic Manuscripts and Scrolls Micro-filmed at the Library of the Monastery of St. Catherine, Mount Sinai*, Baltimore, 1955, p. 19, and plates II-V, showing Syriac, Greek, and Old Kufic layers of text. Cf. also A. S. ATIYA, «The Arabic Palimpsests of Mount Sinai», in J. KRITZECK and R. B. WINDER (eds.), *The World of Islam; Studies in Honour of Philip K. Hitti*, New York, 1960, p. 109-120.

reference to the efforts of a monk educated to write in Syriac, who has set down the story of ʿAbd al-Masīḥ in what for him was a second language, the spoken Arabic dialect of southern Palestine, using the only scribal conventions known to him, i.e., those of the writer of Syriac. As is obvious from the text, he struggled to find appropriate Arabic vocabulary and phraseology. And it is precisely in this matter that his text was immeasurably improved by the later scribe of *BM Or. MS* 5019, as one may confirm by a brief glance at the variants cited in the notes to the edition of the text in the appendix below.

III. The hagiography of encounters between Christians and Muslims

Although, until modern times, the story of ʿAbd al-Masīḥ an-Naǧrānī has had only the local audience of the church at Sinai to read it, the account of his martyrdom is not without analogues from its own time and place which did gain a hearing in the wider world. There are almost a half dozen other stories with Palestinian connections, which come from the eighth and ninth centuries and which share some of the principal motifs of the account of ʿAbd al-Masīḥ. These principal motifs are conversion from Islam to Christianity, the attempt to proselytize among Muslims, and seeking martyrdom at the hands of the Muslim authorities. It will be useful in the present context, very briefly to mention these other stories.

The closest analogue to ʿAbd al-Masīḥ's story, as has already become clear, is the account of St. Anthony Ruwaḥ. The saint is represented as a noble Arab, a relative of the caliph, Harūn ar-Rašīd (786-809). According to the narrative, as a young warrior for Islam, the hero enjoys harassing Christians in Damascus. But a number of miracles cause him to reflect on his religious situation, and finally he resolves to convert to Christianity. He goes to Jerusalem for an interview with patriarch Elias II (d.c. 800), and proceeds from there to a monastery by the Jordan, where he is baptized and receives the name Anthony. He returns home to Damascus dressed in a monk's habit, a circumstance which leads to his arrest and eventual transport to Raqqa, where on the order of the caliph, after giving public testimony to his Christianity, Anthony is executed on Christmas day, in the year 799[51]. His story achieved a wide currency in Christian circles within the realm of Islam. Theodore Abū Qurrah refers to it as a well known fact in

[51] Cf. Dick, *art. cit.*, n. 8 above.

the course of his Arabic treatise on the Christian practice of venerating images[52]. And even the Muslims, in the person of al-Birūnī, are aware of the story as it is told among the Christians, albeit with a certain skepticism about its veracity[53].

As Ignace Dick, the modern editor of the Arabic account of St. Anthony has written, there is nothing improbable or unlikely about the basic elements of the story, leaving aside any judgment about visions and miracles. In its earliest Arabic form, buttressed by the testimony of Abū Qurrah, and the skeptical testimony of al-Bīrūnī, it is a straightforward account of a young Muslim who paid with his life for his illegal conversion to Christianity. The penalty is perfectly well in accord with what one knows of the statutory punishment for such a conversion in the law books of the Muslim jurists of the period[54]. And this much alone constitutes an important bit of evidence for the historical reconstruction of the social relationships which obtained between Muslims and Christians in the eighth and ninth centuries. Conversion was a real option, which elicited strong governmental sanctions against it. As a matter of fact, it was for proselytism among his fellow prisoners, who had become Muslims, that Romanos, the captive Byzantine monk, had been executed under al-Mahdī, a generation before St. Anthony Ruwaḥ[55]. And it was for the same reason, Christian proselytism, that yet another enthusiast, named Bacchus, was executed in Jerusalem, around the same time. This young man, whose Arabic name was Daḥḥāq, had become a monk at Mar Sabas monastery after his father had led the rest of his family into Islam. According to his story, Bacchus, fired with devotion, had returned from the monastery and re-converted his brothers to Christianity; all but one, who denounced him to the Muslim authorities, with the expected result[56]. Like both Romanos and Anthony Ruwaḥ, Bacchus' memory was also celebrated among the Georgians[57]. Unlike the other two,

[52] ARENDZEN, *op. cit.*, n. 42 above, p. 33 (Arabic), p. 34-35 (Latin).

[53] Cf. R. GRIVEAU (ed.), «Sur la célébration des jours de l'année chrétienne chez les chrétiens melchites», *Patrologia Orientalis*, 10 (1915), p. 299.

[54] Cf. A. FATTAL, *Le Statut légal des non-musulmans en pays d'islam*, Beyrouth, 1958, p. 163-168; A.S. TRITTON, *The Caliphs and their Non-Muslim Subjects*, London, 1930, p. 12. Cf. also the account of a similar incident outside of Palestine in K. SCHULTZE, «Das Martyrium des heiligen Abo von Tiflis», in *Texte und Untersuchungen zur Geschichte der Altchristlichen Literatur*, n. F., 13 (1905), p. 1-41.

[55] Cf. PEETERS, *art. cit.*, n. 37 above.

[56] Cf. R. JANIN, «Bacchus», *DHGE*, vol. VI, col. 50.

[57] Cf. G. GARITTE, *Le Calendrier palestino-georgien du Sinaiticus 34 (Xe siècle)* (*Subsidia Hagiographica*, 30), Bruxelles, 1958, p. 197.

however, Bacchus' feast was even commemorated by the Byzantines[58], who may have learned about him from the Georgians.

These stories of Christian converts and proselytes, simple in outline, and unadorned in the telling, buttressed as they are with documentary evidence to support them, even though they are told for purposes of edification in the Christian community, have a verisimilitude which allows them to serve as historical evidence for one who studies the life of the Palestinian church and its influence in the early Islamic period. But they are obviously also grist for the mill of hagiographic fiction. And true to one's expectations, there are stories from the Palestinian area in this period which have elicited skepticism not only from the likes of al-Birūnī, who found Anthony Ruwaḥ's story simply incredible, but also from modern critical hagiographers such as P. Paul Peeters. Peeters found fictional elements even in the story of Anthony Ruwaḥ, especially in its Ethiopic, Georgian, and later Arabic forms[59]. But he also studied two other narratives, in which, in his judgment, later fictional accretions have all but completely obscured the kernel of historical reality which he believes to lie under them. They are the stories of Peter of Capitolias, and Michael of Mar Sabas[60]. Here is not the place to discuss these stories in any detail. Suffice it to say that in both of them the hero is executed by the Muslim authorities, after defaming Islam and delivering a defense of Christianity in full court. The suspected accretions and fictional embellishments appear particularly in the speeches which the characters deliver. And in this connection it is worth mentioning that in Peeters' judgment the story of Michael is eventually taken up into the story of another fictional character, Theodore of Edessa, whose story in turn was modelled by its Greek writer on the well known career of the Arabic and Syriac apologist, Theodore Abū Qurrah[61]. It seems clear that anti-Islamic polemic and pro-Christian apologetic were the primary motivations

[58] Cf. F. HALKIN, *Bibliotheca Hagiographica*, *op. cit.*, n. 41 above, vol. I, p. 75.

[59] Cf. P. PEETERS, «S. Antoine le néo-martyr», *Analecta Bollandiana*, 31 (1912), p. 410-450; *idem*, «L'Autobiographie de s. Antoine le néo-martyr», *Analecta Bollandiana*, 33 (1914), p. 52-63.

[60] Cf. P. PEETERS, «La Passion de s. Pierre de Capitolias», *Analecta Bollandiana*, 57 (1939), p. 299-333; *idem*, *«La Passion de s. Michel le Sabaite»*, *Analecta Bollandiana*, 48 (1930), p. 65-98.

[61] Cf. PEETERS, «S. Michel», *art. cit.* For an opposing view cf. A. VASILIEV, «The Life of St. Theodore of Edessa», *Byzantion*, 16 (1942-1943), p. 165-225. However, the two facts which Vasiliev advances in support of the historicity of a Theodore of Edessa, distinct from Theodore Abū Qurrah, viz., the saint's visit to Constantinople, and his ordination at an alleged synod of the oriental patriarchs in Jerusalem in 836, are themselves doubtful. Cf. GRIFFITH, «Stephen of Ramlah», *art. cit.*, n. 29 above.

of the Greek writer of the *Vita* of Theodore of Edessa[62], and one might suppose that a similar motivation would have lain behind the alleged fictional embellishments of the other Georgian and Greek accounts as well. What is pertinent to the present inquiry is to recall that under all of the proposed embellishments which Peeters saw in the Georgian and Greek versions of these stories, he posited the existence of simpler, more straightforward «souvenirs authentiques» in Arabic or Syriac, which would have furnished the raw material for the Byzantine hagiographers of a later period, active after the reconquest of Syria/Palestine in the late tenth century[63]. The early Arabic stories of Anthony Ruwaḥ and ʿAbd al-Masīḥ an-Nağrānī are cases in point, in which unobjectionable, trustworthy narratives have in fact survived. However, in the instance of the latter Christian hero, there are as yet no known Greek or Georgian hagiographic novels which have taken him for their leading character.

Before passing on to a consideration of the historical information which one might glean from the Arabic account of ʿAbd al-Masīḥ an-Nağrānī, it is worthwhile quickly to take note of another Palestinian monk who, like one or two mentioned already, deliberately sought martyrdom at the hands of the Muslim authorities. His name is George, originally of Bethlehem, who spent twenty-seven years in Mar Sabas monastery. He was sent by his abbot on business for the monastery to North Africa. Finding the church there under a severe persecution, he proceeded to Spain. And there, according to the account of Eulogius of Toledo, an eyewitness of the affair, George joined up with a group of four other Christians who deliberately provoked the Cadi of Cordoba to order their execution on 27 July 852[64]. From the narrative one learns that when George was at Mar Sabas, he had five hundred confreres in the monastery[65]. Leaving room for a considerable exaggeration, the testimony still suggests a fully functioning, populous community. And Eulogius' boast that George was proficient in Greek, Latin, and Arabic[66], testifies not only to the cultivation of Greek

[62] Cf. A. Abel, «La Portée apologétique de la 'vie' de s. Théodore d'Edesse», *Byzantinoslavica*, n. 60, 10 (1949), p. 229-240.

[63] Cf. Peeters, «S. Michel», *art. cit.*, n. 60, p. 91 ; *idem*, «S. Pierre», *art. cit.*, n. 60, p. 316, 322-323.

[64] Cf. Eulogius of Toledo, *Memoriale Sanctorum, Documentum Martyriale, Apologeticus Martyrum*, *PL*, vol. 115, col. 777-792. Cf. also Edward P. Colbert, *The Martyrs of Cordoba (850-859) : a Study of the Sources* (The Catholic University of America Studies in Medieval History, New Series, vol. XVII), Washington, 1962, p. 239-242.

[65] Eulogius, *op. cit.*, col. 787.

[66] *Ibid.*

among the learned monks at the monastery in the ninth century, but suggests to the reader one route by which Latin speaking «Franks» may have come to be found in the east even prior to the crusades, in early Abbasid times. For not only did George himself travel all the way to Spain without any insuperable impediment, but before contriving his own martyrdom he left with Eulogius a testament to be sent back to Mar Sabas monastery, without any indication that this might be a difficult or impossible request[67]. Of course, the whole question of «Franks» in the Holy Land in Abbasid times has its own associated controversies[68], but Eulogius' account of George of Bethlehem reminds the reader that there was a route linking Christian speakers of Latin with their Arabic speaking brothers in the east, running wholly within the territories of *dār al-Islām*. Perhaps this route may even explain how «Franks» came to be in prison with Romanos in Baghdad around the year 780[69].

IV. History and Hagiography

The account of 'Abd al-Masīḥ an-Nağrānī is simple and straightforward. There are in it none of the fantastic elements which invite the skepticism of the critical scholar and set him in search of another agenda on the part of the writer, beyond the bound of edifying biography. It is a memoir, probably written by a Sinai monk, which tells what happened to one of his earlier confreres, who had risen to high monastic office, probably, as the the narrative suggests, because of his success in dealing with the Arab overlords. His own life was in jeopardy because he was a former Muslim. And this circumstance in point of fact is what in the end made him a martyr, because he refused to apostatize from Christianity. Such in essence is the whole story. Accordingly, given the relatively early date of the account, it may be examined as a historical document, with its own peculiar witness to

[67] *Ibid.*, cols. 788-789.

[68] Cf. S. Runciman, «Charlemagne and Palestine», *The English Historical Review*, 50 (1935), p. 606-619. Of course, pilgrims continued to come to Palestine from the west and from Byzantium, but they seem to have paid little attention to the local church in Palestine. Cf. the studies of John Wilkinson, *Jerusalem Pilgrims Before the Crusades*, Warminster, 1977.

[69] Cf. Peeters, «S. Romain», *art. cit.*, n. 37 above, p. 398, and the *caveat* of I. Ševčenko, «Hagiography of the Iconoclast Period», in A.J. Bryer and J. Herrin, *Iconoclasm*, Birmingham, 1977, p. 114, n. 9.

the circumstances of life under Muslim rule during ʿAbd al-Masīḥ's life-time.

The period of time during which ʿAbd al-Masīḥ an-Naǧrānī lived must be reckoned from the clues which are to be found in the narrative. Some of them have been mentioned earlier, in connection with the problem of determining whether or not the narrative was composed at a time when Greek would have been a likely language option for the original writer. But now the issue of chronology must be discussed more fully. And by way of an introduction to the discussion, one may establish the temporal parameters within which ʿAbd al-Masīḥ's life-time must fall. As mentioned earlier, the *terminus post quem* is provided by the date of the establishment of the Islamic city of ar-Ramlah, i.e., after the time of the caliph Sulayman ibn ʿAbd al-Malik (d. 717)[70]. And since the mosque of ar-Ramlah is mentioned in the story, one may suppose that the date may even be brought down to the time of the caliph caliph Hišām ibn ʿAbd al-Malik (724-743), during whose reign the building was completed with the addition of the minaret[71]. As for the *terminus ante quem*, the Arabic hand employed to write Sinai Arabic MS 542 supplies a somewhat fluid limit, which cannot be far removed in either direction from the turn of the ninth and tenth centuries[72]. When one takes into consideration the likelihood that the account of ʿAbd al-Masīḥ in this manuscript is a copy, one comes to the conclusion that the original story should have been composed sometime before the end of the ninth century. Therefore, ʿAbd al-Masīḥ's *floruit* might reasonably be sought in an interval during the century and a half from 750 to 990 A.D., give or take a decade or so at either end of the period.

The narrative mentions John as the name of the patriarch whom ʿAbd al-Masīḥ met in Jerusalem just after his re-conversion to his ancestral Christianity. There are only two patriarchs of this name who reigned in Jerusalem at times when it would have been possible for one of them to have met ʿAbd al-Masīḥ, and in this writer's judgment the first of them, John V (705-735), should be disqualified, in spite of the scribe's additional note in BM 5019 that the martyrdom took place «during the reign of the Umayyads»[73]. While the scribe of BM 5019 probably thought immediately of John V, and hence

[70] Cf. n. 45 above.

[71] Cf. the testimony of al-Muqaddasi, quoted in Le Strange, *op. cit.*, in n. 45 above, p. 304-305.

[72] Cf. the paleographical dates assigned by Atiya and Kamil, cited in n. 11 above.

[73] Cf. the earlier discussion, and n. 1 to the Arabic text below.

of the time of the Umayyads, there are other considerations which make his choice of the patriarch unlikely. The first of them is the fact that there are no known Greek or Georgian records of the martyrdom of ʿAbd al-Masīḥ an-Nağrānī. It seems higly unlikely, therefore, that the martyrdom could have occurred at a time when both of these languages were still flourishing in Palestine, without some mention of the martyr being preserved in them. Moreover, John V died in the year 735, a circumstance which would put the latest possible date for ʿAbd al-Masīḥ's martyrdom in the early 750's, still some twenty years before the earliest recorded date for the adoption of Arabic in the monasteries of Palestine. As mentioned earlier, the date of the martyrdom of St. Anthony Ruwaḥ is 799, and his memory is celebrated in Georgian and other languages of the Christian communities, while no mention of ʿAbd al-Masīḥ is to be found outside of Arabic before modern times, a fact which is best explained if his lifetime came about a century after the time of Patriarch John V. So, the patriarch John whom ʿAbd al-Masīḥ met must have been John VI (839-843). And the latest time when the execution could have been carried out would then have been in the early 860's, as explained earlier. This date, of couse, puts the whole affair at a time which suits all of the circumstances so far discussed, and the very suitability of it all constitutes good grounds for assuming the probability of this dating.

According to Eutychius of Alexandria, John VI became patriarch of Jerusalem in the seventh year of the caliph, al-Muʿtasim (833-842), and he reigned such a short time, three to four years, because «they spoke all manner of infamy about him and he became frightened of them, and at their dictation he wrote out his own document and resigned from the throne»[74]. While no one any longer knows for sure what were the troubles which precipitated this action, or who were the protagonists who instigated the patriarch's resignation, it may not be farfetched to suppose that the Muslim authorities were behind it. Eutychius goes on to say that John's successor, who was made patriarch in the second year of the reign of the caliph, al-Wāthiq (842-847), was Sergios ibn Manṣūr (843-859), a descendant of the Manṣūr «who had helped the Muslims at the conquest of Damascus, and been cursed throughout the world»[75]. The Manṣūr in question was John Damascene's grandfather, who was in fact widely disdained among some Christians

[74] L. Cheikho et al., *Eutychii Patriarchae Alexandrini Annales* (*CSCO*, 51), Beirut and Paris, 1909, p. 60-61.

[75] *Ibid.*, p. 61-62.

for his role in the Muslim appropriation of Damascus[76]. This very fact, of course, would probably have made Manṣūr's descendant, Sergios, a more acceptable Patriarch of Jerusalem in the eyes of the Muslims, which may be why Eutychius mentioned his lineage. Furthermore, there is evidence that in earlier years the patriarchs of Jerusalem did indeed go in fear of the Muslims. For example, Patriarch Elias II did not want personally to baptize Anthony Ruwaḥ because, as he reportedly said, «I am afraid to baptize you. For abuse would come upon me for it, and fear of the Sultān»[77]. If, on the other hand, John VI was willing to arrange for such things as ʿAbd al-Masīḥ's becoming a monk at Mar Sabas monastery, it is no wonder that the Islamic authorities would have found him to be an unacceptable patriarch.

According to the Arabic account of his martyrdom, ʿAbd al-Masīḥ was twenty years old when he left home with the Muslim raiders, and he stayed with them for thirteen years, according to the account, which would have made him thirty-three years old when he experienced his conversion, and came to Patriarch John. This age instantly attracts the suspicious eye of the hagiographer, because it is Jesus Christ's reputed age when he was crucified, and a favorite age in hagiographical fiction for major events in the heroes' lives. It is impossible to tell, of course, whether this device has any bearing on the present story. The writer goes on to report that ʿAbd al-Masīḥ spent five years at Mar Sabas before undertaking the monastic tour which eventually brought him to Mt. Sinai, where, after an unspecified period of time spent in service to the monastery, he became its *oeconome*, and held this post for another five years. Finally, after his unsuccessful attempt to become a martyr during his first visit to ar-Ramlah, the narrative says that ʿAbd al-Masīḥ served as superior at Sinai for seven years, before the fateful events which brought about his execution. Following these calculations, ʿAbd al-Masīḥ would have been in his early fifties when he died. Since he would have met Patriarch John between 839 and 843, his execution would have taken place around 860, and his birth would therefore have been around the year 810.

The narrative says that ʿAbd al-Masīḥ was from among the Christians of Nağrān, and that his given name was Rabīʿ ibn Qays (or Qays ibn Rabīʿ) ibn Yazīd al-Ghassānī. Of course, the Christians of Nağrān are the well known group who were originally from the South Arabian

[76] Cf. J. NASRALLAH, *Saint Jean de Damas, son époque, sa vie, son œuvre*, Harissa, 1950, p. 10-29.

[77] DICK, «La Passion arabe», *art. cit.*, n. 8 above, p. 123.

city of that name who, in Islamic sources are known for having once sent a delegation to the prophet Muḥammad, and who are said to have reconciled themselves to his hegemony[78]. In Christian sources they are remembered for their martyrs, who suffered in pre-Islamic times at the hands of the Jewish king of Ḥimyar, Dhū Nuwās[79]. Under the caliph 'Umar I (634-644), the Christians of Nağrān were dispersed to Iraq[80] and, also to Syria[81]. In both places they established settlements which carried the name of their former South Arabian home-town.

All of the elements of 'Abd al-Masīḥ's given name are attested among the Christians of Nağrān, with the exception of Rabī', which may be considered his own *ism* and which is certainly itself a traditional Arab name[82]. His sobriquet al-Ghassānī on the other hand indicates that in all likelihood he was himself originally from among the Christians of Nağrān who had settled in Syria, and who, as Prof. Irfan Shahid has shown, cast in their lot with the remaining Ghassanids of the area[83]. As for his religious name, 'Abd al-Masīḥ, which al-Ghassānī adopted on becoming the superior of the monastery at Mt. Sinai, it too had ancestral, as well as confessional significance, in that on Ibn Isḥāq's testimony, this was also the name of the *'Āqib*, or leader, of the Nağrān Christians who had visited Muḥammad[84]. The coincidence of all these details, therefore, is a testimony at the very least to the hagiographer's concern to exploit the Arab geneological significance of the names of 'Abd al-Masīḥ an-Nağrānī al-Ghassānī.

There is another element in 'Abd al-Masīḥ's story which is of interest to the historian of the early Islamic period, and it has to do with the remarks in the text about taxation (*al-ḫarāğ*). The first of

[78] Cf. Muḥammad Muḥyī d-Dīn 'Abd AL-ḤAMĪD (ed.), *Sirat an-Nabī li Abī Muhammad 'Abd al-Malik ibn Hišām* (4 vols.), Cairo, 1356, vol. II, p. 204ff.; A. GUILLAUME, *The Life of Muhammad; a Translation of Ibn Ishaq's Sirat Rasūl Allah*, Oxford, 1955, p. 270-277.

[79] Cf. Irfan SHAHID, *The Martyrs of Najran; New Documents* (*Subsidia Hagiographica*, 49), Bruxelles, 1971.

[80] Cf. J.M. FIEY, *Assyrie Chrétienne* (3 vols.), Beyrouth, 1968, p. 226-229; esp. p. 227, n. 2, for sources regarding the action of 'Umar I.

[81] Cf. R. DUSSAUD, *Topographie historique de la Syrie antique et médiévale*, Paris, 1927, p. 378, locating the Syrian town of Nağrān in the south of the Leğā region of the Haurān.

[82] Cf. 'Abd AL-ḤAMĪD, *op. cit.*, vol. II, where Qays and Yazīd are listed among the fourteen chief men of Nağrān. GUILLAUME, *op. cit.*, p. 271.

[83] Cf. Irfan SHAHID, «Byzantium in South Arabia», *Dumbarton Oaks Papers*, 33 (1979), p. 78-80.

[84] Cf. 'Abd AL-ḤAMĪD, *op. cit.*, vol. II, p. 204 and 206; GUILLAUME, *op. cit.*, p. 170 and 171.

them tells of the martyr's duties when he first came to Mt. Sinai. The text says, «He used to frequent Aylah in connection with the tax on the estate of Qasr at-Ṭūr, and in connection with the tax of the Christians of Pharān and Rā'yah». In the first place, it is interesting to note that there was a Muslim tax official at Aylah in the ninth century. This should perhaps not be surprising, in view of the fact that al-Muqaddasī, writing in the latter part of the tenth century (c. 985), calls the city, «the great port of Palestine and the emporium of the Hijjāz»[85]. Furthermore, one knows from the Nessana papyri that tax problems had been a constant source of difficulties for Christians in southern Palestine since the conquest[86]. ʿAbd al-Masīḥ's services in this connection probably had to do with his insider's knowledge of how to deal with the Arab officials, on the part of the Christians of the Mount (*aṭ Ṭur*), as it was called, and of the neighboring Christian towns as well[87]. One may conclude from this account that in the ninth century the officials of the monastery were responsible for all the Christians in the area, in regard to their relationships with the Islamic government.

Tax difficulties were also the reason for ʿAbd al-Masīḥ's final trip to the provincial capital, ar-Ramlah. In explanation of the journey, the writer of the account says, «The minister of the tax treated the Mount unjustly. At that time their tax went to Palestine. So he set out with a company of monks for ar-Ramlah». What strikes the reader immediately in this remark is the phrase, «At that time their tax went to Palestine». It means that by the time of ʿAbd al-Masīḥ's death, which is here dated to the early 860's, there had been no interruption in the traditional fiscal arrangements of the Islamic province of Palestine, but that by the time when the story of his martyrdom was written, or copied, a change in the direction of finances had come about. Given the chronological considerations discussed above, the most likely agency of change would have been the seizure of power in the area by Aḥmad ibn Tūlūn (835-883). He was sent to Egypt as deputy-governor in 868, and was directed by the caliph in 869 to quell the revolt in Palestine by the governor, Amāǧūr. By 877, Aḥmad had taken control of Syria/

[85] Guy LE STRANGE, *Description of Syria, Including Palestine, by Mukaddasi* (*Palestine Pilgrims Text Society*), London, 1896, p. 64. For other texts describing Aylah, cf. MARMARDJI, *op. cit.*, n. 45 above, p. 11-12; H.W. GLIDDEN, «Ayla», *EI*², vol. I, p. 783-784.

[86] Cf. C. J. KRAEMER, *Excavations at Nessana*, vol. III. Non-Literary Papyri, Princeton, 1958, esp. nos. 69-77.

[87] Cf. E. HONIGMANN, «al-Ṭūr», *EI*¹, vol. IV, p. 913-914.

Palestine, and annexed the area to Egypt[88]. It does not seem unreasonable to suppose that after this event, Sinai's tax went to Egypt. Perhaps Amāğūr's revolt had been responsible for the unjust treatment which was the occasion for ʿAbd al-Masīḥ's journey to ar-Ramlah in the first place. The governor may have attempted to raise extra revenues to support his revolt. In any event, since the Arabic account of the martyrdom of ʿAbd al-Masīḥ was copied into Sinai Arabic MS 542 in the late ninth century, the Ṭūlūnids would already have been in power, and this circumstance would be enough to explain a copyist's remark about a change in the destination of Sinai's taxes. And it may even be the case that the original Arabic writer of the account made the remark, since not more than ten or fifteen years separated ʿAbd al-Masīḥ's death from Aḥmad ibn Ṭūlūn's definitive seizure of power.

ʿAbd al-Masīḥ's bones, according to the martyrdom, were divided between the Sinai monastery and the church of St. Cyriacus at ar-Ramlah, which had been the scene of earlier action in the story. The only other record of this church of St. Cyriacus in ar-Ramlah is in Eutychius of Alexandria's *Annales*, and specifically in his account of the events during the reign of the caliph, al-Muqtadir (908-932). At that time, says Eutychius, «the Muslims rioted in ar-Ramlah, and they tore down two churches of the Melkites, the Church of Mār Cosmas, and the church of Mār Cyriacus»[89]. Although Eutychius goes on to say that the Christians were eventually given permission to rebuild these churches, there is apparently no trace of them left today[90].

One cannot now be sure about which St. Cyriacus was the titular saint of the church visited by ʿAbd al-Masīḥ, and where some of his relics were venerated. Perhaps it was the martyr St. Cyriacus (Cyricus, Quiricus), the son of St. Julitta, whose story is told in one of the earliest Christian Arabic manuscripts from Palestine, Sinai Arabic MS 514 (Kamil, 507)[91]. Or perhaps the titular saint of the church at ar-Ramlah was the Cyriacus who in the sixth century had been a monk of the so-called «Old Lavra», the monastery of St. Charitōn, and whose feast was in fact celebrated in the Palestinian church[92].

A *suasio* in favor of the martyr St. Cyriacus (Cyricus, Quiricus) as the patron saint of the church at ar-Ramlah may be seen in the identical

[88] Cf. Zaky M. Hassan, «Aḥmad b. Ṭūlūn», *EI*², vol. I, p. 278-279.

[89] Cheikho, *op. cit.*, p. 82.

[90] Cf. B. Bagatti, *Antichi Villaggi Cristiani di Samaria*, Jerusalem, 1979, p. 156.

[91] Cf. Atiya, «The Arabic Palimpsests», *art. cit.*, p. 117. Cf. also Halkin, *Bibliotheca Hagiographica Graeca*, I, p. 111-112.

[92] Cf. Garitte, *Le calendrier palestino-géorgien*, p. 325 and 344; Sauget, *Premières recherches*, p. 343-344.

spelling of the saint's name in Sinai Arabic MS 542 and Sinai Arabic MS 514, i.e., قرقس. The reading in BM Or. MS 5019 is قورقس, which Zayat changed to قورقوس, and interpreted as جرجس, i.e., St. George[93]. Apparently Zayat thought that the church which ʿAbd al-Masīḥ visited, and where some of his relics were kept, was the famous church of St. George in Lydda, a neighboring city to ar-Ramlah, and this supposition led him to accept such an unlikely spelling of the name 'George'. Subsequently, Sauget accepted this identification without objection[95]. However, in view of Eutychius of Alexandria's testimony to the presence of the church of كورقس in ar-Ramlah, which was mentioned above, Zayat's and Sauget's reading of قورقس / قرقس as an alternative spelling for جرجس would seem to be unjustified. Furthermore, if either the writer of the *Vita* of ʿAbd al-Masīḥ, or Eutychius of Alexandria, meant to designate St. Cyriacus, the monk, as the patron saint of ar-Ramlah's church, the chances are they would have spelled his name كيرياكوس (κυριακός), as the name in fact appears in the later Melkite synaxaries[96]. So the most probable suggestion remains that the patron saint of the church was the martyr son of Julitta, whose name is variously spelled in the sources as Cyriacus, Cyricus, Cirycus and Quiricus[97].

It remains only to consider what the martyrdom of ʿAbd al-Masīḥ has to tell the modern inquirer about its author and his milieu. Of course, one does not know the author's name. But it is reasonable to suppose that he was himself a monk of the Sinai monastery, perhaps from the generation after the time of ʿAbd al-Masīḥ. In all probability, like Theodore Abū Qurrah before him, and the copyist who wrote *Sinai Arabic Ms* 542 after him, the author was an original speaker of Syriac, with ties to Edessa. One recalls that somewhat improbably, even ʿAbd al-Masīḥ is said to have made a quick journey to Edessa after his first visit to ar-Ramlah, and just before his election as superior at Mt. Sinai. Furthermore, it is clear from other considerations that Melkite Syrians played a large role in the Palestinian monasteries during the ninth and tenth centuries, particularly in the undertaking to trans-

[93] Cf. n. 90 to the edition of the Arabic text in the appendix below.

[94] Cf. C. Clermont-Ganneau, *Archaeological Researches in Palestine* (3 vols.), London, 1896-1902, vol. II, p. 102-109; A. Ovadiah, *Corpus of the Byzantine Churches in the Holy Land* (*Theophaneia*, 22), Bonn, 1970, p. 130-131; Bagatti, *Antichi Villaggi*, p. 160-169.

[95] Sauget, *Premières recherches*, p. 367.

[96] *Ibid.*, p. 343-344.

[97] Cf. R. Van Doren, «Cyrice», *DHGE*, vol. XIII, col. 1168.

late the ecclesiastical books into Arabic[98]. So the author of the martyrdom, with all his evident Syriacisms, was probably among their number. Unlike most of his colleagues, however, he took the adventuresome step of composing in Arabic, on the model of the traditional stories of the saints and martyrs, the account of the exploits of 'Abd al-Masīḥ, a recent hero of his own monastery. It is clear from the telling, that while the author's Arabic usage was not good enough either lexically, syntactically, or grammatically to pass muster for truly literary purposes, it must have been good enough to allow him some participation in the intellectual life of the caliphate and to give him access to Islamic lore. For it seems perfectly clear that he was anxious to enroll 'Abd al-Masīḥ among the noble Christians of Nağrān, as they were portrayed by Ibn Isḥāq in his biography of Muḥammad. And this apologetic dimension to the martyrdom is perfectly well in accord with what one would expect from the author's position within what has been called «the sectarian milieu»[99]. Inevitably, in Arabic, he had to commend the social standing of his main character by reference to tribal associations which had immediate social and religious implications within the Islamic polity. So one may conclude that the author of the story of 'Abd al-Masīḥ al-Ghassānī an-Nağrānī was motivated not only to extol the perseverance in faith of the former superior of Mt. Sinai, but he was also concerned to accent the nobility of his lineage in terms calculated to elicit the respect of Muslims and Christians alike. In the years after the mid-tenth century when more monks of Greek culture returned to Palestine and Sinai, with the reassertion of some Byzantine power in the area, 'Abd al-Masīḥ's feast was certainly celebrated, and his name duly appears in the Melkite synaxaries of later times[100]. But no one was ever moved to write his *Vita* in Greek, or any other western language.

[98] Cf. the forthcoming study cited in n. 3 above.

[99] Cf. John WANSBROUGH, *The Sectarian Milieu. Content and Composition of Islamic Salvation History*, Oxford, 1978. As the subtitle indicates, Wansbrough is interested in how Islamic thought adjusted itself to the necessity to state its religious claims in an idiom intelligible in the context of the discourse of other religious groups. After the establishment of Islam, Christian writers in Arabic, *mutatis mutandis*, faced the same challenge.

[100] Cf. SAUGET, *Premières recherches*, p. 366-367.

APPENDIX

TEXT AND TRANSLATION

The Martyrdom of ʿAbd al-Masīḥ al-Ghassānī an-Naǧrānī

The following edition of the Arabic text of the martyrdom of ʿAbd al-Masīḥ is presented in harmony with the purposes discussed in the foregoing article. A particular aim is to highlight the ongoing project among the scribes and writers in the Palestinian monasteries in the ninth century and thereafter to improve the Arabic diction of their compositions. Accordingly, *Sinai Arabic MS* 542 (Kamil, 576), f. 65r-67r, provides the base-text for the edition.

The text is copied as it appears in *Sinai Arabic MS* 542, in terms of spelling, orthography, syntax and grammar. The case of *alif otiosum*, however, presents a special difficulty. The writer of *Sinai Arabic MS* 542, as expected in Palestinian manuscripts, writes *alif otiosum* often, even when by classical standards it should not appear. However, in thirteen instances in the present piece, following another Palestinian scribal convention, he omits this *alif* when it would appear before *lam* or another *alif*. But in this usage the scribe was not consistent; in five or six instances he writes *alif otiosum* even preceding *lam* or another *alif*. In the edition which follows, the omission of *alif otiosum* is marked by the plus sign (+), to call attention to this scribal usage. In two instances, cited in notes 108 and 137 respectively, the scribe seems to have omitted *alif otiosum* by mistake, so it is restored in the edited text. (On the *alif otiosum* in these MSS see G. Graf, *Sprachgebrauch der ältesten christlich-arabischen Literatur*, Leipzig, 1905, p. 8; Blau, *Grammar*, vol. 267, p. 127-128; B. Knutsson, *Studies in the Text and Language of Three Syriac-Arabic Versions of the Book of Judicum, with Special Reference to the Middle Arabic Elements*, Leiden, 1974, p. 113-116.)

Paragraph division, punctuation, diacritical points and vowelling are at the discretion of the editor. The attempt has been to aid clarity, while at the same time preserving what may be the closest available approximation to the text which left the pen of the original writer, given the limitations of the manuscript witness to the original text. Textual variations from the base-manuscript are cited from the text preserved in the *British Museum MS* 5019, f. 103v-105v. Here too the text is presented as it appears in the manuscript.

The citations from the text in BM 5019 which are quoted in the notes, along with other remarks in the notes, refer to the word or phrase which immediately precedes the note-number in the edited text of the base-manuscript. The limit of the phrase in the edited text to which a reference in the notes applies is indicated by the supralinear right-angle mark (˺) at the beginning of the phrase, meaning that the text cited in the note refers to the text running from this right-angle mark to the note-number in the edited text. When such a phrase is involved, instead of a single word, the right-angle mark is repeated alongside the note-number in the edited text. For several note-numbers one must look as far as the foregoing paragraph to find the appropriate right-angle mark. In at least one instance, n. 135, the note refers to a word which is included in a phrase to which the following note, n. 136, refers inclusively.

The following *sigla* are used:

S	=	*Sinai Arabic MS* 542
L	=	*British Museum Or.* MS 5019
Z	=	Zayat's text edited in *al-Machriq* 36 (1938), pp. 473-475.
>	=	Word or phrase omitted in the MS cited.
+	=	In the notes, the sign indicates that a word or phrase is added in the MS cited; in the edited text, as discussed above, + designates the omission of *alif otiosum*.
*	=	In n. 136, * notes changes in Z, not found in L.

˺بسم الاب والابن وروح القدس، اله واحد.

هذه شهادة ابونا القديس عبد المسيح، ريس طور سينا، الذى استشهد بالرملة[١].

كان رجل من نصارا نجران يقال له ربيع بن قيس بن يزيد الغسانى، من خيار عرب نصاراها، حسن العبادة، ˺فهم بما له وعليه[٢]. وانه[٣] خرج مرة[٤]، وهو بن[٥]

١ المسيح الهى ورجاى والسيدة مارتمريم شفيعتى هذه قصة عبد المسيح الذى استشهد بالرملة فى ملك الاموية L .

٢ فى النصرانية عالم بما له وعليه L .

٣ الى ان L .

٤ مدة من الزمان L .

٥ ابن L .

عشرين سنة، يريد الصلاة ببيت المقدس، مع[٦] مسلمين من اهل نجران، ˹عازمين على الغزوا[٧]. فلم ˹يزلوا، فى صحبته لهم، يغروه ويسترلوّه الى ان ذهب معهم فى الغزوا[٨].

˹وكان ارما الناس بسهم، واضرب الخلق بسيف، واطعنه برمح[٩]. فحملته الجهالة والحداثة وخبث الصحابة[١٠] الى الدخول مع الغزاة الى ارض الروم. فجاهد معهم وقاتل وقتل ونهب[١١] واحرق، ووطى كل محرم كفعلهم[١٢]، وصلّا معهم. وصار على الروم اشد منهم[١٣] غيظا واقسا قلبا[١٤]. فدام[١٥] على ذلك ثلثة عشر سنة، ˹مدمن على الغزوا فى كل سنة[١٦].

˹فلما تمت له هذه السنين[١٧]، خرج الى[١٨] بعض مدن الشام ليشتوا[١٩] فيها. فدخل ˹الى بعلبك نصف النهار[٢٠]. فاستقام على فرسه ˹الى كنيسة بها[٢١]، ˹وانه دخل فيها. فنظر الى قس جالس على باب الكنيسة وهو يقرا فى الانجيل. وانه جلس الى جانبه تسمعه قال له، «ايش تقرا يا قس»؟ اجابه القس وقال، «فى الانجيل اقرا»[٢٢]. فقال له[٢٣]، «فسّر لى ما تقرا»[٢٤]. ففسّر له قايلا[٢٥]،

[٦] + قوم L.

[٧] يريدون الغزوا L.

[٨] يزالوا فى صحبتهم له يغروه ويستهولوه الى ان صير طريقه الى الغزوا معهم L.

[٩] وكان من ارمى الناس بسهم واشده فى قتال بسيف او رمح L.

The writer in S seems to have formulated the elatives اطعن and اضرب on the analogy of ارمى, an attested form in the classical language. Cf. W. E. Lane, *An Arabic-English Lexicon* (7 vols.), London, 1863-1893, vols. I, p. 309 under تقن ; III, p. 1163.

[١٠] اصحابه L.

[١١] وانتهب L.

[١٢] كصنعتهم L.

[١٣] > L.

[١٤] + منهم L.

[١٥] فاقام L.

[١٦] يغزوا الروم كل سنة ولا يبرح الثغور L.

[١٧] فلما مضت له ثلثة عشر سنة L.

[١٨] يريد L.

[١٩] يسبى L.

[٢٠] نصف النهار الى مدينة بعلبك L.

[٢١] حتى نزل الى جانب كنيسة L.

[٢٢] ثم دخل لينظر الى الكنيسة فاذا القسيس جالس على باب الكنيسة يقرا فى الانجيل فجلس وتسمعه ثم قال له اى شى تقرا فقال الانجيل L.

[٢٣] > L.

[٢٤] + بالرومية L.

[٢٥] ان L.

«من احبˋ ام او اب[٢٦] او اخ[٢٧] او شيˋ افضل مني[٢٨] فليس هو لي باهل»[٢٩].
وما يتلوا ذلكˋ حينيذا بكا[٣٠] وتذكر ما كان فيه والىˋما قد صار اليه[٣١]. فلما اكثر من[٣٢] البكا، قال لهˋ القس، «ايش امرك[٣٣] يا فتا»؟ فقال له الغساني، ˋ«لا تلمني على بكاي، فاني[٣٤] كنت مرة من اصحاب هذا الانجيل، فاما اليوم فمن[٣٥] اعداه. ˋاسمع قصتي حتا اخبرك بها»[٣٦].

ˋفلما اعلم القس بخبره[٣٧]، فقال لهˋ القس، «فايش[٣٨] يمنعك، ان كنت[٣٩] نادم، ان ترجع وتتوب»؟ فقال له الغساني[٤٠]، «ان الامر عظيم جدا، وانا اعرف[٤١] من نفسي ما لا تحتمله الجبالˋولا الارضين»[٤٢]. فقال له القس[٤٣]، «الم تسمع الانجيل يقول[٤٤]، «ان الذي لاˋيطيقوا الناس هو على الله سهل»[٤٥]؟ وقال[٤٦] ايض،

٢٦ اب او اما L.

٢٧ + او اخت L.

٢٨ على الله L.

٢٩ The Gospel reference is a conflation of elements from Mt. 10:37 and Lk. 14:26. It is interesting to note that the text in S has obvious similarities to the text of Mt. 10:37a in *Sinai Arabic MSS* 72 and 74, f. 13r and 21v respectively, من احب ابا او اما افضل مني فليس هولي باهل. *Sinai Arabic MS* 72, presumably the more recent of these two Gospel MSS, was written in the year 897 A.D. Cf. Sidney H. GRIFFITH, «The Gospel in Arabic: an Inquiry into its Appearance in the First Abbasid Century», *Oriens Christianus*, to appear; idem, «Stephen of Ramlah and the Christian Kerygma in Arabic in Ninth Century Palestine», *The Journal of Ecclesiastical History*, 36 (1985), p. 23-45.

٣٠ فبكا L.

٣١ اى شي صار L.

٣٢ > L.

٣٣ القسيس اى شي دينك L.

٣٤ فاني for انا + L Phrase omitted in

٣٥ فانا من L.

٣٦ وانه قص على القسيس قصته كلها L.

٣٧ > L.

٣٨ القسيس فاى شي L.

٣٩ + كما ذكرت L.

٤٠ الرجل L.

٤١ اعلم L.

٤٢ والارضين L.

٤٣ اقسيس + ان الله هو احمل من الجبال لنا والارضين L. لنا Z omits.

٤٤ تسمعه كيف يقول في الانجيل L.

٤٥ يستطاع عند الناس فهو عند الله يستطاع L.
A reference to Mt. 19:26. The corrected text in L is similar to the Arabic version in *Sinai Arabic MSS* 72 and 74, f. 24r and 42v respectively.

٤٦ فاذ قال L.

«ان الله[٤٧] يفرح برجعة خاطى واحد اكثر من ماية صديق»[٤٨]. نعم ˹ياخى الحبيب اعلم[٤٩] ان˺ الله اسرع الينا منا اليه[٥٠]. انت[٥١] قد قرات˺ الانجيل، كما ذكرت لى[٥٢]، فاذكر اللص والابن الشاطر».

˹فقام ذلك الشاب[٥٣] فصلّا فى الكنيسة واخرج صلاحه فرماه[٥٤] قدام المذبح وعاهد الله انه لا يعود الى شى مما كان فيه. وان القس[٥٥] صنع له˺ اصمون لغفران الذنوب[٥٦]. خرج[٥٧] وباع فرسه ˹وسلاحه وصدق به[٥٨] على المساكين. وقدس˺ القس وقربه[٥٩]. ˹وانه سلم عليه[٦٠] وخرج الى اورشلم[٦١] قاصدا.

فلما وصل، لبس السواد ودخل على[٦٢] البطريرك، انبا ينه، فاخبره بقصته. ˹فعزّاه البطريرك وشدده وفرح به وصلّا عليه وبعثه[٦٣] الى سيق سابا[٦٤]، الى ريس[٦٥] الدير ليرهبه. ˹فذهب الى هناك[٦٦] وتراهب ˹وصير عند معلم قديس روحانى[٦٧]. ˹فلبث هناك خمسة سنة.

[٤٧] لله L. الله Z.

[٤٨] + الذين لم يخطوا L. An inexact allusion to Lk. 15:7+10.

[٤٩] يا حبيب فاعلم L.

[٥٠] الينا اسرع تعطفا منا الى الرجعة اليه L.

[٥١] وانت L.

[٥٢] كما تخبرنى الانجيل L.

[٥٣] وان ذلك الشاب قام L.

[٥٤] > L.

[٥٥] القسيس L.

[٥٦] يسمونى اعنى تمحيص غفران من الذنوب L. يسمون (ἁγιασμός) اى تمحيص Z.

[٥٧] وانه خرج L.

[٥٨] وتصدق بثمن سلاحه وفرسه L.

[٥٩] له القسيس وقربه وصلا عليه L.

[٦٠] وودعه L.

[٦١] ياروسليم L.

[٦٢] الى L.

[٦٣] فبسطه وفرح به وصلا عليه وارسله L.

[٦٤] مارى سابا L.

[٦٥] راس L.

[٦٦] فمضى الى ثم L.

[٦٧] وصيره راس الدير الى معلم روحانى قديس L. In S the ه of وصيره is written above the line, suggesting that it was a later contribution to the text. The correction presumes *ṣayyara* instead of *ṣīra*, with ريس الدير as presumed subject.

وبعد ذلك خرج وطاف[٦٨] الديارات التى حول بيت المقدس. ˹وبعد ذلك خرج[٦٩] الى طور سينا. فاقام ثمّ ايضا[٧٠] سنين فى عبادة شديدة وخدمة الرهبان[٧١] وحرص عليهم، حتا[٧٢] انه كان يتردد الى ايلة، منجل[٧٣] خراج ضيعة قصر الطور، ˹ومنجل خراج نصارى فاران وراية. فلما ارو + الرهبان من حرصه، صيره عليهم اقنوم. فدام على ذلك خمسة سنين[٧٤].

˹وبعد ذلك[٧٥] احب ان يظهر امره فخرج[٧٦] الى الرملة ومعه راهبين فاضلين[٧٧]، قد وهبو + [٧٨] انفسهم له[٧٩] ومعه ودونه. فكتب كتاب فيه هكذا[٨٠]،

«انا هو[٨١] قيس بن ربيع بن يزيد الغسانى النجراني، من[٨٢] قصتى كذا وكذا، وقد تنصرت وتراهبت[٨٣]. ˹شوق منى[٨٤] ورغبة فى النصرانية. وانا فى ˹ الكنيسة نازل. ان[٨٥] اردتمونى فاطلبونى هناك»[٨٦].

٦٨ فلما اقام خمس سنين خرج فطاف L.

٦٩ وخرج L.

٧٠ < L.

٧١ للرهبان L.

٧٢ حتى L.

٧٣ من اجل L.

٧٤ ومن اجل من هناك من نصارى اهل فاران وراية حتى احبوه اهل تلك البلاد وصيروه اهل الطور اقنوم هليهم حمسة سنين L.

٧٥ ثم انه L.

٧٦ فاتا L.

٧٧ خيرين L.

٧٨ ابذلوا L.

٧٩ < L.

٨٠ < L.

٨١ < L.

٨٢ ومن L.

٨٣ ترهبت L.

٨٤ The reading on the microfilm of S is uncertain, due to smudges on the MS; زهد فى الاسلام L.

٨٥ كنيسة الرملة نازلا فان L.

٨٦ فيها L.

˹ورما بالكتاب[٨٧] فى مسجد الجامع بالرملة. ثم انه مضا ˹مع الراهبين وجلس[٨٨] فى كنيسة[٨٩] السفلا مارى قرقس[٩٠].

فلما قروا الكتاب[٩١] فى المسجد تصايحوا[٩٢]، وخرج منهم ˹خلق حتا صاروا الى[٩٣] الكنيسة السفلا. ˹فداروها كلها داخل وخارج[٩٤] وفوق واسفل، وهو جالس ˹مع الراهبين[٩٥]، ولم يروه لان الله ˹اعماهم عنه. فقام ومشا قدامهم ليروه فلم يروه. فذهبوا الى الكنيسة الفوقا يطلبوه ورجعو + الى السفلا. فما قدروا عليه. وكانوا يزحموه، وقد اعماهم الله عنه. فقالو + له الراهبين،

˹«يابونا[٩٦] ان الله لم يحب[٩٧] يظهر امرك[٩٨] لهم. ولو علم انك ˹تصبر اليوم لعرّفهم بك. فاذ كان الله لم يهوا ذلك، فلا تقاوم[٩٩] امر الله».

فقام ˹بالرملة ثلثة ايام[١٠٠]. ثم انطلق الى الرها، ورجع[١٠١] الى الطور.

فوافوا[١٠٢] ريس[١٠٣] الدير قد تنيّح، ˹فطلبوا اليه الرهبان وتحملوا عليه حتا صيره ريس على الطور[١٠٤] وكان اسمه عند الرهبانية عبد المسيح. فاقام ˹ريس على طور سينا سبعة سنين[١٠٥].

٨٧ والفا الكتاب L.

٨٨ هو والراهبين فجلسوا L.

٨٩ الكنيسة L.

٩٠ قورقس L. قورقوس (جرجس) Z. كورقس Cheikho, *Eutychii Annales*, p. 82

٩١ + المسلمين L.

٩٢ تصلحوا (تسلحوا) Z.

٩٣ جماعة يطلبوا فاتوا الى مارى قورقس L. (يطلبوه) Z.

٩٤ فدروا فيها كلها خارج وداخل L.

٩٥ والراهبين معه L.

٩٦ غطا اعينهم فلم يروه وكانوا يرجموه ويصيبوه ولا يريهم الله اياه فلما راوا ذلك الرهبان قالوا له L. وكانوا يرجموه (من الرجم اى الظن غيبا) ولا يصيبوه .... Z.

٩٧ + ان L.

٩٨ + اليوم L.

٩٩ تصير بصيرا لهم لهذا لا ظهرك فاذا لم يريد الله ان يظهر امرك فلا تقابلن L. تقاتلن Z.

١٠٠ ثلثة ايم بالرملة L.

١٠١ فصلا ورجعوا L.

١٠٢ فصادفوا L؛ وصادفوا Z.

١٠٣ راس L.

١٠٤ فتحمل عليه كلهم وصيروه راس على طور سينا وقسيس L.

١٠٥ ريس الدير سبعة سنين على طور سينا L.

فتحامل صاحب الخراج على الطور. ˈوكان خراجهم يوميذ[١٠٦] الى فلسين. ˈوانه خرج مع جماعة رهبان الى الرملة. فلما صاروا فى موضع يقال له غضيان، وافوا رفاق الحاج قادمين من حجهم[١٠٧]. فبينما هم يدوروا[١٠٨] فى الرفقة، ˈنظر انسان منهم يعرفه[١٠٩]، ˈواذاه من بعض رفقاه اذ كان بالغزوا سنين[١١٠]. فتعلق به وقال له،

ˈ«اليس انت الغسانى»[١١١]؟

فقال له، «ما ادرى ما تقول».

فصيّح وجلب ˈفالتأم على صياحه عامّة[١١٢] اهل الرفقة. فقال للناس[١١٣]، «هذا الراهب كان معى فى الغزوا سنين، ˈيصلى بنا، وهو رجل من العرب[١١٤]، وكان[١١٥] رفيق لى. وقد ˈكان اصابه ضربة فى راس كتفه. ففتّشوه، فان لم تجدوا كما قلت[١١٦] فانا كاذب».

وانهم ˈنزعوا عنه كساه وثوبه فاوجدو + الاثر كما قال لهم. وانهم قيدوه[١١٧] بقيود الدواب ˈوضمّوه مع الرهبان[١١٨] اصحابه، وكانوا ثلثة. ˈوانهم فكوّا قيده[١١٩]. ˈوطلبوا اليه فى الليل ان يفر وقالوا له،

«نحن نقيم معهم، يعملوا بنا ما ارادوا، ونبذل انفسنا دونك».

اجابهم قايلا، «انا احق ان اكون فداكم نفسى»[١٢٠].

١٠٦ سنة من تلك السنين فى الخراج وعلى جوره وكان اذذاك الخراجهم L.

١٠٧ فخرج هو ورهبان معه يريد الرملة حتى اذا صاروا بمرحلة يقال لها عصيان لنى رفاق الحجاج قد انصرفوا من حجهم L.

١٠٨ فبين ما هو يدور L؛ يدورو S.

١٠٩ اذا قد لقيه انسان من الحجاج فعرفه L.

١١٠ واذا هو قد كان رفيق له بالغزوا سنين L.

١١١ الست انت قيس الغسانى L.

١١٢ فاجتمع لصياحه جميع L.

١١٣ لهم L.

١١٤ يصلى معنا ويصلى بنا رجل من العرب L.

١١٥ وقد كان L.

١١٦ اصابته ضربة فى عنقه ففتشوا عنقه فان لم تجدوه كذلك

١١٧ وثبوا عليه كلهم وكلموه وانكر وراوا الاثر فى عنقه فقيدوه L.

١١٨ وضمنوه الرهبان L.

١١٩ فحلوه L.

١٢٠ وقالوا له S. فلما كان الليل طلبوا اليه الرهبان ان يفر ويدعهم يعملوا بهم ما ارادوا وقالوا له نحن يابونا نضع انفسنا دونك فابا وقال انا احق ان اقتل دونكم L.

فلما صاروا بالقرب[١٢١] من الرملة، ركب[١٢٢] ذلك الملعون دابته وسبق[١٢٣] الى الرملة. فجمع خلق[١٢٤] ودخل الى الوالى واعلمه بما[١٢٥] كان من امر الراهب. فوجه[١٢٦] معه خيل ˹حتا تلقاه[١٢٧] فى الطريق، ودخلوا[١٢٨] به الى الرملة وادخلوه[١٢٩] على الوالى. ˹فقال له الوالى[١٣٠]،

«استحى لنفسك ˹لانك رجل ذوا شرف وقدر»[١٣١].

فقال له عبد المسيح، «الحيا من الاهى المسيح اوجب ˹من الحيا منك[١٣٢]. فافعل ما احببت».

فطلب عليه من شهد[١٣٣]. فشهد عليه ˹خلق بما لم يعرفوا[١٣٤]. فحبسه ثلثة ايام. ثم اخرجه ˹فاعرض عليه الاسلام لله[١٣٥] قبل منه، واسا سماعه الجواب. فاغتاظ لذلك فامر بضرب رقبته، فتموّا ذلك بالفعل. وانه امر ان يواروه عن النصارى ويحرق. فحملوه حتا صاروا به الى بير فى بالغة، كان قد خرب. فرموا بجسده فيه وطرحوا عليه حطب كثير واشعلوا فيه النار، حتا فنى الحطب، واقاموا عليه حراس ليلا يسرقوه النصارى[١٣٦].

١٢١ > L.

١٢٢ على مرحلة ركب L.

١٢٣ > L.

١٢٤ جماعة L.

١٢٥ بالذى L.

١٢٦ فارسل L.

١٢٧ حتى تلقوه L.

١٢٨ واتوا L.

١٢٩ فادخل L.

١٣٠ فكلمه وقال له L.

١٣١ فانك رجل من اهل بيت L.

١٣٢ علىّ من الحيا من الناس L.

١٣٣ الشهادة L.

١٣٤ كثيرين زور لا يعرفوه على شهادة الذى عرفه L.

١٣٥ لله: In right margin in S.

١٣٦ فاعرض عليه ايضا دينه * فلم يسمع منه الا ما نكره فامر يضرب عنقه فلما ضرب عنه * امر ان يوارا عن النصارا * ويحرق فاخذوه وحملوه الى بير ببالغة * كانت قد خربت والقوا جسده فيها والقوا عليه حطب كثير ونار فاحرقوه فلما يروا ومضوا وتركوه وكانوا كثيرين الارصاد له الا ياتى احد من النصارا * فيخرجه L. فعرض عليه دينه ... فلما ضرب عنقه ... يوارى ... النصارى بير بالغة ... النصارى Z.

فلما مضا لذلك تسعة اشر، ⌐خرجوا رهبان من[١٣٧] طور سينا فكلموا اقوام من اهل الرملة ⌐فى سبره[١٣٨]. فجزعوا من ذلك جدا ⌐خوف من السلطان ولطول[١٣٩] البير. لان طوله[١٤٠] كان نحوا[١٤١] من ثلثين ⌐باع. فخاطره فى ذلك عشرة احداث شباب اشدا[١٤٢]. فهيّوا حبال وقفّة[١٤٣] كبيرة وصارو + [١٤٤] الى الكنيسة السفلا فباتوا ⌐ فيها حتا[١٤٥] اذا ناموا الناس. اخذوا شمعة ⌐ونار وذهبوا[١٤٦]. ومعهم الرهبان. فربطو + الراهب الواحد فى الحبل والقفّة[١٤٧] ودلوّه. وفى يده ⌐نار وشمعة[١٤٨]. فلما وصل الى[١٤٩] اسفل. اسرج الشمعة وفتّش على قدر ركبه رماد ⌐من الحطب الذى[١٥٠] كانو + القوا عليه. فاول ما ظهر[١٥١] له منه جمجمة راسه. وهى تضى[١٥٢] كالثلج. ⌐واخرج باقى جسده. ولم تحرقه النار ولا اذته بتة. فرح بذلك جدا وكثر تعجبه. وانه اخذ ذراعه الواحد فخباه. وكذلك اخذ بعض عظامه. وجعل الباقى فى الزنبيل وصاح اليهم ليصعدوه[١٥٣].

فلما ⌐ اصعدوه اتخاطفوه جميع من كان فوق، تهاربوا به الى كنيسة السفلا وتخلف منهم ثلثة فاطلعو + الراهب. فلما اطلعوه، ذهبو + الى مارى قرقس فاوجدوهم

١٣٧ خرجو S. رهبان S. Added in right marg. اقبلوا رهبان L.

١٣٨ < L. سبـ. Unclear word, S.

١٣٩ للسلطان ولبعد L.

١٤٠ طولها L.

١٤١ نحو L.

١٤٢ قامة الى ان خاطر فى ذلك عشرة رجل اشدا L.

١٤٣ + قفير L.

١٤٤ واتوا L.

١٤٥ حتى L.

١٤٦ وانطلقوا L.

١٤٧ والقفير L.

١٤٨ الشمعة والنار L.

١٤٩ < L.

١٥٠ < L.

١٥١ بدا L.

١٥٢ + بيضا L.

١٥٣ ثم اخرج البقية فاصابه لم يحترق من النار البتة منه جزو ففرح وعجب فخبا معه ذراع واحد من عظامه ثم القا كل شى فى الزنبيل L.

يتنازعوا عليه. فلم يزل الراهب، الذى كان اسفل. يقاومهم حتا اخذ راسه[١٥٤].
وتركو + له الذراع الذى كان[١٥٥] اخذه فى البير. فدفنوه فى الدياقنقون[١٥٦]، ما
خلا[١٥٧] الساعد وساق. امسكوه[١٥٨] ليخرجوه للناس يتباركون[١٥٩] به. 'وانصرفو +
الرهبان الى الطور براسه وعيّدو + له هناك[١٦٠].

وكان شهادته فى تسعة ايام خلت من اذار منجل ذلك نسبح للاب والابن وروح القدس الى دهر الادهار امين.

In the name of the Father, the Son, and the Holy Spirit, one God.

This is the martyrdom of our father, the holy ʿAbd al-Masīḥ, the superior of Mount Sinai, who was martyred at ar-Ramlah.

There was a man of the Christians of Nağrān, whose Christians were noble Arabs, called Rabīʿ ibn Qays ibn Yazīd al-Ghassānī[1]. He was correct in worship, knowlegeable in what was his right and in what was his duty. Once upon a time, when he was twenty years old, wanting to pray in Jerusalem, he set out with some Muslims of the people of Nağrān bent on raiding. On account of his association with them, they were continually beguiling him and misleading him, to the point that he went with them on the raid.

He was the best of men to shoot an arrow, the most expert of people in striking with a sword, and the most skilled in thrusting with a spear. Igno-

١٥٤ اصعدوا العظام تخاطفوها كلهم وهربوا به الى الكنيسة السفلا وتخلفوا ثلثة من القوم فرفعوا الراهب فلما صعد انطلق حتى اتوا جميع الى مارى قورقس فوجدهم يتنازعون عليه فلم يزال ينازعهم حتى اعطوه راسه L .

١٥٥ > L .

١٥٦ دياقونيقون الكنيسة L .

١٥٧ الا L .

١٥٨ وامسكوه L . امسكوه Z .

١٥٩ يتبركوا L .

١٦٠ وانطلقوا الرهبان بما اخذوا حتى وصلوا به الى الطور وعملوا له عيد فى الطور وبالرملة فى السر وسبحوا جميع المسيح الذى له التسبحة مع ابيه وروح قدسه الى الدهر امين L .

[1] Below, in both MSS, cf. p. 372, the name is given with Qays and Rabīʿ in reverse order, viz., Qays ibn Rabīʿ ibn Yazid al-Ghassānī. It is in all likelihood simply a scribal error in S, faithfully copied in L. The awkward phrase, «whose Christians were noble Arabs», may not be unrelated to the fact that according to Ibn Isḥāq, the leading men of Nağrān who visited Muḥammad were said to be Christians, «according to the religion of the king». Cf. ʿAbd al-Ḥamīd, *op. cit.*, n. 75 above, vol. II, p. 206; Guillaume proposes that the phrase in question means «they were Christians according to the Byzantine rite». *Op. cit.*, n. 78, p. 271. In the present instance the hagiographer is probably establishing the connection between his hero and the group which even the Muslims knew to be of honorable Arab reputation.

rance, youth, and bad companions brought him to enter Roman territory[2] with the raiding party. He fought and did battle along with them. He killed, he plundered, he burned, and following their example, he engaged in everything forbidden. He prayed with them, and he became even more furious and harder of heart against the Romans than they. He persevered in this for thirteen years, devoting himself to raiding every year.

When these years were finished, he set out for certain cities of Syria to pass the winter in them. One noonday he entered Baalbek, and on his horse he headed straight for a church there. He entered it and saw a priest sitting there at the door of the church, reading in the Gospel. He sat down beside him to listen. He said, «What are you reading O priest? The priest said in answer, «I am reading in the Gospel». He said, «Translate for me what you are reading»[3]. So he translated for him saying,

«Whoever loves mother, or father, or brother, or anything more than me, is not worthy of me». (Cf. Mt. 10:37 and Lk. 14:26)

When this was read, right then he wept and recalled what had been his estate, and to what he had come. Then, when he had wept copiously, the priest said to him, «What is your business, young man?» Al-Ghassānī said to him, «Do not chide me for my weeping. I once was of the adherents of this Gospel. But today I am of its enemies. Hear my story, while I recount it to you».

When he had informed the priest of his situation, the priest said to him, «What prevents you, if you are contrite, from coming back and doing penance?» Al-Ghassānī said to him, «It is an exceedingly grievous matter. Of my own accord, I would be admitting what neither the mountains nor the lowlands will endure». The priest said to him, «Have you not heard the Gospel saying, 'What men cannot bear is easy for God?' (Cf. Mt. 19:26) It also says, 'God will be glad at the return of a single sinner more than at a hundred just'. (Cf. Lk. 15:7 & 10) Yes, my beloved brother, know that God is swifter to us than we are to Him. You told me you have read the Gospel. Remember the thief and the prodigal son».

So the young man got up and went to pray in the church. He took out his weapon, and threw it down before the altar, and made a covenant with God that he would not go back to the thing in which he had been involved. And when the priest had performed the rite for the forgiveness of sins for him[4],

[2] The Romans, *ar-rūm*, are, of course, the Byzantines. Presumably the raiding expeditions in question were taking place in those areas of Asia Minor under Byzantine control, where annual military shirmishes were the rule in the eighth and ninth centuries. Cf. A. A. Vasiliev, *Byzance et les arabes* (4 vols.), Bruxelles, 1935-1968.

[3] It is interesting to note that the Gospel requires translation. L adds «what you are reading in Greek». On the program at the Palestinian monasteries in the ninth century to translate the Gospel into Arabic for pastoral purposes, cf. Sidney H. Griffith, «The Gospel in Arabic», *art. cit.*, n. ٢٩ to text above.

[4] Both Zayat and the scribe of *BM Or. MS* 5019 suppose that one has to do here with an Arabic transliteration of the Greek word ἁγιασμός. Although this term may be used broadly to mean 'sacrament', or 'rite', one presumes that here it refers to a rite of abjuration and absolution. Cf. G. W. H. Lampe, *A Patristic Greek Lexicon*, Oxford, 1961, p. 17. Such a rite may have involved an imposition of hands, anointing with chrism, and a profession of faith. Cf. V. Ermoni, «Abjuration», *DACL*, vol. I, col. 98-

he went out, sold his horse and his weaponry, and for it he gave alms to the poor. The priest celebrated the liturgy and gave him communion, whereupon he bade him good-bye, and he set out straight away for Jerusalem.

When he arrived, he put on black[5] and visited the patriarch, Abba John, and told him his story. The patriarch sympathized with him, encouraged him, rejoiced on his account, prayed over him, and sent him to the cloister of Mar Sabas, to the superior of the monastery, to accept him as a monk. So he went there, became a monk, and was assigned to a holy, spiritual teacher. He remained there for five years.

After that he set out and made the circuit of the monasteries which are around Jerusalem, and then he went off to Mt. Sinai. He stayed there too some years, in rigorous devotion, and service of the monks, and solicitude for them, to the point that he used to frequent Eilat in connection with the tax of the village of Qaṣr at-Ṭūr, and in connection with the tax of the Christians of Pharan, and Ra'yah. When the monks took note of his solicitude, they made him *oeconome* over them, and he remained at it for five years.

Subsequently, he wanted to divulge his situation, so he set out for ar-Ramlah. With him were two distinguished monks; they had already committed themselves to him, to be with him, and to be under him. So he wrote a message as follows, «I am Qays ibn Rabīʿ ibn Yazīd al-Ghassānī an-Nağrānī[6]. My story is such and such, but now I have become a Christian, and a monk. There is a yearning on my part, and a desire for Christianity. I am lodging in the church. If you want me, seek me there».

He tossed the message into the community mosque in ar-Ramlah[7]. Then he proceeded with the two monks and sat in the lower church of Mar Cyriacus. When they read the message in the mosque, they raised a clamor. Some people set out to go to the lower church. They went around the whole of it, inside and out, above and below, while he was sitting with the two monks. But they did not see him because God had blinded them to him. He stood up, walked around in front of them so they would see him, but they did not see him. They left for the upper church in search of him, and came back to the lower one. They did not get him. They had been crowding around him, but God blinded them to him. The monks said to him, «Father, God did not want to divulge your situation to them. If He had it in mind that you should be apprehended today, He would have made them notice you. Since God did not desire this, you should not resist God's decree».

So he stayed in ar-Ramlah for three days, then he left for ar-Ruhāʾ[8], and he returned to the mountain.

103. The abjuration of Islam required of ʿAbd al-Masīḥ may not have been unlike the one preserved from later times in Byzantium, in *PG*, vol. CXL, cols. 124-136.

[5] ʿAbd al-Masīḥ presumably put on a monk's black garb, to signify his intention in fact to become a monk. St. Anthony Ruwaḥ donned the monastic habit after his baptism. Cf. Dick, «La passion arabe de s. Antoine Ruwaḥ», *art. cit.*, n. 8, p. 124.

[6] Cf. n. 1 above. Note the inclusion of the *niṣbah*, an-Nağrānī.

[7] On the mosque at ar-Ramlah cf. K.A.C. Creswell, *Early Muslim Architecture; Umayyads, A.D. 622-750* (2nd ed.), Oxford, 1969, vol. I, pt. II, p. 482-483.

[8] *Ar-Ruhāʾ*, i.e., Edessa, in Syria.

They discovered the superior of the monastery already having gone to his rest. The monks then besought him and bore upon him until they made him superior over the mountain. And his name in monastic life became ʿAbd al-Masīḥ. He stayed as superior over Mount Sinai for seven years.

The minister of the tax treated the Mount unjustly. At that time their tax went to Palestine. So he [i.e., ʿAbd al-Masīḥ] set out with a company of monks for ar-Ramlah. When they got to a place called Ghaḍyān[9], they came upon companies of pilgrims arriving from their pilgrimage. While they were passing company by company one of their men looked and recognized him. He had been one of his companions when he had been in the raiding party years ago. He held onto him and said to him, «Are you not al-Ghassānī?» He said, «I do not know what you are saying». So he called out and raised a din, and at his shouting all the folk of the company came together. He said to the people, «This monk used to be with me years ago in the rading party. He used to lead us in prayer. He was a man of the Arabs and a companion of mine, and he was hit a blow on the top of his shoulder. Examine him. If you do not discover as I have said, I am a liar». Then they stripped off his dress and his coat from him, and they discovered the scar, just as they had been told. So they tied him up with the animals' straps and arrested him, together with the monks, his companions. There were three of them, and they undid his bonds.

During the night they implored him to flee, and they said to him, «We will stay with them. They may do with us what they will. We will give ourselves in exchange for you». He answered them saying, «I am more entitled myself to be a ransom for you». Then, when they arrived in the vicinity of ar-Ramlah, that scoundrel mounted his animal and came first to ar-Ramlah. He collected a crowd of people and went into the presence of the governor and informed him of the affair of the monk. He dispatched with him horsemen to go meet him on the road, and they escorted him into ar-Ramlah, and brought him into the presence of the governor. The governor said to him, «Save your life, for you are a man of honor and standing». ʿAbd al-Masīḥ said to him, «Life from my God, Christ, is more imperative than life from you. Do what you want». So he sought someone to testify against him, and people testified against him what they did not know. He confined him for three days and then he brought him out. He put the proposal to become a Muslim before him, but the answer aggrieved his ear, and he got angry at it and gave the command to behead him. They carried it out in fact, and then he gave the order that they should hide him from the Christians and that he be burned. So they carried him until they came with him to a well in Bāliʿah[10], which had been ruined. They hurled his body into it and threw a large quantity of wood on it, and kindled a fire in it until

[9] Ghaḍyān is probably ʿAyn Ghaḍyān, a site in the valley of ʿArabah which was long a watering station for travellers taking the eastern route to the north from Sinai. Cf. Alois Musil, *Arabia Petraea* (3 vols.), Wien, 1907-1908, vol. II, pt. 1, p. 18-24, 241 and 254; pt. 2, p. 179-189, 198-199; M. Lejeune, «Les routes du désert hier et aujourd'hui», in L. Prevost, (ed.), *Le Sinai, hier ... aujourd'hui*, Paris, 1937, p. 58-61. Cf. also C. Leonard Woolley and T. E. Lawrence, *The Wilderness of Zin*, New York, 1936, p. 32-33.

[10] A village in the vicinity of ar-Ramlah. Cf. Le Strange, *op. cit.*, n. 85 above, p. 305-306.

the wood was consumed, and then they stationed sentries over it so that the Christians would not steal him.

When nine months had passed, monks came from Mount Sinai and spoke to the most prominent citizens of ar-Ramlah about getting down to him. They were exceedingly worried about this for fear of the authorities, and because of the depth of the well, since its depth was around thirty fathoms. Ten strong young men took on the risk of it. They got ready ropes and large baskets, and came to the lower church. They stayed there until, when people had gone to sleep, they took candles and fire and departed, the monks with them. They tied the one monk onto the rope, and the basket too, and they let him down. In his hand was fire and candle. When he got to the bottom he lighted the candle and explored the ashes up to his knees from the wood which had been thrown on him [i.e., ʿAbd al-Masīḥ]. The first part of him to come to notice was the skull of his head, and it shone like snow. Then he brought out the rest of his body. The fire had not burned it, nor had it harmed it at all. He was exceedingly happy at this, and his astonishment was great. He took one of the arms and concealed it, and likewise he took some other bones. He put the remainder in the basket and shouted to them to bring it up. When they had brought it up, all who were above were snatching at it; they fled with it to the lower church. Three of them stayed behind and they raised up the monk. When they had raised him up, they too left for Mar Cyriacus, and they found them disputing with one another over him [i.e., ʿAbd al-Masīḥ]. The monk who had gone down did not cease arguing with them until he got the head. And they also let him have the arm which he had taken in the well. They buried him [i.e., ʿAbd al-Masīḥ] in the *Diakonikon*, with the exception of the forearm and thigh. They kept it back to bring out to the people seeking his blessing. The monks departed for the Mount with his head, and they observed a feast for him there.

His martyrdom took place during nine days which elapsed in Adhār (March). Therefore, let us give praise to the Father, and to the Son, and to the Holy Spirit, forever and ever, Amen!

XI

Anthony David of Baghdad, Scribe and Monk of Mar Sabas: Arabic in the Monasteries of Palestine

Forty years ago George Every called the attention of the scholarly world to the likelihood that in the oriental patriarchates after the time of John of Damascus the Arabic language increasingly became the language of the Melkite, or Roman (*rūmī*), community of Christians in the caliphate. They came to use Arabic, Every suggested, not only for scholarly purposes, but even for the divine liturgy, at least for the Scripture lessons.[1] In the years since Every made these observations it has become increasingly clear that not only was there such an increase in the use of Arabic in the church during the first Abbasid century, but that the crescendo in the use of Arabic went hand in hand with the diminishment of Greek as a language of church scholarship in the monasteries of the Holy Land from early Abbasid times, perhaps even until the Ottoman period, when the so-called "Rūm Millet" reintroduced the control of Greek speakers in the Jerusalem patriarchate.[2] Accordingly, one might speak of the first flowering of Christian life in Arabic in the Holy Land as having occurred during the three centuries stretching from 750, the beginning of the Abbasid caliphate, to around the year 1050, the eve of the crusader period in Near Eastern history.[3] And the documentary evidence for the literary activity of the Holy Land monks who wrote in Arabic during this period is largely the archive of "old south Palestinian texts" which Joshua Blau studied for his *Grammar of Christian Arabic*.[4]

1. See George Every, "Syriac and Arabic in the Church of Jerusalem," *The Church Quarterly Review* 145 (1947–1948): 230–239. See also Every's "Syrian Christians in Palestine in the Early Middle Ages," *The Eastern Churches Quarterly* 7 (1946): 363–372.
2. See Every's remarks in "Syriac and Arabic," pp. 236–237. On the diminishment of Greek and the growth of Arabic, see the remarks of S. H. Griffith, "Greek into Arabic: Life and Letters in the Monasteries of Palestine in the Ninth Century, the Example of the *Summa Theologiae Arabica*," *Byzantion* 56 (1986): 117–138; idem, "The Monks of Palestine and the Growth of Christian Literature in Arabic," *The Muslim World* 78 (1988): 1–28.
3. Rachid Haddad has studied the works of the writers of this period in his *La Trinité divine chez les théologiens arabes (750–1050)* (Paris, 1985).
4. Joshua Blau, *A Grammar of Christian Arabic*, vols. 267, 276, 279 (Louvain, 1966–1967). See the list of "old south Palestinian" texts in volume 267, pp. 21–33. Additional manuscripts, to which Blau had no access in earlier catalogs, are listed in J. Meimarēs, *Katalogos tōn neōn Arabikōn Cheirographōn tēs hieras monēs hagias aikaterinēs tou orous Sina* (Athens, 1985), Greek and Arabic.

Today, one knows the names of only a few of the ninth-century Melkite scribes and writers of Arabic in Syria, Jerusalem, and in the monasteries of Palestine. Among those whose careers modern scholars have discussed are Theodore Abū Qurrah, Abraham of Tiberias, Stephen of Ramlah, Bishr ibn as-Sirrī, and now Anthony David of Baghdad.[5] The purposes of this article are to call the attention of the modern scholarly community to Anthony David's scribal activity, to discuss his career in the context of the monastic milieu in which he functioned, and briefly to consider the works which he copied in Arabic for the benefit of the monks of his day.

1.

Anthony David of Baghdad left the only personal notices we have of him in the colophons of two Arabic manuscripts which he copied in the monastery of Mar Sabas in the late ninth century (A.D. 885/886). The first of them is the Vatican Arabic MS 71. The contents of this manuscript have been analyzed and published since the early nineteenth century.[6] More will be said about them below. The colophon, which has been published since 1914, reads as follows:[7]

> The poor sinner, Anthony David the son of Sulayman of Baghdad, copied this volume in the *laura* of the holy Mar Saba. The monk Abba Isaac asked him to copy it for the monastery of the hallowed Mt. Sinai. I, the weakly sinner who has copied it, ask and beseech everyone who reads of the holy fathers and others in it to beseech and ask Jesus Christ, our God and saviour, to forgive my many sins and offenses. By the intercession of the honorable Lady Mary, and of our father Saba and all his pious holy ones, may God have mercy on the ones who have produced, copied, asked for a copy, read, heard or said 'Amen' to [this work]. It was copied in the month Rabī^{c} al-Awwal, of the year 272.[8]

The second manuscript bearing the signature of Anthony David is the Strasbourg Oriental MS 4226 (Arabic 151), which has been a focus of scholarly concern several times over the past century as researchers have

5. See Ignace Dick, "Un continuateur arabe de saint Jean Damascène: Théodore Abuqurra, évêque melkite de Harrān, la personne et son milieu," *Proche-Orient Chrêtien* 12 (1962): 209–223, 319–332; 13 (1963): 114–129; K. Vollers, "Das Religionsgespräch von Jerusalem (um 800 D) aus dem Arabischen Übersetzt," *Zeitschrift für Kirchengeschichte* 29 (1908): 29–71, 197–221; G. Vajda, "Un traité de polémique christiano-arabe contre les Juifs attribué à 'Abraham de Tiberiade,'" *Bulletine de l'Institut de Recherche et d'Histoire des Textes* 15 (1967–1968): 137–150; S. H. Griffith, "Stephen of Ramlah and the Christian Kerygma in Arabic in Ninth-Century Palestine," *Journal of Ecclesiastical History* 36 (1985): 23–45; J. Nasrallah, "Deux versions Melchites partielles de la bible du ixe et du xe siècles," *Oriens Christianus* 64 (1980): 203–206.
6. A. Mai, *Scriptorum Veterum Nova Collectio e Vaticanis Codicibus Edita*, vol. 4 (Rome, 1831), pp. 143–145. Note the mistaken date on page 145 and the fact that the current folio numbers do not correspond to those quoted by Mai.
7. E. Tisserant, *Specimina Codicum Orientalium* (Bonnae, 1914), pp. xxxviii–xxxix.
8. Ibid., and G. Garitte, "Homélie d'Éphrem 'Sur la Mort et le Diable,'" *Le Muséon* 82 (1969): 135.

succeeded in tracking down the manuscript's final fourteen leaves, in libraries in Russia and England. J. Oestrup analyzed the contents of the Strasbourg manuscript in 1897.[9] Unaware of any relationship, I. Kračkovsky in St. Petersburg in 1907 published the manuscript's colophon along with five of its final leaves.[10] It was not until 1969 that G. Garitte recognized the fact that these leaves, and the colophon, belonged to the Strasbourg manuscript.[11] Meanwhile, in 1927 W. Heffening had published eight more of the manuscripts's missing leaves, which had made their way to the Mingana collection in Birmingham, England.[12] And, finally, in 1978 M. van Esbroeck announced the location of yet another leaf of this manuscript in the Mingana collection, one which had last been reported by H. L. Fleischer in the mid-nineteenth century in Leipzig, among items brought to Europe by Constantine Tischendorf.[13] So once again the manuscript is complete, at least in the sense that its complete contents are now available to the modern reader. More will be said about them below. The present concern, however, is with the manuscript's colophon, which reads as follows:

> Abba Anthony of Baghdad, David the son of Sīnā [*sic*], copied this volume in the *laura* of the holy Mar Saba. Abba Isaac asked him to write it for Mount Sinai. Through the intercession of the honorable mother of the Light, the pure, blessed Lady Mary, the prayers of all his apostles, disciples, prophets and martyrs, and the prayers of our holy father, Mar Saba, and all his holy friends, we ask Christ, our God and Savior, to have mercy and to forgive the sins of the one who has copied, and the one who has asked for a copy. Amen. I, the poor sinner who has copied this volume, ask everyone who reads it, I beseech him, to pray and to ask the Christ for the forgiveness of my sins. I ask the Christ, our God, in his graciousness and mercy, to have mercy on the ones who have copied, asked for a copy, read, or said 'Amen' to [this work]. It was copied in the year 272 of the years of the Arabs.[14]

9. J. Oestrup, "Über zwei arabische codices sinaitici der Strassburger Universitäts- und Landesbibliothek," *Zeitschrift der Deutschen Morgenländischen Gesellschaft* 51 (1987): 455–458.
10. I. Kračkovsky, "Novozavetniy apokrif v arabskoy rukopisi 885–886 goda," (A New Testament Apocryphon in an Arabic MS of the Year A.D. 885–886) *Vizantijskij Vremennik* 14 (1907): 246–275. Kračkovsky was particularly excited by his encounter with these manuscript leaves. It was one of his first dealings with Arabic manuscripts as a new scholar. He told the story years later in his reminiscences. See I. Y. Kratchkovsky, *Among Arabic Manuscripts: Memories of Libraries and Men* (Leiden, 1953), pp. 2–3.
11. G. Garitte, "Homélie d'Éphrem 'Sur la mort et le diable,' version géorgienne et version arabe," *Le Muséon* 82 (1969): 127–129.
12. W. Heffening, "Die griechische Ephraem-Paraenesis gegen das Lachen in arabischer Übersetzung," *Oriens Christianus* 23 (1927): 94–119.
13. M. van Esbroeck, "Un feuillet oublié du codex arabe or. 4226, à Strasbourg," *Analecta Bollandiana* 96 (1978): 383–384; H. L. Fleischer, "Beschreibung der von Prof. Dr. Tischendorf im J. 1853 aus dem Morgenlande zurückgebrachten christlich-arabischen Handschriften," *Zeitschrift der Deutschen Morgenländischen Gesellschaft* 8 (1854): 584–587 (reprinted in H. L. Fleischer, *Kleinere Schriften*, vol. 3 [Leipzig, 1888], pp. 389–394).
14. See the Arabic text published in Kračkovsky, "New Testament Apocryphon," p. 261; Garitte, "Homélie d'Éphrem," p. 128.

One quickly notices the common elements in these two colophons. The two manuscripts were copied in the same year, 272 "of the Arabs," or A.D. 885/886. Both manuscripts were copied at the request of a monk named Isaac for the monastery of Mar Sabas in Judea. Both manuscripts were copied by Anthony David of Baghdad, although the elements of his name are arranged slightly differently in the two manuscripts. Given the differences, one suspects that Anthony was the copyist's monastic name, while David was his given name. The only real discrepancy to be observed in the two colophons is the variation in the name of Anthony David's father, Sulaymān or Sīnā. At one time this discrepancy led W. Heffening to postulate two contemporary monks of the same name at Mar Sabas, both of different fathers.[15] But G. Garitte, followed by J.-M. Sauget, argued against the likelihood of there having been two monks of the same name working as copyists at Mar Sabas, suggesting that it is easier to believe that the discrepancy is a simple anomaly in the writing of the colophon of Strasbourg 4226.[16] Pursuing this suggestion, one might make the further observation that in fact the name Sīnā in Arabic writing is an exact duplicate of the spelling of the Arabic form of the name Sinai, which appears in the very next line of the colophon. So the conditions are right to suspect a scribal error. And now one knows, due to the researches of Michel van Esbroeck in the Leningrad manuscript, that there is in fact a misprint in Kračkovsky's copy of the scribe's name.[17] Both manuscripts actually say that the monk Anthony is David, the son of Sulaymān. So we may know for certain that the same Anthony David of Baghdad wrote both manuscripts.

Two lines of inquiry now lie open before us. One is to discuss the career of Anthony David of Baghdad within the context of what one knows of monastic life in Palestine in the ninth century A.D. The second line of inquiry is to examine the texts and their contents which Anthony David copied in Arabic with a view to determining the audience for which they were intended.

2.

Anthony David's roots in Baghdad attract one's attention. Of course, throughout their history the monasteries of Palestine were populated by monks from outside the patriarchate of Jerusalem. But for the most part in earlier times, until well into the eighth century, their important ties were with

15. Heffening, "Die griechische Ephraem-Paraenesis," pp. 100–101.
16. Garitte, "Homélie 'Sur la mort et le diable,' " p. 136; J.-M. Sauget, "Le dossier Éphrémien du manuscrit arabe Strasbourg 4226 et de ses membra disiecta," *Orientalia Christiana Periodica* 42 (1976): 430.
17. See M. van Esbroeck, "Le Codex Rescriptus Tischendorf 2 à Leipzig et Cyrille de Scythopolis en version arabe," in *Actes du deuxième congrès international d'études arabes chrétiennes*, ed. K. Samir (Rome, 1986), p. 84.

Cappadocia, Constantinople, and other centers of Greek thought in Byzantium.[18] In the ninth century, however, the monks whom one comes to know from the few personal notices available from the old Palestinian archive of Arabic manuscripts had ties with Edessa (Abū Qurrah), Damascus (Bishr ibn as-Sirrī), and Baghdad (Anthony David), as well as with Palestinian towns such as Tiberias (Abraham), and ar-Ramlah (Stephen of Ramlah). And their languages are Syriac and Arabic, rather than Greek.

While it is incontestable that the theological and liturgical heritage of the Melkite community in the Oriental patriarchates was largely Greek, it is also clear that Syriac had long been an important language in their milieu. Theodore Abū Qurrah himself admitted to having written thirty treatises in Syriac—almost double the number of the clearly authentic Arabic works known from his pen.[19] Bishr ibn as-Sirrī translated Saint Paul's epistles into Arabic, not from Greek, but from Syriac.[20] And, while the Arabic translations of Saint Ephraem's works that circulated in the Palestinian monasteries were the works of Ephraem Graecus, compositions by James of Sarūg were translated from Syriac.[21] Finally, it is noteworthy that Isaac of Nineveh's popularity in Byzantium is owed to the fact that his ascetical homilies were translated from Syriac into Greek by monks of Mar Sabas.[22]

The point to be made by this recitation of items in the Syriac heritage of the Arabophone monks of ninth-century Palestine is that one must learn that

18. See R. P. Blake, "La littérature grecque en Palestine au viiie siécle," *Le Muséon* 78 (1965): 367–380. For Mar Sabas monastery, see A. Ehrhard, "Das griechische Kloster Mar-Saba in Palaestina, seine Geschichte und seine litterarischen Denkmäler," *Römische Quartalschrift* 7 (1893): 32–79; S. Vailhé, "Les écrivains de Mar Saba," *Échos d'Orient* 2 (1898): 1–11, 33–47; Otto F. A. Meinardus, "Historical Notes on the Lavra of Mar Saba," *Eastern Churches Review* 2 (1968–1969): 392–401. See also the appropriate sections of Derwas J. Chitty, *The Desert a City* (Crestwood, N.Y., 1966); and Bernard Flusin, *Miracle et histoire dans l'oeuvre de Cyrille de Scythopolis* (Paris, 1983). See also the important work of Yizhar Hirschfeld, "The Judean Desert Monasteries in the Byzantine Period: An Archeological Investigation" (Ph.D. diss., Hebrew University, Jerusalem, 1987).

19. See C. Bacha, *Les Oeuvres arabes de Théodore Aboucara, évêque d'Haran* (Beirut, 1904), pp. 60–61.

20. Harvey Stahl, *Mt. Sinai Arabic Codex 151; I, Pauline Epistles*, vols. 452–453 (Louvain, 1983).

21. See Sauget, "Le Dossier Ephrémien." See also Samir Khalil, "L'Ephrem arabe, état des travaux," in *Symposium Syriacum 1976 célébré du 13 au 17 septembre 1976 au Centre Culturel "Les Fontaines" de Chantilly* , ed. F. Graffin and A. Guillaumont (Rome, 1978), pp. 229–240; and Samir Khalil, "Un example des contacts culturels entre les églises syriaques et arabes: Jacques de Saroug dans la tradition arabe," in *III*[e] *Symposium Syriacum 1980. Les contacts du monde syriaque avec les autres cultures (Goslar, 7–11 septembre 1980)*, ed. R. Lavenant (Rome, 1983), pp. 213–245.

22. See the English translation and introduction in *The Ascetical Homilies of St. Isaac the Syrian* [trans. Dana Miller] (Brookline, Mass., 1984). For a general orientation to Isaac of Nineveh, see Sebastian Brock, "St. Isaac of Nineveh and Syriac Spirituality," *Sobornost* 7 (1975): 79–89; idem, "Isaac of Nineveh: Some Newly-Discovered Works," *Sobornost* 8 (1986): 28–33.

their intellectual horizon was broader than what may be read in Greek, and their social interests were not completely absorbed by Byzantium. Anthony David's roots in Baghdad call all of this to mind.

As for Baghdad, the Abbasid capital and presumably the home of Anthony David's family, there was a Melkite presence there throughout the ninth century.[23] Baghdad was also the site of the imprisonment of the Byzantine martyr-monk Romanos, prior to his execution at ar-Raqqa in the year 780. According to his martyrology, members of the Melkite community there had cared for him and his companions during their imprisonment. And their story was later told by a monk of Mar Sabas named Stephen of Damascus. It survives only in a Georgian version which seems clearly to have been translated from Arabic. There is no trace of the story in Greek hagiography.[24]

The connections which one can trace in the prospography of the old south Palestinian archive of Christian texts in Arabic, as we have said, document a pattern of intercourse between Baghdad, Edessa, Damascus (sometimes Alexandria), and the monasteries in the Holy Land. Time and space do not allow one to lay out all the details of the evidence here. The single example of Anthony David's associations gives one an idea of the sort of geographical network that the manuscripts allow one to observe. It seems clear that for the Melkites, from early Abbasid times to the Crusades, the Holy Land monasteries, particularly those of Mar Sabas and Mar Charitōn, were the chief intellectual centers for the nascent Arabophone Christianity.[25]

It remains only to speak of the monastery at Mount Sinai, the de facto depository of most of the old Palestinian archive of Christian Arabic manuscripts and the source of most of those manuscripts from the archive which are now found scattered among a few European libraries, including the two written by Anthony David of Baghdad.[26] The colophons explicitly say that the manuscripts were written (copied) for Mount Sinai at the request of one Abba Isaac. Therefore, we may conclude that in the ninth century officials at Sinai were making a purposeful effort to build up the Arabic holdings of their library.

Anthony David of Baghdad copied Vatican Arabic MS 71 and Strasbourg Oriental MS 4226 for the library at Sinai from copies available at the

23. See J. M. Fiey, " 'Rūm' à l'est de l'Euphrate," *Le Muséon* 90 (1977): 365–420. See also the very general survey by M. Allard, "Les chrétiens à Bagdad," *Arabica* 9 (1962): 375–388.
24. P. Peeters, "S. Romain le néomartyr (d. 1 mai 780) d'après un document gérgien," *Analecta Bollandiana* (1911): 393–427.
25. See S. H. Griffith, "Stephen of Ramlah," and "Greek into Arabic."
26. Vatican Arabic MS 71 was purchased in Cairo by Andreas Scandar, who was sent on an expedition to purchase manuscripts for the Vatican library in 1718. See J. S. Assemani, *Bibliotheca Orientalis*, vol. 2 (Rome, 1721), pp. 485, 510–511. Strasbourg Oriental MS 4226 was likewise purchased in Cairo by an agent for the library, a certain Dr. Reinhart; see Oestrup, "Über zwei arabische Codices," p. 453 n. 1.

monastery of Mar Sabas. Presumably, he was not responsible for translating their contents from Greek into Arabic. He admits as much in the colophon to Vatican Arabic MS 71, where he distinguishes between those who have "produced, copied, asked for a copy, or said 'Amen' to" the contents of the work he himself copied.[27] So one must conclude that the Arabic versions were made earlier, perhaps at Mar Sabas. And this consideration brings one to an interest in the contents of the manuscripts which Anthony David copied.

3.

The contents of the Arabic manuscripts which Anthony David copied at Mar Sabas monastery have long been known to scholars. Lists of them have long been published. All of the works in the two manuscripts are translations from Greek into Arabic, and all of them are of an ascetical character, either lives of monastic saints, homilies, or tales of the spiritual feats of monastic heroes. Few of these works have been published or studied in detail.

From Vatican Arabic MS 71 Georg Graf published the Arabic text of the life of Saint Xenophon and his family, and J.-M. Sauget has published the Arabic text and a French translation of an ascetical homily attributed to one Stephen of Thebes.[28] From the Leningrad leaves of Strasbourg Oriental MS 4226 I. Kračkovsky published the Arabic text and a Russian translation of most of a homily on Jesus's victory over death and the devil.[29] In the manuscript the homily is attributed to Saint Ephraem, as one now knows from G. Garitte's publication of the first leaf of the homily, which is kept in the Mingana collection in Birmingham, England.[30] And, from leaves now kept in the same collection, W. Heffening published the Arabic text and a German translation of a homily against laughing also attributed to Saint Ephraem.[31] It remains only to mention J.-M. Sauget's investigation of the nineteen works ascribed to Saint Ephraem in the reassembled Strasbourg 4226, and the list of the few scholarly studies of the manuscript's contents is complete.[32]

The ascetical and monastic texts in Vatican Arabic MS 71 include a life of Epiphanius of Salamis by John of Constantinople, lives of Saint Euthymius and Saint Sabas by Cyril of Schythopolis, a homily on Psalm 6 by Anastasius of Sinai, the aforementioned life of Saint Xenophon and his family, stories of Cassian and the fathers of Scetis, two homilies of Saint Nilus, two reports of

27. Tisserant, *Specimina*, p. xxxix; Garitte, "Homélie d'Éphrem," p. 135.
28. G. Graf, "Iǧtimāᶜ l-ahl baᶜda šatāt aš-šaml [*sic*]," *al-Machriq* 12 (1909): 695–706; J.-M. Sauget, "Une version arabe du 'sermon ascétique' d'Étienne le Thébain," *Le Muséon* 77 (1964): 367–406.
29. See n. 10 above.
30. Garitte, "Homélie d'Éphrem," pp. 156–157.
31. See n. 12 above.
32. Sauget, "Le Dossier Ephrémien," pp. 426–458.

the sayings of the abbot Saint Isaiah, two pieces from the pen of the abbot Saint Macarius, the aforementioned treatise of Stephen of Thebes, and some sayings of the monastic fathers.[33]

Strasbourg Oriental MS 4226, in addition to the nineteen works attributed to Saint Ephraem which already have been mentioned, includes four pieces attributed to Basil of Caesarea, the miracles of St. Nicholas, excerpts from Gregory of Nyssa's history of Gregory the Wonder Worker, some questions and answers attributed to Saint Athanasius, two homilies in praise of the Virgin Mary, one by John of Damascus, a homily of Proclus of Constantinople, extracts from the works of Isaac of Nineveh, an exhortation to monks, and a prayer of Mar Serapion.[34]

From this quick recitation of the contents of Anthony David's two manuscripts it should be clear that they would be of interest principally to the monastic community. And in this connection one notices in particular in Vatican Arabic MS 71 the lives of Saint Euthymius and Saint Sabas by Cyril of Schythopolis, himself an earlier member of the community of Mar Sabas.[35] One will also recall that in his colophons Anthony David specifically asks for the prayers of Saint Sabas and calls him "our holy father." Clearly, therefore, the copyist and his Arabic-speaking community had a special concern for the classic monastic texts of the Palestinian ascetic communities.

By way of a conclusion to the observation that the contents of Anthony David's two manuscripts are peculiarly of monastic interest, one should mention another Arabic manuscript written at Mar Sabas monastery which also contains extracts from Cyril of Schythopolis's lives of the Palestinian monastic fathers. It is the so-called *Codex Rescriptus Tischendorf 2*, a manuscript in which the Arabic translation of Cyril's lives is written over an erased Greek text which Tischendorf dated to the eighth century.[36] Paleographically, the Arabic text belongs with those works in the old south Palestinian archive which are characteristic of the ninth century.[37] The fact that it is a palimpsest simply underscores the shift from Greek to Arabic in the monastic community in ninth-century Palestine.

What is of particular interest to the present discussion in the *Codex Rescriptus Tishchendorf 2* is the fact that there is a postscript at the end of the excerpt from the life of Saint Sabas which sounds a lot like the colophons we have from Anthony David's manuscripts. It reads: "The poor sinner David

33. Mai, *Scriptorum Veterum*, pp. 143–145. Note that Mai's folio numbers do not correspond to those now on the MS.
34. Oestrup, "Über zwei arabische codices," pp. 455–458.
35. On Cyril and his work, see particularly Flusin, *Miracle et histoire*.
36. See H. L. Fleischer,"Über einen griechisch-arabischen Codex rescriptus der Leipziger Universitäts-Bibliothek," in Fleischer, *Kleinere Schriften*, pp. 378–388. The manuscript is now in Leningrad. See Georg Graf, *Geschichte der christlichen arabischen Literatur*, 5 vols. (Rome, 1944–1953), 1:407.
37. See the facsimile published in Fleischer, *Kleinere Schriften*, vol. 3, plate 1, and in G. Graf, "Athar naṣrānī qadīm; aw tarǧamah mār Abramiūs al-quiddīs bi l-ʿarabiyyah," *al-Machriq* 8 (1905): opp. p. 260.

has done the writing. He gives praise to God who has given good help, and he asks everyone who reads this volume to pray for him, for the mercy and forgiveness consequent upon the love of Christ, our God and master. May God be pleased with the one who has produced this. Amen."[38] In this manuscript the text which the writer has produced is perhaps not simple copying. At the beginning of the excerpt from the life of Saint Sabas he wrote: "Here is what we have thought it appropriate to interpret [*nufassir*] from the story of the holy Mar Saba, the star of the desert, and from his good lifestyle—for the profit of whoever reads it or hears it."[39] Here the "interpretation" (*at-tafsīr*) of which the writer speaks, as H. L. Fleischer suggested, is undoubtedly a translation of Mar Saba's biography from Greek into Arabic.[40] So the David who wrote the manuscript may have been the translator as well as the scribe of at least one of the biographies in the text.

At one time Georg Graf thought that the David who wrote the *Codex Rescriptus* was none other than Anthony David of Baghdad.[41] Subsequently, Graf withdrew this suggestion.[42] In fact, the name is spelled differently in the *Codex Rescriptus* (*Dhâwîdh*) than in Anthony David's two manuscripts (*Dâ'ûd*). It seems not unreasonable, therefore, to suppose that the *Codex Rescriptus* is the earlier text, dating from the time when the Arabic translations from Greek were first undertaken, perhaps as far back as the turn of the eighth and ninth centuries.[43]

Since the Arabic monastic texts we have been discussing are almost all translations from Greek, one might suppose that there is nothing essentially new to learn from them. But the fact is that of the works of Cyril of Schythopolis the *Codex Rescriptus* preserves a fuller text of the life of Saint Abramios than does any known manuscript of the Greek original. Recent versions of his life in modern languages have thus benefited from what the Palestinian monks of the ninth century preserved in Arabic.[44]

One might conclude from what one knows of the contents of Anthony

38. Fleischer, *Kleinere Schriften*, p. 381.
39. Ibid., p. 380.
40. Ibid., p. 380 n. 2. For other instances of the use of forms of the verb *tafsīr* to mean "to translate," see S. H. Griffith, "The Arabic Account of ʿAbd al-Masīh an-Nağrānī al-Ghassānī," *Le Muséon* 98 (1985): 338–339.
41. G. Graf, *Die christlich-arabische Literatur bis zur fränkischen Zeit* (Freiburg im Breisgau, 1905), pp. 13, 16; idem, "Die arabische Vita des hi. Abramias," *Byzantinische Zeitschrift* 14 (1905): 509.
42. Graf, *Geschichte*, 1:407 n. 1.
43. See van Esbroeck, "Le Codex Rescriptus Tischendorf 2," pp. 81–91.
44. The Arabic text of the life of St. Abramios was first published by G. Graf, "Athar nasrānī qadim," pp. 258–265. Graf also published a German translation of the text in "Die arabische Vita des hl. Abramios," pp. 509–518. A Latin version appears in P. Peeters, "Historia S. Abramii ex apographo arabico," *Analecta Bollandiana* 24 (1905): 349–356. See the remarks of S. Vailhé, "Saint Abraham de Cratia," *Échos d'Orient* 8 (1905): 290–294. Finally, what is preserved in Arabic is incorporated into the French version of the life of Abramios in A. J. Festugière, *Les moines d'orient*, vol. 3, part 3, *Les moines de Palestine* (Paris, 1963), pp. 69–79.

David's manuscripts, and from some dozen other manuscripts in the old south Palestinian archive, that monasticism was alive and well in the Holy Land during the ninth and tenth centuries, at least in such monasteries as those of Mar Sabas, Mar Charitōn, and the monastery at Sinai.[45] Currently, the old south Palestinian archive is our best evidence of this thriving Arabophone monasticism. As irony would have it, however, if one reads the history of these great monasteries only in Greek or Latin sources, one gets the impression that these institutions were virtually abandoned during the three centuries or so preceding the Crusades.

4.

Theophanes the Confessor (d. ca. 818) reported near the end of his *Chronography* that in 812/813, as modern scholars would reckon it, the Arabs wreaked havoc in the Christian centers in the Holy Land. He said specifically: "The famous *lauras* of Sts. Khariton and Sabas in the desert, as well as other churches and monasteries, were devastated. Some men became martyrs, others got to Cyprus, and from there to Byzantium."[46] The conclusion might be drawn from such a notice as this one that after the first decade of the ninth century the monasteries were virtually dead in the Holy Land until the return of Christian political hegemony to the area in the twelfth century. Certainly, one gets little hint from Greek or Latin sources that during the ninth, tenth, and eleventh centuries the famous old monasteries were populated by Arabic-speaking monks whose influence extended to all the centers of Christian life in the caliphate. The exception to this rule of silence is the report of George of Bethlehem that one finds recorded in Eulogius of Toledo's account of the martyrs of Cordoba, who were executed on 27 July 852. George boasted that he had lived at Mar Sabas monastery for twenty-seven years with some 500 confreres before being sent to North Africa on monastery business by his abbot, yet another monk of Mar Sabas named David. Moreover, Eulogius noted that George was proficient in Greek and Latin, as well as Arabic.[47]

45. With Mar Sabas, the monastery of St. Charitōn was also the site of scribal work in Arabic. See Griffith, "Stephen of Ramlah," and the colophons in P. Cachia and W. M. Watt, *Eutychius of Alexandria, the Book of the Demonstration (Kitāb al-Burhān)*, vols. 192, 193, 209, 210 (Louvain, 1960–1961). Eutychius of Alexandria had nothing to do with this work, which is the product of the monks of the Holy Land. See now M. Breydy, *Études sur Sa'īd ibn Batrīq et ses sources*, vol. 450 (Louvain, 1983). See also Samir Arbache, "Sentences arabes de saint Basil," *Le Muséon* 98 (1985): pp. 315–329.

46. Carolus De Boor, ed. *Theophanis Chronographia*, 2 vols. (Lipsiae, 1883–1885), 1:499. See also Harry Turtledove, *The Chronicle of Theophanes: An English Translation of Anni Mundi 6095–6305 (A.D. 602–813), with Introduction and Notes* (Philadelphia, 1982), p. 178.

47. See Eulogius of Toledo, "Memoriale Sanctorum, Documentum Martyriale, Apologeticus Martyrum," *Patrologia Latina*, ed. J. P. Migne, vol. 115, cols. 786–788. See also Edward P. Colliert, *The Martyrs of Cordoba (850–859): A Study of the Sources* (Washington, 1962), pp. 239–242.

For the rest, there is little further mention in Greek or Latin sources of the active, indigenous monastic life of Palestine in the centuries before the Crusades. There were of course the pilgrims from Rome and Byzantium. But, as John Wilkinson has put it in his study of western pilgrimage to the Holy Land prior to the Crusades, "Despite occasional expressions of gratitude for courtesy and kindness, most of our pilgrims appear to regard local people with curiosity and little more."[48] The Constantinopolitan monk Epiphanius, for example, passed by the monasteries of Mar Sabas and Mar Charitōn on his pilgrimage to the Holy Land. He mentions them, but he gives no hint of the indigenous Christian monasticism thriving there at the very time of his visit. He was interested in the "Holy Places" and not in the monastic communities of the Holy Land.[49]

Even in the days of Charlemagne's alleged interest in the Holy Land, when the Frankish authorities were in possession of a list of the monasteries of Palestine with some indication of the number of their inhabitants, one finds only a quick mention of Mar Charitōn and Mar Sabas, with the notice that the latter housed 150 monks.[50] As for Arabic, the *Commemoratorium* mentions the language only in connection with one monk at the monastery on the Mount of Olives, "Qui Sarracenica lingua psallit ("who sings Psalms in the Saracen language").[51]

This attitude of virtual disinterest in the monasteries of the Holy Land for their own sakes that one finds in the pilgrims's reports of their journeys to the holy places during the Islamic centuries contrasts with the high regard the monastic communities enjoyed in earlier times. For almost three centuries before the Islamic conquest of Palestine the Holy Land had been a magnet for the ascetically minded citizens of the Roman Empire. Communities of monks and nuns grew up there in profusion, and some of them could trace their origins back as far as the first half of the fourth century.[52]

In the fifth and sixth centuries people came from all over the empire to live as monks in Palestine, as the biographies of the famous monks of the Judean desert by Cyril of Schythopolis abundantly show.[53] They were actively engaged in the theological controversies of the day, to the degree that their

48. J. Wilkinson, *Jerusalem Pilgrims Before the Crusades* (Warminster, 1977), p. 32.
49. H. Donner, "Die Palästinabeschreibung des Epiphanius Monachus Hagiopolita," *Zeitschrift des Deutschen Palästina-Vereins* 87 (1971): 71.
50. See the *Commemoratorium de Casis Dei vel Monasteriis* in T. Tobler and Molinier, *Itinera Hierosolymitana et Descriptiones Terrae Sanctae*, vol. 1 (Geneva, 1879), p. 303. See also K. Schmid, "Aachen und Jerusalem," in *Das Einhardkreuz*, ed. K. Hauck (Göttingen, 1974), pp. 122–142; M. Borgolte, *Der Gesandtenaustausch der Karolinger mit den abbasiden und mit den Patriarchen von Jerusalem* (München, 1976).
51. *Commemoratorium*, p. 302.
52. See Chitty, *Desert a City*; E. D. Hunt, *Holy Land Pilgrimage in the Later Roman Empire, A.D. 312–460* (Oxford, 1982).
53. E. Schwartz, *Kyrillos von Skythopolis* (Leipzig, 1939); A. J. Festugière, *Les moines d'Orient*, 3 vols. (Paris, 1962).

influence was empire-wide.[54] And the size and proportions of their establishments in the desert in early Byzantine times are only now becoming evident, due to intensive investigations in the area by modern archaeologists.[55]

An interesting feature in the accounts of the monks and monasteries of the Holy Land is their occasional reference to the indigenous Arabs. There are, to be sure, complaints about the "Saracens" (or "Ishmaelites" or "Hagarenes").[56] But there are also reports of the role the monks played in the conversion of the Arabs to Christianity. One thinks especially of Cyril of Schythopolis's "Life of Saint Euthymius," according to which the saint instigated the inauguration of an Arab tribal bishopric on the empire's *limes arabicus*.[57]

After the Islamic conquest and well into the ninth century, monks from the Holy Land, Jerusalem, and the Judean desert, especially Mar Sabas monastery, were still important in Byzantium. One need only mention some of their names to make the point: John of Damascus, Theodore and Theophane Graptoi, George Synkellos, Michael Synkellos, and Saint Anthony the Younger. But these men—except for John of Damascus— were all refugees in Constantinople.[58] Theophane the Chronicler was right in this respect: he suggests in the passage quoted above that there was no one left in the Holy Land after the early ninth century who could claim the attention of the *literati* in Byzantium.

The later reports of the Holy Land come mostly from pilgrims. They were interested in the *loca sancta* and hardly at all in monasteries except as points of reference in the narratives of their visits to pilgrims' sites.[59] And they

54. See Flusin, *Miracle et histoire*; L. Perrone, *La chiesa di Palestina e le controversie cristologiche* (Brescia, 1980).
55. The ground-breaking work in this area is Hirschfeld, "Judean Desert Monasteries in the Byzantine Period."
56. See V. Christides, "Arabs as *barbaroi* before the Rise of Islam," *Balkan Studies* 10 (1969): 315–324; idem, "Pre-Islamic Arabs in Byzantine Illuminations," *Le Muséon* 83 (1970): 167–181. See also I. Shahid, *Rome and the Arabs* (Washington, 1984), pp. 123–141; idem, *Byzantium and the Arabs in the Fourth Century* (Washington, 1984), pp. 277–283.
57. See Schwartz, *Kyrillos von Skythopolis*, pp. 15–19; R. Genier, *Vie de saint Euthyme le grand* (Paris, 1909).
58. See Ihor Ševčenko, "Hagiography of the Iconoclast Period," in *Iconoclasm*, ed. A. Bryer and J. Herrin (Birmingham, 1977), pp. 112–118; S. Vailhé, "Saint Michel le syncelle et les deux frères Grapti, saint Théodore et saint Théophane," *Revue de l'Orient Chrétien* 9 (1901): 313–332, 610–642; J. Featherstone, "Theophane of Caesarea, Encomium of Theodore Graptos," *Analecta Bollandiana* 98 (1980): 93–150; F. Halkin, "Saint Antoine le jeune et Pétronas le vainquer des arabes en 863," *Analecta Bollandiana* 62 (1944): 187–225. See also J. Gouillard, "Un 'quartier' d'emigrés palestiniens à Constantinople au ixe siècle?" *Revue des Études Sud-Est Européenes* 7 (1969): 73–76.
59. On the *loca sancta*, see H. Busse and G. Kretschmar, *Jerusalem Heiligtumstraditionen in altkirchlicher und frühislamischer Zeit* (Wiesbaden, 1987). A Christian Arab writer of the ninth/tenth centuries composed a list of sites associated with the life of Christ that were also pilgrimage sites. See P. Cachia and W. M. Watt, *Eutychius of Alexandria, the Book of Demonstration*, vol. 192 (Louvain, 1960), pp. 165–197. At least one monk from Byzantium visited Jerusalem, with no mention at all of local monasteries. See E. Martini, "Supplementa ad Acta S. Lucae Iunioris," *Analecta Bollandiana* 13 (1894): 87.

mention Arabs only as agents of brigandage. In fact, the danger of Arabs as perpetrators of robberies, kidnappings, and murders is a theme one finds with some frequency in Byzantine texts of the period between the conquest and the Crusades.[60] One finds no hint at all in them that there ever existed a vibrant Arabophone church in the Holy Land in this period.

The Arabic language the Christians of the Holy Land spoke and wrote in the ninth and tenth centuries seems to have cut them off from communication with their fellows in "Christendom" as effectively as the borders of the *dār al-Islām* (Islamdom) barred the governments of the Franks and the Byzantines from the political control of the holy places they venerated. In later times, when the Crusaders were in power in the Holy Land, Jacques de Vitry, the Latin bishop of Acre, noted in his *History of Jerusalem* that the "Syrians," as he called the local Arabophone Christians, used Arabic only for their secular business. In religious matters, the bishop alleged, they were totally dependent on the Greeks. He says: "The Syrians use the Saracen language in their common speech, and they use the Saracen script in deeds and business and all other writing, except for the Holy Scriptures and other religious books, in which they use the Greek letters; wherefore in Divine service their laity, who only know the Saracenic tongue, do not understand them. . . . The Syrians exactly follow the rules and customs of the Greeks in Divine service and other spiritual matters, and obey them as their superiors."[61]

It is disheartening to find the Latin bishop of Acre denying the very existence of the Arabic literary accomplishment represented by the old south Palestinian archive only a century or so after the last of it was written. Perhaps our consideration of Anthony David's Christian Arabic manuscripts will help in a small way to redress the imbalance of our history of Christianity in the Holy Land, which seems to have suppressed all effective memory of the Arabophone Christian culture that flourished there between the conquest and the Crusades.

60. See, for example, F. Halkin, "Saint Jean l'érémopolite," *Analecta Bollandiana* 86 (1968): 14, 20; T. Detorakis, "Vie inédite de Cosmas le mélode," *Analecta Bollandiana* 99 (1981): 102, 108.

61. Jacques de Vitry, *The History of Jerusalem: A.D. 1180*, trans. Aubrey Stewart (London, 1896), pp. 68–69.

ADDITIONS

Study I.

P. 99 For further discussion of these Syriac and Arabic Christian texts, along with additional bibliographical information, see S.H. Griffith, "Jews and Muslims in Christian Syriac and Arabic Texts of the Ninth Century", *Jewish History* 3 (1988), pp. 65–94; *idem*, "Disputes with Muslims in Syriac Christian Texts: from Patriarch John (d.648) to Bar Hebraeus (d.1286)", forthcoming in the proceedings of the 25th Wolfenbütteler Symposion, "Religionsgespräche im Mittelalter/Religious Disputations in the Middle Ages", 11 to 15 June, 1989; *idem*, "Christians in the Caliphate in Early Islamic Times: Apologetics and the Problem of Conversion", forthcoming in the proceedings of a conference at The Center for Judaic Studies at Wayne State University, "The Jews of Islamic Lands", October 1990. Since the appearance of this essay, a number of the Arabic Christian texts have been published. Among the more significant publications are: Khalil Samir & Paul Nwyia, *Une correspondance islamo-chrétienne entre Ibn al-Munağğim, Ḥunayn Ibn Isḥāq et Qusṭā Ibn Lūqā* (Patrologia Orientalis, 40,4 = No. 185; Turnhout: Brepols, 1981); G.B. Marcuzzo, *Le Dialogue d'Abraham de Tiberiade avec ʿAbd al-Rahman al-Hašîmî à Jérusalem vers 820: étude, édition critique et traduction annotée d'un texte théologique chrétien de la littérature arabe* (Textes et études sur l'Orient chrétien, 3; Roma, 1986); Bo Holmberg, *A Treatise on the Unity and Trinity of God by Israel of Kashkar (d.872): Introduction, Edition and Word Index* (Lund Studies in African and Asian Religions, 3; Lund: Plus Ultra, 1989); Ignace Dick, *Théodore Abuqurra, Traité de l'existence du Créateur et de la vraie religion; introduction et texte critique* (Patrimoine Arabe Chrétien, 3; Jounieh & Rome, 1982); *idem*, *Théodore Abuqurra, Traité du culte des icones; introduction et texte critique* (Patrimoine Arabe Chrétien, 10; Jounieh & Rome, 1986).

P. 111 For early Muslim appraisals of Christians and Christian teachings see now Jane Dammen McAuliffe, *Qur'ānic Christians: an Analysis of Classical and Modern Exegesis* (Cambridge & New York: Cambridge University Press, 1991).

Study II.

P. 132 An earlier colophon date of 859 A.D. has been reported for a Gospel text among the new Sinai Arabic manuscripts described by Iōannēs Meimarēs, *Katalogos tōn neōn aravikōn cheirographōn tēs Hieras Monēs Hagias Aikaterinēs tou Orous Sina* (Athēnai: Ethnikon Hidryma Ereunōn, 1985), p. 27.

Study IV.

P. 190 Regarding the origin of iconoclasm in Byzantium see now the evidence of a Muslim Arabic text in S.H. Griffith, "Bashīr/Bēsḗr: Boon Companion of the Byzantine Emperor Leo III; the Islamic Recension of his Story in Leiden Oriental MS 951(2)", *Le Muséon* 103 (1990), pp. 293–327.

Study V.

P. 54 An updated list of published works of Theodore Abū Qurrah, along with descriptions of manuscripts of unpublished works in Arabic and Greek attributed to him can be found in J. Nasrallah, *Histoire du mouvement littéraire dans l'Église melchite du Ve au XXe siècle: contribution à l'étude de la littérature arabe chrétienne* (Vol. II, tome 2. 750–Xe S.; Louvain: Peeters, 1988), pp. 104–134. See too George Hanna Khoury, "Theodore Abu Qurrah (c.750–820): Translation and Critical Analysis of his 'Treatise on the Existence of the Creator and on the True Religion' ", (Ph.D. diss., Graduate Theological Union, Berkeley, Calif.; Ann Arbor, Michigan: University Microfilms, 1990); Guy Monnot, "Abu Qurra et la pluralité des religions", *Revue de l'Histoire des Religions* 208 (1991), pp. 49–71.

P. 56 This text has now been edited by Ignace Dick, *Théodore Abuqurra, Traité du culte des icones; introduction et texte critique* (Patrimoine Arabe Chrétien, 10; Jounieh & Rome, 1986). An English translation of this work by S.H. Griffith is forthcoming. Abū Qurrah's treatise on the veneration of icons is also the subject of another essay by S.H. Griffith, "Images, Islam and Christian Icons; a Moment in the Christian/Muslim Encounter in Early Islamic Times", forthcoming in the acts of a colloquium held at Lyon, "La Syrie de Byzance à l'Islam, colloque international", 12–16 September, 1990.

Study VI.

P. 79 This discussion is continued in S.H. Griffith, "Free Will in Christian *Kalām*: Chapter XVIII of the *Summa Theologiae Arabica*", in Regine Schulz & Manfred Görg (eds.), *Lingua Restituta Orientalis: Festgabe für Julius Assfalg* (Ägypten und Altes Testament, Bd. 20; Wiesbaden: Harrassowitz, 1990), pp. 129–134.

P. 92, n. 44 See now S.H. Griffith, "Free Will in Christian Kalām: Moshe bar Kepha against the Teachings of the Muslims", *Le Muséon* 100 (1987), pp. 143–159.

Studies VIII and IX.

Discussion of the text of the *Summa Theologiae Arabica* is continued in S.H. Griffith, "Islam and the Summa Theologiae Arabica; Rabīʿ I, 264 A.H.", *Jerusalem Studies in Arabic and Islam* 13 (1990), pp. 225–264; *idem*, "The First Christian *Summa Theologiae* in Arabic: Christian *Kalām* in Ninth-Century Palestine", in Michael Gervers and Ramzi Jibran Bikhazi, *Conversion and Continuity: Indigenous Christian Communities in Islamic Lands Eighth to Eighteenth Centuries* (Papers in Mediaeval Studies, 9; Toronto: Pontifical Institute of Mediaeval Studies, 1990), pp. 15–31.

INDEX